W9-CAU-721

The American Paradox

A History of the United States

SINCE 1945

Steven M. Gillon

University of Oklahoma
and
The History Channel

HOUGHTON MIFFLIN COMPANY

BOSTON   NEW YORK

This book is dedicated with love to the Ryan Family—Jim, Kate, Will, Sam, and Ben

Editor-in-Chief: Jean Woy
Sponsoring Editor: Mary Dougherty
Development Editor: Leah Strauss
Senior Project Editor: Florence Kilgo
Production Editorial Assistant: Marlowe Shaeffer
Production/Design Coordinator: Lisa Jelly Smith
Senior Manufacturing Coordinator: Jane Spelman
Senior Marketing Manager: Sandra McGuire

Cover Design: © Bettmann/Corbis

Copyright © 2003 by Houghton Mifflin Company. All rights reserved.

No part of this work may be reproduced or transmitted in any form or by any means, electronic or mechanical, including photocopying and recording, or by any information storage or retrieval system without the prior written permission of Houghton Mifflin Company unless such copying is expressly permitted by federal copyright law. Address inquiries to College Permissions, Houghton Mifflin Company, 222 Berkeley Street, Boston, MA 02116-3764.

Printed in the U.S.A.

Library of Congress Control Number: 2001133264

ISBN: 0-618-15014-5

3456789-CS-06 05

Contents

7 | The Kennedy Presidency, 1961–1963   157

8 | Lyndon Johnson's Ordeal: The Great Society and Vietnam, 1964–1968   184

12 | America's Crisis of Confidence, 1974–1980   310

13 | The Reagan Presidency, 1981–1989   335

14 | The Culture Wars, 1980–1992   364

15 | The Triumph of Consumerism, 1980–1992   387

16 | The End of the Cold War, 1988–1992   402

Maps and Graphs

Preface

My approach to the study of modern America grows out of my experience growing up in suburban Philadelphia in the late 1970s. As an undergraduate at Widener University (class of 1978), I was introduced to many of the classics in modern American history, and I was often struck by how many of these books, and the authors who wrote them, used the 1930s and the New Deal as their reference point. They emphasized the success of major reform movements and the achievements of progressive presidents to chart the steady triumph of liberal values in America. In many of these accounts, the expanding power of the federal government represented the clearest evidence of the triumph of liberal values.

But these books made little sense of the political events that I was witnessing all around me. My racially divided local community revolted against large-scale busing initiatives. My neighbors, mainly working class Irish and Italians, who had once worshiped Roosevelt, now voted Republican. By the time I entered graduate school at Brown University in 1980, the conservative movement was at high tide: Jerry Falwell was a national celebrity, Ronald Reagan was president, tax revolts were spreading like wildfire across the country, and the once powerful New Deal coalition was in full retreat. But of course the story was not that simple. The decade also witnessed the emergence of a number of important empowerment movements, which fed off the momentum created by the civil rights movement of the 1960s. Women were demanding the Equal Rights Amendment, post-Stonewall gays were fighting against discrimination, and other racial minorities, especially Asians and Hispanics, whose numbers had swelled because of massive immigration, were raising their voices in protest. Nothing I was reading was making sense of this polarized, confused, and contentious national environment.

It was around that time that I came across an observation by the British journalist Godfrey Hodgson who said that "Americans love change, but they hate to be changed." We change our clothing style, our homes, and our hairstyles more than any people on earth, but we resist altering our attitudes about the way we view the world. He was simply recasting a question that Robert Kennedy had asked in the months before his death in 1968: "How do we seek to change a society that yields so painfully to change?" That question captured for me the central contradiction of post-war politics and society: Americans had come to expect government to solve most major social problems, but they retained a traditional fear of federal power. In the abstract, Americans believed in equal rights and opposed discrimination of any kind; but they clung tenaciously to deeply held values about limited government, self-help, and racial and gender stereotypes. Especially in the years since the 1960s, the tension between rising expectations of government and deep-seated fear of federal power has shaped public debate in America. Hence the title of this book: *American Paradox*.

It seems to me that a new framework for understanding modern America must do two things: first, it needs to recognize the role of paradox and irony in understanding public attitudes toward government and in charting the evolution of state power; second, the narrative has to be opened to include groups that had been previously excluded and to consider questions long neglected. The definition of politics must be expanded beyond the realm of elite actors and powerful institutions to include both public and private culture, and an appreciation of how differences of race, class, and gender have shaped our past. It also recognizes the need for synthesis in historical writing, and for weaving together the threads of individual experiences into the broader fabric of American history.

This book also includes a number of stylistic and pedagogical devices that are designed to make it both practical and readable. I have integrated into the narrative important primary documents that are designed to provoke debate and discussion. Especially in upper-division courses, students need to develop the skill to analyze and interpret evidence. Students have under one cover some of the key documents in modern America: from George Kennan's famous Mr. X article, to the Supreme Court's decision in *Brown* v. *Board of Education* (1956), to Phyllis Schlafly's attack on the Equal Rights Amendment (ERA). Ample graphs, charts, and photographs provide visual support for some of the important points raised in the text.

In an effort to animate the narrative, I included lots of colorful quotations, personality sketches, and anecdotes. I also chose to omit the names of people who appear only once in the narrative. As a result, there are lots of references to "a congressman said," or "a journalist noted." The important players and figures, however, are all properly identified. In addition, while the narrative makes reference to key historical debates, specific references to historians are confined to the selected bibliography at the end of each chapter. The bibliography contains both standard works and, when appropriate, the most recent books on major issues raised in the chapter.

A number of people helped make this book possible. My first debt is to the scholars of modern America whose work provides the intellectual foundation for this book. I would also like to thank the colleagues who reviewed the manuscript: J. Lee Annis, Jr., Montgomery College; Shirley Eoff, Angelo State University; Brian Greenberg, Monmouth University; Richard Newman, Rochester Institute of Technology; G. David Price, Santa Fe Community College; and Jessica Wong, University of California–Los Angeles. At Houghton Mifflin, I would like to thank Mary Dougherty and Leah Strauss for taking on the project, and the talented production editors Carla Thompson and Florence Kilgo for seeing it through to publication. I thank also Lisa Jelly Smith, production/design coordinator, and Jane Spelman, senior manufacturing coordinator. Of course, I am indebted to Sandi McGuire for spending countless hours to market the book. I could not have completed the project without the help of a team of talented graduate research assistants at the University of Oklahoma: Dan Cobb, George Milne, and especially, Heather Clemmer. The book is dedicated to the Ryan family. Jim and Kate Ryan have welcomed me into their lives, allowing me to enjoy all the benefits of raising three wonderful kids—Will, Sam, and Ben—without ever once asking me to change a diaper. Not a bad deal.

Introduction: The American Paradox

At 7 P.M. on Tuesday, August 14, 1945, President Harry S Truman invited reporters to the Oval Office for a brief, informal press conference. For weeks rumors had circulated about an imminent Japanese surrender. As the horde of reporters rushed into the room, a solemn Truman rose from his desk to greet them. Reading from a prepared text, he announced that he had received a message of surrender from the Japanese government. "Arrangements are now being made," he said, "for the formal signing of surrender terms at the earliest possible moment." The president then smiled and sat down.

The nation erupted in celebration. Across the country church bells rang, air-raid sirens screeched, horns honked, and bands played. The celebrations, however, were clouded by fears about America's role in the postwar world and the quality of Truman's leadership in shifting America to a peacetime economy. Perhaps most of all, Americans brooded about the legacy of the atomic bomb, which had produced such a swift and dramatic end to the war. "For all we know," warned popular radio host H. V. Kaltenborn, "we have created a Frankenstein." The bomb, which President Truman hailed as "the greatest achievement of organized science in history," also possessed the power to destroy the world. A few weeks after the United States dropped the first bomb on Hiroshima on August 6, the *Washington Post* editorialized that the life expectancy of the human race had "dwindled immeasurably."

Despite these worries, most Americans had high hopes for the postwar world. In 1945 the influential columnist Walter Lippmann predicted that "what Rome was to the ancient world, what Great Britain has been to the modern world,

1

America is to be to the world of tomorrow." There were many reasons for such optimism. The nation, mired in depression during the 1930s, was experiencing an unprecedented economic expansion. Unemployment, which stood at 17 percent when Japanese planes attacked Pearl Harbor, later dropped to nearly unmeasurable levels. National income more than doubled from $81 billion in 1940 to $181 billion five years later, or from $573 to $1,074 per capita. The war improved the distribution of income—an accomplishment lured that had eluded New Deal planners. The share of income owned by the richest 5 percent declined from 23.7 to 16.8 percent, while the average wages of workers employed full-time in manufacturing rose from $28 per week in 1940 to $48 in 1944.

An expansion of federal power played the central role in the prosperity. A growing centralization of power in Washington, begun during the New Deal, accelerated during World War II. Between 1940 and 1945 the number of civilian employees in government posts rose from 1 million to 3.8 million. Federal expenditures from 1940 to 1945 rose from $9 billion to $98.4 billion. The final bill for the war came to more than $330 billion, a sum twice as large as the total of all government spending in the history of the United States to that point. By comparison, Roosevelt's New Deal responded to the 1938 recession by spending $3 billion on public works.

The spending was matched by regulations that made the federal government a part of the fabric of life for most Americans. Congress dramatically expanded the federal income tax during the war. Most Americans had never filed an income-tax return before World War II because the income tax, on the books since 1913, had been a small tax on upper-income families. Starting with 1942, anyone earning $600 or more annually had to file a return. Income-tax withholding from paychecks went into effect in 1943. But it was the draft that brought the federal government into the homes of millions of Americans. Following the Japanese attack on Pearl Harbor, Congress ordered the registration of all men between the ages of twenty (lowered to eighteen in 1942) and forty-four for war service. During the war the nation peacefully registered 49 million men, selected 19 million, and inducted 10 million, twice the number who volunteered.

World War II also refigured social relations in America, providing African-Americans and other racial minorities with new opportunities. The war lured millions of blacks into war plants and labor unions in the North and West.

Wartime experience raised the expectations of African-American veterans who had risked their lives to guarantee freedom in Europe and were unwilling to accept second-class citizenship in their own country. "I spent four years in the army to free a bunch of Dutchmen and Frenchmen, and I'm danged if I'm going to let the Alabama version of the Germans kick me around when I get home," a discharged army corporal from Alabama said. "No siree-bob! I went into the Army a nigger; I'm comin' out a man." World War II also inspired a drive for equal rights among Asian-American, Native American, and Hispanic-American veterans who returned home to their communities determined to secure full access to American life.

With men being drafted for the service, employers looked to women to maintain the mobilization at home. "Rosie the Riveter," who, according to a popular song of the time, was "making history working for victory," became the media symbol of the woman at work. She could do a man's job without compromising her feminine qualities. Over the next four years nearly 6 million women responded to the call. By the end of the war almost 19 million women (or 36 percent) were working, many at jobs from which they had previously been excluded. Nearly 2 million women—about 10 percent of female workers—took up jobs in defense plants. For many women, working in the factories represented "the first time we got a chance to show that we could do a lot of things that only men had done before."

The war was responsible for producing the striking paradox that would define postwar America: World War II revolutionized American society, but it did not produce a corresponding change in public attitudes. The war may have transformed America's relationship with Washington, producing a dramatic expansion of federal power, but it did little to challenge deeply rooted fears of centralized power. At the same time that the war contributed to the growth of big government, it reaffirmed Americans' faith in limited government and individualism. In all of the major initiatives of the war—building an army, mobilizing industry, controlling wages and prices—Americans tried to balance the needs of war with the values of democracy. In fact, the brutality of Adolf Hitler's regime made Americans more skeptical of state power. In a war depicted as a struggle between good and evil, the victory over fascism seemed to confirm the continuing relevance of America's democratic experiment.

Although social relations had been transformed by war, American attitudes about race and gender remained remarkably resilient in the wake of extraordinary changes. Women, African-Americans, and other racial minorities may have emerged from the war with expanded expectations, but the majority of Americans showed little interest in questioning old stereotypes or changing past practices. Though Rosie the Riveter became a popular symbol of working women during the war, polls showed that majorities of men and women disapproved of working wives, and most women of traditional child-bearing age (twenty through thirty-four) remained at home. As a result, the war did little, in the short run, to challenge traditional notions that a women's proper place was in the home raising the children. "The housewife, not the WAC or the riveter, was the model woman," observed the historian D'Ann Campbell.

The war gave African-Americans a glimpse of a better life, but it did little to change deeply imbedded racial attitudes or undermine the structure of segregation. The army remained rigidly segregated. In 1940 the army had just five African-American officers, three of them chaplains. Black soldiers had to watch the army segregate the blood plasma of whites and blacks. Regulations restricted blacks to their own barracks, movie houses, and commissaries. Conditions on the home front were not much better. Management and labor joined forces to limit black access to the war boom. "We will not employ Negroes," declared the president of North American Aviation. "It is against company policy."

This tension between American ideals and social realities, which had roots deep in the nation's past, was sharpened in the years following World War II by what the historian James T. Patterson has described as America's "grand expectations." These expectations touched on nearly every aspect of American society: economists believed they had discovered the tools to guarantee growth, promising a better life for all Americans; marginalized groups—especially African-Americans and women—gained new wartime opportunities, which they hoped would translate into tangible peacetime gains; and victory convinced policy makers of the universal appeal of American values and the need to project U.S. power abroad.

While Americans entered the postwar world with high hopes about the possibilities of change, they remained deeply ambivalent about the consequences of change. The

British journalist Godfrey Hodgson once observed that "Americans love change, but they hate to be changed." This paradox is essential to understanding the dynamics of American history since 1945. Franklin Roosevelt's leadership during the Great Depression and World War II had altered America's relationship with the federal government. Once the war ended, Americans continued to look to Washington, especially the president, to satisfy their expectations of a better life. The result was a dramatic and sustained expansion of federal power. By the end of the century Washington played a role in the daily lives of most Americans. This expansion of government power, however, did not produce a corresponding change in attitudes toward government power. The tension between expectations of government as a vehicle of change and traditional fears of encroaching state power provides the central narrative of this book.

This paradox has its roots in the nation's revolutionary past. The Founders rebelled against the imperial designs of a distant and impersonal British government. Believing that "power" was antithetical to "liberty," they created a system of government that made it difficult for power to concentrate in any one branch of government. "The constant aim," James Madison explained in *The Federalist Papers*, "is to divide and arrange the several offices in such a manner that they may be a check on the other—that the private interest of every individual may be a sentinel over the public rights."

Despite these inhibitions, Americans have witnessed a dramatic increase in the size and scope of government power. This trend was especially pronounced in the years after World War II when Americans, their expectations whetted by prosperity and rising expectations of the "good life," placed enormous pressure on government to increase services and benefits. By the 1990s, 48 percent of all American households, including many with high incomes, received some form of federal entitlement check—unemployment compensation, Medicare, social security, food stamps, pension, veteran's benefits, or welfare allotment. (The *Federal Register,* which lists government rules and regulations, grew from 5,307 pages in 1940 to 68,101 in 1995.)

The irony is that Americans have come to accept the benefits of a modern welfare state without accepting the legitimacy of federal power. Polls, for example, show overwhelming support for the large entitlement programs that make up a significant portion of domestic spending. Yet the same surveys show a clamoring for cuts in government spending, a reduction in Washington's power, and a demand for local control. A bellwether poll conducted by Princeton Survey Associates in 1995 found that by a margin of 61 to 24 percent Americans trusted state government to "do a better job running things" than the federal government. The poll results confirm the historian Arthur Schlesinger Jr's assertion that America is "operationally liberal and philosophically conservative." Americans are against big government, for example, yet also want Washington to provide for social security, Medicare, Medicaid, clean air and water, and safe streets.

The same paradox of grand expectations shaped America's postwar foreign policy. The American victory in the fight against Hitler shattered the myth of isolationism that had dominated thinking during the 1930s and introduced a new consensus in favor of internationalism. America emerged from the struggle as the leading economic and military power in the world. Flush with victory, the United States prepared to launch a new crusade against communism armed with enormous military might and confidence in the universal relevance of American values. But the experience of total war against absolute evil did little to prepare Americans for the prospect of limited war or for the moral ambiguity of many Third World conflicts. The Cold War raised troubling new questions: How could the United States balance its support for democracy with its fear of communism? Did the expansion of the national security state, and the fear of subversion, threaten democracy and liberty at home? It would take a tragic war in Vietnam to expose the tension between American expectations of the postwar world and the realities of international power.

A further dimension of the paradox of expectations and social realities shaped many of the cultural assumptions of postwar America. The wartime experience produced a celebration of civic nationalism, an outpouring of patriotism that bridged social divisions and produced unprecedented unity. The war reinforced the image of the melting pot, a singular American identity that transcended racial and class differences. "Never before in its history," the historian John Diggins has written, "and never again in its immediate future, would America enjoy such unity in time of war." Most Americans emerged from the war with a renewed faith in consensus, a belief in a common American identity and culture. But the war also sowed the seeds of cultural pluralism—a belief in many different American identities based on racial, gender, religious, and cultural differences—by promoting racial consciousness and by raising the expectations of groups that had been excluded from the nation's political and economic life. The clash between these two competing definitions of American identity—civic nationalism and cultural pluralism—remained an enduring feature of postwar American culture.

The war forged the foundation of postwar America, but it was an ambiguous legacy that rested on a paradox. The war, and the prosperity that came with it, stimulated America's appetite for a better life, producing an ever-widening cycle of expectations about the possibility of change. But the war also produced a celebration of American values that emphasized national unity, limited government, and traditional ideas abut race relations and gender roles. The tension between rising expectations and traditional attitudes would define the nature of social and political conflict in America for the remainder of the century.

SELECTED READINGS

▪ John Morton Blum's *V Was for Victory* (1976) is a colorful analysis of American culture and society during World War II. William O'Neill's *A Democracy at War* (1993) is a fascinating look at the impact of American political ideology on the mobilization of the country for war. David M. Kennedy's lucid *Freedom from Fear* (1999) provides the best overview of the war at home and abroad.

▪ I relied heavily on Gary Gerstle's *American Crucible* (2001) for his insight into American identity and the problem of race. David Kryder's *Divided Arsenal* (2000) explores the government's dealings with the race issue as a whole. Mario T. Garcia's *Mexican-Americans* (1989) examines the Hispanic experience during the war. Kenneth Townsend addresses the impact of the war on Native Americans in *At the Crossroads* (2000). Sherna Berger Gluck's *Rosie the Riveter Revisited* (1987) is a compelling oral history of women workers during World War II. Ronald Takaki's *Double Victory* (2000) is a general history of the wartime experiences of Asians in America.

▪ The starting point for understanding America's attitudes toward government is Gordon Wood, *The Radicalism of the American Revolution* (1992). Also useful in understanding the contradictions in American views of government are Joseph Nye, "In Government We Don't Trust," *Foreign Policy* 108 (September 22, 1997); James Morone, *The Democratic Wish: Popular Participation and the*

Limits of American Government (1990); Michael Kazin, *The Populist Persuasion* (1995); and Samuel P. Huntington, *American Politics: The Promise of Disharmony* (1981).

■ James T. Patterson's *Grand Expectations* is the finest synthesis of the gap between postwar hopes and reality. Also valuable is the very readable Robert J. Samuelson, *The Good Life and Its Discontents: The American Dream in the Age of Entitlement, 1945–1995* (1995). Steven M. Gillon analyzes the unintended consequences of reform in postwar America in *"That's Not What We Meant to Do"* (2000).

1

The Specter of Appeasement: The Cold War, 1945–1949

On February 22, 1946, the State Department's telex machine began clattering with a secret eight-thousand-word telegram from Moscow. The cable, written by George Frost Kennan, a forty-two-year-old Soviet specialist in the U.S. embassy, tried to explain Soviet aggression to puzzled officials in Washington. Since the end of World War II, U.S. policy makers had grown increasingly alarmed as the Soviets violated wartime agreements and tightened their military grip over Eastern Europe. Worried officials were all asking the same questions: What were Soviet intentions? And how should the United States respond to them? They turned to Kennan for the answers.

Kennan laid out a frightening picture of an aggressive Soviet Union intent upon world domination. The Soviets, he wired, were driven by a "neurotic view of world affairs" that emerged from an "instinctive Russian sense of insecurity." They compensated for their insecurity by going on the attack "in patient but deadly struggle for total destruction of rival power, never in compacts and compromises with it." Moscow, he suggested, was "highly sensitive to logic of force. For this reason it can easily withdraw—and usually does—when strong resistance is encountered at any point." According to Kennan's analysis, the Soviets were solely to blame for international tensions, negotiations and compromise had reached an impasse, and only military and economic pressure could tame the Russian bear.

Kennan's telegram caused a sensation in Washington. "Splendid analysis," exclaimed Secretary of State James

Byrnes. "Magnificent . . . to those of us here struggling with the problem," said H. Freeman Matthews, head of the State Department's Office of European Affairs. The following year Kennan published an expanded public version of the telegram in an article written under the pseudonym "Mr. X." The Soviets, he argued, saw the world divided into hostile capitalist and communist camps between which there could be no peace. He recommended a U.S. foreign policy based on the "long-term, patient but firm and vigilant containment of Russian expansive tendencies." From Kennan's essay a word emerged to characterize a new experiment in American foreign policy: *containment.*

PRIMARY SOURCE

1.1 | *The Sources of Soviet Conduct*

GEORGE KENNAN

George Kennan recognized the possibilities of serious ideological and geographic conflict between the United States and the Soviet Union in the postwar world. In July 1947 *Foreign Affairs* published an article by Kennan, which he had submitted under the pseudonym "Mr. X." The article outlined Kennan's suggestions for a new American policy toward the Soviets, the foreign policy that became known as containment.

The political personality of Soviet power as we know it today is the product of ideology and circumstances: Ideology inherited by the present Soviet leaders from the movement in which they had their political origin, and circumstances of the power which they have now exercised for nearly three decades in Russia. . . .

5   It is difficult to summarize the set of ideological concepts with which the Soviet leaders came into power. Marxian ideology . . . has always been in process of subtle evolution. . . . But the outstanding features of Communist thought as it existed in 1916 may perhaps be summarized as follows: (a) that the central factor in the life of man, the fact which determines the character of public life and the

10 "physiognomy of society," is the system by which material goods are produced and exchanged; (b) that the capitalist system of production is a nefarious one which inevitably leads to the exploitation of the working class by the capital-owning class and is incapable of developing adequately the economic resources of society or of distributing fairly the material goods produced by human labor;

15 (c) that capitalism contains the seeds of its own destruction and must, in view of the inability of the capital-owning class to adjust itself to economic change, result eventually and inescapably in a revolutionary transfer of power to the working

class; and (d) that imperialism, the final phase of capitalism, leads directly to war
20 and revolution. . . .

These considerations make Soviet diplomacy at once easier and more difficult to deal with than the diplomacy of individual aggressive leaders like
Napoleon and Hitler. On the one hand it is more sensitive to contrary
force. . . . On the other hand it cannot be easily defeated or discouraged by a sin-
25 gle victory on the part of its opponents. And the patient persistence by which it is
animated means that it can be effectively countered not by sporadic acts which
represent the momentary whims of democratic opinion but only by intelligent
long-range policies on the part of Russia's adversaries—policies no less steady in
their purpose, and no less variegated and resourceful in their application, than
30 those of the Soviet Union itself.

In these circumstances it is clear that the main element of any United States
policy toward the Soviet Union must be that of a long-term, patient but firm and
vigilant containment of Russian expansive tendencies. It is important to note,
however, that such a policy has nothing to do with outward histrionics: with
35 threats or blustering or superfluous gestures of outward "toughness." While the
Kremlin is basically flexible in its reaction to political realities, it is by no means
unamenable to considerations of prestige. Like almost any other government, it
can be placed by tactless and threatening gestures in a position where it cannot
afford to yield even though this might be dictated by its sense of realism. The
40 Russian leaders are keen judges of human psychology, and as such they are highly
conscious that loss of temper and of self-control is never a source of strength in
political affairs. They are quick to exploit such evidences of weakness. . . .

In the light of the above, it will be clearly seen that the Soviet pressure against
the free institutions of the Western world is something that can be contained by
45 the adroit and vigilant application of counter-force at a series of constantly shifting geographical and political points, corresponding to the shifts and maneuvers
of Soviet policy, but which cannot be charmed or talked out of existence. The
Russians look forward to a duel of infinite duration, and they see that already
they have scored great successes. . . .

50 It is clear that the United States cannot expect in the foreseeable future to
enjoy political intimacy with the Soviet regime. It must continue to regard the
Soviet Union as a rival, not a partner, in the political arena. It must continue to
expect that Soviet policies will reflect no abstract love of peace and stability, no
real faith in the possibility of a permanent happy coexistence of the Socialist and
55 capitalist worlds, but rather a cautious, persistent pressure toward the disruption
and weakening of all rival influence and rival power.   ■ ■ ■

The "Long Telegram" and the "Mr. X" article provided the ideological justification for a new "get-tough" approach with the Soviets. The strategy of containment fundamentally transformed American foreign policy. It ripped the United
States from its isolationist roots, imposed new international obligations on the
American people, and created a massive national security state. World War II had
reconfigured the international environment and America's place in it, but it

had failed to produce a corresponding change in American attitudes toward the world. Once the war ended, most American soldiers planned to return home and most policy makers planned to reduce the nation's military commitments abroad. Victory raised expectations of a peaceful postwar world shaped by American commerce and influenced by American values. But the Cold War confronted America with a paradox: How could the nation assume its new position of world power, and justify the dramatic enlargement of the national security state, while also being true to its democratic faith in limited government?

Roots of the Cold War

Who started the Cold War? This question has inspired passionate debate among historians. Some scholars place most of the blame on the Soviet Union, charging that its aggressive foreign policy was the logical outgrowth of an ideological commitment to world revolution. Other scholars contend that Russian aggression reflected a legitimate fear of American economic imperialism. In recent years historians studying the origins of the Cold War have emphasized that both nations shared responsibility for the conflict, though these same historians differ greatly on how much responsibility to assign each side. Rather than seeing the Cold War as the product of conspiracies hatched in the Kremlin or in Washington, post–Cold War historians stress how history, ideology, and national interest created serious misperceptions, limited the range of options on both sides, and made confrontation nearly inevitable.

The Cold War between the Soviet Union and the United States had its genesis in the past. In 1917 relations between the two nations plummeted into the deep freeze when the Bolsheviks seized control of the Russian government. Under V.I. Lenin, the Soviets pulled out of World War I, leaving the West to fight the Central Powers alone. More importantly, the Soviets committed the new state to the goal of world revolution and the destruction of capitalism. Communism challenged the basic tenets of the American dream: it threatened democratic government, supported state power over individual freedom, and cut off free markets.

The brutality of the Soviet regime added to American hostility. Joseph Stalin, who seized control of the Soviet Union following Lenin's death in 1924, consolidated his power through a series of bloody purges that killed nearly 3 million citizens. He initiated a massive effort to collectivize agriculture that led to the deaths of 14 million peasants. In 1939 after Stalin signed a prewar nonaggression treaty with Adolf Hitler, he sent troops pouring into Finland, Estonia, Latvia, and Lithuania. By then most Americans agreed with the *Wall Street Journal* that "the principal difference between Mr. Hitler and Mr. Stalin is the size of their respective mustaches."

Likewise, the Soviets had reason to distrust the United States. The rhetoric and actions of American policy makers appeared to support one of the principal teachings of Marxist-Leninist doctrine: the incompatibility of capitalism and communism. Western leaders, including President Woodrow Wilson, made no secret of their contempt for Lenin or their desire to see him ousted. Wilson's decision to send American troops on a confused mission to north Russia in 1918 confirmed the Soviets' suspicion of a western conspiracy to topple their government. Indeed, the United States did not extend diplomatic relations to the Soviets until 1933—sixteen years after the new government came to power.

Hitler's invasion of Russia in 1941 forced the United States and the Soviet Union into a brief alliance to defeat Germany. Wartime cooperation greatly improved the Soviet Union's image in America. Confronted with evidence that the Russian people were willing to fight for their government, many Americans jumped to the conclusion that the Soviet Union had suddenly become a democracy. In the best-selling book *Mission to Moscow* (1943), former Ambassador Joseph E. Davies proclaimed that "the Russia of Lenin and Trotsky—the Russia of the Bolshevik Revolution—no longer exists." *Life* magazine declared in 1943 that Russians "look like Americans, dress like Americans and think like Americans."

The war may have softened American public opinion, but it did little to ease the mistrust between leaders. Franklin Roosevelt, though hopeful about a postwar settlement, recognized that "a dictatorship as absolute as any . . . in the world" ruled Moscow. At the same time, Roosevelt's agreement with Winston Churchill in delaying a second front in Europe, and his refusal to share information about the development and testing of the atomic bomb, convinced Stalin that the western Allies could not be trusted.

As the war ground to an end, it became clear that the United States and Soviet Union possessed fundamentally different visions of the postwar world. Since the early days of the republic, Americans considered it their mission to spread their revolutionary ideology of democracy, individual rights, and open markets, but they differed on how to fulfill that mission. Some Americans advocated a policy of active intervention in the affairs of other nations, while others suggested that America should keep to itself and lead by example. In the nineteenth century America's sense of mission translated into a "manifest destiny" to expand to the Pacific and to civilize the Indians. During World War I Woodrow Wilson expanded the notion to include spreading democracy and liberal capitalism around the globe. President Roosevelt extended that vision into the postwar world in the Atlantic Charter (1941), which affirmed the right of all people to choose their own form of government and assured all nations equal access to trade and raw materials.

America's vision of universal rights clashed with Stalin's insistence on maintaining a Soviet "sphere of influence" in Eastern Europe. Since historians have not yet examined most of the documents in Soviet archives (opened for research in the 1990s after the Soviet Union's collapse), it is hard to know Stalin's intentions at the end of the war. Most of the available evidence, however, suggests that the Soviets had one overriding goal: to secure their borders from foreign invaders. Twice in the twentieth century German armies had swept over Russia like hungry locusts. In the most recent assault by Hitler's Germany, as many as 20 million Russians died. Six hundred thousand starved to death in the battle and siege of Leningrad alone. Along with the millions of deaths, the war caused enormous physical destruction. The Soviets, determined to head off another attack, insisted on defensible borders and friendly regimes on their western flank. As early as December 1941 Stalin asked the British and Americans to accept Soviet influence in Eastern Europe. "All we ask for," he told the British foreign minister, "is to restore our country to its former frontiers."

Europe emerged as the key battleground between these rival visions of the postwar world. The war had devastated Europe, weakened established powers, and created a power vacuum that the United States and the Soviet Union moved to fill. "The odor of death," recalled an American diplomat, "was everywhere." Fifty million people had perished. Great cities had been reduced to rubble. Tens of millions of people had no shelter. On the walls of Germany's Reichstag someone wrote, "Blessed are the dead, for their hands do not freeze." Everywhere farmlands had been despoiled, animals slaughtered. In Poland almost three-fourths of the horses and two-thirds of the cattle were gone.

The wretched conditions in Europe precipitated a historic shift in American foreign policy. The United States could not withdraw to its side of the Atlantic as it had after World War I. "We are for all time deisolated," wrote an observer. With the world's largest navy and air force, a monopoly on nuclear weapons, and a thriving economy, the United States seemed poised to fulfill its historic mission to spread the values of democracy and free enterprise to the rest of the world. "We are going forward to meet our destiny—which I think Almighty God intended us to have—and we are going to be the leaders," Harry Truman told his Missouri neighbors in 1945.

Yet despite the global military might of the United Sates, it was unable to control events in the Soviet sphere of influence. In 1945, with a 10-million-man army in control of most of Eastern Europe, the Soviets were in a position to enforce their will with force. Within weeks of the Yalta Conference, where Stalin had agreed to hold "free and unfettered elections," he installed a pro-Soviet puppet government in Poland. With Poland firmly in his grasp, Stalin moved to strangle the rest of Eastern Europe. He appointed a communist-led government in Rumania and reoccupied Latvia, Estonia, and Lithuania.

American officials viewed Soviet actions as a real threat to U.S. interests. No policy maker worried about a direct Soviet assault on the United States, and few believed the Soviets could muster the resources—military, financial, or psychological—for an invasion of Western Europe. The danger was that the Soviets would extend their influence politically by capitalizing on social and economic chaos in Europe, which created a fertile breeding ground for Soviet-dominated Communist parties. In France, Italy, and Finland, 20 percent of the public voted communist in elections after the war; in Belgium, Denmark, Norway, Holland, and Sweden, the figure was nearly 10 percent. If the trend continued, the Soviet Union could capture vital strategic resources and cut the United States off from potential markets.

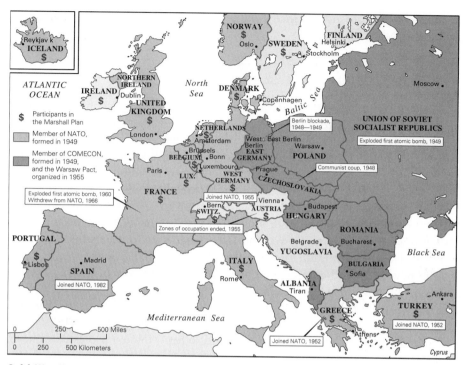

Cold War Europe   With the end of World War II, political ideologies divided Europe. While Eastern Europe received its orders from the Soviet Union, the United States worked to maintain noncommunist governments in the West by means of the Marshall Plan and the North Atlantic Treaty Organization.

The Soviet view of American foreign policy was almost a mirror image of Washington's fears about Moscow. In 1946 the Soviet ambassador to the United States, Nikolai Novikov, sent a memorandum to the Kremlin warning of America's imperialist impulses and urging Moscow to be vigilant in protecting its national security. Soviet ambassador Anatoly Dobrynin, who arrived in the United States a few years later, admitted that his mind "was clogged by the long years of Stalinism, by our own ideological blinders, by our deep-seated beliefs and perceptions, which led to our misconstruing all American intentions as offensive."

By 1945 the battle lines were clearly drawn. Stalin interpreted U.S. calls for free elections and democratic reform in Eastern Europe as part of a capitalist plot to surround the Soviet Union. The Americans viewed the Soviet Union's effort to consolidate its control over Eastern Europe as the first step of a larger plan of global conquest. "We can't do business with Stalin," Roosevelt complained three weeks before his death. "He has broken every one of the promises he made at Yalta." Moscow and Washington became ensnarled in a "security dilemma": each step taken by one side to enhance its security appeared an act of provocation to the other.

Harry Truman Takes Charge

When Harry Truman assumed the presidency in April 1945, he knew little about Roosevelt's growing hard line toward the Soviets. He learned quickly when he sought the recommendations of Roosevelt's advisers, most of whom favored a tougher policy toward the Soviets. "We had better have a showdown with them now than later," declared Secretary of the Navy James Forrestal.

A combative posture fit Truman's temperament. Impulsive and decisive, he lacked Roosevelt's talent for ambiguity and compromise. "When I say I'm going to do something, I do it," he once wrote. On his desk he displayed a sign: "The Buck Stops Here." Truman viewed the Yalta Accords as contracts between East and West. He was committed to seeing that Stalin honored the agreements.

The new president, emboldened by America's monopoly of atomic bombs and eager to show critics and the nation that he was in charge, matched Stalin's inflexibility with calls for self-determination and free elections in Eastern Europe. In office less than two weeks, he scolded Soviet foreign minister Vyacheslav Molotov for Soviet aggression in Poland. When Molotov protested, "I have never been talked to like that in my life," Truman retorted, "Carry out your agreements and you won't get talked to like that."

The Russians interpreted Truman's tongue-lashing as proof that the new administration had abandoned Roosevelt's policy of cooperation. When a bureaucratic blunder led to the abrupt termination of lend-lease shipments to the Soviets, a bitter Stalin complained that the United States was trying to use economic pressure to force political concessions. Despite reassurances that the decision resulted from a bureaucratic error, the incident likely reinforced the Soviet leaders' deep suspicion of the West. In May former Undersecretary of State Sumner Welles charged that "our Government now appears to the Russians as the spearhead of an apparent bloc of the western nations opposed to the Soviet Union."

Although Truman believed the United States needed to confront Soviet aggression, he also recognized that U.S.–Soviet cooperation was necessary to guarantee a lasting peace. In July 1945 Truman carried these conflicting goals to Potsdam, outside Berlin, for the final meeting of the Grand Alliance. Truman and Stalin squabbled over the sensitive issues of reparations and implementation of the Yalta Accords, but by the end of the meeting the leaders reached tentative agreements. The USSR would permit Anglo-American observers in Eastern Europe to monitor free elections and would withdraw its troops from oil-rich Azerbaijan in Iran. In return, the West reluctantly accepted Soviet occupation of eastern Germany and approved Russian annexation of eastern Poland. On the key issue of reparations, the leaders agreed that each power would extract reparations from its own zone in occupied Germany and that the western powers would transfer 15 percent of the capital equipment in their zones to the Soviet Union in return for food, coal, and other raw materials. Despite obvious differences, Truman left Potsdam hopeful that he could develop a working relationship with Stalin. "I can deal with Stalin," he wrote in his diary. "He is honest—but smart as hell."

The Fall of the Iron Curtain

Truman's optimism proved unfounded. With the Red Army occupying half of Europe at the end of the war, Stalin moved decisively to establish his control over Eastern Europe. Violating his pledge at Potsdam to allow free elections, Stalin tightened his grip over Poland, Bulgaria, Hungary, and Rumania. He denied western observers access to Eastern Europe and continued his occupation of Azerbaijan.

Soviet actions in Germany did little to ease U.S. suspicions. Yalta had divided Germany into four zones and Berlin into four sectors (U.S., USSR, British, and

Truman and Stalin at the Potsdam Conference In office only two months, Truman traveled to Potsdam, Germany, in July 1945 where he met with Winston Churchill and Joseph Stalin to finalize plans for the division of Germany. While at the conference, Truman received word that an atomic bomb had been successfully tested in New Mexico. Toward the end of the conference the Allies gave Japan an ultimatum—surrender or face absolute destruction. In this picture, Truman and Stalin visit on the balcony of Stalin's quarters during the conference.

French). The Soviets, wanting to punish Germany for its aggression, planned to impose a harsh peace. By April 1946 the Soviets had stripped their zone of industry and started to make heavy demands for factories, power plants, and tools from the American and British zones. The Truman administration feared that the Soviets would cripple Germany, produce widespread famine, and require a massive infusion of American resources. Truman halted reparations for the Soviets in May 1946. In September Secretary of State James Byrnes stated that the United States would no longer seek agreement with the Soviet Union on the future of Germany.

Disagreements over the control of nuclear technology further divided the former allies. In December 1945 the Big Three foreign ministers established an atomic energy commission to deal with the question of nuclear weapons in the postwar world order. In June 1946 the Americans proposed a plan that allowed the United States to retain its nuclear monopoly while the United Nations implemented a system of international control. In the most controversial part, the plan

Occupation Zones of Postwar Germany   At the Yalta Conference in early 1945, the Allied powers decided that after Germany surrendered unconditionally the Allies would dismember the enemy, dividing Germany and its capital, Berlin, into zones of occupation. After Germany's official surrender May 8, the Soviet Union, Great Britain, the United States, and France established control over their zones, with the hope of keeping their policies relatively uniform so that Germany could remain a single nation once disarmament and demilitarization took place. However, as the Cold War intensified, conflicting political and economic systems made compatible zone standards impossible. In December 1946, the American and British zones merged and in 1948 France agreed to join them, resulting in the Soviet Union's blockade of West Berlin.

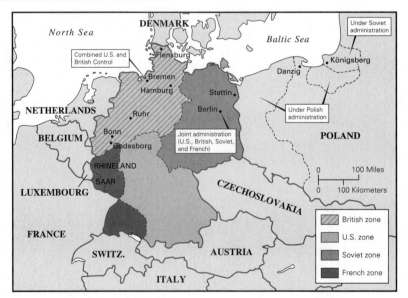

stipulated mandatory UN inspection of Soviet nuclear facilities—a condition the administration knew Stalin would never accept.

By the summer of 1946 neither Truman nor Stalin was interested in making a deal. Truman did not want to relinquish America's nuclear monopoly. We "should not under any circumstances," he declared, "throw away our gun until we are sure the rest of the world cannot arm against us." Stalin, for his part, wanted no place in an international scheme that would prevent development of the Soviet Union's own atomic bomb. Unable to reach agreement, the United States put aside plans for international cooperation. In 1946 Congress created the Atomic Energy Commission to control research and development of nuclear energy.

Both the Soviets and the Americans heightened tensions by engaging in a war of words. On February 9, 1946, Stalin delivered a rare public speech in which he

Atomic Detonation at Bikini Atoll, July 1, 1946 In December 1945, Truman issued a directive to the military, ordering them to determine the effect of atomic bombs on the nation's warships. The military chose Bikini Atoll, located in the Marshall Islands at some distance from regular air and sea routes, as the place to conduct their tests. After removing the 167 residents of the island, the navy moved more than 200 ships into the area, along with thousands of goats, pigs, and rats to determine the bomb's effect on living beings. The military conducted two tests, one detonation above the surface and one underwater.

explained the fundamental incompatibility of communism and capitalism. The American system, he stressed, needed war for raw materials and markets. The Second World War had been the most recent in a chain of conflicts that could be broken only when the world's economy made the transformation to communism. *Time* magazine concluded that the remarks were "the most warlike pronouncement uttered by any top-rank statesman" since the war had ended.

A few weeks later Winston Churchill returned fire. Speaking in March 1946 in Fulton, Missouri, with Truman on the platform, the former prime minister declared of Europe that "from Stettin in the Baltic to Trieste in the Adriatic, an iron curtain has descended across the Continent." To counter this threat, he called for an association of English-speaking peoples to remain vigilant at all times.

Polls suggested that the American public agreed with Churchill's assessment. Shortly after the speech a survey showed that 60 percent of the public believed that the United States was being "too soft" on the Russians. Soviet actions and hardening public attitudes pushed many isolationists into the internationalist camp. Most conservatives, distrusting European leaders and fearing that active involvement in world affairs would enlarge presidential power, had hoped to resurrect traditional isolationist sentiment after the war. By 1946, however, the threat of Soviet expansion forced many to reconsider their views. "I am more than ever convinced," said powerful Republican Senator Arthur Vandenberg of Michigan, "that communism is on the march on a world-wide scale which only America can stop." For Vandenberg, fear of Soviet domination outweighed deeply held ideas about American self-reliance.

Americans supported a tougher line with the Soviets, but they remained deeply ambivalent about assuming the responsibility of world power. Many of the same people who feared Soviet aggression also clamored for the president to bring home American soldiers and to convert to a peacetime economy. Congress delivered this contradictory message directly to the president. Legislators eager to reestablish their control over foreign policy called on Truman "to get tough with Russia." Yet they also pushed for lower taxes and for a rapid demobilization of the armed forces. By mid-1946 the total number of American forces in active duty had dropped from 12 million at the end of the war to less than 3 million.

PRIMARY SOURCE

1.2 | *The Last Chance for Peace*

HENRY WALLACE

President Truman's postwar get-tough policy with the Soviet Union troubled many liberals, such as Secretary of Commerce Henry Wallace. In July 1946 Wallace sent Truman a twelve-page, single-spaced letter expressing his concern and hope that a continuation of Roosevelt's wartime cooperation with Stalin was still possible.

I should list the factors which make for Russian distrust of the United States and of the Western world as follows. The first is Russian history, which we must take into account because it is the setting in which Russians see all actions and policies of the rest of the world. Russian history for over a thousand years has
5 been a succession of attempts, often unsuccessful, to resist invasion and conquest. . . . The Russians, therefore, obviously see themselves as fighting for their existence in a hostile world.

Second, it follows that to the Russians all of the defense and security measures of the Western powers seem to have an aggressive intent. Our actions to expand
10 our military security system . . . appear to them as going far beyond the requirements of defense. I think we might feel the same if the United States were the only capitalistic country in the world, and the principal socialistic countries were creating a level of armed strength far exceeding anything in their previous history.

Finally, our resistance to her attempts to obtain warm-water ports and her
15 own security system in the form of "friendly" neighboring states seems, from the Russian point of view, to clinch the case. After twenty-five years of isolation and after having achieved the status of a major power, Russia believes that she is entitled to recognition of her new status. Our interest in establishing democracy in Eastern Europe, where democracy by and large has never existed, seems to her an
20 attempt to reestablish the encirclement of unfriendly neighbors which was created after the last war, and which might serve as a springboard of still another effort to destroy her.

If this analysis is correct, and there is ample evidence to support it, the action to improve the situation is clearly indicated. The fundamental objective of such
25 action should be to allay any reasonable Russian grounds for fear, suspicion and distrust. . . .

We should make an effort to counteract the irrational fear of Russia which is being systematically built up in the American people by certain individuals and publications. The slogan that communism and capitalism, regimentation and
30 democracy, cannot continue to exist in the same world is, from a historical point of view, pure propaganda. . . .

. . . We are by far the most powerful nation in the world, the only Allied nation which came out of the war without devastation and much stronger than before the war. Any talk on our part about the need for strengthening our
35 defenses further is bound to appear hypocritical to other nations. . . .   ■ ■ ■

Containing Communism: The Truman Doctrine and the Marshall Plan

Reflecting his growing impatience with the Russians and frustration with his own government's response to Cold War pressures, Truman replaced Secretary of State James Byrnes with General George C. Marshall in January 1947. While Byrnes was a largely ineffectual and absent leader, Marshall, who served as army chief of staff during the war, had earned a well-deserved reputation as a distinguished military officer and skilled manager. "He is the great one of the age,"

Truman claimed. As secretary of state, Marshall presided over the process that transformed America's approach to the world.

For advice Marshall turned to two State Department professionals who had long harbored deep suspicions of the Soviets: Undersecretary of State Dean Acheson and Moscow diplomat George Kennan. An elegant and arrogant man, Acheson rejected suggestions that morality should drive American policy; he instead stressed that American power was essential to peace. By 1946 Acheson was urging Truman to employ the full range of American power—economic, military, and diplomatic—to tame the Soviet Union. "I think it is a mistake to believe that you can, at any time, sit down with the Russians and solve questions," he told the Senate in 1947, echoing many of the ideas Kennan had espoused in his Long Telegram.

By 1947 a communist insurgency was battling the right-wing monarchy in Greece. Stalin was also pressuring Turkey to share control of the strategic Dardanelles Strait, the waterway linking the Black Sea and the Mediterranean. In February 1947 the British ambassador informed the U.S. State Department that his country could no longer afford to support Greece and Turkey with economic and military aid. The Truman administration, fearful that the Soviet-backed insurgents might gain the upper hand, wanted to fill the vacuum. But the administration first needed to overcome deep-seated American fears of getting involved in European affairs. Senator Vandenberg suggested that the administration build support by "scaring hell out of the country."

The administration accepted the challenge. On March 12, 1947, Truman stood before a joint session of Congress to make his case for American aid to Greece and Turkey. "I believe that it must be the policy of the United States to support free peoples who are resisting attempted subjugation by armed minorities or by outside pressures," he declared. The future of the "free world," he insisted, rested in America's hands. After setting the stage, Truman requested that Congress appropriate $400 million for Greek and Turkish military and economic aid. The American people responded by rallying around the cause of freedom. Public opinion strongly supported the request, and Truman's poll ratings leaped 10 points.

PRIMARY SOURCE

1.3 | *The Truman Doctrine*

HARRY TRUMAN

Looking to hinder the growth of Soviet-supported insurgency in Greece and Turkey, President Truman wanted to provide American military and economic aid, but many Americans wanted to stay out of European affairs. To garner support, Truman spoke before a joint session of Congress on March 12, 1947, and explained why Americans should assist the free peoples of the world.

Mr. President, Mr. Speaker, Members of the Congress of the United States:

The gravity of the situation which confronts the world today necessitates my appearance before a joint session of the Congress. The foreign policy and the national security of this country are involved.

5   One aspect of the present situation, which I wish to present to you at this time for your consideration and decision, concerns Greece and Turkey.

The United States has received from the Greek Government an urgent appeal for financial and economic assistance. Preliminary reports from the American Economic Mission now in Greece and reports from the American Ambassador in 10 Greece corroborate the statement of the Greek Government that assistance is imperative if Greece is to survive as a free nation.

I do not believe that the American people and the Congress wish to turn a deaf ear to the appeal of the Greek Government. . . .

The very existence of the Greek state is today threatened by the terrorist activ-15 ities of several thousand armed men, led by Communists, who defy the government's authority at a number of points, particularly along the northern boundaries. A Commission appointed by the United Nations Security Council is at present investigating disturbed conditions in northern Greece and alleged border violations along the frontier between Greece on the one hand and Albania, Bul-20 garia, and Yugoslavia on the other.

Meanwhile, the Greek Government is unable to cope with the situation. The Greek army is small and poorly equipped. It needs supplies and equipment if it is to restore the authority of the government throughout Greek territory. Greece must have assistance if it is to become a self-supporting and self-respecting 25 democracy.

The United States must supply that assistance. We have already extended to Greece certain types of relief and economic aid but these are inadequate.

There is no other country to which democratic Greece can turn.

No other nation is willing and able to provide the necessary support for a 30 democratic Greek government. . . .

Greece's neighbor, Turkey, also deserves our attention.

The future of Turkey as an independent and economically sound state is clearly no less important to the freedom-loving peoples of the world than the future of Greece. The circumstances in which Turkey finds itself today are con-35 siderably different from those of Greece. Turkey has been spared the disasters that have beset Greece. And during the war, the United States and Great Britain furnished Turkey with material aid.

Nevertheless, Turkey now needs our support.

Since the war Turkey has sought financial assistance from Great Britain and 40 the United States for the purpose of effecting that modernization necessary for the maintenance of its national integrity.

That integrity is essential to the preservation of order in the Middle East. . . .

At the present moment in world history nearly every nation must choose 45 between alternative ways of life. The choice is too often not a free one.

One way of life is based upon the will of the majority, and is distinguished by free institutions, representative government, free elections, guarantees of individual liberty, freedom of speech and religion, and freedom from political oppression.

The second way of life is based upon the will of a minority forcibly imposed
50 upon the majority. It relies upon terror and oppression, a controlled press and radio, fixed elections, and the suppression of personal freedoms.

I believe that it must be the policy of the United States to support free peoples who are resisting attempted subjugation by armed minorities or by outside pressures.

55 I believe that we must assist free peoples to work out their own destinies in their own way.

I believe that our help should be primarily through economic and financial aid which is essential to economic stability and orderly political processes.

The world is not static, and the status quo is not sacred. But we cannot allow
60 changes in the status quo in violation of the Charter of the United Nations by such methods as coercion, or by such subterfuges as political infiltration. In helping free and independent nations to maintain their freedom, the United States will be giving effect to the principles of the Charter of the United Nations.

It is necessary only to glance at a map to realize that the survival and integrity
65 of the Greek nation are of grave importance in a much wider situation. If Greece should fall under the control of an armed minority, the effect upon its neighbor, Turkey, would be immediate and serious. Confusion and disorder might well spread throughout the entire Middle East.

Moreover, the disappearance of Greece as an independent state would have a
70 profound effect upon those countries in Europe whose peoples are struggling against great difficulties to maintain their freedoms and their independence while they repair the damages of war.

It would be an unspeakable tragedy if these countries, which have struggled so long against overwhelming odds, should lose that victory for which they sacri-
75 ficed so much. Collapse of free institutions and loss of independence would be disastrous not only for them but for the world. Discouragement and possibly failure would quickly be the lot of neighboring peoples striving to maintain their freedom and independence.

Should we fail to aid Greece and Turkey in this fateful hour, the effect will be
80 far reaching to the West as well as to the East.

We must take immediate and resolute action. . . .

If we falter in our leadership, we may endanger the peace of the world—and we shall surely endanger the welfare of our own nation.

Great responsibilities have been placed upon us by the swift movement of
85 events.

I am confident that the Congress will face these responsibilities squarely.   ■ ■ ■

The Truman Doctrine articulated before Congress represented a turning point in American foreign policy. By rooting America's response to a local conflict in traditional rhetoric of good and evil, free and unfree, Truman hoped to prepare the American people for their responsibility as a world power. Presidential aide Clark Clifford called it "the opening gun in a campaign to bring the people up to [the] realization that the war isn't over by any means." Truman's announcement also highlighted the tension between public moralism and private realism that often characterized postwar foreign policy. In an effort to rally the public to assume a more active role in the world, policy makers occasionally exaggerated the nature of the threat.

The administration realized that military assistance might deter the Soviets in Greece and Turkey, but it would not save war-torn Western Europe from economic disaster. Europe, Churchill declared, had become "a rubble heap, a charnel house, a breeding ground of pestilence and hate." To challenge the strength of Communist parties and Soviet influence, administration officials moved to shore up Europe's battered economy.

On June 5, 1947, Secretary of State Marshall offered his prescription for recovery. He chose the Harvard University commencement ceremony to announce a bold new plan of economic assistance to Europe. Marshall explained that the aid program was "directed not against any country or doctrine but against hunger, poverty, desperation, and chaos." Marshall invited the participation of any country, including the Soviet Union, that was "willing to assist in the task of recovery." But Truman realized that Stalin would never accept a plan that required him to share vital economic information with the United States while western leaders controlled how funds would be distributed. In December 1947 Truman submitted the plan to Congress, with a recommendation that the United States spend $17 billion over four years.

At first, congressional leaders were cool to the idea. Critics condemned the plan as "a bold Socialist blueprint." "I've been out on the hustings, and I know, the people don't like it," said House Republican leader Charles Halleck of Indiana. Vandenberg led the bipartisan supporters, calling the plan a "calculated risk" to "help stop World War III before it starts." While Congress held hearings during the fall, Europe sank deeper into its economic abyss. England announced it was cutting individual meat rations to twenty cents' worth per week.

Inadvertently, the Soviet Union provided the Marshall Plan with the boost it needed. During the summer of 1947 Stalin established the Communist Information Bureau (Cominform) to coordinate communist party activity around the globe. The Cominform tightened Stalin's control in the Eastern bloc and within Russia at the same time that it called upon communists in the underdeveloped world to accelerate "their struggle" for liberation. A U.S. diplomat called the creation of the Cominform "a declaration of political and economic war against the U.S. and everything the U.S. stands for in world affairs."

In February 1948 communists staged a coup in Czechoslovakia, overthrowing a freely elected coalition government. Two weeks later that government's popular foreign minister, Jan Masaryk, died in a fall from a bathroom window. The Soviets said it was suicide; almost everyone else said it was murder. Western leaders interpreted the coup as part of an aggressive Soviet plan to conquer Europe before it could be revived. According to Kennan, a "real war scare" swept

Washington. Once again, top policy makers were aware that the hysteria was exaggerated and war was unlikely. But they were not above using fear to help sell their new approach to the Soviets. Sometimes, said Dean Acheson, "it is necessary to make things clearer than the truth."

Opposition to the Marshall Plan wilted in the heated atmosphere. On April 2 the House approved the plan by the lopsided vote of 318 to 75. The Senate roared its approval by an overwhelming voice vote. In April the SS *John H. Quick* sailed from its port in Galveston, Texas, with 19,000 tons of wheat for starving Europeans. Within months it was joined by 150 ships carrying food and fuel to Europe every day. Between 1948 and 1951 American aid to Europe amounted to a staggering $12.5 billion. As a program to revitalize Europe's troubled economy, the Marshall Plan was a dramatic success. Thanks in part to the plan, European industrial production increased 200 percent between 1948 and 1952. Perhaps the Marshall Plan's greatest export was hope. British foreign secretary Ernest Bevin called the plan "a lifeline to a sinking man."

The Marshall Plan added to the mutual misperception that contributed to the Cold War. The plan reassured America's European allies but worried Stalin, who was convinced that the United States designed the aid program to lure Eastern European nations out of the Soviet orbit and to rebuild Germany. In response, the Kremlin cracked down on dissent in Poland, Rumania, and Bulgaria; encouraged the coup in Czechoslovakia; and blockaded Berlin. "For Stalin," concluded two scholars familiar with new archival information in Moscow and Eastern Europe, "the Marshall Plan was a watershed."

The Soviet moves in turn magnified the sense of threat in Washington, leading to a massive expansion of federal power in the traditionally anti-statist United States. In 1947 Congress institutionalized the Cold War with passage of the National Security Act. This legislation created the skeleton of what would become an overpowering national security apparatus. The act expanded executive power by centralizing previously dispersed responsibilities in the White House. It established the Department of Defense to oversee all branches of the armed services and formed the Joint Chiefs of Staff, which included the generals of the three services and the marines. The act also created the National Security Council (NSC), a cabinet-level body to coordinate military and foreign policy for the president. Led by the president, the NSC included the head of the Joint Chiefs of Staff, the secretaries of state and defense, the vice president, and any other members the president chose to appoint. The act also created the Central Intelligence Agency, which carried out espionage operations directly under the authority of the NSC. Following passage of the act, a journalist noted an ominous trend toward "militarization of [the] government and of the American state of mind." By blurring the line between peace and war, the Cold War led the government to adopt a constant state of readiness.

In March 1948 Truman wrote his daughter, Margaret, "We are faced with exactly the same situation with which Britain and France were faced in 1938–39

The Marshall Plan at Work in Austria In the war's aftermath, the United States sent $17 billion to Europe in the form of money and supplies to bolster relief and rebuilding efforts. The European landscape and economy were devastated, creating a dangerous political and social vacuum that the United States feared the Soviet Union might exploit. Secretary of State George Marshall and other policy makers believed that massive aid would enable European nations to resist communism and would build loyalty to the United States among the European people. They certainly won a friend in this little boy, who is obviously thrilled with his new shoes, brought by American planes and distributed by Red Cross workers. *(American Red Cross, Falls Church, Va.)*

with Hitler. Things look black. A decision will have to be made. I am going to make it. . . . Our present policy for world peace has thus settled into the formula of reconstruction plus containment."

Mounting Tensions, Precarious Solutions

In June 1948 the West consolidated its hold on Germany by fusing the French zone with the British and American areas, thereby creating "Trizonia," which contained Germany's richest industrial resources and a population of 50 million. The western powers also invited the Germans to create a new government in West Germany and initiated financial reforms that produced a remarkable economic revival.

The Russians responded on June 24 to this unilateral action by the western powers by clamping a tight blockade around West Berlin, which lay 110 miles within the Soviet occupation zone. The western powers had failed to write clear arrangements for land access to Berlin into their agreement with the Soviets. Taking advantage of the legal confusion, the Soviets blocked all surface

Truman and His National Security Advisers Events such as the detonation of the Soviet Union's first atomic bomb and the communist victory in China made it clear to the Truman administration in 1949 that the United States needed a more well-defined and coordinated national security policy. Several of the developers of this policy are seen with President Truman in this photograph, taken on July 13, 1951. They are Secretary of State Dean Acheson, Mutual Security Administrator Averell Harriman, and Secretary of Defense George Marshall.

transportation into West Berlin, depriving some 2.5 million people of food and fuel.

Since the Soviets possessed an overwhelming military advantage in Germany—175 fighting divisions compared with 2⅓ American divisions—many Pentagon officials advised Truman to concede to the Soviet demands and withdraw from Berlin. Admiral William D. Leahy, chairman of the Joint Chiefs of Staff, wrote in his diary: "American military position in Berlin is hopeless. . . . It would be advantageous to United States prospects to withdraw from Berlin." But General Lucius D. Clay, commander of U.S. occupation forces in Europe, recommended confrontation, calling for a 200-truck convoy escorted by tanks and infantry. "It is our view," he wrote of the Soviets, "that they are bluffing and that their hand can and should be called now."

Truman and Secretary of State Marshall rejected both options. If the United States retreated from Berlin, Marshall warned, it would mean the "failure of the rest of our European policy." But an effort to break the blockade might lead to armed confrontation, and Truman searched for a safer response that would demonstrate American resolve. His answer was a massive airlift operation. For the next 324 days, American and British planes dropped 2.5 million tons of provisions to sustain the 10,000 troops and the 2 million civilians in Berlin. Truman threatened publicly to use "the bomb" if the Soviets shot down the relief planes. He wrote in his diary that "we are very close to war." On May 12, 1949, however, the Russians accepted defeat and ended the blockade.

The Berlin crisis further catalyzed western leaders to present a unified front to the Soviets. Already Great Britain, France, Belgium, the Netherlands, and Luxembourg had signed the Brussels Treaty (1948), which provided for collective self-defense. In January 1949 Truman proposed expanding the alliance by committing the United States to the defense of Europe. In April he pledged American involvement in the North Atlantic Treaty Organization (NATO), a mutual-defense pact that bound its twelve signatories to fight against aggression. Article 5 provided "that an armed attack against one or more . . . shall be considered an attack against them all."

The treaty still needed Senate approval, and Truman anticipated a heated debate. Since George Washington first warned against "entangling alliances" with Europe, the United States had avoided peacetime involvement in collective security agreements with other countries. But NATO supporters, led by Vandenberg, argued that the Soviet threat required the country to develop a new approach to the world. On July 21, 1949, in a clear indication of the shift in American thinking from isolationism to internationalism, the Senate approved the NATO treaty by a wide 82-13 margin. In 1950 Truman appointed General Dwight D. Eisenhower to serve as NATO supreme commander and ordered four American divisions stationed in Europe.

While challenging the Soviets claim to a sphere of influence in Europe, the United States consolidated its own sphere in the Western Hemisphere. In 1947 in the Rio Treaty, U.S. and Latin American signatories agreed that "any armed attack by any state against an American state shall be considered an attack against all the American states." The following year North and Latin American countries created the Organization of American States.

Despite these professions of unity, however, U.S. relations with Latin America were based on suspicion. Most Latin American countries remained politically unstable, suffering from wide gaps between rich and poor and governed by repressive military dictatorships. For now, American policy makers were more concerned about preventing Soviet military influence than offering economic assistance.

The Cold War also shaped American policy in the Middle East. After World War II many Jews who had survived Nazi concentration camps resettled in British-controlled Palestine. In 1947 the British, weakened by World War II, turned over control of Palestine to the United Nations, which voted to partition the region into separate Jewish and Arab states. The president's military advisers, including Secretary of State Marshall and Secretary of Defense Forrestal, feared that recognition of the Jewish state of Israel would anger Arab oil-producing nations. On an emotional level, however, the president empathized with the suffering of Jews during World War II. And as a practical matter, since Stalin had already announced his support for Israel, Truman worried about the possibility of a close Soviet-Israel relationship that would exclude the United States. Truman also respected the political clout of Jewish voters at home. "In all of my political experience," Truman remarked during the presidential campaign of 1948, "I don't ever recall the Arab vote swinging a close election." On May 14, 1948, Israel declared its independence. Within a few hours the United States recognized the new state.

The Soviets matched all these western initiatives by intensifying their domination of Eastern Europe. In October 1949 Stalin created a separate government in East Germany, the German Democratic Republic. Moscow tightened its economic grip on Eastern Europe by sponsoring the Council for Mutual Economic Assistance (1949) and its military grasp by forming the Warsaw Pact (1955). The Soviets poured massive aid into Poland, Czechoslovakia, and Bulgaria to accelerate industrialization and increase Soviet control. The only exception to Soviet domination was Yugoslavia, which stubbornly resisted Soviet influence and gradually managed to develop as an independent socialist state.

Debating Containment

The adoption of the containment policy thrust upon the United States political and military responsibilities as a "world policeman" that went far beyond anything ever contemplated by the American people. It also raised new and troubling questions that went to the heart of American identity. The Cold War, and the need for an expanded military, presented the American people with a conundrum: Could the nation adapt to the demands of total war without losing its democratic identity? Or, as the *New York Times* asked in 1947, "how can we prepare for total war without becoming a 'garrison state' and destroying the very qualities and virtues and principles we originally set out to save?"

Many conservatives believed it was impossible to reconcile the administration's new national security goals with the nation's democratic traditions. The new military bureaucracy, built on the foundation of the New Deal's expansion of federal power, threatened to regiment American life and take the nation down the same road as Nazi Germany. Military planners would undermine civilian control of government. "We are having our initial experience with the garrison state," complained a congressman, "in which the conduct of our lives is made secondary to the demands of the Military Establishment." Concentration of power in the hands of the executive would inevitably lead to higher levels of taxation and an erosion of the traditional American commitment to fiscal responsibility and a balanced budget. "We must not let our fear of Communism blind us to the danger of military domination," complained a Republican congressman. A senator expressed similar sentiments, saying, "We can wipe out all traces of communism in the world, but if we lose the Constitution we are doomed to slavery."

Many conservatives feared that an expansive foreign policy would distort national and international priorities. Powerful Republican senator Robert Taft of Ohio observed that the traditional purpose of U.S. involvement in the world was "to maintain the liberty of our people" rather than "reform the entire world or spread sweetness and light and economic prosperity to peoples who have lived and worked out their own salvation for centuries." The country should expand the national security state only "as far toward preparing for war as we can go in time of peace without weakening ourselves . . . and destroying forever the very liberty which war is designed to protect."

A few voices on the Left joined the chorus of criticism, though often for different reasons. In a series of newspaper columns, later published in book form as *The Cold War*, the journalist Walter Lippmann charged that containment would increase executive power at the expense of the other branches of government and divert energy and resources away from domestic needs. The policy of containment, he wrote, "can be implemented only by recruiting, subsidizing and supporting a heterogeneous array of satellites, clients, dependents, and puppets." Most of all, he argued, containment would militarize American foreign policy and force the United States to support corrupt dictators. Unlike many conservatives, however, Lippmann supported the administration's effort to strengthen the western alliance and criticized conservatives as outdated isolationists.

The administration argued that a new era of total war required the country to take unprecedented steps to defend its interests. "Total war" could not be confined to the battlefield; it required the full participation of the home front as well. All of the nation's resources had to be mobilized to defeat the enemy, blurring the line between civilian and military. Every citizen was a soldier, responsible for defending the American way of life. In an age of total war Americans had to abandon traditional objections to a standing army and enlarged federal power. "Wars are no longer fought solely by armed forces," explained navy admiral Ernest J. King. "Directly or indirectly, the whole citizenry and the entire resources of the nation go to war."

Since the United States faced a enemy possessing a "messianic" ideology, it needed to be prepared to fight at any time. America had assumed the role of leader of the free world. In urging the American people to fight against communism, Kennan said that "Providence" had "made their entire security as a nation dependent on their pulling themselves together and accepting the responsibilities of moral and political leadership that history plainly intended them to bear."

Supporters of containment won the argument by claiming that Americans faced a new situation that required unprecedented steps. "A drastic departure from the anti-militaristic tradition of our peace-loving America is now necessary," argued a congressman. "We cannot have business as usual," agreed another, especially when the "free world" was "watching mighty America today and wondering if she has the determination to meet the challenge of the times." The greatest threat to American liberty came not from the expansion of state power produced by national security needs, but from the threat from abroad. "The loss of Europe, Asia, and Africa," claimed Democratic senator Paul Douglas of Illinois, "would bring an irresistible drive toward isolationism in the United States and the consequent erection of a garrison state. The effort to build an unconquerable bastion while surrounded by a Communist world would bring in its train the suppression of many of our precious liberties."

SELECTED READINGS

■ Walter LaFeber's *America, Russia, and the Cold War* (9th ed., 2001) provides a good overview of Cold War–era politics, while Stephen Ambrose and Douglas Brinkley's *Rise to Globalism* (8th ed., 1997) focuses on Cold War foreign policy. Melvyn Leffler's *A Preponderance of Power* (1992) is the most comprehensive history of the early Cold War, with John L. Gaddis providing the most up-to-date synthesis in *We Now Know* (1997). The Cold War from the Soviet Union's perspective, using recently declassified materials, is contained in *Inside the Kremlin's Cold War* (1996), by Vladislav Zubok and Constantine Pleshakov.

■ Bernard Weisberger's *Cold War, Cold Peace* (1984) is a good standard account of the immediate postwar period. John L. Gaddis, in his Bancroft Prize–winning book, *The United States and the Origins of the Cold War* (1990), illuminates the many factors—domestic, political, bureaucratic—that influenced American foreign policy regarding the Soviet Union. In *Debating the Origins of the Cold War* (2002), Ralph Levering examines the beginnings of the conflict from both the Soviet and American perspectives. Lloyd C. Garner's *Architects of Illusion* (1970) has biographical vignettes of America's leading foreign policy makers and explores mistakes that contributed to the Cold War.

■ In *The Specter of Communism* (1994), editors Melvyn Leffler and Eric Foner have collected essays that discuss the inconsistent policy of both nations and their interaction, from the Bolshevik Revolution to 1953, as each sought to protect its spheres of influence and ideology. Another collection of essays, *Victory in Europe 1945* (2000), edited by Arnold Offner and Theodore Wilson, explores the difficult transition from war to peace, while James Gormly's *From Potsdam to Cold War* (1990) retraces the diplomacy pursued by the Big Three in their last meeting together.

■ George Mazuzan and J. Samuel Walker collected a wealth of information for their book on nuclear regulation and the Atomic Energy Commission, *Controlling the Atom* (1985). The part played by the Soviet military in maintaining control of the Eastern bloc nations is the focus of Christopher Jones's *Soviet Influence in Eastern Europe* (1981), and Peter Grose's *Operation Rollback* (2000) discusses America's secret programs to encourage resistance behind the Iron Curtain.

- Lawrence Wittner focuses on the Greek civil war in *American Intervention in Greece* (1982). Howard Jones examines the reasons for the development of the Truman Doctrine, its application in the Greek civil war, and its long-lasting effect on American foreign policy in *A New Kind of War* (1989). Richard Freeland's *The Truman Doctrine and the Origins of McCarthyism* (1972) links Truman's policies with the later Red Scare. Michael Hogan's *The Marshall Plan* (1987) is a good one-volume history of that ambitious initiative. Imanuel Wexler's *The Marshall Plan Revisited* (1983) offers a more critical analysis of the plan. The development of the Marshall Plan is seen through the life of one of its creators, Will Clayton, in Gregory Fossedal's *Our Finest Hour* (1993). Timothy P. Ireland examines the formation of NATO in *Creating the Entangling Alliance* (1981). A 1989 conference at the Truman Library on the birth of NATO and its first decade of operation served as the basis for editors Francis Heller and John Gillingham's work *NATO* (1992). Joyce Kolko and Gabriel Kolko's *The Limits of Power* (1972) discusses how the complexity of foreign affairs stymied American attempts to dictate world politics.

- Bruce R. Kuniholm's *The Origins of the Cold War in the Near East* (1980) has good material on the formation of Israel, as does Linda Jacobs Altman's *The Creation of Israel* (1998). The division of Germany is the subject of Carolyn Eisenberg's *Drawing the Line* (1996), while W. R. Smyser's *From Yalta to Berlin* (2000) traces the history of the German question from the division to the collapse of communism. A detailed history of the Berlin blockade can be found in Thomas Parrish's *Berlin in the Balance* (1998). The history of the National Security Council from its inception by Truman as a channel for collective advice to its massive expansion as an institution that dictates foreign policy can be found in John Prados's *Keeper of the Keys* (1991).

- George Kennan's *American Diplomacy* (exp. ed., 1985) and Dean Acheson's *Present at the Creation* (1970) offer intriguing insider accounts of the early Cold War, while John L. Harper compares these two men to FDR in *American Visions of Europe* (1994). Walter Isaacson and Evan Thomas's *The Wise Men* (1986) is a study of Truman's advisers and their impact on American foreign policy.

2

In the Shadow
of FDR

It was nearly 2:00 A.M. before Harry Truman and his running mate, Alben Barkley, made their way to the podium at the Democratic National Convention in Philadelphia. An accidental president, Truman presided over a deeply divided party convinced that it had no chance of defeating the Republicans in November. "We are here to honor the honored dead," a Democratic official declared, reflecting on the party's chances in the 1948 presidential contest. Wearing a double-breasted white suit and black tie, Truman nevertheless appeared cool and confident despite the oppressive July heat. He understood the deep sense of loyalty many Americans felt toward Franklin Roosevelt and the New Deal. Truman's task was to convince his party, and the countless Americans who were seeing him on television for the first time, that he was the true heir of the Roosevelt legacy.

Instead of highlighting his own agenda, Truman attacked the hypocrisy of a Republican Party that talked like FDR but acted like Herbert Hoover. "The Republican platform is for extending and increasing social security benefits. . . . I wonder if they think they can fool the people of the United States with such poppycock as that," he thundered. Truman decided to call his opponents' bluff. "On the 26th day of July, which out in Missouri we call 'Turnip Day,' I am going to call Congress back and ask them to pass laws to halt rising prices, to meet the housing crisis—which they say they are for in their platform." How the Republican Congress responded, he said, "will be the test," and "the American people . . . will decide on the record." The speech electrified convention delegates and put the Republicans on the defensive—which is where they would stay through election day.

Truman managed to pull together the New Deal coalition to score a surprising victory in the 1948 election. But the icy winds of the Cold War froze Truman's drive to expand Roosevelt's agenda. Many liberals hoped that the postwar world would see a revival of the New Deal at home. But a host of new problems—the emerging Cold War, labor unrest, inflation, and a powerful conservative coalition in Congress—dimmed many of these aspirations. These new issues divided the once-powerful Democratic coalition, which had carried Roosevelt to four successive victories. In an effort to institutionalize and expand the New Deal, Truman confronted the central paradox of American postwar politics: Americans had come to expect the president to offer solutions to pressing social problems, but they also feared the expansion of federal power. During the 1948 campaign Truman successfully managed the tension between expectations of government and fear of Washington by tying his administration to the legacy of Roosevelt. After the election, however, growing fear of the Cold War made Truman's balancing act even more precarious.

From War to Peace

"We are completely unprepared for a Japanese collapse," the journalist I. F. Stone wrote a few weeks before the war ended, "and unless we act quickly and wisely [we] may face an economic collapse ourselves." As Stone predicted, the sudden end of the war sent shock waves through the American economy. Within a month the government canceled $35 billion in war contracts and slashed war-related production by 60 percent. The cuts produced massive layoffs. Within ten days of the Japanese surrender 2.7 million men and women lost their jobs. Economists predicted that more than 10 million Americans would be thrown out of work by peace.

At the same time, a flood of servicemen returned home looking for civilian jobs. Both Roosevelt and Truman planned to maintain a strong American military presence overseas at the end of the war. General George Marshall warned of the need for "strong American forces abroad to protect the fruits of victory." The public, however, demanded immediate demobilization. "We are getting 10,000 letters a day" about the slow pace of demobilization, complained a senator. Liberals and organized labor formed a "Bring the Boys Home by Christmas" campaign that flooded the White House with sixty thousand postcards in one day. An Oklahoma constituent made his threat explicit in a letter to his representative: "You put us in the army, and you can get us out. Either demobilize us, or, when given the next shot at the ballot box, we will demobilize you." Truman gave in to the public pressure, releasing almost 7 million men and women from the armed forces by April 1946. "The program we were following was no longer demobilization—it was disintegration of our armed forces," Truman reflected in his memoirs.

Soaring inflation added to public anxiety. During the war speculation had pushed property values and stock prices to new highs. Between 1941 and 1945 the national debt climbed from $61 billion to $253 billion; government spending rose from $9 billion to $98 billion. Savings accounts multiplied, increasing liquid assets of individuals and corporations to almost $200 billion. A postwar rush to spend the savings threatened to unleash a spiral of rising prices as too many dollars chased too few consumer goods. In August 1945 Office of Price Administration (OPA) chief Chester Bowles said the nation was in "one of the most dangerous periods in our country's economic history."

Most liberals wanted Truman to limit inflation by continuing wartime price controls. But a coalition of Republicans and conservative Democrats in Congress, eager to eliminate most wartime controls, slashed the OPA budget. Truman fought the effort, but he lacked the votes in Congress to keep an effective OPA alive. During the first week that controls ended in July 1946, prices increased 16 percent. Steak increased in price from fifty-five cents to one dollar a pound. Staples such as milk, butter, and vegetables all showed huge increases overnight. A headline in the *New York Daily News* screamed, "Prices Soar, Buyers Sore, Steers Jump over the Moon." The public blamed the president, even though he personally opposed ending price controls. Truman's popularity fell from a peak of 87 percent to 32 percent in just a few months.

The combination of high prices and job losses squeezed organized labor. During the war labor unions had for the most part honored a voluntary no-strike pledge. With the war ended and prices rising, labor demanded steep wage increases. By October 1945 a half-million workers had walked out on strike. In April 1946 John L. Lewis, the tenacious and relentless head of the mine workers, lead four hundred thousand coal miners out of the pits. The unions represented one of the Democratic Party's most valuable interest groups. Moreover, their members were irreplaceable in the American economy. "When we control the production of coal," Lewis said, "we hold the vitals of our society right in our hands. . . . I can squeeze, twist, and pull until we get the inevitable victory." For forty days the strike cut off the nation's supply of fuel and threatened European recovery. On May 21 Truman ordered government troops to take over the mines. "Let Truman dig coal with his bayonets," Lewis said. On May 25 Truman went before Congress to ask for the authority to draft strikers into the army. The threat was effective: the strike ended after only a few days. But the president's tough talk did little to assure liberals that he would continue FDR's legacy. *The New Republic* called Truman's congressional message the "most vicious piece of anti-union legislation ever introduced by an American President."

With liberals carping and labor-management disputes sweeping the nation, Truman's popularity plummeted. With the president's approval rating dipping below 50 percent, journalists wrote about "the cult of mediocrity" in the White House, and one newspaper ran a series entitled "The Tragedy of Truman." The Republicans, capitalizing on the pervasive dissatisfaction with

John L. Lewis Interviewed by the Press   President of the United Mine Workers from 1920–1960 and leading organizer of the CIO, John Lewis often defied the wishes of Washington and other labor unions in his efforts to improve conditions for the nation's miners, including conducting a strike during World War II, which led to accusations that Lewis was disloyal. By 1948, Lewis and his coal miners had won significantly higher wages, but their combative tactics brought down the wrath of Congress on all labor unions in the form of the Taft-Hartley Act.

rising prices, labor strikes, and the anxieties aroused by the Cold War, pounced on the hapless Democrats in the 1946 congressional elections. Their campaign slogan was as simple as it was effective: "Had enough?" The Republicans gained control of both Houses of Congress for the first time since 1930. Voters returned only thirty-seven of the seventy-seven liberal members of Congress to office. The arrival of staunch conservative members of the class of 1946 such as Representative Richard Nixon of California and Senator Joseph McCarthy of Wisconsin foreshadowed the coming of a new political and cultural phase of the Cold War.

The Rise of Harry Truman

Truman's plunging popularity and the Republican success in the 1946 election left liberals sour and disillusioned. Cold War with the USSR and conservative resurgence at home frustrated their hopes for the postwar world. Most blamed Truman for their plight, agreeing with the liberal *Nation*'s characterization of the president as a "weak, baffled, angry man." The columnists Joseph and Stewart

Alsop, looking toward the 1948 election, predicted that "if Truman is nominated, he will be forced to wage the loneliest campaign in history."

Truman, the last American president who had not been to college, lacked the grace and magnetism liberals had come to expect from the White House. Born in 1884, he spent most of his youth in rural Missouri. His poor eyesight—doctors called it "flat eyeballs"—prevented him from joining other children in sports. Instead, Harry worked long hours at a local drugstore, studied piano, and read books—though not as many as he later claimed. After high school he moved to Kansas City, where he worked as a banker. In 1906 he returned to help with the family farm. Over the next eleven years, while keeping the farm afloat, Truman devoted considerable effort to courting Bess Wallace, whom he later married.

In 1917, with war waging in Europe, Truman left the farm and enlisted in the army. Not only did his service as commander of the 193 men of Battery D convince him that he could be a leader; it also provided him with a cadre of loyal followers who helped launch his political career. "My whole political career," he said, "is based upon my war service and war associates."

Business, not politics, was on Truman's mind when he returned home from the war. Truman set up a haberdashery and sold men's clothing in Kansas City until a steep recession in 1921 destroyed the business. A few years shy of his fortieth birthday, Truman confronted a bleak future: he had to contend with a failed business and the real threat of bankruptcy, and he had few career options. Then one day in the summer of 1921 a representative of the notorious Pendergast political machine, which dominated Kansas City politics, invited Truman to run for county judge. Truman won election in 1922 and served on the court for most of the next twelve years, fighting a constant struggle to serve his patron while also providing good government for his constituents. "Three things ruin a man," he liked to say: "power, money, and women. I never wanted power, I never had any money, and the only woman in my life is up at the house right now."

In 1934 Truman won election to the U.S. Senate. Many people, including his fellow senators, treated him with contempt, dismissing him as the "Senator from Pendergast." Truman cast aside the criticism and threw himself into his work. With the nation mired in depression, Truman supported most of Franklin Roosevelt's New Deal agenda. It was during World War II, as head of a committee to investigate the national defense program, that Truman distinguished himself. In 1943 *Time* put Truman on its cover, calling him "a crusader for an effective war effort." The following year *Look* named Truman as one of the ten most valuable officials in the nation—and the only one in Congress. That exposure, along with his border-state background, helped gain him the vice-presidential nomination in 1944 when the Democrats were looking for a compromise choice.

In April 1945 a cerebral hemorrhage brought Franklin Roosevelt's life to a tragic end and elevated Harry Truman to the presidency. "For a time he walked," observed a journalist, "in the long shadow of the dead President." Many New Dealers distrusted Truman, believing he lacked FDR's grace, dignity, and patrician vision. Many viewed the new president as a provincial man incapable of transcending his modest roots. David E. Lilienthal, who served as chairman of the Tennessee Valley Authority, captured the mood of many Roosevelt loyalists when he wrote in his journal that he felt "consternation at the thought of that Throttlebottom, Truman. . . . The country and the world doesn't deserve to be left this way." Compounding the problem, Truman frequently replaced liberals with his political friends. I. F. Stone said that "the Truman era was the era of the moocher. The place was full of Wimpys who could be had for a hamburger."

Most of these criticisms were unfair. Truman often made distinguished appointments, especially in the foreign policy area. The president's critics underestimated his decisiveness and his shrewd instincts. "A man of immense determination," Winston Churchill said of him, "he has direct methods of speech and a great deal of self-confidence and resolution." Dean Acheson, a man not easily impressed, called his boss "straight forward, decisive, simple, entirely honest."

Perhaps most of all, liberals misjudged the public mood and ignored the institutional obstacles that confronted Truman. Many on the Left hoped the end of the war would result in a revival of the New Deal, a return to the ambitious social experimentation that had characterized the 1930s. But the war had dramatically altered the political climate in America. By 1945 many groups that had turned to the federal government for help during the depression had benefited from wartime prosperity, supported the status quo, and often complained about excessive government controls. This new attitude found expression in Congress, where a powerful coalition of conservative Democrats and Republicans planned to scale back existing government regulations.

In September 1945 Truman tried to put to rest doubts about his leadership by announcing his support for a range of new domestic initiatives, including laws to increase the minimum wage, broaden social security, and establish a national health program. The House Republican leader fumed, "Not even President Roosevelt ever asked so much at one sitting." Even many Democrats grumbled that the president was asking Congress to move too quickly on too many different fronts. As a result, over the next few years Congress frustrated most of Truman's domestic agenda.

Most significantly, Congress passed, over Truman's veto, the Labor-Management Relations Act of 1947, better known as the Taft-Hartley Act. The measure, a major blow to organized labor, outlawed the closed shop, which had required that all hiring be done through a union hall; permitted states to pass so-called right-to-work laws allowing nonunion members to work in unionized plants; empowered authorities to issue federal injunctions against strikes that jeopardized public health or safety; and gave the president power to stave off strikes by proclaiming a "cooling-off" period of up to eighty days. The legislation also required union leaders to swear that they were not communists. "We have got to break with the corrupting idea that we can legislate prosperity, legislate equality, legislate opportunity," declared Senator Robert Taft (D-Ohio), the chief spokesman for economic conservatism.

Creators of the Taft-Hartley Act The bill, sponsored by Representative Fred Hartley Jr. and Senator Robert Taft (seen here), amended the New Deal's Wagner Act. Officially known as the Labor-Management Relations Act, the bill sought to curb the activities of labor unions. Passed over President Truman's veto, the Taft-Hartley Act gave the government the power to prevent strikes for the sake of national security.

Truman and the Divided Democrats

These political setbacks further frustrated liberals, who were unanimous in their disaffection with Truman's domestic leadership but divided over how to respond to Cold War tensions. Many liberals, who called themselves progressives, believed that continued American-Soviet cooperation was essential to the preservation of the wartime antifascist alliance. Believing that legitimate security needs inspired Joseph Stalin's actions in Eastern Europe, they opposed Truman's growing hard line with the Soviets. Many progressives also hoped to rebuild the left-of-center Popular Front of the mid-1930s by forging a powerful coalition that would include labor, small farmers, intellectuals, communists, and socialists. Only by combining to fight the forces of reaction, they argued, could liberals retain power in the postwar period.

Progressives looked to former Vice President Henry Wallace for leadership. Born on a small farm in 1888, Wallace served first as secretary of agriculture from

1933 to 1940, then as vice president until January 1945, and finally as secretary of commerce under Truman. While Truman seemed to be moving away from Roosevelt's domestic and international policies, Wallace lifted liberal hopes with calls for economic development, full employment, and cooperation with the Soviet Union. In September 1946 Wallace criticized both U.S. and Soviet policy. Under pressure from Secretary of State James Byrnes and Republican senator Arthur Vandenberg, Truman fired Wallace. In December 1947 Wallace announced that he would run for president on a third-party progressive ticket, exhorting his "Gideon's Army, small in number, powerful in convictions," to force Truman from office. Few people believed Wallace could win the election, but many Democrats feared that he could siphon liberal votes away from Truman in key states.

By then Stalin's repressive regime and Soviet aggression in Eastern Europe were making any coalition with communists at home less attractive to many liberals. In 1946 Walter Reuther purged communists from the United Auto Workers. Following his lead, in 1949 the Congress of Industrial Organizations expelled nine unions, representing nine hundred thousand workers, for refusing to purge themselves of communist leaders. Similar housecleaning occurred in Popular Front political organizations. In Minnesota the young Democratic mayor of Minneapolis, Hubert Humphrey, gained control of the Minnesota Farmer-Labor party and purged communists from its ranks. In 1947 many leading anticommunist liberals met in Washington and created the Americans for Democratic Action, an independent political organization.

Confronted by a revolt among liberals, Truman turned to his advisers Clark Clifford and James Rowe for advice on how to hold the party together. They prepared a brilliant campaign blueprint, a forty-three-page memorandum entitled "The Politics of 1948." The memo argued that Truman should pursue a strategy of militant liberalism, which would undercut Wallace's support, and strident anticommunism. The key to victory, they reasoned, was winning the major interest groups—blue-collar workers, blacks, Jews, farmers, and the poor—that had provided the backbone of Roosevelt's coalition. Running on a liberal platform would also allow the president to exploit the differences within the Republican Party between the moderate national party, led by New York governor and likely nominee Thomas E. Dewey, and its conservative wing in Congress, led by Ohio senator Robert Taft.

Truman took the recommendations to heart. Over the next few months he championed an aggressive liberal reform agenda, calling for a far-reaching housing program, stronger rent control, a sweeping enlargement of social security coverage, and federal aid to education. Before Congress had a chance to act, he went on the offensive, blaming Republicans for not supporting his program. At the same time, the president highlighted his hard line with the Soviets to underscore his anticommunist credentials.

Truman made support for civil rights a centerpiece of his fighting liberal program. In 1946 Truman had established the President's Committee on Civil Rights, the first presidential committee ever created to investigate race relations in America. The following year the committee released its report, *To Secure These Rights,* which called for an end to segregation and discrimination and advocated legislation to abolish lynching and the poll tax. In February 1948 Truman hailed the report as "an American charter of human freedom" and asked Congress to support the committee's recommendations.

In July Truman signed Executive Order 9981, which set up procedures for ending racial discrimination in the military. Top military leaders opposed the measure, claiming that it would undermine morale and discipline. "The Army is not out to make any social reform," complained army chief of staff Omar Bradley. Organized resistance from within the ranks of the military prevented implementation until the Korean War, when the army had to scramble to find troops. For many African-Americans, however, the order symbolized Truman's commitment to civil rights. The *Chicago Defender,* a black newspaper, called the order "unprecedented since the time of Lincoln."

Truman's advocacy of civil rights in 1948 exposed the deep ideological and sectional strains in his party. The New Deal coalition consisted of groups that shared a common sense of class solidarity but were deeply divided on social issues such as race relations. During the 1930s, fearing the potential of a white backlash, Roosevelt avoided tackling sensitive civil-rights issues. But the war elevated racial tension, both in the North and the South, and increased white anxiety about the future of race relations. In the North industrial expansion lured African-Americans there to fill a desperate labor shortage. During the 1940s Chicago experienced a 77 percent increase in its black population. In Detroit, where Ford, Chrysler, and General Motors served as the "arsenal of democracy," the African-American population doubled. To preserve white neighborhoods, many locals refused to sell goods to blacks, established restrictive covenants, and used intimidation to discourage any movement away from black enclaves. In June 1943 race riots in Harlem and Detroit cut swaths of devastation across the urban landscape.

African-Americans—many of whom anticipated a "double victory" over fascism abroad and racism at home—grew less patient with rhetorical and symbolic actions. The National Association for the Advancement of Colored People railed against lynching and sought a federal law making it illegal. At the same time, black veterans began to challenge the disfranchisement of African-Americans. In 1944 the Supreme Court in *Smith* v. *Allwright* struck down the white Democratic primary. Signs of growing black activism, combined with indications that the federal government would support blacks' cause, produced a wave of anxiety and fear across the white South.

Truman and his advisers, however, were convinced that party loyalty would outweigh racial fear. In the 1948 campaign memorandum Clifford and Rowe suggested that by adopting a strong civil-rights stance, Truman could win black votes without alienating whites. Like many Americans, they tended to view race as primarily a southern issue. "As always the South can be considered safely Democratic," the two advisers wrote. "And in formulating national policy, it can be safely ignored."

But not all Democrats agreed. Some thought the president had made a major miscalculation. Senator James Eastland of Mississippi warned that Truman's civil-rights proposals "would destroy the last vestige of the South's social institutions and mongrelize her people." He and other southerners in Congress threatened to boycott the national convention if Truman included a civil-rights plank in the platform.

As early as 1948 the civil-rights issue was revealing its potential for unraveling the New Deal coalition. In July when Democrats assembled in sultry Philadelphia for their convention, Truman was feeling the southern heat on civil rights. Fearful of a revolt, he backtracked, endorsing a weak plank that made no mention of his own proposals. Northern liberals, however, whom Truman needed to ward off the threat from Henry Wallace, made civil rights the litmus test of their support for the president. Only if the president included a strong civil-rights plan in the Democratic platform would they endorse him.

When Truman hedged, liberals took their fight to the floor. In a dramatic and emotional speech Humphrey, who was seeking a Senate seat, called upon the party to enact a "new emancipation proclamation." "The time has come," he declared, "to walk out of the shadow of states' rights and into the sunlight of human rights." Humphrey's emotional appeal carried the day. Convention delegates rejected Truman's compromise measure and approved a strong civil-rights plank.

Rejected by the national party, southern delegates stormed out of the convention; formed the States' Rights Democratic, or "Dixiecrat," party; and nominated J. Strom Thurmond, governor of South Carolina, for the presidency. "We stand for the segregation of the races and the racial integrity of each race," the party's platform declared. For his part, Thurmond avoided direct racial appeals and instead focused on states' rights. The civil-rights program, Thurmond declared, and the expansion of federal power that it required, had their "origin in communist ideology" and sought "to excite race and class hatred," thereby "creat[ing] the chaos and confusion which leads to communism."

PRIMARY SOURCE

2.1 | *Acceptance Speech, 1948*
HARRY TRUMAN

On July 15, 1948, just hours after a bitter debate on civil rights had split the Democratic Party, President Truman stepped before the delegates at the Democratic National Convention in Philadelphia to accept the party's presidential nomination.

This convention met to express the will and reaffirm the beliefs of the Democratic Party. There have been differences of opinion, and that is the democratic way. Those differences have been settled by a majority vote, as they should be.

5   Now it is time for us to get together and beat the common enemy. And that is up to you.

We have been working together for victory in a great cause. Victory has become a habit of our party. It has been elected four times in succession, and I am convinced it will be elected a fifth time next November.

10   The reason is that the people know that the Democratic Party is the people's party, and the Republican Party is the party of special interest, and it always has been and always will be.

The record of the Democratic party is written in the accomplishments of the last 16 years. I don't need to repeat them. They have been very ably placed before

15 this convention by the keynote speaker, the candidate for Vice President, and by the permanent chairman.

Confidence and security have been brought to the people by the Democratic Party. Farm income has increased from less than $2½ billion in 1932 to more than $18 billion in 1947. Never in the world were the farmers of any republic

20 or any kingdom or any other country as prosperous as the farmers of the United States; and if they don't do their duty by the Democratic Party, they are the most ungrateful people in the world!

Wages and salaries in this country have increased from $29 billion in 1933 to more than $128 billion in 1947. That's labor, and labor never had but one

25 friend in politics, and that is the Democratic Party and Franklin D. Roosevelt.

And I say to labor what I have said to the farmers: they are the most ungrateful people in the world if they pass the Democratic Party by this year.

The total national income has increased from less than $40 billion in 1933 to $203 billion in 1947, the greatest in all the history of the world. These ben-

30 efits have been spread to all the people, because it is the business of the Democratic Party to see that the people get a fair share of these things.

This last, worst 80th Congress proved just the opposite for the Republicans.

The record on foreign policy of the Democratic Party is that the United

35 States has been turned away permanently from isolationism, and we have converted the greatest and best of the Republicans to our viewpoint on that subject. . . .

I would like to say a word or two now on what I think the Republican philosophy is; and I will speak from actions and from history and from experi-

40 ence.

The situation in 1932 was due to the policies of the Republican Party control of the Government of the United States. The Republican Party, as I said a while ago, favors the privileged few and not the common everyday man. Ever since its inception, that party has been under the control of special privilege;

45 and they have completely proved it in the 80th Congress. They proved it by the things they did *to* the people, and not *for* them. They proved it by the things they failed to do. . . .

My duty as President requires that I use every means within my power to get the laws the people need on matters of such importance and urgency.

50   I am therefore calling this Congress back into session July 26th.

On the 26th day of July, which out in Missouri we call "Turnip Day," I am going to call Congress back and ask them to pass laws to halt rising prices, to meet the housing crisis—which they are saying they are for in their platform.

At the same time I shall ask them to act upon other vitally needed mea-
55 sures such as aid to education, which they say they are for; a national health program; civil rights legislation, which they say they are for; an increase in the minimum wage, which I doubt very much they are for; extension of the social security coverage and increased benefits, which they say they are for; funds for projects needed in our program to provide public power and cheap elec-
60 tricity. By indirection, this 80th Congress has tried to sabotage the power policies the United States has pursued for 14 years. That power lobby is as bad as the real estate lobby, which is sitting on the housing bill.

I shall ask for adequate and decent laws for displaced persons in place of this anti-Semitic, anti-Catholic law which this 80th Congress passed. . . .
65 In 1932 we were attacking the citadel of special privilege and greed. We were fighting to drive the money changers from the temple. Today, in 1948, we are now the defenders of the stronghold of democracy and of equal opportunity, the haven of the ordinary people of this land and not of the favored classes or the powerful few. The battle cry is just the same now as
70 it was in 1932, and I paraphrase the words of Franklin D. Roosevelt as he issued the challenge, in accepting nomination in Chicago: "This is more than a political call to arms. Give me your help, not to win votes alone, but to win in this new crusade to keep America secure and safe for its own people."
75 Now my friends, with the help of God and the wholehearted push which you can put behind this campaign, we can save this country from a continuation of the 80th Congress, and from misrule from now on.

I must have your help. You must get in and push, and win this election. The country can't afford another Republican Congress. ■ ■ ■

A few hours after the bitter civil-rights fight, Truman accepted his party's nomination. As his running mate, Truman selected the seventy-five-year-old Senator Alben Barkley of Kentucky. Truman gave a rousing acceptance speech, but he could do little to lift the spirits of Democratic leaders who feared that defections of Democratic voters to Wallace and Thurmond spelled doom in November. At a nearby convention hotel a group of Democratic leaders called for room service. "Send up a bottle of embalming fluid," they said. "If were going to hold a wake, we might as well do it right."

The 1948 Election

The Republicans, in contrast, were united and hopeful. They were certain of victory against Truman, whom they saw as a small-town politician lacking Roosevelt's grace and charisma. With little fanfare and even less debate, they nominated New York governor Thomas E. Dewey, who had run a strong race against Roosevelt in 1944 and seemed certain to beat Truman. The convention, which was the first ever televised, picked California governor Earl Warren for the second place on the ticket and adopted a platform promising a foreign policy based on "friendly firmness which welcomes cooperation but spurns appeasement."

Confident of election, Dewey spent much time campaigning for other Republican candidates in states that were not crucial to his own election. Ignoring Truman and avoiding specific issues, Dewey concentrated on convincing voters that he was an efficient administrator who could bring unity to the country and effectiveness to its foreign policy. According to the *Louisville Courier Journal,* Dewey's speeches could be boiled down "to these historic four sentences: Agriculture is important. Our rivers are full of fish. You cannot have freedom without liberty. The future lies ahead." Many observers found Dewey a lackluster campaigner. According to one observer, Dewey sought the presidency "with the humorless calculation of a Certified Public Accountant in pursuit of the Holy Grail."

Dewey's weakness was his personality: chilly and aloof. He was, according to a long-time associate, "cold—cold as a February icicle." He disliked other politicians, seemed uncomfortable campaigning, and preferred to spend lots of time alone. He did, however, have two great assets: personal integrity and a clear sense of purpose. Despite heavy pressure from leaders in his own party, he refused to use the communists-in-government issue during the campaign. "If I'm going to lose, I'm going to lose on something I believe in," he told critics. Polls showed overwhelming support for outlawing the Communist party, but Dewey refused to pander to hysteria. "You can't shoot an idea with a gun," he said. When party leaders pleaded with him to downplay his strong commitment to civil liberties, Dewey responded that he was not "going around looking under beds."

While Dewey tried to stay above the partisan fray, Truman waged a tough, bare-knuckled campaign. The president went on a whirlwind, transcontinental railroad trip in which he gave 351 speeches to an estimated 12 million people. He blamed the "do-nothing, good-for-nothing 80th Congress" for everything from high prices to poor health care. "If you send another Republican to Washington," he told audiences, "you're a bigger bunch of suckers than I think you are."

Truman tied himself to Roosevelt's legacy, reminding voters that the Democratic Party had led the nation through depression and world war. He peppered his speeches with references to "Republican gluttons of privilege" who had "stuck a pitch fork in the farmer's back" and "begun to nail the American consumer to the wall with spikes of greed." His speeches pictured politics as a struggle between the "people," represented by the Democrats, and "special interests," represented by the Republicans. Enthusiastic crowds shouted, "Give 'em hell, Harry!" Truman responded: "I don't give 'em hell. I just tell the truth and they think it's hell." Truman even summoned the ghosts of the Great Depression. "Herbert Hoover once ran on the slogan: 'Two cars in every garage,'" he taunted. "Apparently the

Truman on the Campaign Trail   Considered the underdog in 1948, President Truman ran an aggressive campaign, touring the country on a train called the *Ferdinand Magellan*. Truman covered 31,000 miles and spread his message to an estimated 12 million Americans. Surrounded by the press, Harry and Bess Truman prepare to pull out of Washington's Union Station.

Republican candidate this year is running on the slogan: 'Two families in every garage.' "

Despite his energetic campaign, Truman lagged behind Dewey in the polls. In October *Newsweek* polled fifty top political journalists; they were unanimous in predicting a Dewey victory. The day before the election the Gallup poll gave Dewey 49.5 percent of the popular vote and Truman, 44.5 percent. On election night, long before the votes were in, the *Chicago Tribune* ran the headline "DEWEY DEFEATS TRUMAN."

Instead, Truman scored the most dramatic upset victory in the history of presidential elections, winning 24.1 million votes to Dewey's 22 million. How did Truman pull off such a surprising victory? First, both Wallace and Thurmond were hurt by the public's reluctance to waste their vote on a third-party candidate with little chance of victory. At the same time, their campaigns actually helped Truman. With Wallace being openly supported by the communists, and with Truman denouncing him, the president was much less vulnerable than he might otherwise have been to charges of being "soft" on communism. The Dixicrat rebellion against Truman's civil-rights program encouraged the loyalty of liberals and most black voters, many of whom might otherwise have been attracted to Wallace or even to Dewey.

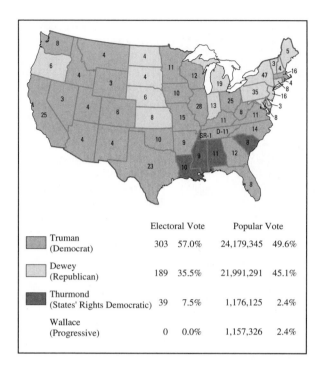

The Election of 1948

Thomas Dewey was the favorite in the polls, in large part due to the Dixiecrat split from the Democratic Party, but it was not enough to win him the election. "Give 'em hell, Harry" Truman made an impressive 31,000-mile whistle-stop tour of the country promoting the continuation of New Deal programs at home and support of democracy abroad. Such aggressive campaigning propelled him past his opponent with 50 percent of the popular vote.

	Electoral Vote		Popular Vote	
Truman (Democrat)	303	57.0%	24,179,345	49.6%
Dewey (Republican)	189	35.5%	21,991,291	45.1%
Thurmond (States' Rights Democratic)	39	7.5%	1,176,125	2.4%
Wallace (Progressive)	0	0.0%	1,157,326	2.4%

Second, Dewey's bland campaign failed to excite voters. Dewey was vague and unclear on the issues, and he ignited little grass-roots enthusiasm. Fewer Republicans went to the polls in 1948 than in either 1940 or 1944.

Finally, the election demonstrated the enduring appeal of the New Deal. As Clifford and Rowe had predicted, the president assembled the key groups of the New Deal coalition: urban workers, Jews, and African-Americans. Like Roosevelt, Truman carried the nation's thirteen largest cities, scoring well in the poorest neighborhoods. The president's aggressive campaigning in the Great Plains and the West helped maintain the support of farmers. "I talked about voting for Dewey all summer, but when the time came I just couldn't do it," said one farmer. "I remembered the depression and all the other things that had come to me under the Democrats."

Trying for a Fair Deal

Liberals had high hopes that the newly elected president would use his mandate to revive the New Deal. The Democrats, by picking up nine seats in the Senate and seventy-five in the House, regained control of Congress. "The party that Roosevelt formed has survived his death," Walter Lippmann observed, "and is without question the dominant force in American politics." Truman certainly viewed his victory as a mandate for liberalism, and he outlined his ambitious

The Campaign of Henry Wallace Once a Democratic Party insider and Franklin Roosevelt's vice president, Henry Wallace left the party in opposition to Truman's foreign policy and in 1948 helped organize the Progressive Party and became its presidential candidate. Wallace's platform, which called for greater cooperation with the Soviets and support of labor at home, was unacceptable to most Americans in the new Cold War environment. Labeled a communist, Wallace often faced hostile crowds during the campaign; during this speech the crowd pelted him with eggs.

social and economic agenda in his 1949 State of the Union message. "Every segment of our population and every individual," he declared, "has a right to expect from our Government a fair deal." Truman implored Congress to expand many New Deal programs while launching new initiatives in civil rights, national health insurance, and federal aid to education. The liberal *New Republic* called Truman's Fair Deal "one of the boldest reform programs ever presented by an American President."

The eighty-first Congress often complied with Truman's pleas to expand existing programs. In the most ambitious burst of reform since 1935, Congress increased the minimum wage from forty to seventy-five cents per hour, extended rent controls, and approved a displaced persons act admitting some four hundred thousand refugees to the United States. It passed the National Housing Act of 1949, which authorized the construction of 810,000 low-income housing units and provided funds for slum clearance and rural housing. In 1950 Congress increased social security benefits by an average of 80 percent, extending the system's coverage to an additional 10.5 million people.

Congress, however, showed little desire to support Truman's calls for new programs that moved beyond the New Deal. It rejected the president's proposals for federal aid to education, a crop-subsidy system, and the repeal of Taft-Hartley. When Truman proposed a system of national health insurance, the American Medical Association (AMA) hired an advertising agency to fight against the measure. "Would socialized medicine lead to socialization of other phases of American life?" asked an AMA leaflet. The answer: "Lenin thought so." Most Americans agreed, and the bill died in Congress. Congress also stymied Truman's efforts to enact civil rights legislation. Truman proposed creating a civil-rights division in the Department of Justice to protect the right to vote, to abolish the poll tax in federal elections, and to establish a permanent fair employment practices committee. Southern Democrats and Republicans killed the bill before it reached the floor for debate.

To some extent, Truman's Fair Deal was a victim of the Cold War, which drained attention and resources away from domestic initiatives. The Cold War also strengthened the power of conservatives, whose support Truman needed to maintain his foreign and defense policies. "Any illusion that the liberal Democrats dominate either the House or the Senate has been completely blasted," Hubert Humphrey observed. The 1948 election was "not so much a victory as a reprieve."

The Vital Center

Truman may have governed in the shadow of Roosevelt, but his administration produced a limited redefinition of American liberalism and marked an important shift in the evolution of the Democratic Party. The liberalism that emerged in America after World War II rested on a foundation of shared assumptions forged during the depression and World War II. Arthur Schlesinger Jr., in a popular book published in 1949, referred to the new liberalism as *The Vital Center,* which he defined as a middle way between the tyranny of the Left and of the Right.

Three basic assumptions undergirded the vital center. The "gospel of economic growth" formed the first pillar. By 1949 most Americans believed that economic growth would eliminate class division, guarantee social harmony, and provide a constant source of revenue for necessary social programs. This faith in capitalism marked an important shift from the New Deal. During the 1930s many liberals had been convinced that the Great Depression signaled the death of capitalism. They spent most of the decade experimenting with different plans for restructuring the economy. All included large-scale government planning and controls. But the enormous productivity during the war, which saw the gross national product double in four years, revitalized liberal faith in capitalism and fostered new confidence in government's ability to regulate the economy. Full employment was possible, liberal economists believed, and they now felt they knew how to use their tools to achieve that end.

Within the Truman administration, Leon Keyserling, who served as the chairman of the Council of Economic Advisors, emerged as the most forceful proponent of the Fair Deal's economic philosophy. Rather than creating a large welfare state, which shifted resources from the rich to the poor, government policy should, he argued, focus on using fiscal and monetary policy to promote economic growth. The government would continue to provide essential services not offered by the private sector—low-cost housing, medical insurance, and funds for education—but its emphasis would be on expanding the economic pie, not reslicing it.

Foreign-policy issues had been largely absent from the New Deal agenda, but the question of America's role in the world formed the second pillar of the vital center. Since Russian aggression of the 1940s was seen as the same as the German belligerence of the 1930s, American policy makers reacted toward the Soviet Union as they believed their predecessors should have behaved toward the expansionist states of their time. "The image of Hitler," wrote the historian Gaddis Smith, "seared itself on the eye of all who fought him. When Hitler was gone, his image lingered." Between 1946 and 1948 Truman shifted liberals and the Democratic Party toward an aggressive internationalism based on fear of Soviet expansion and an enlarged definition of American interests. Truman's victory in the 1948 election signaled the triumph of liberal anticommunism.

Prosperity served as the third pillar of the vital center. Economic growth, and the constant tax revenue that it generated, would provide the nation with the resources it needed to fund necessary social problems at home while also paying for the military needs of the Cold War. The nation, in other words, could have both guns and butter. Prosperity also guaranteed social harmony. The contrast with Adolf Hitler's fascism and Joseph Stalin's totalitarianism convinced Americans of their common faith in the values of freedom and democracy and underscored the importance of consensus. Prosperity maintained that consensus by muting ideological differences and by blurring the lines of potential conflict based on race or gender. Everyone benefited from abundance: business reaped high profits, labor received better wages, farmers earned larger incomes, and the poor—both black and white—gained the opportunity to lead a better life.

The vital center, a blend of liberal goals and conservative means, represented an accommodation with the new political realities of postwar America. It recognized the need for an activist federal government and an internationalist foreign policy, but it rested on conservative assumptions about the power of private capital to solve social problems and to forge consensus. The vital center promised to raise the standard of living, promote social justice, and guarantee U.S. interests abroad, but with a minimum of social dislocation or sacrifice. The nation could fulfill its grand expectations of the future while remaining faithful to its conservative values.

In the end, this new liberalism created unrealistic expectation about the possibilities of change and thus intensified the American paradox. Though general prosperity increased the quality of life for most Americans, it did not produce meaningful redistribution of income. Economic growth not only failed to erase class division; it also was unable to mute ideological conflict in America. At the same time, the promise of gradual reform failed to satisfy the rising expectations of African-Americans, who demanded an end to segregation in the South. The bipolar view of the world, born in the heat of the Cold War, quickly became obsolete as nationalist movements in the Third World complicated the global balance of power. America's zero-sum view of the world also failed to account for differences among communist countries or appreciate the limits of American power.

SELECTED READINGS

▌ Jack S. Ballard's *The Shock of Peace* (1983) recounts the economic trauma of demobilization at war's end. The conflict that arose between labor and government is described in George Roukis's *American Labor and the Conservative Republicans* (1988). In *Beyond the New Deal* (1973), Alonzo L. Hamby assesses Truman's effort to preserve and expand the New Deal. Stephen K. Bailey chronicles the adoption of the Employment Act of 1946 in his *Congress Makes a Law* (1957). Robert J. Donovan captures the 1940s feeling of upheaval in *Tumultuous Years* (1982). Susan Hartmann outlines Truman's first-term frustrations in *Truman and the 80th Congress* (1971). Monte S. Poen details the defeat of national health insurance in *Harry S Truman Versus the Medical Lobby* (1979).

▌ David G. McCullough's *Truman* (1992) is a generally uncritical appraisal of Truman's life and policies. Alonzo L. Hamby provides the best biographical treatment of Truman in *Man of the People* (1995). Donald R. McCoy's *The Presidency of Harry S Truman* (1984) is more balanced. Graham White and John Maze's biography of *Henry A. Wallace* (1995) traces the life of this controversial figure, as does John Culver and John Hyde's *American Dreamer* (2000), which examines not only Wallace's political career, but also his ground-breaking work in agricultural economics. The work of Leon Keyserling, Truman's economic policy adviser, is analyzed in W. Robert Brazelton's biography of Keyserling, *Designing U.S. Economic Policy* (2000).

▌ The 1948 election is detailed in Everett C. Ladd and Charles Hadley's *Transformation of the American Party System* (1978). Zachary Karabell argues in *The Last Campaign* (2000) that the 1948 election was the last to provide Americans with choices across the ideological spectrum. William C. Berman's *The Politics of Civil Rights in the Truman Administration* (1970) covers the controversy within the Democratic Party.

▌ Arthur Schlesinger Jr. argues the virtues of Fair Deal liberalism in *The Vital Center* (1949). The tension within the liberal community in the early Cold War years is described in Jim Tuck's *The Liberal Civil War* (1998). Steven M. Gillon's *Politics and Vision* (1985) examines the new political environment that liberals of the Cold War era faced.

3

The Cold War Heats Up

O n September 17, 1947, the "Freedom Train" pulled out of its Philadelphia station, beginning a nearly two-year journey across America during which it would visit 326 cities and welcome more than 3.5 million visitors. The seven cars—all painted red, white, and blue—housed ninety-eight historical American documents, including the Declaration of Independence, the Bill of Rights, and the Emancipation Proclamation. The chairman of the American Heritage Foundation, the private group that sponsored the touring exhibit, said the pilgrimage was designed to reaffirm America's faith in liberty and freedom. "Without faith in the individual," he declared in christening the new streamliner, "you cannot have millions of free, educated, resourceful, independent, self-reliant men and women."

The arrival of the train in towns and cities across the country produced a carnival-like atmosphere. Schools and businesses declared a holiday. People decorated the streets in patriotic banners and organized colorful parades. City officials called for a "week of rededication" to American freedom, and local ministers preached about freedom of religion. Nearly one-half of the residents of Burlington, Vermont, turned out to see the exhibit. About one hundred thousand people lined the tracks in Washington, D.C., and in New York City nearly fifty thousand people had to be turned away. The Freedom Train took its message of nonsegregation to the South, where blacks and whites stood together in long lines to wait for their opportunity to view the exhibit. "They'll say we just came to see the free show," said an elderly man who had waited in line for hours. "But I know better. We have particular interest when you talk about freedom."

The Freedom Train highlighted the nation's uneasiness about the Cold War and the threat of communist subversion. In 1949 America's unrealistic faith in the universal appeal of American values left it unprepared for the dramatic news that the communists had triumphed in China's civil war. The shock led to accusations of subversion at home. The Red Scare forced Americans to confront a fundamental question of identity: What did it mean to be an American? Fears of communist subversion produced a narrow definition of Americanism, isolated potential radicals, and reinforced the postwar consensus. "You can call it nationalism. Or you can call it patriotism, love of country, loyalty—anything you like," said a Nashville man who had weathered rain and cold to view the Freedom Train exhibit.

The Korean War intensified the debate over American identity, but it also exposed the gap between American expectations of the postwar world and the realities of international power. The war underscored the limits of American power and revealed the nation's discomfort with the demands of limited war. Meanwhile, the Cold War in general pressured Americans to balance their commitment to freedom and individual rights with their sense of patriotism and national security. This conflict between freedom and security, which was intensified by the Korean War, presented Americans with a painful choice.

The Cold War in Asia

During the 1930s many Americans viewed China as America's junior partner in the Pacific. *Time* chose its Christian leader Jiang Jieshi (Chiang Kai-shek) and his American-educated wife as the magazine's "Man and Wife of the Year" in 1938. World War II enhanced China's reputation in the United States, with wartime propaganda depicting the Chinese people as democratically inclined and desirous of an American way of life. The Office of War Information asked Hollywood to portray China as "a great nation, cultured and liberal, with whom, inevitably, we will be closely bound in the world that is to come." The effort worked: by 1942, 82 percent of Americans believed that China would be a strong ally after the war.

When World War II ended, however, Jiang Jieshi's Nationalists in the south faced a serious challenge from Mao Zedong's (Mao Tse-tung) Communists in the north. At first the Nationalists had the upper hand, but Jiang's corrupt and incompetent government failed to inspire public support or stem the tide of Chinese communism. In 1945–46 Harry Truman, anxious to work out a peaceful settlement between Jiang and Mao, sent General George C. Marshall to China in a failed attempt to negotiate a compromise. U.S. efforts continued, but by 1949 Truman had grown weary of Jiang's refusal to undertake necessary reforms or attack corruption in his government. The president wrote in his diary that Jiang's government "was one of the most corrupt and inefficient that ever made an attempt to govern a country."

Deciding there was little the United States could do to salvage the noncommunist government, Truman stopped all aid to Jiang in 1949. Shortly afterward Jiang's forces collapsed, sending the Nationalist leader scurrying to the offshore island of Formosa (Taiwan), where Nationalists set up the independent Republic of China. The Soviet Union consolidated its power in Asia by extending diplomatic recognition to Mao's government and signing a "mutual-assistance" agreement.

The communist victory precipitated a firestorm of criticism at home against those responsible for "losing China." How could a communist peasant army have wrested America's Asian prize and turned it into what a government official described as "a colonial Russian government, a Slavic Manchukuo on a large scale"? Friends of Jiang in the Republican Party complained that Democrats had let the Communists win. Led by publisher Henry Luce, the "China Lobby," an influential group that advocated U.S. intervention in China, wondered aloud why the Truman administration had stopped supplying weapons to Jiang after the Marshall mission of 1946. Years later John F. Kennedy and Lyndon Johnson, remembering the bruising assault Truman endured for losing China, would determine never to lose another inch to the communists.

The emotional reaction to the communist triumph in China focused U.S. attention on Asia. At the end of World War II the United States occupied Japan and, under the leadership of General Douglas MacArthur, transformed the vanquished country into a model of western democracy where women could vote, trade unions were encouraged, and land was redistributed among the peasants. Wanting to make sure that Japan would never reemerge as a military threat, the United States wrote a Japanese constitution, adopted in 1946, that renounced war, promising that "land, sea and air forces, as well as other war potential, will never be maintained." The growing communist threat in Asia, however, forced a dramatic shift in American policy. Now, viewing Japan as a potential military counterweight against China, policy makers negotiated a new treaty in 1951 that terminated the U.S. occupation and conceded to Japan "the inherent right of individual or collective self-defense."

The "fall" of China also transformed a local nationalist struggle against French rule in Indochina into a globally strategic battleground. During World War II Franklin Roosevelt had expressed support for Vietnamese nationalist forces led by Ho Chi Minh, a communist educated in Paris and Moscow, and called for an end to French colonial rule. After Jiang's collapse American policy shifted. Fearing that a communist "victory" in Indochina would become a sweep of Southeast Asia and tilt the global balance of power, the United States abandoned its pretense of neutrality and openly endorsed French policy in Asia. In 1950 when the Soviet Union and China extended diplomatic recognition to Ho's government, Truman supplied military aid to the French. America had taken its first step into the Vietnam quagmire.

While debating the consequences of the fall of China, Americans experienced another Cold War setback. On September 23, 1949, Truman issued a terse press release: "We have evidence that within recent weeks an atomic explosion occurred in the U.S.S.R." The report sent shock waves through Washington. The American military believed the Soviets were at least five years away from producing the bomb. Though the administration publicly downplayed the significance of the Soviet breakthrough, it realized that, in Senator Arthur Vandenberg's words, "this is now a different world." Since the United States could not match the Soviets in manpower, military planners had depended on "the bomb" to deter Soviet aggression. According to one general, Joe One, as military officials called the Russian bomb, ended "the era when we might have destroyed Russia completely and not even skinned our elbows in doing it."

Together, the fall of China and the Soviet nuclear test forced American policy makers to rethink U.S. strategic doctrine. A fierce debate erupted in the administration over the development of a hydrogen bomb, potentially a thousand times more powerful than the atomic weapons that had destroyed Hiroshima and Nagasaki. J. Robert Oppenheimer, the "father" of the atomic bomb, questioned the morality of such a powerful weapon and feared the consequences of an escalating arms race. "We may be likened to two scorpions in a bottle," he wrote, "each capable of killing the other, but only at the risk of his own life." In January 1950 Truman sided with German-born physicist Edward Teller, who argued that the Soviets would eventually develop the weapon and use it to blackmail the United States.

PRIMARY SOURCE

3.1 | ## NSC-68
NATIONAL SECURITY COUNCIL

After the Soviet Union detonated its first atomic bomb and China fell to communism, President Truman ordered his advisers to study America's role in world affairs and the nation's military capability. Their report, submitted to the National Security Council in April 1950, predicted that the conflict with the Soviet Union would continue indefinitely and recommended a dramatic increase in America's military capabilities.

The issues that face us are momentous, involving the fulfillment or destruction not only of this Republic but of civilization itself. They are issues which will not await our deliberations. With conscience and resolution this Government and the people it represents must now take new and fateful decisions. . . . The
5   fundamental design of those who control the Soviet Union and the international

communist movement is to retain and solidify their absolute power, first in the Soviet Union and second in the areas now under their control. In the minds of the Soviet leaders, however, achievement of this design requires the dynamic extension of their authority and the ultimate elimination of any effective opposi-
10 tion to their authority.

The design, therefore, calls for the complete subversion or forcible destruction of the machinery of government and structure of society in the countries of the non-Soviet world and their replacement by an apparatus and structure subservient to and controlled from the Kremlin. To that end Soviet efforts are now
15 directed toward the domination of the Eurasian land mass. The United States, as the principal center of power in the non-Soviet world and the bulwark of opposition to Soviet expansion, is the principal enemy whose integrity and vitality must be subverted or destroyed by one means or another if the Kremlin is to achieve its fundamental design.

20 The Kremlin regards the United States as the only major threat to the achievement of its fundamental design. There is a basic conflict between the idea of freedom under a government of laws, and the idea of slavery under the grim oligarchy of the Kremlin, which has come to a crisis with the polarization of power described in Section I, and the exclusive possession of atomic weapons by the two
25 protagonists. The idea of freedom, moreover, is peculiarly and intolerably subversive of the idea of slavery. But the converse is not true. The implacable purpose of the slave state to eliminate the challenge of freedom has placed the two great powers at opposite poles. It is this fact which gives the present polarization of power the quality of crisis. . . .

30 Thus unwillingly our free society finds itself mortally challenged by the Soviet system. No other value system is so wholly irreconcilable with ours, so implacable in its purpose to destroy ours, so capable of turning to its own uses the most dangerous and divisive trends in our own society, no other so skillfully and powerfully evokes the elements of irrationality in human nature everywhere,
35 and no other has the support of a great and growing center of military power. . . .

Our overall policy at the present time may be described as one designed to foster a world environment in which the American system can survive and flourish. It therefore rejects the concept of isolation and affirms the necessity of our positive participation in the world community.

40 This broad intention embraces two subsidiary policies. One is a policy which we would probably pursue even if there were no Soviet threat. It is a policy of attempting to develop a healthy international community. The other is the policy of "containing" the Soviet system. . . .

A more rapid build-up of political, economic, and military strength and
45 thereby of confidence in the free world than is now contemplated is the only course which is consistent with progress toward achieving our fundamental purpose. The frustration of the Kremlin design requires the free world to develop a successfully functioning political and economic system and a vigorous political offensive against the Soviet Union. These, in turn, require an adequate military
50 shield under which they can develop. It is necessary to have the military power to deter, if possible, Soviet expansion, and to defeat, if necessary, aggressive Soviet or

Soviet-directed actions of a limited or total character. The potential strength of the free world is great; its ability to develop these military capabilities and its will to resist Soviet expansion will be determined by the wisdom and will with which
55 it undertakes to meet its political and economic problems. . . .

In summary, we must, by means of a rapid and sustained build-up of the political, economic, and military strength of the free world, and by means of an affirmative program intended to wrest the initiative from the Soviet Union, confront it with convincing evidence of the determination and ability of the free
60 world to frustrate the Kremlin design of a world dominated by its will. Such evidence is the only means short of war which eventually may force the Kremlin to abandon its present course of action and to negotiate acceptable agreements on issues of major importance.

The whole success of the proposed program hangs ultimately on recognition by
65 this Government, the American people, and all free peoples, that the cold war is in fact a real war in which the survival of the free world is at stake. Essential prerequisites to success are consultations with Congressional leaders designed to make the program the object of non-partisan legislative support, and a presentation to the public of a full explanation of the facts and implications of the present interna-
70 tional situation. The prosecution of the program will require of us all the ingenuity, sacrifice, and unity demanded by the vital importance of the issue and the tenacity to persevere until our national objectives have been attained. . . . ■ ■ ■

In April 1950, after months of deliberation, the National Security Council (NSC) recommended that the president initiate a massive rebuilding of the American military, both nuclear and conventional forces, to confront the new Soviet nuclear threat. The council's report, National Security Council Memorandum 68 (NSC-68), presented a frightening portrait of a Soviet system driven by "a new fanatic faith" that "seeks to impose its absolute authority over the rest of the world." To deter the Russians and inspire confidence in U.S. allies, the report called for an extraordinary increase in the defense budget, from $13 billion to $50 billion a year. The report heightened the tension between security and freedom by making clear that the new demands of national security required Americans to abandon their fear of enlarged federal power.

On November 1, 1952, the United States exploded the first H-bomb, obliterating an uninhabited island in the Pacific. The bomb blast created a fireball 5 miles high and 4 miles wide and left a hole in the Pacific floor 1 mile long and 175 feet deep. The following year the USSR exploded its first hydrogen bomb. Britain and France soon joined the nuclear club. The arms race had entered a frightening new phase.

The Korean War: From Invasion to Stalemate

In January 1950 Secretary of State Dean Acheson omitted any mention of Korea when he outlined the "defensive perimeter" that the United States would protect in Asia. At the end of the Second World War, the United States and the Soviets had temporarily divided the Korean peninsula, previously dominated by Japan, at the thirty-eighth parallel. Cold War tensions, however, ended any hope of unification. The Russians installed Kim Il Sung to lead the communist North, while Syngman Rhee, a conservative nationalist, emerged as the American-sponsored ruler in the South. Korea was not a top American priority, however, and the United States withdrew its troops from Korea in June 1949.

That changed on June 25, 1950, when 110,000 North Korean soldiers crossed the thirty-eighth parallel and within hours overpowered South Korean forces. The circumstances surrounding the invasion remain unclear, but documents in Soviet archives, made available to historians at the end of the Cold War, suggest that the North Koreans, not the Soviets, pushed for the invasion. Kim Il Sung pestered Joseph Stalin with forty-eight telegrams seeking his approval for an attack on the South. Stalin, fearful of a military conflict with the United States, refused many times, but he finally gave his approval in January 1950. Why the change of mind? Most historians speculate that he believed that the United States would not respond. "According to information coming from the United States, it is really so," Stalin told Kim in a Kremlin meeting in April 1950. "The prevailing mood is not to interfere." The new information included Acheson's speech excluding South Korea from the U.S. "defense perimeter" and a top-secret government document, which Soviet spies in London had stolen, that reinforced Acheson's statement.

Truman viewed the situation in a dramatically different light. He interpreted the invasion as a Soviet-engineered assault, the opening salvo in a broader Soviet attack on America's global allies. With memories of western appeasement of Adolf Hitler fresh in mind, Truman immediately ordered American air and naval forces to support the South Koreans. "If this was allowed to go unchallenged," he wrote in his memoirs, "it would mean a third world war, just as similar incidents had brought on the second world war." Two days later, on Tuesday, June 27, 1950, Truman asked the UN Security Council to condemn North Korea as an aggressor and to send forces to South Korea. The resolution passed because the Russian delegate, who could have used his veto to defeat the measure, was boycotting the meetings. The defense effort was theoretically a UN venture, but in the end the United States provided half the ground troops and most of the sea and air support.

In the first few weeks it appeared that North Korean forces might win a decisive victory. Their troops pushed the South Koreans and the entire U.S. Eighth Army all the way down to the peninsula's tip around the port city of Pusan. Then on September 15 General Douglas MacArthur, a seventy-year-old World War II hero and commander of the U.S. forces in Korea, turned the war around with a daring amphibious invasion behind enemy lines at Inchon, near the South Korean capital of Seoul. At the same time, the American and South Korean armies attacked in force at Pusan. The dual tactic fooled the North Koreans, who suffered heavy losses and quickly retreated beyond the thirty-eighth parallel. By the end of the month American troops had liberated Seoul and reestablished Syngman Rhee's government in the South.

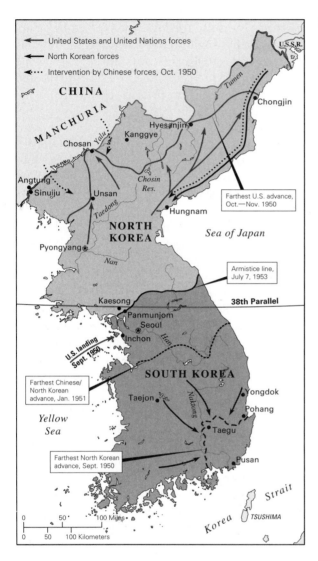

United States and United Nations forces
North Korean forces
Intervention by Chinese forces, Oct. 1950

The Korean War, 1950–1953 After the initial wave of North Korean troops swept through the South in the summer of 1950, United Nations' forces under General Douglas MacArthur countered at Inchon and Pusan. By November, UN troops occupied most of Korea, but Chinese troops quickly repulsed the advance and pushed MacArthur's men south of the thirty-eighth parallel. There the fighting remained until the armistice in 1953.

The dramatic victory on the ground raised hopes that U.S. forces could advance beyond the thirty-eight parallel, overthrow Kim Il Sung, and unite Korea under a noncommunist government. On September 27 Truman authorized MacArthur to cross into North Korea. Within a few weeks, MacArthur's forces had advanced within 50 miles of the Yalu River, the boundary between Korea and the Chinese province of Manchuria.

When the Communist Chinese condemned the U.S. invasion of North Korea and threatened retaliation, Truman began to have second thoughts about his strategy. In October the president flew to Wake Island in the Pacific to consult with MacArthur. The general assured Truman that the Chinese Communists, despite their buildup of troops on the border and their loud warnings, would not intervene in the war, which MacArthur said was over. Acheson agreed with MacArthur's assessment. "I should think it would be sheer madness for the Chinese to intervene," he said. The president, uplifted by MacArthur's optimistic assessment and Acheson's support, returned home confident that the war had been won.

MacArthur and Acheson were wrong. On November 27, 1950, a Chinese army of 400,000 men, armed with Soviet tanks and aircraft, attacked American forces in North Korea. The Chinese forces overwhelmed UN forces, attacking day and night, engaging Americans in terrifying hand-to-hand combat. MacArthur, at his headquarters in Tokyo, refused to accept that the tide of the war had shifted and continued barking orders for his troops to advance to the North. On December 15 Truman went on television to call for a full mobilization to meet the threat. "Our homes, our nation, all the things we believe in are in great danger," he told the America people. "This danger has been created by the rulers of the Soviet Union."

By Christmas the massive wave of Chinese troops had pushed MacArthur south of the thirty-eighth parallel again. Shaken, the general pressured Truman for permission to attack Chinese military bases in the North. This time Truman rejected MacArthur's strategy, fearing that direct attack on Chinese installations would antagonize the Russians and precipitate a global conflict. In January 1951 the U.S. Eighth Army halted the communist advance and, by March, pushed back to the thirty-eighth parallel. The war then bogged down, with neither side able to gain the advantage.

The Korean War underscored the paradox of American power in the post–World War II era. Although the nation possessed the most powerful weapons of mass destruction, it was often powerless to use them. Between 1950 and 1953 the air force dropped vast numbers of explosives, destroying nearly every building in the northern and central parts of Korea, driving much of the population underground. Naval ships sat offshore bombarding coastal cities. Navy shells rained down on the city of Wosun for forty-one days and nights, which one navy official called "the longest sustained naval or air bombardment of a city in history." Twice the United States publicly threatened North Korea and China with atomic attack. In April 1951 the military flew B-29s on Hiroshima-like bombing raids over the North, often dropping dummy bombs to intimidate the enemy.

The Truman administration believed that nuclear weapons could guarantee a military victory. But administration officials soon realized that these new weapons of mass destruction did little to enhance the nation's ability to wage conventional war. Since most of the world considered the use of nuclear bombs "immoral," the administration could not use them without eroding America's image in the world. "An immoral weapon," said an air force general, "is one too big for your service to deliver." In the end, neither the nation's massive conventional advantage nor its nuclear monopoly could intimidate the enemy or produce victory. It was not the last time the United States would learn this painful lesson.

Truman-MacArthur and the Trials of Containment

With the public growing weary of war and the threat of continued bloody fighting, Truman looked for a diplomatic solution to the conflict. MacArthur opposed a settlement and insisted that U.S. forces had to attack Chinese bases north of the thirty-eighth parallel. He criticized his civilian commander-in-chief in the press, sabotaged Truman's efforts to achieve a negotiated settlement, and sent long-winded telegrams to veterans' groups outlining his own personal foreign policy for Asia. In April he wrote a letter to Republican House minority leader Joseph J. Martin of Massachusetts denouncing the stalemate. As MacArthur hoped, Martin read the letter on the floor of the House. Truman, fed up with his general's insubordination, exploded. On April 11, 1951, he relieved MacArthur of his command.

Truman miscalculated the warrior's grip on the public imagination. Within twelve days the White House received over twenty-seven thousand angry letters of protest. MacArthur returned from Korea to a hero's welcome in San Francisco, and millions crowded downtown Manhattan for one of New York's largest ticker-tape parades. Republican leaders clamored for a congressional investigation and threatened to impeach Truman. On April 19 MacArthur gave an impassioned farewell address to a joint session of Congress. He concluded by repeating a line from a West Point ballad: "Old soldiers never die, they just fade away." The words moved many congressmen to tears. "We saw a great hunk of God in the flesh, and we heard the voice of God," said one congressman. Truman's assessment was blunter and more accurate: "It was nothing but a bunch of damn bullshit."

The general's appeal transcended mere sentimentality. The public response to MacArthur's critique of Washington's handling of the Korean conflict revealed the frustration and confusion of a nation struggling to adjust to the idea of a limited war. An old man when the Korean War started, MacArthur had been trained in the military doctrine of total war. "Here in Asia is where the Communist conspirators have elected to make their play for global conquest," he wrote. "If we lose the war to Communism in Asia the fall of Europe is inevitable. . . . We must win. There is no substitute for victory."

Truman and his advisers argued that the Cold War forced America to develop a new strategy suited to fighting limited wars. MacArthur, they argued, failed to recognize that the real enemy was not North Korea but the Soviet Union. The fighting in Korea was a strategic diversion, a Russian maneuver to draw American strength away from Europe. Larger strategic goals—namely, containing Moscow—required the United States to avoid squandering its resources on the pursuit of "victory" in proxy wars in remote places.

The administration won the debate with MacArthur, but the questions raised by the confrontation would continue to haunt policy makers. With World War II as the frame of reference, most Americans were accustomed to waging total war and reaping the benefits of total victory. The fight against Hitler did little to prepare Americans for the demands of limited war. Containment required Americans to settle for fighting limited, protracted wars; seeking diplomatic solutions

Douglas MacArthur Addresses Congress   As commander of the UN forces in Korea, General Douglas MacArthur was expected to accept the decisions made by his commander-in-chief, President Harry Truman. However, in the spring of 1951, MacArthur publicly expressed his approval of bombing China to end their advance into North Korea, an idea Truman had already rejected. As a result, Truman dismissed MacArthur for insubordination on April 11 and MacArthur returned to the United States where he received a hero's welcome. On April 19, 1951, MacArthur addressed a joint session of Congress, announcing the end of his long, and at times controversial, military career.

rather than military victory; and enduring the hardship of an uncertain peace. As the MacArthur experience revealed, American expectations of both war and peace were in conflict with the new international realities of the Cold War era.

Consequences of Korea

The stalemated fighting in Korea would drag on, amid cease-fire talks, for more than a year, ending soon after Truman left office. Despite the limited nature of the war, it resulted in 36,940 American deaths and left 103,284 American soldiers wounded. It also brought significant change within the United States. It produced a huge escalation of defense spending from approximately $14 billion in 1949 to $44 billion in 1953. As government spending created millions of new jobs, unemployment dropped to its lowest level in years. Federal expenditures, together with special tax incentives, encouraged industries to expand production. From 1950 to 1954 steel capacity increased by 24 percent, electrical generating capacity by 50 percent, and aluminum capacity by 100 percent.

UN Forces in Korea, 1953 Although talks to end the Korean War began in the summer of 1951, both sides agreed the fighting would continue until they signed the armistice. For two more years the fighting persisted as the UN and North Korean forces fought to improve their position at the negotiating table by winning battles on the field. For the soldiers on the ground, the hope of peace seemed remote as they repeatedly found themselves ordered into combat; and the number of dead, wounded, and missing continued to mount.

The Korean War also accelerated the desegregation of the armed services. By mid-1950 the navy and air force had taken strides toward desegregation, but the army still maintained separate black and white units. Critics had complained that segregation, besides being morally wrong, was also wasteful and inefficient. Korea exposed another problem with segregation: assigning African-Americans to noncombat duty led whites to suffer a disproportionate share of casualties. When white troops experienced heavy losses in the early days of the war, field commanders in Korea broke with existing policy and used black soldiers as replacements. In March 1951 the Pentagon announced the integration of all training facilities in the United States. By the end of the war nearly all African-American soldiers were serving in integrated units.

The war continued the expansion of presidential power begun under Franklin Roosevelt. When North Korea invaded, Truman made a unilateral decision to intervene, acting with neither Congress's approval nor its declaration of war. Only after he had authorized American force did Truman meet with Congress to inform members about what he had done. This expansion of presidential power, and the consequent dramatic increase in government spending, however, produced little public debate or discussion. The war only sharpened the inconsistencies in America's attitude toward government. The structure of government expanded during the Korean War, but public fear of federal power persisted. In the short run conservatives tapped into those fears to fan the flames of anticommunism, but in the long run the tension between expectations of government and fear of government only sharpened during the 1950s.

The Politics of Fear

The Korean War intensified suspicions of communist subversion at home. Americans viewed communism as a double threat. Ideologically, communist doctrine challenged basic American notions of private property and individual rights. Strategically, its chief supporter, the Soviet Union, was engaged in a global struggle against the United States. Rumors that Soviet spies had infiltrated the upper echelons of American society, especially government, ignited a wildfire of fear and suspicion. Anxious Americans rushed to prove their loyalty and to punish potential subversives, who seemed to be un-American. Ferreting out disloyalty became a duty of both citizens and government. But in their efforts to prove their loyalty and assert their patriotism, Americans supported policies that contradicted the very values of individual liberty and freedom they claimed were so central to American identity.

In March 1945 government agents found numerous classified government documents in the Manhattan offices of the allegedly pro-communist *Amerasia* magazine. A year later a Canadian investigation led to the arrest of twenty-two men and women for passing classified U.S. documents to the Soviets. Together the cases proved that Soviet spies had gained access to secret government documents. "The disloyalty of American Communists is no longer a matter of conjecture," declared J. Edgar Hoover, head of the Federal Bureau of Investigation (FBI).

Americans cried out for protection against communist influence in government. In an attempt to quell public concern, President Truman in March 1947 issued Executive Order 9835, which established the Federal Employee Loyalty Program. The Truman program allowed dismissal of any federal employee where "reasonable grounds exist for belief that the person involved is disloyal." The question of loyalty and disloyalty touched on a recurring issue in American history: What does it mean to be an American? Most loyalty review boards imposed a narrow definition of loyal citizenship, using the fear of communism to intimidate people who had different ideas. Civil rights activists came under intense scrutiny, and homosexuals were automatically dismissed as security threats. The head of one government loyalty board noted, "The fact that a person believes in racial equality doesn't prove he's a Communist, but it certainly makes you look twice, doesn't it?"

Truman also used a high-profile court case to convince the public that his administration was tough on communism. In July 1948 the administration charged eleven top communist party members with violating the Smith Act of 1940, which made it a crime to conspire to "advocate and teach" the violent overthrow of government. After ten months of trial and deliberation, a lower court declared the Smith Act constitutional and the communists guilty. The Supreme Court, in *Dennis* v. *U.S.* (1951), upheld the conviction, clearing the way for prosecution of other communist leaders.

Perhaps the most talked about loyalty case occurred in August 1948 when Whittaker Chambers, an editor at *Time* magazine, accused Alger Hiss, who had served as a high-ranking aide to Franklin Roosevelt at Yalta, of having been a communist. Chambers claimed that in 1938 Hiss had given him microfilm of classified State Department documents. For many conservatives, Hiss was a symbol of the generation of young, idealistic, Ivy League liberals who had masterminded the New Deal. By attacking him, they hoped to undermine faith in the Democratic Party and remove some of the luster from Roosevelt's memory.

It seemed unlikely that the charges would stick. Chambers was a confessed former underground member of the Communist party and a homosexual ("a pervert," according to FBI director Hoover). The man Chambers was accusing was a striking patrician with impeccable credentials and extensive political contacts. To prove these charges, Chambers produced microfilm of supposedly secret documents taken from a hollowed-out pumpkin on his Maryland farm. (The documents, quickly labeled the "Pumpkin papers," were later revealed to contain information on navy life rafts and fire extinguishers.) Testifying before a grand jury in New York, Hiss denied all the charges. Since the statute of limitations on espionage had expired, Hiss was indicted for perjury instead. After one mistrial Hiss was found guilty in a second trial and sentenced to five years in jail. More than any other event, the Hiss trial convinced many Americans that the Roosevelt and Truman administrations had been oblivious to the dangers of communist espionage. California congressman Richard Nixon, among the most aggressive investigators of subversion, described the case as "the most treasonable conspiracy in American history."

Two weeks after Hiss's conviction, the British government announced the arrest of Klaus Fuchs, an atomic physicist who had worked at the Los Alamos atomic energy laboratory in New Mexico. Shortly afterward the FBI arrested Julius and Ethel Rosenberg for conspiring with Fuchs to pass secrets to the Russians. The Rosenbergs denied the allegations, insisting they were the victims of anticommunist hysteria and anti-Semitism. Recent declassified documents suggest that the government knew Ethel was innocent of espionage but charged her in an effort to squeeze a confession out of her husband. In 1951 after a two-week trial, a jury pronounced them guilty of espionage. The presiding judge, Irving Kaufman, arguing their crime was "worse than murder" because it furthered the goal of "godless" communism, sentenced the Rosenbergs to death. In June 1953, despite personal pleas from the pope and worldwide protests, they were executed.

Well before this time actions against communists and their sympathizers had spread into American culture. In 1947 the House Un-American Activities Committee (HUAC) opened a series of investigations into the Hollywood entertainment industry. "Large numbers of moving pictures that come out of Hollywood carry the Communist line," declared Democratic committee member John Rankin of Mississippi. In September the committee subpoenaed forty-one witnesses. Most cooperated with the committee by offering names of suspected communists. A small group of screenwriters, the "Hollywood Ten," served prison terms for refusing to answer questions about their ties to the Communist party. Shaken by the hearings, the studios initiated a policy of "blacklisting" writers, directors, technicians, and actors who refused to denounce communism. Industry executives assured Congress that they would not "employ a Communist or a member of any party or group which advocates the overthrow of the Government by force or by any illegal or unconstitutional means."

The government used the widespread fear of a communist takeover to expand its power to spy on its own citizens. By 1953 almost one in five Americans working in government or defense-related industries had gone through the loyalty review program. The government created millions of secret files on private

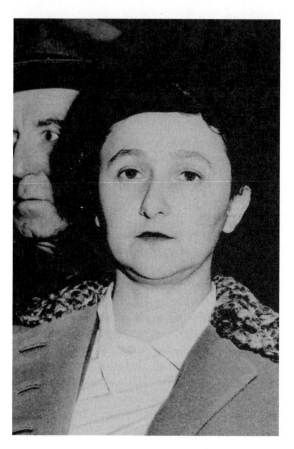

Ethel Rosenberg Going to Court Ethel Rosenberg, who appeared to most to be the typical wife and mother, was arrested in August 1950 and charged with espionage; her husband, Julius, had been charged with the same crime two months earlier. At Ethel's trial, her brother, David Greenglass, and his wife, Ruth, testified that Ethel had been an integral part of Julius's plan to sell American secrets to the Soviets. Despite two years of appeals and public outcry against the execution of an American mother, including an appeal from the pope, Ethel was put to death in the electric chair at Sing Sing Prison just minutes after her husband on June 19, 1953.

Bogey and Bacall Attend the Hollywood Ten Trials Anticommunist hysteria infiltrated all walks of American life, including the film industry, which the House Un-American Activities Committee (HUAC) began investigating in 1947. Actors, writers, and directors faced the difficult decision of cooperating with the investigation or risking their careers. When called before the committee, the Hollywood Ten refused to answer questions, claiming that, even if they were communists, the First Amendment gave them that right. Humphrey Bogart and Lauren Bacall, seen here going into the hearings, joined other stars to form the Committee for the First Amendment in support of those who refused to cooperate. However, most studio heads, fearing a public backlash against Hollywood, blacklisted the Ten and over two hundred others. *(Corbis-Bettmann.)*

citizens. HUAC alone had 1 million secret files. At the same time, the National Security Administration intercepted up to 150,000 cables a month and listened to countless phone calls.

J. Edgar Hoover skillfully manipulated the communist issue to enhance his personal reputation as a tough crime fighter and to expand his power in Washington. Between 1947 and 1952 the number of FBI agents increased from 3,559 to 7,029. Hoover manipulated public fear in pursuit of a program of widespread political surveillance that included both government employees and many private citizens. By the mid-1950s Hoover expanded his operations from intelligence gathering to harassment. In 1956 he created the Counterintelligence Program to neutralize perceived "enemies." Agents leaked damaging information to the media, falsified documents, used Internal Revenue Service audits to harass people, and spread rumors to produce dissension within the ranks.

Hoover and other government officials often used disease metaphors to describe the communist menace. These "poisonous germs," an FBI official warned in 1948, infected "every phase of American life." Liberal anticommunists focused on the threat communists presented to labor and civil rights groups, arguing that the best defense against communist subversion was to solve America's social problems. Conservatives like Hoover stressed the spiritual threat, fearing that communism preyed on the nation's moral fiber. "The danger of Communism," Hoover said, "lies . . . in the awesome fact that it is a materialistic religion inflaming in its adherents a destructive fanaticism. Communism is secularism on the march. It is a moral foe of Christianity."

Congress responded to the hysteria by passing the Internal Security Act of 1950. Among other restrictions, the act required communist and communist-front organizations to register with the government and to identify as communist all their official mail and literature. The act's most severe provisions authorized the government to place all communists in concentration camps whenever a national emergency should occur. Truman vetoed the bill, denouncing it as "the greatest danger to freedom of speech, press, and assembly, since the Alien and Sedition Laws of 1798." But Congress garnered enough votes to override the veto and enact the measure into law.

Was this fear of domestic communism justified? Previously secret American reports of decoded Soviet intelligence traffic during these years—called the Venona Intercepts—reveal that the Soviets had planted as many as one hundred spies in high-level government positions; the intercepts also offer incriminating evidence against Alger Hiss and Julius Rosenberg. Declassified files from Soviet and Eastern European archives support these conclusions while also suggesting that the Communist party in America took its orders directly from Moscow. "Not every American communist was a spy," noted the historian Harvey Klehr, "but almost every spy was a communist."

These recently released documents have fed the historical debate over the nature of the Communist party in the United States. Was it part of a long-standing American radical tradition, or was it simply a functionary of the Soviet Union and a profound threat to American security? A large group of scholars believe that, while the party owed a debt to its Soviet sponsors, members had the opportunity to adapt their ideology to American political traditions and practice. During the 1930s communists emerged as the unofficial left wing of the New Deal, supplying labor and resources to progressive social movements. American communists, noted the historian Maurice Isserman, shaped "the Party to fit their own needs and expectations." Other scholars argue that the Communist party exercised little independence from its Soviet leaders; in fact, its sole reason for existence was to do Moscow's bidding. During the 1930s and 1940s communists had infiltrated important government agencies, stolen classified documents, and tried to influence policy.

It is impossible to settle the argument about the nature of the American Communist party until scholars gain greater access to Soviet archives. But the available evidence suggests that, even though a handful worked as spies, most communists, and their liberal sympathizers, did not threaten national security. In fact, the party was disintegrating in the wake of Cold War fears, evidence of Stalin's tyranny, and Truman's loyalty program. Party membership dropped from an estimated high of eighty thousand in 1944 to only forty thousand in 1949. As Arthur Schlesinger observed, international communism was a threat to America, not in America. Ironically, it was the anticommunist crusaders who, in their reckless disregard for civil rights and liberties, posed a more serious threat to American society. "Whatever our mistakes," playwright and left-wing sympathizer Lillian Hellman wrote, "I do not believe we did our country any harm. And I think they [those who persecuted the Left] did."

Cold War Popular Culture

By taking in movies, reading magazines and novels, and watching television, Americans imbibed the culture of the Cold War. After a brief period of celebrating the Soviet Union as an American ally during the war, a dramatic swing toward anticommunism developed in the film industry, which produced such films as *The Red Menace* (1949), *The Iron Curtain* (1948), and *The Steel Fist* (1952). All painted dark portraits of the Soviets, created gross stereotypes of Russians, and underscored the menace of communist espionage. *I Was a Communist for the FBI* (1951) purported to be based on the real-life experiences of Matt Cvetic, who exposed the hypocrisy of Soviet leaders. While the Soviet power elite spoke of redistributing wealth and uplifting the working class, in reality its members lived in luxury and sought to exploit the world's laborers to further their extravagant lifestyles. The film so captured the public imagination that it was nominated for an Oscar in 1951 as a feature-length documentary.

Meanwhile, Mickey Spillane's best-selling novels about the exploits of detective Mike Hammer highlighted the need to be vigilant in the fight against the communist menace. In action-packed stories such as *The Big Kill* (1951), *My Gun Is Quick* (1950), *One Lonely Night* (1951), and *I, the Jury* (1947), World War II veteran Mike Hammer bashed heads, infiltrated communist cabals, and warded off (but only occasionally) the advances of seductive women. Hammer regularly cast aspersions on wimpy intellectuals, impotent bureaucrats, homosexuals, and no-good criminals. *One Lonely Night* climaxed with Hammer strangling his foe Oscar Deamer. "You were a Commie, Oscar, because you were batty," he growls. "It was the only philosophy that would appeal to your crazy mind."

The fear of subversion produced a culture of suspicion and mistrust. In 1948 *Look* magazine asked, "Could the Reds Seize Detroit?" The answer, which included "enacted" photos, was yes. "Many factors," the magazine claimed, "make Detroit a focal point of Communist activity." In the hysteria over communist subversion, many Americans went to extreme lengths to prove their loyalty. Indiana required professional boxers and wrestlers to take a noncommunist oath before entering the ring. A small town in New York required residents to take a loyalty oath before getting a permit to fish in the local reservoir. The Cincinnati Reds baseball team proved its patriotism by changing its name to the Cincinnati Redlegs. The desire to prove one's Americanism often produced unusual responses. On July 4, 1951, a reporter in Madison, Wisconsin, asked people to sign a petition that contained the words of the Declaration of Independence and the Bill of Rights. More than one hundred people read the petition. Only one signed it. The others dismissed it as communist propaganda.

Communities across the country organized public displays of patriotism. By 1950 most cities bragged annual loyalty day parades designed, in the words of Los Angeles organizers, for Americans "to renew their allegiance to the democratic institutions which have made our country great." The town of Mosinee, Wisconsin, went a step farther by orchestrating a mock communist takeover of the city. The Red invaders—actually members of the American Legion—arrested the mayor and police chief, locked churches, nationalized private business, purged the library of unacceptable books, and rechristened the town center "Red Square." Patriotic citizens quickly displaced the communists, however, and the day ended with the singing of the national anthem. The purpose of the exercise, editorialized the *Mosinee Times,* was "to present a message on Americanism that can be the beginning of an awakening as to the privileges inherent in our way of life."

The nation's schools and universities did not escape the ravages of the Red Scare. In June 1948 the University of California required all of its four thousand faculty members to profess their loyalty to America. Some three hundred New York City schoolteachers were fired as security risks. Zealots forced libraries to purge their shelves of "subversive" works. A librarian in Bartlesville, Oklahoma, lost her job for shelving such magazines as *The New Republic, Consumer's Research,* and *Negro Digest* and for taking part in "group discussions on race relations." A member of the Indiana State Textbook Commission tried unsuccessfully to ban from school libraries any reference to Robin Hood. The reason, he said, was that Robin Hood "robbed the rich and gave . . . to the poor. That's the Communist line. It's just a smearing of law and order."

Joseph McCarthy

In the midst of this cultural Red Scare, Joseph McCarthy became the most feared demagogue of his time. Born in 1908 to poor Irish-American farmers in northeastern Wisconsin, McCarthy earned a degree in 1935 and entered politics in 1939, running successfully for circuit judge in Wisconsin's Tenth Circuit. With the outbreak of World War II, McCarthy decided to join the glamorous marines. For three years he served as an intelligence officer debriefing American pilots following raids over the Pacific. Not satisfied with his low-profile role but unwilling to risk injury in combat, McCarthy fabricated his military record for the folks back home. He bragged about his exploits as a tail gunner flying dangerous missions and shooting down enemy planes. He claimed to have been injured when his plane crash-landed. During his Senate campaigns he walked with a limp and complained about having "ten pounds of shrapnel" in his leg. In reality, he injured his leg not while flying on a dangerous mission, but during a hazing ceremony aboard a navy ship when he slipped as he was running a gauntlet of paddle-wielding sailors.

In 1946, armed with phony wartime press releases, McCarthy ran for the Senate. During his campaign to unseat sitting Republican Robert LaFollette Jr, McCarthy crisscrossed the state attacking the New Deal, criticizing wartime controls, and pleading with voters to send a "tail gunner" to the Senate. His energetic campaign style worked: McCarthy scored a surprising victory over LaFollette in a GOP primary and went on to win easily against his Democratic opponent in the fall.

During his first few years in the Senate, McCarthy supported Truman's foreign-policy initiatives but voted with the conservative wing of his party on domestic issues. He developed a close relationship with many corporate lobbyists. His efforts to end price controls on sugar earned him the nickname "the Pepsi-Cola kid." In Senate debates McCarthy frequently distorted facts and manipulated evidence to prove his point. He reduced political issues to personal terms and turned Senate debates into angry brawls. "He can be the most affable man in the world," one senator reflected, "and suddenly he will run the knife into you—particularly if the public is going to see it."

PRIMARY SOURCE

3.2 | *Final, All-Out Battle*
JOSEPH MCCARTHY

Wisconsin senator Joseph McCarthy, speaking to the Republican Women's Club of Wheeling, West Virginia, at its annual luncheon honoring Abraham Lincoln, announced that he had uncovered the names of current government employees involved with the Communist party. The speech, given on February 9, 1950, capitalized on the growing fear of espionage and communist infiltration of the government.

A t war's end we were physically the strongest nation on earth and, at least potentially, the most powerful intellectually and morally. Ours could have been the honor of being a beacon in the desert of destruction, a shining living proof that civilization was not yet ready to destroy itself. Unfortunately, we have
5 failed miserably and tragically to rise to that opportunity.

The reason why we find ourselves in a position of impotency is not because our only powerful potential enemy has sent men to invade our shores, but rather because of the traitorous actions of those who have been treated so well by this nation. It has not been the less fortunate or members of minority groups who
10 have been selling this nation out, but rather those who have had all the benefits that the wealthiest nation on earth has had to offer—the finest homes, the finest college education, and the finest jobs in government we can give.

This is glaringly true in the State Department. There the bright young men who are born with silver spoons in their mouths are the ones who have been
15 worst. . . . In my opinion the State Department, which is one of the most important government departments, is thoroughly infested with communists.

I have here in my hand a list of 205—a list of names that were made known to the secretary of state as being members of the Communist Party and who nevertheless are still working and shaping policy in the State Department.
20 One thing to remember in discussing the communists in our government is that we are not dealing with spies who get thirty pieces of silver to steal the blueprints of a new weapon. We are dealing with a far more sinister type of activity because it permits the enemy to guide and shape our policy. . . .

This brings us to the case of one Alger Hiss, who is important not as an individ-
25 ual anymore, but rather because he is so representative of a group in the State Department. It is unnecessary to go over the sordid events showing how he sold out the nation which had given him so much. Those are rather fresh in all of our minds.

However, it should be remembered that the facts in regard to his connection with this international communist spy ring were made known to the then Under
30 Secretary of State Berle three days after Hitler and Stalin signed the Russo-German alliance pact. At that time one Whittaker Chambers, who was also part of the spy ring, apparently decided that with Russia on Hitler's side, he could no longer betray our nation to Russia. He gave Under Secretary of State Berle—and this is all a matter of record—practically all, if not more, of the facts upon which
35 Hiss's conviction was based. . . .

As you know, very recently the secretary of state proclaimed his loyalty to a man guilty of what has always been considered as the most abominable of all crimes—of being a traitor to the people who gave him a position of great trust. The secretary of state, in attempting to justify his continued devotion to the man
40 who sold out the Christian world to the atheistic world, referred to Christ's Sermon on the Mount as a justification and reason therefore, and the reaction of the American people to this would have made the heart of Abraham Lincoln happy. When this pompous diplomat in striped pants, with a phony British accent, proclaimed to the American people that Christ on the Mount endorsed commu-
45 nism, high treason, and betrayal of a sacred trust, the blasphemy was so great that it awakened the dormant indignation of the American people.   ■ ■ ■

By 1950 McCarthy was searching for an issue that would grab the public's attention. He found it in Wheeling, West Virginia, where he had traveled to speak to the Republican Women's Club. His speech, standard Republican rhetoric of the time, charged that traitors and spies had infiltrated the State Department.

What was different about the speech was McCarthy's claim to have proof. "I have here in my hand," he blustered, ". . . a list of names that were made known to the secretary of state . . . and who nevertheless are still working and shaping policy in the State Department." Though few people paid him much notice at first, he repeated, expanded, and varied his charges in succeeding speeches. By March he was front-page news across the country. McCarthy, observed a journalist, "was a political speculator who found his oil gusher in Communism."

Democrats tried to knock out McCarthy before he could do any damage to the president. Senate Democrats established a special committee to investigate McCarthy's charges and stacked it with administration loyalists. "Let me have him for three days in public hearings," boasted Maryland's powerful Millard Tydings, who chaired the committee, "and he'll never show his face in the Senate again." Tydings underestimated his opponent. McCarthy used the attention to make wild accusations. The hearings established to destroy McCarthy helped transform him into a towering national figure.

McCarthy shrewdly manipulated the press, which treated his sensational charges as page-one news. He held press conferences early in the morning to announce that he would soon release dramatic information on domestic spying. The nation's afternoon papers then printed banner headlines; "McCarthy's New Revelations Expected Soon." When reporters hounded him for details, McCarthy announced that he would soon produce a key witness. Headlines the following day would read, "Delay in McCarthy Revelations: Mystery Witness Sought." McCarthy never produced the evidence to support his accusations, but his tactics gained him the publicity he needed and thus fueled his attacks. The rules of objective journalism dictated that the press cover McCarthy's charges even if reporters knew they were not true. "Joe couldn't find a Communist in Red Square," reflected one journalist, "he didn't know Karl Marx from Groucho—but he was a United States Senator."

PRIMARY SOURCE

3.3 | *Declaration of Conscience*
MARGARET CHASE SMITH

Senator McCarthy's allegations promoted him to a position of political power that made opposition to his actions dangerous; McCarthy could easily make those against him the target of his next inquiry and in the process ruin political careers. Despite the risk, Senator Margaret Chase Smith (R-Maine), the only female senator at the time, questioned McCarthy's practices in a speech she gave before her colleagues on June 1, 1950.

I think that it is high time for the United States Senate and its members to do some real soul searching and to weigh our consciences as to the manner in which

we are performing our duty to the people of America and the manner in which we are using or abusing our individual powers and privileges. I think that it is high
5 time that we remembered that we have sworn to uphold and defend the Constitution. I think that it is high time that we remembered that the Constitution, as amended, speaks not only of the freedom of speech but also of trial by jury instead of trial by accusation. Whether it be a criminal prosecution in court or a character prosecution in the Senate, there is little practical distinction when the life of a per-
10 son has been ruined.

Those of us who shout the loudest about Americanism in making character assassinations are all too frequently those who, by our own words and acts, ignore some of the basic principles of Americanism: the right to criticize, the right to hold unpopular beliefs, the right to protest, the right of independent thought.
15 The exercise of these rights should not cost one single American citizen his reputation or his right to a livelihood, nor should he be in danger of losing his reputation or livelihood merely because he happens to know someone who holds unpopular beliefs. Who of us does not? Otherwise none of us could call our souls our own. Otherwise thought control would have set in.

20 The American people are sick and tired of being afraid to speak their minds lest they be politically smeared as communists or fascists by their opponents. Freedom of speech is not what it used to be in America. It has been so abused by some that it is not exercised by others.

The American people are sick and tired of seeing innocent people smeared
25 and guilty people whitewashed. But there have been enough proved cases—such as the Amerasia case, the Hiss case, the Coplon case, the Gold case—to cause nationwide distrust and strong suspicion that there may be something to the unproved, sensational accusations. . . .

The nation sorely needs a Republican victory. But I do not want to see the
30 Republican Party ride to political victory on the Four Horsemen of Calumny— Fear, Ignorance, Bigotry, and Smear. I doubt if the Republican Party could do so, simply because I do not believe the American people will uphold any political party that puts political exploitation above the national interest. Surely we Republicans are not that desperate for victory. I do not want to see the Republi-
35 can Party win that way. While it might be a fleeting victory for the Republican Party, it would be a more lasting defeat for the American people. Surely it would ultimately be suicide for the Republican Party and the two-party system that has protected our American liberties from the dictatorship of a one-party system.

As members of the minority party, we do not have the primary authority to
40 formulate the policy of our government. But we do have the responsibility of rendering constructive criticism, of clarifying issues, of allaying fears by acting as responsible citizens. As a woman, I wonder how the mothers, wives, sisters, and daughters feel about the way in which members of their families have been politically mangled in Senate debate—and I use the word *debate* advisedly. As a
45 United States senator, I am not proud of the way in which the Senate has been made a publicity platform for irresponsible sensationalism. I am not proud of the reckless abandon in which unproved charges have been hurled from this side of the aisle. I am not proud of the obviously staged, undignified countercharges which have been attempted in retaliation from the other side of the aisle. . . .

50   As an American, I am shocked at the way Republicans and Democrats alike are playing directly into the communist design of "confuse, divide, and conquer." As an American, I do not want a Democratic administration white-wash or cover-up any more than I want a Republican smear or witch hunt.

As an American, I condemn a Republican fascist just as much as I condemn a 55 Democrat communist. I condemn a Democrat fascist just as much as I condemn a Republican communist. They are equally dangerous to you and me and to our country. As an American, I want to see our nation recapture the strength and unity it once had when we fought the enemy instead of ourselves.   ■ ■ ■

By the fall of 1950 McCarthy was the most feared man in American politics. His face appeared on the cover of *Time* and *Newsweek*. Republican candidates begged him to make appearances on their behalf. By October he had received more than two thousand speaking requests, more than all other senators combined received. Though he campaigned around the country, McCarthy spent most of his time in Maryland, where Millard Tydings faced a tough reelection challenge. "Joe was so preoccupied with Tydings," a friend recalled, "that he'd sit by the hour figuring ways to get revenge."

Accusing his target of "protecting communists for political reasons," McCarthy distributed a widely reproduced photograph showing Tydings having a friendly conversation with deposed Communist party head Earl Browder. The "conversation" never took place: McCarthy had combined two separate pictures. When Tydings lost the election, the media credited McCarthy with the victory. *Newsweek* spoke of the "political scalps dangling from his belt." Another journalist saw "a political landscape . . . littered with the wreckage of anti-McCarthy careers." A new word entered the language: *McCarthyism.*

Why did McCarthy have such appeal? McCarthy's charges against the established elite tapped into a deep populist impulse in the American character. McCarthy called Dean Acheson a "pompous diplomat in striped pants, with a phony British accent." He denounced the "egg-sucking phony liberals" who defended "communists and queers." In focusing on liberal thinkers, homosexuals, and others who did not fit with Americans' traditional view of themselves, McCarthy exploited America's unease with its new international stature and its discomfort with alien ideas and lifestyles. In this sense McCarthyism was part of a recurring pattern in American history. In 1798 Federalists had tried to silence critics by introducing the Alien and Sedition Acts, targeting dissenters as traitors. Waves of prejudice against foreigners swept the country during the 1850s and again in the 1870s. Following World War I, the United States tried to drown "radical" thoughts in a Red Scare wave of "100 percent Americanism."

McCarthyism was also the product of partisan politics at midcentury. McCarthy had the support of conservative Republicans, who saw him as a useful means to reassert their authority in the country. Embittered by their stunning loss in the 1948 election, Republicans saw McCarthy as a way to undermine support for Truman and the Democrats and guarantee victory in the 1952 presidential campaign. So long as McCarthy wielded his anticommunist club against Democrats, many

McCarthy Investigates the State Department   Although Senator Joseph McCarthy focused much of his attention on the weaknesses of the Democrats during the 1952 presidential election, Eisenhower's victory in November did not end the Red Scare leader's quest to root out communism in the federal government. After his inauguration, Eisenhower quickly sought to expand Truman's security investigation of federal employees, but that action did not stop McCarthy from continuing his search. Journalists recognized the administration's frustration with McCarthy's continued accusations, as depicted in this cartoon in which Secretary of State John Foster Dulles attempts to coax McCarthy out of his probe into the State Department.

Republicans were willing to overlook his offensive tactics. Many GOP members repeated the refrain "I don't like some of McCarthy's methods but his goal is good."

Most of all, McCarthy capitalized on Cold War anxieties. He offered simple answers to the complex questions of the time. Strong faith in the righteousness of their position left Americans ill-prepared to comprehend the foreign-policy setbacks of the immediate postwar years. McCarthy reassured a troubled nation that the string of bad news resulted from the traitorous actions of a few individuals, not from a flawed view of the world or the strengths of communist opponents. China turned communist, he explained, because "traitors" in the State Department had sold out American interests, not because of the internal weakness of the Nationalist regime. The Soviets developed the atomic bomb because spies sold them America's secrets, not because they had talented scientists capable of developing their own bomb. The paradox of demagogues like Joseph McCarthy was that they eroded individual liberty in the name of freedom and used legitimate security concerns to undermine support for the very values they claimed to be upholding.

SELECTED READINGS

■ Akira Iriye's *The Cold War in Asia* (1974) is a good introduction for developments on that continent. Russell D. Buhite's *Soviet-American Relations in Asia*

Roy Cohn and Senator McCarthy at the Army-McCarthy Hearings From April to June 1954, Senator Joseph McCarthy made his last great attempt to root out communism in the nation's government, this time targeting the U.S. Army. McCarthy's investigation of the army began when the army drafted one of his assistants and refused to give the man a deferral so he could continue his anticommunist work with McCarthy. At the height of the Army-McCarthy hearings, which were televised live, the army's attorney, Joseph Welch, tenaciously cross-examined McCarthy's associate, Roy Cohn (seated to the left of Senator McCarthy in this picture). In retaliation, McCarthy attacked one of the young lawyers in Welch's law firm who had been a member of a communist organization for a brief time in college, but who was not involved in the Army-McCarthy hearings. Watching McCarthy's vicious attack on a young man who had long ago rejected communism led many Americans to question McCarthy's motives for the hearings and to doubt McCarthy's ability to find any real communist infiltration into the American government.

(1982) details the superpowers' conflict over the region. Michael Schaller's *The American Occupation of Japan* (1985) and John Dower's *Embracing Defeat* (1999) both study the American role in postwar Japan. The fall of China and the domestic reaction to it are the subject of Kenneth Shewmaker's *Americans and the Chinese Communists* (1971), while the widening ideological gulf between the two nations is the focus of *Useful Adversaries* (1996), by Thomas J. Christensen. Daniel Yergin's *Shattered Peace* (1977) demonstrates both the American and the Soviet motives that contributed to the arms race. Gregg Herken critiques U.S. leaders' reliance on the bomb in *The Winning*

Weapon (1980), and Richard Rhodes's *Dark Sun* (1995) examines the development of the hydrogen bomb. Ernest May's *American Cold War Strategy* (1993) places NSC-68 in historical context and provides analysis of the document by over twenty former government officials and scholars.

■ Clay Blair's *The Forgotten War* (1988) offers a moving account of the first limited war and the people who fought in it, while the best treatment of the causes and consequences of the conflict is William Stueck's *The Korean War* (1995). Rosemary Foot's *The Wrong War* (1985) explores America's unpreparedness to fight a war in Asia. Bruce Cummings's two-volume *Origins of the Korean War* (1981, 1990) is a detailed study of the politics around the conflict. For General MacArthur, William Manchester's *American Caesar* (1979) is the classic work; Michael Schaller's *Douglas MacArthur* (1989) is also helpful.

■ E. J. Kahn Jr covers the *Amerasia* controversy in *The China Hands* (1975). Allen Weinstein's *Perjury* (1978) explores the Hiss case. John E. Haynes and Harvey Klehr's *Venona* (1999) offers a new interpretation of the case based on declassified Soviet documents. Walter Schneir and Miriam Schneir detail the Rosenberg trial in *Invitation to an Inquest* (1983). Interviews with Ethel Rosenberg's brother, David Greenglass, are the basis of Sam Roberts's *The Brother* (2001). Victor S. Navasky surveys the world of informants and blacklists in *Naming Names* (1980). Larry Ceplair and Steven Englund's *The Inquisition in Hollywood* (1980) analyzes the Red Scare's impact on popular culture, while the story of one member of the Hollywood Ten is described in the autobiography of Edward Dmytryk, *Odd Man Out* (1995). Athan Theoharis and John S. Cox study the role of J. Edgar Hoover and the FBI in the Red Scare in *The Boss* (1988).

■ John Diggins surveys U.S. culture and politics in the 1940s and 1950s in *The Proud Decades* (1989). George Lipsitz studies popular culture during the era in *Class and Culture in Cold War America* (1981), as does Stephen J. Whitfield's *The Culture of the Cold War* (1996). Two of the most valuable studies of Joseph McCarthy are Richard Fried's *Nightmare in Red* (1990) and Stanley Kutler's *The American Inquisition* (1982). David M. Oshinsky's *A Conspiracy So Immense* (1983) portrays Joseph McCarthy as a product of the political conditions of the era. Ellen Schrecker's *The Age of McCarthyism* (1994) uses primary documents from the period to show how most politicians from both parties aided and abetted the Red Scare.

4

The Consumer Society, 1945–1960

As shocked journalists looked on, Vice President Richard Nixon and Soviet premier Nikita Khrushchev stood toe to toe in the hottest personal confrontation of the Cold War. The exchange took place in July 1959 as Nixon escorted the Soviet leader through the U.S. National Exhibition, a two-week exhibit in Moscow that celebrated American life. After playing with the new TV equipment and sipping soda from a bottle of Pepsi-Cola, they moved on to the most publicized display of American affluence: a six-room, model suburban ranch house filled with shining new furniture. "I want to show you this kitchen," Nixon said. "It is like those of our houses in California." "We have such things," Khrushchev retorted. But in the United States any worker could afford this house, Nixon replied. Later, when Nixon turned the topic to the new consumer devices making life easier in American homes, Khrushchev became enraged. "You Americans think that the Russian people will be astonished to see these things!" They were, he blustered, worthless gadgets.

Within minutes the conversation about television sets and washing machines escalated into an ideological clash between communism and capitalism. A defensive Khrushchev charged that the American military wanted to destroy the Soviet Union. Jamming his thumb into Nixon's chest to underscore his point, Khrushchev warned, "If you want to threaten, we will answer threat with threat." Not to appear intimidated, Nixon brazenly waived his finger in Khrushchev's face, retorting that it was the Soviets, not the Americans, who threatened the world's peace. Later that evening at a state dinner Nixon, still gloating over the display of American affluence, told his Soviet hosts that the United States had achieved "the ideal of prosperity for all in a class-less society."

This "Kitchen debate," appropriately set in the simulated kitchen of a suburban house, captured the conflicting currents of the decade. During the 1950s the United States experienced a "consumer revolution" as millions of Americans scrambled to buy a new home in the suburbs and fill it with the latest consumer gadgets. Television, the most popular of the new products, reinforced the celebration of traditional values under way by offering Americans a steady diet of shared images. America's love affair with the material benefits of prosperity bred contentment, especially among the expanding white middle classes, and reinforced traditional American optimism about the future.

What many Americans failed to realize at the time was that all these celebrations of prosperity and national unity raised expectations among groups that had been excluded from mainstream society. These years sharpened the paradox between expectations and social realities and laid the background for the social turmoil to come in the 1960s.

The Baby Boom and the Rise of Mass Consumption

The United States experienced an unprecedented economic boom following World War II. Between 1940 and 1960 the gross national product (GNP) more than doubled from $227 billion to $488 billion. The median family income rose from $3,083 to $5,657, and real wages rose by almost 30 percent. By 1960 a record 66.5 million Americans held jobs. And unlike in earlier boom times, runaway prices did not eat up rising income: inflation averaged only 1.5 percent annually in the 1950s. "Never had so many people, anywhere, been so well off," the editors of *U.S. News and World Report* concluded in 1957.

At the heart of the new prosperity was a dramatic increase in consumer spending. A postwar "baby boom" created an enormous demand for new consumer goods that propelled the economy forward as Americans experimented with new ways of living and spending. To provide more room for growing families, millions of Americans moved to the new suburban communities sprouting up around major cities.

"It seems to me," observed a British visitor to America in 1958, "that every other young housewife I see is pregnant." Americans in the postwar period were marrying younger and having more children then ever before. Between 1940 and 1955 the United States experienced the largest population increase in its history—27 percent, from 130 million to 165 million. The baby boom peaked in 1957, when 4.3 million babies were born, one every seven seconds.

Why the rush to have babies? Several reasons can be identified. First, young couples who had delayed getting married during World War II decided to make up for lost time. Indeed, as the decade progressed, the median age of those

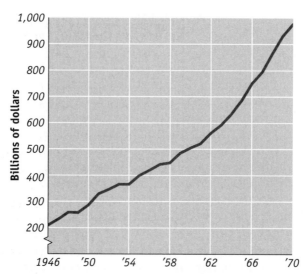

Gross National Product A number of factors, including pent-up consumer demands and profuse military spending, spurred the GNP upward after World War II. The climbing GNP figures reflect the prosperity of the 1950s and 1960s, with the numbers almost doubling from 1945 to 1960 and showing even more dramatic growth during the 1960s. (Source: Adapted from U.S. Bureau of the Census, *Historical Statistics of the United States, Colonial Times to 1970,* Bicentennial Edition, Washington, D.C.: U.S. Government Printing Office, 1975, 224.)

getting married hit historic lows—20.1 years for women and 22.5 for men. Young couples were starting families earlier and continuing to have children over a longer period of time.

Second, changing cultural attitudes toward sexuality and pregnancy created a "procreation ethic" that encouraged young couples to have children. Popular television shows and magazine stories celebrated the joys of pregnancy and motherhood, as did advertisers: "I'm Alice Cook," declared a suburban housewife in one aspirin commercial. "I have six children, and they come in all shapes and sizes. So do their colds."

Third, a general spirit of confidence about the future convinced young couples they could afford the demands of parenthood. Government policies played a key role in promoting the new optimism. The Serviceman's Readjustment Act, popularly known as the GI Bill, which Congress passed in 1944, pumped millions of dollars into the economy by providing veterans with unemployment compensation, medical benefits, loans to start new businesses, and tuition benefits for continuing education.

Fourth, modern science contributed to the fertility euphoria by conquering diseases that had plagued human beings for centuries. Antibiotics and other new drugs subdued diseases such as tuberculosis, diphtheria, whooping cough, and measles. The most significant achievement was the victory over poliomyelitis

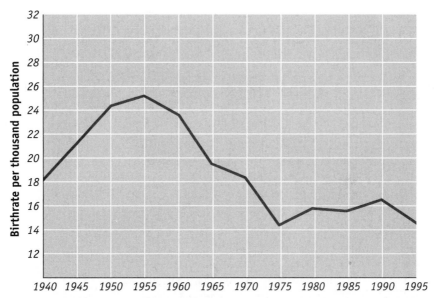

American Birthrate   The bulge in the birthrate from the end of World War II to the mid-1960s marks the height of the "baby boom." By their sheer numbers, the members of this generation could not help but shape every aspect of American culture for the rest of the twentieth century. (Source: National Center for Health Statistics, U.S. Dept. of Health and Human Services, as reported in *Statistical Abstract of the U.S., 1997* and *World Almanac, 1998.*)

(polio), most of whose victims were children. Between 1947 and 1951 this crippling disease struck an annual average of thirty-nine thousand Americans. In 1955 Dr. Jonas Salk of the Pittsburgh Medical School developed the first effective vaccine against polio, and by 1960 vaccines had practically eliminated the disease in the United States.

The consumer revolution traced its roots back to the 1920s, but postwar affluence and the baby boom allowed it to blossom in the years following World War II. In 1958 *Life* magazine called children the "Built-in Recession Cure," concluding that all babies were potential consumers who spearheaded "a brand-new market for food, clothing, and shelter." Signs in the New York City subway read: "Your future is great in a growing America. Everyday 11,000 babies are born in America. This means new business, new jobs, new opportunities." Parents purchased an endless number of products to raise their families. In 1957 Americans spent $50 million on diapers. Toy sales skyrocketed. By the end of the decade Americans were buying over 2 million bicycles a year. Many Americans turned to new discount stores to get the latest products at the lowest prices.

Advertising whetted America's appetite for these new products. The amount of money spent to advertise products doubled during the decade from $6 billion to over $12 billion. TV screens and the pages of *Life, Collier's,* and the *Saturday Evening Post* glittered with ads. Advertising helped promote the rise of a credit

The End of Polio   By the 1950s, polio had killed or disabled thousands of children and young adults, and two epidemics in 1950 and 1952 afflicted ninety thousand more. A massive effort by medical researchers and ordinary Americans who contributed to the March of Dimes finally yielded success when on April 12, 1955 (the anniversary of polio-patient FDR's death), Dr. Jonas Salk, himself a victim of the disease, announced his vaccine was effective. By the end of the decade, most children had been inoculated, and the disease was virtually eradicated. Here six-year-old Michael Urnezis of San Diego reluctantly receives his vaccine while his twelve-year-old sister and polio survivor, Joanne, joyfully looks on. *(Corbis-Bettmann.)*

society: if people did not have the money to purchase products, they borrowed it. "Buy Now, Pay Later," General Motors (GM) declared. The credit card business began in 1950 with the introduction of the Diner's Club card. Oil companies, motel and hotel chains, and many other companies introduced credit cards in the 1950s as well. By the end of the decade Sears Roebuck, a large department store, had more than 10 million accounts. "Capitalism is dead—consumerism is king," declared a sales executive. And *Newsweek* announced in 1953, "Never before have so many owed so much to so many." As a result, total private debt in the United States increased from $104.8 billion to $263.3 billion during the 1950s.

The emergence of the credit card symbolized the evolving societal change from independence and frugality to consumption and debt. For generations many Americans had followed the advice of Benjamin Franklin: "A penny saved is a penny earned." But in the 1950s advertisers encouraged Americans to buy now and pay later. One observer commented, "Thrift now is un-American." But older attitudes died hard. The challenge for advertisers, noted a social scientist, was resolving "the conflict between pleasure and guilt;" not just to sell the product, but to give consumers "moral permission to have fun without guilt." Much of the advertising of the decade focused on consumer goods as rewards for years of hard work and sacrifice. "Here is the man who has earned the right to sit at this wheel," a Cadillac ad declared. McDonald's slogans ended by stating, "You deserve a break today."

Consumer demand for new products was just one force contributing to the postwar prosperity. Government spending played an important role as well. Overall government spending, which amounted to only 1 percent of the GNP in 1929, ballooned to more than 25 percent in 1960. Governments directly employed more than 8 million people by 1957, double the number in 1940. The military alone spent almost $40 billion a year, accounting for approximately 60 percent of the federal budget and 10 percent of the GNP. In addition, government programs, such as the Marshall Plan, opened new markets to American goods or, like the GI Bill, added millions of dollars directly to the economy.

The Rise of the Suburbs

The return of American servicemen following World War II produced a severe housing shortage. In 1945, 98 percent of American cities reported housing shortages. By 1947, 6 million families (or 35 million nationwide) were doubling up with friends or family. People were living in trolley cars, abandoned missile silos, and army barracks left over from World War II.

Many urban Americans looked to the suburbs to provide the additional space needed for their growing families, while rural residents and farmers moved to these same suburbs in search of better jobs and more opportunity. In New York City 1.5 million people moved to the suburbs in the 1950s, while outside Los Angeles, Orange County more than tripled in population. Similar growth occurred around many other cities across the country until by 1960 almost 60 million people, making up about one-third of the total population, resided in suburban areas.

Builders plowed under more than 1 million acres of farmland every year to make way for new communities. Of the 13 million homes built in the decade before 1958, 85 percent were built in the suburbs. Inexpensive housing in the suburbs led to a boom in home ownership, which by 1960 was double that of any other industrialized country in the world.

Builder William Levitt made the suburban dream a reality for millions of Americans. In 1949 Levitt bought 4,000 acres of potato fields in Hempstead, Long Island. Using mass-production methods, he produced affordable suburban homes for young families. Every house was identical: one story high, with a 12-by-16-foot living room, a kitchen, two bedrooms, and a tiled bathroom. The price: $7,990, or $60 a month with no money down. Buyers snapped up 1,400 houses in the first three hours after sales began in March 1949. Levitt built a new home every sixteen minutes, as many as 150 homes a week. The *New York Times* wrote that Levittown houses "turned the detached, single-family house from a distant dream to a real possibility for thousands of middle-class American families." Levitt eventually built three northeastern Levittowns: in Long Island, New York (1947); Bucks County, Pennsylvania (1952); and in Burlington County, New Jersey (1958). Builders throughout the country quickly followed his example.

Levitt built the houses, but government made the homes affordable for millions of young families. Congress approved higher spending for home loans provided by the Federal Housing Administration (FHA) and the Veterans Administration (VA). These agencies revolutionized home ownership in the United States. In the past prospective homeowners had had to produce a significant downpayment, often 50 percent or more, and pay off the rest of the loan in less than ten years. The FHA and VA required only a 10 percent downpayment and allowed homeowners to pay off the mortgage over thirty years at a low interest rate. By 1955 these two agencies insured 41 percent of all new nonfarm mortgages.

The suburbs fed the consumer society's appetite for new products. The average suburban family earned 70 percent more income than the rest of the nation. "Suburbia," *Fortune* magazine observed in 1953, is "the cream of the market." But suburbanites were not the only Americans filling their homes with new furniture and the latest in electrical gadgetry. By 1960, 96 percent of the nation's families owned refrigerators, 87 percent their own TV set, and 75 percent their own washing machine. The swimming pool, in the past affordable only by the rich, began to appear in the yards of more and more middle-class homeowners.

For all the opportunities opened by the development of suburbia, it was not the dream come true for all Americans. Blacks were excluded from many of the new suburban communities. Levitt banned African-Americans from Levittown. "I have come to know," he said, "that if we sell one house to a Negro family, then 90 or 95 percent of our white customers will not buy into the community." Suburban communities used a variety of formal and informal methods to exclude blacks. In many cases, local real estate agents refused to sell houses to blacks and bankers rejected their mortgage applications. Some communities adopted zoning regulations designed to exclude lower income groups. The methods proved effective: by the end of the decade African-Americans made up less than 5 percent of suburban residents.

The Changing World of Work

Meeting the demands of the new consumer society produced enormous changes in the economy and in the nature of work. The 1950s witnessed an acceleration of the trend toward concentration of power in the hands of fewer corporations. By the end of the decade some 600 corporations, which made up only 0.5 percent of all

U.S. companies, accounted for 53 percent of total corporate income. In the Cold War defense buildup the government contributed to the growth of big business by awarding military contracts to a handful of large corporations. Industrial giants used their vast resources to gobble up smaller competitors. Between 1950 and 1961 the 500 largest American corporations merged with 3,404 smaller companies.

In addition to mergers, U.S. corporations extended their reach by establishing themselves abroad. Boosted by government programs such as the Marshall Plan, U.S. corporate investment overseas increased by nearly 300 percent during the decade. After World War II the most successful corporations developed new products and moved into new markets.

Expanding computer use represented the decade's most significant technological development. First developed to aid the defense effort during World War II, the original machines were massive: the Mark I, completed in 1944, stretched 50 feet in length and stood 8 feet high. In 1946 engineers at the University of Pennsylvania marketed the first commercial computer. International Business Machines, already a leader in the office-equipment industry, produced its first computer in 1953. The new technology was at the forefront of a wave of automation that promised to boost productivity and cut labor costs. By 1957 more than 1,250 computers were in use making airline reservations, forecasting elections, and helping banks process checks.

At the same time, important economic changes were disrupting the lives of millions of Americans. From 1947 to 1957 the number of factory workers dropped 4 percent. Automation alone eliminated an estimated 1.5 million blue-collar workers, most of them union members, between 1953 and 1959. Those jobs were replaced by new service-sector positions. In 1956, for the first time in U.S. history, white-collar workers outnumbered their blue-collar counterparts. In the two decades after 1950, 9 million jobs opened up for secondary-school teachers, hospital support staff, and local government office workers. Consumer demand spurred the creation of new department stores and supermarkets staffed by 3 million additional employees.

The consumer economy presented organized labor with new challenges. At first glance, unions appeared to make tremendous gains during the decade. The number of union members in the United States climbed from 14.7 million in 1945 to 18 million in the mid-1950s. In 1955 the two most powerful labor organizations, the American Federation of Labor, headed by George Meany, and the Congress of Industrial Organizations, led by Walter Reuther, merged into one great federation. But unions faced serious problems making inroads into the fastest growing segment of the work force: white-collar employees. By 1960 unions had organized less than 184,000 of 5 million public employees and only 200,000 of 8.5 million office workers.

During this time, however, the significance of low white-collar unionization was not apparent. Labor-management relations became far less antagonistic than they had been in the 1930s, with few strikes or work stoppages. In 1950 General Motors and the United Automobile Workers signed a contract containing two provisions that would become standard in postwar contracts: (1) an automatic cost-of-living wage increase for workers and (2) a guarantee that wages would rise with productivity. Critics charged that the new accord between labor and management bred contentment and stagnation as union leaders who joined the middle class lost touch with the problems plaguing the working class. "The young, class-conscious workingmen who had fought the battles of River Rouge and Flint in the 1930s," wrote the historian William Leuchtenburg, "had become middle-aged, enbourgeoised members of the PTA."

Shaping National Culture: The Shared Images of Television

Television emerged as the most visible symbol of the new consumer society. TV transformed the cultural landscape in America by bringing people from diverse backgrounds together in a shared experience. Along with the automobile, which broke down the geographical distance separating rural and urban, television helped promote a national culture.

Although television had been invented in the 1920s, it did not gain widespread acceptance until the 1950s. Mass production and technological advances in the 1950s allowed most American families to own a set. The size of the screen expanded from 12 inches to 19 and 21 inches. Even as color was introduced in 1953, the cost of the sets declined from $700 in the late 1940s to as little as $200 by 1955. In 1946 about one of every eighteen thousand people owned a TV set. By 1960 nine out of every ten American homes had a TV. Its appeal was universal: designed for a mass audience, television did not honor race or class divisions.

Most shows avoided controversy and celebrated traditional American values. Families were intact, men worked during the day, women stayed at home. No one was ever sick. No one was poor. No one was African-American. "We never had any blacks on television," said the casting director for CBS. Shows such as *Ozzie and Harriet, Father Knows Best,* and *Leave It to Beaver* presented a glossy image of middle-class suburban life. Supportive wives spent their days minding the household and the clean-cut kids while their husbands provided for the family and solved the family crisis of the day. Millions of families gathered around the television set each week to watch as Superman, a comic-book hero turned television star, fought for "truth, justice, and the American way." Only a few shows, such as Jackie Gleason's *The Honeymooners,* which described life in a bleak urban apartment, hinted at the world beyond suburbia.

Television shows, often produced in cooperation with the armed services, reinforced the Cold War ethos by glorifying the military and America's role in the world. During the 1952–53 television season every Sunday afternoon families gathered around the television set to watch *Victory at Sea.* "From island to island," intoned the narrator, "continent to continent, the children of free peoples move the forces of tyranny from the face of the earth. . . . It is, it will be so, until the forces of tyranny are no more." In some cases the Defense Department produced shows for the networks. The *Armed Forces Hour* aired documentaries from each branch of the service, like the navy's *Take 'Er Down* or the air force's *Air Defense.* The army's *Big Picture* documentary was the most popular. "From Korea to Germany, from Alaska to Puerto Rico, all over the world the United States Army is on the alert to defend our country—you, the American people—against aggression."

Television viewers also tuned into quiz shows that offered excitement and instant success. The format, which frequently saw taxi drivers and bricklayers outwit doctors and lawyers for huge cash prizes, reaffirmed the rags-to-riches notion that anybody could strike it rich in America. Charles Van Doren, a young Columbia University professor, dazzled millions of television viewers with his knowledge of everything from opera to chemistry on the popular show *Twenty-one.* In 1959, however, congressional investigators exposed Van Doren as a fraud: he had been given all the answers in advance. The scandal killed the quiz shows but did little to dampen public enthusiasm for television.

TV transformed American social habits. Studies showed that the average household watched five hours of television a day. Most viewers confessed to reading fewer books and magazines after purchasing a TV set. When a popular show was on, all the toilets in the nation flushed at the same time: during commercial breaks and when the program ended. Saturated by commercials, children recited the Pepsi-Cola theme song before they learned the national anthem and recognized the word *detergent* before they could read. As the poet T. S. Eliot observed, television provided a valuable shared experience, but it was "a medium of entertainment which permits millions of people to listen to the same joke at the same time, and yet remain lonesome."

By promoting national brand names, advertising helped standardize purchasing decisions. By 1956 companies were spending over $488 million a year on network advertising. Advertising executives discovered that television could do what radio never could: "Show the product," one adman exclaimed, "and show it in use." Many advertisers did just that: a Remington razor shaved the fuzz off a peach, and a Band-Aid, as a demonstration of its strength, lifted an egg. Advertisers frequently used subtle psychological appeals to create consumer demand for their products. The Phillip Morris tobacco company, for example, created the Marlboro Man to create a link in the public mind between cigarette smoking and masculinity. "At a time when many Americans feared losing their individualism to the norms of suburbia, the myth of the cowboy, celebrated by Hollywood in a thousand films, was powerful stuff," observed David Halberstam.

But advertising was not without its challenges. In 1952 Washington ordered Philip Morris to stop claiming that its cigarettes were "recognized as being less irritating to the nose and throat by eminent nose and throat doctors." A few years later *Reader's Digest* published an article linking smoking with certain forms of cancer. For that reason tobacco companies became especially sensitive about how their product was presented on television. On the *Camel News Caravan* cameras were forbidden to show "No Smoking" signs. Camel cigarettes, which also sponsored *Man Against Crime,* issued specific instructions that criminals could never be shown with a cigarette, fires and arson were out since they might suggest that cigarettes produced fires, and no one was ever allowed to cough on the show. When an actor on another show sponsored by a cigarette manufacturer said that his wife's astrological sign was Cancer, the advertiser ordered the scene refilmed, with Cancer changed to Aries.

In order to target products more effectively, advertisers needed information about their audience. In 1950 the Neilsen Company launched its "Television Index," issuing daily ratings of shows. The Neilsen ratings transformed the family into a commodity to be identified, measured, and sold the right "show." The new rating system convinced television advertisers that they could direct their products specifically to children. "Never underestimate the buying power of a child under seven," the star of the television show *Ding Dong School* told a 1954 advertising conference. "He has brand loyalty and the determination to see that his parents purchase the product of his choice."

Not surprisingly, toys fashioned after military weapons were among the most popular children's items during the 1950s. Advertisers sold toys that allowed youngsters to fantasize about shooting nuclear weapons or buy "an exact automatic action replica of our Navy's newest atomic sub, or fire a water-powered 'ICBM.' " In 1955 Mattel, a small toy company, spent an unheard-of $500,000 to sell its new Burp Gun, which it described as a cap gun "modeled after the machine guns used in WWII jungle fighting." Orders flooded in so fast that the toy maker sold out before Christmas, creating a national panic. President Dwight D. Eisenhower had to write to Mattel to request one for his grandchild.

The combination of advertising, prosperity, and television produced overnight national fads. In 1954 the popular Disneyland show *Davy Crockett* produced the first fad of the decade. The "king of the wild frontier" became an instant hero among millions of children. Enterprising manufacturers flooded the market with Davy Crockett coonskin caps, knives, bow and arrow sets, and records of the show's theme song, "The Ballad of Davy Crockett." Before the fad was over, more than $100 million worth of Crockett paraphernalia had been sold.

Likewise, professional sports flowered under the sympathetic eye of the camera. Television exposed more people to sports, making popular figures out of athletic heroes and pouring money into team coffers. "The golden age is now," declared *Sports Illustrated* in its premier issue in August 1954. The leading spectator sport was baseball. In 1953 the sixteen major league teams drew 14.3 million into their parks, while millions more watched on television. Thanks to television, professional football became a new supersport, the first true rival to major league baseball for the nation's affection. Attendance at professional football games rose steadily for eight straight years, going from 1.9 million in 1950 to 2.9 million in 1957.

As television absorbed millions of dollars of advertising money, it squeezed out other entertainment sources. Radio suffered most, losing nearly one-half of its audience between 1948 and 1956. Thousands of motion picture houses were forced to close their doors. "Why go to the movies," asked film executive Samuel

A Family of Television Viewers   By the mid-1950s, most homes in America had a television in their living room, which quickly replaced the dining room as the center of family activity. While the screen was much smaller than on later televisions, families circled the "boob tube" to watch their favorite westerns, comedies, dramas, and variety shows. There were also numerous children's cartoons and shows, the most popular of which was *Howdy Doody.* Once a week, when the announcer of the show asked America's television audience, "What time is it?", children across the country shouted in unison, "It's Howdy Doody time!" *Howdy Doody* not only came into the nation's homes via the television; images of Howdy Doody and other members of the cast were plastered on lunch boxes, dolls, and TV tray place mats.

Goldwyn in 1955, "when you can stay home and see nothing worse?" Many large-circulation magazines suffered a similar fate. General-interest magazines such as *Life,* the *Saturday Evening Post, Look,* and *Women's Home Companion* lost circulation and eventually ceased publication.

Television transformed religious preachers into overnight celebrities. The first clergyman to become a television star was the Most Reverend Fulton J. Sheen, who warned viewers that godless communism was infiltrating American institutions, especially government, and advised against making peace with the Soviets. At the height of his popularity Sheen's *Life Is Worth Living* show played to an audience of 10 million people.

Sheen competed for airtime with ordained Methodist minister Norman Vincent Peale, who reached millions of people every week with his television and radio shows and his own magazine. Peale preached a gospel of reassurance and comfort by mixing religion with traditional American ideas of success. Published at $2.95 in 1952, his book *The Power of Positive Thinking* stayed at the top of the nonfiction best-seller list for 112 consecutive weeks. In 1954 it sold more copies than any other book except the Bible.

The most popular evangelist of the 1950s was undoubtedly Billy Graham. In 1954 *Time* magazine described Graham as "the best known, most talked about Christian leader in the world today, barring the Pope." Handsome and dynamic, Graham used the mass media to reach millions of people. Like other popular preachers of the day, he downplayed doctrinal differences, emphasized the common link between Christian teachings and American values, and warned of the evils of communism, which he called "a great sinister anti-Christian movement masterminded by Satan." When critics complained that Graham sold religion like Madison Avenue sold consumer products, the preacher responded, "I am selling the greatest product in the world; why shouldn't it be promoted as well as soap?"

PRIMARY SOURCE

4.1 | *America's Greatest Sin*
BILLY GRAHAM

During the religious revival of the 1950s, no minister had a greater national audience than Billy Graham. In his sermon "America's Greatest Sin," first preached on September 24, 1958, in Charlotte, North Carolina, Graham explored the sins of a consumer society that needed to repent.

Americans are considered all over the world as materialistic, worldly, secular, greedy, and covetous. We are guilty of that sin as a nation, as a people, and as individuals. Americans have the highest standard of living the world has ever known. Never in history—in Rome, in Babylon, in the great nations of the past—
5 has there ever been a standard of living like we enjoy in America.

You say, "But, Billy, I'm not a rich person." You have shoes, don't you? You have a suit of clothes; you have a dress. Then you are rich by the world's standards. You had something to eat, didn't you? In India tonight, over a hundred million people will go to bed hungry tonight—if they have a bed to go to. And
10 when they drive the trucks down the streets of Calcutta tomorrow morning, they will pick up people that died of starvation, as I have seen them in India. The poorest person in this audience tonight is rich by the world's standards.

Billy Graham's Revival at Madison Square Garden   The 1950s brought a major upswing in church attendance in the United States and a growing awareness of the importance of religion in the lives of Americans facing the anxieties of the Cold War. Among the leaders of the religious revival movement was Billy Graham, a young minister from North Carolina who spent the decade organizing and preaching at evangelical rallies in every major city in the nation and also in Africa, Europe, Asia, and South America. One of his most successful revivals was his New York Crusade of 1957, which began as an eight-week series of revival meetings, but which was quickly extended to sixteen weeks because of the overwhelming demand to hear Graham preach.

And in spite of our riches, in spite of our high standard of living, our whole
15 economy is geared to getting more. The capitalist wants more profit. The laboring man wants more wages for less hours. And all of us are engaged in a mad race—trampling over each other, cheating each other, lying, stealing, any way we can get it—to get another dollar. The Bible says it's the sin of covetousness. "Thou shall not covet."
20 The word "covetousness" means to delight in something. It's the object of your attention—to wish for, to desire it, to love, to set your heart on. Something that fascinates, something that you long for, something that you are looking for; to get more of this world's goods, even if it means the starvation of your own soul.
25 You are a rich man, and you are a rich person now. I'm not talking about the millionaire now. I'm talking about the man that makes twenty-five dollars a week. I am talking about a rich American.

This man went out, looked over his fields and he saw his barn. And he said, "Soul, take thine ease, drink and be merry, you've laid up enough goods. You've
30 got economic security now. You've got money in the bank. You've got good insurance policies. You've got a good job. You've got a good business. Take it easy. Go and get you a little cottage in Florida and take it easy." God says, "Wait a minute."

That man went to his room that night and retired in his soft bed. About midnight, the servants heard a scream. They ran to the master's room and they found
35 him on the floor, writhing and dying, and his hands folded in a strange manner as though he had been holding on to something and suddenly it had slipped away. And they heard a voice from heaven that said, "Thou fool, this night thy soul is required of thee."

God said that any man that will give himself to the making of money over
40 and against the development and nature of his own soul is a fool, and doesn't deserve to live. Jesus said, "Out of the heart proceeds covetousness. These evil things come from within, in defilement of man" [see Mark 7:21–23].

The Scripture again says in Ephesians 5:3 that "fornication, and all uncleanness, or covetousness, let it not be once named among you." Also, in verse 5, "Nor
45 covetous man, who is an idolater, hath any inheritance in the kingdom of . . . God."

God says that covetousness is actually idolatry, and He says a covetous person has no place in the kingdom of God. No place in the kingdom of God—the Bible says that in Ephesians 5:3 and 5. I just read it to you. If words mean anything, it means that a covetous person shall not go to heaven, shall not be saved. You say,
50 "Well, Billy, isn't a man supposed to take care of his family?" Yes. The Bible says "Give me not poverty lest I steal" [see Proverbs 30:8, 9].

We are to have enough, but we're not to give our full attention to the things of the world. Our first attention is to be on Christ. We are to seek first the kingdom of God and his righteousness, then all of these things shall be added unto us [see
55 Matthew 6:33].

Is that what you're doing? Are you seeking God's kingdom first? Are you seeking the things of Christ first? Or is your business, your pleasure, your amusement—the things of this world—first in your life? . . .

You can't work your way to heaven if you join every church in town. You
60 could work from now on, and you could never save yourself. Salvation is by the grace and mercy of God. Ladies and gentlemen, we are all sinners. We all deserve hell, and we are going to get hell, unless we are willing to repent and come to the cross; hell in this life, and in the life to come. ■ ■ ■

Graham's ecumenical message helped transform Christianity into a national religion. Church membership and professions of faith became popular methods of affirming "the American way of life" during the Cold War.

"Today in the U.S.," *Time* magazine claimed in 1954, "the Christian faith is back in the center of things." Considerable evidence existed to support the claim. Church membership skyrocketed from 64 million in 1940 to 114 million in 1960. Sales of Bibles reached an all-time high. In 1954 Congress added the phrase "under God" to the Pledge of Allegiance and the next year mandated "In God We Trust" on all U.S. currency. The return to religion found expression in religious songs such as "I Believe" and movies such as *The Robe* (1953) and *The Ten Commandments* (1956). "Everyone I knew went to church," Eisenhower reflected. "The only exception were people we thought of as the toughs—pool room sharks, we called them."

However, in an influential 1955 study the theologian Will Herberg complained that modern religion was "without serious commitment, without real inner conviction, without genuine existential decision." Polls showed that a majority of Americans could not distinguish the New Testament from the Old or even name one of the Gospels. Religion offered Americans what they needed most in the 1950s: a sense of belonging in a rapidly changing society and divine support for traditional American values in the battle with communism. As the *Christian Century* noted in 1954, it had become "un-American to be unreligious."

The paradox of television was that an essentially conservative medium would, in time, produce such revolutionary changes in American society. By celebrating American prosperity, television contributed to America's grand expectations for the postwar world. The contrast between the idealized image of America as seen on the screen and the often harsh reality of everyday life for the nation's poor, women, and minorities contributed to the broad social movement in the 1960s to extend opportunity to all groups in society. Television avoided challenging racial stereotypes, but news coverage of white violence against blacks in the South would touch the nation's conscience and propel forward the civil-rights movement.

The Car Culture

Television nationalized culture by projecting a common set of images, a shared language, that Americans experienced in the comfort of their homes. At the same time, a dramatic increase in the number of automobiles and new highways narrowed the physical gap between rural and urban communities.

Manufacturers had halted the production of automobiles during World War II, but once the war was over, car sales boomed. Car registrations soared from 26 million in 1945 to 60 million in 1960. The number of two-car families doubled between 1951 and 1958. By 1956 an estimated 75 million cars and trucks were on American roads. During these years General Motors developed a strategy of breaking down the consumer market into niches defined by economic and social status. The car was no longer just a means of transportation; it was now a reflection of status. GM cars in the 1950s, observed a critic, "were brought about by a deliberate corporate policy of encouraging dreams." GM designed the Chevy to appeal to blue-collar workers or young couples buying their first car; the Pontiac, to attract young professional types who wanted a sportier car; the luxurious Cadillac, to fit the ambitions of top executives. In order to keep people buying cars, GM instituted the annual model change, designed to make car owners eager for the latest equipment.

What Americans wanted most of all were style, horsepower, and convenience. The decade witnessed the introduction of a number of innovations that made

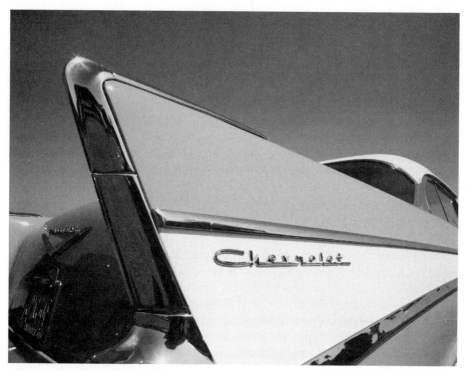

The Transformation of the Chevrolet Tail Fin The pent-up demand for consumer goods led many Americans on a quest to fulfill those purchasing needs after World War II, and car manufacturers looked for ways to draw consumers to their automobiles. As consumer spending skyrocketed in the 1950s, automobile makers worked diligently to construct the most modern and desirable car. By the end of the decade, Chevy was changing the style of the car's tail fin each year, making it longer and more detailed as the decade wore on. For consumers concerned with keeping up the appearance of personal wealth and prosperity, it was necessary to purchase a new car every couple of years so as not to be labeled behind the times.

driving both exciting and comfortable. By 1960 most cars boasted power brakes and steering, automatic transmission, a high-compression V-8 engine that reached over 400 horsepower, a padded dashboard and seat backs, a fiberglass body, and air conditioning. Consumer demands led car makers to develop over 350 varieties of styles. The prospective car buyer could pick a long car, a lower car, more or less chrome, tail fins, multiple taillights, bright colors, a plush interior, and an endless array of gadgets. The one innovation car makers seemed least concerned with was safety. Even though cars were involved in 5 million accidents a year, manufacturers were convinced that "a square foot of chrome sells ten times more cars than the best safety-door latch."

With millions of new cars on the road, Americans demanded better roads and highways. The Eisenhower administration backed the building of a nationwide network of four-lane highways to allow for the massive evacuation of urban areas in case of a nuclear war. Congress responded in 1956 by passing the Interstate Highway Act. The largest public works project in American history, this act appropriated $32 billion to build 41,000 miles of highway. The new highway system made travel easier, faster, and more convenient. By the end of the decade the nation had over 3 million miles of roads, almost 75 percent of which were paved. In 1950 Americans traveled 458 billion miles by car; by the early 1960s that number had nearly doubled to 800 billion.

The car had a profound impact on American life during the 1950s. By the end of the decade the automobile was directly or indirectly responsible for one-sixth of the GNP and millions of jobs. In turn, the auto industry spurred production in related industries: petroleum, steel, tourism and travel, service stations, and highway construction and maintenance. The automobile also promoted the decline of metropolitan areas by accelerating the move to the suburbs, added to the decay of public transportation, and produced higher levels of air pollution.

Cars and new roads contributed to a massive population shift from the Northeast to the South and West. Florida's population boomed, fed by the tourist industry, an influx of retirees, and a rapid expansion of the fruit industry. The fastest growth occurred in California, which added 3.1 million residents and accounted for an astounding 20 percent of the nation's population growth in the fifties. By 1963 California had moved past New York as the nation's most populous state. By 1960 half of the people living in the West were living in a state different from the one in which they had been born.

By opening the development of suburban retail commerce, the automobile also made the United States a more homogeneous nation. "Our new roads, with their ancillaries, the motels, filling stations and restaurants advertising Eats, have made it possible for you to drive from Brooklyn to Los Angeles without a change of diet, scenery, or culture," observed critic John Keats. In metropolitan areas across the country small mom-and-pop stores gave way to mammoth shopping malls housing national retail chains on the edges of the city. Korvettes, the largest chain of discount stores, opened its first suburban store in 1953; by the end of the decade twenty-five stores were operating in four states. Interchangeable motels and fast-food chains materialized nearby. In August 1952 Kemmons Wilson opened the first Holiday Inn in Memphis, Tennessee. The hotel offered all the amenities needed by tired travelers and businessmen: a restaurant, a gift shop, a swimming pool, and a room with an air conditioner and television set. The cost was four dollars a night for a single; six dollars for a double.

In 1955 an ambitious salesman, Ray Kroc, established a chain of burger joints called McDonald's, which would become the symbol of the fast-food industry. "Our whole concept was based on speed, lower prices, and volume," noted Dick McDonald, who sold his name to Kroc. By the end of the decade Kroc had franchised 228 restaurants across the nation. Whether eating in California or Connecticut, customers would be served the same-sized hamburger,

Crossing the Moat at Disneyland   Disneyland, which cost $17 million to build, opened its doors in Anaheim, California, in 1955. Its accessibility to the ordinary American made it a contemptible emblem of the "mass society," whose packaged commercialism and mindless entertainment intellectuals despised. But for American families, who had more kids and more money than ever before, Disneyland was a modern marvel. Its combination of nostalgia for the past (Main Street) and excitement for the future (Tomorrowland) captured the mood of postwar culture. *(Wide World Photos, Inc.)*

with ¼ ounce of onion, 1 teaspoon of mustard, 1 tablespoon of ketchup, and a pickle 1 inch in diameter. "I put the hamburger on the assembly line," Kroc boasted.

The automobile boosted the travel industry and made possible new forms of entertainment. In July 1955 the vast Disneyland theme park opened in Southern California. The park attracted more than 1 million visitors in its first six months. Over 40 percent of the guests came from outside California, most of them by car. Inside the park Main Street USA recalled America's small-town past, Frontierland brought back the thrill of the pioneers, and Tomorrowland suggested the future frontier of space. While enjoying the thrill of Disneyland's amusements, visitors shared in the celebration of common cultural images that reaffirmed the nation's mythic past and its promised future.

Teenagers and the Rise of Rock and Roll

During the 1950s there were more young people in America than at any previous time in history. The word *teenager* entered the American language, and parents and educators worried about the emergence of a national youth subculture. American teens now had the purchasing power to taste the fruits of abundance and to do so without having to seek parental approval. Postwar prosperity provided America's 13 million teenagers with more money than ever before. In 1956 teenage income from allowances and part-time jobs reached $7 billion a year. Between 1944 and 1958 the average teenager's weekly income quadrupled from $2.50 to $10.55. The expansion of public education contributed to the development of a teenage culture. A high-school education was supposed to inculcate middle-class values. But by segregating young people with many others of the same age, universal education gave teenagers the opportunity to develop their own values.

PRIMARY SOURCE

4.2 | ### *The New Teen Market*
     | LIFE

A writer for the August 31, 1959, edition of *Life* magazine examined the new demands of America's teenagers and their growing influence on the economy as consumers.

The time is past when a boy's chief possession was his bike and a girl's party wardrobe consisted of a fancy dress worn with a string of dime-store pearls. What Depression-bred parents may still think of as luxuries are looked on as necessities by their offspring. Today teen-agers surround themselves with a fantas-
5 tic array of garish and often expensive baubles and amusements. They own 10 million phonographs, over a million TV sets, 13 million cameras. Nobody knows how much parents spend on them for actual necessities nor to what extent teen-agers act as hidden persuaders on their parents' other buying habits. Counting only what is spent to satisfy their special teen-age demands, the youngsters and their parents
10 will shell out about $10 billion this year, a billion more than the total sales of GM.

Until recently businessmen have largely ignored the teen-age market. But now they are spending millions on advertising and razzle-dazzle promotional stunts. Their efforts so far seem only to have scratched the surface of a rich lode. In 1970, when the teen-age population expands from its present 18 million to 28
15 million, the market may be worth $20 billion. If parents have any idea of organized revolt, it is already too late. Teen-age spending is so important that such action would send quivers through the entire national economy. . . .

Some Fascinating Facts About a Booming Market

20 FOOD: Teen-agers eat 20% more than adults. They down 3½ billion quarts of milk every year, almost four times as much as is drunk by the infant population under 1. Teen-agers are a main prop of the ice cream industry, gobble 145 million gallons a year.
BEAUTY CARE: Teen-agers spent $20 million on lipstick last year, $25 mil-
25 lion on deodorants (a fifth of total sold), $9 million on home permanents. Male teen-agers own 2 million electric razors.
ENTERTAINMENT: Teen-agers lay out more than $1.5 billion a year for entertainment. They spend about $75 million on single pop records. Although they create new musical idols, they are staunchly faithful to the old.
30 Elvis Presley, still their favorite, has sold 25 million copies of single records in four years, an all-time high.
HOMEMAKERS: Major items like furniture and silver are moving into the teen-age market because of [the] growing number of teen-age marriages. One third of all 18- and 19-year-old girls are already married. More than 600,000 teen-
35 agers will be married this year. Teen-agers are now starting hope chests at 15.
CREDIT RISKS: Some 800,000 teen-agers work at full-time jobs and can buy major items on credit. ■ ■ ■

Writers, directors, and advertisers appealed directly to the teenager's sense of alienation from the adult world. The publication of J. D. Salinger's *The Catcher in the Rye* (1951) marked the beginning of the youth culture. The novel traced the thoughts and actions of sixteen-year-old Holden Caulfield, who roams around New York City recording his rejection of the phoniness and corruption of the adult world. In *Rebel Without a Cause* (1955), teen idol James Dean abandons the middle-class values of his parents for the excitement of a lower-class car culture. Television made its contribution to the youth culture in 1957 with the debut of *American Bandstand*. The daily show, hosted by Dick Clark, showed clean-cut teenagers dancing with each other while others watched from the bleachers.

Reassuring images of boys in jackets and ties and girls in dresses did little to ease adult concern about juvenile delinquency. Between 1948 and 1953 the number of teenagers charged with crimes increased by 45 percent. Especially troubling were the organized gangs that roamed the streets in many larger cities. As early as 1953 the federal government's Children's Bureau predicted that the exploding teenage population would soon produce an increase of 24 percent in car thefts, 19 percent in burglaries, and 7 percent in rapes. "Younger and younger children commit more and more serious and violent acts," wrote psychiatrist Fredric Wertham in his popular book, *Seduction of the Innocent* (1953).

Perhaps the most obvious symbol of the new youth culture was the emergence of rock and roll. Young adults used their added purchasing power to change musical taste in America by propelling "rock 'n' roll" to the top of the charts. At the beginning of the decade a few popular singers like Perry Cuomo and Frank Sinatra held broad appeal, but most radio stations played to the musical tastes of a specific segment of the market. Educated whites tuned into classical stations; rural whites listened to country and western music; middle-class whites kept to pop; blacks embraced jazz or rhythm and blues. Teenagers played the key role in breaking down these self-imposed musical barriers.

A mix of rhythm and blues, country, and white gospel music, rock and roll had gained enormous popularity among African-Americans in the late forties. Because of its association with blacks and its strong sexual overtones, most whites dismissed the new sound as "race music." At the beginning of the decade it was being recorded only by small record companies and played only on African-American radio stations. In 1951 a white disc jockey named Alan Freed began playing race music on his popular Cleveland radio station, renaming it "rock and roll," an urban euphemism for dancing and sex. By bringing race music to a white teenage audience, Freed's *Moondog's Rock and Roll Party* shattered musical barriers and helped begin a national music craze.

Initially, most white radio stations refused to play rock and roll music that was performed by black singers. Pressed by growing teenage demand, major record companies produced white versions of songs originally recorded by black singers. In 1955 twelve of the year's top fifty songs were rock and roll, including "Rock Around the Clock," written by two white songwriters and recorded by an all-white group, Bill Haley and the Comets.

The Comets' success opened the door for the most popular rock and roll star of the decade: Elvis Aaron Presley. A nineteen-year-old truck driver from Tupelo, Mississippi, Presley emerged in 1956 with his hit single "Heartbreak Hotel." The young entertainer adapted race music's powerful rhythms and raw sexual energy to create his own unique style and sound. The new white star enthralled screaming audiences of white teens. In April 1956 he already owned six of RCA's all-time top-twenty-five records and was selling $75,000 worth of records a day. Between 1956 and 1958 Presley had ten number-one hit records, including "Heartbreak Hotel," "Hound Dog," "All Shook Up," and "Jailhouse Rock." Many parents were aghast at watching "Elvis the Pelvis," with his tight pants, swinging his hips while young female fans screamed in excitement.

By the end of the decade white audiences were rushing to record stores to buy the original black versions of songs. *Billboard* magazine noted that race music was "no longer identified as the music of a specific group, but can now enjoy a healthy following among all people, regardless of race and color." Radio stations and record companies now featured black artists. Little Richard (born Richard Wayne Penniman) sang, shouted, danced, gyrated, and sweated profusely through "Tutti Frutti." Antoine "Fats" Domino, less threatening to whites than Little Richard, belted out songs such as "Blueberry Hill" (1956) and "Whole Lotta Loving" (1958). Chuck Berry, who developed a famous "duck walk" across the stage, hit the charts with "Roll over Beethoven" (1956) and "Johnny B. Goode" (1957).

The emergence of rock and roll produced a boom in national record sales. In 1950 Americans purchased 189 million records; by the end of the decade that number soared to over 600 million. Teenagers accounted for nearly 70 percent of all record sales. In 1956 alone Elvis Presley sold over 3.75 million albums.

Mass Culture and Its Critics

Many writers during the 1950s began to complain that mass culture promoted conformity and contributed to the homogenization of American society. Critics further complained that mass culture had promoted an American identity based solely on consumerism, which had created a nation of ugly shopping strips, mindless entertainment, and rampant commercialization. In the popular book *The Lonely Crowd* (1950), the sociologist David Riesman suggested that consumerism had moved America from an "inner-directed" culture in which people developed individualized goals to an "other-directed" society molded by peer-group pressures. Other critics took aim at the new service economy, which emphasized teamwork and frowned on mavericks. "When white-collar people get jobs, they sell not only their time and energy but their personalities as well," wrote the sociologist C. Wright Mills in *White Collar* (1951).

Television received much of the blame for debasing American culture. Scores of articles and books suggested that television promoted violence, stifled communication in families, and suppressed intellectual creativity and independence of thought. In 1955 a best-selling book, *Why Johnny Can't Read,* blamed television for high rates of child illiteracy.

These critics pointed to the suburbs as evidence of the harmful impact of mass culture on contemporary society. Suburban communities, with their row after row of identical homes and well-manicured lawns, suggested a community that valued uniformity over individualism. "For literally nothing down," wrote John Keats, "you too can find a box of your own . . . inhabited by people whose age, income, number of children, problems, habits, conversations, dress, possessions, perhaps even blood types are almost precisely like yours." Everyone in the suburbs, a hostile observer noted, "buys the right car, keeps his lawn like his neighbor's, eats crunchy breakfast cereal, and votes Republican." Critic Lewis Mumford denounced Levittown as an "instant slum." Levittown, he suggested, represented the worst vision of America's future: bland people living in bland houses and leading bland lives.

PRIMARY SOURCE

4.3 | *Perils of Mass Culture*

U.S. NEWS AND WORLD REPORT

In an article entitled "What TV Is Doing to America," a journalist with *U.S. News and World Report* sought to assess the impact of the medium on the mental and physical health of the nation's viewers in the magazine's September 2, 1955, edition.

The biggest of the new forces in American life today is television. There has been nothing like it in the postwar decade, or in many decades before that—perhaps not since the invention of the printing press. Even radio, by contrast, was a placid experience. . . .

5 Everywhere, children sit with eyes glued to screens—for three to four hours a day on the average. Their parents use up even more time mesmerized by this new marvel—or monster. They have spent 15 billion dollars to look since 1946.

Now, after nearly 10 years of TV, people are asking: "What hath TV wrought? What is this thing doing to us?"

10 Solid answers to this question are very hard to get. Pollsters, sociologists, doctors, teachers, the TV people themselves come up with more contradictions than conclusions whenever they start asking.

But almost everybody has an opinion and wants to air it.

What do these opinions add up to? People have strong views. Here are some 15 widely held convictions, both against and for television:

That TV has kept people from going places and doing things, from reading, from thinking for themselves. Yet it is said also that TV has taken viewers vicariously into strange and fascinating spots and situations, brought distinguished and enchanting people into their living rooms, given them a new perspective.

20 That TV has interfered with schooling, kept children from learning to read and write, weakened their eyesight and softened their muscles. But there are those who hold that TV has made America's youngsters more "knowing" about life, more curious, given them a bigger vocabulary. Teaching by TV, educators say, is going to be a big thing in the future.

25 That TV arouses morbid emotions in children, glorifies violence, causes juvenile crime—that it starts domestic quarrels, tends to loosen morals and make people lazy and sodden. However, it keeps families together at home, provides a realm of cheap entertainment never before available, stimulates new lines of conversation.

That TV is giving the U.S. an almost primitive language, made up of 30 grunts, whistles, standardized wisecracks and clichés—that it is turning the average American into a stereotype. Yet it is breaking down regional barriers and prejudices, ironing out accents, giving people in one part of the country a better understanding of people in other parts. That TV is making politics "a rich man's game," turning statesmanship into a circus, handing demagogues a new 35 weapon. But it is giving Americans their first good look at the inside of their

40 Government, letting them judge the people they elect by sight as well as by sound and fury.

That TV has distorted and debased Salesmanship, haunting people with singing "commercials" and slogans. However, because or in spite of TV, people are buying more and more things they never before thought they needed or 45 wanted.

These are just some of the comments that people keep on making about TV. The experts say that it probably will be another generation before there is a firm basis of knowledge about television's impact on America.

Today's TV child, the boy or girl who was born with a TV set in his home, is 50 too young to analyze his feelings. Older people, despite their frequent vehemence about TV, are still far from sure whether they have all Aladdin's lamp or hold a bear by the tail. . . .

What Is It?

55 Why do people want TV? A $67.50-per-week shoe repairman in San Francisco, puts it about as plainly as anyone can. "TV," he says, "is the only amusement I can afford." That was the reason he gave for paying four weeks' wages for his set.

The cobbler's comment explains TV's basic lure. It is free entertainment 60 except for the cost of [the] set, and repairs and electricity. It becomes so absorbing that a broken set is a family catastrophe. People will pay to have the set fixed before they will pay the milk bill, if necessary. . . .   ■ ■ ■

While these critics were correct in highlighting the importance of mass culture, they frequently overplayed their hand. The public was not as passive, nor the dominant culture as monolithic, as they suggested. Despite dire warnings that television would overshadow other forms of information, Americans enjoyed a greater variety of cultural sources than at any time before. Book sales doubled during the decade. A dramatic increase in the number of specialized magazines, such as *Sports Illustrated* and *The New Yorker,* compensated for the decline of general-readership publications. Innovative newspapers increased their circulation by playing to the changing taste of suburban readers.

It is also difficult to measure how viewers interpreted the images they saw on their TV screens. Americans tended to filter the "messages" of mass media through the prism of their own experience. Italians in Boston's North End may have watched the same television show as African-Americans in rural Alabama, but they responded to the images in different ways. By depicting America as a satiated and affluent society, television may actually have served as an unwitting vehicle of social change. TV's nightly diet of product advertising whetted the appetite of groups excluded from the consumer cornucopia, namely, the poor and minorities, and added momentum to their drive for inclusion.

Finally, suburbs, which appeared to some as manifestations of the growing conformity of modern life, were more diverse than critics recognized. Suburban communities included managers and workers, Democrats and Republicans, as well as a variety of ethnic and religious groups. Besides, most people viewed the move to the suburbs as a step up in life, the opportunity to own a piece of the American dream. One suburban resident reflected on the thrill of moving from an apartment in Brooklyn to Levittown. "We were proud," he recalled. "It was a wonderful community—and still is."

The rise of the consumer society reinforced America's optimism about the future and seemed to offer proof of the vital-center faith that economic growth could solve all social problems. During the 1950s many Americans believed that prosperity had muted ideological differences at the same time that the automobile and television were forging a common identity as consumers. By the end of the decade, however, clear signs emerged that the celebrations of consensus and prosperity were premature. The rise of teen culture and the emergence of rock and roll offered clear evidence of the social conflict that would consume the nation in the 1960s. Perhaps television offered the best insight into the impact of the consumer culture on the American paradox: while it trumpeted traditional values and the wonders of prosperity, it sowed the seeds of conflict by raising the expectations of groups excluded from the consumer culture.

SELECTED READINGS

▪ William E. Leuchtenberg's *A Troubled Feast* (3rd ed., 1987) highlights the contradictions and anxieties of American society during the period, while James T. Patterson focuses on the role of prosperity and the baby boom in transforming postwar ambition in *Grand Expectations* (1996). David Halberstam's *The Fifties* (1993) traces the major events and anxieties of the decade. The transformation of America's self-image is the focus of Tom Englehardt's *The End of Victory Culture* (2nd ed., 1998).

▪ David P. Calleo's *The Imperious Economy* (1982) surveys the economic changes of the 1950s. John Kenneth Galbraith explores the postwar consumer culture in *The Affluent Society* (40th anniv. ed., 1998) and *The New Industrial State* (3rd ed., 1978). Martin Campbell-Kelly and William Aspray study the rise of computers and automation in *Computer* (1996). Alfred D. Chandler chronicles the rise of the modern corporation in *The Visible Hand* (1977).

▪ Richard Easterlin's *Birth and Future* (2nd ed., 1987) provides a longitudinal study of the baby boomers and their impact on America. Landon Y. Jones tracks the largest generation through adolescence and early adulthood in *Great Expectations* (1980). Jane S. Smith recounts the development of the polio vaccine in *Patenting the Sun* (1990). Kenneth T. Jackson's *Crabgrass Frontier* (1985) is a valuable survey of American suburbia. Dolores Hayden's *Redesigning the American Dream* (1984) discusses the social engineering behind the suburbs. Herbert Gans's *The Levittowners* (1967) is a nuanced study that focuses on the diversity of suburban communities. Tom Lewis's

Divided Highways (1997) examines how the United States became an auto-oriented nation and the political support for highway projects. The rise of the motel industry along the nation's new highways is told in Michael Witzel's *The American Motel* (2000), and Eric Schlosser traces the growth of fast-food chains and their impact on American diets in *Fast-Food Nation* (2001).

■ Erik Barnouw's *Tube of Plenty* (2nd rev. ed., 1990) tracks the rise of television, with emphasis on its impact on American culture and politics. Lynn Spigel's *Make Room for TV* (1992) considers the transformation wrought by television on family life, as does Karal A. Marling's *As Seen on TV* (1994). Biographies of influential religious leaders include Carol George's *God's Salesman* (1994) about Norman Vincent Peale and William Martin's *A Prophet with Honor* (1991), which examines the work of Billy Graham. The history of rock and roll is examined in James Miller's *Flowers in the Dustbin* (1999), and the role of teens in the Cold War era is discussed by Grace Palladino in *Teenagers* (1996).

5

The Politics of Moderation, 1951–1960

In 1952 advertising pioneer Rosser Reeves asked a simple question: if television spots could be used to sell consumer products, why not use them to win votes for politicians? After all, Reeves would develop some of the most memorable commercials of the decade. To demonstrate how pain reliever Anacin performed, he showed how the pill quieted hammers pounding against the brain. Reeves once bragged about his Anacin spot that it "made more money [for Anacin] in seven years than *Gone with the Wind* did for . . . MGM in a quarter of a century." To convince viewers to buy Bic Pens, he shot the ball-points from rifles and crossbows, and to attract candy lovers, he announced that "M&M's melt in your mouth, not in your hands." Reeves proposed using the same method to sell Republican presidential candidate Dwight Eisenhower to the American people.

The centerpiece of the strategy was a series of fifty twenty-second commercials, called "spots," showing Eisenhower responding to questions from ordinary Americans. In early September Eisenhower met Reeves at a film studio in New York. For the next few hours Ike sat patiently, reading answers to hypothetical questions from giant cue cards. Uncomfortable with the whole process, Ike at one point remarked, "To think that an old soldier should come to this!"

Armed with Eisenhower's answers, Reeves needed to find a diverse group of people to ask the questions. He went to New York's Radio City Music Hall, chose a group of "everyday Americans," brought them to the studio, and filmed them asking questions of Eisenhower. When edited together, the spot showed Ike responding directly to the concerns of average Americans. An elderly woman remarked: "You know what things cost today. High prices are just driving me crazy." "My wife, Mamie," Ike answered, "worries about the same thing. I tell her it's our job to change that on November fourth." Though simplistic and devoid of any substance, such spots would become a standard feature of American politics.

Eisenhower's opponent, Illinois governor Adlai Stevenson, was uncomfortable with the new medium of television. Although he came across well on camera—a critic said he was "a television personality the like of which has not been seen before"—he did not like talking to an invisible audience of millions. "This is the worst thing I've ever heard of," he complained when he learned about the Eisenhower spots, "selling the president like cereal. Merchandising the presidency. How can you talk seriously about issues with one-minute spots!"

In the short run the ads carried Eisenhower's reassuring smile into millions of living rooms. In style and manner President Dwight D. Eisenhower served as a political symbol of the age. As one historian commented, "If he sought not to arouse the people to new political challenges, he was suited to reassure them that their elemental convictions were safe from doubt and confusion." At home Eisenhower's philosophy of dynamic conservatism reassured conservatives at the same time that it consolidated New Deal programs. Abroad Eisenhower's tough anti-Soviet rhetoric belied a policy that reflected caution and prudence in dealing with the Cold War adversary. The Republicans controlled the White House, but the basic ideas of the vital center still dominated thinking in Washington.

The Election of 1952

Eisenhower had not taken the typical route into politics. Born in Denison, Texas, on October 4, 1890, Eisenhower grew up in Abilene, Kansas, before becoming a career military officer. He was a diligent student, an eager reader, and a talented writer. His high-school yearbook predicted that Ike would become "a professor of history at Yale." After graduating from West Point in 1915, he rose within the ranks of the army, serving with distinction on the War Department staff in Washington. He began World War II as a brigadier general and ended it as supreme commander in Europe. After leading the Anglo-American military forces that defeated Germany in 1945, Eisenhower remained in the army as chief of staff until 1948, when he accepted the presidency of Columbia University. Three years later he was called back to serve as the first supreme commander of North Atlantic Treaty Organization (NATO) forces in Europe.

Eisenhower's status as a war hero made him a popular choice to run for president in 1952. Independent Ike for President clubs were springing up across the country. Everywhere bumper stickers proclaimed, "I Like Ike." At first Eisenhower, who had never registered a party affiliation or voted in an election, expressed little interest, but he feared that if he did not run, the Republican Party would nominate Ohio senator Robert Taft. Though Taft enjoyed a large following among the party's Old Guard, his isolationist views and uninspiring manner limited his appeal to mainstream voters. When in February 1952 Taft advocated bringing American troops home from Europe, Eisenhower decided to run. He resigned from NATO and entered his name for the Republican nomination.

After a bitter convention struggle, Eisenhower won the nomination. To appease the party's right wing, he selected thirty-nine-year-old Senator Richard Nixon of California as his running mate. Besides hailing from an important western state, Nixon had close ties to party conservatives. He was also a ferocious, frequently unscrupulous campaigner who could keep the Democrats on the defensive while Eisenhower took the high road. Hailing from California, Nixon added regional balance and was expected to deliver the state's electoral votes.

The Democrats faced a more difficult choice. In March a beleaguered President Harry Truman announced that he would not seek a second term. Recent investigations had linked appointees in Truman's administration to influence peddling and other corrupt practices. The scandals, added to the stalemate in Korea and Senator Joseph McCarthy's persistent accusations that the administration was "soft on communism," drove Truman's popularity to an all-time low of 26 percent. With Truman out of the picture, many Democrats looked to the popular Adlai Stevenson. Along with being an incumbent governor of a large and powerful state, Stevenson had endeared himself to party loyalists by taking strong positions on civil rights and civil liberties. Like Eisenhower, Stevenson expressed little interest in the nomination, but he bowed to party leaders' insistence. To balance the ticket, Stevenson selected a segregationist senator, John Sparkman of Alabama, as his running mate.

The candidates possessed strikingly different styles. Intellectuals and liberals found Stevenson's speeches eloquent and inspirational, but his aristocratic manner failed to arouse the support of the New Deal coalition, composed, as it was, of working-class, black, ethnic, and urban voters. "He ran for President not to rescue the downtrodden but to assume the responsibilities properly belonging to the privileged," observed the liberal economist John Kenneth Galbraith. Eisenhower, in contrast, endeared himself to the public. With a serene, confident manner and what one reporter called a "leaping and effortless smile," he seemed above partisan politics. Billboards in California proclaimed, "Faith in God and Country; that's Eisenhower—how about you?"

Few substantive issues separated the two candidates. Ike and Stevenson subscribed to the basic precepts of the vital center. Both men were ardent Cold Warriors who feared the expansion of federal power at home. Stevenson abandoned many of the controversial programs of the Fair Deal, including public housing and national health insurance. On civil rights the Democratic nominee felt that it was the states' responsibility to address the problem and that the federal government should not "put the South completely over a barrel."

The GOP campaign correctly identified Korea, communism, and corruption as key issues. The Republicans complained of "plunder at home, blunder abroad" and promised to "clean up the mess in Washington." Nixon referred to "Adlai the Appeaser," who was a "Ph.D. graduate of Dean Acheson's cowardly College of Communist Containment." Eisenhower, just ten days before the election, declared, "I shall go to Korea." Though he did not say what he would do when he got there, his pledge was a masterful stroke. In a break with most presidential elections, which are decided primarily on domestic issues, more than one-half of the electorate regarded the war as the country's single most important problem, and most people believed Eisenhower's military background made him the best candidate to end the conflict.

While Eisenhower was free to speak in vague terms about ending the war, lowering taxes, and easing inflation, Stevenson needed to defend the Truman administration's record. High taxes, inflation, and a budget deficit, he argued, were the price America had to pay to maintain freedom around the world. Korea, he declared, "was the testing point for freedom throughout the world. . . . Everyone of us knows in his heart why he had to stand up and fight in Korea." Stevenson also forcefully defended himself against charges of being soft on communism and continued his strong opposition to redbaiting at home. At one point he appeared before the American Legion to condemn those who for "political or personal reasons" attacked the loyalty of faithful government servants.

The Republicans did have to endure an embarrassing scandal of their own, however. In September the *New York Post* revealed that a group of wealthy California businessmen had provided Nixon with an $18,000 private "slush fund" to pay for personal campaign expenses. On September 23 Nixon went on national television to defend himself, citing the emotional and material needs of his family, not personal ambition, as his reason for accepting the money. Near the end of the talk Nixon told the story of one special gift he had received—a "little cocker spaniel dog," which his daughter Tricia had named Checkers. He vowed his family would keep the dog "regardless of what they say about it." The address revealed the growing importance of television in politics. Over 9 million sets were tuned into Nixon's speech, and popular reaction was overwhelmingly favorable. Eisenhower, recognizing the positive response, assured Nixon, "You're my boy."

Nixon's Televised "Checkers" Speech Just days after Eisenhower selected Richard Nixon as his running mate in the fall of 1952, the *New York Post* reported that Nixon had received substantial gifts from wealthy businessmen. To save his political career, Nixon decided to plead his case to the American people with a televised speech. On September 23, Richard Nixon, with his wife sitting close by, explained to the American people that he had never accepted lavish gifts from friends, but that he had accepted a cocker spaniel for his daughters, one of whom named it Checkers, and that "we're going to keep it." At the end of the speech, Nixon turned the tables on his opponents, questioning their ethics and challenging them to be as open with their finances as he had been. The American people rallied behind Nixon and Eisenhower kept him on the ticket. The two went on to win by a landslide in November.

PRIMARY SOURCE

5.1 | *The Checkers Speech*
RICHARD NIXON

During the 1952 election Republican vice-presidential nominee Richard Nixon found himself at the center of a possibly embarrassing scandal when the *New York Post* reported that Nixon had taken $18,000 from supporters to pay for personal campaign expenses. Utilizing the power of the new medium of television, Nixon made a passionate appeal for understanding from viewers as he explained his family's economic situation and confessed to accepting a dog for his daughters.

My Fellow Americans,

I come before you tonight as a candidate for the Vice Presidency and as a man whose honesty and integrity has been questioned.

Now, the usual political thing to do when charges are made against you is to
5   either ignore them or to deny them without giving details. I believe we have had enough of that in the United States, particularly with the present Administration in Washington, D.C.

To me the office of the Vice Presidency of the United States is a great office, and I feel that the people have got to have confidence in the integrity of the men
10   who run for that office and who might attain them.

I have a theory, too, that the best and only answer to a smear or an honest misunderstanding of the facts is to tell the truth. And that is why I am here tonight. I want to tell you my side of the case.

I am sure that you have read the charge, and you have heard it, that I, Senator
15   Nixon, took $18,000 from a group of my supporters.

Now, was that wrong? And let me say that it was wrong. I am saying it, incidentally, that it was wrong, just not illegal, because it isn't a question of whether it was legal or illegal, that isn't enough. The question is, was it morally wrong. I say that it was morally wrong—if any of that $18,000 went to Senator Nixon, for my
20   personal use. I say that it was morally wrong if it was secretly given and secretly handled. And I say that it was morally wrong if any of the contributors got special favors for the contributions that they made.

And now to answer those questions let me say this: Not a cent of the $18,000 or any other money of that type ever went to me for my personal use. Every
25   penny of it was used to pay for political expenses that I did not think should be charged to the taxpayers of the United States. . . .

. . . And so now, what I am going to do—and incidentally this is unprecedented in the history of American politics—I am going at this time to give to this television and radio audience, a complete financial history, everything I have
30   earned, everything I have spent and everything I own, and I want you to know the facts.

I will have to start early, I was born in 1913. Our family was one of modest circumstances, and most of my early life was spent in a store out in East Whittier. It was a grocery store, one of those family enterprises.
35   The only reason we were able to make it go was because my mother and dad had five boys, and we all worked in the store. I worked my way through college, and, to a great extent, through law school. And then in 1940, probably the best thing that ever happened to me happened. I married Pat who is sitting over here.

We had a rather difficult time after we were married, like so many of the
40   young couples who may be listening to us. I practiced law. She continued to teach school. Then, in 1942, I went into the service. Let me say that my service record was not a particularly unusual one. I went to the South Pacific. I guess I'm entitled to a couple of battle stars. I got a couple of letters of commendation. But I was just there when the bombs were falling. And then I returned. I returned to the

45 United States, and in 1946, I ran for the Congress. When we came out of the war—Pat and I—Pat during the war had worked as a stenographer, and in a bank, and as an economist for a Government agency—and when we came out, the total of our savings, from both my law practice, her teaching and all the time I was in the war, the total for that entire period was just a little less than
50 $10,000—every cent of that, incidentally, was in Government bonds—well, that's where we start, when I go into politics. . . .

I own a 1950 Oldsmobile car. We have our furniture, we have no stocks and bonds of any type. We have no interest, direct or indirect, in any business. Now that is what we have. What do we owe?

55 Well, in addition to the mortgages, the $20,000 mortgage on the house in Washington and the $10,000 mortgage on the house in Whittier, I owe $4,000 to the Riggs Bank in Washington, D.C. with an interest at 4½ percent.

I owe $3,500 to my parents, and the interest on that loan, which I pay regularly, because it is a part of the savings they made through the years they
60 were working so hard—I pay regularly 4 percent interest. And then I have a $500 loan, which I have on my life insurance.

Well, that's about it. That's what we have. And that's what we owe. It isn't very much. But Pat and I have the satisfaction that every dime that we have got is honestly ours.

65 I should say this, that Pat doesn't have a mink coat.

But she does have a respectable Republican cloth coat, and I always tell her she would look good in anything.

One other thing I should probably tell you, because if I don't they will probably be saying this about me, too. We did get something, a gift, after the
70 election.

A man down in Texas heard Pat on the radio mention the fact that our two youngsters would like to have a dog, and, believe it or not, the day we left before this campaign trip we got a message from Union Station in Baltimore, saying they had a package for us. We went down to get it. You know
75 what it was?

It was a little cocker spaniel dog, in a crate that he had sent all the way from Texas, black and white, spotted, and our little girl Tricia, the six year old, named it Checkers. And you know, the kids, like all kids, loved the dog, and I just want to say this, right now, that regardless of what they say about it, we
80 are going to keep it. . . .

And now, finally, I know that you wonder whether or not I am going to stay on the Republican ticket or resign. Let me say this: I don't believe that I ought to quit, because I am not a quitter. And, incidentally, Pat is not a quitter. After all, her name is Patricia Ryan and she was born on St. Patrick's Day,
85 and you know the Irish never quit.

But the decision, my friends, is not mine. I would do nothing that would harm the possibilities of Dwight Eisenhower to become President of the United States. And for that reason I am submitting to the Republican National Committee tonight, through this television broadcast, the decision

90 which it is theirs to make. Let them decide whether my position on the ticket will help or hurt. And I am going to ask you to help them decide. Wire and write the Republican National Committee whether you think I should stay on or whether I should get off. And whatever their decision is, I will abide by it.

But let me just say this last word. Regardless of what happens, I am going 95 to continue this fight. I am going to campaign up and down America until we drive the crooks and the Communists and those that defend them out of Washington, and remember folks, Eisenhower is a great man, believe me. He is a great man, and a vote for Eisenhower is a vote for what is good for America. . . . ■ ■ ■

Nixon had saved his spot on the ticket, but at a high price. Eisenhower remained suspicious of him, and although the public responded warmly to Nixon's speech, opinion makers found the whole episode unsavory. They were turned off by his self-pity and his willingness to use his wife, children, and even his dog to save his political life. Journalist Walter Lippmann called the speech "a disturbing experience . . . with all the amplification of modern electronics, simply mob law." For many people the episode underscored their perception of Nixon as a ruthless opportunist who would do almost anything to get what he wanted. That image would linger long after election night.

Few people were surprised on election day when Eisenhower scored a landslide victory. Ike won 55.1 percent of the popular vote and carried thirty-nine states. His vote total, 33.9 million, was nearly 12 million more than Dewey had received in 1948. Sweeping the electoral college 442 to 89, Eisenhower made inroads into the once solidly Democratic South by winning Florida, Tennessee, Texas, and Virginia. Stevenson, with 27.3 million votes, won 44.4 percent of the popular vote and carried nine states, all southern or border states. Most significantly, Eisenhower offset Democratic strength in major urban areas by scoring well in the growing suburbs. The Republicans gained majorities in both houses of Congress, 48 to 47 in the Senate and 221 to 211 in the House. Republicans were in control of the White House and Capitol Hill for the first time since 1930.

Dynamic Conservatism at Home

Unlike most modern presidents, who use their honeymoon with Congress to push through an ambitious agenda, Eisenhower planned to use his first months in office for study and reflection. "It is a mistake for a new Administration to be talking so soon after the inauguration," he wrote in his diary. "Time for study, exploration and analysis is necessary." Eisenhower may have felt that he needed more time to master the details of the job, but he certainly came to office with a general idea of what he wanted to accomplish and where he wished to move the nation.

Eisenhower called his political philosophy "dynamic conservatism," which he interpreted as "conservative when it comes to money and liberal when it comes

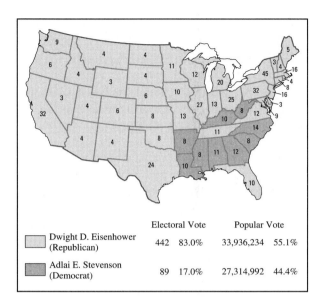

	Electoral Vote		Popular Vote	
Dwight D. Eisenhower (Republican)	442	83.0%	33,936,234	55.1%
Adlai E. Stevenson (Democrat)	89	17.0%	27,314,992	44.4%

The Election of 1952

Though a political novice, Dwight D. Eisenhower's persona as a war hero and man of the people gave him the edge over his more experienced, yet less-well-known opponent, Adlai Stevenson. Eisenhower's popularity and his promise to end the Korean War even swayed many southern Democrats to vote Republican for the first time.

to human beings." The approach represented Ike's way of dealing with the paradox of rising expectations and traditional values. Like many conservatives, Eisenhower believed that the executive branch had grown too strong under Franklin Roosevelt and Harry Truman. Government regulation had strangled business, while the growth of executive power had disrupted the delicate constitutional balance among the branches of government. The solution, Ike argued, was to take a more restrained approach to the presidency. "I am not one of those desk-pounding types that likes to stick out his jaw and look like he is bossing the show," he said.

The new president was determined to reverse the direction taken by the New Deal and Fair Deal or, in his words, to remove "the Left-Wingish, pinkish influence in our life." The key was to control government spending—even on defense—and balance the budget. He believed that expanded federal power threatened individual liberty. The role of government was to tame special interests, restraining their excess demands and forcing them to work together for common purposes. The president should not use the federal budget to reward friends and punish enemies—as Eisenhower believed FDR and Truman had done—but instead to promote domestic harmony and economic stability. His strongest supporters referred to Eisenhower's approach to government as "modern Republicanism."

To help carry out his program, Eisenhower selected a conservative cabinet and gave it wide discretion. "The White House will stay out of your hair," he said. Secretary of Agriculture Ezra Taft Benson vowed to get the government out of the business of supporting farm prices. Treasury chief George Humphrey, a former corporate executive and an old-fashioned fiscal conservative, considered it his job to reduce spending. Millionaire businessmen or corporate lawyers held every cabinet office except that of secretary of labor, which was reserved for the head of the plumbers union. Liberals accused Eisenhower of appointing a cabinet of "eight millionaires and a plumber."

Acting on his conservative impulses, the president removed Truman's moderate wage and price controls, lowered price supports for farm products, cut the government payroll by two hundred thousand workers, and trimmed federal spending by 10 percent, or $6 billion, in his first year. Eisenhower's position on natural resource development clearly revealed his desire to limit federal involvement in the private sector. He reversed Truman's decision to proceed with federal construction of a hydroelectric plant in Hell's Canyon, Idaho, and licensed a private firm to complete the work. He opposed the Tennessee Valley Authority's request to build a new plant to furnish power for the Atomic Energy Commission. In May 1953 Eisenhower signed the Submerged Lands Act, which transferred control of about $40 billion worth of oil lands from the federal government to the states. The *New York Times* called it "one of the greatest and surely the most unjustified give-away programs in all the history of the United States."

Despite the hopes of many conservatives, and the fears of liberals, Eisenhower did not undermine the foundation of the modern welfare state. Political and economic realities prevented such a drastic step. "Should any political party attempt to abolish Social Security, unemployment insurance, and eliminate labor and farm programs," Ike warned, "you would not hear of that party again in our political history." In addition, congressional Democrats, who recaptured control of both houses in 1954 and retained it throughout the remainder of Eisenhower's presidency, would have blocked any attempt to repeal established programs. Meanwhile, sharp recessions in 1954 and 1958 led the president to abandon his budget-balancing efforts and to accelerate government spending.

Indeed, in the end Eisenhower's policies consolidated and strengthened the New Deal's economic and social programs. During his presidency spending on social welfare programs rose steadily, from 7.6 percent of the gross national product (GNP) in 1952 to 11.5 percent in 1961. The president and Congress agreed in 1954, and again in 1956, to increase social security benefits and to broaden the federal system to include an estimated 10 million new workers. In 1955 Congress and Eisenhower compromised on a new law that increased the minimum wage from seventy-five cents to one dollar an hour. Between 1953 and 1961 the federal government spent some $1.3 billion for slum clearance and public housing. In health and medical welfare Eisenhower carried forward the programs begun by Roosevelt and Truman. On April 1, 1953, Eisenhower signed a bill that raised the Federal Security Agency to cabinet rank as the Department of Health, Education, and Welfare. Barry Goldwater, a rising conservative star from Arizona, complained that Ike ran a "Dime Store New Deal."

Taking on McCarthy

While consolidating the New Deal, Eisenhower outflanked his party's right wing by intensifying the campaign against internal subversion. Soon after taking office, he issued Executive Order 10450, which toughened the government loyalty program. The new guidelines included not only loyalty and security but also an open-ended category called "suitability." Under his new guidelines almost ten thousand federal employees resigned or were dismissed. The president gave Federal Bureau of Investigation (FBI) director J. Edgar Hoover a free hand to wiretap suspected communists. The administration also supported the Communist Control Act. Passed by Congress in 1954, the law prohibited communists from running for public office.

Among those removed from the government was the scientist J. Robert Oppenheimer. The nation's leading scientists testified to his loyalty and dedication. But it did little good. "Quite possibly no American public figure had been bugged and shadowed by the FBI more relentlessly than Robert Oppenheimer," observed the journalist David Halberstam. Oppenheimer was on the witness stand for twenty exhausting hours. "There hadn't been a proceeding like this since the Spanish Inquisition," noted an observer.

Eisenhower hoped that his aggressive loyalty program would steal the limelight from Joseph McCarthy. But McCarthy had other ideas. In October 1953 McCarthy blasted the administration for conducting a foreign policy of "whiny, whimpering appeasement." At the same time, his investigations subcommittee conducted seventeen hearings, including ten that focused on current subversion in government.

Eisenhower had had enough. In March 1954 the president leaked to the press an army report that documented attempts by McCarthy and his staff to win preferential treatment for David Schine, a former staff member drafted into the army. The Senate, embarrassed by the army's accusations, decided to hold investigative public hearings carried live on national television. Beginning on April 27, as many as 20 million Americans watched the proceedings for thirty-five days. Toward the end McCarthy savagely attacked a lawyer for having once belonged to a left-wing organization. Outraged, attorney Joseph Welch berated McCarthy, concluding: "Have you no sense of decency, sir, at long last? Have you left no sense of decency?" After watching McCarthy on television, a majority of Americans were asking the same question. As his appeal ebbed, the Senate roused itself against McCarthy, voting in December 1954, 67-22, to "condemn" him for bringing Congress into disrepute. Three years later, at the age of forty-eight, Joseph McCarthy, once the most feared man in America, died of hepatitis and other health problems caused by alcoholism.

McCarthy's fall removed a major source of embarrassment and virtually guaranteed Eisenhower's reelection in 1956. Polls showed Ike leading all Democratic challengers by wide margins. The president's enormous popularity had as much to do with his style and personality as it did with his policies. Most people viewed Eisenhower as a strong leader and a likable man who embodied traditional American values. He often spoke of old-fashioned virtues such as honor, duty, patriotism, and hard work. The White House seemed home to a traditional family, with First Lady Mamie Eisenhower playing the proper role of dutiful wife. "Ike took care of the office," she declared. "I ran the house."

Eisenhower used television not only when campaigning but also when building public support for his administration. Realizing that television allowed politicians to project themselves into the homes of millions of potential voters, Eisenhower hired movie star Robert Montgomery to help craft his media image. By 1955 Ike was so confident in his ability to perform for the cameras that he became the first president to allow television coverage of his press conferences.

The president's critics often poked fun at Eisenhower's apparent intellectual laziness. They pointed out that he spent an inordinate amount of time golfing, reading western novels, and playing poker and bridge. Liberals accustomed to the take-charge leadership of FDR complained that Ike did not work hard at his job. "Eisenhower is no fire-eater," observed the liberal journalist I. F. Stone, "but seems to be a rather simple man who enjoys his bridge and his golf and doesn't like to be too much bothered." Liberals often objected to the president's inarticulateness in press conferences, where he mumbled and often confused his thoughts. His love of golf became a subject of public ridicule. A contemporary joke had Ike asking golfers ahead of him: "Do you mind if we play through? New York has just been bombed."

These critics often underestimated Eisenhower and failed to appreciate his strong bond with the American people. Ike's engaging personality and dominating presence more than compensated for his passive presidency. He radiated sincerity. "He has this power of drawing the hearts of men towards him as a magnet attracts the bits of metal," noted one observer. "He has merely to smile at you, and you trust him at once." Eisenhower's appeal transcended the politics of personality: his modern Republicanism effectively straddled the contradiction between postwar expectations that government would do more to address social problems and the fear of expanding federal power.

The 1956 Presidential Campaign

The public demonstrated its satisfaction with Ike's leadership in the 1956 presidential election. After a spirited primary campaign, Democrats turned again to Adlai Stevenson to lead their party. Stevenson ran an energetic campaign for a "New America" where "poverty is abolished" and "freedom is made real for everybody." The central issue of the election, he said, is "whether America wants to stay on dead center, mired in complacency and cynicism; or whether it wants once more to move forward—to meet our human needs, to make our abundance serve all of us and to make the world safer." Yet fatigue and repetition made the speeches read better than they sounded. "Adlai Stevenson, the lilt gone from his voice, ran with all the zest and decisiveness of a man taking the final steps to the gas chamber," observed a contemporary.

Most commentators had trouble even pretending the race would be close. "The Republican mood," wrote a journalist, "is one of supreme conviction of victory." The confidence was well founded. The Eisenhower-Nixon ticket won with the largest popular vote in U.S. history up to that time. Eisenhower's support of 57.6 percent of the voters had been exceeded only by FDR's in 1936. The popular president carried such Democratic strongholds as Chicago and Jersey City, along with Baltimore, Milwaukee, Los Angeles, and San Francisco. He carried a majority of the Catholic vote and did well among African-Americans. The victory was, however, an endorsement of Eisenhower, not of his party. The Democrats actually increased their majorities in Congress and their governorships.

The "New Look" Abroad

Eisenhower came to the White House better prepared to handle foreign policy than any other twentieth-century president. He had toured the globe and served as supreme commander of Allied forces and NATO. He came to office with a clear vision of America's role in world affairs. Like most Americans, Ike was convinced of the superiority of American values, committed to spreading the gospel of democracy and free enterprise around the globe, and determined to use American military might to limit Soviet expansion. He devoted his inaugural address to denouncing communism. "Freedom," he said, "is pitted against slavery; lightness against dark." In his first State of the Union message

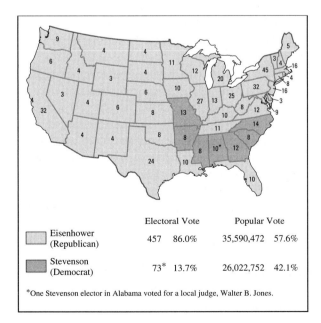

	Electoral Vote		Popular Vote	
Eisenhower (Republican)	457	86.0%	35,590,472	57.6%
Stevenson (Democrat)	73*	13.7%	26,022,752	42.1%

*One Stevenson elector in Alabama voted for a local judge, Walter B. Jones.

The Election of 1956
The 1956 election again pitted Dwight Eisenhower against Adlai Stevenson, and again Eisenhower won—by an even greater margin of victory than in 1952. This election also marked the first time that a state in the Deep South had voted Republican since Reconstruction.

he added that the United States would "never acquiesce in the enslavement of any people."

But Eisenhower was also a practical man who appreciated the dangers of excessive idealism and understood the need for compromise in the international arena. Ike was wiser and more subtle in his approach to the Soviets than his rhetoric suggested. He understood that world communism was not monolithic, that tensions between Russia and China exposed the divisions within the communist world. Ideology, he recognized, was not the force driving Soviet international behavior; Russian leaders wanted desperately to avoid a conflict with the United States.

Eisenhower's fiscal conservatism shaped his views of American foreign policy. The Korean conflict taught him that the United States could not afford to fight local wars with conventional troops. America, he believed, should instead take advantage of its overwhelming superiority in nuclear weapons, attacking enemy forces with small nuclear weapons or even striking at the source of the aggression—Moscow or Beijing. Being cheaper than conventional forces, nuclear weapons offered "more bang for the buck." The administration called its defense strategy the "New Look."

Although his private thinking was far more sophisticated than that of many of his contemporaries, Ike did little to educate the public about the complexity of the postwar world. Politically he needed to reassure hard-liners in his own party that he would stand tough against the Russians. Leading defense contractors, and many labor unions, pressed for higher defense spending to increase profits and maintain job security. Most members of his own administration shared these tough anticommunist views. In 1954 and 1955 numerous government committees, including the National Security Council, warned the president that the Soviets had dramatically increased their spending on nuclear weapons in order to deliver a "knockout" blow to the United States. Under these circumstances Eisenhower felt obliged to keep his guard up.

Eisenhower delegated a great deal of authority to his secretary of state, John Foster Dulles, but never relinquished control to him. The grandson of John Foster, President Benjamin Harrison's secretary of state, Dulles had been involved in international affairs for almost fifty years. "There's only one man I know who has seen more of the world and talked with more people and knows more than he does, and that's me," Eisenhower said before making the selection. Dulles possessed supreme confidence, faith in the righteousness of his position, and a domineering personality. Winston Churchill said that Dulles was "the only case of a bull I know who carried his own china shop with him." Dulles, people said, carried foreign policy under his hat.

He possessed deeply held convictions about America's role in the world. He believed in a monolithic "world Communist movement," the "unholy alliance of Marx's communism and Russia's imperialism." He came into office denouncing Truman's containment policy. The Eisenhower administration, he vowed, was committed to "liberation" of nations under communist rule. He favored a policy

"Don't Be Afraid—I Can Always Pull You Back"

---from <u>Herblock's Special For Today</u> (Simon & Schuster, 1958)

of "brinkmanship"—pushing the Soviet Union to the brink of war before considering negotiations. The "ability to get to the verge without getting into war is the necessary art," Dulles said. "If you try to run away from it, if you are scared to go to the brink, you are lost."

Though Dulles often dominated the rhetoric during the decade, Eisenhower maintained control of policy. A number of features distinguished Eisenhower's New Look strategy. First, the administration committed itself to a policy of "massive retaliation." The "Free World," Dulles announced in 1954, could not match "the mighty land power of the Communist world." Therefore, the United States would rely on nuclear weapons, which would provide "more basic security at less cost." Eisenhower not only reviewed the speech ahead of time, but also penned the key passage calling for a policy based on a "capacity to retaliate, instantly, by means and at places of our own choosing."

Second, to make credible the threat to use atomic arms, the administration dramatically increased the nation's nuclear arsenal. Between 1952 and 1959 the number of nuclear weapons in the American arsenal grew from around one thousand five hundred to over six thousand. The navy introduced submarine-based intermediate-range Polaris missiles. The Strategic Air Command, headed by General Curtis LeMay, whom the historian James T. Patterson has called "a kind of airborne George Patton," replaced its aging propeller-driven B-36 bombers with jet-propelled B-47s that could fly 600 miles an hour and hit targets in the Soviet heartland.

The New Look defense policy, coupled with the end of the Korean War, enabled Eisenhower to slash defense spending by some 20 percent in his first two years in office. As a percentage of the GNP, defense spending decreased from 14 percent to 9 percent during Eisenhower's presidency. Only the air force saw its budget rise, from $15 billion to $19 billion, between 1953 and 1959. Lowering spending and balancing the budget were especially important goals for Eisenhower, who feared that high levels of defense spending would shift power from the people to the military and to defense contractors. "Every gun that is made," he said, "every warship launched, every rocket fired signifies, in the final sense, a theft from those who hunger and are not fed, those who are cold and not clothed."

Third, in its efforts to surround the Soviet Union strategically, the Eisenhower administration negotiated a number of regional defense treaties. By the end of the 1950s the United States had signed agreements to defend forty-three different nations against "communist aggression."

Finally, the administration dramatically expanded the role of the Central Intelligence Agency (CIA), which provided an inexpensive method of protecting American interests abroad. Headed by Allen Dulles, the brother of the secretary of state, the CIA by 1955 employed almost fifteen thousand people, triple what it had in 1950. Among the employees were thousands of covert agents stationed in "trouble spots" around the world. The CIA expanded its role beyond intelligence gathering to a wide range of political activities, including the overthrow of foreign governments.

The Rhetoric and Reality of Liberation

Despite the tough language about brinkmanship and liberation, Eisenhower and Dulles discovered that the realities of international power and domestic politics prevented a radical departure from past practices. The first indication of the continuity in their approach to the world came in Korea, where Eisenhower was determined to end American involvement. But on what terms? Dulles and conservative Republicans objected to any peace proposal that left the communists in control of North Korea and divided the nation into two societies—one "free," one communist. But Eisenhower was more interested in ending the war and saving lives than in proving his fidelity to the Republican platform. As promised, he flew to Korea after the 1952 election to nudge the cease-fire talks. He also dropped hints to China that he was ready to use nuclear weapons in Korea. In July 1953 he agreed to terms that called for a division of Korea at approximately the same lines that had existed in June 1950— the thirty-eighth parallel—with a demilitarized zone separating the two Koreas.

The president showed similar restraint in dealing with a potentially dangerous situation in China. During the fall of 1954 the Communist Chinese began to shell the offshore islands of Quemoy and Matsu, which were occupied by the Nationalist Chinese. The Nationalists fired back. Conservatives urged Eisenhower to respond forcefully, perhaps by bombing the mainland. "We must be prepared," declared Senate majority leader William Knowland of California, "to go it alone in China if our allies desert us. . . . We must not fool ourselves into thinking we can avoid taking up arms with the Chinese Reds. If we don't fight them in China and Formosa, we will be fighting them in San Francisco, in Seattle, in Kansas City." Some military advisers recommended using tactical nuclear weapons against the Communists.

Fortunately, calmer heads prevailed. Realizing that it would be politically dangerous to do nothing, Eisenhower signed a security agreement with the Nationalists that committed the United States to protect the strategically important island of Formosa (Taiwan), but left ambiguous America's commitment to Quemoy and Matsu, which he believed to be of limited strategic value. When the Chinese renewed their bombing of Quemoy and Matsu later that spring, Ike issued public statements hinting about the possibility of using nuclear weapons to stem communist attacks. "In any combat where these things [tactical nuclear weapons] can be used on strictly military targets and for strictly military purposes, I see no reason why they shouldn't be used, just exactly as you would a bullet or anything else." Chinese leaders, uncertain whether Eisenhower was bluffing, stopped the attacks.

Eisenhower also pursued a moderate course in his dealings with the Soviet Union. In March 1953, only ninety-five days after Eisenhower's election, Soviet leader Joseph Stalin died, raising hopes of a thaw in relations between the two countries. Nikita Khrushchev became Soviet premier and secretary of the Communist party in March 1958. A shrewd politician, Khrushchev planned to lessen Cold War tensions so that his country could spend less money on the military and more on consumer goods. He also hoped that lowering the heat of the Cold War would weaken ties between the United States and its western allies.

Eisenhower approached the new regime cautiously. In a major speech on April 16, 1953, he invited the Soviets to end the arms race. And in a dramatic address to the United Nations on December 8, he proposed that the major scientific nations of the world jointly contribute to a UN pool of atomic power to be used solely for peaceful purposes. "Let no one think," he said, "that the expenditure of vast sums for systems and weapons of defense can guarantee absolute safety."

The Soviets responded by settling their differences with Germany over war prisoners; by establishing diplomatic relations with Greece, Israel, and Yugoslavia; and by withdrawing troops from neutral Austria. These initiatives led to the first U.S.–Soviet summit meeting in a decade. Churchill was the first to suggest a meeting between the Soviets and the Americans. Dulles forcefully opposed the idea, but Ike overruled him and agreed to attend. A popular Herblock cartoon captured the Ike-Dulles split. It showed a smiling Ike telling the Kremlin on the phone, "Yes, we'll be there, rain and shine." Next to him a dour Dulles stands outfitted in layers of military clothing.

In July 1955 Eisenhower and Khrushchev, with their British and French counterparts, met in Geneva for the first top-level conference of the wartime Allies since the 1945 meeting at Potsdam. "The United States will never take part in an aggressive war," Eisenhower told the Soviets. Eisenhower then won a propaganda victory with his "Open Skies" proposal, which called for aerial surveillance of both countries' nuclear facilities. The suggestion was neither as bold nor as innovative as many at the time thought. Since American skies were already open, Eisenhower was asking the Soviets to make a unilateral concession—something they refused to do. "In our eyes," Khrushchev told the president, "this is a very transparent espionage device. . . . You could hardly expect us to take this seriously."

Although Eisenhower returned from the summit with no tangible victory, he felt the United States had made an important first step toward a new era of coexistence with the USSR. Ignoring advice by Dulles that he maintain an "austere countenance" in all photographs taken at Geneva, Ike flashed his famous grin while posing with his Soviet counterpart. The cordial atmosphere produced a brief thaw in superpower tensions, which the press labeled "the spirit of Geneva." Ike returned from his trip claiming that "the prospects of a lasting peace" were "brighter" and the "dangers of the overwhelming tragedy of modern war are less." The American public certainly appreciated his efforts. His popularity rose to 79 percent in August 1955.

The friendly words and smiling faces of Geneva could not mask the serious differences between the two countries, however. The thaw ended on October 29, 1956, when 200,000 Soviet soldiers and hundreds of tanks swept into Hungary to repress a popular uprising demanding democratic reforms. The Soviet juggernaut killed 40,000 Hungarian freedom fighters and forced 150,000 refugees to flee the country. The invasion shocked the world and soiled Khrushchev's image as a reformer.

Conservatives expected the administration to intervene to support the rebels. After all, Eisenhower and Dulles had campaigned on a platform that called for the "liberation" of "captive peoples." When the CIA recommended parachuting arms and supplies to the Hungarian freedom fighters, Eisenhower refused. He understood the military risks of attempting to intervene in a country so close to the Soviet border. Hungary, he observed sadly, was "as inaccessible to us as Tibet." Once again Eisenhower had confronted the paradox of American power: U.S. defense policy relied upon atomic attack, or massive retaliation, which was too dangerous a weapon to use in this situation.

The Threat of Third World Nationalism

Hungarians were not alone in their struggle for independence. Between 1945 and 1960 almost forty nations with 800 million people fought nationalist struggles against colonial rulers. The leaders of these countries tried to exploit superpower tensions to win concessions from both Washington and Moscow. These newly independent nations in Asia, the Middle East, Latin America, and Africa became the new battlegrounds of the Cold War. Henry Cabot Lodge, U.S. ambassador to the United Nations, first asked the question that plagued American policy makers in the years following World War II: "The U.S. can win wars," but "can we win revolutions?"

The Middle East confronted the administration with its first serious nationalist challenge. In 1954 Egyptian leader Colonel Gamal Abdel Nasser increased trade with the Soviet bloc and officially recognized China. Two years later Dulles, in an attempt to punish Egypt for its growing ties with communists, abruptly canceled American financing to build the Aswan Dam across the Nile. In response, Nasser seized control of the Suez Canal, the vital waterway between the Mediterranean and the Gulf of Suez, and used the revenue to complete the Aswan project. Arabs hailed Nasser as a hero for his strong stand against western imperialism. Eisenhower worked behind the scenes to craft a compromise, but the British, who had controlled the canal, and the French, angered by Nasser's aid to rebels against French rule in Algeria, conspired to regain control of the canal and teach Nasser a lesson.

They got their chance on October 29, 1956, when, provoked by eight years of border attacks and fear of the Egyptian arms buildup, Israel invaded Egypt's Sinai Peninsula, advancing to within 10 miles of the Suez Canal. In an attack carefully coordinated with the Israelis, the British and French bombed Egyptian military targets and seized the northern third of the canal. The Soviets escalated tensions, claiming they were prepared to use military force to expel the Israeli-British-French forces. Eisenhower responded by placing American troops on alert, warning that the United States would respond to any Soviet move into the region. "If those fellows start something," he said, "we may have to hit 'em—and if necessary, with *everything* in the bucket."

The Anglo-French military action enraged Eisenhower, who feared it would alienate nationalist elements in the Middle East and drive the entire Arab world, and its lucrative oil fields, closer to the Soviet Union. The president publicly condemned the attacks on Egypt and worked with the Soviets through the United Nations for a cease-fire and the creation of a special UN emergency force to supervise withdrawal of all outside forces from Egypt. By December 1956 the crisis was over, but the Suez affair had shaken the western alliance to its foundations, provided the Russians with a foothold in the Middle East, and increased antiwestern sentiment in the region. In 1957 Eisenhower asked for, and both houses of Congress passed, a resolution that came to be called the "Eisenhower Doctrine." The new plan provided the president with broad authority to provide economic and military assistance to defend any Middle East ally from "international communism."

In other regions of the world the administration relied upon the CIA to quell nationalist uprisings that appeared to threaten American interests. In Iran when the government of Mohammed Mossadegha nationalized the Anglo-Iranian Oil Company in 1953, the CIA planned, financed, and orchestrated a coup to overthrow him. To replace him, the CIA worked with Iranian army officers to consolidate power behind the prowestern shah Reza Pahlavi. "I owe my throne to God, my people, my army—and to you!" exclaimed a grateful shah. The easy success of the operation in Iran encouraged the administration to use the CIA in other Third World hotspots.

The next opportunity came in 1954 when the administration used the CIA to topple the new leftist government of Jacob Arbenz Guzman in Guatemala. In 1953 the Arbenz government launched an ambitious land-reform program, which included seizing more than 200,000 acres controlled by the American-owned United Fruit Company. With an annual profit of $65 million, double the total revenue of the government, United Fruit became an obvious target of nationalist sentiment. Warning that the country could become an outpost for communism in the Western Hemisphere, the CIA trained a rag-tag liberation army in Honduras. On June 18 the army crossed the border into Guatemala while the CIA provided the planes and pilots to support the assault. At the same time, the agency jammed the government's radio station and broadcast its own version of the fighting, one that emphasized how government troops were laying down their arms and refusing to fight (they were not). A few days later Dulles told the media that the coup represented "a new and glorious chapter for all the people of the Americas." A new government, approved by the CIA, took power and restored the appropriated lands to United Fruit.

Eisenhower's experiments in intervention revealed the flaws in the vital center's approach to nationalist revolutions. Viewing local struggles as part of the superpower competition and threats to U.S. security, Americans confused indigenous nationalist movements with Soviet-inspired aggression. America's attitude revealed an arrogance of power, a belief that U.S. power could and should shape the internal affairs of distant nations. In time America would pay a heavy price for its mistakes.

Eisenhower and Vietnam

The administration's foreign policy faced another test in Indochina, where Ho Chi Minh's nationalist movement controlled a part of northern Vietnam and continued to battle French colonial authority. Eisenhower, like Truman, viewed Ho as a communist puppet and believed that if southern Vietnam fell to the communists, all Southeast Asia would be at risk. The administration's approach to Vietnam was also influenced by its priorities in Europe. Ike supported the French effort, providing up to 75 percent of the cost of the war by 1954, because he wanted France to join NATO.

The poorly led French army, however, was no match for the resourceful Vo Nguyen Giap, the commander-in-chief of the Vietminh troops in the South. In 1954 Vietnamese and Communist Chinese forces surrounded 12,000 French troops at Dien Bien Phu, a remote jungle fortress. The French pleaded for direct American intervention to rescue their troops. For weeks the administration debated a course of action. Dulles wanted to take the nation to the brink of war by launching air strikes against the North Vietnamese. Vice President Nixon went further, suggesting the introduction of ground troops or even the use of tactical nuclear weapons. He was supported by the air force chief of staff, who favored dropping "small tactical A-bombs," to clean those Commies out of there" so that "the band could play the Marseillaise and the French would come marching out of Dienbienphu in fine shape."

PRIMARY SOURCE

5.2 | *Dwight Eisenhower to Swede Hazlett, 1954*

In 1954 the French fighting in Indochina found themselves surrounded by Vietnamese and Communist Chinese forces at the remote camp of Dien Bien Phu. Even though the American government had been sending military and economic assistance to the French for years, Eisenhower's administration debated whether to aid the French in this crisis. Eisenhower's questions regarding American intervention on behalf of the French are evident in a letter written to friend Everett "Swede" Hazlett on April 27, 1954.

In my last letter I remember that I mentioned Dien Bien Phu. It still holds out and while the situation looked particularly desperate during the past week, there now appears to be a slight improvement and the place may hold on for another week or ten days. The general situation in Southeast Asia, which is rather
5 dramatically epitomized by the Dien Bien Phu battle, is a complicated one that has been a long time developing. . . .

For more than three years I have been urging upon successive French governments the advisability of finding some way of "internationalizing" the war; such action would be proof to all the world and particularly to the Viet Namese that
10 France's purpose is not colonial in character but is to defeat Communism in the region and to give the natives their freedom. The reply has always been vague, containing references to national prestige, Constitutional limitations, inevitable effects upon the Moroccan and Tunisian peoples, and dissertations on plain political difficulties and battles within the French Parliament. The result has been
15 that the French have failed entirely to produce any enthusiasm on the part of the Vietnamese for participation in the war. . . .

In any event, any nation that intervenes in a civil war can scarcely expect to win unless the side in whose favor it intervenes possesses a high morale based

upon a war purpose or cause in which it believes. The French have used weasel
20   words in promising independence and through this one reason as much as anything else, have suffered reverses that have been really inexcusable.   ■ ■ ■

But once again Eisenhower preferred caution. The president had little faith in
the military capability of the French, whom he called "a hopeless, helpless mass
of protoplasm." European allies, especially the British, opposed American intervention. At home leading Democrats, including Senators Lyndon Johnson of
Texas and John F. Kennedy of Massachusetts, warned against using American soldiers in Indochina. Eisenhower also worried about the moral implications of
using tactical nuclear weapons in Asia. "You boys must be crazy," Eisenhower
replied. "We can't use those awful things against Asians for the second time in ten
years. My God." Without American support the French garrison surrendered in
May 1954.

Eisenhower was not opposed to some form of intervention, however. When
asked a question about Indochina at a press conference, Ike spelled out for the
first time what would become known as the "domino theory." "You have a row of
dominoes set up, you knock over the first one, and what will happen to the last
one is the certainty that it will go over very quickly. So you could have the beginning of a disintegration that would have the most profound influences."

PRIMARY **SOURCE**

5.3 | *The Domino Theory*
Dwight Eisenhower

With the growing unrest in Indochina, President Eisenhower recognized the
need for stronger American resolve to prevent communism from spreading
throughout Southeast Asia. During the president's news conference on April 7,
1954, Eisenhower explained why support of the French in Indochina was vital to
American interests in the entire region, promoting what became known as the
domino theory.

Q: Robert Richards, Copley Press: Mr. President, would you mind commenting on
the strategic importance of Indochina to the free world? I think there has been,
across the country, some lack of understanding on just what it means to us.

The President: You have, of course, both the specific and the general when you
5   talk about such things.
First of all, you have the specific value of a locality in its production of materials that the world needs.

Then you have the possibility that many human beings pass under a dictatorship that is inimical to the free world.

10　　Finally, you have broader considerations that might follow what you would call the "falling domino" principle. You have a row of dominoes set up, you knock over the first one, and what will happen to the last one is the certainly that it will go over very quickly. So you could have a beginning of a disintegration that would have the most profound influences.

15　　Now, with respect to the first one, two of the items from this particular area that the world uses are tin and tungsten. They are very important. There are others, of course, the rubber plantations and so on.

Then with respect to more people passing under this domination, Asia, after all, has already lost some 450 million of its people to the Communist dictator-
20　ship, and we simply can't affort greater losses.

But when we come to the possible sequence of events, the loss of Indochina, of Burma, of Thailand, of the Peninsula, and Indonesia following, now you begin to talk about areas that not only multiply the disadvantages that you would suffer through loss of materials, sources of materials, but now you are talking really
25　about millions and millions and millions of people.

Finally, the geographical position achieved thereby does many things. It turns the so-called island defensive chain of Japan, Formosa, of the Philippines and to the southward; it moves in to threaten Australia and New Zealand.

30　　It takes away, in its economic aspects, that region that Japan must have as a trading area or Japan, in turn, will have only one place in the world to go—that is, toward the Communist areas in order to live.

So, the possible consequences of the loss are just incalculable to the free world.　　　　　　　　　　　　　　　　　　　　　　　■ ■ ■

In July the French government signed the Geneva Accords, which temporarily divided Indochina at the seventeenth parallel until the holding of free democratic elections in 1956. Realizing that the popular Ho Chi Minh would win in a free election, the administration installed as head of state in South Vietnam Ngo Dinh Diem, an ardent Vietnamese nationalist who hated the French. Diem was also a staunch anticommunist and devout Catholic. The United States poured economic and military aid into the South in hopes of making Diem a viable leader. In 1954, in an effort to stem Soviet and Chinese influence in the area, Dulles set up yet another anticommunist military alliance, the Southeast Asia Treaty Organization. The treaty pledged the United States to defend Australia, New Zealand, Thailand, Pakistan, and the Philippines against communist aggression.

The Geneva Accords gave the administration two years to develop a viable government in South Vietnam. Between 1954 and 1956 the CIA launched plans to harass the North, destroying printing presses, contaminating the fuel supply, and distributing leaflets designed to undermine support for Ho Chi Minh. At the same time, U.S. officials poured economic and military aid into the South.

Critics pointed out that Diem was a weak leader, "a messiah without a message" whose goal was "to ask immediate American assistance in every form." But Diem was the only option, and the administration feared the consequences of abandoning his government.

With American support, Diem announced that the South would not participate in free elections as mandated by the Geneva Accords. Publicly he claimed that his government had never signed the accords and that free elections would be impossible given the repressive nature of the North Vietnamese government. The real reason was that he knew the North would win an overwhelming victory. It would turn out to be one of the most fateful decisions of the Cold War.

Eisenhower's response to the postwar paradox was to provide rhetorical support to conservative notions of limited government at home and muscular anticommunism abroad while pursuing moderate policies that institutionalized New Deal programs and accommodated the realities of the U.S.–Soviet relationship. Despite differences in style and tone from the Truman administration, the Republican president governed within the broad parameters of the vital center, attempting to promote growth at home, placing a premium on social harmony, and fighting the spread of communism abroad. Politically Ike used his personality to steer a middle course between the growing gap between American ideals and social realities. But beneath the surface important changes were forcing Americans to confront the contradiction.

SELECTED READINGS

▪ Gary W. Reichard's *Politics as Usual* (1988) surveys politics at midcentury. Stephen E. Ambrose's *Eisenhower* (2 vols., 1983, 1984) is a comprehensive scholarly biography of the president, as is Geoffrey Perret's *Eisenhower* (1999). Fred I. Greenstein's *The Hidden-Hand Presidency* (1982) has good material on Eisenhower's campaigns against Adlai Stevenson; the use of television advertisements for the first time in the 1952 campaign is discussed in Wil Benoit's *Seeing Spots* (1999). Nicol Rae's *The Decline and Fall of the Liberal Republicans* (1989) chronicles the struggle between conservatives and moderates in the Republican Party.

▪ Eisenhower's efforts to protect national security by promoting a healthy economy is the basis of Gerard Clarfield's *Security with Solvency* (1999). *Who Killed Joe McCarthy?* (1984), by William Ewald, recounts the circumstances surrounding the Army-McCarthy hearings and the behind-the-scenes role played by Eisenhower. Jeff Broadwater, in *Eisenhower and the Anti-Communist Crusade* (1992), argues that Eisenhower, while opposed to McCarthy's tactics, frequently failed to protect civil liberties in the name of national security.

▪ Robert Divine's *Eisenhower and the Cold War* (1981) provides an excellent survey of U.S.–Soviet relations in the 1950s. The impact of Eisenhower's historic meeting with Khrushchev at the Geneva Summit is discussed in *Cold War Respite* (1999), edited by Gunter Bischof and Saki Dockrill. The essays collected by editors Richard Melanson and David Mayers in *Reevaluating Eisenhower* (1986) examine America's foreign policy around the globe. Ray Takeyh's *The Origins of the Eisenhower Doctrine* (2000) traces the emergence of Eisenhower's foreign policy as he attempted to balance Cold War theory with the forces of nationalism in the Middle East. Burton Kaufman's *The Arab Middle East and the United States* (1996) serves as an introduction to the American role in Middle East affairs.

▮ Stephen E. Ambrose's *Ike's Spies* (1981) details the rise of the American intelligence establishment, and the impact of a daring few in the CIA's early years is examined in Evan Thomas's *The Very Best Men* (1995). Richard Immerman provides a valuable case study of the CIA's actions in *The CIA in Guatemala* (1982). Andrew Rotter focuses on America's early Indochina policy in *The Path to Vietnam* (1987), as does David L. Anderson in *Trapped by Success* (1991).

American Ideals and Social Realities, 1952–1960

The Reverend George W. Lee devoted his life to his community. As vice president of the Regional Council of Negro Leadership, an active member of the National Association for the Advancement of Colored People (NAACP), and a clergyman, he stood as a pillar of the small Mississippi Delta town of Belzoni. By the mid-1950s Lee had set his sights on registering black voters to deliver an African-American to Congress. After Lee helped organize a huge voter registration rally in Mound Bayou that attracted more than ten thousand citizens, the local White Citizen's Council began issuing death threats in a futile attempt to intimidate him and frustrate his campaign for racial equality.

One steamy Mississippi night in May 1955, a convertible raced up to Reverend Lee's car as he drove through the center of town. Suddenly, the crackle of gunfire ripped through the air. A fatally wounded Lee slumped in his seat, and the car swerved off the road and crashed. No one was ever arrested for Lee's murder. Local white officials even denied that a crime had been committed. The headline in a local newspaper read, "Negro Leader Dies in Odd Accident."

Similar incidents of violence were part of the fabric of everyday life for many southern blacks. Over 180 years after independence and some 90 since the abolition of slavery, Lee and other African-Americans found themselves still fighting for a most basic American right: freedom. At a time when intellectuals and politicians proclaimed that prosperity had muted class and racial differences, the contradiction between American ideals and American reality provided the central paradox of the 1950s.

Intellectuals and the Celebration of Consensus

The tension went unnoticed by most intellectuals during the 1950s. Prosperity, the lure of suburbia, the stifling effects of McCarthyism, and the oppressive atmosphere of the Cold War discouraged critical social analysis, muted vigorous political debate, and reinforced the vital-center consensus. Intellectuals gave their scholarly blessing to the self-satisfied images that pervaded mass culture. In 1956 *Time* magazine observed that the intellectual "found himself feeling at home" in America.

Most intellectuals, ensconced in comfortable positions at major universities, foundations, and mass communication, benefited from the postwar prosperity and believed that capitalism was transforming America into a land of plenty. "American capitalism works," declared Harvard economist John Kenneth Galbraith early in the decade. Meanwhile, McCarthy's attacks against leftist intellectuals intimidated many of them, who sought refuge in moderate liberalism. Many opinion makers, determined not to leave themselves vulnerable to right-wing attacks on their patriotism, expressed enthusiastic support for the Cold War, viewing it as a struggle between the free world and totalitarian communism.

Historians, sociologists, and political scientists heralded an "age of consensus," a time when prosperity, social programs, and fear of communism rendered social protest obsolete. At the end of the decade the sociologist Daniel Bell declared all radical alternatives dead in *The End of Ideology* (1960). Such historians as Daniel Boorstin and Henry Steele Commager minimized the role of conflict and change in American history and stressed the importance of continuity and consensus. Commager claimed that the New Deal "was no revolution, but rather the culmination of half a century of historical development," and that FDR was "the greatest conservative since Alexander Hamilton." Surveys showing that 75 percent of Americans considered themselves part of the middle class contributed to a growing sense that the nation was evolving toward a classless society.

Liberals joined in the celebration of consensus, abandoning or moderating the arguments born during the Great Depression for sweeping changes in the nation's economic institutions. Like earlier reformers, liberals in the 1950s believed that government needed to play a role in regulating the economy and guaranteeing social justice. But they also shared with many conservatives a reverence for the enormous potential of the free enterprise system and a fear of expansive federal power. Reflecting the broader consensus, liberals believed that sustained economic growth, with a minimum of government regulation, would eliminate class divisions, create opportunity for all citizens, and ensure a stable society.

A sizable number of intellectuals went even further, abandoning the pretense of moderation and embracing conservatism. While critical of the growth of government power in the years after World War II, these intellectuals celebrated the success of American capitalism and accepted the U.S. mission to redefine the world in its own image. Many conservative thinkers, fearful that the expanded state power would lead the nation down "the road to serfdom," and confident in the power of capitalism, offered a powerful defense of free market capitalism.

Others, most notably Russell Kirk, worried about the decline of moral standards and called for a revival of traditional religious values. Finally, ex-communists who converted to conservatism, including Whittaker Chambers and James Burnham, carried into the postwar period a profound conviction that the West was involved in a titanic struggle with a ruthless adversary that sought nothing less than the conquest of the world.

The New Poverty

The celebration of a classless society proved unfounded. In spite of the widening prosperity, the distribution of income remained uneven. In 1960 the top 1 percent of the population held 33 percent of the national wealth, while the bottom 20 percent held only 5 percent. In 1959, 25 percent of the population had no liquid assets; over 50 percent had no savings accounts. "If we made an income pyramid out of child's blocks, with each portraying $1,000 of income," the economist Paul Samuelson observed, "the peak would be far higher than the Eiffel Tower, but almost all of us would be within a foot of the ground."

Although poverty had declined significantly since the Great Depression, about 40 million Americans representing 25 percent of the population were poor in 1960. The elderly, people over sixty-five, made up one-fourth of the poor. One-fifth were people of color, including 45 percent of African-Americans. Conditions were especially bad on Indian reservations, where unemployment soared to over 80 percent during the winter and averaged near 50 percent the rest of the year. The average Indian family income of $1,500 fell far below the national average of $5,000. Poverty, however, was not restricted to disadvantaged groups. The white working poor made up about one-fifth of those families living in poverty. These families were headed by a white male who worked a full-time job but simply did not make enough money to stay above the poverty line.

The majority of these poor people received little help from the meager welfare system. About one-half of America's poor families were not covered by social security in 1960. Only about one-fifth received assistance from the federal government. Money spent on them represented less than 1 percent of the gross national product.

What was new about poverty in the 1950s was that it had moved from the rural farm to the inner city. By 1960 some 55 percent of the poor lived in cities. African-Americans made up a majority of the new urban residents. Before World War II, 80 percent of African-Americans lived in the South. During the war defense-related jobs lured almost 3 million southern workers to the nation's cities. In 1943 the mechanical cotton picker displaced perhaps 2.3 million family farm workers, many of whom traveled north looking for jobs. At one point in the

1950s the black population of Chicago swelled by more than two thousand two hundred new arrivals each week. By 1960 half of all African-Americans lived in central cities.

African-Americans, and other minorities, flooded the nation's cities just as the white middle class, and many jobs, were fleeing to the suburbs. Discrimination prevented minorities from following the same route. Many private developers refused to sell homes to African-Americans. The Federal Housing Administration, which financed 30 percent of all new homes in the 1950s, endorsed "restrictive covenants" prohibiting sales to minorities. It also contributed to the declining quality of urban housing by supporting "redlining," the refusal to write mortgage loans to central-city areas.

At the same time, many cities adopted ambitious "urban renewal" projects, which demolished neighborhoods and displaced poor people in the name of progress. By 1963 urban renewal had uprooted 609,000 Americans, two-thirds of whom were minority-group members. When planning the route of new superhighways to speed the commute between the suburbs and the central city, Los Angeles officials bypassed wealthy neighborhoods such as Beverly Hills and plowed through densely populated Chicano communities in East Los Angeles and Hollenbeck. In October 1957 the city displaced the Chicano community in Chavez Ravine to make room for the building of Dodger Stadium.

Women During the 1950s

A gap between popular perceptions and social realities also plagued women during the decade. In a special 1956 issue on American women, *Life* magazine concluded that the ideal modern woman married, cooked and cared for her family, and kept herself busy by joining the local Parent-Teacher Association and leading a troop of the Campfire Girls. The magazine praised the "increasing emphasis on the nurturing and homemaking values among women who might have at one time pursued a career."

As the *Life* magazine article revealed, women faced enormous social pressure to conform to traditional gender roles. Many people viewed marriage and child bearing as keys to a stable society and a bulwark against communism. Federal Bureau of Investigation (FBI) director J. Edgar Hoover lectured that marriage and motherhood would help in the fight against "the twin enemies of freedom—crime and Communism." Popular culture often reinforced the message as Hollywood screenwriters, still smarting from their confrontation with Red-hunters, required career women to acknowledge marriage as their top priority. "Marriage is the most important thing in the world," Debbie Reynolds said in *The Tender Trap* (1955). "A woman isn't really a woman until she's been married and had children."

Advertisers tapped into women's insecurities as wives, mothers, and house-keepers in order to sell new products. The "professional" housewife scoured and sanitized her home to keep her children healthy, sewed her own clothes, and chauffeured her children around the neighborhood. She still had time to entertain guests in her family's suburban house and work out on the trampoline "to keep her size 12 figure." Psychologists instructed manufacturers on how to make a housewife feel professional. "When a housewife uses one product for washing clothes, a second for dishes, a third for walls, a fourth for floors, a fifth for venetian blinds, rather than an all-purpose cleaner, she feels less like an unskilled laborer and more like an engineer."

The publication of Dr. Benjamin Spock's best-selling *The Common Sense Book of Baby Care* (1946) placed all the burden of child care on the mother. Children, he argued, needed constant motherly affection; otherwise they languished or would grow up to be juvenile delinquents. For Spock, a woman's place was in the home raising children. "If a mother realizes clearly how vital this kind of care is to a small child," he explained, "it may make it easier for her to decide that the extra money she might earn, or the satisfaction she might receive from an outside job, is not so important after all."

Many leading educators discouraged women from seeking a college education. In 1950 the president of Mills College announced that education "frustrated" women. Instead of studying science and math, college women should learn the "theory and preparation of a basque paella, of a well-marinated shish-kebab, lamb kidney sauteed in sherry, an authoritative curry." In keeping with this philosophy, the college instituted a "marriage" major and introduced a course on "volunteerism." The president of Radcliffe College suggested changing the curriculum so that it would not "encourage women to compete with men." This oppressive atmosphere shaped the expectations of female students. "We don't want careers," explained one student. "Our parents expect us to go to college. Everybody goes. But a girl who got serious about anything she studied—like, wanting to go on and do research—would be peculiar, unfeminine. I guess everybody wants to graduate with a diamond ring on the finger. That's the important thing."

However, the decade's celebration of the American housewife failed to account for important changes in women's lives. Between 1940 and 1960 the number of women in the work force doubled, rising from 15 percent to 30 percent. Even more striking, the proportion of married working mothers jumped 400 percent. By 1952, 2 million more women were at work than during World War II. Many of the women who joined the work force were middle-aged wives looking for a second income to help their suburban families pay for their new consumer goods. By the early 1960s one worker in three was a woman and three of five women workers were married.

The expanding economy provided jobs for women, especially in the growing service sector. Businesses sought out educated middle-class married mothers to fill secretarial and clerical jobs. At the same time, the definition of "economic necessity" changed, as middle-class families now dreamed of a new house in the suburbs, two cars, a college education for their children, and leisure money for a family vacation every year. Increased expectations of the "good life" forced women into the work force to earn extra money.

While millions of women went to work every day, they found themselves segregated in low-paying positions. The job ads that appeared in newspapers were divided by sex. On one side of the page were jobs for men; on the opposite page were ads that funneled women into "pink-collar work." In 1959 a white man with a high-school education earned an average of $4,429, while a white woman earned only $3,458. A greater portion of women's jobs than men's jobs were not covered by minimum wage or social security. In 1960 women represented only 3.5 percent of lawyers and 6.1 percent of physicians. But they made up 97 percent of nurses and 85 percent of librarians. Of high-school principals, 90 percent were male, while of elementary-school teachers, 85 percent were female.

Evidence of changing sexual behavior challenged the celebration of traditional family life. In 1947 Alfred Kinsey, an Indiana University zoologist best known as the world's foremost authority on the North American gall wasp, decided to abandon his work on bees and turn his attention to human sexuality. He became so obsessed by the topic that his wife remarked, "I hardly see him at night since he took up sex." His studies on *Sexual Behavior in the Human Male* (1948) and *Sexual Behavior in the Human Female* (1953) rocketed to the top of the best-seller list, where they stayed for twenty-seven weeks. The statistics shocked the nation: 86 percent of men said they had engaged in premarital sex, 50 percent said they had committed adultery before turning 40, 37 percent reported at least one episode of homosexual sex, and 17 percent who had grown up on farms claimed to have had sex with animals.

The Kinsey report exposed the contradiction between private behavior and public morality. Perhaps the most surprising revelation was about the promiscuity of women. Each generation of women, he reported, was more sexually active than the last. In addition, many women were engaging in sexual acts that previous generations of Americans had deemed immoral and illegal. Sexual activity previously labeled "deviant" or "immoral" seemed rampant among the very people who outwardly condemned it. All this was too much for many traditionalists. *Life* magazine condemned Kinsey's results as an "assault on the family as a basic unit of society, a negation of moral law, and a celebration of licentiousness."

In the last few years of the decade a housewife and former journalist named Betty Friedan began interviewing other women who had graduated from her alma mater, Smith College. Most of these women seemed to possess all the material needs that society deemed important—nice suburban homes, the latest home appliances, healthy children. But they were all unhappy. Unaware that other women shared their feelings, they suffered in silence and blamed themselves for their misery. Friedan later wrote about this unhappiness, which she called "the problem that has no name," in her ground-breaking book, *The Feminine Mystique* (1963). Friedan challenged women to confront the problem and change their lives. "We can no longer ignore the voice within women that says: 'I want something more than my husband and my children and my home.' " The book, which sold more than 3 million copies, had finally broken the silence and forced Americans to deal with the reality of women's lives.

The Struggle for Black Equality

Nowhere was the contradiction between ideals and reality more striking than in the lives of African-Americans. The South's racially segregated schools formed only one piece in a vast mosaic of institutionalized racism. Wherever one looked in early postwar America, blacks were treated as second-class citizens.

Yet following World War II a combination of forces began undermining the structures of racial segregation in the South. For the previous half-century the NAACP had focused on fulfilling the constitutional promise of civil and political rights for African-Americans by doggedly pursuing test cases in the courts. Gradually, the Supreme Court began to chip away at the legal bases of segregation. In 1951 the Reverend Oliver Brown tried to enroll his eight-year-old daughter, Linda, in an all-white elementary school in Topeka. School officials refused to admit her, citing a law in force in Kansas and in sixteen other states requiring black children to attend segregated educational facilities. Instead of walking the four blocks to her neighborhood school, Linda had to board a bus every morning for the 5-mile journey to an all-black school across town. With the help of a small team of skilled black lawyers from Howard University and the NAACP, led by Thurgood Marshall, Reverend Brown took the case to court.

The suit claimed that refusal to admit Linda Brown violated the equal protection clause of the Fourteenth Amendment, which states that "no State . . . shall deprive any person of life, liberty, or property, without due process of law; nor deny to any person within its jurisdiction the equal protection of the laws." The case quietly worked its way up the appeal system and reached the Supreme Court in 1954. The Court overturned the legal justification for one of the principal pillars of white supremacy in a unanimous decision popularly known as *Brown* v. *Board of Education*. The *Brown* decision declared segregation in public schools to be illegal, claiming that "in the field of public education the doctrine of 'separate but equal' has no place." Two days after *Brown* the *Washington Post* declared, "It is not too much to speak of the court's decision as a new birth of freedom." A year later the Supreme Court instructed federal district courts to require local authorities to show "good faith" and to move with "all deliberate speed" toward desegregation of all public schools.

6.1 | *Brown* v. *Board of Education*

On May 17, 1954, Chief Justice Earl Warren read the Supreme Court's unanimous ruling in the case of *Brown* v. *Board of Education* and the reasons for this decision. Overturning the doctrine of "separate but equal" established by *Plessy* v. *Ferguson* in 1896, the Court declared that segregation in public schools was unconstitutional.

The plaintiffs contend that segregated public schools are not "equal" and cannot be made "equal," and that hence they are deprived of the equal protection of the laws. . . .

5 In approaching this problem, we cannot turn the clock back to 1868 when the Amendment was adopted, or even to 1896 when *Plessy* was written. We must consider public education in light of its full development and its present place in American life throughout the Nation. Only in this way can it be determined if segregation in public schools deprives these plaintiffs of the equal protection of the laws. Today, education is perhaps the most important function of state and local

10 governments. Compulsory school attendance laws and the great expenditures for education both demonstrate our recognition of the importance of education to our democratic society. . . . In these days, it is doubtful that any child may reasonably be expected to succeed in life if he is denied the opportunity of an education. Such an opportunity, where the state has undertaken to provide it, is a right which

15 must be made available to all on equal terms.

We come then to the question presented: Does segregation of children in public schools solely on the basis of race, even though the physical facilities and other "tangible" factors may be equal, deprive the children of the minority group of equal educational opportunities? We believe that it does. . . .

20 To separate [children] from others of similar age and qualifications solely because of their race generates a feeling of inferiority as to their status in the community that may affect their hearts and minds in a way unlikely ever to be undone. The effect of this separation on their educational opportunities was well stated by a finding in the Kansas case by a court which nevertheless felt compelled

25 to rule against the Negro plaintiffs: "Segregation of white and colored children in public schools has a detrimental effect upon the colored children. The impact is greater when it has the sanction of the law; for the policy of separating the races is usually interpreted as denoting the inferiority of the Negro group. . . . Segregation with the sanction of law, therefore, has a tendency to retard the educational

30 and mental development of Negro children and to deprive them of some of the benefits they would receive in a [racially] integrated school system." Whatever may have been the extent of psychological knowledge at the time of *Plessy* v. *Ferguson,* this finding is amply supported by modern authority. . . .

We conclude that in the field of public education the doctrine of "separate

35 but equal" has no place. Separate educational facilities are inherently unequal. . . . ■ ■ ■

This historic decision triggered massive resistance to ending Jim Crow among state and local politicians in the South. They and newly formed White Citizens Councils employed legal maneuvers, economic reprisals, and outright defiance against blacks who challenged segregation. Democratic Senator James Eastland of Mississippi denounced the Court's "monstrous crime," which would result in "the mongrelization of the white race." Nineteen southern senators and seventy-seven representatives signed a manifesto in 1956 that bound them to "use all lawful means to bring about a reversal of this decision which is contrary to the Court and to prevent the use of force in its implementation."

PRIMARY SOURCE

6.2 | *The Southern Manifesto, 1956*

A year after the *Brown* decision, the Supreme Court ordered public schools desegregated with "all deliberate speed," thereby angering many southern whites, who vowed to fight back. Unable to obtain enough votes for a congressional resolution denouncing *Brown,* Virginia senator Harry Byrd composed the Southern Manifesto in March 1956 to express his dissatisfaction with the Court's ruling. Nineteen southern senators and seventy-seven representatives signed the manifesto, encouraging white defiance of desegregation.

We regard the decision of the Supreme Court in the school cases as clear abuse of judicial power. It climaxes a trend in the Federal judiciary undertaking to legislate, in derogation of the authority of Congress, and to encroach upon the reserved rights of the states and the people.

5   The original Constitution does not mention education. Neither does the Fourteenth Amendment nor any other amendment. The debates preceding the submission of the Fourteenth Amendment clearly show that there was no intent that it should affect the systems of education maintained by the states. . . .

When the amendment was adopted in 1868, there were thirty-seven states of

10 the Union. Every one of the twenty-six states that had any substantial racial differences among its people either approved the operation of segregated schools already in existence or subsequently established such schools by action of the same law-making body which considered the Fourteenth Amendment. . . .

This unwarranted exercise of power by the court, contrary to the Constitution, is

15 creating chaos and confusion in the states principally affected. It is destroying the amicable relations between the white and negro races that have been created through ninety years of patient effort by the good people of both races. It has planted hatred and suspicion where there has been heretofore friendship and understanding. . . .

With the gravest concern for the explosive and dangerous condition created

20 by this decision and inflamed outside meddlers:

We reaffirm our reliance on the Constitution as the fundamental law of the land.

We decry the Supreme Court's encroachments on rights reserved to the states and to the people, contrary to established law and to the Constitution.

We commend the motives of those states which have declared the intention to
25 resist forced integration by any lawful means.

We appeal to the states and people who are not directly affected by these decisions to consider the constitutional principles involved against the time when they too, on issues vital to them, may be the victims of judicial encroachments.

■ ■ ■

The first outright defiance of the federal courts occurred in Little Rock, Arkansas. Desegregation of Central High School was scheduled to begin in September 1957. But many whites wished to obstruct the plan, and the state's ambitious governor, Orville Faubus, believed that supporting desegregation would mean political suicide. Faubus called out the National Guard to prevent black students from entering Central High. The guardsmen, with bayonets drawn, turned back the nine young African-American students who planned to attend Central and thereby mainlined segregation for nearly three weeks until a federal judge ordered the guard removed.

The students managed to enter the school, but only after a mob of unruly whites outside pelted and pushed the police who tried to protect the students. National television cameras recorded the ugly events. President Dwight Eisenhower, who privately deplored the *Brown* decision, responded by sending federal troops to uphold the court order. The president told a southern senator that "failure to act in such a case would be tantamount to acquiescence in anarchy and the dissolution of the union." For the first time since Radical Reconstruction, the federal government demonstrated that it would use military force to protect rights guaranteed to blacks by the Constitution. Troops patrolled the high school for months, but the controversy over desegregation convulsed the city for two more years.

The *Brown* decision and Eisenhower's forceful response in Little Rock offered hope that Washington had finally decided to join the black struggle for civil rights. African-Americans, however, were not going to wait for the federal government in their effort to end the daily humiliation of legal segregation. Even before *Brown,* African-Americans living in the South had laid the foundation of a powerful social movement that would challenge white supremacy.

The Montgomery Bus Boycott

What would become one of the most dramatic symbols of the civil-rights movement occurred in Mississippi in 1955. In September Emmett Till, a fourteen-year-old black youth from Chicago, visited relatives near Greenwood, Mississippi. After buying some candy at a rural store, Till allegedly said, "Bye, baby" to the white female clerk. Three days later, after midnight, her husband and brother dragged

Till from his home, shot him through the head, cut off his testicles, and dumped his body in the Tallahatchie River. Till's mother insisted on an open casket at the funeral so that, in her words, "all the world can see what they did to my boy."

The image of Till's mutilated body, captured by television, seared itself into the consciousness of a generation of black leaders. The subsequent trial did little to boost confidence in southern justice. "Your ancestors will turn over in their graves," one of the defense lawyers told the jury in his summation, if these men "are found guilty and I'm sure every last Anglo-Saxon one of you has the courage to free these men in the face of that [outside] pressure." Despite overwhelming evidence of guilt, an all-white, all-male jury deliberated for sixty-seven minutes before finding the two white suspects innocent of kidnapping.

The image of Emmett Till was fresh on people's minds when on December 1, 1955, a forty-two-year-old civil-rights advocate named Rosa Parks boarded a city bus in Montgomery, Alabama. When asked to give up her seat to a white person as required by Alabama law, Parks refused. "I felt it was just something I had to do," Parks said. Her simple act of courage became a challenge to the edifice of racial injustice in the South. After police arrested Parks for her defiance, black leaders decided to boycott the city bus system and sought the support of black ministers, the traditional leaders of African-American communities. One of the key organizations supporting the boycott was the Women's Political Council (WPC). Made up of middle-class African-American women, the WPC organized a "telephone tree" to inform members of developments and to coordinate activities. The night that Parks was arrested, JoAnn Robinson, the chair of the WPC, composed and printed more than thirty thousand mimeographed copies of a leaflet pleading with Montgomery's citizens to "please stay off all buses on Monday."

Twenty-six-year-old Martin Luther King Jr., pastor of the Dexter Baptist Church, agreed to head the Montgomery Improvement Association (MIA), created to promote and support the boycott. King had grown up in Atlanta, the son of a prosperous minister of one of the largest Baptist congregations in the country. After graduating from Atlanta's Morehouse College, he attended Crozer Seminary in Pennsylvania and earned his doctorate at Boston University. A brilliant speaker, he could inspire blacks and whites alike with his words. King preached a philosophy of nonviolent resistance that represented a synthesis of the teachings of Jesus and Mohandas Gandhi. His goal was to use the power of love and the tactic of nonviolence—boycotts, strikes, marches, and mass civil disobedience—to combat social evil. "We must meet the forces of hate with the power of love; we must meet physical force with soul force." King planned to use nonviolent confrontations to expose to the nation the viciousness of southern society, and to highlight the compelling moral contrast between peaceful blacks demanding basic American rights and a violent white political leadership determined to deny them those rights.

To deal with the loss of public transportation, the bus boycotters organized a massive and complicated system of car-pools that involved twenty thousand people every day. Some preferred to walk, as far as 12 miles a day, to underline their determination and hope. "I'm not walking for myself," said an elderly woman turning down a ride. "I'm walking for my children and my grandchildren." Another elderly woman, known as Mother Pollard, vowed to King that she would walk until it was over. "But aren't your feet tired?" he asked. "Yes," she said, "my feets is tired, but my soul is rested."

The city used intimidation tactics to try breaking the will of blacks. Policemen stopped car-pool drivers, writing tickets for imaginary violations of the law. In January the White Citizen's Council drew ten thousand people to the Montgomery Coliseum for what was described as the largest segregation rally of the century. The Ku Klux Klan marched in full garb through the center of black parts of town in an attempt to intimidate blacks. The intimidation tactics failed. King attracted the attention of the national news media, which flooded into Montgomery to cover the story. The presence of so many reporters made it difficult for the city's white leadership to inflict physical violence on blacks, provided the rest of the nation with its first real glimpse of conditions in the South, and transformed King into a national celebrity.

Montgomery Bus Boycotters In the 1950s, the civil rights movement moved into a new, more determined phase dominated by ordinary people, such as seamstress Rosa Parks, who sparked the Montgomery bus boycott in 1955 by refusing to give up her seat on a segregated bus. For months, African-Americans in the city refused to ride public buses, instead forming car-pools and even walking miles to work each day. These black workers are waiting for their ride at a car-pool pickup site. Their sacrifices reduced the profits on city buses by 65 percent and produced a Supreme Court decision that declared segregation on city buses unconstitutional. *(Dan Weiner, Courtesy Sandra Weiner.)*

With media attention came money from across America, which allowed the MIA to buy a new fleet of cars. The momentum had clearly shifted in favor of the boycotters. The final blow came from the courts. In June 1956 a panel of federal judges struck down Montgomery's segregation ordinances. The state appealed to the Supreme Court, which upheld the lower court decision a few months later. On December 21 a bus pulled up to a street corner where King was standing. The white driver greeted him with a smile. "I believe you are Reverend King." "Yes, I am," King responded. "We are glad to have you with us this morning," the driver said.

The Montgomery boycott demonstrated that intimidation, which had served for so long to repress black aspirations, would no longer work. In doing so, the boycott laid the foundation for the civil-rights struggle of the 1960s. It also established Martin Luther King as a persuasive and articulate spokesman for the movement. In the past white leaders in the South had served as both judge and jury, but the news media nationalized the struggle, exposing the South to the critical eye of public opinion. The boycott forced changes in one institution that mistreated blacks, but it could not attack the most important problem facing blacks in the South—segregation.

Civic Nationalism/Cultural Pluralism

African-Americans were not the only minority group challenging the fragile Cold War consensus. During the 1940s and 1950s a combination of technological innovation and a population explosion in Mexico produced massive new waves of immigrants across America's southern border. Meanwhile, when Puerto Rico mechanized its sugar-cane production, many workers who lost their jobs migrated to the mainland. Between 1940 and 1960 the Puerto Rican population of New York City increased from 70,000 to 613,000.

At the same time, the United States recruited millions of Mexican laborers through the Bracero Program. Created to address the agriculture labor shortage during World War II, the program continued for more than two decades. At its peak in 1957 more than 450,000 Mexicans worked in the seasonal program, primarily in Texas and California, often sending money to their families back in Mexico. The volume of illegal immigration also rose steadily. By 1960 Spanish-speakers, almost all of them of Mexican origin, made up 12 percent of the population in the Southwest. Between 1950 and 1960 the Mexican-American population of Los Angeles County doubled, from 300,000 to more than 600,000. By 1960 Hispanics made up 16 percent of California's population. Nearly 80 percent of Hispanic-Americans lived in urban centers.

Hispanic veterans, inspired by their service in World War II and by the evolving African-American freedom struggle, spearheaded their own civil-rights movement. "We had earned our credentials as American citizens," observed Hispanic veteran Sabine R. Ulibarri. "We had paid our dues on the counters of conviction and faith. We were not about to take any crap." In 1948 when a funeral home in Three Rivers, Texas, refused to conduct a burial service for a Mexican-American veteran, local leaders formed the American GI Forum (AGIF) to protest discrimination. Over the next decade, under the leadership of Dr. Hector Pérez, a World War II combat surgeon with a distinguished service record, AGIF broadened its agenda. It led voter-registration drives, filed lawsuits to end discrimination, and helped educate Mexican-American veterans about their rights under the GI Bill.

Like AGIF, many of the new Hispanic organizations established after World War II were made up of middle-class leaders who worked to remove the barriers preventing integration into American life. The League of United Latin American Citizens, which had chapters in cities with large Hispanic populations between Texas and California, filed a series of lawsuits to end segregation of Hispanic students in public schools. In Chicago the Spanish-Speaking People's Council and the Pan-American Council, often with the support of local Catholic church leaders, fought discrimination and provided services to help new arrivals assimilate into American life. Other groups, like the Community Service Organization, helped register voters and elect Hispanic political candidates.

Native Americans faced renewed pressure after World War II to abandon their tribal associations and integrate into mainstream society. Leading politicians from both parties stressed the need to terminate the tradition of Indian self-rule on the reservation. "All Indians are citizens of the United States and no longer should be denied full enjoyment of their rights of citizenship," the Republican platform declared in 1952. As "domestic dependent nations," the tribes had the right to govern their own affairs, were exempt from most local and state laws, and lived under federal jurisdiction. Over the next few years Congress passed, and the president signed into law, a series of bills designed to "terminate" federal oversight of Indian reservations. According to Utah senator Arthur V. Watkins, the legislation "emancipated" Native Americans by getting "the government out of the Indian business."

In 1951 the Bureau of Indian Affairs, often with the support of local tribal councils, began relocating Indians from the reservations to cities. The federal government recruited Indians, paid the cost of moving, and provided housing and jobs. By 1957 more than one hundred thousand Indians had left the reservations to start a new life in places like Chicago, Los Angeles, and Denver. By the end of the decade more than six hundred thousand Indians, about one-third of the native population, were living in major cities.

The harsh realities of urban life often crushed hopes that burgeoning cities would offer better opportunities. Instead of integrating into American society, many Native Americans established small, often poor, enclaves in large cities. Most of the jobs were low-paying, entry-level positions that were the first ones cut when business slowed down. "You get placed on the job, and your first job don't work out, where are you?" asked a frustrated Indian. "Several thousand miles from your home and broke."

The Quest for National Purpose, 1957–1960

As the 1950s drew to a close, many Americans began to question their view of themselves as a prosperous, satisfied, and secure society. The Soviets' successful launch of a satellite to orbit the Earth shocked the American public's confidence in Eisenhower's New Look. On October 4, 1957, the Soviet Union launched a 184-pound space satellite called *Sputnik,* or "Little Traveler." One month later it launched a second satellite, this one carrying a small dog, the first living creature to leave Earth's atmosphere.

The Soviets gloated, claiming the achievement demonstrated the superiority of their "socialist society." The Soviet success in space dealt a serious blow to American national pride and created a widespread and unfounded fear of a "mis-

Sputnik I   On October 4, 1957, the Soviet Union added a new dimension to the Cold War by launching *Sputnik I,* an artificial satellite the size of a basketball and weighing 183 pounds. Americans were stunned by the Soviet's ability to send a satellite into orbit and feared this technology might be translated into a ballistic missile that could carry a nuclear warhead from Europe to the United States. In response, the United States developed the *Explorer* project and created the National Aeronautics and Space Administration to coordinate America's research in space travel. The launching of *Sputnik I* marked the beginning of the space race as both nations sought to gain supremacy in space exploration.

sile gap" between the United States and the Soviet Union. Asked by reporters what Americans would find should they ever reach the moon, Edward Teller, "father" of the hydrogen bomb, replied, "Russians."

The United States responded by trying to launch its own satellite into space. The rocket lifted briefly, toppled over, and exploded into flames. "The fire died down and we saw America's supposed response to the 200-pound Soviet satellite—our four pound grapefruit—lying amid the scattered glowing debris," observed a scientist who worked on the project. The Soviet success and the U.S. failure brought to the surface America's underlying anxiety about atomic power. If the USSR had rockets powerful enough to launch satellites, it could also bombard the United States with nuclear weapons. Newspaper articles, books, and government studies reminded people they were vulnerable to Soviet nuclear bombs. A generation of schoolchildren learned to "duck and cover" in drills for a nuclear attack. A 1959 congressional study concluded that 28 percent of the population likely would be killed by such an attack.

In response, federal and state governments encouraged people to build bomb shelters for protection in the event of a nuclear war. Government manuals such as *You Can Survive* and *Atomic Attack* downplayed the dangers posed by radiation and firestorms and offered advice on how to build a shelter in the backyard and stockpile food and water. In the event of a nuclear attack Americans were advised to "shut windows and doors, pull down shades, turn off pilot lights, close stove and furnace doors," and seek shelter below ground. They were promised that "a thick wall or overhead covering will protect you from the prompt radioactivity of the bomb, even if you are close to it." Advertisers created a variety of shelter styles to fit every consumer, ranging from a "$13.50 foxhole shelter" to a "$5,000 deluxe suite with telephone, escape hatches, bunks, toilets, and a geiger counter." In 1959 *Life* magazine celebrated a couple's honeymoon of "unbroken togetherness" spent in a 8-by-14-foot steel and concrete shelter 12 feet underground.

PRIMARY SOURCE

6.3 | *How to Respond to a Nuclear Attack, 1950*

During the height of America's anxiety concerning atomic strikes by the Soviet Union, the federal Civil Defense Agency sought to relieve fears by publishing tips on how to survive a nuclear attack, like this one printed in 1950.

Survival Secrets for Atomic Attacks

ALWAYS PUT FIRST THINGS FIRST

Try to Get Shielded

If you have time, get down in a basement or subway. Should you unexpectedly be caught out-of-doors, seek shelter alongside a building, or jump in any handy ditch or gutter.

Drop Flat on Ground or Floor

To keep from being tossed about and to lessen the chances of being struck by falling and flying objects, flatten out at the base of a wall, or at the bottom of a bank.

Bury Your Face in Your Arms

When you drop flat, hide your eyes in the crook of your elbow. That will protect your face from flash burns, prevent temporary blindness and keep flying objects out of your eyes.

NEVER LOSE YOUR HEAD

DIRECTION OF
HEAT FLASH

If you are caught outdoors in a sudden attack, a hat will give you at least some protection from the 'heat flash'.

CIVIL DEFENSE GROUPS

Men	Women
FIRE-FIGHTING	MEDICAL TEAMS
RESCUE WORK	CAR-DRIVING
MEDICAL TEAMS	AIR-RAID WARDEN
GEIGER CREW	GEIGER CREW
STREET CLEARING	CHILD CARE
POLICE AUXILIARY	HOSPITAL WORK
AIR-RAID WARDEN	SOCIAL WORK
REBUILDING	EMERGENCY FEEDING

Here are some of the civil defense jobs open to men and women.

SECLUDED 15 ACRE ESTATE

on fair sized lake beyond Luzerne. 25 minutes from Saratoga. Large well furnished and equipped main house. 4-room guest house, large garage, accessory buildings, woods, gardens, boats, fishing, swimming. Good bomb immunity. Attractive summer home or could be converted for resort or institutional purposes. $30,000.

Box H 70, The Wall Street Journal.

Americans also feared the by-products of the nuclear age—in particular, the health consequences of radioactive fallout from bomb tests. The United States exploded 217 nuclear weapons over the Pacific and in Nevada between 1946 and 1962. The Soviet Union conducted 122 tests in the 1950s, Great Britain at least 50. By the mid-1950s Americans were growing increasingly alarmed by radioactive substances turning up in the soil and in food. The federal government downplayed the possible health consequences, reassuring Americans that ordinary citizens received more radiation from dental x-rays than from nuclear testing fallout. At the same time, however, military scientists used unsuspecting civilians as human guinea pigs in secret experiments on the consequences of prolonged exposure to radioactive substances.

The fears of atomic energy found creative outlet in popular culture. *Mad,* a favorite humor magazine among teens, fantasized that after a nuclear war the "Hit Parade" would include songs that lovers would sing as they "walk down moonlit lanes arm in arm in arm." Science fiction writers such as Ray Bradbury, Isaac Asimov, and Arthur C. Clarke penned imaginative novels about space travel, time travel, and the dangers of atomic weapons.

Hollywood produced a series of monster and mutant movies suggesting that nuclear tests had either dislodged prehistoric monsters or created new genetically altered creatures. Though universally panned for their cinematic quality, movies such as *The Beast from 20,000 Fathoms* (1953) played to public concern about life in the nuclear age. In the movie an atomic blast in the Arctic melts an iceberg, releasing a "rhedosaurus" that decides to visit Brooklyn's Coney Island. In *The Day the Earth Stood Still* (1951) a superior race of aliens invades Earth to warn humans of the dangers of nuclear weapons, threatening to destroy the planet if all nations do not abolish atomic weapons. *On the Beach* (1959), perhaps the best science fiction film of the decade, presented a chilling picture of the final days of the human race after a nuclear war. The film ended showing a tattered Salvation Army poster declaring, "THERE IS STILL TIME, BROTHER."

Public sightings of unidentified flying objects (UFOs), or "flying saucers," were another manifestation of America's atomic anxieties. The modern era of American UFO sightings began in 1947 when a pilot reported seeing nine aircraft resembling flying saucers moving across the sky at approximately 1,200 miles an hour, making a motion "like a saucer skipping over water." In these anxious days of the Cold War, Americans speculated that the saucers had either come from outer space or were a new Soviet weapon. Whatever the explanation, the number of UFO sightings skyrocketed during the decade. More than one thousand people reported seeing flying saucers in 1952 alone.

Political and Economic Uncertainties

Sputnik was only the first of a series of blows to Americans' pride and stature at the end of the decade. At home a persistent recession contributed to the sense of unease. Unemployment, which had held steady at 4 percent from 1955 to 1957, jumped to 8 percent in 1959. Since fewer people were working and paying taxes, the floundering economy produced huge budget deficits.

Potentially the greatest threat to American pride occurred 90 miles off the coast of Florida on the small island of Cuba. On January 1, 1959, a young lawyer turned revolutionary, Fidel Castro, led a successful insurrection against the American-supported dictatorship of Fulgencio Batista. American economic interests expressed concern when Castro began breaking up large cattle ranches and sugar plantations. When the United States threatened to cut off economic aid, Castro responded by declaring his support for communism and confiscating about $1 billion in U.S. property. In February 1960 the Cuban leader signed a trade agreement with the Soviet Union. In 1961 Dwight Eisenhower severed diplomatic relations with Cuba and authorized the Central Intelligence Agency to train Cuban expatriates for an invasion of the island.

These blows to American pride spurred a debate over national purpose. Critics viewed the consumer revolution and American prosperity, so frequently celebrated earlier in the decade, as the main culprits in producing a society that had grown soft and complacent. The poet Carl Sandberg expressed contempt for America's "fat-dripping prosperity." In 1958 in the best-selling book *The Affluent Society,* Harvard economist John Kenneth Galbraith complained that the consumer culture had produced a materialistic society that valued private wealth over public needs. In an article titled "Have We Gone Soft?" the author John Steinbeck raged, "If I wanted to destroy a nation I would give it too much and would have it on its knees, miserable, greedy, and sick." The National Goals Commission, created by President Eisenhower to develop national objectives, supported the opinion of social critics that the consumer society had weakened America's moral fiber. By calling for increased government support for education and scientific research, the commission rejected Eisenhower's dynamic conservatism and signaled the dawn of more activist government.

Eisenhower's commitment to restraining defense spending was called into question by another government study, the Gaither Report, which released its findings in 1957. The evidence, it stated, "clearly indicates an increasing threat which may become critical in 1959 or early 1960." Claiming that the Russians had opened a missile gap, the report recommended spending an additional $19 billion on new weapons. The committee did not, however, have access to the top-secret information produced by U-2 spy planes. If committee members had, they would have known, as Eisenhower did, that no missile gap existed: the Soviets lagged far behind the United States in nearly every weapons category. Ike was in a frustrating position: he knew the panic about a missile gap was not true, but going public would have compromised America's chief intelligence-gathering operation.

Many people blamed the educational system for allowing the Soviet Union to pass America in the development of space-age rockets. To remedy the situation, Congress passed the National Defense Education Act of 1958. The legislation provided loan funds for college students and fellowships for advanced study, and it promised more resources to strengthen instruction in mathematics, the sciences, and foreign languages at the elementary- and secondary-school levels. The government decided that it was time to educate both girls and boys. "A great national resource of feminine brain power is being lost," Washington declared, "because potential mathematicians, scientists, writers and artists marry early, have large families, and never put their higher education to public use."

Concern about Soviet missiles pushed Congress to accept the statehood applications of Alaska and Hawaii, areas positioned to provide an early-warning system for potential Soviet rocket attacks. Alaska entered the Union as the forty-ninth state on January 3, 1959. Hawaii followed as the fiftieth state on August 21, 1959.

In his final years in office Eisenhower tried to block out the criticism and focus on producing a thaw in Soviet-American relations. In 1959 he invited Nikita Khrushchev for a ten-day visit to the United States. The meeting went well, and Khrushchev reciprocated by inviting the president to visit Moscow. "I'll bring along the whole family," Ike said. "You'll have more Eisenhowers than you know what to do with." The plan was to attend a summit meeting with the French, British, and Russians in Paris and from there fly to Moscow. In late April, as he prepared for the summit, Eisenhower wanted to cancel all U-2 flights over Soviet territory, fearing one could be shot down and ruin the summit. Secretary of State John Foster Dulles pleaded with him to allow one more. Against his better judgment, Eisenhower agreed.

The president's fears were soon realized. In May the Soviets shot down an American U-2 spy plane and its pilot, Gary Powers. Believing the pilot had died in the crash, Eisenhower initially called the flight a weather data–gathering mission that had strayed off course, but when the Soviets produced Powers and his spying equipment, Eisenhower confessed responsibility for the U-2 flight. An angry Khrushchev, who paraded the captured American pilot before the world media, canceled the summit and withdrew the invitation for Eisenhower to visit Moscow. His administration ended without real progress. "I had longed," Ike said years later, "to give the United States and the world a lasting peace. I was able only to contribute to a stalemate."

Kennedy and the 1960 Presidential Election

Politically, Democrats planned to capitalize on the growing unease about national purpose. They sharpened their arguments in the 1958 congressional races when they gained thirteen Senate seats and a massive majority in the House. Indicting a failure of leadership in Washington, Democratic congressional candidates won 56 percent of votes cast—the highest figure since 1936. They planned to continue on to capture the White House in 1960.

The Republicans, forced by the Twenty-second Amendment—which limited a president to two terms—to seek a new leader, turned to Vice President Richard Nixon to counter the Democratic offensive. "To your hands," President Eisenhower wrote to the GOP's new standard-bearer, "I pray that I shall pass the responsibility of the office of the Presidency." At Nixon's request, Henry Cabot Lodge, ambassador to the United Nations, was drafted as his running mate.

After a tough primary campaign the Democrats turned to the youthful and attractive John F. Kennedy. The forty-two-year-old senator was the first Catholic to contend for the presidency since Al Smith in 1928. "Jack" Kennedy grew up in a conservative Boston Irish family. After graduating from Harvard, he enlisted in the navy during World War II. When a Japanese destroyer rammed his patrol boat, *PT-109,* Kennedy spent hours swimming in shark-infested waters trying to save his crew. He returned from the war a hero, ready to fulfill the ambitions of his father, Joseph P. Kennedy, a wealthy businessman who had served under Franklin Roosevelt as ambassador to Great Britain. "It was like being drafted," Kennedy reflected. "My father wanted his eldest son in politics. 'Wanted' isn't the right word. He demanded it." The political journey began in 1946 when Kennedy won a congressional seat. He served three terms in the House before winning election to the Senate in 1952. Six years later voters reelected him to the Senate by the widest popular margin in Massachusetts history.

Kennedy attracted considerable media attention. With the help of his talented group of advisers, he carefully cultivated the image of a youthful, robust leader; hero of *PT-109;* and brilliant author of the Pulitzer Prize–winning book *Profiles in Courage* (1956). In later years historians would discover that Kennedy had manufactured much of the image. In reality he suffered from various illnesses, including Addison's disease, which required regular doses of cortisone. A speechwriter had written most of *Profiles in Courage,* and his

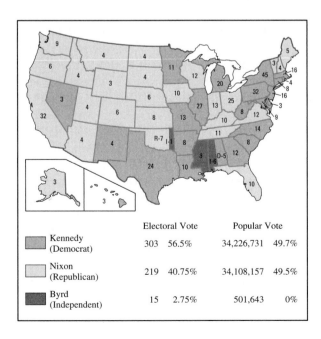

	Electoral Vote		Popular Vote	
Kennedy (Democrat)	303	56.5%	34,226,731	49.7%
Nixon (Republican)	219	40.75%	34,108,157	49.5%
Byrd (Independent)	15	2.75%	501,643	0%

The Election of 1960

The 1960 election was not only the closest presidential race in the twentieth century, it also had the highest voter turnout (63 percent). Yet the discontent of white southerners over the issue of civil rights was evident as all of Mississippi's delegates and some of Alabama's rejected both parties and voted for prosegregationist Senator Harry Byrd of Virginia.

father's intervention had secured Jack Kennedy the Pulitzer Prize. Many liberals also complained that Kennedy's failure to vote with other Democrats to censure Joseph McCarthy revealed that he was long on profile and short on courage.

Whatever his shortcomings, Kennedy possessed considerable political skill and broad popular appeal. He revealed his shrewd political instincts at the 1960 Democratic National Convention. Realizing he needed a running mate who could provide regional balance and help diminish criticism of his religion, Kennedy asked Texas senator Lyndon Johnson to join the ticket. The move startled the convention, especially liberals who felt the selection of a conservative southerner betrayed the party's New Deal heritage. In fact, Kennedy's decision represented a brilliant political stroke that revealed both his pragmatism and his moderation.

Few substantive differences separated Kennedy and Nixon. Both candidates reflected the widespread belief that American institutions were fundamentally sound, that economic growth had alleviated the need for social conflict, and that Soviet aggression presented the greatest threat to American security. Kennedy, however, understood better than Nixon the public's desire for dynamic leadership. Throughout the campaign he struck the right tone with his calls for positive leadership, public sacrifice, and a bold effort to "get America moving again." "I run for the Presidency because I do not want it said that in the years when our generation held political power . . . America began to slip," Kennedy declared with a crisp Boston accent.

Despite Kennedy's appeal, the election remained close. Nixon skillfully played to public concern about Kennedy's inexperience, especially in foreign affairs. Most of all, many Americans were reluctant to vote for a Catholic for president. In a bold stroke Kennedy appeared on September 12 before the Protestant Ministerial Association of Houston, Texas, to emphasize that he placed his oath to the Constitution above the dictates of his Church. "I am not the Catholic candidate for President," he said, "I am the Democratic party's candidate for President who happens also to be a Catholic." Kennedy also energized the African-American community when he intervened to help secure Martin Luther King's release from a Montgomery jail.

The turning point in the campaign came in a series of four televised debates between September 26 and October 24. Kennedy used the debates—the first ever televised between presidential contenders—to demolish the Republican charge that he was inexperienced and badly informed. And he succeeded far better than his opponent in communicating the qualities of boldness, imagination, and poise. Kennedy appeared alert, aggressive, and cool. Nixon, who perspired profusely, looked nervous and uncomfortable. Radio listeners divided evenly on who had won the debate. Television viewers, the overwhelming majority, gave Kennedy a decisive edge. The performance energized Kennedy's campaign, and the debates institutionalized television's role as a major force in American politics. "That night," the journalist Russell Baker reflected, "image replaced the printed word as the natural language of politics."

The momentum from the debate carried Kennedy to victory—though just barely. Of the nearly 68,500,000 popular votes cast, Kennedy won 34,226,731 and Nixon, 34,108,157. Kennedy's popular majority of two-tenths of 1 percent was the smallest since 1880. His vote in the electoral college was only slightly more convincing, 303 to 219.

Kennedy's victory signaled a desire for change, but the narrowness of his triumph reflected the caution with which Americans approached the challenges of the new decade. The consumer culture reinforced America's celebration of consensus at the same time that it stimulated the appetite for change among groups excluded from the benefits of prosperity. During the campaign Kennedy managed to convey a message of change to Americans who questioned the complacency of the consumer culture, while reassuring conservatives that he would not threaten existing arrangements. The tension between American ideals and social realities, which sharpened during the decade, foreshadowed the difficult balancing act that would confront the new president in the next decade.

SELECTED READINGS

▮ Michael Harrington's *The Other America* (1962) is still a classic exposé of the 1950s have-nots. Thomas Sugrue's *The Origins of the Urban Crisis* (1996) focuses on how blacks were denied houses in the suburbs and confined to inner-city Detroit. Nicholas Lemann covers the postwar black migration in *The Promised Land* (1991). James T. Patterson's *America's Struggle Against Poverty* (1981) is a broad survey of the American underclass, as is the interracial poverty traced in Jacqueline Jones's *The Dispossessed* (1992). Rodolfo Acuna's *Occupied America* (4th ed., 2000) has useful material on Hispanic poverty in the 1950s. In *The Urban Experience in America* (2000), Donald Fixico traces the experiences of Native Americans who relocated to cities in the 1950s and 1960s, and Kenneth Philp's *Termination Revisited* (1999) explains the federal policy of termination that led many Native Americans to leave the reservations.

▮ Glenna Matthews's *Just a Housewife* (1987) explores the world of 1950s homemakers, while Wini Brienes, in *Young, White, and Miserable* (1992), analyzes the conflicting sentiments of their daughters. Susan Strasser's *Never Done* (1982) paints a bleak picture of the demands placed on housewives. The essays in Joanne Meyerwitz's *Not June Cleaver* (1994) examine women who did not fit the domestic stereotype. Elaine Tyler May's *Homeward Bound* (1988) is a valuable study of the American family during the Cold War. The unrealistic image of the ideal family is the theme of Stephanie Coontz's *The Way We Never Were* (1992).

▮ Aldon D. Morris's *The Origins of the Civil Rights Movement* (1984) details the black-community organizing that presaged the upheaval of the 1960s. Mark Tushnet's *Making Civil Rights Law* (1994) examines the goals and legal work done by the NAACP. In *The Turning Tide* (1995), editors Margaret Dornfeld and Clayborne Carson follow the developing civil-rights movement from the desegregation of the armed forces to the Montgomery bus boycott. Editor Stewart Burns provides a well-documented account of the bus boycott in Montgomery in *Daybreak of Freedom* (1997). The death of Emmitt Till and the subsequent trial and protest are the focus of Stephen Whitfield's *A Death in the Delta* (1991). Robert F. Burk evaluates Eisenhower's performance on race issues in *The Eisenhower Administration and Black Civil Rights* (1984).

▌ Robert Divine's *The Sputnik Challenges* examines Eisenhower's inability to suppress the American belief in a missile gap. David Snead analyzes the impact of the Gaither Report on the acceleration of the arms race in *The Gaither Committee, Eisenhower, and the Cold War* (1999). Diane Ravitch describes the "crisis" in American education in *The Troubled Crusade* (1983). Howard Ball's *Justice Downwind* (1986) studies the nuclear testing programs. Thomas Paterson's *Contesting Castro* (1994) examines U.S.–Cuban relations during Castro's uprising and successful revolution. The U-2 spy plane incident is related in Michael Beschloss's *Mayday* (1986). The heightened awareness of the destructive force of nuclear weapons and its impact on popular culture is analyzed in Margot Henriksen's *Dr. Strangelove's America* (1997) and Joyce Evans's work on the movie industry of the 1950s, *Celluloid Mushroom Clouds* (1999). John Kennedy's ability to grasp the reins of leadership sets the tone of Theodore White's classic on the art of modern campaigning, *The Making of the President, 1960* (1961).

7

The Kennedy Presidency, 1961–1963

In November 1963 President John F. Kennedy began laying the foundation for his 1964 reelection campaign by visiting the key state of Texas. Shortly after noon on the twenty-second his entourage arrived at Dallas's Love Field airport. Kennedy, handsomely attired in a gray suit and pin-striped shirt, exited the plane with his wife, Jacqueline, who was wearing a strawberry-pink wool outfit and matching pillbox hat and cradling a bouquet of red roses. After shaking a few hands, the president, the first lady, and Texas governor John Connally and his wife, Nellie, hopped into the back of their open-top Lincoln limousine. Since it was a bright autumn day, Kennedy chose not to use the bulletproof bubble top.

Friendly crowds greeted the president's motorcade—eighteen cars and three buses—as it traveled along a 10-mile route through downtown Dallas. The crowds became denser when the cars turned into Main Street and moved westward toward Dealey Plaza. People were everywhere, waving from office buildings, filling the streets, cheering. At the corner of Main and Houston the motorcade turned right and headed north. As it approached Elm Street, Nellie Connally said, "Mr. President, you can't say Dallas doesn't love you." Kennedy answered, "That's obvious." The time was 12:30 P.M.

Suddenly, the sound of gunfire ripped through the air. "Oh no!" Jacqueline Kennedy cried. The president clutched his neck with both hands and slumped down in his seat. One bullet had passed through his throat; another had shattered his skull. Governor Connally had also been hit, seriously but not mortally. The driver pulled the limousine out of the motorcade line and sped to Parkland Hospital. Nine minutes later a bulletin flashed over the news wires: "Kennedy wounded. Perhaps seriously. Perhaps fatally by assassin's bullet."

The president's limousine arrived at the hospital's emergency entrance at 12:36 P.M. A Secret Service agent lifted Kennedy from his wife's arms, placed him on a stretcher, and rushed him into Trauma Room 1. Doctors were shocked by the extent of his wounds. "I looked at the President's head," recalled one physician. "A considerable portion of the skull, of the brain, was gone. It looked like a wound we just could not salvage." As a grieving Jacqueline Kennedy looked on, doctors worked feverishly to revive her husband. Their efforts were in vain. The president was pronounced dead at 1 P.M.

Secret Service agents placed the slain president's body in a casket and loaded it onto the presidential plane for the trip back to Washington. In the central compartment of the plane Judge Sarah T. Hughes of the Northern District of Texas administered the oath of office to Lyndon Johnson. A stunned and blood-soaked Jackie Kennedy stood to the left of the new president. Within hours of the assassination Dallas police arrested Lee Harvey Oswald and charged him with assassinating the president of the United States. Two days later Jack Ruby, a Dallas nightclub owner, shot and killed Oswald as police were transferring him to another prison.

For a generation of Americans Kennedy's assassination served as a symbolic marker separating a confident age of consensus from the period of social conflict that followed. The president's death may have been the most traumatic, but it was only one of a series of shocks that challenged the pervasive optimism of the consumer society. By the summer of 1963 Kennedy was questioning some of the assumptions of vital-center liberalism. The possibility of nuclear war, brought home in dramatic fashion by the Cuban missile crisis, led to a softening of Cold War attitudes and a new emphasis on cooperation. More importantly, the confrontation between the black freedom struggle and the intransigence of southern whites threatened to expose the gap between expectations and social realities and to undermine the fragile vital-center consensus. The president's tragic death in November 1963 cut short his evolution and left future generations asking, What if Kennedy had lived?

JFK and the New Frontier

At the age of forty-two John F. Kennedy was the youngest man ever elected president and the first American president born in the twentieth century. Kennedy's inaugural address, delivered on a cloudless and cold January day in 1961, captivated the nation's imagination and captured the hope and expectations of the decade. His vigor and youth stood in sharp contrast with the staid and stodgy Eisenhower style. Calling for "a struggle against the common enemies of man: tyranny, poverty, disease, and war," he promised a "New Frontier" of opportunity and challenge.

Kennedy's youth and charm suited him to the new medium of television. "Memories of the Kennedy days are memories of television," recalled a prominent television producer. Kennedy was the first president to allow live broadcast of his press conferences. By May 1961 nearly 75 percent of the public had seen one, and the vast majority—over 91 percent—gave him high marks for his performance. With the help of a media-conscious staff, the administration produced a constant flow of captivating Kennedy images. His sophisticated and glamorous wife, Jacqueline, and two handsome children, Caroline and John, added to the Kennedy mystique.

The King and Queen of Camelot   The Kennedys captivated the American people with their youth, style, and elegance. The First Lady in particular drew admiration; she served as the gracious hostess for lavish White House balls, wore beautiful designer gowns, worked tirelessly to restore the White House's interior, and of course took care of her young children, themselves favorites of Americans. The fresh breath the Kennedys brought to the presidency earned the administration the nickname "Camelot," after the mythic reign of King Arthur. Here they leave a performance at Ford's Theater looking every bit like American royalty. *(National Archives.)*

Kennedy surrounded himself with bright young men who shared his faith in activist government. Among "the best and the brightest" were McGeorge Bundy, a forty-one-year-old former Harvard dean who became Kennedy's chief foreign-relations counselor. As secretary of defense Kennedy chose Robert McNamara, a past president of Ford Motor Company with a passion for systems analysis and organizational management. To head the State Department, Kennedy chose Dean Rusk, a Rhodes scholar and former diplomat. The most controversial choice was Robert Kennedy, the president's brother, as attorney general. Critics complained about his lack of legal experience, but the president trusted his brother's shrewd political instincts, clear judgment, and firm support.

The liberals who surrounded Kennedy shared the widely held belief that America had entered an age of consensus. Building on the ideas developed by liberal intellectuals during the 1940s and 1950s, they argued that economic growth, when combined with prudent government social programs, would provide every American with a minimum standard of living and boundless opportunity for success. Prosperity offered the added benefit of rendering obsolete ideological conflict and social struggle. "Politics," Kennedy said in 1962, was to avoid "basic clashes of philosophy and ideology" and be directed to "ways and means of achieving goals." Proponents of consensus believed that international communism presented the greatest threat to American institutions and values. "The enemy," Kennedy declared with typical flourish, "is the Communist system itself—implacable, insatiable, increasing in its drive for world domination." Convinced that Dwight Eisenhower had failed to fight the Cold War with sufficient vigor, Kennedy moved to sharpen ideological differences and to increase military pressure on the Soviet Union.

Acting on the assumptions of the consensus, the new president focused much of his energy at home on revitalizing a stagnant economy. During the last two years of the Eisenhower administration, economic growth had slowed to about 2 percent and unemployment had started creeping upward. At Kennedy's request, Congress extended unemployment benefits, raised the minimum wage, broadened social security benefits, increased the defense budget by almost 20 percent, and approved over $4 billion in long-term spending on federally financed housing. It also approved the Area Redevelopment Act, which provided federal aid for poor regions, and the Manpower Retraining Bill, which appropriated $435 million for the training of workers. Kennedy prodded Congress to double the budget of the National Aeronautics and Space Administration and approved a plan to put an American on the Moon by 1970. Finally, Congress passed the Revenue Act of 1962, which granted $1 billion in tax breaks to businesses.

While using government spending to increase economic growth, Kennedy moved to keep a lid on price increases and control inflation by enlisting the aid of business leaders. When Roger Blough, the head of U.S. Steel, announced that he was raising prices $6 a ton in defiance of a previous agreement with the White House, Kennedy complained about the "unjustifiable and irresponsible defiance of the public interest" by a "tiny handful of steel executives." After a well-orchestrated White House campaign, Blough retreated.

By 1963 a brief economic downturn convinced Kennedy that he needed to take bolder action. In January the president proposed a tax reduction of $13.5 billion that he hoped would stimulate consumer spending, create new jobs, and generate economic growth. His support of a tax cut revealed Kennedy's willingness to experiment with unconventional ideas. Many liberals, who wanted higher government spending, not more tax cuts, opposed the plan. Conservatives blustered at the idea of intentionally running a budget deficit. Ignoring criticisms from the Left and the Right, Kennedy submitted his proposal to Congress, claiming that "the unrealistically heavy drag of federal income taxes on private purchasing power" was the "largest single barrier to full employment."

Kennedy gave tepid support to efforts to address gender inequities in the workplace. The president appointed Ester Peterson to head the Women's Bureau, a division of the U.S. Labor Bureau. Peterson used her position to mobilize a coalition of women and labor organizations to pressure the president to create a special commission to explore the status of women. In 1961 Kennedy responded by issuing an executive order establishing the President's Commission on the Status of Women, which was chaired by former First Lady Eleanor Roosevelt. Kennedy had little personal interest in the issue of women's rights, and he viewed the commission as a way of rewarding Roosevelt for her support during the 1960 presidential campaign. The commission, however, took its responsibilities seriously. Its final report, presented in October 1963, documented the discrimination that women faced in the workplace and helped legitimize public debate about the role of women in American society. Within a year of its publication the national commission spawned dozens of state commissions. By 1967 all fifty states boasted one.

Kennedy faced many obstacles in his effort to fulfill his campaign promise to "get the country moving again." His narrow victory denied him a clear mandate. He presided over a divided party. Democrats controlled Congress, but conservative southern Democrats who were unsympathetic to Kennedy's liberal proposals controlled key congressional committees. "Franklin Roosevelt was thwarted by nine old men," observed one historian. "Kennedy must deal with a Congress full of them." Congress enacted only seven of twenty-three bills that the president submitted in his early months in office. Among the bills defeated were an ambitious health care plan for the elderly and a proposal for federal aid to education. But Kennedy shares part of the blame for this record. He showed little interest either in domestic issues or in the political brokering necessary to court Congress. "Foreign affairs is the only important issue for a President to handle, isn't it?," he once remarked. "I mean, who gives a shit if the minimum wage is $1.15 or $1.25, compared to something like Cuba."

JFK and Civil Rights

Civil rights confronted Kennedy with the most important test of his domestic policy. Late in the afternoon on Monday, February 1, 1960, four well-dressed black students sat down at a segregated lunch counter at a Woolworth's department store in Greensboro, North Carolina, and ordered a cup of coffee. "I'm sorry," the waitress said, "we don't serve you here." The next day twenty-seven black students occupied the Woolworth's lunch counter; on Wednesday, sixty-three. By Friday more than three hundred protesters jammed the store and the nearby Kress's five-and-dime. As news of the sit-ins reached other cities, the protest spread "like a fever." By the end of 1960 more than seventy thousand people in over 150 southern cities and towns had participated in the protests. "I guess everybody was pretty well fed up at the same time," observed a Greensboro activist. Lunch counters were the most popular focus of action, but protesters also organized "wade-ins" at segregated pools and beaches, "kneel-ins" at churches, "read-ins" at public libraries, and "bowl-ins" at recreational areas.

The sit-in movement represented an important change in the strategy of civil-rights protesters. It revealed the growing frustration of many younger blacks who were impatient with the slow pace of change and convinced that more aggressive

Greensboro Sit-in, February 1, 1960 On February 1, 1960, four young black men, all freshmen at North Carolina A&T State University, walked into the Woolworth store in downtown Greensboro and sat at the whites-only lunch counter, defying the city's segregation ordinances. In the subsequent days, an ever-growing number of students joined the original four at the lunch counter, waiting for service that never came, but showing the nation (thanks to the arrival of news crews) their perseverance and desire to hold out for integration, as well as interrupting the usual business of the Woolworth. On and off for five months, hundreds of students staged these sit-ins, which eventually led to the integration of the local Woolworth. The sit-ins also inspired people across the country to stage their own peaceful protests, using Greensboro as their model.

tactics could force the government to take bolder action to redress existing wrongs. In April 1960 these younger, more militant protestors formed the Student Nonviolent Coordinating Committee (SNCC). The sit-ins also underscored the decentralized, "grass-roots" approach of the civil-rights movement. The success of national figures such as Martin Luther King Jr. rested on a foundation forged by the courage and commitment of ordinary "local people" such as Fannie Lou Hamer, Robert Moses, Amelia Boynton, and Fred Shuttlesworth.

PRIMARY SOURCE

7.1 | *Statement of Purpose, 1960*
SNCC

In April 1960 leaders of the southern sit-in movement met at Shaw University in Raleigh, North Carolina, where they organized what would become the Student Nonviolent Coordinating Committee. SNCC's Statement of Purpose, written by the Reverend James Lawson and dated May 14, 1960, outlines the organization's goals and beliefs.

We affirm the philosophical or religious ideal of nonviolence as the foundation of our purpose, the presupposition of our faith, and the manner of our action. Nonviolence as it grows from Judaic-Christian tradition seeks a social order of justice permeated by love. Integration of human endeavor represents the 5 crucial first step toward such a society.

Through nonviolence, courage displaces fear; love transforms hate. Acceptance dissipates prejudice; hope ends despair. Peace dominates war; faith reconciles doubt. Mutual regard cancels enmity. Justice for all overthrows injustice. The redemptive community supersedes systems of gross social 10 immorality.

Love is the central motif of nonviolence. Love is the force by which God binds man to Himself and man to man. Such love goes to the extreme; it remains loving and forgiving even in the midst of hostility. It matches the capacity of evil to inflict suffering with an even more enduring capacity to absorb evil, all the while 15 persisting in love.

By appealing to conscience and standing on the moral nature of human existence, nonviolence nurtures the atmosphere in which reconciliation and justice become actual possibilities. ■ ■ ■

In 1961 members of the Congress of Racial Equality (CORE) decided to challenge another aspect of racial segregation. By 1960 the Supreme Court had barred racial segregation in bus and train stations, airport terminals, and other facilities related to interstate transit. But southerners widely ignored these decisions. In May 1961 seven black and six white "freedom riders" left Washington on two buses headed for Alabama and Mississippi. "Our intention," declared CORE national director James Farmer, "was to provoke the southern authorities into arresting us and thereby prod the Justice Department into enforcing the law of the land."

As the vehicles moved into the Deep South, white racists mobilized. At stops along the way the Freedom Riders were assaulted by gangs of thugs brandishing baseball bats, lead pipes, and bicycle chains. A white mob in Birmingham, Alabama, beat the riders so badly that an informant for the Federal Bureau of Investigation (FBI) reported that he "couldn't see their faces through the blood." President Kennedy, fearful that the violence would undermine American prestige abroad, negotiated a compromise with southern authorities: if local officials would guarantee the safety of the riders, the federal government would not protest their arrest. During the next few months over three hundred Freedom Riders were arrested. In September 1961, after hundreds of Freedom Riders had risked their lives, the Interstate Commerce Commission enforced the ban against segregation in interstate terminals.

In the fall of 1961 SNCC chose Albany, Georgia, as the site of its next campaign. Attempting to rally opposition to continuing segregation in bus and train terminals, schools, libraries, and parks, local leaders called in Martin Luther King. But wily local police chief Laurie Pritchett avoided the overt violence King needed in order to arouse national indignation, while the Kennedy administration agreed not to intervene if local authorities managed to keep the peace. By the summer of 1962 King had left town and the movement had suffered its first defeat.

Even though the Albany campaign failed, it left an important legacy to the movement. It was here that African-American spiritual and cultural power found its fullest expression. The sounds of freedom songs, which traced their roots to slave music of the nineteenth century, rocked black churches in Albany, inspiring spiritual commitment to the cause. "A transformation took place inside of the people," recalled one participant. "The singing was just the echo of that." One African-American slave spiritual—"We Shall Overcome"—became the anthem of the movement. When people rose to sing it, recalled one participant, "nobody knew what kept the top of the church on its four walls. It was as if everyone had been lifted up on high."

From Albany the movement moved to Oxford, Mississippi, where James Meredith, a twenty-eight-year-old black air force veteran, attempted to register at the all-white University of Mississippi. When Governor Ross Barnett, a segregationist demagogue, personally blocked Meredith's attempt to register, many white people in the state interpreted Barnett's actions as encouragement to take up arms to fight desegregation. To maintain the peace, Attorney General Robert Kennedy sent 500 federal marshals to the Ole Miss campus on September 20, 1962. "The eyes of the nation and all the world are upon you and upon all of us," President Kennedy admonished Mississippians. But the federal presence failed to intimidate Barnett and his supporters. On September 30 a white mob attacked the federal marshals, killing 2 and injuring 375. Outraged by the violence, the president ordered 30,000 regular army troops and federalized national guardsmen to Oxford to restore order. The massive show of force worked: Barnett backed down, and Meredith enrolled.

President Kennedy nevertheless moved cautiously on the issue of civil rights. Despite the rising tide of protest, the public outside the South remained largely indifferent to the black struggle, and powerful southern Democratic congressmen fiercely opposed the demands to end segregation. Kennedy feared that pushing too hard would alienate the South, risk his domestic agenda, and siphon off votes he needed for reelection in 1964. One civil-rights leader complained that the "New Frontier looks like a dude ranch with Senator Eastland as the general manager." The president also worried that social unrest at home would diminish U.S. prestige in the world and undermine his negotiating position with the Soviets. During the Freedom Riders campaign Robert Kennedy pleaded for a "cooling-off" period, claiming the need for national unity at a critical stage in the Cold War. One civil-rights leader responded that blacks "have been cooling off for 150 years. If we cool off any more, we'll be in a deep freeze."

From Birmingham to Montgomery

In March 1963 the civil-rights struggle focused on Birmingham, Alabama, perhaps the most segregated city in the South. The city's segregation code outlawed even the most innocent interaction between blacks and whites. "It shall be unlawful for a Negro and a white person to play together," the segregation code declared, "in any game of cards or dice, dominoes or checkers." White terrorists had blown up so many buildings there that some called the town "Bombingham." King's immediate focus was on ending discrimination at the city's department stores and lunch counters, but his larger goal was to send a strong signal across the South that racial intolerance was no longer acceptable. "As Birmingham goes, so goes the South," King declared.

When King and fifty other protest marchers violated a state court injunction against protest marches, they were promptly arrested and thrown into jail. He spent his week behind bars responding to criticism from white Alabama clergy that his tactics were too militant, asking him to cancel his "unwise and untimely" demonstrations. King used a smuggled yellow, legal-sized pad to produce his powerful argument for civil disobedience, "Letter from Birmingham Jail." "I submit," he wrote, "that an individual who breaks a law that conscience tells him is unjust, and who willingly accepts the penalty of imprisonment in order to arouse the conscience of the community over its injustice, is in reality expressing the highest respect for law."

King's passionate defense of nonviolence energized the Birmingham movement. In May after his release from jail, King organized a peaceful march to City Hall. In response, the police commissioner, Eugene ("just call me 'Bull' ") Connor, and his officers set upon the marchers with dogs, clubs, and fire hoses, making martyrs of his victims and assuring their triumph. "Let those people come to the corner, Sergeant," shouted Connor to a group of whites gathered to watch the spectacle. "I want 'em to see the dogs work. Look at those niggers run." Television coverage of the clubbings aroused the indignation of the nation. Kennedy went on national television calling upon the citizens of Birmingham to "maintain standards of responsible conduct that will make outside intervention unnecessary." Behind the scenes Robert Kennedy called dozens of corporate leaders whose companies had local offices in Birmingham, urging them to pressure their employees to cooperate with the demand for desegregation. Eventually, the business community, stung by the national publicity and a black boycott, broke with the city government and agreed to most of King's demands.

In June 1963 the stage shifted to Montgomery, where Governor George Wallace planned to fulfill his campaign promise to "stand in the schoolhouse door" if the courts ordered the integration of his alma mater, the University of Alabama. Wallace started politics as a progressive Democrat who avoided race-baiting and advocated higher taxes on corporations and expanded social programs for the poor. In 1962 he won election by playing on white fears about integration. His

Children's Crusade in Birmingham, Alabama   In March 1963, Martin Luther King Jr. and leading members of the African-American community in Birmingham organized a series of demonstrations to bring attention to the city's strong adherence to the policy of segregation. While the early demonstrations led to the arrest of King and the subsequent publication of his "Letter from a Birmingham Jail," the nation's attention was captured by the activities of the city's children in early May. Following in their parents' footsteps, the children staged marches through the city, carrying signs denouncing segregation. Birmingham Police Chief Eugene "Bull" Connor responded by calling out the Fire Department, which turned fire hoses on the children to disperse them, and by ordering his officers to use police dogs to attack the peaceful protestors. Police arrested close to nine hundred children during the demonstrations. Photographs and video of the events shocked the nation, increasingly aware of the violence white southerners were willing to use to prevent integration.

inaugural address helped earn him a reputation as America's leading spokesman for white supremacy. "In the name of the greatest people that have ever trod this earth," he announced, "I draw the line in the dust and toss the gauntlet before the feet of tyranny. And I say, segregation now! Segregation tomorrow! Segregation forever!"

For weeks the Kennedy brothers tried negotiating with Wallace, and a federal judge warned him against defying a court order demanding the students be accepted. On the morning of June 11, under such a court order, two black students arrived to register at the Huntsville branch of the state university. With television cameras recording the drama, Wallace stood in the doorway, where a deputy attorney general confronted him. Having made his point, Wallace made a brief speech for the television cameras and then allowed the students to register.

That evening Kennedy delivered one of the most eloquent, moving, and important speeches of his presidency. For the first time he referred to civil rights as a moral issue, one that was, he said, "as old as the scriptures and as clear as the American constitution." The confrontations between blacks demanding civil rights and local white leaders insisting on preserving the status quo underscored the postwar paradox. Kennedy now realized that the liberal promise to provide equal opportunity to all citizens could not be accomplished within the framework of consensus. Economic growth and promises of gradual reform failed to satisfy African-American expectations of a better life. The growing militancy of the movement exposed the gap between liberal promises and social realities and forced Kennedy to make a difficult choice. Eight days after his speech Kennedy asked Congress for laws to support voting rights, to provide assistance to school districts that were desegregating, to ban segregation of public facilities, and to empower the attorney general to initiate proceedings against the segregation of schools.

To build support for the legislation and to appeal to the conscience of the nation, black leaders organized a march on Washington for August 1963. Polls showed that the vast majority of Americans opposed the proposed march. Some feared the possibility of racial violence, but most white Americans were simply uncomfortable with African-American demands. Responding to the public concerns, President Kennedy tried unsuccessfully to convince the organizers to call off the demonstration. City residents fled for the day. Anticipating violence, the Pentagon readied more than 4,000 troops in the event of trouble.

On August 28 more than a quarter-million people gathered under a cloudless sky at the Lincoln Memorial for the largest civil-rights demonstration in the nation's history. The high point of the sweltering afternoon came when Martin Luther King took the speakers' podium. "Even though we face the difficulties of today and tomorrow," King intoned in his powerful cadence, "I still have a dream. It is a dream chiefly rooted in the American dream . . . that my four little children will one day live in a nation where they will not be judged by the color of their skin but by the content of their character." For a brief moment the nation embraced King's vision of interracial brotherhood, but no speech, no matter how moving, was going to tame the pent-up demands of the freedom struggle.

The March on Washington as Seen from Within the Lincoln Memorial On August 28, 1963, hundreds of thousands of Americans—black and white, young and old, rich and poor, famous and unknown—made their way to the mall between the Washington Monument and the Lincoln Memorial for a day of singing and speeches that called for the immediate passage of the pending civil rights bill and showed the mounting support for equal rights for all Americans. The morning's music, performed by artists like Joan Baez and Bob Dylan, gave way in the afternoon to numerous speeches by leading members of the civil rights movement, closing with King's famous "I Have a Dream" speech. From inside the Lincoln Memorial, the throngs of people are evident, all pressing toward the stage located at the entrance to the memorial.

New Frontiers Abroad

Frustrated by a stubborn Congress at home, Kennedy was freer to express his activist instincts in foreign affairs. The president believed that instability in the Third World presented the greatest threat to American security in the 1960s. He took seriously Nikita Khrushchev's warning that the Soviets would continue support for "wars of national liberation" in Asia, Africa, and Latin America. The president, and the men who surrounded him, believed that Eisenhower's approach of massive retaliation prevented the United States from responding to communist insurgents trying to topple pro-American governments.

The administration called its new defense strategy "flexible response" because it expanded the options for fighting the communist threat. The new strategy had three components. First, it called for a dramatic increase in America's strategic and tactical nuclear capability, including rapid development of the Polaris submarine and Minuteman missiles systems. Between 1961 and 1964 the defense budget increased by 15 percent, from $47.4 billion to $53.6 billion. By 1963 the United States had 275 major bases in thirty-one nations, sixty-five countries hosted U.S. forces, and the American military trained soldiers in seventy-two countries. In 1961 the United States had 63 intercontinental ballistic missiles (ICBMs); by 1963, 424. During 1961–1963 the nuclear firing power of the North Atlantic Treaty Organization (NATO) increased 60 percent.

Second, flexible response increased economic assistance to troubled parts of the Third World. Kennedy established the Agency for International Development to coordinate Washington's foreign-aid program. In 1962 the president created the Alliance for Progress, which called for a massive development program in Latin America. The most successful program was the Peace Corps. Established by executive order in 1961, this volunteer group of mostly young Americans numbered five thousand by early 1963 and ten thousand a year later. The volunteers went into developing nations as teachers, agricultural advisers, and technicians.

Third, to deter aggression, the Pentagon and the Central Intelligence Agency (CIA) increased the training of paramilitary forces. The Pentagon established the Jungle Warfare School, which taught Latin American policemen how to infiltrate leftist groups. Kennedy personally elevated the status of the American Special Forces units, or "Green Berets," who were trained to fight unconventional wars. As the president declared in 1961, "We intend to have a wider choice than humiliation or all-out war."

Kennedy often described the Cold War as a clash between good and evil. His inaugural address, which focused almost exclusively on foreign affairs, underscored the urgency of the moment and the need to stand strong against an aggressive Soviet Union. His soaring rhetoric both captured and expanded the nation's sense of destiny and its grand expectations of America's role in world affairs. "We shall pay any price, bear any burden, meet any hardship, support any friend, oppose any foe to assure the survival and success of liberty," he thundered in his crisp New England twang. Kennedy also preferred tough action, having little patience with the "striped-pants boys" in the State Department who often counseled quiet negotiations over dramatic gestures. The president possessed an intense desire to prove his mettle. To prevail in a confrontation, he believed, was to prove one's manhood. The poet Robert Frost described Kennedy as "young ambition eager to be tried." A disillusioned diplomat complained that the men in Kennedy's inner circle were "full of belligerence." They were "sort of looking for a chance to prove their muscle."

The Bay of Pigs

Kennedy's instinctive activism and strong anticommunism led him into the first blunder of his presidency. As president-elect, Kennedy learned of a secret plan, approved by Eisenhower in the spring of 1960, for the invasion of Cuba by anti-Castro refugees. A few aides expressed doubts about the plan. Cuba, after all, observed Senate Foreign Relations chairman J. William Fulbright (D-Ark.), was "a thorn in the flesh, but not a dagger in the heart." Nevertheless, the CIA and most military advisers assured Kennedy the plan was sound. Having criticized the Eisenhower administration for being soft on communism, Kennedy decided to support this initiative.

The operation began on April 15 with an air strike by American planes painted over to look like stolen Cuban aircraft. At the same time, an American invasion fleet carried a landing force to the island. Shortly before midnight on April 17, 1961, over 1,600 American-trained Cuban exiles landed on Cuba's southern coast at *Bahia de Cochinos* (Bay of Pigs). There, Castro's army, which had anticipated the attack, lay in ambush. His planes sunk ships carrying essential communications equipment and ammunition, while his well-trained army prevented the invaders from establishing a beachhead. At the last minute Kennedy called off a planned air strike, fearing it would expose U.S. involvement in the attack. After three days of intense fighting the rebels surrendered.

"How could I have been so stupid to let them go ahead?" Kennedy asked. In retrospect the invasion's poor planning became obvious. News stories had predicted the invasion. White House press secretary Pierre Salinger described the invasion as the "least covert military operation in history." In a mistake that would be repeated throughout the postwar period, officials overestimated the universal appeal of American values and underestimated the nationalist roots of revolution. The administration hoped that as news of the rebel landing swept across the island, the Cuban people would rise up in rebellion. Instead, the invasion aroused Cuban nationalist sentiment, strengthened Castro's control over the nation, and pushed him closer to the Soviet Union. The United States suffered widespread international condemnation and humiliating loss of prestige in Latin America. The affair represented an embarrassing disaster for the Kennedy administration.

The public rallied behind the president, but Kennedy remained deeply shaken by the Bay of Pigs' fiasco. Both the president and his brother were intent upon getting rid of Castro. Within six months they launched Operation Mongoose, a secret CIA-coordinated program to destabilize the Cuban government. "My idea," Robert Kennedy said, "is to stir things up on the island with espionage, sabotage, general disorder." Over the next few years hundreds of American and Cuban agents tried to contaminate Cuban sugar exports, explode bombs in factories, and sponsor paramilitary raids on the island. The program also developed at least thirty-three plans to assassinate Castro. Operation Mongoose not only failed either to topple Castro or undermine support for his administration; like the Bay of Pigs invasion, it also may have increased popular support for his regime and driven him into the arms of the USSR.

Kennedy and Khrushchev

Hoping to prove himself a leader on the world stage, the president agreed to a summit meeting in Vienna with Soviet premier Khrushchev in June 1961. The meeting did little to boost Kennedy's spirits. Khrushchev was especially militant about Berlin, a divided city deep in Soviet-controlled East Germany. The Soviet position in Germany had deteriorated in recent years. Thousands of skilled workers were pouring out of East Germany seeking refuge and jobs in the more prosperous West. Khrushchev was determined to stop the exodus. Yet Kennedy was just as committed to maintaining the autonomy of West Berlin. The American public seemed to support taking a hard line. A poll showed that 57 percent of Americans believed that Berlin was "worth risking total war [for]."

Khrushchev continued to heighten the tension over access to Berlin, and by July a war of words and nerves had developed. Kennedy decided to make Berlin, in the words of a speechwriter, "a question of direct Soviet-American confrontation over a shift in the balance of power." On July 25 Kennedy announced that he was increasing draft calls, extending enlistments, and mobilizing some National Guard units. The real threat of imminent war led to a surge in construction of bomb shelters in the United States. International Business Machines gave each of its employees $1,000 to build one. New companies, such as Acme Bomb and Fallout Shelter Company and Peace-o-Mind Shelter Company, sprang up to satisfy the demand.

Before dawn on August 13, 1961, the Soviets responded by starting construction of a wall separating East and West Berlin. American and Soviet tanks stared at each other across the rising wall. A false move or miscalculation could lead to fighting, perhaps escalating to a nuclear confrontation. Hawks wanted Kennedy to take a dramatic step, perhaps knocking down the wall. The president refused to react. Instead he sent a token force of 1,500 troops to Berlin, making clear that the United States would defend the beleaguered city. The troops managed to avoid an incident, and Khrushchev backed down from his threat to block American supply routes. Tensions between the superpowers eased—but only temporarily.

The Cuban Missile Crisis

On October 14 an American U-2 spy plane discovered offensive nuclear missile sites in Cuba. Khrushchev "can't do that to me!" Kennedy declared. Two days later Kennedy convened a meeting of his top advisers to consider how to respond to this bold strategic move. The military warned that the missiles would soon be operational and able to strike cities up and down the East Coast of the United States.

In fact, the missiles provided the Soviets with few strategic benefits since they already had enough nuclear missiles to obliterate every major American city. But

Kennedy and Khrushchev at Vienna In June 1961, President Kennedy, in office only six months and already plagued by the failure of the Bay of Pigs invasion, met with Soviet premier Nikita Khrushchev in Vienna. The main topic for discussion at the summit meeting was the future of Berlin, but it was also the first face-to-face meeting for the two leaders. Both men used the meetings to judge the character and resolve of the opposition. During the two-day meeting no agreements were reached, and in mid-August, the Soviet Union began building a wall around East Berlin.

Kennedy recognized that the presence of Soviet missiles in the Western Hemisphere, in open defiance of the Monroe Doctrine, presented the administration with an untenable political problem. Failure to mount a forceful response would bolster Soviet prestige in the Third World and, more importantly, provide Khrushchev with a powerful bargaining chip. The Soviet's U.S. ambassador wrote years later that Khrushchev's move "was part of a broader geopolitical strategy to achieve parity with the United States that could be used not only in the dispute over Berlin but in negotiations on other issues." Kennedy understood the Soviet motive. "What's basic to them is Berlin," Kennedy is overheard saying in a secretly taped White House meeting. "Berlin—that's what Khrushchev's committed himself to personally."

The question was, How should the United States respond? Kennedy initially supported an air strike to destroy the missile sites, but an air strike alone would

Duck-and-Cover Drill While Americans had faced the threat of nuclear attack from the Soviet Union since 1949, the fear of such an attack never seemed as real or possible as it did in October 1962 during the Cuban missile crisis. Missiles in Cuba, if launched, could easily reach most of the United States, leading Americans across the country to prepare for the possibility that their community could be a target. The number of bomb shelters built skyrocketed during the fall, as did the diligence with which the nation's schools practiced their air raid drills. Known as duck-and-cover drills, teachers trained children to scramble under their desks and cover their faces as quickly as possible when an alarm sounded.

not destroy all of them. Attorney General Robert Kennedy, who played an important role in the discussions, warned that the Soviet response to a military action "could be so severe as to lead to general nuclear war." He also worried that an air strike would diminish America's moral position in the world. "I now know how Tojo felt when he was planning Pearl Harbor," he said. The hawks objected to Kennedy's analogy to Japanese militarism, but RFK persisted, pointing out that air strikes would kill Cuban and Soviet civilians, provoking Khrushchev to retaliate, perhaps in Berlin.

On October 22 President Kennedy decided on a more moderate course of action: he would impose a naval quarantine of the island. A blockade would provide more time for each side to contemplate the costs of its actions and possibly provide the Russians with a graceful way to back out of the crisis. Later that evening Kennedy delivered a nationwide television address to the American

Location of Missiles in Cuba, 1962   In the summer of 1962, Soviet premier Nikita Khrushchev began secretly sending troops and weapons into Cuba. When American intelligence discovered the military buildup, Khrushchev explained to Kennedy that it was simply a defensive measure, a way to protect the government of Fidel Castro from further American attempts to overthrow his government. However, by sending medium-range ballistic missiles (MRBM) and intercontinental-range ballistic missiles (IRBM), Khrushchev was also ensuring the Soviet Union's first-strike capability. Cuban and Soviet technicians assembled the missiles on the western end of Cuba, as close to the U.S. Florida Keys as possible and as far from the prying eyes of the American military at Guantanamo Bay in southeastern Cuba as they could. On October 15, 1962, an American U-2 spy plane photographed the missile complexes, sparking the Cuban missile crisis.

people. Declaring the Russian tactic in Cuba "deliberate, provocative and unjustified," he insisted the United States had to respond "if our courage and our commitments are ever again to be trusted by either friend or foe." Announcing establishment of a "strict quarantine of all offensive military equipment under shipment to Cuba," Kennedy asserted that the United States would demand "prompt dismantling and withdrawal" of all offensive missiles.

The nation, and the world, teetered on the edge of nuclear war. Tension mounted when Khrushchev denounced the blockade as "outright banditry" and accused Kennedy of driving the world to nuclear war. The crisis intensified as a dozen Soviet ships headed toward a possible confrontation with the U.S. Navy off the coast of Cuba. Raising the stakes, Kennedy ordered B-52 aircraft carrying nuclear weapons to stand ready and moved troops south to prepare for a possible invasion. Then he and his advisers waited for the Soviets' response.

Khrushchev believed Kennedy lacked the backbone to force a nuclear confrontation, but as the cargo ships pushed toward the American navy, his intelligence told him the Americans were holding firm. On October 28 Khrushchev retreated, ordering the Soviet ships to turn around. Secretary of State Rusk remarked, "We're eyeball to eyeball and I think the other fellow just blinked." Over the next few days the two superpowers hammered out an agreement to end the confrontation. The United States promised not to invade Cuba if the missiles were quickly withdrawn and if a number of Russian medium-range bombers were returned from Cuba to the USSR. Privately, Kennedy also agreed that American missiles in Turkey would be removed.

Years later American officials learned just how close the nation had come to nuclear war. The White House had been working under the assumption that the nuclear weapon sites were not fully operational. In fact, the Soviets had already installed nine tactical nuclear missiles, each with a range of about 30 miles. The local commander had the authority to fire the weapons in the event of an American invasion. Also, some 42,000 Soviet personnel were on the island, nearly twice the number estimated by American intelligence.

In the short run the missile crisis set the stage for a gradual improvement in U.S.–Soviet relations. Both nations, traumatized by their close brush with nuclear war, appeared ready to lessen tensions. Taking the initiative in a speech at American University in June 1963, Kennedy called for a reexamination of American attitudes toward the Soviet Union and the Cold War. "In the final analysis," he said, "our most common link is that we all inhabit this small planet. We all breathe the same air. We all cherish our children's future. And we are all mortal." He proposed a joint Soviet-American expedition to the Moon and approved the sale of $250 million worth of surplus wheat to Russia. The White House and the Kremlin agreed to install a "hot line" to establish direct communications between the leaders of the world's two superpowers. Perhaps the most tangible evidence of the new thaw in relations was the Nuclear Test Ban Treaty. Initialed on July 25, it banned atmospheric and underwater nuclear testing.

JFK and Vietnam

Kennedy had less success in dealing with a deteriorating situation in Vietnam. Between 1955 and 1961 the United States had provided over $1 billion in aid to South Vietnam and sent more than 1,500 advisers to provide economic and military assistance. The American effort, however, focused on transforming Ngo Dinh Diem's government into an effective anticommunist fighting force, not on helping him to establish a firm base of public support.

Diem had inherited from the French a crippled economy, a poorly trained army, and a corrupt and incompetent government bureaucracy. Ho Chi Minh, the nationalist leader of the communist forces in North Vietnam, added to Diem's problems by creating the communist National Liberation Front, called Vietcong, in the South to fight a guerrilla war against the Diem government.

Diem's aloof personality and authoritarian style contributed to his failure to win popular support. Indifferent to the concerns of peasants living in the country-side, he ruthlessly suppressed dissenters, including powerful Buddhist groups.

Kennedy had once described Vietnam as the "cornerstone of the free world in Southeast Asia." During the 1950s he publicly supported the Eisenhower admin-istration's decision to maintain a noncommunist South by funneling aid to the Diem government. Like others of his generation, Kennedy accepted the domino theory of communist conquest. If the United States abandoned Vietnam to the communists, he said in September 1963, "pretty soon Thailand, Cambodia, Laos, Malaya would go and all of Southeast Asia would be under control of the Com-munists and under the domination of the Chinese."

The president believed that American credibility was at stake in Vietnam. The United States needed to demonstrate its strength in order to reassure its allies and discourage potential adversaries. Yet Kennedy also harbored doubts about whether Diem could unite the country, and he questioned the wisdom of using American ground forces in the jungles of Southeast Asia. In fact, with the excep-tion of an occasional crisis, Vietnam was never a high priority for Kennedy. "Once in a while," the *New York Times* observed in October 1963, "Washington remembers that there is a war in South Vietnam."

PRIMARY SOURCE

7.2 | *Diem to JFK, 1961; JFK to Diem, 1961*

America's foreign policy of containment made economic and military aid to South Vietnam appear necessary, especially as tensions escalated into war with North Vietnam. Inheriting this program of assistance from Eisenhower, President Kennedy struggled with decisions concerning the role of the United States in Viet-nam and the effectiveness of the South's leader, President Ngo Dinh Diem. On December 7, 1961, Diem sent Kennedy a letter urging an increase in America aid to prevent communism from spreading; Kennedy responded on December 14.

President Diem to President Kennedy

December 7, 1961

Dear Mr. President:

Since its birth, more than six years ago, the Republic of Vietnam has enjoyed the close friendship and cooperation of the United States of America.

5   Like the United States, the Republic of Vietnam has always been devoted to the preservation of peace. My people know only too well the sorrows of war. We have honored the 1954 Geneva Agreements even though they resulted in the par-tition of our country and the enslavement of more than half of our people by

Communist tyranny. We have never considered the reunification of our nation by
10 force. On the contrary, we have publicly pledged that we will not violate the
demarcation line and the demilitarized zone set up by the Agreements. We have
always been prepared and have on many occasions stated our willingness to
reunify Vietnam on the basis of democratic and truly free elections.

The record of the Communist authorities in the northern part of our country
15 is quite otherwise. They not only consented to the division of Vietnam, but were
eager for it. They pledged themselves to observe the Geneva Agreements and during the seven years since have never ceased to violate them. They call for free elections but are ignorant of the very meaning of the words. They talk of "peaceful
reunification" and wage war against us.

20 From the beginning, the Communists resorted to terror in their efforts to
subvert our people, destroy our government, and impose a Communist regime
upon us. They have attacked defenseless teachers, closed schools, killed members
of our anti-malarial program, and looted hospitals. This is coldly calculated to
destroy our government's humanitarian efforts to serve our people.

25 We have long sought to check the Communist attack from the North on our
people by appeals to the International Control Commission. Over the years, we
have repeatedly published to the world the evidence of the Communist plot to
overthrow our government and seize control of all of Vietnam by illegal intru-
sions from outside our country. . . .

30 . . . The Vietnamese nation now faces what is perhaps the gravest crisis in its
long history. For more than 2,000 years my people have lived and built,
fought and died in this land. We have not always been free. Indeed, much of our
history and many of its proudest moments have arisen from conquest by foreign
powers and our struggle against great odds to regain or defend our precious in-
35 dependence. But it is not only our freedom which is at stake today, it is our
national identity. For, if we lose this war, our people will be swallowed by the
Communist bloc, all our proud heritage will be blotted out by the "Socialist society" and Vietnam will leave the pages of history. We will lose our national soul.

Mr. President, my people and I are mindful of the great assistance which the
40 United States has given us. Your help has not been lightly received, for the Vietnamese are proud people, and we are determined to do our part in the defense of
the free world. It is clear to all of us that the defeat of the Vietcong demands the
total mobilization of our government and our people, and you may be sure that
we will devote all of our resources of money, minds, and men to this great task.

45 But Vietnam is not a great power and the forces of international Communism
now arrayed against us are more than we can meet with the resources at hand. We
must have further assistance from the United States if we are to win the war now
being waged against us.

We can certainly assure mankind that our action is purely defensive. Much as
50 we regret the subjugation of more than half of our people in North Vietnam we
have no intention, and indeed no means, to free them by use of force.

I have said that Vietnam is at war. War means many things, but most of all it
means the death of brave people for a cause they believe in. Vietnam has suffered
many wars, and through the centuries we have always had patriots and heroes
55 who were willing to shed their blood for Vietnam. We will keep faith with them.

When Communism has long ebbed away into the past, my people will still be here, a free united nation growing from the deep roots of our Vietnamese heritage. They will remember your help in our time of need. This struggle will then be a part of our common history. And your help, your friendship, and the strong
60 bonds between our two peoples will be a part of Vietnam, then as now.

President Kennedy to President Diem

December 14, 1961

Dear Mr. President:

I have received your recent letter in which you described so cogently the dangerous condition caused by North Vietnam's efforts to take over your country. The
5 situation in your embattled country is well known to me and to the American people. We have been deeply disturbed by the assault on your country. Our indignation has mounted as the deliberate savagery of the Communist program of assassination, kidnapping, and wanton violence became clear.

Your letter underlines what our own information has convincingly shown—
10 that the campaign of force and terror now being waged against your people and your Government is supported and directed from the outside by the authorities at Hanoi. They have thus violated the provisions of the Geneva Accords designed to ensure peace in Vietnam and to which they bound themselves in 1954.
15 At that time, the United States, although not a party to the Accords, declared that it "would view any renewal of the aggression in violation of the Agreements with grave concern and as seriously threatening international peace and security." We continue to maintain that view.

In accordance with that declaration, and in response to your request, we are
20 prepared to help the Republic of Vietnam to protect its people and to preserve its independence. We shall promptly increase our assistance to your defense effort as well as help relieve the destruction of the floods which you describe. I have already given the orders to get these programs underway.

The United States, like the Republic of Vietnam, remains devoted to the
25 cause of peace and our primary purpose is to help your people maintain their independence. If the Communist authorities in North Vietnam will stop their campaign to destroy the Republic of Vietnam, the measures we are taking to assist your defense efforts will no longer be necessary. We shall seek to persuade the Communists to give up their attempts of force and subversion. In any case,
30 we are confident that the Vietnamese people will preserve their independence and gain the peace and prosperity for which they have sought so hard and so long. ■ ■ ■

During these early years the cost of losing Vietnam far outweighed the price the nation had to pay to maintain stability. Kennedy had little doubt that the United States would prevail, that its vast military might would intimidate the North Vietnamese at the same time that counterinsurgency measures would help stabilize the South. Kennedy never seriously considered that the conflict would escalate into a wider war. In 1961 when Undersecretary of State George Ball warned Kennedy that Vietnam could lead to the deployment of hundreds of thousands of American troops, Kennedy laughed: "George, you're supposed to be one of the smartest guys in town, but you're crazier than hell. That will never happen."

During his nearly three years in office, Kennedy increased both economic aid and the number of American military advisers. The infusion of American support did little to stabilize the Diem regime, however. The North Vietnamese–supplied Vietcong established control over large portions of the countryside. At the same time, American officials watched helplessly as Diem gradually lost control. He squandered millions of dollars in American aid, refused to call free elections, and used the army to crush even peaceful noncommunist demonstrations.

Most of Kennedy's senior advisers recommended expanding the American role in Vietnam. With the exception of the U.S. ambassador to Vietnam, who advocated a policy of "sink or swim with Ngo Dinh Diem," both the State Department and the Pentagon believed that the United States needed to take a tougher line with Diem and introduce combat troops to stabilize the government. Without the introduction of 8,000 troops, claimed General Maxwell Taylor, who served as the president's military adviser, "I do not believe that our program to save SVN [South Vietnam] will succeed." The chairman of the Joint Chiefs of Staff went further than Taylor, urging Kennedy to "grind up the Vietcong with 40,000 American ground troops. . . . Grab 'em by the balls and their hearts and minds will follow." Robert McNamara supported the introduction of combat troops but stressed that the military had to avoid fighting a conventional war and instead develop a counterinsurgency strategy to battle the communists. Ball counseled caution, claiming that Vietnam was not a vital American interest.

Caught in the middle, Kennedy initially tried taking a hard line with Diem, insisting that American aid was contingent on his willingness to reform his corrupt government and seek accommodation with dissident groups in South Vietnam. When Diem ignored the pressure, the administration backed down. Kennedy, however, was deeply skeptical about the proposal to send combat troops to Vietnam. He worried about the difficulty of fighting in the jungles of Southeast Asia, the lack of support from major U.S. allies, and the possibility of Chinese intervention in the conflict. While he accepted the domino theory, Kennedy doubted whether Vietnam was the place to draw a line in the sand. "We are not sending combat troops," Robert Kennedy declared during a 1961 meeting discussing Vietnam.

In the summer and fall of 1963 the situation in South Vietnam seriously deteriorated when Diem ordered his troops to fire on Buddhist leaders holding banned religious celebrations. Anti-Diem forces immediately rallied to the Buddhists, and civil war threatened within the principal cities. Several Buddhists responded by publicly burning themselves to death, an act that Diem's government ridiculed as a "barbecue show." The deaths, flashed on the evening news in the United States, dramatized the growing opposition and grabbed the administration's attention.

Buddhist Monks Protest the Diem Government   From the beginning of American involvement in Vietnam, the United States found itself aiding less-than-democratic regimes in the South in order to thwart communism in the North. President Ngo Dinh Diem ruled autocratically, abolishing local elections, curbing the press, and harassing his enemies. By 1963, his actions literally drew fire from devout Buddhist priests, who set themselves ablaze to protest his administration. Photographs such as this one horrified the American public, who questioned why the United States supported a government that provoked this kind of defiance. President Kennedy, also disturbed, gave his tacit approval to a military coup that overthrew the hated government and assassinated the deposed Diem. *(Wide World Photos, Inc.)*

The communists tightened their grip on the countryside while Diem floundered, refusing to enact changes that might strengthen his support among noncommunists in the cities. Confronted by the possibility of a massive revolt against the Diem government, Kennedy reconsidered his support of the beleaguered ally. He replaced the previous ambassador, who had supported Diem, with the hard-line Henry Cabot Lodge, who was determined to force the regime to make changes. In addition, Kennedy twice sent Robert McNamara to Vietnam with instructions to "press the need for reform and change as a pragmatic necessity and not as a moral judgement." Nothing seemed to work. "They can send ten Lodges," a defiant Diem declared, "but I will not permit myself or my country to be humiliated, not if they train their artillery on this Palace." When South Vietnamese generals approached Washington with plans for a coup, Kennedy reluctantly agreed. On November 1, 1963, the generals seized key military and communications installations and demanded Diem's resignation. Later that day Diem was captured and, despite American assurances of safe passage, murdered.

Although Kennedy resisted pressure to commit American troops, he spent nearly $1 billion in South Vietnam and increased the number of American military "advisers" to more than 16,000. But the Vietcong was stronger than ever. Two weeks after the coup Kennedy ordered a "complete and very profound review of how we got into this country, what we thought we were doing, and what we now think we can do." Kennedy would never see the report.

The Life of Kennedy's Death

Within months of Kennedy's assassination polls showed a majority of Americans questioning whether Lee Harvey Oswald had acted alone. To quell the doubts, President Johnson appointed a blue-ribbon commission of seven prominent public figures chaired by Chief Justice Earl Warren. On September 24, 1964, only ten months after the events in Dallas, the President's Commission on the Assassination of President Kennedy, popularly known as the Warren Commission, presented its 888-page report. There was no conspiracy, foreign or domestic; it declared that Lee Harvey Oswald had acted alone.

The Warren Commission's findings failed to convince skeptics. A *Newsweek* poll taken in 1983 on the twentieth anniversary of the assassination showed that 74 percent of Americans believed that "others were involved." Critics charged that Oswald could not have fired three shots in 5.6 seconds from a mail-order, bolt-action rifle. More improbable was the contention that one bullet, dubbed the "magic bullet," could have traveled through the president's body, inflicted extensive injury to Governor Connally, and remained in nearly pristine condition. Skeptics charged that in a "rush to judgment" the Warren Commission ignored witnesses who claimed to hear more than three shots and repressed evidence that could have implicated other groups with a motive to shoot the president. Such suspicions would gain a new lease on life in 1992 with the release of the Hollywood film *JFK,* directed by Oliver Stone. The film portrayed an elaborate web of conspiracy involving Vice President Johnson, the FBI, the CIA, the Pentagon, defense contractors, and assorted other officials and agencies.

While critics have poked holes in the Warren Commission's findings, they have failed either to undermine its final conclusion that Oswald acted alone or to develop a convincing alternative interpretation of events on November 22, 1963. Numerous re-enactments, along with new computer-enhanced models, have confirmed the core of the ballistic evidence: Oswald could have fired all three shots, and a single bullet could have cut its deadly path through both the president and Governor Connally. The opening of nearly all records related to the assassination undercuts suggestions of a government coverup.

If the evidence supports the Warren Commission, why do the conspiracy theories persist? Sloppiness on the part of the Warren Commission, intense media interest, and Cold War paranoia all played a part in keeping Kennedy's death alive. Perhaps most of all, people find the theories of conspiracy attractive because they imbue Kennedy's death with meaning. Believing that great tragedies require great causes, Americans reject the notion that a single lunatic can change history. By making Kennedy a victim of some sinister, powerful force, conspiracy theories transform Kennedy's death into something more than a senseless act of violence.

Kennedy's death, and the debate that it generated, would fascinate Americans for decades. Television played a role in cementing Kennedy's image with the public. Kennedy was the first president to use television to bypass the Washington opinion makers and communicate directly with the American public. The trauma of his death, played over seventy-five straight hours on television, was burned into the national consciousness. Four of five Americans felt "the loss of someone very close and dear," and more than one-half cried.

More than anything else, however, Kennedy's inspiring rhetoric and youthful style projected an image of America moving forward to a better future. The consensus was unraveling all around him, but for many Americans Kennedy represented a time when the United States stood strong in the world, the nation felt united, and life seemed simpler. Events in the years following his death—the defeat in Vietnam, campus unrest, urban rioting, Watergate, and stagflation—would shatter that faith. As the nation's faith in government and hope for the future diminished, Americans clung more tenaciously than ever to a mythic view of Kennedy.

Ultimately, America's fascination with Kennedy revealed more about the nation's tenacious belief in progress and its need for heroes than it did about the man. Kennedy was mortal, very much a product of his times, and he offered few solutions to the day's pressing issues. Like his postwar predecessors, JFK relied upon the vital-center consensus to deal with the American paradox. By 1963 the seams of the consensus were already beginning to split under the strain of the civil-rights movement, which exposed the tension between expectations and reality.

SELECTED READINGS

▮ John Blum's *Years of Discord* (1991) surveys the broad sweep of political strife that marked the Kennedy, Johnson, and Nixon administrations. Arthur Schlesinger Jr.'s epic *A Thousand Days* (1965) compounds the sympathy of a former Kennedy administration official with the perspective of a historian. With *JFK: The Presidency of John F. Kennedy* (1983), Herbert Parmet steps back from the ebullience of the Schlesinger generation to survey the major events of the Kennedy administration, balancing accomplishments against limitations. He is joined in that effort by James Giglio, *The Presidency of John F. Kennedy* (1991).

▮ The best recent account of Kennedy's presidency, providing assessment of foreign policy and his agenda as a reformer, is Hugh Brogan's *Kennedy* (1997). Irwin Unger's *Best of Intentions* (1996) traces the evolution of the Great Society programs from Kennedy's efforts to Johnson's ability to get them through Congress. Gary Wills's *The Kennedy Imprisonment* (1982) is a critical meditation on the troubling aspects of Kennedy's charismatic leadership. Thomas Brown casts a skeptical eye on the use of the media to create an aura surrounding the Kennedy image in his *JFK: The History of an Image* (1988). Irvin Bernstein's *Promises Kept* (1990) focuses on the domestic programs, such as civil rights, that provided Kennedy with opportunities to act.

■ A detailed account of the sit-ins at the Woolworth in Greensboro, North Carolina, is found in Miles Wolff's *Lunch at the 5 and 10* (1990), while Clayborne Carson traces the evolution of black consciousness through the process of grass-roots mobilization and protest in his definitive history of SNCC, *In Struggle* (1981). In *An American Insurrection* (2001), William Doyle examines the tumultuous events surrounding James Meredith's admission to the University of Mississippi and its impact on southern resistance. Diane McWhorter's *Carry Me Home* (2001) tells the story of her own white, middle-class family, but in the context of the wider civil-rights struggle occurring in her hometown of Birmingham. A detailed biography of Alabama's governor George Wallace and his anti-integration movement is Dan Carter's *The Politics of Rage* (1995). Taylor Branch's *Parting the Waters* (1989) is a Pulitzer Prize–winning examination of the civil-rights movement up through 1963, with an emphasis on the work of Martin Luther King.

■ The early history of the Peace Corps and its role as one of Kennedy's foreign-policy tools is depicted in Gerard Rice's *The Bold Experiment* (1985). *Kennedy's Wars* (2000), by Lawrence Freedman, examines Kennedy's foreign policy in the light of his response to problems in Berlin, Cuba, Laos, and Vietnam. Mark White's *Missiles in Cuba* (1997) provides a chronological narrative of the event, while Robert Weisbrot analyzes the role of public perception and Kennedy's leadership qualities during the crisis in *Maximum Danger* (2001). David Kaiser's *American Tragedy* (2000) argues that Kennedy's foreign policy in Vietnam was a retraction of Eisenhower's escalating policy, which would be resurrected by Johnson. David Halberstam, who made his name reporting from Vietnam, reveals in *The Best and the Brightest* (1972) the atmosphere of brash optimism and technocratic assurance that accompanied the U.S. commitment.

CHAPTER 8

Lyndon Johnson's Ordeal: The Great Society and Vietnam, 1964–1968

A t about 2:00 P.M. on February 7, 1965, the sentry at Camp Holloway, an American air base outside the Vietnamese city of Pleiku, spotted the shadows of men moving along the perimeter of the base. Seconds later a series of explosions shattered the concrete wall surrounding the installation, dozens of mortar shells rained from the sky, and thousands of rounds of small-arms fire pelted the area. By the time the attack ended, 7 men were dead, 109 wounded. Three days later the Vietcong hit a U.S. Army barracks at Qui Nhon, killing 8 Americans and wounding 21.

Over the next several days President Lyndon Johnson met with the National Security Council (NSC) to discuss the American response. NSC adviser McGeorge Bundy, sent to Vietnam after the attacks, returned with a startling report. "The prospect in Vietnam is grim," he informed the president. "The stakes in Vietnam are extremely high." the president's leading civilian and military advisers had been eager to expand U.S. military involvement in Vietnam by initiating a campaign of sustained bombing of selected targets. The attack on Pleiku provided the administration with the justification for escalation. "Pleikus are like streetcars," Bundy told a reporter, meaning that you jump onto one when you need it.

Following the attack on Pleiku, the administration committed the nation to its fateful course in Vietnam. Not only did the United States decide to begin a program of sustained bombing; it also agreed to commit American ground troops to protect air bases from attacks similar to Pleiku. In order to launch a bombing campaign, Johnson said the only way to stop the attacks was by "sending a very large number of U.S. troops to Vietnam." Secretary of Defense Robert McNamara told the president that guarding American bases would require "at least 100,000 men, 44 battalions." The president also made another key decision: he would keep the change in policy a secret. When William Bundy, an assistant secretary of state and brother of McGeorge, suggested that "at an appropriate time we could publicly announce that we have turned a corner and changed our policy," Johnson said that since the United States was already committed to helping the South Vietnamese, he did not have to announce any change in strategy.

At the same time, with his massive congressional majorities, President Johnson planned to revive the liberal agenda, implementing many of the assumptions of the vital center. With unbound optimism in the possibility of change, LBJ planned to launch a war abroad to tame communism and a war at home to end poverty. The American paradox frustrated Johnson's ambitious agenda: liberals raised expectations about the possibilities of change but, fearful of inciting a conservative backlash, offered only modest proposals for reform. By the end of the decade Johnson's cherished consensus had unraveled, exposing the fatal flaw in the new liberalism. Americans wanted to eradicate poverty without a dramatic expansion of federal power and to defeat communist aggression in Vietnam without the sacrifices of war—mobilization, draft, soaring taxes.

Lyndon Johnson Takes Charge

John Kennedy's death brought to the White House a man with a strikingly different background and temperament. Lyndon Baines Johnson was born in 1908 in Stonewall, Texas, a depressed rural area of the Texas hill country. Johnson, the eldest of five children born to Sam and Rebekah Johnson, lived his early years in poverty. "When I was young," Johnson said, "poverty was so common that we didn't know it had a name." After completing his education at Southwest Texas State Teachers College in nearby San Marcos, Johnson taught school for a few years. In 1931 he traveled to Washington, where he worked as a clerk to a Texas congressman.

As a young man in Washington during the depression, Johnson developed deep admiration for Franklin Roosevelt, whom he described as "like a daddy to me." In 1937 he won election to Congress on a "Franklin D. and Lyndon B.

ticket." He lost a Senate race in 1941 before serving as a lieutenant commander in the navy. In 1948 he earned the nickname "Landslide Lyndon" following his election to the Senate by a margin of eight votes.

Once in the Senate Johnson impressed powerful Democrats with his energy and ambition. As minority leader and then as majority leader, he became a master of parliamentary maneuver and a skillful behind-the-scenes negotiator. A tall, physically imposing man, Johnson was not afraid to twist arms to bend recalcitrant senators to his will. Two journalists described this process as "the Johnson treatment." "He moved in close, his face a scant millimeter from his target, his eyes widening and narrowing, his eyebrows rising and falling." Hubert Humphrey once described an encounter with Johnson as "an almost hypnotic experience. I came out of that session covered with blood, sweat, tears, spit—and sperm." In 1955 Johnson, who drank recklessly and smoked heavily, suffered a near-fatal heart attack, but he recovered to seek the Democratic nomination in 1960. Overshadowed by the charismatic Kennedy, he reluctantly accepted second place on the ticket.

For someone who had been a leader of the Washington establishment for so long, Johnson was surprisingly insecure. He believed that people from distinguished families, old money, and Ivy League educations would scorn a self-made Texan. His insecurity was obvious to those who worked with him. "Dubious whether people liked him," observed one historian, "he pleaded, clawed, and maneuvered to have them love him." His insecurity was accentuated by the frequent comparisons between him and Kennedy. "Why don't people like me?" Johnson asked in a rare moment of introspection. "Because Mr. President," an aide responded, "you are not a very likeable man." His press secretary observed later that Johnson "as a human being was a miserable person—a bully, sadist, lout, and egoist."

Doubts about Johnson's character damaged his relations with the press. The Washington establishment did not know how to deal with a president as vulgar and egotistical as Johnson. He swam naked in the White House swimming pool and pulled up his shirt to show newsmen the scar from his gallbladder operation. He scratched his private parts, belched loudly at meals, and speckled his speech with profanity. At state banquets he sometimes helped himself to food on other people's platters. He frequently spoke about "my Supreme Court." On one occasion, after receiving some Vietnam-bound marines, he started walking toward a helicopter when an officer stopped him, pointed to another location, and said, "That's your helicopter over there, sir." "Son," LBJ said, "they are all my helicopters." In Rome he once met the pope, who presented Johnson with a fourteenth-century painting as a gift. In return, the president gave the pontiff a bust of himself.

More seriously, Johnson's penchant for bending the truth to suit his purposes raised doubts about his integrity and created a credibility gap that eventually undermined public trust in his presidency. Johnson told so many small lies that many people began to question everything he said. At one point Johnson claimed that his great-great-grandfather had died defending the Alamo. When a reporter informed him that none of his relatives had ever fought at the Alamo, Johnson exclaimed, "God damn it, why must all those journalists be such sticklers for detail?" In April 1965 Johnson sent the marines to quell an insurrection in the Dominican Republic. When reporters suggested that the president had overreacted to a situation that offered no threat to American security, Johnson responded by exaggerating the magnitude of the crisis. He told stories—all proven false—of fifteen hundred innocent people being murdered and beheaded and of the American ambassador being forced to seek cover from stray bullets spraying the U.S. embassy. Almost nothing Johnson said about the crisis had been true, prompting renewed questions about his honesty. "How do you know when Johnson is telling the truth?" a skeptic asked. "When he scratches his head, rubs his chin or knits his brow, he's telling the truth. When he begins to move his lips, he's lying."

The War on Poverty

The new president, however, displayed a quiet dignity in the traumatic days following Kennedy's assassination. Lyndon Johnson convinced a grieving nation to honor its slain president by passing his stalled reform agenda. After winning a landslide election in 1964, Johnson pushed through Congress liberal legislation that had been backlogged since the days of Franklin Roosevelt and Harry Truman. Ironically, at the same time that events were eroding the foundation of consensus, Johnson was constructing a reform agenda based on its assumptions.

On November 26, 1963, he addressed Congress, committing himself to fulfilling the slain president's intentions for reform. "We would be untrue to the trust he reposed in us," he told a joint session of Congress, "if we did not remain true to the tasks he relinquished when God summoned him." Always the political tactician, Johnson realized that Kennedy's death provided him with a powerful symbol to build political support for an expansive liberal agenda. "Everything I had ever learned in the history books taught me that martyrs have to die for causes," he reflected. "John Kennedy had died. But his 'cause' was not really clear. That was my job. I had to take the dead man's program and turn it into a martyr's cause."

Johnson used his political talent to push Congress into enacting a number of Kennedy's initiatives. In February 1964 Congress passed the Kennedy tax package, reducing personal income taxes by more than $10 billion. To win support for the tax cut, Johnson promised to keep the federal budget under $100 billion. "If you don't get this budget down to around 100 billion," he told an economic adviser, "you won't pee one drop." Many economists believe the tax cut contributed to an economic boom that saw the nation's gross national product (GNP) rise from $591 billion in 1963 to $977 billion in 1970. Johnson also pushed through Congress Kennedy's stalled housing and food-stamp programs.

Johnson was not content merely to pass Kennedy's agenda, however. He sought to create a program that would bear his personal brand. In January 1964 in his first State of the Union message, Johnson declared "unconditional war on poverty. . . . We shall not rest until that war is won. The richest Nation on earth can afford to win it. We cannot afford to lose it." Reflecting the grand expectations that animated liberals in the 1960s, Johnson believed that a constantly expanding economy could fund needed social problems and solve nearly all of the nation's domestic problems. "I'm sick of all the people who talk about the things we can't do," he said in 1964. "Hell, we're the richest country in the world, the most powerful. We can do it all."

The resulting war on poverty actually had its roots in the Kennedy administration. Like many Americans, Kennedy took office believing that economic growth alone would solve the problems of poverty. In 1962 the social activist Michael Harrington passionately challenged that notion in a popular book entitled *The Other America*. Estimating the ranks of the poor at 40 to 50 million, or as much as 25 percent of the U.S. population, Harrington argued that poverty resulted from long-term structural problems, such as unemployment and low wages, which only the federal government could address. On November 19, 1963, just three days before his death, Kennedy asked Walter Heller, the chairman of the Council of Economic Advisors, to design a legislative proposal for fighting poverty. "I want to go beyond the things that have already been accomplished," he told Heller. The day after the assassination Johnson enthusiastically endorsed the plan. "That's my kind of program," the president said. "Move full speed ahead."

Johnson initiated his war on poverty with a legislative proposal that Congress passed in the summer of 1964. This poverty legislation, called the Economic Opportunity Act, authorized almost $1 billion dollars for a wide range of antipoverty programs, including Head Start for preschoolers and the Job Corps for inner-city youth. Volunteers in Service to America, a domestic version of the Peace Corps, provided volunteers with the opportunity to work in poor urban areas and depressed rural communities. The law also authorized creation of the Office of Economic Opportunity (OEO) to coordinate the antipoverty battle. Johnson chose Peace Corps director R. Sargent Shriver, a Kennedy brother-in-law, to administer the OEO.

The centerpiece of the new legislation was the community action program (CAP). The initiative, intended to stimulate sustained involvement among the poor, called for the "maximum feasible participation" of local community members in shaping antipoverty programs. But as the historian Allen Matusow has noted, there was one significant problem with the heralded legislation: no one had any idea what community action meant. "Thus in August 1964, when the Economic Opportunity Act was enacted," he wrote, "neither the president who sponsored it, the director-designate who would administer it, nor the congressmen who passed it really knew what they had done."

By some measures the various programs that made up the war on poverty succeeded. The proportion of Americans below the federal poverty line fell from 20 percent in 1963 to 13 percent in 1968. For African-Americans, who faced the most desperate conditions, the statistics were even more impressive. The percentage of blacks living below the poverty line dropped from 40 percent to 20 percent between 1960 and 1968. However, a booming economy contributed to these statistics as much as did the antipoverty program.

Johnson had promised that his program would offer people jobs, not relief. "We want to offer the forgotten fifth of our people opportunity and not doles," Johnson said in the signing ceremony. During the 1960s the unemployment rate was cut by one-half, but the number of recipients of Aid to Families with Dependent Children (AFDC) increased by two-thirds and the cost of the program doubled. New York, which saw its unemployment rate drop to 3.2 percent in 1969, watched as the relief rolls swelled to over 1 million. In many urban communities, CAP funded local service centers, which encouraged the eligible poor to sign up for welfare. The individual service centers gave birth to a coordinated national welfare movement. In 1967 the civil-rights activist George Wiley founded the National Welfare Rights Organization (NWRO), claiming that "the poor at the grass roots needed a new voice." By 1968 the NWRO had established chapters in thirty-five states and was representing about twenty-five thousand welfare clients. The success of the welfare-rights movement depended heavily on the work of legal aid lawyers, who were funded by CAP.

Like many of the social programs of the 1960s, the war on poverty was characterized by grand ambition and limited gains. In submitting his bill to Congress, Johnson called for "total victory." "Conquest of poverty is well within our power," he declared. Sargent Shriver, the president's chief evangelist, predicted that the program "will in the end eliminate poverty from the United States." But ingrained conservative attitudes toward the poor, and toward government's role in promoting social welfare, limited the choice of weapons used to fight the war. With polls showing that large numbers of Americans believed that poverty resulted from "lack of effort" and that the poor were partly to blame for their plight, the administration developed a program that emphasized opportunity and promised to help the poor to help themselves. From 1965 to 1970 OEO spent an average of $1.7 billion per year—less than 1.5 percent of the federal budget, or one-third of 1 percent of the GNP. If all OEO money had gone directly to the poor, it would have amounted to between $50 and $70 per person.

The administration camouflaged the conceptual problems with the program by wrapping it in language familiar to most Americans. Describing the effort as a war on poverty appealed to American faith in social progress, while the emphasis on community control and local initiative reassured a public leery of an enlarged federal presence. Underlying the initiative was a naïve notion about the malleability of American society, a false faith in consensus, a belief that all groups in society—the poor, the middle class, and big business—shared a common agenda and could work together to achieve similar goals. Convinced of the healing power of economic growth, policy makers believed they could solve the age-old problems of poverty by tinkering with the welfare system. The problem, however, was that poverty was not a local problem and "the people" were fragmented into competing groups that battled one another for limited social resources.

The ultimate irony of the war on poverty was that a program launched as the result of renewed faith in the power of government was to undermine public faith in Washington's ability to solve social problems. "Perhaps no government program in modern American history promised so much more than it delivered," noted the historian James T. Patterson. The contrast between promise and performance infuriated some of the poor. In 1967 when rioting hit Detroit, Mayor Jerome Cavanagh blamed the OEO and other federal programs. "What we've been doing, at the level we've been doing it, is almost worse than nothing at all. . . . We've raised expectations, but we haven't been able to deliver all we should have." The experience also soured a generation of intellectuals who viewed the war on poverty as a metaphor for government ineptitude. "There are limits to the desirable reach of social engineering," observed the sociologist Nathan Glazer. Increasingly, the public shared many of these doubts. By 1967 more than 67 percent of the public thought the administration had gone "too far." In 1969 a total of 84 percent agreed with the statement "There are too many people receiving welfare who ought to be working."

The 1964 Election

While launching his war on poverty, Johnson was laying the foundation for the 1964 presidential election. At the party's Atlantic City convention, Johnson won the nomination by acclamation. As his running mate, he chose Minnesota senator Hubert Humphrey, a passionate proponent of civil rights and a leading liberal.

To oppose Johnson in November, the Republicans nominated Arizona senator Barry Goldwater. Tall, trim, and handsome, Goldwater was an outspoken critic of liberal reform who hoped to rally millions of conservative voters in the South and West with his calls for smaller government and aggressive anticommunism. During the 1950s Goldwater had developed a loyal group of conservative followers, but he burst on the national scene in 1960 with publication of *Conscience of a Conservative*. The book challenged the prevailing faith in consensus, arguing that government intervention had restricted individual freedom and that coexistence with Russia had rewarded unchecked Soviet aggression. "A tolerable peace . . . must *follow* victory over Communism." *Conscience* debuted at number fourteen on the *New York Times* best-seller list and was especially popular on college campuses.

In 1962 Goldwater loyalists developed elaborate plans to seize control of the Republican Party at the grass roots. Instead of winning the support of governors and senators, conservatives would organize precinct by precinct to control the delegates at the 1964 convention. Rather than cultivating traditional Republican votes in the Northeast, they would focus their efforts in the white South. "We're not going to get the Negro vote as a bloc in 1964 and 1968," Goldwater declared, "so we ought to go hunting where the ducks are." As civil-rights tensions mounted in the South, and Kennedy's approval rating among whites dropped, pundits began speculating that Goldwater could ride the discontent into the White House. By 1963 he had become, according to *Fortune* magazine, "the favorite son of a state of mind."

PRIMARY **SOURCE**

8.1 | *Acceptance Speech, 1964*
BARRY GOLDWATER

Capitalizing on the growing right-wing conservatism of the Republican Party in the early 1960s, Barry Goldwater garnered the party's nomination for president in 1964. In his acceptance speech, delivered on July 17, 1964, Goldwater focused on the deterioration of America's moral purpose under the Democratic Party and the results of such decay.

Rather than useful jobs in our country, people have been offered bureaucratic "make work," rather than moral leadership, they have been given bread and circuses, spectacles, and, yes, they have even been given scandals. Tonight there is violence in our streets, corruption in our highest offices, aimlessness among our
5 youth, anxiety among our elders and there is a virtual despair among the many who look beyond material success for the inner meaning of their lives. Where examples of morality should be set, the opposite is seen. Small men, seeking great wealth or power, have too often and too long turned even the highest levels of public service into mere personal opportunity.
10 Now, certainly, simple honesty is not too much to demand of men in government. We find it in most. Republicans demand it from everyone. They demand it from everyone no matter how exalted or protected his position might be. The growing menace in our country tonight, to personal safety, to life, to limb and property, in homes, in churches, on the playgrounds, and places of business, par-
15 ticularly in our great cities, is the mounting concern, or should be, of every thoughtful citizen in the United States.
Security from domestic violence, no less than from foreign aggression, is the most elementary and fundamental purpose of any government, and a government that cannot fulfill that purpose is one that cannot long command the
20 loyalty of its citizens. History shows us—demonstrates that nothing—nothing prepares the way for tyranny more than the failure of public officials to keep the streets from bullies and marauders.
Now, we Republicans see all this as more, much more, than the rest: of mere political differences or mere political mistakes. We see this as the result of a fun-
25 damentally and absolutely wrong view of man, his nature and his destiny. Those who seek to live your lives for you, to take your liberties in return for relieving

you of yours, those who elevate the state and downgrade the citizen must see ultimately a world in which earthly power can be substituted for divine will, and this
Nation was founded upon the rejection of that notion and upon the acceptance
30 of God as the author of freedom.

Those who seek absolute power, even though they seek it to do what they
regard as good, are simply demanding the right to enforce their own version of
heaven on earth. And let me remind you, they are the very ones who always create the most hellish tyrannies. Absolute power does corrupt, and those who seek
35 it must be suspect and must be opposed. Their mistaken course stems from false
notions of equality, ladies and gentlemen. Equality, rightly understood, as our
founding fathers understood it, leads to liberty and to the emancipation of creative differences. Wrongly understood, as it has been so tragically in our time, it
leads first to conformity and then to despotism.

40 Fellow Republicans, it is the cause of Republicanism to resist concentrations
of power, private or public, which enforce such conformity and inflict such
despotism. It is the cause of Republicanism to ensure that power remains in the
hands of the people. And, so help us God, that is exactly what a Republican president will do with the help of a Republican Congress.

45 It is further the cause of Republicanism to restore a clear understanding of
the tyranny of man over man in the world at large. It is our cause to dispel the
foggy thinking which avoids hard decisions in the illusion that a world of conflict will somehow mysteriously resolve itself into a world of harmony, if
we just don't rock the boat or irritate the forces of aggression—and this is
50 hogwash.

It is further the cause of Republicanism to remind ourselves, and the world,
that only the strong can remain free, that only the strong can keep the peace. . . .

Today, as then, but more urgently and more broadly than then, the task of
preserving and enlarging freedom at home and safeguarding it from the forces of
55 tyranny abroad is great enough to challenge all our resources and to require all
our strength. Anyone who joins us in all sincerity, we welcome. Those who do not
care for our cause, we don't expect to enter our ranks in any case. And let our
Republicanism, so focused and so dedicated, not be made fuzzy and futile by
unthinking and stupid labels.

60 I would remind you that extremism in the defense of liberty is no vice. And
let me remind you also that moderation in the pursuit of justice is no virtue. . . .

■ ■ ■

Goldwater's extremism may have energized the party's vocal right wing, but it
alienated Republican moderates and liberals. "Extremism in the defense of liberty is no vice," he orated. "Moderation in the pursuit of justice is no virtue." He
suggested that nuclear weapons be used against Cuba, China, and North Vietnam
if they failed to accede to American demands. "Our job, first and foremost," he
wrote, "is to persuade the enemy that we would rather follow the world to Kingdom Come than consign it to Hell under communism." GOP campaign posters
asserted, "In Your Heart You Know He's Right." (Democrats retorted, "In Your
Guts You Know He's Nuts.")

By waging a campaign to win over the Right, Goldwater conceded the broad middle ground to Johnson, who brilliantly exploited the opportunity. He played the role of the fatherly figure committed to continuing the policies of the nation's fallen leader. Campaigning eighteen hours a day, he reminded voters of his party's past accomplishments and promised to carry the nation to new heights.

The election was never close. Johnson's portion of the popular vote, 61 percent, matched Roosevelt's in 1936. Voters gave Johnson 43.1 million votes to Goldwater's 27.2 million. Carrying all but six states, Johnson gathered 486 electoral votes to Goldwater's 52. Congressional Democrats coasted to victory on the president's coattails, providing the administration with large majorities in both houses: 68 to 32 in the Senate and 295 to 140 in the House. The *New York Times* opined that Goldwater had "wrecked his party for a long time to come," while *The New Yorker* predicted that Johnson's landslide victory had "finished the Goldwater school of political reaction."

The Democrats may have triumphed on election day, but Goldwater won the debate in the long run. He was a prophet of the new conservatism. While mainstream Republicans were still debating balanced budgets, Goldwater tapped into a growing discontent with the unfulfilled expectations of postwar liberalism. In the final months of the campaign Goldwater taught Republicans how to appeal to the cultural frustrations of white voters by addressing such issues as racial quotas, law and order, and fear of moral decline. The message helped the Republicans make dramatic inroads into the once solidly Democratic South. He received 70 percent of the vote in Alabama and 87 percent in Mississippi. Even in southern states that he lost, Republicans won a majority of white voters.

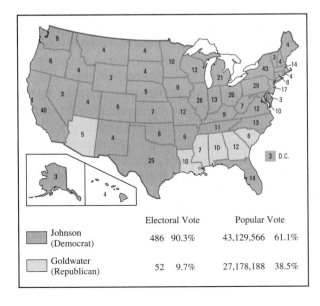

	Electoral Vote		Popular Vote	
Johnson (Democrat)	486	90.3%	43,129,566	61.1%
Goldwater (Republican)	52	9.7%	27,178,188	38.5%

The Election of 1964
Republicans tried a new political strategy with their candidate Barry Goldwater, attacking the liberal domestic policies of Democratic presidents, including the New Deal and the war on poverty. Lyndon Johnson retaliated by campaigning to as wide an audience as possible and urged people at every point of the political spectrum to join him. This broad appeal led to a Johnson landslide.

The Goldwater campaign revealed the fragile nature of the postwar consensus. The new liberalism had raised expectations of a secular utopia: prosperity would solve the problems of poverty and racism without challenging traditional values of limited government or individual rights. By 1964 the contradiction between expectations and social realities was becoming apparent to those on both the Left and the Right. African-Americans, realizing that southern racism could not be uprooted without the use of coercive federal power, grew disillusioned by Washington's halfhearted response to their plight. At the same time, conservatives were becoming resentful of federal activism, complaining that it had usurped rights reserved to individuals and the states. It was becoming apparent that Lyndon Johnson planned to build the foundation of his reform agenda on the quicksand of the American paradox.

The Great Society

In the spring of 1964 Johnson coined a phrase meant to define his vision for the presidency. In a commencement speech at the University of Michigan he announced that he hoped to build a great society "where men are more concerned with the quality of their goals than the quantity of their goods." At the heart of the Great Society was a belief that economic growth provided all Americans—rich and poor, urban blacks and rural whites, young and old—with the historic opportunity to forge a new national consensus. Growth would eliminate the need for higher taxes at the same time that it produced a social surplus that would replenish new social programs. Social progress would be painless. *Time* Magazine declared that Johnson added two new phrases to the American vocabulary—"let us reason together," and "I want to be President of all the People."

Not surprisingly, many observers viewed the Great Society as a "second New Deal." The comparisons pleased Johnson, who, on the first day after the election, declared, "I am a Roosevelt New Dealer." Following his victory over Goldwater in November, Johnson and the massive new majority in both Houses launched his Great Society. "Hurry, boys, hurry," he told his aides. "Get that legislation up to the Hill and out. Eighteen months from now ol' Landslide Lyndon will be Lame-Duck Lyndon." The administration's top priorities were to rescue two staples of the Democratic agenda since the Fair Deal that had been held hostage by congressional conservatives: medical insurance for the elderly and education funding for the young. Johnson and his new allies in Congress overwhelmed the opposition. Along with providing medical assistance to people on social security (Medicare), the legislation included a Medicaid program that would pay the medical expenses of the poor regardless of age. "No longer will older Americans be denied the healing miracle of modern medicine," a triumphant Johnson declared. The president also managed to quiet opponents of federal aid to education and convince Congress to pass his Elementary and Secondary Education Act of 1965. Its heart was Title I, which provided more than $1 billion for textbooks, library materials, and special-educational programs for poor children.

Signing a Piece of the Great Society into Law   Lyndon Johnson went further than any previous president to employ the federal government to meet people's needs and solve social problems. Key to his program was ensuring that every American child had an adequate education, from preschool through high school. Johnson, raised in poor, rural Texas, justified his generous education package by claiming that "education is the only valid passport from poverty." Here he signs the bill, accompanied by his first grade teacher at the site of the one-room schoolhouse he attended as a boy. (*Wide World Photos, Inc.*)

Mounting momentum enabled Johnson to push through a wide range of legislation. "The legislation rolled through the House and Senate in such profusion and so methodically," recalled one White House official, "that you seemed part of some vast, overpowering machinery, oiled to purr." In the first six months of 1965 the administration submitted eighty-seven bills to Congress and saw eighty-four of them become law. Congress passed consumer protection acts and provided aid for mass transit, urban development, and slum clearance.

In July, standing in the shadow of the Statue of Liberty, Johnson signed the Immigration Act of 1965. "The bill that we sign today is not a revolutionary bill," he said, but it did "repair a very deep and powerful flaw in the fabric of American justice." Since 1924 the United States had allocated visas in ratios determined by the number of persons of each nationality in the United States in 1890. Not surprisingly, the "national origins" clause favored people from northern Europe, who consumed 98 percent of the quota, leaving only 2 percent for the rest of the world. The new legislation replaced national origins with a family preference system. Congress believed the new law would eliminated discriminatory quotas without producing an increase in the overall number of immigrants or significantly altering the sources of immigration.

In a classic case of unintended consequences, the Immigration Act of 1965 opened the door to an increased flow of immigrants from Asia and Latin America that would profoundly affect American life in the decades ahead. Legislators never considered how family unification could produce a chain of migration that would confound efforts to control immigration. Under the new preference system an engineering student from India could come to the United States to study, find a job after graduating, get labor certification, and become a legal resident alien. His new status would then entitle him to bring over his wife, and six years later, after being naturalized, his brothers and sisters. They in turn could begin the process all over again by sponsoring their wives, husbands, children, and siblings. Within a dozen years one immigrant entering as a skilled worker could generate dozens of visas for distant relatives.

Despite large numbers in the United States, many northern European immigrants lacked the close family ties needed to benefit from the new system. Many came over as single men, applied for jobs, married Americans, and raised families. However, immigrants from southern Europe and especially from Asia emigrated as families and were therefore better positioned to take advantage of the family unification provisions. In the twenty years following the 1965 Immigration Act, the Asian population in the United States soared from 1 million to 5 million; nearly four times as many Asians entered the country during that period as had emigrated in the previous hundred years. Most of these came from a handful of countries: the Philippines, China, Korea, and India.

Johnson made concern for the environment a central tenet of his Great Society. Prodded by the White House, Congress passed legislation mandating tougher regulation of water and air pollution. The Wilderness Act of 1964 set aside over 9 million acres of national forest to be preserved in their unspoiled state. A companion measure, the Wild and Scenic Rivers Act of 1968, similarly protected a number of rivers from the threat of development. The first lady, Lady Bird Johnson, supported environmental awareness as an eloquent and effective leader of a campaign for national beautification.

Whether the Great Society programs were successful is a subject of heated scholarly debate. Supporters point out that programs such as Medicare and Medicaid provided essential medical benefits to the elderly and the poor. One scholar concluded that the combination of social insurance and public aid during the Great Society had a "highly egalitarian effect on income distribution." Critics, however, point out that the middle class, not the poor, was the chief beneficiary of many Great Society programs. By refusing to impose restrictions on what doctors could charge patients, Medicare and Medicaid contributed to spiraling medical costs that benefited doctors. "Medicare-Medicaid," observed the historian Alan Matusow, "primarily transferred income from middle-class taxpayers to middle-class health professionals." A similar problem plagued Johnson's compensatory education program. To avoid raising fears of encroaching government power, Johnson gave local school districts authority for developing and implementing education programs. In a classic case of the "curse of localism," school officials skirted federal guidelines and redirected money toward middle-class students.

Johnson and Civil Rights

After Kennedy's death in November civil-rights supporters looked to Lyndon Johnson for leadership. "For Lyndon Johnson as for John Kennedy," Anthony Lewis wrote in the *New York Times,* "the great challenge from within this country is the cry for justice in race relations." Johnson heard the pleas for reform. Using the skills he had learned from years on the Hill, the president assumed personal control of the fight to pass the civil-rights package. A few days after Kennedy's funeral Johnson called King and told him, "I'm going to try to be all of your hopes." At the same time, he informed Congress that he would not accept any compromise. "I'm not going to cavil and I'm not going to compromise," he told Georgia Democratic senator Richard Russell. "I'm going to pass it just as it is, Dick, and if you get in my way I'm going to run you down."

The president was true to his word. In the House opponents of the legislation attempted to divide liberal forces by adding a provision that would bar employment discrimination against women as well as blacks. But the measure backfired when Congress adopted the amendment without controversy. Still, for seventy-five days opponents filibustered against the bill, until, on June 10, Senate minority leader Everett Dirksen (R-Ill.) announced his support for allowing a vote. The next day, by a 73-27 tally, the Civil Rights Act of 1964 passed the Senate. Three weeks later the House followed suit. On July 2 President Johnson signed the measure into law.

The Civil Rights Act of 1964 was the most far-reaching law of its kind since Reconstruction. The *Congressional Quarterly* called it "the most sweeping civil rights measure to clear either house of Congress in the 20th century." At its heart was a section guaranteeing equal access to public accommodations. The legislation created the Equal Employment Opportunity Commission and charged it with investigating discrimination in employment and included sex, along with race, color, religion, and national origin, as a protected class. Though slow to act, the commission later became a major bulwark in the effort to abolish practices that discriminated against women workers. The law also empowered the government to file school desegregation suits and cut off funds wherever racial discrimination was practiced in the application of federal programs.

Many black leaders believed that racism would never be overcome until blacks exercised political power. In 1964 only 2 million of the South's 5 million voting-age blacks were registered to vote. The Fifteenth Amendment, passed almost a century earlier, had guaranteed the right to vote, but the U.S. system of federalism had allowed states to deny voting privileges through such measures as the poll tax, literacy tests, and grandfather clauses (until 1939). When laws failed to keep blacks off the rolls, segregationists resorted to physical violence and economic intimidation.

In 1964 the Student Nonviolent Coordinating Committee (SNCC) organized a voting rights campaign in Mississippi, where only 5 percent of blacks were registered to vote. The volunteers working to help blacks register included many white college students, and they encountered fierce and sometimes fatal resistance. In June federal agents pulled the decaying bodies of three such workers, Michael Schwerner, James Chaney, and Andrew Goodman, from an earthen dam near Philadelphia, Mississippi. Autopsies showed that Schwerner and Goodman had been shot in the head. Chaney, the only black, had been shot three times and savagely beaten. Before the summer ended, opponents of this Freedom Summer had burned or bombed thirty-five houses, churches, and other buildings. "It was the longest nightmare I have ever had," recalled one organizer.

Despite daily beatings and arrests, the volunteers expanded their program to challenge the state's lily-white Democratic organization. They formed their own Mississippi Freedom Democratic party (MFDP) and elected a separate slate of delegates to the 1964 Democratic National Convention. On August 22 the credentials committee listened to the MFDP's emotional appeal: "Is this America, the land of the free and the home of the brave, where we are threatened daily because we want to live as decent human beings?" asked Fannie Lou Hamer, the daughter of sharecroppers who had lost her job and been evicted from her home because of her organizing efforts. When the regular all-white delegation threatened to walk out if the convention seated the protestors, Johnson feared the controversy would hurt his election in the South. "If you seat those black buggers," Texas governor John Connally warned, "the whole South will walk out." In response, the president offered the dissidents two at-large seats and agreed to bar from future conventions any state delegation that practiced discrimination. The Freedom Democrats rejected the compromise. "We didn't come all this way for no two seats," protested Hamer. In the end, however, Johnson and his liberal allies prevailed and the convention voted to accept the compromise.

The "compromise" at Atlantic City angered many blacks, who no longer felt they could achieve justice through the system, pushing many toward more militant politics. SNCC leader Stokely Carmichael believed that the defeat of the MFDP challenge indicated the need for racial power. The experience showed "not merely that the national conscience was generally unreliable but that, very specifically, black people in Mississippi and throughout this country could not rely on their so-called allies." "Things could never be the same," SNCC's Cleveland Sellers wrote. "Never again were we lulled into believing that our task was exposing injustice so that the 'good' people of America could eliminate them. We left Atlantic City with the knowledge that the movement had turned into something else. After Atlantic City, our struggle was not for civil rights, but for liberation."

A Former Slave Finally Gets the Vote Although the Fifteenth Amendment gave African-Americans the right to vote in 1869, that right was effectively withheld from them through loopholes and discriminatory state legislation. The Voting Rights Act of 1965 authorized the attorney general to suspend local and state regulations that interfered with voter registration. The act transformed southern politics in particular, admitting hundreds of thousands of citizens into the political process for the first time. One hundred years after he was freed from slavery, this 106-year-old Mississippi man registers to vote in Batesville. He is escorted by members of the Mississippi Freedom Democratic Party. *(Corbis-Bettmann.)*

The growing militancy of the movement further complicated King's efforts, making it essential that he score a quick victory in order to restore confidence in his moderate approach. In 1965 King chose Selma, Alabama, as the site of a renewed voting rights campaign. "We are not asking, we are demanding the ballot," he declared, just weeks after accepting the Nobel Peace Prize. Selma was home to 14,400 whites and 15,100 blacks, but its voting roles were 99 percent white and 1 percent black. SNCC workers had spent several frustrating months organizing local residents to vote. But their efforts had reaped few rewards. The chief obstacle was Sheriff Jim Clark, a bulldog-visaged segregationist who led a group of deputy volunteers, many of them members of the Ku Klux Klan. In response to blacks singing "We Shall Overcome," Clark penned a button reading, "Never."

Clark, however, fell into King's trap, the purpose of which was to provoke confrontation. The sheriff steadfastly turned away the waves of blacks who tried to register. During one week more than three thousand protesters were arrested. As police patience wore thin, police actions became more violent. In February a mob of state troopers assaulted a group of blacks, fatally shooting twenty-six-year-old Jimmie Lee Jackson as he tried to protect his mother and grandmother.

Jackson's death inspired black leaders to organize a 54-mile march from Selma to Montgomery to petition Governor George Wallace for protection of blacks registering to vote. On March 7, ignoring an order from Wallace forbidding the march, 650 blacks and a few whites began walking through Selma. Conspicuously absent from the march was Martin Luther King, who, after private pressure from the White House, had returned to Atlanta.

On the other side of the Alabama River a phalanx of 60 state policemen, wearing helmets and gas masks, stood at the foot of the Edmund Pettus Bridge waiting to greet the marchers. After a few tense minutes the patrolmen moved on the protesters, swinging bullwhips and rubber tubing wrapped in barbed wire. White spectators cheered the police on, while Sheriff Clark bellowed, "Get those God Damn niggers!" The marchers stumbled over each other in retreat. The images, shown that evening on all the networks, horrified the nation and pushed the administration into action.

The strategy of massive demonstrations had paid off. Supporters staged marches in Detroit, New York, Chicago, and Los Angeles. Sympathizers in Washington conducted sit-ins at the White House, at the Capitol, and along Pennsylvania Avenue. On March 15 Johnson went before Congress to make his case for a powerful new voting rights bill. Selma, he told the hushed chambers, marked a turning point in American history equal to Lexington and Concord. "Because it is not just Negroes, but really all of us who must overcome the crippling legacy of bigotry and injustice. And," he concluded, "we shall . . . overcome." Martin Luther King called Johnson's speech one of "the most eloquent, unequivocal and passionate pleas for human rights ever made by a President of the United States."

Five months later, on August 6, in the President's Room of the Capitol, where 104 years earlier Abraham Lincoln had signed a bill freeing slaves impressed into the service of the Confederacy, Johnson signed into law the Voting Rights Act of 1965. With a statue of Lincoln to his right, Johnson reflected on when blacks had first come to Jamestown in 1619. "They came in darkness and chains. Today we strike away the last major shackles of those fierce and ancient bonds." The legislation authorized federal examiners to register voters, and it banned the use of literacy tests.

The Voting Rights Act permanently changed race relations in the South. The most dramatic result was in Mississippi. In 1965 just 28,500 blacks, a mere 7 percent of the voting-age population, had been registered; three years later 250,770 blacks were registered. Between 1964 and 1969 the number of black adults registered to vote increased from 19.3 percent to 61.3 percent in Alabama and from 27.4 percent to 60.4 percent in Georgia. One of the many white officerholders removed from office by the surge in black voting was Sheriff Jim Clark, who was defeated in the 1966 Democratic primary.

The legislation also had the unintended consequences of increasing mobilization of white voters and undermining support for the Democratic Party in the South. On the night that Congress passed the act, a somber Johnson told an aide, "I think we've just handed the South over to the Republican Party for the rest of our lives." The prediction proved painfully accurate for Democrats. Despite the massive mobilization of black voters between 1960 and 1980, the increase of white registration surpassed black by almost five to one. Before 1964 nearly 55 percent of all southern counties voted consistently Democratic in presidential elections. By 1980 that number had dropped to only 14 percent. While many forces conspired to erode Democratic support in the once-solid South, race ranked at the top of the list.

The Reforms of the Warren Court

The same activist spirit that guided the president and Congress infused the third branch of government—the courts. Under the leadership of Chief Justice Earl Warren, the Supreme Court asserted its right to review and declare unconstitutional legislation that it believed infringed on individual rights. A group of liberal judges—especially William O. Douglas, Hugo Black, and William J. Brennan Jr.—formed a powerful coalition in favor of liberal ideas. Kennedy's 1962 appointment of Secretary of Labor Arthur Goldberg to the Court guaranteed a liberal majority. Acting on its philosophy, the Court issued several landmark rulings.

On civil rights liberal justices built on the foundation of *Brown* v. *Board of Education* (1954) by upholding the right of demonstrators to participate in public protests. The Court disallowed the use of the poll tax in state and local elections and in 1967 struck at the core of white supremacy doctrine in *Loving* v. *Virginia* by declaring laws prohibiting interracial marriages to be unconstitutional.

The Court extended the definition of individual rights to other explosive social issues. In the early 1960s twelve states required Bible reading in public schools. Children in New York State recited a nonsectarian Christian prayer: "Almighty God, we acknowledge our dependence upon Thee, and we beg Thy blessings upon us, our parents, our teachers and our country." The Supreme Court, in *Engel* v. *Vitale* (1962), ruled the New York prayer unconstitutional on the grounds that it was a religious activity that placed an "indirect coercive pressure upon religious minorities."

Nowhere did the Court break more decisively with the past than in the area of sexual freedom. In 1965, in *Griswold* v. *Connecticut,* the Court struck down a Connecticut statute banning the sale of contraceptives. In a ruling that would influence future debates about a woman's right to an abortion, Justice William O. Douglas wrote that the Constitution guaranteed "a right to privacy." In *Jacobellis* v. *Ohio* (1964), the Court ruled that states could not ban sexually explicit material unless "it is found to be utterly without redeeming social value." Under that standard nearly all restrictions on the right of an adult to obtain sexually explicit material vanished.

A number of decisions overruled local electoral practices that had prevented full participation in the political process. In 1962 the Court ruled in *Baker* v. *Carr* that the state of Tennessee had to reapportion its legislature to reflect changes in the population. The Court expanded on the ruling two years later when, in *Reynolds* v. *Sims,* it established the principle of "one man, one vote." Legislative districts, the Court ruled, had to be apportioned so that they represented equal numbers of people. "Legislators represent people, not acres or trees," Warren said.

Perhaps the Court's most controversial decisions concerned criminal justice. In *Gideon* v. *Wainwright* (1963), the Court ruled that a pauper accused in state courts of a felony had to be provided an attorney at public expense. The following year, in *Escobedo* v. *Illinois,* it voided the murder confession of a man who had been denied permission to see his lawyer. In the most controversial criminal-rights case, *Miranda* v. *Arizona* (1966), a divided Court required police to inform suspected criminals of their right to remain silent and to have an attorney present during interrogation.

This expansion of judicial activism touched a raw nerve among Americans fearful of encroaching federal power. One congressman said that the justices were "a greater threat to this Union than the entire confines of Soviet Russia." Rulings on pornography, school prayer, and contraception outraged Catholics, fundamentalists, and other religious groups. Reverend Billy Graham called the decision banning school prayer part of a "diabolical scheme" that was "taking God and moral teaching from the schools" and ushering in a "deluge of juvenile delinquency." The Court's involvement in apportionment offended traditionalists, who charged that questions of representation were best handled by elected leaders. The Court's rulings on criminal rights irked white, middle-class Americans worried about rising crime. A 1966 poll showed that 65 percent of Americans opposed recent rulings on criminal rights.

Vietnam: The Decision to Escalate

Like Kennedy, Johnson was torn between his commitment to preventing a communist victory in Vietnam and his reluctance to get pulled into a major confrontation in Southeast Asia. Like others of his generation, Johnson had learned the lessons of Munich. Johnson, in a press conference in 1965, explained that America's defeat in South Vietnam "would encourage and spur on those who seek to conquer all free nations within their reach. This is the clearest lesson of our time." He continued, "From Munich until today we have learned that to yield to aggression brings only greater threats."

The president's key advisers, all leftovers from the Kennedy administration, expressed no doubts. They urged a strong U.S. military response to the deteriorating situation in Saigon. In March 1964 North Vietnam sent 23,000 fresh recruits south, swelling the ranks of the Vietcong. North Vietnam improved and extended the Ho Chi Minh Trail, a network of trails and roads on which supplies flowed south. The increased military pressure added to the political instability in the South. Desertions in South Vietnam's military, the Army of the Republic of Vietnam, reached epidemic levels, exceeding 6,000 a month in 1964. The Central Intelligence Agency estimated that the Vietcong controlled up to 40 percent of the territory of South Vietnam and more than 50 percent of the people.

The president's senior advisers believed the war could not be won without severing the flow of supplies from North Vietnam. They recommended a campaign of strategic bombing both to shore up the government in the South and to send a clear signal of U.S. resolve to the North. In March the Joint Chiefs of Staff advocated a "progressive and selective attack" against targets in North Vietnam.

Like Kennedy, Johnson dreaded getting mired in a protracted ground war in Southeast Asia. A wider war, he feared, would distract attention from his Great Society programs and provide critics with ammunition to scale back domestic spending. He told biographer Doris Kearns "that bitch of a war" would destroy "the woman I really loved—the Great Society." Remembering the chastising Harry Truman had received when China "fell" to the communists, Johnson told the U.S. ambassador to Vietnam, "I am not going to be the president who saw Vietnam go the way China went."

Privately, Johnson anguished over the war, often questioning whether the United States could win a military struggle in Southeast Asia. In private conversations he recorded on the White House taping system, made public in 2001, the president described himself as "depressed" and "scared to death" about the conflict. On the one hand he was convinced that the United States needed to expand the war in order to maintain its credibility, but on the other hand he doubted whether the nation could win a war in Vietnam. "If you let a bully come in and chase you out of your front yard," he said, "tomorrow he'll be on your porch, and the next day he'll rape your wife in your own bed." But Johnson feared that the United States could not defeat the Vietcong "bully" without using nuclear weapons and "kicking off World War III." At one point early in the conflict he cried to Lady Bird; "I can't get out [of Vietnam], and I can't finish it with what I have got. And I don't know what the hell to do!" Trying to decide what to do about Vietnam, he told her, was "like being in an airplane—and I have to choose between crashing the plane or jumping out. I do not have a parachute."

Despite his private doubts, the president approved the recommendation of his military advisers calling for an incremental escalation in Vietnam. Before implementing the new tactics, Johnson wanted to neutralize potential critics by securing congressional support for a wider war. He needed a dramatic incident to convince the nation to support his plans. He did not have to wait long. On August 4, 1964, while operating in heavy seas about 60 miles off the North Vietnamese coast in the Tonkin Gulf, the U.S. destroyers *C. Turner Joy* and *Maddox* reported they were under attack by North Vietnamese torpedo boats. Neither saw any enemy boats, however, and afterward crew members speculated that poor weather conditions may have contributed to the confusion. Johnson expressed doubts. "For all I know our navy might have been shooting at whales out there," he said.

The reported attack nonetheless gave Johnson the opportunity he needed to establish congressional support for his actions in Vietnam. With little debate and strong public support, Congress overwhelmingly ratified the Gulf of Tonkin Resolution, which authorized the president to take "all necessary measures to repel any armed attacks against the forces of the United States and to prevent further aggression." The resolution provided the legislative foundation for the Vietnam War. As Lyndon Johnson observed, it was "like Grandma's nightshirt, it covers everything."

PRIMARY SOURCE

8.2 | *The Gulf of Tonkin Resolution, 1964*

After the reported attacks on the *Maddox* and the *C. Turner Joy,* Congress voted in favor of the Gulf of Tonkin Resolution. Passed on August 7, 1964, the resolution gave President Johnson permission to expand America's mission in Vietnam and opened the way for Johnson to send ground troops.

Whereas naval units of the Communist regime in [North] Vietnam, in violation of the principles of the Charter of the United Nations and of international law, have deliberately and repeatedly attacked United States naval vessels lawfully present in international waters, and have thereby created a serious threat
5 to international peace; and

Whereas these attacks are part of a deliberate and systematic campaign of aggression that the Communist regime in North Vietnam has been waging against its neighbors and the nations joined with them in the collective defense of their freedom; and

10 Whereas the United States is assisting the peoples of southeast Asia to protect their freedom and has no territorial, military, or political ambitions in that area, but desires only that these peoples should be left in peace to work out their own destinies in their own way: Now, therefore, be it

Resolved by the Senate and House of Representatives of the United States of
15 *America in Congress assembled,* That the Congress approves and supports the determination of the President, as Commander in Chief, to take all necessary measures to repel any armed attack against the forces of the United States and to prevent further aggression.

Sec. 2. The United States regards as vital to its national interest and to world
20 peace the maintenance of international peace and security in southeast Asia. Consonant with the Constitution of the United States and the Charter of the United Nations and in accordance with its obligations under the Southeast Asia Collective Defense Treaty, the United States is, therefore, prepared, as the President determines, to take all necessary steps, including the use of armed force, to
25 assist any member or protocol state of the Southeast Asia Collective Defense Treaty requesting assistance in defense of its freedom.

Sec. 3. This resolution shall expire when the President shall determine that the peace and security of the area is reasonably assured by international conditions created by action of the United Nations or otherwise, except that it may be termi-
30 nated earlier by concurrent resolution of the Congress. ■ ■ ■

Armed with congressional support for a wider war, Johnson considered further action, asking his civilian and military leaders for recommendations that would produce "maximum results and minimum danger." On August 27 the Joint Chiefs of Staff declared that "an accelerated program of actions" was now "essential to prevent a complete collapse of the U.S. position in Southeast Asia." Seeing the conflict as a military problem with its roots in North Vietnam, they recommended intense air strikes and the commitment of a large American ground force. Senior civilian advisers viewed the conflict as a political issue resulting from the weakness of the South Vietnamese government. As a result, they stressed pacification programs combined with an effective counterinsurgency program in the South. But Undersecretary of State George Ball rejected the premise of intervention, arguing that Vietnam was not a vital American interest. In a brilliant sixty-page, single-spaced memorandum he systematically challenged every argument used to support the U.S. commitment to South Vietnam. He took special aim at the logic for bombing. "Once on the tiger's back," he observed, "we can not be sure of picking the place to dismount."

PRIMARY SOURCE

8.3 | *Memorandum for the President*

GEORGE BALL

While many members of Johnson's staff supported escalation of the war in Vietnam, Undersecretary of State George Ball did not. In a July 1965 memorandum to President Johnson, Ball warned of the futility of American military intervention and recommended an alternative solution, which Johnson rejected.

A Compromise Solution in South Vietnam

(1) A Losing War: The South Vietnamese are losing the war to the Viet Cong. No one can assure you that we can beat the Viet Cong or even force them to the conference table on our terms, no matter how many hundred thousand *white, foreign* (U.S.) troops we deploy.

5   No one has demonstrated that a white ground force of whatever size can win a guerrilla war—which is at the same time a civil war between Asians—in jungle terrain in the midst of a population that refuses cooperation to the white forces (and the South Vietnamese) and thus provides a great intelligence advantage to the other side. Three recent incidents vividly illustrate this point: (a) the sneak

10   attack on the Da Nang Air Base which involved penetration of a defense perimeter guarded by 9,000 Marines. This raid was possible only because of the cooperation of the local inhabitants; (b) the B-52 raid that failed to hit the Viet Cong who had obviously been tipped off; (c) the search and destroy mission of the

15 173rd Air Borne Brigade which spent three days looking for the Viet Cong, suffered 23 casualties, and never made contact with the enemy who had obviously gotten advance word of their assignment.

   (2) The Question to Decide: Should we limit our liabilities in South Vietnam and try to find a way out with minimal long-term costs?

20   The alternative—no matter what we may wish it to be—is almost certainly a protracted war involving an open-ended commitment of U.S. forces, mounting U.S. casualties, no assurance of a satisfactory solution, and a serious danger of escalation at the end of the road.

   (3) Need for a Decision Now: So long as our forces are restricted to advising
25 and assisting the South Vietnamese, the struggle will remain a civil war between Asian peoples. Once we deploy substantial numbers of troops in combat it will become a war between the U.S. and a large part of the population of South Vietnam, organized and directed from North Vietnam and backed by the resources of both Moscow and Peiping.

30   The decision you face now, therefore, is crucial. Once large numbers of U.S. troops are committed to direct combat, they will begin to take heavy casualties in a war they are ill-equipped to fight in a non-cooperative if not downright hostile countryside.

   Once we suffer large casualties, we will have started a well-nigh irreversible
35 process. Our involvement will be so great that we cannot—without national humiliation—stop short of achieving our complete objectives. *Of the two possibilities I think humiliation would be more likely than the achievement of our objectives—even after we have paid terrible costs.*

   (4) Compromise Solution: Should we commit U.S. manpower and prestige to
40 a terrain so unfavorable as to give a very large advantage to the enemy—or should we seek a compromise settlement which achieves less than our stated objectives and thus cut our losses while we still have the freedom of maneuver to do so.

   (5) Costs of a Compromise Solution: The answer involves a judgment as to the cost to the U.S. of such a compromise settlement in terms of our relations with the
45 countries in the area of South Vietnam, the credibility of our commitments, and our prestige around the world. In my judgment, if we act before we commit a substantial U.S. force to combat in South Vietnam we can, by accepting some short-term costs, avoid what may well be a long-term catastrophe. I believe we tended grossly to exaggerate the costs involved in a compromise settlement. An apprecia-
50 tion of probable costs is contained in the attached memorandum.   ■ ■ ■

By the end of 1964 Johnson had agreed to a phased escalation of the Vietnam War. He waited for the right opportunity to implement his new strategy. When the Vietcong launched the mortar attack against Pleiku, Johnson initiated "a carefully orchestrated bombing attack" against the North. The bombing accomplished none of its objectives. The enemy intensified its efforts, and the political situation in the South continued to deteriorate. In March 1965 the administration responded by launching Operation Rolling Thunder, the sustained bombing of North Vietnam that would last until 1968. Once again Johnson privately expressed doubts that an expanded military effort in Vietnam would produce an

American victory. "Now we're off to bombing these people," he was recorded telling McNamara as he gave the bombing order on February 26. "We're over that hurdle. I don't think anything is going to be as bad as losing, and I don't see any way of winning."

At first the president kept tight control of the bombing, claiming that the pilots "can't even bomb an outhouse without my approval." However, by spring he had loosened his control, authorized the use of napalm, and allowed pilots to drop their deadly cargoes without prior approval. Instead of intimidating the North Vietnamese, the bombing raids only stiffened their resolve; the flow of arms into the South actually increased. By the spring of 1965 more than 6,500 regular North Vietnamese troops were moving south to join the indigenous Vietcong. In March 1965 the U.S. military estimated that Vietcong forces totaled about 48,000 troops, a significant increase in one year. America believed that its commitment to South Vietnam would deter Chinese aggression. Just the opposite occurred: Chinese leader Mao Zedong promised assistance to the North, beginning a flow of arms that would continue throughout the war. The South Vietnamese government, weakened by corruption and constant political intrigue, seemed incapable of stemming the communist advance. "The situation is very disturbing," McNamara informed the president at the end of 1964. "Current trends, unless reversed in the next 2–3 months, will lead to neutralization at best and more likely to a Communist-controlled state."

The deteriorating military situation frustrated Johnson, who complained that a "raggedy-ass, fourth rate country like North Vietnam [could] be causing so much trouble." In April 1965 Johnson tried another tact, offering the Vietnamese a foreign version of his Great Society. At a speech at Johns Hopkins University Johnson promised "an investment" of $1 billion to rebuild the Mekong River in the North. The river, he said, could "provide food and water and power on a scale to dwarf even our own TVA." After the speech Johnson assured his press secretary that "old Ho can't turn me down." Just in case Ho rejected the offer, which he did, Johnson still believed the United States could impose a military solution on the problem.

The Joint Chiefs of Staff pressed the president for both unlimited bombing of the North and the aggressive use of American ground troops in the South. "You must take the fight to the enemy," declared the chairman of the Joint Chiefs. "No one ever won a battle sitting on his ass." In mid-July McNamara recommended sending 100,000 combat troops, more than doubling the number already there. Again Ball was the lone voice of dissent in the administration, telling the president he had "serious doubt that an army of westerners can successfully fight Orientals in an Asian jungle."

In July 1965 Johnson, enacting a decision made months earlier, announced that he was committing American ground forces to offensive operations in Vietnam. He scaled back McNamara's request for 100,000 troops to 50,000, though privately he assured the military that he would commit another 50,000 before the end of the year. While planning for war, Johnson talked about peace, deliberately misleading Congress and the American people about his intended escalation of the conflict. While confidently predicting victory in public, he privately feared defeat. Unwilling to distract attention from his Great Society programs, he refused to admit that he had dramatically increased America's involvement in Vietnam.

America's War

To lead the combat troops in Vietnam, Johnson chose General William West-moreland, a veteran of World War II and former superintendent of West Point. Westmoreland planned to limit ground action to "search-and-destroy" missions launched from fortified bases in the countryside. Rather than confronting the enemy in large-scale ground assaults, he would depend on firepower from ground artillery, helicopter gunships, fighter aircraft, and B-52 bombers. "We'll just go on bleeding them," he said, "until Hanoi wakes up to the fact that they have bled their country to the point of national disaster for generations."

Westmoreland's optimism proved premature. The air war failed to sever the flow of supplies between North and South. Thousands of peasants worked daily to rebuild parts of the Ho Chi Minh Trail damaged by American bombs. By the time the war ended, the Ho Chi Minh Trail had 12,500 miles of roads, complete with

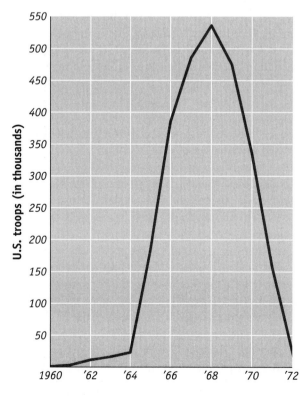

American Troop Levels in Vietnam After Johnson's decision to send marines to Danang in 1965, the American presence in Vietnam skyrocketed. Not until the Tet Offensive in 1968, though, did Americans begin loudly to demand an end to the war. The outcry led to the election of a new president in 1968 and the de-escalation of American ground forces in Vietnam.

portable bridges, underground fuel storage tanks, hospitals, and supply warehouses. By 1967 some 6,000 tons of supplies arriving in North Vietnam daily from China and the Soviet Union diluted the effects of the bombing. Since the North had an agricultural economy with few industries vital to the war effort, aerial sorties against cities in North Vietnam had little impact on supplies. The civilian toll, however, was heavy. All told, U.S. bombs killed an estimated 100,000 North Vietnamese civilians.

Vietnam, to 1968   Despite the number of soldiers (see graph, page 208): and military bases in South Vietnam and Thailand, American troops could not confine and fight an enemy as mobile as the North Vietnamese. With a constant supply line, known as the Ho Chi Minh trail, the North Vietnamese circumvented the border between the North and South, smuggling men and supplies through Laos and Cambodia to supporters in the South. The Tet Offensive of 1968 showed the effectiveness of the trail and perseverance of the North.

Unable to win the war from the air, the administration gradually increased the number of ground troops, from 184,000 in late 1965 to more than 500,000 in 1968. The Vietcong continued its guerrilla tactics, avoiding fixed positions and striking from ambush. By the end of 1967 more than 16,000 U.S. soldiers had lost their lives, with more than 10,000 killed in the previous twelve months alone. Hanoi's strategy was to fight a war of attrition, confident that American public opinion would sour on an inconclusive war. As the U.S. death count mounted, North Vietnamese general Vo Nguyen Giap predicted, "their mothers will want to know why. The war will not long survive their questions."

Along with trying to crush the enemy with massive bombing and a ground war, the United States launched a pacification and nation-building program in South Vietnam to build support for the noncommunist regime in Saigon. But the military effort directly undermined the political goals. By the end of 1968 almost 4 million South Vietnamese had lost their homes in aerial bombardments. Between 1965 and 1972 more than 1.4 million civilians died or were wounded by American forces. One American official observed, "It was as if we were trying to build a house with a bulldozer and wrecking crane."

The military's failure in Vietnam, despite its enormous advantages in firepower, underscored the fundamental problem with America's Vietnam policy. Blinded by a rigid anticommunism, American policy makers rejected the nationalist impulse behind the Vietnamese revolution. Insisting on viewing Ho as a puppet of Soviet and Chinese aggression, the United States aided in the transformation of a local struggle into a superpower conflict. "We both overestimated the effect of South Vietnam's loss on the security of the West and failed to adhere to the fundamental principle that, in the final analysis, if the South Vietnamese were to be saved, they had to win the war themselves," the contrite former Secretary of Defense Robert McNamara reflected in 1995.

The Soldier's War

Who fought in Vietnam? From 1964 to 1973, 2.2 million men were drafted, 8.7 million enlisted, and 16 million did not serve. The average age of American soldiers in Vietnam was nineteen. In World War II the average American solider was twenty-six years old. The estimated total of women who served in Vietnam, including those employed by private organizations like the Red Cross, ranged from 33,000 to over 50,000.

The majority of the young men who fought in Vietnam came from either poor or working-class backgrounds. Many youth from middle-class families used a liberal student deferment policy to avoid the draft. In 1969 *Newsday* traced the family backgrounds of 400 men from Long Island who had been killed in Vietnam. "As a group," the newspaper concluded, "Long Island's war dead have been overwhelmingly white, working-class men. Their parents were typically blue collar or clerical workers, mailmen, factory workers, building tradesmen, and so on." Class was far more important than race in determining the overall social composition of American forces. Beginning in 1965 when African-Americans accounted for 24 percent of all army combat deaths, the Defense Department undertook a concerted campaign to reduce the minority share of the fighting. By 1970 blacks made up only 9 percent of combat troops in Vietnam.

Early in the war most men went to Vietnam confident they were doing the right thing. "There was nothing we could not do because we were Americans," wrote Philip Caputo, who joined the Marines in 1960 looking forward to a "splendid little war." At one end of the spectrum service in Vietnam could be easy for the those working in the rear handling paperwork, moving supplies, helping the wounded. For soldiers in the field it could be hell. Climate and country imposed horrible conditions. Malaria, blackwater fever, and dysentery took their toll. "Our days were spent hacking through mountainous jungles," Caputo remembered. "At night we squatted in muddy holes, picked off the leeches that sucked on our veins, and waited for an attack to come rushing at us from the blackness beyond the perimeter wire."

An American Soldier Crawling Through a Vietnamese Rice Paddy American soldiers in Vietnam experienced an untold number of challenges in the jungles of Vietnam. The military rotated soldiers in and out of Vietnam every twelve months, meaning that just as a soldier became acclimated to the region and began to understand the military's objectives, his tour of duty ended. High humidity, months of rain, dense jungle forests, and tangled rice paddies added to the frustration and misery soldiers (like this soldier, photographed in 1966) endured as they sought an enemy they could not find and fought a war that a growing number of Americans did not support.

Combat involved constant patrolling, days and days of suspense waiting for an ambush or a booby trap, and then a short, intense firefight followed by more suspense. The war was fought not on set battlefields but in villages and rice paddies. The strategy for victory eluded most ground soldiers. No clear objectives were set; no territory was captured. Units swept across the same area repeatedly, taking casualties each time, never seeming to achieve any lasting effect. One day they were trying to win the "hearts and minds" of local villagers; the next day they had orders to destroy the village. A chopper pilot commented bitterly: "Vietnam, man. Bomb 'em and feed 'em, bomb 'em and feed 'em." Repeated over and over, such actions bred a sense of hopelessness.

In a war of attrition, as Vietnam had become, the "body count" was the primary measure of success. It inflicted a terrible emotional toll on the nineteen-year-olds ordered to fight. "What am I doing here?" asked a young solider. "We don't take any land. We don't give it back. We just mutilate bodies." The tragic consequences of that policy played out in March 1968 when an American platoon led by Lieutenant William L. Calley descended on the tiny village of My Lai. Not a single shot was fired at them, and almost no men of military age were present in the village. Nonetheless, the American soldiers slaughtered more than 450 people. In an orgy of violence they gang-raped girls, blew apart children with hand grenades, slaughtered domestic animals, and burned the village to the ground.

In the final years of the war as American troop withdrawals increased, many soldiers refused to risk their lives in what they believed was a futile effort. Who wanted to be, asked Lieutenant John Kerry, "the last man to die in Vietnam?" Desertion and absent-without-leave rates skyrocketed. Incidents of *fragging*—the term soldiers used to describe the assassination of overzealous officers—multiplied. Drug abuse reached epidemic proportions. In 1969 the Pentagon estimated that nearly two-thirds of combat soldiers had used marijuana, while one-third had tried heroin. "What the hell is going on?" asked a bewildered general. "Is this a goddamned army or a mental hospital?"

The change in tone from the expansive optimism of JFK, who promised to "bear any burden" to defend freedom around the world, to a frustrated Johnson, burdened by a war that he could not understand or win, symbolized the perils of the American paradox. Johnson had the misfortune of presiding over a nation that was forced to confront the contradiction between its expansive expectations of change and its commitment to older notions of limited government. At home Johnson's war on poverty served as a fitting symbol of a reform approach that tried to solve major social problems without challenging existing notions of government power. Abroad Johnson struggled to uphold America's global commitment to resisting the spread of communism in Vietnam without sacrificing his domestic agenda or requiring full mobilization. Perhaps the greatest victim of the 1960s was the cherished notion of an American consensus.

The irony was that Johnson's desire to preserve a fragile consensus by obscuring the true nature of the war divided the nation. His yearning to maintain credibility by fighting in Vietnam eroded his authority and diminished America's stature in the world. And his faith that economic growth could sustain reform at home and a war abroad produced spiraling inflation that crippled the economy. The decade exposed not only Johnson's personal limitations but also the flawed assumptions of the vital center.

SELECTED READINGS

▌ Irving Bernstein's comprehensive *Guns or Butter* (1996) chronicles the many significant accomplishments of Johnson's Great Society and balances them against the compromises necessitated by the escalation of the Vietnam War. John A. Andrew offers a brief overview in *Lyndon Johnson and the Great Society* (1998). Robert Caro's critical biography, *The Years of Lyndon Johnson: Path to Power* (1982) and *Means of Ascent* (1990), needs to be balanced with Robert Dalleck's masterful volumes, *Lone Star Rising* (1991) and *Flawed Giant* (1998). James T. Patterson's *America's Struggle Against Poverty, 1900–1994* (1995) analyzes the fateful consequences of the Great Society's "welfare explosion" from the longer-term perspective of modern poverty policy and its implementation. Michael Beschloss uses White House tape recordings to provide a rare glimpse inside the Johnson administration in *Taking Charge* (1997). The media's role in the Johnson presidency and the war in Vietnam is the focus of Kathleen Turner's *Lyndon Johnson's Dual War* (1986).

▌ J. Harvie Wilkinson discusses the evolution of Supreme Court decisions concerning school integration in his instructive *From Brown to Bakke* (1979), underlining the increasingly expansive definition of the Court's role in national life. Alexander Bickel's collected lectures, *The Supreme Court and the Idea of Progress* (rev. ed., 1978), critique the Court's "subjective" approach to jurisprudence, arguing that the judiciary had become overburdened in its attempt to redress social problems. Lucas Powe in *The Warren Court and American Politics* (2000) argues that the Court worked to impose national liberal-elite values on the country. In *Earl Warren* (1982), G. Edward White discusses the formative influences on Warren's progressive world-view and the ways they revealed themselves in public life. Anthony Lewis brings to life the personal stakes of judicial activism in his classic account of one man's extraordinary involvement in a landmark criminal-rights decision, *Gideon's Trumpet* (1964).

▌ John Dittmer's history of the civil-rights movement in Mississippi, *Local People* (1994), reveals the commitment and grit of ordinary people that sustained an extraordinary social movement. Doug McAdam's *Freedom Summer* (1988) studies the impact of SNCC's watershed moment on a generation of activists. David Garrow's *Bearing the Cross* (1986) is a Pulitzer Prize–winning biography that digs deep into the complex life of Martin Luther King. Robert Loevy examines the civil rights events that stirred Kennedy and Johnson to action and the strategies for getting Congress to pass the Civil Right Act of 1964 in *To End All Segregation* (1990).

▌ The literature on the conduct of the Vietnam War is immense. George Herring's *America's Longest War* (2nd ed., 1986) and Stanley Karnow's *Vietnam* (1983) are good starting points. On the fateful decision to send troops, see Larry Berman's *Planning a Tragedy* (1982). Neil Sheehan captures the tragic dimensions of Americans' commitment to winning the war in his elegantly written *A Bright Shining Lie* (1988). *In Retrospect* (1995) offers Robert McNamara's reflections on mistakes made and lessons learned, while H. R. McMaster picks apart the decisions McNamara made that contributed to the disaster in Vietnam in *Dereliction of Duty* (1997). The impact of the war on the American men who fought in it, especially those from poor families, is detailed in Christian Appy's *Working-Class War* (1993).

Challenging the Consensus, 1960–1969

On August 15, 1969, a half-million like-minded young people gathered on Max Yasgur's 600-acre farm near Bethel, New York, for a weekend festival of "peace and love and music." Known as Woodstock, the festival included a stellar lineup of musical talent: Jimi Hendrix, the Who, the Grateful Dead, Joe Cocker, Janis Joplin, and Sly and the Family Stone, among others. "It was a very magical, once-in-a-lifetime thing to be part of," said guitarist Carlos Santana. Whether they attended the concert or not, those who came of age during the 1960s embraced Woodstock's freedom-espousing spirit: Hendrix's screaming guitar rendition of the national anthem, rampant drug use, sexual freedom, long hair and bell-bottoms. "Everyone swam nude in the lake," recalled one participant, "balling was easier than getting breakfast, and the 'pigs' just smiled and passed out the oats."

Not everyone experienced the magic of Woodstock, however. Organizers, who had expected about 150,000 people, were overwhelmed by the size of the crowds. Tickets were priced to sell for $18, but the organizers had failed to have fences installed or ticket booths set up, so it turned into a free event. Heavy rains turned the grounds into a mud pit. There were traffic jams that led many people to abandon their cars miles from the site. There was such a severe shortage of water, food, and medical and sanitation facilities that New York governor Nelson Rockefeller declared a state of emergency. "I went to Woodstock and I hated it," recalled singer Billy Joel. "I think a lot of that community 'spirit' was based on the fact that everybody was so wasted."

Many contemporary observers congratulated Woodstock for its celebration of community and its clear statement about the power of young people. The three-day celebration

The Counterculture at the Woodstock Music Festival For three days, August 15–17, 1969, the counterculture took center stage at the Woodstock music festival, held on a farm outside Bethel, New York. Organizers booked some of the greatest music artists of the baby-boom generation, but failed to anticipate the number of rock music fans that would descend on Woodstock. As a result the crowd, estimated at around 400,000, found that there were few facilities available. Despite the crowded conditions and the persistent rain that turned the festival's grounds into a muddy mess, those assembled enjoyed themselves in the true spirit of the counterculture—with three days of sex, drugs, and rock and roll.

could hardly capture the diversity of an entire generation, but it did serve as a metaphor for the younger generation's desire to challenge the political and cultural establishment. Lyndon Johnson had built his vision of a great society on the vital-center belief that America had forged a national consensus in favor of gradual change achieved through economic growth and activist government. The 1960s shattered the consensus, produced intense ideological clashes between the New Left and New Right, exposed profound racial conflict, and polarized American politics and culture for the rest of the century. Violent confrontations over Vietnam and race relations clarified the tension between American ideals and social realities and uncovered the painful paradox of postwar America.

The Youth Culture

Young Americans in the 1960s were not the first to speak against the injustice and hypocrisy of their elders, but social and demographic forces provided this generation with new clout. The postwar baby boom had dramatically increased the number of college-age students in America. In 1965, 41 percent of all Americans were under the age of twenty. College enrollments soared from 3.6 million in 1960 to almost 8 million in 1970. Because colleges contained the largest concentration of young people in the country, they became the seedbed of youth protest.

In the 1950s "Beat" poets and artists had begun to decry American materialism and complacency. Writer Jack Kerouac, author of the best-selling novel *On the Road* (1957), coined the term *Beat* to express the "weariness with all the forms of the modern industrial state." In 1955 poet Allen Ginsberg, a Jew and homosexual who was deeply versed in Zen Buddhism, emerged as one of the leaders of the movement when he recited his poem "Howl" to a small audience in San Francisco. "Howl" railed against "robot apartments! invincible suburbs! skeleton treasuries! blind capitals! demonic industries!" The Beats embraced open sexuality and free drug use as keys to spiritual liberation.

By the early 1960s the Beat message, popularized in inexpensive paperback novels, television, and movies, had gained wide acceptance among young people and formed the backbone of the "counterculture" movement. The movement lacked a coherent ideology but shared a core of attitudes and beliefs. In search of a "higher consciousness," the counterculture rejected the tenets of modern industrial society: materialism, self-denial, sexual repression, and the work ethic. To the alarm of many older Americans, counterculture fashion promoted long hair for men, eastern symbols, and clothes purchased from the Salvation Army.

Drug use was part of the message. The prophet of the new drug culture was Timothy Leary, a Harvard psychologist who preached to his students (and anyone else who would listen) about the wonders of magic mushrooms and LSD. "Tune in, turn on, drop out," he advised the young. LSD was widely available on college campuses, and many of the world's most popular rock groups used it and wrote songs about it. According to *Life* magazine, by 1966 over 1 million people had experimented with LSD. But the drug of choice for the young remained marijuana. By 1969 more than 30 percent of all college students in the United States had smoked pot.

Sexual expression and freedom were central to the counterculture's rejection of mainstream morality. The media offered extensive coverage of "Summer of Love" festivals. Music, which once celebrated the wonders of dating, soon made explicit reference to sex acts. In 1964 the Beatles topped the charts with "I Want to Hold Your Hand." By 1967 they were singing, "Why don't we do it in the road?" During the decade sexual images became a part of the nation's public culture. By 1970 there were 830 adults-only bookstores and 200 theaters showing hardcore sex films. An estimated 45 million pieces of sexually oriented material were sent through the mail each year. Studies showed that roughly 80 percent of boys and 70 percent of girls had seen visual depictions or read descriptions of sexual intercourse by the age of eighteen.

The ability to enjoy sex without the burden of procreation was enhanced by new methods of birth control. Developed in 1957 and licensed by the Food and Drug Administration in 1960, the birth control pill—which quickly became known as "the pill"—gave women a greater sense of sexual freedom than any previous contraceptive device had done. It was an instant success. By 1962 an estimated 1,187,000 women were using the pill. Ten years later 10 million women were doing so. *Time* magazine called it "a miraculous tablet." The pill divorced sex from the danger of unwanted pregnancy. It gave women the freedom to have sex when and where they wished and made contraception acceptable to the mainstream. "Gone are the days when women live in terror of the sexual embrace because it means still another pregnancy, still another year of sickness, another child to care for," a feminist wrote. The pill put birth control on the front pages of newspapers and on the cover of magazines, forcing people to confront the gap between public morality and private behavior.

The counterculture also defined itself through music. Bob Dylan's rapid rise to fame was emblematic of the newly emerging cultural sensibility. Dylan, born Robert Zimmerman in Hibbing, Minnesota, joined the New York Greenwich Village folk music scene in 1961. Blending poetic economy with poetic diction, Dylan accompanied himself on an acoustic guitar and wore a harmonica supported by a shoulder brace. His hugely successful second album, *The Freewheelin' Bob Dylan* (1963), which included political songs such as "A Hard Rain's Gonna Fall," "The Times They Are A-Changin'," and "Blowin' in the Wind," sold two hundred thousand copies in two months. The last song, with its call to political action and challenge to consensus—"How many times can a man turn his head pretending he just doesn't see?"—sold more than 1 million copies. The following month the folk group Peter, Paul, and Mary released their own single of "Blowin' in the Wind" that sold over three hundred thousand copies in less than two weeks.

After 1964 Dylan had to compete with a host of new rock bands from England. The most popular, the Beatles, captured the hearts of teenage America following a TV appearance on the popular *Ed Sullivan Show* in 1964. Initially, the Beatles, with ties, jackets, and well-kempt, if long, hair, hoped to reach a mass consumer market by avoiding a clear association with the counterculture. But their music, which seemed to mock the adult world, contained a message of freedom and excitement that belied their sometimes subdued lyrics. By 1967, however, with the release of *Sergeant Pepper's Lonely Hearts Club Band,* the Beatles were celebrating their new role as cultural antagonists. "When the Beatles told us to turn off our minds and float downstream," recalled one fan, "uncounted youngsters assumed that the key to this kind of mind-expansion could be found in a plant or a pill."

The Beatles changed their tune, in part, to keep ahead of other groups that were gaining widespread popularity by preaching a more potent message. In 1967 Mick Jagger, lead singer of the Rolling Stones, also a British import, was arousing young audiences with a mixture of anger and sexual prowess. During concerts Jagger would thrust the microphone between his legs and whip the floor with a leather belt in a blatantly erotic demonstration. "The Beatles want to hold your hand," said one critic, but "the Stones want to burn your house."

The New Left and the Antiwar Movement

At the heart of the youth rebellion of the 1960s was a desire to challenge the established political and cultural order. "The New Left," observed the historian Stewart Burns, "was a direct response to the cold, conformist culture of the 1950s, with its ethic of acquisitiveness and its model, the unquestioning 'organization man.' " In 1962 Students for a Democratic Society (SDS), the leading New Left organization on college campuses, composed the Port Huron Statement. The founding document of the New Left, it called for tackling the nation's problems through "self cultivation, self direction, self understanding, and creativity." While recognizing the need to address issues of poverty and racism, the statement suggested the crisis of modern life was primarily moral. "A new left," SDS proclaimed, "must give form to the feelings of helplessness and indifference, so that people may see the political, social, and economic source of their personal troubles and organize to change society." Despite many differences, both the New Left and the counterculture rejected their parents' definition of reality and searched for ways to express their individuality and find self-fulfillment in an age of mass conformity.

PRIMARY SOURCE

9.1 | *Port Huron Statement*
SDS

Founded in 1960 by college students Tom Hayden and Al Haber, Students for a Democratic Society became the preeminent New Left organization in the country. In June 1962 Hayden, Haber, and sixty other activists met in Port Huron, Michigan, and created the organization's statement of purpose.

We are people of this generation, bred in at least modest comfort, housed now in universities, looking uncomfortably to the world we inherit.

When we were kids the United States was the wealthiest and strongest country in the world; the only one with the atom bomb, the least scarred by modern
5 war. . . . Many of us began maturing in complacency.

As we grew, however, our comfort was penetrated by events too troubling to dismiss. First, the permeating and victimizing fact of human degradation, symbolized by the Southern struggle against racial bigotry, compelled most of us from silence to activism. Second, the enclosing fact of the Cold War, symbolized

10 by the presence of the Bomb, brought awareness that we ourselves, and our friends, and millions of abstract "others" we knew more directly because of our common peril, might die at any time. . . .

We witnessed, and continue to witness, other paradoxes. With nuclear energy whole cities can easily be powered, yet the dominant nation-states seem more

15 likely to unleash destruction greater than that incurred in all wars of human history. Although our own technology is destroying old and creating new forms of social organization, men still tolerate meaningless work and idleness. While two-thirds of mankind suffers undernourishment, our own upper classes revel amidst superfluous abundance. Although world population is expected to double in

20 forty years, the nations still tolerate anarchy as a major principle of international conduct and uncontrolled exploitation governs the sapping of the earth's physical resources. Although mankind desperately needs revolutionary leadership, America rests in national stalemate, its goals ambiguous and tradition-bound instead of informed and clear, its democratic system apathetic and manipulated rather

25 than "of, by, and for the people." . . . The worldwide outbreak of revolution against colonialism and imperialism, the entrenchment of totalitarian states, the menace of war, overpopulation, international disorder, supertechnology—these trends were testing the tenacity of our own commitment to democracy and freedom and our abilities to visualize their application to a world in upheaval.

30 Our world is guided by the sense that we may be the last generation in the experiment with living. But we are a minority—the vast majority of our people regard the temporary equilibriums of our society and world as eternally-functional parts. In this is perhaps the outstanding paradox: we ourselves are imbued with urgency, yet the message of our society is that there is no viable alternative to the present. . . .

35 Some would have us believe that Americans feel contentment amidst prosperity—but might it not better be called a glaze above deeply-felt anxieties about their role in the new world? And if these anxieties produce a developed influence to human affairs, do they not as well produce a yearning to believe there *is* an alternative to the present, that something *can* be done to change circumstances in

40 the school, the workplaces, the bureaucracies, the government? It is to this latter yearning, at once the spark and engine of change, that we direct our present appeal. The search for truly democratic alternatives to the present, and a commitment to social experimentation with them, is a worthy and fulfilling human enterprise, one which moves us and, we hope, others today. . . .

45 To turn these possibilities into realities will involve national efforts at university reform by an alliance of students and faculty. They must wrest control of the educational process from the administrative bureaucracy. They must make fraternal and functional contact with allies in labor, civil rights, and other liberal forces outside the campus. They must import major public issues into the cur-

50 riculum—research and teaching on problems of war and peace is an outstanding

example. They must make debate and controversy, not dull pedantic cant, the common style for educational life. They must consciously build a base for their assault upon the loci of power.

55   As students for a democratic society, we are committed to stimulating this kind of social movement, this kind of vision and program in campus and community across the country. If we appear to seek the unattainable, as it has been said, then let it be known that we do so to avoid the unimaginable.   ■ ■ ■

In 1963, 125 SDS members, mostly middle-class white men and women, set up chapters to organize poor whites and blacks in nine American cities. Other members traveled to Mississippi in 1964 as part of the Freedom Summer organized by the Student Nonviolent Coordinating Committee (SNCC). Direct exposure to the brutality of southern justice radicalized many of the students, who returned to campus the following fall searching for an outlet for their fear and anger.

In October 1964 the administration of the University of California at Berkeley provided one outlet. Chancellor Clark Kerr decided to enforce campus regulations prohibiting political demonstrations at the entrance of campus—a traditional site for student political expression. When police tried to arrest protester Jack Weinberg, a crowd of students surrounded the car and organized a sit-in. The next day the university backed down and dropped charges, but the Free Speech Movement (FSM) had been born. In a December rally FSM leader Mario Savio told a spirited crowd that "there is a time when the operation of the machine becomes so odious . . . [that] you can't even passively take part." When he finished, the crowd of eight hundred stormed Sproul Hall, Berkeley's administration building. The movement soon broadened its focus to protest the "multiversity machine." Many students began wearing computer punch cards marked "I AM A STUDENT. DO NOT FOLD, SPINDLE, OR MUTILATE." The revolt quickly spread to other campuses and championed many causes, from opposing dress codes to fighting tenure decisions.

PRIMARY SOURCE

9.2 | *Sproul Hall Steps*
MARIO SAVIO

In the fall of 1964 the chancellor of the University of California at Berkeley, Clark Kerr, banned political demonstrations on the Telegraph Avenue corner where such activity commonly occurred. Students, in turn, formed the Free Speech Movement and organized demonstrations. On December 3, 1964, FSM leader Mario Savio stood on the steps of the administration building and encouraged students to resist the university's position on political activism and join him inside for a sit-in.

The Free Speech Movement at the University of California, Berkeley At the beginning of the fall semester in 1964, the University of California at Berkeley banned student organizations from setting up tables to promote various political activities along Telegraph Hill, located in front of the administration building, Sproul Hall. Student groups banded together, under the leadership of Mario Savio, to form the Free Speech Movement. Though their grievances against the administration varied, undergraduate and graduate students worked together to organize a rally held on December 3, and, after a moving speech by Savio, a thousand people marched into Sproul Hall to stage a sit-in. While eight hundred students were arrested early the next morning, the sit-in prompted change at the university. In early January, the new acting chancellor loosened the rules for political activity on campus and opened up the steps of Sproul Hall to political speeches.

We have an autocracy which runs this university. It's managed. We asked the following: if President Kerr actually tried to get something more liberal out of the Regents in his telephone conversation, why didn't he make some public statement to that effect? And the answer we received—from a well-meaning
5 liberal—was the following: He said, "Would you ever imagine the manager of a firm making a statement publicly in opposition to his board of directors?" That's the answer! Now, I ask you to consider: if this is a firm, and if the Board of Regents are the board of directors, and if President Kerr in fact is the manager, then I'll tell you something: the faculty are a bunch of employees, and we're the
10 raw material! But we're a bunch of raw material[s] that don't mean to have any process upon us, don't mean to be made into any product, don't mean to end up being bought by some clients of the University, be they the government, be they industry, be they organized labor, be they anyone! We're human beings!
    [*Applause*]

15   There is a time when the operation of the machine becomes so odious, makes you so sick at heart, that you can't take part; you can't even passively take part, and you've got to put your bodies upon the gears and upon the wheels, upon the levers, upon all the apparatus, and you've got to make it stop. And you've got to indicate to the people who run it, to the people who own it, that unless you're
20   free, the machine will be prevented from working at all!   ■ ■ ■

President Lyndon Johnson's decision to escalate the conflict in Vietnam fanned the flames of student discontent. On March 24, 1965, students at the University of Michigan organized the first anti-Vietnam teach-in. Organizers planned lectures and discussions about the war in the hope of "educating" students to the dangers of American involvement in Vietnam. This restrained and respectable form of protest spread quickly to other college campuses.

By late 1965 students were planning mass demonstrations, burning draft cards, and chanting, "Hey, hey, LBJ, how many kids did you kill today?" Student anger reached a new level when in January 1966 Johnson ended automatic draft deferments for college students. The threat of the draft pushed a generation of young people to protest the war. The demonstrations swelled in size and intensity as protestors burned draft cards and an occasional American flag. By highlighting the angriest confrontations between students and police, television contributed to a widespread public impression that the nation's campuses had been overrun by radicals. In fact, antiwar protest was largely confined to elite private colleges and large state universities. One study concluded that between 1965 and 1968 only 20 percent of college students participated in antiwar demonstrations.

Antiwar spirits were bolstered by establishment figures who joined the cause. In 1966 Democratic senator J. William Fulbright, the powerful chairman of the Senate Foreign Relations Committee, held nationally televised hearings on the war. Fulbright charged that by displaying an "arrogance of power," the United States was "not living up" to its "capacity and promise as a civilized example for the world." The nation listened as George Kennan, the father of containment, complained that the administration's preoccupation with Vietnam was stretching America's power and prestige. In April 1967 Martin Luther King criticized the government for sending young black men "to guarantee liberties in Southeast Asia which they had not found in Southwest Georgia and East Harlem."

While members of the New Left united in opposition to the Vietnam War, they divided over strategy and tactics. The Port Huron Statement had called for the creation of "a left with real intellectual skills, committed to deliberativeness, honesty, reflection as working tools." Angry and frustrated with an escalating war abroad and exploding cities at home, many SDS leaders abandoned their early hope of building coalitions in pursuit of reform. By 1967 SDS leaders were calling for a strategy of "common struggle with the liberation movements of the world" by means of "the disruption, dislocation and destruction of the military's access to the manpower, intelligence, or resources of our universities." Many members of the New Left openly supported the North Vietnamese, carrying

Vietcong flags during protests and chanting slogans like "Ho, Ho, Ho Chi Minh/the NLF is gonna win." The new militant message angered many Americans and alienated more moderate New Left members, but it resonated with frustrated college students. By the end of 1967 SDS membership had swelled to over thirty thousand.

The New Left also fractured along gender lines. Many women in new left organizations felt marginalized by their male colleagues. The assumption of male superiority, they charged, left many "competent, qualified, and experienced" women relegated to "female kinds of jobs," such as "typing, desk work, and telephone work." By 1967 New Left women were organizing small, independent caucuses and workshops in many major cities where they developed competing visions of liberation. While a few men were sympathetic to these efforts to address gender discrimination in the New Left, most were either indifferent or openly hostile. "What is the position of women in SNCC?" Stokely Carmichael joked in response to the feminist complaint. "The position of women in SNCC is prone!"

How successful was the antiwar movement in changing public attitudes or influencing the administration before 1968? Antiwar sentiment had made the greatest inroads among students, Jews, women, and African-Americans. But important differences emerged even among those who opposed the war. Students viewed the war as immoral, a reflection of fundamental problems in American society. "There is something sick," commented the University of Michigan daily paper, "about a nation that can deploy thousands of soldiers to go off shooting Vietcong . . . but can't spare a few hundred to avert the murder" of civil-rights workers in the South. Students hoped to use opposition against the war to lead a broader assault on American institutions and values.

To the great majority of Americans, however, the war was not immoral. It was simply a tragic mistake. They wanted to end the war because winning no longer seemed worth the price. Class resentment reinforced the ideological differences among war opponents. A large number of working-class Americans opposed the war, but they disliked privileged student protesters even more. "We can't understand," lamented a blue-collar worker, "how all those rich kids—the kids with the beads from the fancy suburbs—how they get off when my son has to go over there and maybe get his head shot off."

In the short run, the administration successfully exploited these divisions by appealing to ingrained habits of patriotism. As late as the summer of 1967 opinion surveys showed that a majority of Americans continued to support the president's Vietnam policy. In the long run, however, the antiwar protesters chipped away at one of the pillars of the postwar consensus: America's policy of global containment. The antiwar movement failed to articulate a unified critique of American foreign policy, yet over time it raised widespread doubts about the nation's anticommunist obsession and forced a rethinking of America's role in the world.

The New Conservatives

While the public focused most of its attention on the Left, conservatives were healing old wounds and mobilizing new recruits. Until the 1950s conservatives had been divided into two rival camps: "libertarians," who opposed all limitations on individual freedom, and "moralists," who believed that maintaining moral standards was more important than defending individual rights. By the end of the decade fear of communism and the growing threat from expanded government forced a fusion of the two strains of conservative thought. At the same time, conservatives abandoned their traditional isolationism and advocated an aggressive internationalism.

With their ideological rift healed, conservatives presented a compelling alternative to the mainstream consensus. Like the New Left, the New Right attacked the moral relativism of the vital center, which they claimed blurred the distinction between right and wrong. Unlike their counterparts in SDS, however, the new conservatives called for an aggressive foreign policy, dramatic increases in military spending, and an end to most social welfare programs. The *National Review,* founded in 1955 by William F. Buckley, played a key role in promoting the new fusionism. "We are in opposition," the magazine declared, "and we have to fight conformity." The message struck a responsive chord. Between 1960 and 1964 the circulation of the conservative monthly magazine tripled to ninety thousand.

Also growing in size was the ultraconservative John Birch Society (JBS), founded in 1958 by Robert Welch. The United States, Welch declared, was at war with "a gigantic conspiracy to enslave mankind." The list of conspirators included Dwight Eisenhower, the justices of the Supreme Court, and just about anyone else who supported nuclear disarmament or civil rights. President John Kennedy's softening position toward the Soviets following the Cuban missile crisis caused alarm among anticommunists and helped swell the JBS membership. By 1964 the JBS claimed about fifty thousand members and received more than $7 million a year in contributions.

During the 1950s and 1960s conservatives developed a base of support in thriving suburban communities, especially in the South and West. In Orange County, California, for example, middle-class whites, worried about the decline of morality and the growth of federal power, organized at the grass-roots level to support right-wing causes. As small property owners, they fought to maintain the racial homogeneity of their communities and to resist Washington's efforts to force integration. Heavily dependent on military contracts for their survival, local residents supported an aggressive anticommunism and opposed efforts to negotiate with the Soviets. Although the federal government supplied the loans used to pay the mortgage and helped build the roads that tied the communities together, many suburban residents developed a virulent hatred of Washington.

The Right also established an energetic presence on college campuses. In 1960 more than one hundred conservative students gathered at William Buckley's family estate in Sharon, Connecticut, to develop an agenda for conservative youth. "Now is the time for Conservative youth to take action to make their full force and influence felt," declared the invitation. The conference marked the birth of the Young Americans for Freedom (YAF). The group issued a statement of principles calling for restrictions on government power to allow "the individual's use of his God-given free will," and urged "victory over, rather than coexistence with," the Soviet Union. By 1961 YAF claimed twenty-four thousand members at 115 schools. Noting the proliferation of conservative clubs on college campuses, one conservative proclaimed a "new wave" of campus revolt. These new campus conservatives, he predicted, would be the "opinion-makers—the people who in ten, fifteen, and twenty-five years will begin to assume positions of power in America."

■ PRIMARY ■ SOURCE

9.3 | *The Sharon Statement*
| YAF

Conservatives had their own organizations on the nation's college campuses. In September 1960 one hundred conservative students met at William Buckley's home in Sharon, Connecticut, and established a set of core beliefs that laid the foundation for the Young Americans for Freedom.

In this time of moral and political crisis, it is the responsibility of the youth of America to affirm certain eternal truths.

We, as young conservatives, believe:

That foremost among the transcendent values is the individual's use of his
5 God-given free will, whence derives his right to be free from the restrictions of arbitrary force;

That liberty is indivisible, and that political freedom cannot long exist without economic freedom;

That the purposes of government are to protect these freedoms through the
10 preservation of internal order, the provision of national defense, and the administration of justice;

That when government ventures beyond these rightful functions, it accumulates power which tends to diminish order and liberty;

That the Constitution of the United States is the best arrangement yet devised
15 for empowering government to fulfill its proper role, while restraining it from the concentration and abuse of power;

That the genius of the Constitution—the division of powers—is summed up in the clause which reserves primacy to the several states, or to the people, in those spheres not specifically delegated to the Federal Government;

20　　That the market economy, allocating resources by the free play of supply and demand, is the single economic system compatible with the requirements of personal freedom and constitutional government, and that it is at the same time the most productive supplier of human needs;

That when government interferes with the work of the market economy, it
25　tends to reduce the moral and physical strength of the nation; that when it takes from one man to bestow on another, it diminishes the incentive of the first, the integrity of the second, and the moral autonomy of both;

That we will be free only so long as the national sovereignty of the United States is secure: that history shows periods of freedom are rare, and can exist only
30　when free citizens concertedly defend their rights against all enemies;

That the forces of international Communism are, at present, the greatest single threat to these liberties;

That the United States should stress victory over, rather than coexistence with, this menace; and
35　　That American foreign policy must be judged by this criterion: does it serve the just interests of the United States?　　　　　■ ■ ■

The fusion of libertarians and moralists, which provided the foundation of the new conservatism, unraveled as the decade progressed. Moralists opposed nearly all forms of protest, applauded aggressive police action to maintain law, and abhorred the counterculture. Libertarians embraced the emphasis on individual freedom that was at the heart of the counterculture and opposed heavy-handed state pressure. Most of all, the two groups stood on different sides of the Vietnam War. In language strikingly similar to the New Left, a libertarian member of YAF said he opposed the "U.S. imperialist venture in Vietnam" because it was "being conducted in a manner that seriously undermines freedom for the Vietnamese and for citizens in our own country, who are being subjected to fascism in the name of freedom."

The New Left and the New Right rejected the emphasis on consensus that had defined their parents' generation. For twenty years Americans had balanced the paradox of rising expectations and social realities by muting social conflict and blurring ideological conflict. But prosperity had produced a new middle class of students who gloried in ideological purity and thrived on social conflict. Viewing politics through the prism of morality, student leaders saw little opportunity to compromise on controversial issues such as Vietnam. But the war in Vietnam was not the only issue that was polarizing Americas in the 1960s.

The Watts Rebellion

Ironically, just when Johnson was legislating into law the most progressive domestic legislation in history, African-American discontent reached a new high. Between 1964 and 1968 the United States experienced the most intense period of civil unrest since the Civil War. In 1964 blacks rioted in Harlem and in the Bedford-Stuyvesant section of Brooklyn. In August 1965, five days after Johnson signed the Voting Right Act into law, the Watts section of Los Angeles exploded in violence. Two-thirds of the 250,000 blacks living in Watts were on welfare, and unemployment stood at 34 percent. Complaints about the police were common. The population was 98 percent black, but only 5 of the 205 police officers were black.

On August 11, 1965, a white police officer stopped a car driven by a twenty-one-year-old, unemployed black man. When the man resisted arrest, a crowd gathered, forcing police to summon reinforcements. Within an hour a thousand blacks were on the street hurling rocks and bottles at the cops and shouting, "Burn, baby, burn!" For four nights marauding mobs in the black suburb burned and killed, while 500 policeman and 5,000 national guardsmen struggled to contain the fury. Before the rioting ended, thirty-four were dead, nearly four thousand were arrested, and property damage had reached $45 million. Fourteen thousand national guardsmen and several thousand local police needed six days to stop the arson, looting, and sniping.

The Watts explosion marked the first of four successive "long hot summers." In the summer of 1966 thirty-eight disorders destroyed ghetto neighborhoods in cities from San Francisco to Providence, Rhode Island. The result was seven deaths, four hundred injuries, and $5 million in property damage. The following year Newark erupted, leaving twenty-five dead and some twelve hundred wounded. In Detroit forty-three were killed, and more than four thousand fires burned large portions of the city. The governor, after viewing the destruction from a helicopter, remarked that Detroit looked like "a city that has been bombed." *Newsweek* called the riots "a symbol of a domestic crisis grown graver than any since the Civil War."

The paradox of American prosperity, and the revolution of rising expectations that it produced, contributed to the success of the civil-rights movement, but it also sowed the seeds of discontent and rebellion. Between 1963 and 1969 blacks were experiencing the most significant gains since the Civil War. The Civil Rights Act of 1964 and Voting Rights Act of 1965 had removed the last vestiges of legal discrimination against African-Americans. In 1967 African-Americans were elected mayors in Gary, Indiana, and Cleveland, Ohio—the first blacks to govern a major city. The same year Thurgood Marshall became the first black to serve on the Supreme Court. Economically, blacks were faring better, thanks to Great Society programs and an overheated economy. Median black family income rose from $5,921 to $8,074; the percentage of black families below the poverty line declined from 48.1 percent in 1959 to 27.9 percent in 1969. Polls showed that the majority of blacks were optimistic about their personal futures.

With expectations of the "good society" stimulated by the acquisition of legal and political rights, many younger northern African-Americans demanded social and economic rights as well. While the struggle in the South raised the

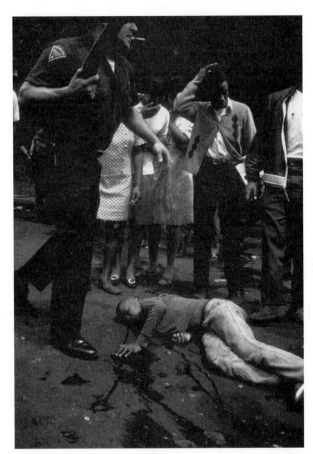

Newark Riot, July 28, 1967 Despite passage of the Civil Rights Act of 1964 and the Voting Rights Act of 1965, the economic conditions for African-Americans across the country remained unchanged. Northern black communities suffered poverty in the ghettos of the nation's larger cities and discrimination at the hands of white police officers. In 1965, the Watts section of Los Angeles exploded in violence. However, it was the summer of 1967 that saw the greatest number of riots, beginning with a riot in Newark, New Jersey, in late July. The four-day riot left more than twenty people dead and approximately twelve hundred wounded, including 12-year-old Joe Bass Jr., who was accidentally hit by fragments from a police officer's shotgun blast. The riot cost over $10 million in property damage, but the Newark riot was only the beginning. A five-day riot in Detroit that same month was even bloodier and more destructive, costing more than forty lives and at least two thousand injuries.

hopes of blacks living in northern ghettos, it did little to improve their condition. Violence became a means of expressing their rage at the limited pace and scope of racial change and their bitterness over increased white opposition to their minimal advances. "The Negro masses are angry and restless," observed the author Louis Lomax, "tired of prolonged legal battles that end in paper decrees."

King in Chicago

Fearing that violence would polarize the movement and prevent further gains, Martin Luther King decided to take his southern movement north to Chicago in 1966. In July King urged blacks to boycott all banks and companies that discriminated against them. The following month he led six hundred followers through a neighborhood of second-generation European immigrants. An angry white mob assaulted the marchers, hurling bottles and rocks. "Go back to Africa. We don't want you here," they shouted. A brick struck King just above the right ear. Afterward King noted: "I've never seen anything like it. I've been in many demonstrations all across the south, but I can say that I have never seen—even in Mississippi and Alabama—mobs as hostile and as hate-filled as I've seen in Chicago."

Over the next few weeks King tried to force the city's powerful mayor, Richard Daley, to make concessions. But Daley was too shrewd to allow himself to become the foil in King's strategy of reform symbolism. Fearful that future marches would produce even more violence and make martyrs of King and his followers, Daley agreed on a ten-point accord to combat residential segregation. By the terms of the agreement, every business and institution in the city pledged to honor the principle of fair housing. King hailed the settlement for producing "the most significant program ever conceived to make open housing a reality in the metropolitan area." In reality, King had been outmaneuvered by Daley, who promised to enforce open-housing laws and disperse low-cost public housing but never agreed to a timetable for change.

King's failed crusade in Chicago exposed some of the basic differences between the struggle for political rights in the South and his new campaign for economic rights in the North. It also highlighted how King's strategy of nonviolence seemed inappropriate for addressing the new problems. In the South King confronted a political system that systematically prevented blacks from exercising rights that most Americans considered essential—the right to vote, the right of access to public facilities. This de jure discrimination was written into law and enforced by the state. An intransigent white power structure allowed King to convey to the nation the sharp moral contrast between the black struggle for rights and the reality of a oppressive society still struggling with the legacy of slavery.

In the North blacks suffered from economic inequality and more informal, but no less pernicious, forms of discrimination. This de facto discrimination developed over years and found expression in profoundly segregated housing, limited job opportunities, poor schools, and minimal health care. Sometimes the discrimination was written into law through various covenants that prevented blacks from moving into white neighborhoods. Sometimes it was practiced by government officials even without the clear sanction of law. For decades school boards consciously redirected resources away from predominately black schools, for example. For the most part, however, the discrimination developed through voluntary habits and custom and served as a reminder of the deep racial divide in America. Blacks in the North could vote, board public buses, and occasionally join unions, but they had little choice in where they worked or lived.

Not only were the issues different; so also were the political leaders. Mayor Daley was no Bull Conner. He was determined to deny King the clear moral contrast he hoped to create for the television cameras. With a united business community and sizable support from many blacks, Daley played political jujitsu with King. To counter King's claims of a serious gap in services between segregated black and white communities, Daley announced a new program to address the problem. The reforms never materialized, but the promise of change deflected King's blows.

Perhaps a more serious problem with King's campaign was his inability to develop a message and a strategy to appeal to poor urban blacks. His success in the South depended on appealing to the conscience of the North, which had always considered race a southern problem. Now that he had brought his campaign into the backyards of his northern supporters, who was going to provide the political support for his campaign? It was more than a failure of tactics; King, like most liberals, was overwhelmed by the size and scope of urban problems and lacked viable solutions to them. Blacks living in northern cities confronted overcrowding, unemployment, crime, and discrimination. In 1966, 41.7 percent of nonwhites in urban America lived below the federal poverty line. The infant mortality rate for African-Americans was 90 percent higher than it was for whites. President Johnson's National Advisory Commission on Civil Disorders, created to investigate the causes of the riots, speculated that despair, black militancy, and white racism combined to create a combustible situation. Ominously, the commission warned, "Our nation is moving toward two societies, one black, one white—separate and unequal."

Black Power/White Backlash

By the mid-1960s many black leaders had repudiated King's message of integration and nonviolence in favor of separatism and self-defense. The change could be seen in the evolution of SNCC, the organization that helped organize sit-ins and freedom rides. By 1965 bruised and angry SNCC members were unwilling to turn the other cheek when confronted by violence. SNCC members felt betrayed when Lyndon Johnson refused to support the Mississippi Freedom Democratic party's challenge to the all-white delegation at the Democratic National Convention in 1964. Believing that liberal white college students only helped to reinforce the feelings of inferiority in southern blacks, SNCC kicked whites out of the organization, ending the biracial coalition that had been so successful in the South.

SNCC leader Stokely Carmichael captured the anger of many urban blacks when he coined the phrase *Black Power*. Instead of integration, which he called "a subterfuge for the maintenance of white supremacy," blacks needed to develop their own cultural heritage and become self-dependent. "We don't need white liberals," Carmichael told supporters. "We have to make integration irrelevant." Rejecting nonviolence, Carmichael said, "Black people should and must fight back."

King urged Carmichael to tone down his rhetoric, arguing that the cry of Black Power would "confuse our allies, isolate the Negro community and give many prejudiced whites . . . a ready excuse for self-justification." Roy Wilkins of the National Association for the Advancement of Colored People (NAACP) branded Black Power "the father of hatred and the mother of violence." Others pointed out that a racial minority could not achieve anything of substance without allies. But Carmichael refused to back down. He was frustrated and angry with the slow pace of progress, disillusioned with King, and eager to build a mass movement that would include young radicals and the urban poor.

In developing his message of Black Power, Carmichael drew on the writings of Malcolm X. A spellbinding preacher and a charismatic leader, Malcolm X offered a compelling alternative vision to King's. In 1946 while in prison for robbery, Malcolm Little converted to the Nation of Islam, or Black Muslims. Upon joining, Little abandoned his "slave name" in favor of Malcolm X; the X stood for his lost African name. Dismissing the aspirations of white civil-rights leaders, he said that black nationalists did not want "to integrate into this corrupt society, but to separate from it, to a land of our own, where we can reform ourselves, lift up our moral standards, and try to be godly." While civil-rights leaders called for nonviolent change, Malcolm insisted on a "black revolution." Moderates like King wanted to desegregate; black revolutionaries demanded land, power, and freedom. King preached the Christian philosophy of "love thy enemy," but black nationalists had no love or respect for their oppressor.

In 1963 Malcolm X broke with the Nation of Islam, and after a 1964 African pilgrimage to Mecca, the holy city of Islam, in Saudi Arabia, his ethical position shifted. He embraced multiracial Islam, rejected racism, spoke of the common bond linking humanity, and suggested that blacks build alliances with like-minded whites. But he emphasized the need for blacks to unify themselves before they reached out for help from whites and liberals. His evolution remained incomplete, however. In February 1965 he was gunned down at a Harlem rally, apparently by Black Muslim loyalists.

PRIMARY SOURCE

9.4 | *The Black Revolution*
MALCOLM X

On April 8, 1964, Malcolm X spoke to a mostly white audience at Palm Gardens in New York. Focusing on increasingly violent protests by young African-Americans, Malcolm X encouraged an international struggle against racism and suggested that a bloody revolution might be necessary.

Friends and enemies: Tonight I hope that we can have a little fireside chat with as few sparks as possible being tossed around. Especially because of the very explosive condition that the world is in today. Sometimes, when a person's house is on fire and someone comes in yelling fire, instead of the person who is awak-
5 ened by the yell being thankful, he makes the mistake of charging the one who awakened him with having set the fire. I hope that this little conversation tonight about the black revolution won't cause many of you to accuse us of igniting it when you find it at your doorstep. . . .

Just as we can see that all over the world one of the main problems facing the
10 West is race, likewise here in America today, most of your Negro leaders as well as the whites agree that 1964 itself appears to be one of the most explosive years yet in the history of America on the racial front, on the racial scene. Not only is this racial explosion probably to take place in America, but all of the ingredients for this racial explosion in America to blossom into a world-wide racial explosion
15 present themselves right here in front of us. America's racial powder keg, in short, can actually fuse or ignite a world-wide powder keg.

There are whites in this country who are still complacent when they see the possibilities of racial strife getting out of hand. You are complacent simply because you think you outnumber the racial minority in this country; what you
20 have to bear in mind is wherein you might outnumber us in this country, you don't outnumber us all over the earth.

Any kind of racial explosion that takes place in this country today, in 1964, is not a racial explosion that can be confined to the shores of America. It is a racial explosion that can ignite the racial powder keg that exists all over the planet that
25 we call earth. I think that nobody would disagree that the dark masses of Africa and Asia and Latin America are already seething with bitterness, animosity, hostility, unrest, and impatience with the racial intolerance that they themselves have experienced at the hands of the white West.

And just as they have the ingredients of hostility toward the West in general,
30 here we also have 22 million African-Americans, black, brown, red, and yellow people, in this country who are also seething with bitterness and impatience and hostility and animosity at the racial intolerance not only of the white West but of white America in particular.

And by the hundreds of thousands today we find our own people have
35 become impatient, turning away from your white nationalism, which you call democracy, toward the militant, uncompromising policy of black nationalism. I point out right here that as soon as we announced we were going to start a black nationalist party in this country, we received mail from coast to coast, especially from young people at the college level, the university level, who expressed com-
40 plete sympathy and support and a desire to take an active part in any kind of political action based on black nationalism, designed to correct or eliminate immediately evils that our people have suffered here for 400 years. . . .

1964 will be America's hottest year; her hottest year yet; a year of much racial violence and much racial bloodshed. But it won't be blood that's going to flow only
45 on one side. The new generation of black people that have grown up in this country during recent years are already forming the opinion, and it's a just opinion, that if there is to be bleeding, it should be reciprocal—bleeding on both sides. . . .

So today, when the black man starts reaching out for what America says are his rights, the black man feels that he is within his rights—when he
50 becomes the victim of brutality by those who are depriving him of his rights—to do whatever is necessary to protect himself. An example of this was taking place last night at this same time in Cleveland, where the police were putting water hoses on our people there and also throwing tear gas at them— and they met a hail of stones, a hail of rocks, a hail of bricks. A couple of weeks
55 ago in Jacksonville, Florida, a young teen-age Negro was throwing Molotov cocktails.

Well, Negroes didn't do this ten years ago. But what you should learn from this is that they are waking up. It was stones yesterday, Molotov cocktails today; it will be hand grenades tomorrow and whatever else is available the next day. The
60 seriousness of this situation must be faced up to. You should not feel that I am inciting someone to violence. I'm only warning of a powder-keg situation. You can take it or leave it. If you take the warning, perhaps you can still save yourself. But if you ignore it or ridicule it, well, death is already at your doorstep. There are 22 million African-Americans who are ready to fight for independence right here.
65 When I say fight for independence right here, I don't mean any nonviolent fight, or turn-the-other-cheek fight. Those days are gone. Those days are over.

If George Washington didn't get independence for this country nonviolently, and if Patrick Henry didn't come up with a nonviolent statement, and you taught me to look upon them as patriots and heroes, then it's time for you to realize that
70 I have studied your books well. . . .

So in this country you find two different types of Afro-Americans—the type who looks upon himself as a minority and you as the majority, because his scope is limited to the American scene; and then you have the type who looks upon himself as part of the majority and you as part of a microscopic minority. And this one uses
75 a different approach in trying to struggle for his rights. He doesn't beg. He doesn't thank you for what you give him, because you are only giving him what he should have had a hundred years ago. He doesn't think you are doing him any favors.

He doesn't see any progress that he has made since the Civil War. He sees not one iota of progress because, number one, if the Civil War had freed him, he
80 wouldn't need civil-rights legislation today. If the Emancipation Proclamation, issued by that great shining liberal called Lincoln, had freed him, he wouldn't be singing "We Shall Overcome" today. If the amendments to the Constitution had solved his problem, his problem wouldn't still be here today. And if the Supreme Court desegregation decision of 1954 was genuinely and sincerely designed to
85 solve his problem, his problem wouldn't be with us today.

So this kind of black man is thinking. He can see where every maneuver that America has made, supposedly to solve this problem, has been nothing but political trickery and treachery of the worst order. Today he doesn't have any confidence in these so-called liberals. (I know that all that have come in here tonight
90 don't call yourselves liberals. Because that's a nasty name today. It represents hypocrisy.) So these two different types of black people exist in the so-called Negro community and they are beginning to wake up and their awakening is producing a very dangerous situation.

You have whites in the community who express sincerity when they say they
95 want to help. Well, how can they help? How can a white person help the black
man solve his problem? Number one, you can't solve it for him. You can help him
solve it, but you can't solve it for him today. One of the best ways that you can help
him solve it is to let the so-called Negro, who has been involved in the civil-rights
struggle, see that the civil-rights struggle must be expanded beyond the level of
100 civil rights to human rights. Once it is expanded beyond the level of civil rights to
the level of human rights, it opens the door for all of our brothers and sisters in
Africa and Asia, who have their independence, to come to our rescue.... ■ ■ ■

The reorientation of the civil-rights movement away from integration and
assimilation and toward separatism and racial pride spread like wildfire across
black America. But this reorientation meant different things to different people. It was more a cry of rage than a systematic doctrine. For some, the
emphasis on black solidarity would allow African-Americans to gain political
power. In order to overcome racism, this argument went, blacks had to work
together. "Before a group can enter the open society," read one manifesto, "it
must first close ranks." In theory, this was similar to the model of liberal pluralism used by European ethnic groups in America and celebrated by political
scientists.

Another theme stressed cultural nationalism as a way for black people to
uncover their roots and recognize the uniqueness of their culture and traditions.
African-American parents pushed school boards to approve the teaching of
black history and culture. College students pressured administrators to recruit black
teachers and students, create Afro-American cultural centers, and institute
Black Studies classes and departments. Young people let their hair grow in what
became known as the "Afro" and began wearing African-styled clothing. Singer
James Brown declared, "Say it loud, I'm black and I'm proud." In this sense the
Black Power movement represented a new spirit of pride and assertiveness.

In the world of sports, within minutes of winning the heavyweight boxing
championship in 1964, Cassius Clay proclaimed his membership in the Nation of
Islam and changed his name to Muhammad Ali. At the 1968 Mexico City Summer Olympics the sprinters Tommie Smith and John Carlos mounted the victory
stand to accept their medals, then lowered their heads and raised black-gloved
fists as the "Star Spangled Banner" was played. The dramatic gesture was a defining moment in the evolving Black Power movement.

In the most radical statement of nationalism blacks stressed the common
struggle of all Third World peoples against western capitalist imperialism. It was
these more militant and violent advocates of Black Power who grabbed the head-
lines and horrified whites. In Cambridge, Massachusetts, in August 1967 H. Rap
Brown told a crowd of angry blacks to "burn this town down." In contrast to
King, he said about the white man, "Don't love him to death, shoot him to death."
Rather than trying to cool racial fires, young black militants used the message of
Black Power to stoke them.

This incendiary black militancy crystalized with the Black Panther party, formed in Oakland in October 1966 following the killing of an unarmed black youth by a San Francisco police officer. Huey Newton and Bobby Seale created the Panthers to embody Malcolm X's doctrine of community self-defense. Above all, the Panthers believed that the black community needed to arm in order to defend itself from the brutality of the white police: "Only with the power of the gun can the black masses halt the terror and brutality perpetuated against them by the armed racist power structure." Black people constituted a colony in the mother country of the American empire, Newton said, and, like all victims of oppression, could legitimately resort to revolution— meaning guns. "The heirs of Malcolm X," Newton rejoiced, "have picked up the gun."

Uninterested in legislative or political reform, the Panthers called themselves "armed revolutionaries." In May 1967 Newton, Seale, and thirty followers armed with shotguns and M-16 rifles marched into the California state legislature in Sacramento in order to protest a bill that would have made it illegal for people to carry unconcealed weapons. In October 1967 Panther Huey Newton went to jail for killing a police officer. In April 1968 thirteen Panthers ambushed an Oakland police car, hitting it with 157 shots and badly wounding one officer. By 1970 the Panthers had killed eleven police officers. Beyond their rhetoric and their shootouts with the police, a few committed Panthers, many of them women, set up free breakfast programs, medical clinics, and other community-based programs in several cities.

Even before the riots and the rise of black nationalism, white America revealed its general discomfort with African-American appeals for racial justice. In 1963 a *Newsweek* magazine survey found that 55 percent of whites objected to having a black family living next to them; 90 percent would object to having their daughters date a black man. "I don't like to touch them. It just makes me squeamish," said one northerner. Over half of the people polled believed that "Negroes laugh a lot," "tend to have less ambition," and "smell different." In 1964 voters in California, who elected Lyndon Johnson in a landslide, also passed by a 2–1 margin a referendum, Proposition 14, repealing the state's new fair housing act. "The essence of freedom is the right to discriminate," observed a leader of the repeal movement.

Most whites responded to the riots and the new militancy with increased fear and anger. In 1966 whites sought revenge against the Democrats at the polls. In California movie actor Ronald Reagan won the governorship by blaming the Watts riot on liberal policy makers. Even his defeated opponent, liberal Pat Brown, declared in his concession speech that "whether we like it or not the people want separation of the races." The biggest change took place in Congress, where Republicans campaigning on a tough "law-and-order" platform gained 47 seats in the House and 3 in the Senate. The Democrats lost more seats in 1966 then they had won in 1964. After November 1966 there were 156 northern Democrats in the House, 62 short of a majority. "I view this election as a repudiation of the President's domestic policies," declared House Republican leader Gerald Ford. Johnson, a meteorologist of the public mood, tailored his program to suit the times. Only once in his 1967 State of the Union message, a thirteen-page, single-spaced text, did he refer to the Great Society.

Tet and the Anguish of Lyndon Johnson

Meanwhile, during the summer of 1967, wrote *Time*, "a profound malaise overcame the American public." In August Johnson sent 45,000 more troops to Vietnam and asked for higher taxes to finance the war. The horror of the war, flashed into the homes of most Americans on the evening newscasts, was matched by that of racial violence in the nation's cities. Flames tore through thirty cities. In one week alone in August forty-five people were killed, thousands were injured, and property damage ran into the billions of dollars. Robert Kennedy called it the "greatest domestic crisis since the war between the states." Critics on the Left made clear that they believed that the violence at home and abroad stemmed from the same problem—the failure of democracy. "One cannot speak of Black Power, or the riots or even Vietnam, in a departmentalized vacuum. They are all part of something larger," declared the journalist Jack Newfield. "Representational democracy has broken down."

With unrest over urban upheaval, the war, and the need to raise taxes, the president's popularity all but vanished. "If I got to believing all the things that had been written about me," Johnson said, "I would pack my suitcase and go home." In October the antiwar movement staged a march on the Pentagon, later celebrated by Norman Mailer's *Armies of the Night* (1968). One thousand angry students converged on the Pentagon in order to shut down "the American military machine" in one act of civil disobedience. By October 1967 only 31 percent of the nation approved of Johnson's handling of the war.

On January 31, 1968, communist troops launched an offensive during the lunar New Year, called Tet in Vietnam. The Vietcong invaded the U.S. embassy compound in Saigon and waged bloody battles in the capitals of most of South Vietnam's provinces. Sixty-seven thousand enemy troops invaded more than one hundred of South Vietnam's cities and towns. The National Liberation Front held parts of Saigon for three weeks and parts of the imperial capital of Hue for almost a month. To retake many urban areas, the United States called in air power to bomb part of Saigon and other cities. The effort produced one of the most infamous quotes of the war when of the battle to regain control of one city a U.S. military official said, "it became necessary to destroy the town to save it."

From a military perspective the Tet Offensive was a failure for the North Vietnamese. They suffered heavy casualties and failed to gain new ground or incite a popular rebellion against the United States. Nevertheless, Tet represented a striking psychological victory. The ferocity of the offensive belied the optimistic reports of General William Westmoreland, who had proclaimed as recently as November 1967 that he had "never been more encouraged in my four years in

Vietnam." Television pictures of marines defending the grounds of the American embassy in Saigon shocked the nation. Television anchorman Walter Cronkite, echoing many Americans, declared that the United States was "mired in stalemate." At that moment Johnson turned to an aide and said, "It's all over." If Johnson had lost Cronkite, he had lost "Mr. Average Citizen."

The Tet Offensive dealt Johnson's credibility a crushing blow. In the month after Tet the number of self-described hawks plummeted from 60 percent to 40 percent while the number of doves doubled to 42 percent. The chief political beneficiary of the shift of opinion was Senator Eugene McCarthy. The Minnesota senator had challenged Johnson in the New Hampshire primary, the first contest of the 1968 presidential campaign. The state's governor had predicted that Johnson would "murder" McCarthy in his state. Instead, McCarthy polled a stunning 42.2 percent of the Democratic vote to Johnson's 49.4 percent by galvanizing both hawks and doves who opposed Johnson's Vietnam policy. New Hampshire transformed McCarthy from a hopeless underdog into a serious challenger and demonstrated Johnson's vulnerability.

Kennedy and King

Four days after Johnson's embarrassment Robert F. Kennedy, who had been a senator from New York since 1964, entered the race for the Democratic nomination. Many Democrats believed that Kennedy was the only politician in America who could pull together the fractured liberal coalition. On Vietnam Kennedy, who had supported his brother's military escalation of the conflict, now called for a negotiated settlement. He focused most of his attention, however, on domestic issues. Kennedy believed that convincing poor people of all colors to pursue their shared class interests offered the only solution to the deep racial hostility that was tearing the nation apart. "We have to convince the Negroes and poor whites that they have common interests," Kennedy told a journalist. "If we can reconcile those two hostile groups, and then add the kids, you can really turn this country around."

Lyndon Johnson, meanwhile, seemed cornered by his own policies. Public support for his Vietnam policy dropped to 26 percent in the aftermath of Tet. His military advisers asked for an additional 206,000 troops, which would have brought the total to 750,000. His civilian advisers, led by veteran presidential adviser Clark Clifford, recommended a negotiated settlement. "We seem to have a sinkhole," Clifford said. Reluctantly, Johnson agreed.

On March 31 the president told a national television audience that he had ordered a temporary halt to the bombing and called for peace talks between the warring sides. His face grown gaunt and tired from years of strain, Johnson concluded his speech by announcing that he would not seek reelection. Three weeks later Vice President Hubert Humphrey announced that he would run in Johnson's place.

The Vietnam War Takes Its Toll on Johnson In a televised speech on March 31, 1968, President Johnson announced he would not run for reelection in November. Still the commander-in-chief, Johnson continued to pursue the war in Vietnam, but he rejected calls from the military for another 206,000 men and limited the bombing of North Vietnam. This picture, taken July 31, shows an exhausted Johnson facing the end of his political career and unable to extract the nation successfully from the quagmire that the Vietnam war had become during his administration.

While Kennedy and McCarthy battled in the Democratic primaries, another outspoken critic of the administration was raising his voice in protest. By 1968 Martin Luther King had abandoned his previous emphasis on dramatic confrontations and accepted SNCC's emphasis on community organizing in an effort to build a class-based, grass-roots alliance among the poor. King spent most of the winter organizing a "poor people's march on Washington." Like Kennedy, King argued that America's racial problems could not be solved without addressing the issue of class. "We must recognize," he said in 1967, "that we can't solve our problems now until there is a radical re-distribution of economic and political power." King now considered himself a revolutionary, not a reformer. "We are engaged in [a] class struggle . . . dealing with the problem of the gulf between the haves and the have nots."

In March 1968 King supported striking garbage workers in Memphis, Tennessee, hoping a peaceful, successful strike would further his new, more militant message of redistribution of power and his enduring commitment to nonviolence. While in

Memphis he reaffirmed his faith in the possibility of racial justice: "I may not get there with you. But we as a people will get to the promised land." The following day, April 4, King died, shot to death by assassin James Earl Ray, a white ex-convict.

King's death touched off a spree of racial violence. Rioters burned twenty blocks in Chicago where Mayor Daley ordered police to "shoot to kill." The worst violence occurred in Washington, D.C., where seven hundred fires burned and nine people lost their lives. For the first time since the Civil War armed soldiers guarded the steps to the Capitol. Nationally the death toll was forty-six. "Martin's memory is being desecrated," said one black leader.

With King dead, Kennedy became for many disaffected people, black and white, the only national leader who commanded respect and enthusiasm. Kennedy may have had the broadest base of support, but party leaders selected most convention delegates. A large majority of these delegates, remaining loyal to the administration, pledged their support to Humphrey. Kennedy's strategy was to sweep the remaining major primaries, showing such support at the polls that the convention delegates would have no choice but to nominate him.

Kennedy won a decisive victory over Humphrey and McCarthy in Indiana but lost in Oregon. The California primary on June 4 was critical, and Kennedy won. But that evening, after giving his victory speech, he was shot by Sirhan Sirhan, a Palestinian who opposed the senator's pro-Israel position. Twenty-five hours later Robert Kennedy died, dimming Democrats' hopes of uniting their disparate coalition of blacks and whites, hawks and doves, young and old.

Robert Kennedy's death assured Humphrey of the nomination on the first ballot. But in the months leading up to the Democratic convention in Chicago, he could not achieve a compromise on a Vietnam plank for the party platform that was acceptable to both the peace forces and the president, who said he would oppose any statement that implied criticism of his policy.

The 1968 Democratic Convention

Johnson added just one combustible ingredient to the explosive atmosphere at the Chicago convention. Antiwar protestors contributed a second. While most protesters planned peaceful marches, many demonstrators had come to Chicago with the clear intent of taunting the police and provoking a violent response. Yippie leaders Abbie Hoffman and Jerry Rubin threatened to let greased pigs loose in the streets of Chicago and to lace the city's water supply with LSD. Mayor Richard Daley contributed the final ingredient. Determined to demonstrate that he was in control of the streets, Daley turned the city into a fortress. He surrounded the convention hall with barbed wire, mobilized 12,000 police, and placed 7,500 national guardsmen on alert.

The explosion took place on August 2 when police dispersed thousands of protesters from Lincoln Park. With demonstrators hurling bricks, bottles, and nail-studded golf balls at the police lines, the Chicago cops decided to charge blindly into the crowd. "The cops had one thing on their minds," one journalist said; "club and then gas, club and then gas, club and then gas." The presence of television cameras and dozens of journalists from around the world did nothing to deter police violence. The police went berserk, a British journalist wrote; "the kids screamed and were beaten to the ground by cops who had completely lost their cool."

The next day the convention debated the Vietnam platform plank. At the end of nearly three hours of heated debate by the party's most distinguished leaders, the majority pro-administration plank won in a close vote. As the session ended, supporters of the minority plank donned black armbands and remained in their seats, singing, "We Shall Overcome."

As dramatic as these events were, the real action was taking place outside the convention hall where the police assaulted a group of peaceful demonstrators seeking to march on the convention headquarters. With no attempt to distinguish bystanders and peaceful protesters from lawbreakers, the police smashed people through plate-glass windows, fired tear gas canisters indiscriminately, and brutalized anyone who got in their way. "These are our children," *New York Times* columnist Tom Wicker cried out as the violence swirled around him.

Television crews filmed the melee as it occurred, and footage of the violence was shown during the nomination speeches. Standing at the podium to nominate George McGovern, Connecticut senator Abraham Ribicoff denounced "Gestapo tactics in the streets of Chicago." An enraged Mayor Daley, sitting with the Illinois delegation, leaped to his feet. Gesturing his contempt for Ribicoff and for his critics, Daley extended his middle finger in full view of a national television audience. The dramatic scenes overshadowed Humphrey's nomination on the first ballot and his selection of Maine senator Edmund Muskie as his running mate.

The public's reaction to the police riot gave an indication of the American mood in 1968. Most Americans sympathized with the police. In a poll taken shortly after the Democratic convention, most blue-collar workers approved the way the Chicago police had handled the protesters; some of them thought the police were "not tough enough." Bumper stickers declaring, "WE SUPPORT MAYOR DALEY AND HIS CHICAGO POLICE" blossomed across the country.

The Center Holds: The Election of 1968

Two candidates were vying for the allegiance of these angry voters. The most direct appeal came from American Independence party candidate George Wallace, whose symbolic stance in a university doorway had made him a hero to southern whites. In 1968 Wallace's anti-establishment populism also appealed to many northern Democrats angry over the party's association with protest and integration. Wallace moved up in the polls by catering to the resentments of his followers. "If a demonstrator ever lays down in front of my car," Wallace told

large and enthusiastic crowds, "it'll be the last car he'll ever lay down in front of."
A ranting orator who seemed to intentionally mangle his syntax and mispro-
nounce his words, Wallace's appeal was blatantly racist and anti-intellectual. One
survey showed that more than half of the nation shared Wallace's view that "liberals, intellectuals, and long-hairs have run the country for too long."

Joining Wallace in pursuit of the hearts and minds of America's angry white
voters was the Republican nominee, Richard Nixon. Just six years earlier, after
losing a race for California governor, Nixon had told reporters, "You won't have
Nixon to kick around anymore, because, gentlemen, this is my last press conference." In the years following Goldwater's defeat in 1964, Nixon had emerged as a
centrist who could appeal to both the liberal and conservative wings of the
Republican Party. Nixon campaigned in 1968 as the candidate of unity, reflecting
his belief that most Americans wanted an end to the civil discord. To capitalize
on the yearning for tranquility, Nixon promised that he had a plan—never spec-
ified—to end the war in Vietnam. But his top priority, he declared, was the
restoration of law and order. Nixon appealed to the "forgotten Americans," those
whose values of patriotism and stability had been violated by student protesters,
urban riots, and arrogant intellectuals. His strategy for the campaign was to stay
above the fray. He refused to debate Humphrey, and he limited his public appearances to televised question-and-answer sessions before audiences of partisan
Republicans.

Humphrey emerged from the debacle in Chicago a badly damaged candidate. Antiwar protesters blamed him for LBJ's Vietnam policies, while many
working-class Democrats associated him with the violent protest and civil unrest
of the convention. "My most serious dilemma," Humphrey said, "is how on the
one hand do you chart an independent course and yet at the same time not
repudiate the course of which you've been a part?" On September 30 Humphrey
discovered his independent voice and announced that he would "stop the bombing of North Vietnam as an acceptable risk for peace." On October 31, less than a
week before election day, Johnson helped Humphrey's cause by announcing a
bombing pause in Vietnam. On the offensive for the first time, Humphrey
appealed to working-class whites by portraying Wallace as a dangerous extremist
and enemy of organized labor, at the same time that he blunted Nixon's message
by emphasizing the themes of togetherness and trust. Suddenly the campaign
picked up steam.

The weekend before the election Humphrey pulled even with Nixon in many
polls. But on election day Nixon won by a razor-thin majority in the popular
vote, receiving 31,785,480 votes compared to Humphrey's 31,275,166. Less than
seven-tenths of 1 percent separated the two candidates. Nixon took only 43 percent of the popular vote, the smallest share of a winning candidate since
Woodrow Wilson in 1912. Nixon scored a more decisive triumph in the electoral
college, however, amassing 301 votes to Humphrey's 191. Wallace carried five
states, receiving 9.9 electoral votes and 13.5 percent of the popular vote—the best
showing for a third-party candidate in forty-four years.

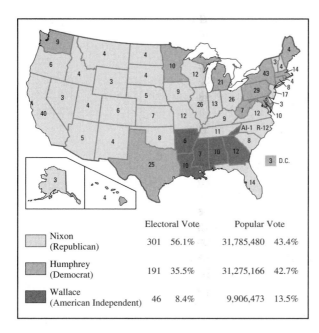

The Election of 1968
With Johnson out of the race, both Richard Nixon and Hubert Humphrey pursued voters with promises to end the war in Vietnam. A third-party candidate, governor of Alabama George Wallace, won the Deep South with a segregationist platform, while Nixon carried all but four states west of the Mississippi. Vice President Humphrey, unable to shake his ties to Johnson, made inroads predominantly in the Northeast.

	Electoral Vote		Popular Vote	
Nixon (Republican)	301	56.1%	31,785,480	43.4%
Humphrey (Democrat)	191	35.5%	31,275,166	42.7%
Wallace (American Independent)	46	8.4%	9,906,473	13.5%

The 1968 election may have produced a conventional political result, but the social conflict that shaped it was anything but conventional. The decade sharpened, and in many ways redefined, the American paradox: consensus and prosperity had sown the seeds of social conflict by producing a generation that rejected the tenets of consensus and stressed the value of ideology. Many middle-class college students were angered by the perceived gap between American ideals and social realities, especially the rhetoric of social justice and the brutality of southern racism, as well as the escalation of violence in Vietnam. For them, the vital center had lost its vitality: gradual change and compromise had done little to improve the lives of African-Americans in the South, narrow the gap between rich and poor, or prevent Lyndon Johnson from escalating the war in Vietnam. Despite extraordinary progress, such as the passage of the most important civil-rights legislation since Reconstruction, expectations far outpaced the possibility of change, producing disillusion and despair.

Perhaps Robert Kennedy best conveyed the spirit of the 1960s when during his presidential campaign he asked, "How do you seek to change a society that yields so painfully to change?" The question captured the contradictions of postwar America. How, in other words, do you reconcile prosperity-bred expectations of reform with the reality of embedded conservative values and practices? That question would remain unanswered, but the cultural civil war that erupted during the 1960s would cast a long shadow over American politics and society for the rest of the century. For now, in a decade marked by bold challenges to established institutions, Americans looked to a familiar face and old values to help forge a new consensus in the troubled days ahead.

SELECTED READINGS

■ Todd Gitlin, a former SDS president and war protester, combines memoir and critical analysis in his *The Sixties* (1987) to portray the social activism that gave the decade much of its dynamism and drama. Allen Matusow's *The Unraveling of America* (1984) offers a more distanced account of the decade that centers on the crisis of liberalism. David Burner captures the failed idealism of the decade in *Making Peace with the 60s* (1996).

■ The tendency to see the student protest movements as harbingers of a profound societywide awakening of political activism and consciousness was influenced early on by two widely read essays, Theodore Roszak's *The Making of a Counter-Culture* (1969) and Charles Reich's *The Greening of America* (1971). Terry Anderson's *The Movement and the Sixties* (1995) looks closely at underground sources to draw connections among the many protests of the period and see in them a much larger overall cultural shift toward activism. David Caute's *The Year of the Barricades* (1988) identifies 1968 as a moment of cultural epiphany when many discrete protests coalesced into something more significant than they had been separately. David Allyn looks at the sexual revolution and its impact in *Make Love, Not War* (2000). George Katsiaficas's *The Imagination of the New Left* (1987) views the protests of the 1960s as part of a world-historical movement. Martin Lee and Bruce Shlain emphasize the distance between the counterculture and the establishment in *Acid Dreams: The CIA, LSD, and the Sixties Rebellion* (1985). For a gripping, dizzying journey into the lives of some pioneers of the counterculture, see Tom Wolfe's *The Electric Kool-Aid Acid Test* (1968).

■ Thomas Sugure uses Detroit to examine black-white tensions in *The Origins of the Urban Crisis* (1996). Works on the violent side of civil rights include Robert Fogelson's *Violence as Protest* (1971) and Robert Conot's *Rivers of Blood* (1967). The Kerner Commission's *Report of the National Advisory Commission on Civil Disorders* (1968) and Stokely Carmichael and Charles Hamilton's *Black Power* (1967) are both important primary sources on the later civil-rights movement.

■ Godfrey Hodgson traces liberalism's cathartic passage through the 1960s in his masterful synthesis, *America in Our Time* (1976). Steven Gillon views the crisis within liberalism through the prism of the ADA (Americans for Democratic Action) in his *Politics and Vision* (1987). John Diggins's *The Rise and Fall of the American Left* (1992) discusses the culmination of the American Left's troubled legacy in the sixties. Maurice Isserman's *If I Had a Hammer* (1987) draws more sanguine connections between the Old Left and the New Left, although his account remains ambivalent. The political rift that dislocated liberalism in 1968 and the collision of paradigms that caused it are nicely encapsulated in David Farber's study of the yippies, the antiwar protesters, and the Daley machine at the Democratic convention in *Chicago '68* (1988). On the decade's political legacy, see Maurice Isserman and Michael Kazin's *America Divided* (1999).

■ Much of the student activism that challenged centrist liberals in the 1960s was inspired by or patterned after the national student movement described by W. J. Rorabaugh in *Berkeley at War* (1989). Kirkpatrick Sales's *SDS* (1973) places the equally influential student organization at the center of the cultural ferment of the sixties. Todd Gitlin unveils the opportunities and constraints the media posed for the New Left in *The Whole World Is Watching* (1980). Charles DeBenedetti's *An American Ordeal* (1990) provides a history of the American peace movement from 1955 to 1975. On Barry Goldwater and the rise of conservatism, see Robert Alan Goldberg's *Barry Goldwater* (1995) and Mary C. Brennan's *Turning Right in the Sixties* (1995)

10

Richard Nixon and the New Republican Majority, 1969–1974

At noon on Monday, May 4, 1970, students at Kent State University in Ohio organized for a antiwar rally on the Commons, a grassy campus gathering spot. For the previous three days the lush lawns and green elms and maple trees of this 790-acre campus had been the site of violent confrontation between students and police. What had ignited the protest was President Richard Nixon's announcement on April 30 of his decision to widen the war in Vietnam by sending American ground troops into neighboring Cambodia. The surprise announcement had come as a shock to a nation lulled into complacency by troop withdrawals and declining body counts.

A National Guard jeep drove onto the Commons, and an officer ordered the crowd to disperse. A platoon of guardsmen, armed with M-1 rifles and tear-gas equipment, followed, moving methodically across the green and over the crest of a hill chasing the protesters. The crowd taunted the poorly trained guardsmen, chanting, "Pigs Off Campus" and hurling stones and bricks. The troops, most of them local townspeople—accountants, bankers, barbers—responded by firing volleys of tear gas into the crowd.

Suddenly, the crackle of gunfire cut through the tear-gas-laced air. A girl screamed, "My God, they're killing us!" Some students fled; others fell to the ground. It took only a few seconds, but by the time the shooting stopped, four students lay dead and another eleven were seriously wounded. None of those hit at Kent State had broken any law, and none was a campus radical. Among them were two women simply walking to class who had never been part of the protest. An investigation by the Federal Bureau of Investigation called the shootings "unnecessary, unwarranted, and inexcusable."

Death at Kent State University   Richard Nixon promised an end to the American involvement in Vietnam with his plan of "Vietnamization," but in April 1970 Nixon expanded America's role in the region by sending U.S. troops into Cambodia to protect that nation's new government from possible North Vietnamese aggression. American opposition to such action was readily apparent as antiwar activists quickly prepared a number of rallies after Nixon's announcement of his Cambodian plan. At Kent State University, student demonstrators were met by National Guard forces that opened fire on the crowd, killing four and wounding eleven. This photograph, of a young woman grieving over the body of one of the victims, stirred opposition to Nixon's Southeast Asia policy and also led administrators to close many state universities before finals, fearing a repeat of Kent State on another college campus.

After the Kent State killings, in what Columbia University president William J. McGill called "the most disastrous month of May in the history of American higher education," over 400 colleges had to cancel some classes and 250 campuses were closed as young people expressed their outrage. But not everyone was sympathetic to the students. One poll indicated that 58 percent of the public blamed the students for the Kent State deaths. A local resident told the town newspaper that the guardsmen "should have fired sooner and longer."

During the late 1960s and early 1970s the American paradox produced unprecedented social strife. On one side of the divide were those Americans, like protesting students at Kent State, who were frustrated by the government's slow and half-hearted response to the civil-rights struggle, angered by the nation's continued involvement in the Vietnam War, and disillusioned by the gap between American ideals and social realities. Made up largely of middle-class baby boomers nurtured on postwar affluence and filled with grand expectations about the possibilities of reform, they took to the streets to challenge the establishment. On the other side of the debate were the millions of Americans whom Richard Nixon called the "silent majority." A broad cross section of Americans, they were united by fears of social disorder, by resentment of middle-class youth who questioned traditional values, and by anxiety about the consequences of dramatic social and political changes. Richard Nixon was elected on a promise to bring harmony to American politics, but his efforts to create a durable base of political support by mobilizing the backlash against protest clarified and hardened the divisions separating Americans.

The Rise of the Middle Americans

For most political observers, the surprising popularity of George Wallace's third-party candidacy and the election of Richard Nixon represented an important shift in the nation's political life. By 1969 it appeared that the radical 1960s were giving way to the mainstream 1970s. The signs were everywhere: car windows were plastered with American flag decals and bumper stickers reading, "Honor America" had replaced the 1960s mantra "Make Love Not War." In big cities fearful voters worried about rising crime rates were turning to elected tough law-and-order mayors like former police officer Frank Rizzo in Philadelphia.

Middle Americans were driving the nation's rightward drift. The journalist Joseph Kraft first coined the phrase in 1967, and Richard Nixon made numerous references to these voters during his 1968 campaign. But who were the Middle Americans? A *Newsweek* reporter defined them in cultural terms as those who felt "threatened by a terrifying array of enemies: hippies, Black Panthers, drugs, the sexually liberated, those who questioned the sanctity of marriage and the morality of work." Others defined them in economic terms—"blue-collar workers, lower-echelon bureaucrats, and white-collar employees who earned between $5,000 and $15,000 a year." Perhaps *Time* described them best when it referred to Middle America as "a state of mind, a morality, a construct of values and prejudices and a complex of fears."

The sources of Middle American discontent were easy to identify: an unresolved war in Vietnam, race riots in major cities, rebellious student protesters, and rising inflation. More than the specific grievances, many Americans were troubled by a general sense that middle-class values were under assault. "They feared that they were beginning to lose their grip on the country," *Time* noted, which named "The Middle Americans" as its "Man and Woman of the Year" for 1969. "The values that we held so dear are being shot to hell," noted a typical Middle American. "Everything is being attacked—what you believed in, what you learned in school, in church, from your parents." *Newsweek* noted in a special October 1969 issue entitled "The Troubled American" that "the average American is more deeply troubled" about the direction in which the nation was headed "than at any time since the Great Depression."

This frustration with American society may have been palpable, but many Middle Americans were conflicted about possible solutions as well. Most wanted peace in Vietnam but refused to accept the possibility of defeat, preferring instead "an honorable withdrawal." They believed that African-Americans deserved a quality education, but they were also appalled by "the idea of sacrificing their own children's education to a long-range improvement for blacks." Middle Americans were a diverse group, divided by sex (women tended to be less hawkish on the war), education (those with college degrees were more tolerant on race issues), and geography (racial attitudes in the South tended to be harsher). According to *Newsweek,* what they all shared was a desire for "stability—or at least the illusion of stability."

The desire to win the allegiance of disaffected white middle-class voters, combined with the goal of forging a new governing coalition, undergirds the logic of Nixon's presidency. He almost succeeded. Nixon's smashing victory in the 1972 election revealed the potential of this "new majority." But Watergate and a sluggish economy destroyed Nixon's presidency and in the short run derailed the Republican appeal to "forgotten Americans." For all of his personal failings, however, Nixon articulated a message and defined an electoral strategy that would shape American politics for the rest of the century.

The Rise of Richard Nixon

Throughout his political career Richard Nixon seemed to have an instinctive feel for the issues that motivated the average, white, largely suburban voter. Many Middle Americans, in turn, identified with Nixon's rise from humble origins, his public professions of support for traditional values and hard work, and his disdain for the eastern establishment. "Nixon himself is the embodiment of Middle America," *Time* noted. From his deprived childhood in suburban Los Angeles Nixon derived both his outsider status and his deep resentment of privilege. He worked his way through college and won a scholarship to Duke University Law School. After a brief stint in the military during World War II, he returned to California and won election to Congress in 1946.

Realizing early on the potential of the communist issue, Nixon waged ruthless campaigns against his liberal opponents, often falsely accusing them of having ties with communists. He earned a national reputation as a communist hunter with his tireless pursuit of Alger Hiss, who for the young congressman represented the evils of wealth and privilege. Nixon's unscrupulous methods and his relentless pursuit of suspected communists in government earned him the enmity of liberals and many journalists, but it endeared him to the Republican Party's right wing and earned him a place on the Eisenhower ticket as vice president in 1952. When accused of maintaining an illegal slush fund, Nixon went on national television in a maudlin "Checkers" speech in which he depicted himself as a member of the hard-working "silent majority" and a victim of a smear campaign by his political enemies.

More than any other politician of his time, Richard Nixon understood the public's longing for stability and order at the end of the tumultuous 1960s. Following the Barry Goldwater debacle in 1964, Nixon positioned himself in the strategic middle of his party, a centrist alternative, flanked by California governor Ronald Reagan on the right and New York governor Nelson Rockefeller on the left. Running against an embattled Democratic administration in 1968, Nixon toned down his tough rhetoric, emphasizing instead his desire to "Bring Us Together." He hammered away at the Democrats for "cities enveloped in smoke and flame" and for "Americans dying on distant battlefields," but he remained intentionally vague and noncommittal about his plans for addressing such problems. He crafted a subdued populist message that appealed to the angry white middle class, but he avoided the direct racial appeals of third-party candidate George Wallace. As president, Nixon promised to listen to "the voice of the great majority of Americans, the forgotten Americans, the nonshouters, the non-demonstrators." As the sociologist Jonathan Rieder noted, "If Wallace offered rollback, Nixon suggested containment."

There emerged a clear political intention to Nixon's conduct of the presidency: he pursued policies that would attract the support of frustrated Middle Americans, allowing him to forge a new majority that was made up of traditional Republicans and angry ex-Democrats. He believed that race riots, student protest, and an unpopular war in Vietnam could do for the Republicans what a depression and world war had once done for the Democrats. And he, Richard Nixon, the man scorned by the eastern establishment, would be the architect of the new coalition, the Roosevelt of the new majority. Though he courted big business and powerful conservative interests, Nixon identified with the fears and resentments of the struggling middle class. "My source of strength," he once observed, "was more Main Street than Wall Street."

Constructing his new majority required Nixon to appeal to the shifting ideological center of American politics. He hoped to reach out to the two-thirds of the country he called the "constituency of uneducated people." They were the angry voters who flirted with George Wallace's antiestablishment populism in 1968. "These are my people," Nixon said. "We speak the same language." Since the days of the New Deal, Democrats had used the language of economic populism to cement the loyalties of the working class, charging that an economic elite was out of touch with the concerns of average voters. Nixon's goal was to articulate a new lexicon of cultural populism, arguing that a cultural elite associated with the Democratic Party had lost touch with the mainstream values of average Americans.

In his early years in office Nixon adopted moderately progressive positions. As the first elected president since 1849 forced to work with a Congress controlled by the opposition party, he favored cooperation over confrontation. In addition to signing Democratic bills raising social security benefits, Nixon increased federal funds for low-income public housing and even expanded the Job Corps. His first term saw steady increases in spending on mandated social-welfare programs, especially social security, Medicare, and Medicaid. His most innovative and surprising proposal was the Family Assistance Plan, which provided a guaranteed minimum income of $1,600 to every U.S. family. Although the proposal died in the Senate, it revealed Nixon's capacity for domestic innovation. Michael Harrington, whose *The Other America* had helped inspire the War on Poverty, called it "the most radical idea since the New Deal."

Vietnam: The War at Home and Abroad

Nixon understood that his administration's success hinged on diffusing the crisis in Vietnam. "It is essential that we end this war, and end it quickly," he declared during the presidential campaign. He believed, however, that the United States could not simply "cut and run"; instead he promised "peace with honor." Nixon wanted to intimidate the North Vietnamese, raising the stakes by threatening an expanded war. Nixon explained his approach as "the Madman Theory." "I want the North Vietnamese to believe I've reached the point where I might do *anything* to stop the war," he confided in 1968.

In developing his strategy for dealing with the conflict, Nixon relied heavily on his national security adviser, Henry Kissinger. Born in Germany in 1923, Kissinger traveled to the United States in 1938. After serving in World War II, he attended Harvard, earned a Ph.D. in government, and joined the faculty. Both men shared a personal style and a similar view of America's role in the world. They possessed a desire for power and a penchant for secrecy and intrigue. Together they concentrated decision making in the White House and excluded even close aides from sensitive diplomatic initiatives. An observer suggested that Kissinger's aides were like mushrooms: "They're kept in the dark, get a lot of manure piled on them, and then get canned." Nixon, who took great pride in his knowledge of international relations, functioned as his own secretary of state until Kissinger assumed the post in 1973. The man who until then actually occupied the position, William Rogers, had little foreign-policy experience and no influence in the White House. Nixon and Kissinger also shared an essentially pessimistic view of the behavior of nations known as realpolitik. Power, they believed, not ideals or moral suasion, counted in international affairs. Nations could be expected to act in their own narrowly defined interest.

For Nixon, Vietnam was a two-front war, with battle lines in Asia and America. He saw himself engaged in a contest "with the antiwar movement for the public mind in the United States and the private mind in Hanoi." In order to make his threats credible to the North Vietnamese, Nixon needed to diffuse domestic opposition. Hostility to the war had forced his predecessor from office, but by the time Nixon entered the presidency, the peace movement was in disarray, demoralized by the Republican victory, splintered into rival factions, and reeling from the public backlash at protest. By the spring of 1969 a majority of Americans—52 percent—opposed peaceful demonstrations and 82 percent believed students who participated in demonstrations should be expelled from school.

The centerpiece of the president's strategy of deflating the peace movement was the policy of Vietnamization. Nixon believed that by reducing the number of combat troops, which stood at 530,000 on the day he took office, he could cut the casualties that fueled home-front protest. In June the White House announced the withdrawal of 25,000 troops in the first large-scale reduction of troop strength. Within weeks U.S. combat losses dropped to their lowest level of the war. In December 1969 Nixon announced a draft lottery system that eliminated many of the inequities of the older system. By 1973 troop withdrawals would allow him to end the draft and create an all-volunteer army.

While official announcements focused on troop withdrawals, the president dramatically enlarged the bombing campaign. In January 1969, in keeping with his madman theory, Nixon authorized Operation Menu—the secret bombing of North Vietnamese bases and supply routes in Cambodia. "Breakfast," was followed by "Lunch," "Snack," "Dinner," "Dessert," and "Supper." Over the next fifteen months American B-52 bombers served up a deadly diet of explosives. "We were dropping a hell of a lot of bombs," said a military official. "I refuse to believe that a little fourth-rate power like North Vietnam does not have a breaking point," Kissinger told his staff.

The bombings not only failed to intimidate the North Vietnamese; they also did little to stem the losses on the ground in South Vietnam. The South's government was failing miserably in its efforts to win popular legitimacy and to build an effective military force. Its army suffered from massive desertions and poor, often corrupt and brutal, leadership. In July Nixon warned Ho Chi Minh that unless significant progress was made, he would be forced to turn to "measures of great consequence and force," later described by Kissinger as a "savage, punishing blow." Operation Duck Hook called for intensive bombing of North Vietnamese population centers and military targets, mining of harbors and rivers in the North, and bombing of the dike and rail system connecting North Vietnam and China.

More troubling for Nixon, by the fall of 1969, were signs of new life in the dormant peace movement. Discontent with the war was mounting. By September 57 percent opposed and only 35 percent supported the president's policies. "You could sense the change in the country," noted a peace organizer. On October 15 in towns and cities across America opponents of the war participated in a massive moratorium protest. More than 2 million people held candlelight vigils, engaged in discussions, and attended church services as part of the largest antiwar demonstration in U.S. history. The media, which provided live coverage of the rallies, highlighted the moderate tone of the moratorium and its middle-class constituency.

Nixon feared that the moratorium would undercut his November ultimatum to Hanoi. White House chief of staff H. R. "Bob" Haldeman noted that Nixon "was as bitter and disappointed as I ever saw him" following the moratorium. With another mass protest scheduled for November 15, Nixon decided to take the offensive, orchestrating a campaign of pro-Americanism that focused public attention on the critics of the war rather than the war itself. Dismissing the peace movement as a "brotherhood of the misguided, the mistaken, the well-meaning, and the malevolent," Nixon tried to buy time for his policy by redirecting public anger against antiwar protesters.

Mobilizing the "Silent Majority"

The centerpiece of Nixon's counteroffensive was a November 3 address to the American people on national television. Considering the speech the most important of his career, Nixon worked through twelve drafts before being satisfied that he had articulated the right message. More than 80 million Americans listened to Nixon outline his Vietnamization policy and explain why the United States could not cut and run. After establishing his war strategy, the president attacked the antiwar movement, saying that he would be "untrue" to his "oath of office" if he allowed national policy to be "dictated" by a "vocal minority" that attempted to "impose" its views on others "by mounting demonstrations in the street." America, he said, had two choices in Vietnam. One was "immediate, precipitate withdrawal." The other was "to search for a just peace through a negotiated settlement." Nixon called for the support of "the great silent majority of my fellow Americans" in his struggle to win the peace. "Let us understand: North Vietnam cannot defeat or humiliate the United States," he said. "Only Americans can do that."

The speech was a brilliant tactical move that undercut public support for the organized antiwar movement. A poll showed that nearly 75 percent of the public considered themselves part of the "silent majority." By a margin of 65 percent to 25 percent, the public agreed with Nixon's point that "protestors against the war are giving aid and comfort to the Communists." Even the liberal *New Republic* referred to the speech as "a political masterpiece." Kissinger claimed that the speech "turned public opinion around completely." As praise for his speech poured into the White House, Nixon gloated, telling aides, "We've got those liberal bastards on the run now."

PRIMARY SOURCE

10.1 | *The Silent Majority*

RICHARD NIXON

Faced with mounting pressure to remove American troops from Vietnam, President Nixon defended his plan of Vietnamization in a televised speech on November 3, 1969. In his address Nixon explained why American troops remained in Vietnam, calling on those Americans not openly protesting the war, whom he called the "silent majority," to support his policy.

My fellow Americans, I am sure you can recognize from what I have said that we really only have two choices open to us if we want to end this war.

I can order an immediate, precipitate withdrawal of all Americans from Vietnam without regard to the effects of that action. Or we can persist in our search
5   for a just peace through a negotiated settlement if possible, or through continued implementation of our plan for Vietnamization if necessary, a plan in which we will withdraw all of our forces from Vietnam on a schedule in accordance with our program, as the South Vietnamese become strong enough to defend their own freedom.

10   I have chosen this second course. It is not the easy way. It is the right way.

It is a plan which will end the war and serve the cause of peace—not just in Vietnam but in the Pacific and in the world.

In speaking of the consequences of a precipitate withdrawal, I mentioned that our allies would lose confidence in America.

15   Far more dangerous, we would lose confidence in ourselves. Oh, the immediate reaction would be a sense of relief that our men were coming home. But as we saw the consequences of what we had done, inevitable remorse and divisive recrimination would scar our spirit as a people.

We have faced other crises in our history and have become stronger by reject-
20   ing the easy way out and taking the right way in meeting our challenges. Our greatness as a nation has been our capacity to do what had to be done when we knew our course was right.

I recognize that some of my fellow citizens disagree with the plan for peace I have chosen. Honest and patriotic Americans have reached different conclusions
25   as to how peace should be achieved.

In San Francisco a few weeks ago, I saw demonstrators carrying signs reading: "Lose in Vietnam, bring the boys home."

Well, one of the strengths of our free society is that any American has a right to reach that conclusion and to advocate that point of view. But as presi-
30   dent of the United States, I would be untrue to my oath of office if I allowed the policy of this nation to be dictated by the minority who hold that point of view and who try to impose it on the nation by mounting demonstrations in the street.

For almost 200 years, the policy of this nation has been made under our Constitution by those leaders in the Congress and the White House elected by all of
the people. If a vocal minority, however fervent its cause, prevails over reason and
the will of the majority, this nation has no future as a free society.

And now I would like to address a word, if I may, to the young people of this
nation who are particularly concerned, and I understand why they are concerned,
about this war.

I respect your idealism. I share your concern for peace. I want peace as much
as you do. There are powerful personal reasons I want to end this war. This week
I will have to sign 83 letters to mothers, fathers, wives and loved ones of men who
have given their lives for America in Vietnam. It is very little satisfaction to me
that this is only one-third as many letters as I signed the first week in office. There
is nothing I want more than to see the day come when I do not have to write any
of those letters.

I want to end the war to save the lives of those brave young men in Vietnam.

But I want to end it in a way which will increase the chance that their younger
brothers and their sons will not have to fight in some future Vietnam someplace
in the world.

And I want to end the war for another reason. I want to end it so that the
energy and dedication of you, our young people, now too often directed into bitter hatred against those responsible for the war, can be turned to the great challenges of peace, a better life for all Americans, a better life for all people on this
Earth.

I have chosen a plan for peace. I believe it will succeed. If it does succeed, what
the critics say now won't matter. If it does not succeed, anything I say then won't
matter.

I know it may not be fashionable to speak of patriotism or national destiny
these days. But I feel it is appropriate to do so on this occasion.

Two hundred years ago this nation was weak and poor. But even then, America was the hope of millions in the world. Today we have become the strongest
and richest nation in the world. And the wheel of destiny has turned so that any
hope the world has for the survival of peace and freedom will be determined by
whether the American people have the moral stamina and the courage to meet
the challenge of free world leadership.

Let historians not record that when America was the most powerful nation in
the world we passed on the other side of the road and allowed the last hopes for
peace and freedom of millions of people to be suffocated by the forces of totalitarianism.

And so tonight—to you, the great silent majority of my fellow Americans—I
ask for your support.

I pledged in my campaign for the presidency to end the war in a way that we
could win the peace. I have initiated a plan of action which will enable me to keep
that pledge.

The more support I can have from the American people, the sooner that
pledge can be redeemed; for the more divided we are at home, the less likely the
enemy is to negotiate at Paris.

80   Let us be united for peace. Let us also be united against defeat. Because let us understand: North Vietnam cannot defeat or humiliate the United States. Only Americans can do that.

    Fifty years ago, in this room and at this very desk, President Woodrow Wilson spoke words which caught the imagination of a war-weary world. He said: "This 85 is the war to end war." His dream for peace after World War I was shattered on the hard realities of great power politics, and Woodrow Wilson died a broken man.

    Tonight I do not tell you that the war in Vietnam is the war to end wars. But I do say this: I have initiated a plan which will end this war in a way that will bring us closer to that great goal to which Woodrow Wilson and every American presi- 90 dent in our history has been dedicated—the goal of a just and lasting peace.

    As president I hold the responsibility for choosing the best path to that goal and then leading the nation along it. I pledge to you tonight that I shall meet this responsibility with all of the strength and wisdom I can command in accordance with our hopes, mindful of your concerns, sustained by your prayers.

95   Thank you and good night.   ■ ■ ■

Nixon's appeal to the "silent majority" tapped into the deep class resentments that shaped attitudes toward the war and toward antiwar protesters. By 1969 many white, middle-class Americans—even those who opposed the war—were convinced that a willful minority of violent youth, militant blacks, and arrogant intellectuals had seized control of the public debate, showing contempt for mainstream values and threatening social stability. At the same time, 55 percent of Americans called themselves "doves" and nearly 80 percent said they were "fed up and tired of the war." Yet as frustrated as Americans were with the war, they disliked protesters even more. Polls showed that more than half of all those who favored immediate and total withdrawal from Vietnam had negative feelings toward those who publicly advocated this same position. Not only did most Americans resent the organized peace movement's public displays of dissent; they also viewed the war itself differently. Antiwar protesters tended to oppose the war for moral reasons, viewing it as an indictment of the entire system. For the vast majority of Americans, however, the war was simply a mistake and a waste of valuable resources.

The "silent majority" speech intensified the cultural clash of the decade. Middle Americans viewed the antiwar movement as an elitist attack on American troops by privileged students who had avoided the war. The journalist Jimmy Breslin condemned the antiwar movement for "its arrogance toward people who work with their hands for a living and its willingness not only to ignore them, but to go even further and alienate them completely." More importantly, by using the antiwar movement as the foil, Nixon managed to transform himself into an antiestablishment figure, a cultural populist fighting for mainstream values against a liberal cultural elite. "By withdrawing U.S. troops while channeling popular resentment against his critics, the president had masterfully secured the national center and reasserted executive control over the politics of war," noted the historian Charles DeBenedetti.

The Cambodian Incursion

Having gained a tactical victory at home, Nixon was ready to send another message to the North Vietnamese. With the war going badly, Nixon talked about a "bold move" in Cambodia, which U.S. military officials believed the North Vietnamese were using as a staging ground for attacks on South Vietnam. At a meeting in April Nixon was warned that if he invaded Cambodia, "the campuses will go up in flames." The president, increasingly isolated from the public and from his own staff, was determined to prove to the North Vietnamese that he was in charge. In the days leading up to the invasion, Kissinger recalled, "Richard Nixon was virtually alone, sitting in a darkened room in the Executive Office Building, the stereo softly playing neoclassical music—reflecting, resenting, collecting his thoughts and his anger."

Nixon ordered American ground troops into the neutral country on April 29, 1970. The next day, in a national televised addressed, a visibly nervous president explained his decision to a war-weary public. Claiming that an American defeat in Vietnam would unleash the forces of totalitarianism around the globe, he insisted that the invasion of Cambodia was a guarantee of American "credibility." "The most powerful nation in the world," he said, could not afford to act "like a pitiful helpless giant."

The raids achieved some of the short-term goals set by military planners, but on the whole the invasion was a strategic failure. At home the invasion reinflamed antiwar sentiment and eroded support for Nixon's policy. Angry senators submitted legislation repealing the Gulf of Tonkin Resolution. South Dakota's Democratic senator George McGovern told his Senate colleagues, "This chamber reeks of blood." Campuses erupted in marches and protests. On May 4 at Kent State University in Ohio panicked national guardsmen fired into a crowd of student protesters. A week later at Jackson State College in Mississippi two black students were killed and eleven wounded when police fired indiscriminately into a dormitory. Student protests reached a fever pitch in the weeks that followed. "The overflow of emotion seemed barely containable," observed the *Washington Post*. "The nation was witnessing what amounted to a virtual general and uncoordinated strike by its college youth."

In public Nixon made a deliberate effort to appear nonchalant about the protest and about the growing signs of discontent with his policies. He made a point of telling reporters that he watched a Washington Redskins football game during one large demonstration outside the White House. Behind the confident façade, however, Nixon was growing increasingly isolated and embattled, paranoid that his enemies in Congress, the press, and the antiwar movement were conspiring to destroy him. "Within the iron gates of the White House, quite unknowingly, a siege mentality was setting in," a Nixon aide recalled. "It was now 'us' against 'them.' Gradually, as we drew the circle closer around us, the ranks of 'them' began to swell."

The circle tightened even further in June 1971 when the *New York Times* began publishing *The Pentagon Papers,* a secret Defense Department study of

American decision making in Vietnam before 1967. Leaked to the press by former Pentagon official Daniel Ellsberg, the report showed that John Kennedy and Lyndon Johnson had consistently misled the public about their intentions in Vietnam. Nixon tried to block further publication, claiming it would damaged national security. The Supreme Court, by a vote of 6 to 3, ruled against the administration, citing the First Amendment freedoms of speech and the press. The decision enraged Nixon.

As support for the war evaporated, and the public appeared more divided than ever, Nixon desperately tried to refocus public anger away from his policies and toward the antiwar movement. Shrewdly playing to the public's mood, Nixon wrapped himself in the flag and questioned the patriotism of those who challenged his policies. After angry construction workers waded into a crowd of protesters in New York City, Nixon invited the leaders of the local union to a White House ceremony, where he donned a hard hat for photographers.

The president's strategy reached a fever pitch in the final weeks of the 1970 midterm elections. In a desperate attempt to unseat Democrats and increase Republican power in Congress, Nixon engaged in a campaign that the historian James T. Patterson described as "among the most aggressive and divisive" in modern politics. Campaigning frantically in twenty-three states during the final days of the campaign, Nixon orchestrated confrontations with protesters as a way of arousing the indignation of his cherished Middle Americans. But this time the public failed to respond to Nixon's shrill rhetoric. The Democrats gained nine House seats, lost two in the Senate, and gained eleven governorships. Overall, Democrats received 4.1 million more votes than their Republican challengers.

Peace with Honor?

The poor showing in the midterm election convinced Nixon that he had to neutralize Vietnam as a political issue before the 1972 presidential campaign. In March 1972 North Vietnam's forces launched a massive invasion of the South. In April the U.S. ambassador in Vietnam cabled Nixon, "ARVN [South Vietnamese] forces are on the verge of collapse." Nixon, refusing to allow South Vietnam to fall, initiated a risky plan to use American air power to give the north a "bloody nose." By approving the campaign, code-named Linebacker, Nixon ran the risk of inflaming public opinion at home and jeopardizing a planned summit with the Russians. The gamble succeeded. The Soviets offered only tepid protest, and most Americans believed the North's invasion required a tough American response.

The North Vietnamese invasion and Nixon's forceful response created an opportunity for negotiations. Both sides had reason to seek accommodation. North Vietnam wanted to end the punishing American bombings; the United States needed to end the war quickly. Since early in 1971 Kissinger had been holding private meetings in a suburb of Paris with his North Vietnamese counterpart, Le Duc Tho. The key stumbling block had been Tho's insistence that

Henry Kissinger Works for Peace in Vietnam Nixon's declaration that he would end American involvement in Vietnam did not prove to be an easy promise to keep. Secretary of State Henry Kissinger and North Vietnamese officials created a tentative agreement for peace in October 1972, but the South Vietnamese government refused to support it, and Nixon intensified the fighting by ordering bombings of North Vietnam during the Christmas season. Negotiations began again in January 1973, with Kissinger threatening to continue the bombing indefinitely if an appropriate solution could not be reached. Kissinger and North Vietnamese envoy Le Duc Tho did reach an agreement that required the removal of U.S. troops from the South and North Vietnamese troops from Laos and Cambodia. Despite the fact that Nixon forced the agreement on the South Vietnamese government and the North had not promised to remove its troops from the South, Nixon proclaimed that peace was at hand. Many Americans, promised for years that the war would soon be over, were not convinced. This cartoon, published in September 1973, shows Kissinger with his fingers crossed that peace would hold and carrying a whip just in case.

South Vietnam's president Thieu be removed from power and that North Vietnamese troops be allowed to remain in the South. For a year neither side budged. The only thing they had agreed on was the shape of the negotiating table.

In September 1972 Kissinger made the first move by agreeing to allow North Vietnamese soldiers to remain in South Vietnam. Tho responded by dropping the long-standing demand that Thieu resign and a coalition government be created. A settlement appeared imminent, and Kissinger announced that "peace is at hand." He had not anticipated, however, the fierce opposition of President Thieu, who adamantly opposed North Vietnamese troops in the South. When Nixon supported Thieu, Kissinger returned to the negotiating table armed with new demands. Feeling betrayed, Tho suspended negotiations and returned to Hanoi.

Nixon decided that only a dramatic demonstration of American power could reassure the South Vietnamese and intimidate the North. On December 18, 1972, he ordered Operation Linebacker II, a massive, eleven-day bombing campaign over North Vietnam. The raids were directed at military targets, but inevitably bombs also fell on schools, hospitals, and prisoner-of-war camps. The American costs were heavy as well: the loss of fifteen B-52 planes and the capture of 98 American airmen. During the previous seven years only one of these high-flying bombers had been downed.

The resumption of bombing, along with pressure from China and the Soviet Union, pushed North Vietnam back to the negotiating table. They did not, however, change the terms for peace. The stumbling block remained the same: Thieu refused to accept a settlement that would allow the North Vietnamese to keep troops in the South. With polls showing overwhelming public support for ending the war and with Congress threatening to cut off funding for the effort, Nixon needed an agreement. This time he privately warned Thieu of grave consequences if he rejected the agreement. Nixon matched the threat with a promise to "respond with full force should the settlement be violated by North Vietnam."

The Paris Peace Accords, signed on January 27, 1973, officially ended U.S. involvement in the Vietnam War. The treaty required the United States to remove its remaining 23,700 troops and the North Vietnamese to return all American prisoners of war. As a face-saving measure for the United States, the accords also called for "free and democratic general elections" to create a government for a unified Vietnam. More importantly, however, was the American and South Vietnamese concession that North Vietnamese troops could remain in the South.

Nixon told a national television audience that the United States had achieved peace with honor. In fact, it had achieved neither peace nor honor. The North Vietnamese had no intention of abandoning their dream of unification. Kissinger hoped that the treaty would provide a "decent interval" between the U.S. military withdrawal and the North's complete military conquest of the South. As Kissinger predicted, the North violated the cease-fire within a few months and continued its relentless drive south. Thieu appealed to the United States for help, but a war-weary Congress refused to provide assistance. By April 1975 when the North's troops captured the South Vietnamese capital of Saigon, America had already turned its attention away from the nation's longest war. In April the House of Representatives voted down the administration's request for $474 million in additional military aid for South Vietnam. The *Washington Post* called it "a stunning defeat" for the administration.

Nixon, Kissinger, and the World

For Nixon and Kissinger, Vietnam was one piece in the global game of chess. The two men shared the belief that changing strategic realities required a new global strategy. For much of the postwar period the United States was preeminent because of its nuclear predominance and economic strength. By the time Nixon took office, however, the nation's nuclear monopoly was dwindling, Europe was regaining vitality, Asia was emerging as a economic power, and independence movements were sweeping Africa. Since each superpower had the capacity to destroy the other, both nations by then shared an interest in self-preservation. This fundamental common interest provided the foundation for erecting a structure of peaceful coexistence and cooperation. Given the apocalyptic dangers of confrontation, each side had to act with restraint, each had to be conscious of the needs and the interests of its adversary, and each had to avoid taking opportunistic advantage of the other side's vulnerabilities.

The Nixon administration called its strategy détente. For Kissinger, the purpose of détente was not to end competition but to manage it and to keep it from flaring into global conflagration. Even as the competition continued, Kissinger hoped that he could propound and codify "principles of responsible relations in the nuclear age," including "respect for the interests of all, restraint in the uses of power, and abstention from efforts to exploit instability or local conflicts for unilateral advantage." Kissinger was confident that through this change of approach and through an elaborate strategy of diplomatic and economic carrots and sticks ("linkage"), the Soviet Union could be induced to behave like a "normal" great power.

Détente was more than an abstract proposition. Circumstances had provided the administration with both an urgent need and a historic opportunity to thaw the Cold War between the United States and the Soviet Union. The American public, weary of foreign involvement, seemed unwilling to provide the emotional or financial resources necessary to continue sustaining the Cold War. The Soviets had reasons of their own to seek closer ties with the United States. Soviet president Leonid Brezhnev presided over a struggling economy in desperate need of western goods and capital. Like his American counterpart, he hoped to divert resources from the arms race to domestic use. The Soviets were also worried about the growing military power of China. Ancient animosities between the Russian and Chinese empires reached a new level of tension in 1964 when the Chinese exploded their first atomic bomb. In the spring of 1969 long-standing border disputes flared into skirmishes between Russian and Chinese regulars.

Shrewdly, Nixon and Kissinger began working to improve relations with Communist China, using the tension between Russia and China to America's strategic advantage. As an incentive Nixon offered the Chinese access to American technology, capital goods, and foodstuffs. With a solid groundwork established, Nixon made a historic trip to China in February 1972, becoming the first sitting American president to visit that nation and reversing more than twenty years of Sino-American hostility. At the end of the meeting Nixon and China's premier Zhou Enlai issued a joint communiqué calling for increased contact between the two nations. "This was the week that changed the world," Nixon proclaimed. In a veiled reference to the Soviets, the two leaders agreed to oppose any nation that tried "to establish hegemony" in "the Asian-Pacific region."

The Soviets watched nervously as anticommunist Richard Nixon embraced the world's largest communist country. Fearing closer ties between the United States and China, they pushed for their own deal with the Americans. Four months after his historic trip to China, Nixon boarded Air Force One for Moscow. "There must be room in this world for two great nations with different systems to live together and work together," Nixon declared. Nixon and Brezhnev signed trade and technology agreements and a statement of "Basic Principles" that called upon both sides to avoid both military confrontations and "efforts to obtain unilateral advantage at the expense of the other."

More importantly, Nixon reached an agreement with the Soviets on the terms of the Strategic Arms Limitation Talks (SALT), an unprecedented breakthrough in Soviet-American relations. Thereafter, the aim of American nuclear doctrine shifted from achieving "superiority" to maintaining "sufficiency." The SALT I agreement limited the building of antiballistic missile systems, and froze for five years the number of strategic offensive weapons in both arsenals, including intercontinental ballistic missiles and submarine-launched missiles. And for the first time improvements in spy satellites made it possible to monitor an arms limitation agreement. When conservative critics complained that the agreement would limit America's ability to maintain its nuclear superiority, Kissinger blustered, "What in the name of God is strategic superiority. What do you do with it."

Nixon Visits the Great Wall of China   Since the formation of a communist government on mainland China in 1949, the United States had refused to extend diplomatic relations to mainland China. As part of Nixon's quest to lessen tensions between the United States and communist nations and possibly gain assistance in ending the war in Vietnam, Nixon traveled to China in February 1972. In what is often considered the greatest foreign policy achievement of his presidency, Nixon put the United States on the road to normalizing relations with China by promising to lift restrictions on trade and travel between the two countries and acknowledged that Taiwan was part of China. On February 24, 1972, surrounded by newspaper and television reporters, Richard and Pat Nixon walked along a portion of the Great Wall of China.

The Limits of Realism

There were limits to the administration's commitment to realism, however. In July 1969 the president announced the Nixon Doctrine, stating that the United States would supply military and economic assistance but not soldiers to help nations defend themselves against invasion. "We must avoid that kind of policy that will make countries in Asia so dependent upon us that we are dragged into conflicts such as the one that we have in Vietnam." Both Kissinger and Nixon, like most postwar U.S. policy makers, were driven by an intense concern for credibility. Kissinger claimed that "displays of American impotence in one part of the world . . . would inevitably erode our credibility in other parts of the world."

Because Nixon believed that a communist victory anywhere in the world tipped the global balance of power away from the United States, he supplied arms to a number of repressive regimes willing to oppose the regional interests of the Soviet Union. Among others, Nixon sent aid and approved arms sales to the shah of Iran, President Ferdinand Marcos in the Philippines, and Balthazar Vorster's white-supremacist regime of South Africa. In 1971 the United States sided with the military dictatorship of West Pakistan in its attempt to prevent the creation of the independent nation of Bangladesh. The Pakistan government slaughtered thousands, but the United States was more interested in the global chess game. Since India, which had signed a treaty of friendship with the Soviet Union, supported independence, Kissinger believed global realities dictated that the United States support West Pakistan. "We can't allow a friend of ours and China's [Pakistan] to get screwed in a conflict with a friend of Russia's [India]," Kissinger concluded.

The Nixon administration also intervened actively in Latin America. Kissinger had once dismissed Chile as "a dagger pointed at the heart of Antarctica," but when a Marxist, Salvador Allende, won election as president, Nixon directed the Central Intelligence Agency to support Allende's opponents. "I don't see why we need to stand by and watch a country go communist due to the irresponsibility of its own people," Kissinger declared. The president cut off economic aid and prevented private banks from granting loans to Chilean concerns. Military leaders in Chile, convinced by Washington's actions that the United States would support them, staged a successful coup and killed Allende in September 1973. The new anticommunist regime, under General Augusto Pinochet, was one of the most repressive in the hemisphere, but it was quickly recognized by the United States and warmly supported.

The Nixon-Kissinger diplomacy faced its toughest challenge in the Middle East. The region represented a tangle of competing interests: the United States supplied military and economic aid to ensure Israel's survival, but it was also heavily dependent on oil from the Arab states. Complicating the picture, the Middle East had become a Cold War battleground between Washington and Moscow. On October 6, 1973—the most sacred Jewish holy day, Yom Kippur—Syria and Egypt attacked Israel. In the first three days of fighting Egyptian troops advanced into the Sinai while Syria's army in the north threatened to cut Israel in half by penetrating through the Golan Heights. With Israel's survival at stake, the United States ordered a massive supply of arms to its ally. The American aid proved decisive. Israel recovered and took the offensive before the fighting ended in late October.

Over the next two years Kissinger pursued "shuttle diplomacy," traveling among capitals in the Middle East to promote peace. He met with limited success. He made progress with Egypt, but the other Arab states, bruised by America's decisive intervention, imposed an oil embargo against the United States, Europe, and Japan. The embargo, which lasted from October 17, 1973, to March 18, 1974, produced dramatically higher energy costs. Thereafter, the member nations of the Organization of Petroleum Exporting Countries continued to raise oil prices, which increased 400 percent in 1974 alone, with devastating consequences for the oil-dependent U.S. economy. Kissinger also found Israel reluctant to return territory gained in the 1967 war. The issue of "land for peace" would prove a source of continuing friction in the region.

In the end, détente produced some meaningful results in U.S. relations with the Soviet Union and China, but failed to produce a reordering of American foreign policy. The administration overestimated the power of Moscow and China to influence their allies and underestimated the importance of regional conflict and nationalist aspirations. Kissinger hoped that his policy of linkage would encourage the Soviets to help end the Vietnam War. Even though Moscow provided Hanoi with arms, it exercised little influence on a nationalist movement that was determined to defeat the United States. Despite arms agreements, the Pentagon demanded more sophisticated weapons and the Soviets continued to modernize their forces and to crack down on internal dissent. Like previous Cold War presidents, Nixon's inclination to view regional conflict as part of a global chess game produced a fascination with credibility and forced him to squander American prestige, especially in Africa and Latin America.

Playing the Race Card

At home Nixon and his advisers developed a multipronged approach to tap into the frustrations of the "silent majority." First, Nixon moved to exploit the Democrats' vulnerability on race issues. Though he came to office on a tough law-and-order platform, Nixon had always been a racial moderate, and in the tense political atmosphere of the late 1960s he was looking for ways to demonstrate his goodwill. During his first two years in office he reached out to black voters, dramatically expanding government enforcement of desegregation and institutionalizing racial quotas in all government contracts. In 1969 the president approved the Philadelphia Plan, which required construction unions in Philadelphia employed on government contracts to establish "goals and timetables" for hiring minorities. The following year the administration expanded the program to include all federal hiring and contracting. The president's motives were not wholly altruistic. Always a shrewd politician, Nixon saw racial preferences as an effective way to pit two Democratic groups—blacks and labor—against each other. In a long memorandum supporting the plan White House adviser John Ehrlichman pointed out that the plan was both "anti-labor and pro-black" and would drive "a wedge between the Democrats and labor."

Nixon proved to be a fair-weather friend of racial quotas, and as political winds shifted to the right, he repudiated one of his administration's major legacies. The pivotal event was the hard hat march in the spring of 1970, during which thousands of New York City construction workers marched in support of Nixon's Vietnam policies. According to journalist William Safire, "Most of the zip went out of [the Philadelphia Plan] after the hard hats marched in support of Nixon and the war." Nixon saw an opportunity to win over the working class to the Republican Party and now viewed his support of quotas as an obstacle. By 1972 Nixon was attacking Democratic nominee George McGovern as "the quota candidate," claiming that a fixed quota system was "as artificial and unfair a yardstick as has ever been used to deny opportunity."

The Pro-War Demonstration by New York's "Hard Hats"   On the morning of May 8, 1970, hundreds of antiwar activists gathered along Wall Street to protest Nixon's sending of U.S. troops into Cambodia. About five minutes to noon, construction workers, often called "hard hats" in New York, began arriving on the scene and started hitting students with their helmets, scattering the crowd. Then the hard hats marched to City Hall and demanded that the American flag, lowered to half-staff to commemorate the Kent State deaths, be fully raised. Nixon used the action of the hard hats as an example of how average working Americans supported their country and Nixon's actions in Southeast Asia. Nixon even received an honorary hard hat from union leaders to show their support for the president.

The president also pounced on the busing issue to win the allegiance of his cherished "silent majority." In 1971 the Supreme Court, losing patience with southern resistance to desegregation, ordered the busing of students to promote racial mixing in the public schools. Court-ordered busing delighted liberals, but it angered most Americans, especially working-class whites who cherished the notion of "neighborhood schools" and who resented the arrogance of unelected judges and government bureaucrats—many of whom sent their children to private schools. Polls showed that by a three-to-one majority, whites opposed busing.

Nixon, who opposed court-ordered busing, was quick to capitalize on white resistance. "Busing provided Nixon with an anvil on which to forge a link for a receptive voter between an intrusive federal government, liberalism, and the national Democratic party," noted the journalist Thomas Edsall. "No other issue brought home so vividly to whites the image of the federal government as intruder and oppressor." In the months leading up to the election the president fired off memos to his staff, insisting that they emphasize his opposition to "forcibly integrated housing or forcibly integrated education."

In an explicit appeal to the white South, Nixon nominated conservative southern judges to fill Court vacancies. In 1969 he successfully nominated conservative Warren Burger to replace departing Chief Justice Earl Warren. Later that year when another vacancy opened on the court, Nixon turned to South Carolina judge Clement Haynsworth. Though no one questioned Haynsworth's legal credentials, his strong opposition to desegregation angered Senate liberals and worried many moderate Republicans. For the first time since the administration of Herbert Hoover, the Senate rejected a Supreme Court nominee. Nixon responded by nominating Judge G. Harrold Carswell, an undistinguished jurist who had once declared his belief in white supremacy. The Senate again refused to confirm the president's nominee. Nixon lost the battle, but he won the political war because he skillfully used the Senate rejection to score political points in the South by playing on Southerners' sense of victimization.

Nixon also unleashed Vice President Spiro Agnew, who traveled the country denouncing the media, radical professors, student protesters, and liberals. Realizing that the administration needed to break the hold of the Democratic Party on white voters, Agnew promised a "positive polarization" of the electorate. "Will America be led by a President elected by a majority of the American people," he demanded, "or will it be intimidated and blackmailed into following the path dictated by a disruptive radical and militant minority—the pampered prodigies of the radical liberals in the United States Senate?" Agnew called the Kent State killings "predictable and avoidable," and he attacked the "elitists" who regarded the Bill of Rights as a protection "for psychotic and criminal elements in our society."

Finally, while denouncing Democrats for being soft on social issues, Nixon tried to co-opt their economic message by intentionally overheating the economy. Nixon began his administration by embracing the monetarist theories of economist Milton Friedman. The conservative Friedman claimed that prices could be lowered by reducing the quantity of money in the economy. If there was less money and it was more expensive to borrow, reasoned Friedman, economic activity would ease and there would be less upward pressure on prices. In practice a reduced money supply did slow economic growth, but it did not stop prices from rising. By 1970 the unemployment rate had increased by 33 percent, from 3.6 percent to 4.9 percent, while the consumer price index rose by 11 percent. This new and troubling phenomenon, dubbed stagflation, haunted the economy for the rest of the decade.

Deeming monetarism a failure, Nixon tried other policies. In August 1971, faced with a combination of rising prices and high unemployment, Nixon shocked conservatives and delighted liberals by declaring, "I am now a Keynesian." Acting on his new faith, the president advocated traditionally liberal solutions: imposing wage and price controls, devaluing the dollar, and abandoning the gold standard. Fearing the political consequences of high unemployment in an election year, Nixon pressured the Federal Reserve Bank, the nation's central institution for setting interest rates and regulating the money supply, to turn on the money spigot. Commenting on Nixon's dramatic switch, a journalist quipped, "It's a little like a Christian crusader saying 'All things considered, I think Mohammed was right!' " Later that year Nixon announced a "new economic policy," imposing a 10 percent surcharge on U.S. imports. "My basic approach," said Secretary of Treasury John Connally, "is that the foreigners are out to screw us. Our job is to screw them first."

The policies realized their short-turn political and economic goals. During the 1972 election year the gross national product grew by 7.2 percent and the unemployment rate plunged from 6 percent to 5.1 percent. In the long run, however, Nixon's policies proved disastrous. By ignoring clear signs of inflation and intentionally expanding the economy, he contributed to a cycle of spiraling inflation that would soon cripple the economy.

The 1972 Presidential Campaign

Nixon had the good fortune to face the perfect foil for his "silent majority" election strategy. In 1972 the Democratic Party nominated as its presidential candidate Senator George McGovern, an outspoken liberal critic of the Vietnam War who sought to win election by directly challenging Nixon's interpretation of American politics and culture. McGovern and the delegates at the Democratic Party convention adopted an aggressively liberal platform. Among its more controversial points were a call for the immediate withdrawal of U.S. troops from Vietnam, amnesty for those who had avoided the draft, busing to achieve integration in the schools, and the abolition of capital punishment. The platform also included a vaguely worded statement—"Americans should be free to make their own choices of lifestyles and private habits without being subject to discrimination"—that many people interpreted as an endorsement of drug use and homosexuality.

The 1972 election turned into a battle to define the "silent majority." Nixon's strategy was to play on public fear of urban violence and social disorder. The party of FDR, he told wavering Democrats, had been hijacked by antiwar protesters and New Left radicals. "The time has come," Nixon declared in a campaign speech, "to draw the line, . . . for the Great Silent Majority . . . to stand up and be counted against the appeasement of the rock-throwers and the obscenity shouters in America." For McGovern, the "silent majority" consisted of the poor and minorities excluded from the system, young people angry about the war, and the educated, socially liberal middle class. Recent passage of the Twenty-sixth Amendment, granting eighteen-year-olds the right to vote, he hoped, would provide a vast source of support for his candidacy. It was in this spirit that George McGovern portrayed the campaign as "a fundamental struggle between the little people of America and the big rich of America, between the average workingman and woman and the powerful elite."

The Democrats badly misread the mood of the electorate. American casualties in Vietnam had declined steadily during Nixon's first term, and the president's assurance that America would achieve a peace with honor in Vietnam was closer to what voters wanted than was McGovern's call for immediate withdrawal. After a would-be assassin critically wounded George Wallace the day before several crucial 1972 primaries, Nixon inherited many of his angry white supporters. Most were former Democrats who thought their party tilted too far to the left. They saw McGovern not as their champion but as the candidate of a liberal, intellectual, northeastern establishment.

On election day Nixon scored a resounding victory, winning 60.7 percent (47,169,911) of the popular vote. McGovern received only 29,170,383 votes, or 37.5 percent. Nixon carried every state except Massachusetts and the District of Columbia, for a margin in the electoral college of 520 to 17. Nixon's shrewd appeals to the "silent majority" touched a responsive chord with many working-class Democrats who felt their party had abandoned them in pursuit of more liberal voters. Almost 10 million Democrats, nearly one-third of all registered Democrats, voted for Nixon. An overwhelming 70 percent of the white working class voted for him. But it was a lonely landslide. The Democrats gained two seats in the Senate, and the Republicans gained only a dozen House seats. Nixon carried 72 percent of the once-solid South. In a clear reflection of the success of his campaign, he won over 90 percent of white southerners who had voted for Wallace in the primaries. Nixon also won 65 percent of middle-income voters, and he scored well with ethnic voters, winning a majority of Italian and Irish voters.

His resounding triumph convinced the president of the potential of his plans to create a new majority. In the months between the election and inauguration day, the White House initiated discussions with conservative Democrats worried about their party's leftward drift. By the end of January as many as forty wavering congressional Democrats, most from cities with large blue-collar constituencies and the South, were involved in discussions with White House staff. The historian Godfrey Hodgson referred to the plan as "the realignment-that-nearly-happened." As the Watergate scandal expanded, many Democrats moved back to the sidelines, thereby undermining public support for the administration.

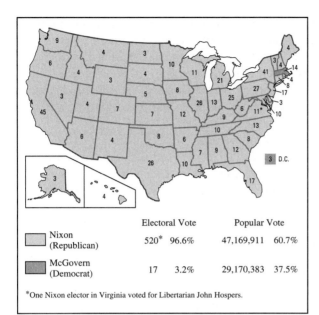

The Election of 1972

The assassination attempt on George Wallace and Edward Kennedy's personal crisis over Chappaquiddick removed two of the leading Democratic candidates for president, leaving Senator George McGovern of South Dakota to take the nomination. The apparent vacillations by McGovern on the campaign trail assisted Nixon in his reelection bid as he focused on his role as "global peacemaker." Nixon won by the largest majority of any Republican in American history.

	Electoral Vote	Popular Vote
Nixon (Republican)	520* 96.6%	47,169,911 60.7%
McGovern (Democrat)	17 3.2%	29,170,383 37.5%

*One Nixon elector in Virginia voted for Libertarian John Hospers.

Watergate and the Downfall of Richard Nixon

The Nixon administration actually began unraveling before the 1972 election. On June 17, 1972, a security guard foiled a break-in at the Democratic Party's national headquarters in the Watergate Hotel. In February 1973 when it learned that one of the men involved in the break-in had once worked for the president's reelection committee, Congress created a bipartisan select committee to probe further into the Watergate affair. Over the next months the committee, headed by North Carolina Democrat Sam Ervin, uncovered a trail of corruption leading to higher and higher levels of the White House staff. Republican senator Howard Baker from Tennessee posed the central question: "What did the president know and when did he know it?"

On June 25 White House counsel John Dean gave a disturbing answer to that question when in flat, unemotional tones he told the committee of the president's personal involvement in a scheme to cover up the Watergate burglary. Dean's proximity to the president and the concrete details he offered in his 245-page testimony made him a compelling witness. Even before he offered his testimony, a large majority of Americans believed that Richard Nixon had either planned or helped cover up the break-in at the Watergate. By June 1973 only 17 percent in one survey believed that Nixon was telling the truth.

While much of official Washington seemed mesmerized by the growing White House scandal, the public was becoming increasingly angry about the economy. The president's wage and price controls had artificially dampened inflation pressures. When he lifted controls, prices climbed. At the same time, higher oil prices raised the inflation rate from 8.4 percent during 1973 to 12.1 percent in 1974. In September 1973, 83 percent reported that "the high cost of living" was the biggest problem facing the nation. Only 14 percent said Watergate. *Time* magazine reported in August that "each costly ring of the check-out cash register seemed to eat away at public patience with the Administration far more than the revelations of the Watergate scandal."

It was Watergate, however, that doomed the Nixon presidency and derailed his strategy of creating a new majority. Former aide Alexander Butterfield revealed to the Ervin committee that Nixon had installed a secret taping system to record, "for posterity," his private conversations in the White House and the Executive Office Building. "Nixon Bugged Himself!" newspaper headlines screamed. A special prosecutor, Harvard law school professor Archibald Cox, asked the courts to order Nixon to release the tapes. Nixon refused. At issue, the president declared, was "the independence of the three branches of our Government." Ervin had a different definition of the question: "Whether the president is above the law."

Cox persisted in his efforts to secure the tapes, and Nixon ordered Attorney General Elliot Richardson to fire the special prosecutor. Richardson refused and then resigned. His deputy, William Ruckelshaus, also refused, and he was fired. Solicitor General Robert H. Bork finally carried out the president's order on October 20, and a dramatic backlash ensued. The press referred to the firings as the "Saturday Night Massacre" and applauded Richardson and Ruckelshaus for their integrity. Members of Congress, citing an outraged public opinion, demanded that a new special prosecutor be appointed and that the tapes be released. Compelled by this unified opposition, Nixon yielded some of the tapes and named a new special prosecutor, Leon Jaworski of Texas. Once again Nixon declared his innocence, this time on television. "I am not a crook," he insisted.

The Saturday night massacre came in the midst of a series of scandals that kept the administration and the American public reeling. Just ten days before, Vice President Spiro Agnew had pleaded no contest in federal court to charges of income-tax evasion and admitted that he had accepted hundreds of thousands of dollars in bribes while governor of Maryland. Agnew resigned from the vice presidency, and Congress quickly confirmed Nixon's choice, House minority leader Gerald R. Ford, a veteran Michigan Republican, to succeed Agnew under the terms of the Twenty-fifth Amendment.

More bad news followed: one of the tapes Nixon had turned over contained a suspicious eighteen-and-one-half-minute gap of a conversation between the president and Haldeman on June 20, three days after the break-in. Nixon's secretary Rosemary Woods took responsibility, claiming that she had accidently erased the tape while transcribing it. Experts testified, however, that the tapes had been deliberately tampered with by "manual" erasures. By December Nixon's own personal finances had come under increasingly critical scrutiny. The Internal Revenue Service disclosed that the president owed more than $400,000 in back taxes and penalties.

The air of scandal and uncertainty continued to hang over the capital until July 24, 1974, when a unanimous Supreme Court ordered President Nixon to turn over all relevant tapes. Just as Dean had contended, the tapes revealed that Nixon had personally intervened to stifle an investigation by the Federal Bureau of Investigation into the Watergate break-in and that he had authorized payments of more than $460,000 in hush money to keep the Watergate burglars from implicating higher-ups in the administration. It was not just the content of the tapes, but Nixon's demeanor and profane language that, in the words of noted columnist Joseph Alsop, engendered "sheer flesh-crawling repulsion."

PRIMARY SOURCE

10.2 | *The Smoking Gun*

In July 1974 the Supreme Court ordered President Nixon to turn over all White House tapes relevant to the Watergate case. One tape recorded a conversation on June 23, 1972, between the president and domestic adviser H. R. Haldeman in which they discussed covering up the Watergate break-in, thereby proving Nixon's culpability.

June 23, 1972

[H. R.] Haldeman: Now, on the investigation, you know the Democratic break-in thing, we're back in the problem area because the FBI is not under control, because [Director Patrick] Gray doesn't exactly know how to control it and they have—their
5 investigation is now leading into some productive area. . . . They've been able to trace the money—not through the money itself—but through the bank sources—the banker. And it goes in some directions we don't want it to go. Ah, also there have been some [other] things—like an informant came in off the street to the FBI in Miami who was a photographer or has a friend who is a photographer who devel-
10 oped some films through this guy [Bernard] Barker and the films had pictures of Democratic National Committee letterhead documents and things. So it's things like that that are filtering in. . . . [John] Mitchell came up with yesterday, and John Dean analyzed very carefully last night and concludes, concurs now with Mitchell's recommendation that the only way to solve this . . . is for us to have [CIA Assistant
15 Director Vernon] Walters call Pat Gray and just say, "Stay to hell out of this—this is ah, [our] business here. We don't want you to go any further on it." That's not an unusual development, and ah, that would take care of it.

President: What about Pat Gray—you mean Pat Gray doesn't want to?

Haldeman: Pat does want to. He doesn't know how to, and he doesn't have any
20 basis for doing it. Given this, he will then have the basis. He'll call [FBI Assistant

Director] Mark Felt in, and the two of them—and Mark Felt wants to cooperate because he's ambitious—

President: Yeah.

Haldeman: He'll call him in and say, "We've got the signal from across the river to
25   put the hold on this." And that will fit rather well because the FBI agents who are working the case, at this point, feel that's what it is.

President: This is CIA? They've traced the money? Who'd they trace it to?

Haldeman: Well, they've traced it to a name, but they haven't gotten to the guy yet.

30   *President:* Would it be somebody here?

Haldeman: Ken Dahlberg.

President: Who the hell is Ken Dahlberg?

Haldeman: He gave $25,000 in Minnesota and, ah, the check went directly to this guy Barker.

35   *President:* It isn't from the Committee though, from [Maurice] Stans?

Haldeman: Yeah. It is. It's directly traceable and there's some more through some Texas people that went to the Mexican bank which can also be traced to the Mexican bank—they'll get their names today.

President: Well, I mean, there's no way—I'm just thinking if they don't cooper-
40   ate, what do they say? That they were approached by the Cubans? That's what Dahlberg has to say, the Texans too.

Haldeman: Well, if they will. But then we're relying on more and more people all the time. That's the problem and they'll [the FBI] . . . stop if we could take this other route.

45   *President:* All right.

Haldeman: [Mitchell and Dean] say the only way to do that is from White House instructions. And it's got to be to [CIA Director Richard] Helms and to—ah, what's his name? . . . Walters.

President: Walters.

50 *Haldeman:* And the proposal would be that . . . [John] Ehrlichman and I call them in, and say, ah—

President: All right, fine. How do you call him in—I mean you just—well, we protected Helms from one hell of a lot of things.

Haldeman: That's what [John] Erhlichman says.

55 *President:* Of course; this [Howard] Hunt [business.] That will uncover a lot of things. You open that scab there's a hell of a lot of things and we just feel that it would be very detrimental to have this thing go any further. This involves these Cubans, Hunt, and a lot of hanky-panky that we have nothing to do with ourselves. Well, what the hell, did Mitchell know about this?

60 *Haldeman:* I think so. I don't think he knew the details, but I think he knew.

President: He didn't know how it was going to be handled though—with Dahlberg and the Texans and so forth? Well who was the asshole that did? Is it [G. Gordon] Liddy? Is that the fellow? He must be a little nuts!

Haldeman: He is.

65 *President:* I mean he just isn't well screwed on, is he? Is that the problem?

Haldeman: No, but he was under pressure, apparently, to get more information, and as he got more pressure, he pushed the people harder.

President: Pressure from Mitchell?

Haldeman: Apparently. . . .

70 *President:* All right, fine, I understand it all. We won't second-guess Mitchell and the rest. Thank God it wasn't [Special White House Counsel Charles] Colson.

Haldeman: The FBI interviewed Colson yesterday. They determined that would be a good thing to do. To have him take an interrogation, which he did, and the FBI guys working the case concluded that there were one or two possibilities—
75 one, that this was a White House (they don't think that there is anything at the Election Committee) they think it was either a White House operation and they have some obscure reasons for it—non-political, or it was a—Cuban [operation] and [involved] the CIA. And after their interrogation of Colson yesterday, they concluded it was not the White House, but are now convinced it is a CIA thing, so
80 the CIA turnoff would—

President: Well, not sure of their analysis, I'm not going to get that involved. I'm (unintelligible).

Haldeman: No, sir, we don't want you to.

President: You call them in.

85   *Haldeman:* Good deal.

President: Play it tough. That's the way they play it and that's the way we are going to play it. . . .

President: O.K. . . . Just say (unintelligible) very bad to have this fellow Hunt, ah, he knows too damned much. . . . If it gets out that this is all involved, the
90   Cuba thing, it would be a fiasco. It would make the CIA look bad, it's going to make Hunt look bad, and it is likely to blow the whole Bay of Pigs thing which we think would be very unfortune—both for CIA, and for the country, at this time, and for American foreign policy. Just tell him to lay off. Don't you [think] so?   ■ ■ ■

On August 8, 1974, facing certain impeachment, a disgraced Richard Nixon became the first American president to resign from office. Following constitutional procedure, he had his formal resignation letter delivered to Henry Kissinger the next morning. "Dear Mr. Secretary: I hereby resign the office of President of the United States. Sincerely, Richard Nixon." He said a tearful farewell to his staff. Just before noon he walked across the south lawn of the White House and climbed on board the presidential helicopter. At noon Vice President Gerald Ford was sworn in as the country's new chief executive. "Our long national nightmare," he declared, "is over."

Many forces conspired to create America's national nightmare. The extraordinary growth of presidential power during the Cold War, the social upheaval and intense partisan divisions of the 1960s and early 1970s, and the emergence of a skeptical and assertive media played important roles in Nixon's downfall. But it is impossible to understand Watergate without coming to terms with the ambitious, paranoid personality of Richard Nixon. Though he occupied the world's most powerful office, Nixon remained surprisingly insecure, fearful that his enemies in the establishment—liberals, media, and Congress—were out to destroy him. Since he equated his own political survival with the fate of the nation, Nixon felt justified in using whatever means necessary to destroy his opponents. "You were either for us or against us," recalled one aide, "and if you were against us we were against you." In a chilling disregard for civil liberties Nixon maintained that to curb domestic dissent, "everything is valid, everything is possible." Perhaps Nixon offered the most insight into his own downfall in his farewell speech to the White House staff. "Never be petty," he said, and "always remember, others may hate

Nixon's Goodbye On August 8, 1974, Richard Nixon became the first American president to resign from office after fellow Republicans made it clear that Nixon would be impeached and removed from office for his role in the Watergate cover-up. Gerald Ford, the House minority leader who had replaced Spiro Agnew as vice president the year before, was then sworn in as president. In this picture, Nixon and his family are boarding the helicopter on the White House lawn for the last time. *(Nixon Presidential Materials Project, National Archives and Record Administration.)*

you, but those who hate you don't win unless you hate them, and then you destroy yourself."

In 1968 Richard Nixon won election preaching social harmony, but he governed by political polarization. Postwar contradictions provided much of the fuel Nixon needed. Affluence, and the rising expectations it produced, had nurtured a younger generation impatient for reform. Rejecting the vital-center faith in slow and gradual progress, the youth culture planned to narrow the gap between American ideals and social realities by forcing a quick end to the Vietnam War and refocusing attention on problems closer to home. Nixon frustrated these plans by playing to the social and cultural anxieties of the "silent majority." Although a majority of Americans opposed the war by 1969, Nixon tapped into the white working class's fear of social disorder, their intense patriotism, and their class resentment. Watergate derailed Nixon's effort to forge a new Republican majority, but it also produced more lasting damage. Nixon not only destroyed himself; he also disgraced the presidency and raised even more doubts about government's ability to produce a meaningful response to the American paradox.

SELECTED READINGS

▋ The history of the Pentagon Papers court case is examined in David Ruden-stine's *The Day the Presses Stopped* (1996); Tom Wells provides a biography of the man who stole the papers, Daniel Ellsberg, in *Wild Man* (2001). William Shawcross indignantly describes Nixon and Kissinger's Cambodia policy in *Sideshow* (1979). Melvin Small outlines the impact of the peace protesters on the administration's policies in *Johnson, Nixon, and the Doves* (1988). Arnold Isaacs critiques Nixon's peace in *Without Honor* (1983), as does Larry Berman in *No Peace, No Honor* (2001). On the influence of the madman theory on Nixon's conduct of the Vietnam War, see Jeffrey Kimball's *Nixon's Vietnam War* (1998). Lewis Sorley offers a revisionist account of the final days of the war in *A Better War* (1999).

▋ Robert S. Litwak's *Detente and the Nixon Doctrine* (1984) is a good intro-duction to Nixon's foreign policy. Tad Szulc's *The Illusion of Peace* (1978) contrasts Nixon's domestic message with his international actions. For Nixon's efforts toward disarmament, see Franz Schurmann's *The Foreign Policies of Richard Nixon* (1987). Edy Kaufman's *Crisis in Allende's Chile* (1988) details the events leading to the 1973 coup. Stephen Rabe covers the crises in the Middle East in *The Road to OPEC* (1982). Raymond Garthoff charts American-Soviet relations in the 1970s in *Detente and Confrontation* (rev. ed., 1994).

▋ Historians are still trying to come to terms with Richard Nixon and his presi-dency. For the best accounts, see Melvin Small, *The Presidency of Richard Nixon* (1999); Joan Hoff, *Nixon Reconsidered* (1995); and Herbert Parmet, *Richard Nixon and His America* (1990). Allen Matusow offers a critical appraisal of the president's economic policy in *Nixon's Economy* (1998). Kim McQuaid analyzes Nixon's mobilization of the "silent majority" in *The Anx-ious Years* (1989). Dean Kotlowski's *Nixon's Civil Rights* (2001) provides a study of Nixon's attempts to redirect the civil-rights debate from integration to economic improvement. Dan Carter examines George Wallace's impact on American politics and the Nixon administration in *The Politics of Rage* (1995). Thomas Edsall describes how Nixon helped mold public anger into a powerful conservative coalition in *Chain Reaction* (1992).

▋ Stanley Kutler's *Abuse of Power* (1997) and The *Wars of Watergate* (1992) are essential reading for understanding Nixon's downfall. Bob Woodward and Carl Bernstein's *All the President's Men* (1974) and *The Final Days* (1976) are both captivating journalistic accounts. See also John Dean's *Blind Ambition* (1976); John Ehrlichman's *Witness to Power* (1982); and John Sirica's *To Set the Record Straight* (1979). For an insightful look at how Americans have remembered the events that led to Nixon's resignation, see Michael Schud-son, *Watergate in American Memory* (1992).

11

The Clash of Cultures, 1970–1980

"**A**rabian Nights," featuring llamas, camels, and a snake charmer, was the theme of the evening at the Enchanted Garden disco in Douglaston, New York. Surrounded by mirrored walls and bathed in colored lights, more than two thousand well-coifed young people crammed onto the rotating dance floor, moving to the rhythmic disco beat. This new musical craze, popularized by the hit movie *Saturday Night Fever* (1977) and by vocalists such as Donna Summer, mesmerized its audiences with glitzy dance halls and pulsating lights. By 1975 there were over ten thousand discos in North America—over two hundred in New York City alone. The music moved millions of young people to dance, while the lyrics, which one critic described as "simple and repetitive to the point of absurdity," left their consciences unscathed.

The extravagant settings and superficial music made popular by disco offered proof to many critics that the 1970s were a cultural wasteland, a time when Americans retreated into personal pursuits and abandoned the higher idealism and public engagement of the 1960s. The journalist Tom Wolfe called it the "me decade." The liberal *New Republic* dismissed the 1970s as "a decade of reaction," while counterculture icon Abbie Hoffman sniffed, "The best thing you can say about the '70s is that they didn't happen." But the critics may have rushed to an unfair judgment, overlooking the central paradox of the decade: while America experienced a political backlash against the 1960s, most Americans absorbed the cultural values of that decade, transforming radical ideas of personal liberation into mainstream values.

Despite popular impressions of the 1970s as shallow and superficial, the decade witnessed an intense cultural clash over the legacy of the 1960s. On one side stood reformers—

homosexuals, Native Americans, Hispanics, and women—who tried to build on the foundation of the "rights consciousness" established during the 1960s. Opposing them were traditionalists—Christian fundamentalists and neoconservative intellectuals—who appealed to traditional values, charging that the emphasis on rights and self-fulfillment had eroded personal responsibility and encouraged a cancerous permissiveness. The tension between reform and traditional values produced a clash between the two sides over a series of contentious issues—busing to achieve racial integration, passage of the Equal Rights Amendment (ERA) to the Constitution, and gay rights—that shaped both the culture and the politics of the decade.

The Me Decade

"In the '70s, hardly anybody was a hippie, because everybody was," declared one observer. Emblems of sixties protest, like long hair and casual dress, gained mainstream appeal during the 1970s. Even notable fashion failures—blue polyester leisure suits and wide, pointy collars—reflected a rebellion against the formality of an older generation. "Many of the changes the hippies spearheaded in the '60s became major cultural phenomena," noted a designer, "particularly the belief that nobody could tell them what to wear." Not everyone rebelled in polyester, however. Many Americans turned to clothes made from natural fabrics, such as cotton caftans and gauze blouses and dresses. The Earth Shoe, designed by a yoga teacher in Denmark, became a big hit, its maker claiming that it provided the natural feel of walking on sand.

Rock and roll, the anthem of the youth rebellion during the 1960s, joined the mainstream in the 1970s. "Rock," noted an observer, "was becoming a common language, the reference point for a splintered culture." Many of the decade's most popular rock and roll artists—David Bowie, Rod Stewart, Elton John, Al Green, the Rolling Stones, and Pink Floyd, among others—wore outrageous costumes, made explicit references to sex and drugs, and often included biting social commentary. But American culture embraced them: young people packed stadiums for concerts and spent millions buying their records. In 1976 presidential candidate Jimmy Carter told audiences that his favorite performers were Bob Dylan, Led Zeppelin, and the Grateful Dead.

The real musical sensation of the decade was disco. Despite all the scorn heaped on it, disco preached a message of inclusion, a blurring of racial and gender differences that were hardening in other areas of American life. In John Updike's *Rabbit Is Rich* (1982), the lead character, Harry Angstrom, marvels over "the Bee Gees [being] white men who have done this wonderful thing of making themselves sound like black women." In addition, disco was music made openly for and by gays as well as straights. Donna Summer and Gloria Gaynor became camp icons, and the Village People presented themselves as cartoon homosexual pinups—a cowboy, a construction worker, a leather man, a Native American, a policeman, and a soldier—who wiggled their way through hits such as "In the Navy" (1979), "YMCA" (1978), and "Macho Man" (1978).

The culture of the 1970s represented a flowering of the youth culture's rebellion, the desire to discover the inner self and find self-fulfillment. The best-selling self-help book of the decade was *Looking Out for #1* (1977). "If we can learn to love and nurture ourselves," said the authors of *How to Be Your Own Best Friend* (1971), "we will find ourselves richer than we ever imagined." Another popular book, *Your Erroneous Zones* (1976), which sold 4 million copies between 1976 and 1980, attacked the "shoulds" that inhibited a person's free spirit and prevented real happiness.

It seemed that everyone wanted to get in touch with her or his true "feelings" in the 1970s. "Feelings" was the title of one of the hit songs of the decade. In 1970 talk-show host Phil Donahue introduced a new form of television journalism, allowing Americans to confess their private sins to the nation. Donahue repeatedly thanked guests for "sharing their feelings" and "sharing their pain" with the audience at home. The desire to share inner feelings led to a spate of tell-all confessional books. Joan Crawford's traumatized daughter wrote about her drunk and crazed mother in the best-selling *Mommie Dearest* (1978). In *The Times of My Life* (1978), Betty Ford discussed her mastectomy and her treatment for pill-and-alcohol dependency. *The David Kopay Story* (1977) recounted the experiences of a former professional football player who publicly announced his homosexuality.

Always sensitive to changing public moods, advertisers told consumers they should buy a product not because it worked, or was a bargain, but because it would make them "feel" better. A popular cereal commercial told housewives that "you feel good about serving your family." Another bragged, "It's nice to feel so good about a meal." In one of the most memorable slogans of the decade, the phone company urged Americans to "reach out and touch someone."

The Flowering of 1960s Culture

The consciousness revolution, once confined to the youthful counterculture, mushroomed into a mass movement, particularly among the white middle class. Drugs remained the method of choice for many Americans trying to escape the drudgery of everyday life. Marijuana use became a right of passage for most college students in the 1970s. Between 1970 and 1979, the proportion of Americans favoring the full legalization of marijuana doubled from 12 to 25 percent. Many young people also experimented with sedatives called Quaaludes. Use of mind-altering drugs spread to older Americans, who managed to get their drugs legally. In 1975 doctors issued 229 million prescriptions. The most popular drug of the decade was the tranquilizer Valium.

Many Americans looked to eastern religions "to get in touch with their feelings," with others, and with the forces of nature. America in the mid-1970s, observed countercultural historian Theodore Roszak, launched "the biggest introspective binge any society in history has undergone." Although techniques of introspection varied, all were directed toward releasing the self from the domination of the ego. Some disciplines focused on liberating emotions in encounter groups, while others used deep massage or physical exercise to restore awareness to the body. Most employed some form of meditation or breathing exercises to expand consciousness beyond the routine of everyday intellectual experience. The most popular fad, Transcendental Meditation (TM), required two twenty-minute periods daily of repeating a word called a "mantra."

In 1977 pollster George Gallup reported that some 6 million Americans had tried TM, 5 million had tried yoga, and 2 million had experimented with one variant or another of eastern religions. "From 1971 to 1975, I directly experienced est, gestalt therapy, bioenergetics, Rolfing, massage, jogging, health foods, tai chi, Esalen, hypnotism, modern dance, meditation, Silva Mind Control, Arica, acupuncture, sex therapy, Reichian therapy—a smorgasbord course in New Consciousness," Jerry Rubin wrote in 1976.

Despite the challenge to convention, the consciousness movement actually reinforced many traditional American beliefs about the innate goodness of people and the ability of individuals to control their own fate. "The new consciousness takes the constitutional right to the pursuit of happiness and gives it a new metaphysical twist," noted an observer. "From 'getting what you want,' the idea of happiness has been transformed into 'changing who you are.' " After conquering the West and exploring outer space, Americans in the 1970s seemed ready to conquer the mysteries of the self. "We were the first to put a man into outer space," noted a supporter. "Now we have the opportunity of launching the first psychenauts into inner space."

Sexual feelings were high on the list of emotions that Americans explored during the decade. By the mid-1970s Americans were bombarded with sexual images. Off-Broadway plays featured frontal nudity, magazines displayed centerfolds, sexual themes pervaded daytime television, and dinner-table conversation revolved around previously taboo subjects such as birth control, abortion, and homosexuality. *The Joy of Sex* (1972), which billed itself as "the first explicitly sexual book for the coffee table," sold more than 3.8 million copies in its first two years. The decade saw the success of new sexually explicit magazines *Penthouse* and *Playgirl,* while mainstream women's publications such as *Cosmopolitan* began featuring centerfolds of nude males. Many cities saw a proliferation in the number of bathhouses, both gay and straight. The most famous, Plato's Retreat in New York City, treated over six thousand men and women every month to an assortment of sexual experiences. By the end of the decade a *Newsweek* columnist noted: "Male prostitutes are now convivial guests on the daytime talk shows. Paperback copies of the *Joy of Sex* are tossed into the grocery shopping bag with the asparagus. Wife-swapping and group sex are such old topics of suburban patio conversation that they are now considered somewhat dreary."

Explicitly sexual messages permeated popular culture. Disco queen Donna Summer moaned her way through "Love to Love You Baby" and followed up that hit with "More, More, More," sung to a backdrop of orgasmic yelps by porn star Andrea True. Among the most popular television shows were *Get Christie Love!, Love, American Style,* and *The Love Boat.* The 1972 release of the pornographic movie *Deep Throat,* starring Linda Lovelace, gained critical acclaim and emerged as one of the year's most popular films, earning more than $25 million in sales. Polls showed that up to 25 percent of the public watched porno films. The most provocative television show of the decade was Norman Lear's eccentric soap opera *Mary Hartman, Mary Hartman.* Its heroine, a befuddled, angst-ridden housewife residing in the mythical blue-collar town of Fernwood, Ohio, deals nearly every day with an impotent husband, a promiscuous sister, and a senile grandfather known to police as "the Fernwood Flasher." "There is something sick, sick and twisted, twisted about 'Mary Hartman, Mary Hartman,' " observed a critic.

The pervasiveness of sexual images reflected a loosening of traditional sexual values. A majority of Americans, both male and female, expressed more liberal views on premarital sex, couples living together outside of marriage, and abortion. In 1973, 74 percent of women saw nothing wrong with premarital sex, up from 53 percent just four years earlier. A survey of female sexuality by *Redbook* magazine revealed that 33 percent of the respondents had extramarital affairs and another 36 percent said they would like to. "Our findings show that women have completely abandoned the role of passive sexual partner," said sociologist Robert J. Levin. "They are now active participants in the sexual relationship." In an age that emphasized personal fulfillment, self-awareness, and sexual freedom, there was less incentive to remain in marriages. The divorce rate, which climbed almost 100 percent in the 1960s, increased another 82 percent in the 1970s. More than two out of five marriages during the decade ended in divorce.

The search for self-fulfillment also found expression in a health and fitness craze. Natural food stores sprouted from coast to coast. Between 1968 and 1972 the number of health food stores in the United States more than doubled, from one thousand two hundred to two thousand six hundred. By the end of the decade Stow-Mills, the largest health food distributor in New England, was selling 12 tons of granola each month. Supermarkets in major cities offered leeks, fresh herbs, and organically grown produce. In 1973 editors revised the *Good Housekeeping Cookbook* to reflect changing eating habits. The newer version cut back on fat and cholesterol and added more natural ingredients. Salad bars, which started as a hippie novelty, became commonplace at fancy restaurants and fast-food eateries.

Americans by the millions started jogging to stay fit and improve their overall health . "If the emblem of the '60s was the angry banner of a protest marcher, the spirit of '79 was the jogger, absorbed in the sound of his own breathing—and wearing a smile button," observed *Newsweek.* In the 1978 bestseller *The Complete Book of Running,* James Fixx suggested that running produced "a trance-like state, a mental plateau where they feel miraculously purified and at peace with themselves and the world." In 1978 Gallup estimated that 15 million American men and women jogged regularly. In 1970, 126 runners participated in the first New York Marathon; by the end of the decade the number had soared to nearly 15,000. In 1977 alone paid circulation of *Runner's World,* the premier joggers' magazine, rocketed from 76,000 to 250,000.

For all its appeal, jogging remained largely a white middle-class, urban phenomenon. Sixty percent of the participants in the 1978 New York Marathon had graduate degrees. Women were a small but growing presence in the marathon. Blacks made up between 1 and 3 percent of runners participating in the race. "For a guy who works hard in a factory all day doing heavy manual labor, it's hard to come home and decide what he needs is to run an hour to relax," observed a New York factory worker. Jogging was especially popular in urban areas that offered few outside forms of recreation. The District of Columbia had more runners in relation to its population than any other area of the country, while rural South Dakota, North Dakota, and Arkansas were at the bottom of the scale.

The jogging craze was part of a larger public fascination with fitness that helped make exercise a very profitable business. The fitness industry generated over $10 billion a year in sales. Jogging and tennis led in popularity, but racquetball, handball, squash, and sailing also found new recruits. Sales of roller skates exploded over 500 percent during the decade. "The only thing that is slowing growth is product availability," said a sporting goods executive. Austrian-born Arnold Schwarzenegger raised bodybuilding to a new art form with the publication of his book *Pumping Iron: The Art and Sport of Bodybuilding* (1974). An older generation displayed its status by wearing expensive clothing and jewelry. In the 1970s the more casual jogging suit became a status symbol. "The jogging suit is a status symbol in the same way that tennis dresses signify something slightly aristocratic," observed an exercise executive. "It implies that the person wearing it has a great deal of leisure time and is in good physical shape."

The anti-authority streak of the 1960s counterculture seeped into the popular culture of the 1970s. The Vietnam War provoked a distrust and cynicism that found expression in such songs as Creedence Clearwater Revival's "Fortunate Son" and Edwin Starr's "War," as well as acclaimed films such as *The Godfather* (1972), *Chinatown* (1974), *Taxi Driver* (1976), and *Midnight Cowboy* (1969). "The common denominator," noted a critic, "is that you can't go to the government and expect justice—you have to do it yourself, which is all linked to the trauma of the war."

Many of the pop icons of the decade, from John Lennon, who performed at peace concerts, to Muhammad Ali, who was stripped of his heavyweight crown for refusing to be drafted, were closely identified with the antiwar movement. At concerts the guitarist Jimi Hendrix dedicated his song "Machine Gun" to "all the soldiers fighting in Chicago, Milwaukee, New York and, yeah, all the soldiers fighting in Vietnam." His irreverent version of "The Star-Spangled Banner" became so identified with the youth revolt that director Francis Ford Coppola hired a Hendrix impersonator to re-create the guitarist's raw style on the sound-track of his film *Apocalypse Now* (1979). Vietnam inspired a new acerbic satire. The originators of *Saturday Night Live,* the comic television hit of the decade, came of age at the height of the Vietnam War and infused their skits with pointed barbs at anyone in a position of authority.

But popular culture also revealed the struggle of a culture attempting to reconcile new ideas with old realities. The popular ABC miniseries *Roots* (1976) provided audiences with a rich portrayal of the African-American experience. Norman Lear's popular sitcom *All in the Family* pitted Archie Bunker, who preferred an older, simpler America, expressed in the theme song "Those Were the Days," against the progressive views of his liberal son-in-law, Michael. "Why fight it?" Michael asked Archie in the first episode. "The world's changing." But Archie, refusing to accept defeat, continued his fight against the forces of change, especially minorities, liberals, and radicals. "I'm against all the right things," Archie shouted, "welfare, busing, women's lib, and sex education."

A number of blockbuster movies also touched on sensitive issues and revealed the decade's conflicting social currents. In the 1976 Academy Award–winning film *Rocky,* filmwriter Sylvester Stallone played a streetwise white rough-neck named Rocky Balboa, "the Italian Stallion," who challenged the outspoken and black Apollo Creed for the heavyweight championship of the world. Movie audiences cheered for the white ethnic underdog who one movie critic called "the most romanticized Great White Hope in screen history." *Breaking Away* (1979), the story of blue-collar youth competing in a bicycle race in Blooming-ton, Indiana, offered a more subtle and sensitive portrayal of working-class frus-tration. *Kramer vs. Kramer,* the biggest box-office hit of 1979, used the story of a painful divorce and child custody battle to deal with changing gender roles and the breakup of the family.

Hollywood, and the nation, struggled during the decade to come to terms with Vietnam. The film *M*A*S*H* (1970), later made into a television sitcom, used the backdrop of an army field hospital in Korea to present a black comedy about Vietnam. In 1978 two Vietnam films, *Coming Home* and *The Deer Hunter,* swept the Oscars with their vivid portrayals of how the war traumatized ordinary Americans. The message of *Coming Home,* which starred peace activist Jane Fonda, was solidly antiwar. *The Deer Hunter* was more ambiguous. In tracing the tragic journey of three friends from a steel-mill town in western Pennsylvania who volunteered for the war, director Michael Cimino showed the tremendous price, both physical and psychological, many Americans paid during the conflict. At the same time, critics charged that by depicting the Vietcong as "brutes and dolts" and the Americans as "innocents in a corrupt land," the movie took a sub-tle prowar position.

African-Americans: Progress and Poverty

Dreams of social change did not end with the changing of the calendar. "The rise of rights-consciousness, having flourished in the early and mid-1960s, became central to the culture of the 1970s," observed the historian James T. Patterson. African-Americans were once again at the center of that movement, building on the success of the civil-rights movement of the 1960s, moving beyond demands for political rights and calling for expanded economic opportunities. The Civil Rights Act of 1964 and the Voting Rights Act of 1965 had destroyed the last vestiges of legal discrimination. The courts gave legal sanction to the demands of civil-rights groups for affirmative action programs that sought to achieve equality by reserving opportunities for minorities. In 1978 a white man, Allan Bakke, sued the University of California Medical School at Davis, claiming that the university had rejected him in favor of less-qualified minority candidates. A divided Supreme Court, in *Bakke* v. *University of California* (1978), ruled that the university's absolute quota for minorities was illegal, but it also agreed that schools could consider race as a "plus factor" in admissions so as to foster "diversity" in the classes.

With vigorous government enforcement of the Voting Rights Act of 1965, African-Americans began voting in unprecedented numbers and dramatically increased their representation in Congress, in statehouses, and in town halls across the nation. The most dramatic gains took place on the local level. In 1964 there were 70 elected black officials at all levels of government; by 1980, there were 4,600, including more than 170 mayors. During the 1970s black mayors were elected in Los Angeles, Detroit, Cleveland, Birmingham, Oakland, and Atlanta.

The end of legal segregation opened up new opportunities for African-Americans. Many took white-collar jobs and held union memberships for the first time, earning higher incomes and enjoying advances in job security. In the 1970s the earnings of between 35 and 45 percent of African-American families rose to middle-class levels. By 1977 more than 1 million blacks were attending college, a 500 percent increase since 1960. In 1980 the University of Michigan's National Opinion Research Center concluded that American society had "a truly visible black middle class" for the first time in its history.

Unfortunately, legal and economic gains took place against a backdrop of increasing misery for many African-Americans. In the 1970s black America increasingly divided into a two-class society: while some black families rose to middle-class income levels during the decade, about 30 percent slid deeper into poverty. African-Americans had long suffered disproportionately from poverty, but that of the 1960s and 1970s was in many ways new, marked by a deeper isolation and hopelessness. The economic gap between blacks and whites also widened during the decade. Between 1975 and 1980 the number of unemployed white workers declined by 562,000, while the number of unemployed black workers increased by 200,000. Those African-Americans who held jobs earned less than their white counterparts. In 1970 blacks working in the Northeast made seventy-five cents for every dollar whites made; by 1979 that number had dropped to fifty-eight cents. In 1978 only 8.7 percent of white families lived below the poverty line, compared to 30.6 percent of African-American families.

Frustrated by the persistence of discrimination, many African-Americans abandoned the integrationist ideal of the early civil-rights struggle. In the words of African-American scholar Harold Cruse, discussions about race in America shifted from a "politics of civil rights" to a "politics of black ethnicity." "The Negro Integrationist runs afoul of reality in pursuit of an illusion," Cruse noted. Even though the vast majority of African-Americans rejected militant expressions of Black Power, they did embrace expressions of black cultural nationalism.

The New Cultural Pluralism

The black freedom struggle inspired other groups to reassess their relationship with the larger society. Young Native American, Chicano, and Asian activists asserted a new message of cultural pluralism that rejected the assimilationist hopes of their parents. During the 1960s and 1970s Native Americans invoking "Red Power" protested against Washington's effort to force them off reservations and "assimilate" into mainstream society. In December 1972 members of the American Indian Movement (AIM) orchestrated the seizure of the headquarters of the Bureau of Indian Affairs in Washington, D.C., and held it for a week. In February 1973 when local whites who had murdered a Sioux were lightly punished, two hundred AIM members occupied the town of Wounded Knee, South Dakota. They held the area for over two months, demanding that the government honor hundreds of broken treaties and calling for major changes in reservation government.

Other Native Americans used more traditional tactics to win a series of legal actions that restored violated treaty rights and extended legal rights. Armed with copies of old treaties, Native Americans marched into courts and won the return of land wrongly taken from them. They also won legal battles to block strip mining and to preserve rights to fishing and mineral resources of reservation land. In 1970 President Richard Nixon's "Special Message to Congress on Indian Affairs" helped produce two important pieces of legislation: the 1975 Indian Self-Determination and Education Assistance Act and the 1976 Indian Health Care Improvement Act. These two laws, along with future amendments, ensured tribal sovereignty and increased tribes' ability to control programs affecting their welfare.

Despite impressive gains, Native Americans faced overwhelming obstacles. Reservations, shrunken by treaty violations and far from employment opportunities, were dismal places. In 1971 unemployment among reservation Indians ranged from 40 to 75 percent and annual family incomes averaged about $1,500.

© Owen Luck 1973. All Rights Reserved

Native American Seizure of the Wounded Knee Church, April 1973 The American Indian Movement (AIM), inspired by the African-American civil rights movement, seized the trading post and Catholic church at Wounded Knee, on the South Dakota Pine Ridge Reservation, on February 28, 1973. Site of the last Native American resistance to white rule in the nineteenth century, Wounded Knee was seen as the perfect place to air the grievances of twentieth-century Native Americans living on reservations and suffering from staggering poverty and poor health facilities. Members of AIM and local Ogala Lakota people fought attempts by the FBI to extricate them from the church, and the ensuing violence led to the deaths of two agents. After seventy-one days, AIM surrendered, but their actions forced public discourse about the civil rights of Native Americans and began the debate over tribal self-governance.

Life expectancy was only forty-six years, compared to the national average of seventy. Infant mortality rates were the highest in the nation. Educational opportunities on reservations, according to a Harvard study, were "by every standard . . . the worst in the nation," and the dropout rate among Indian high-school students was the highest of any ethnic group in the nation.

Many young Mexicans and Puerto Ricans were inspired by the militancy of the civil-rights struggle and by the early victories of labor organizers who appealed to the ethnic pride of Hispanics. In 1965 César Chávez and the United Farm Workers (UFW) organized a strike against powerful California grape growers. Despite the UFW gaining the support of Walter Reuther and the United Auto Workers, and of influential politicians such as Robert F. Kennedy, the growers continued to import workers to replace the strikers. In 1966 Chávez organized a 250-mile march from Delano to Sacramento to call attention to the strike, or *la huelga*. The cry *huelga* became symbolic of a broad, nonviolent crusade for civil rights—*la Causa*. Between 1968 and 1970 Chávez orchestrated a national boycott of California grapes, which eventually forced the growers to recognize the UFW.

United Farm Workers on Strike   Led by César Chávez, Filipino farm workers in Delano, California, protested the horrible conditions of migrant labor camps, the corrupt labor contracts, and the intense racism of the San Joaquin region in 1965. By 1970, protests and boycotts forced twenty-six grape growers to the bargaining table, improving conditions for migrant workers in the West. *(Matt Herron/Take Stock.)*

PRIMARY SOURCE

11.1 | *The Grape Boycott*
CÉSAR CHÁVEZ

During a UFW boycott of grape growers, union founder César Chávez initiated a hunger strike in February 1964 as a show of solidarity with the UFW. On March 10, after three weeks of fasting, a weak Chávez met with eight thousand farm workers and political leaders, including Senator Robert Kennedy, to pray and end the fast. Because Chávez was unable to deliver his prepared speech, a minister who worked with the UFW read the address to the assembled crowd.

I have asked the Reverend James Drake to read this statement to you because my heart is so full and my body too weak to be able to say what I feel.

My warm thanks to all of you for coming today. Many of you have been here before, during the fast. Some have sent beautiful cards and telegrams and made
5 offerings at the Mass. All of these expressions of your love have strengthened me, and I am grateful.

We should all express our thanks to Senator Kennedy for his constant work on behalf of the poor, for his personal encouragement to me, and for taking the time to break bread with us today.

10 I do not want any of you to be deceived about the fast. The strict fast of water only which I undertook on February 16 ended after the twenty-first day because of the advice of our doctor, James McKnight, and other physicians. Since that time I have been taking liquids in order to prevent serious damage to my kidneys.

We are gathered here today not so much to observe the end of the fast but 15 because we are a family bound together in a common struggle for justice. We are a union family celebrating our unity and the nonviolent nature of our movement. Perhaps in the future we will come together at other times and places to break bread and to renew our courage and to celebrate important victories.

The fast has had different meanings for different people. Some of you may 20 still wonder about its meaning and importance. It was not intended as a pressure against any growers. For that reason we have suspended negotiations and arbitration proceedings and relaxed the militant picketing and boycotting of the strike during this period. I undertook this fast because my heart was filled with grief and pain for the sufferings of farm workers. The fast was first for me and then for 25 all of us in this union. It was a fast for nonviolence and a call to sacrifice.

Our struggle is not easy. Those who oppose our cause are rich and powerful and they have many allies in high places. We are poor. Our allies are few. But we have something the rich do not own. We have our own bodies and spirits and the justice of our cause as our weapons.

30 When we are really honest with ourselves we must admit that our lives are all that really belong to us. So it is how we use our lives that determines what kind of men we are. It is my deepest belief that only by giving our lives do we find life. I am convinced that the truest act of courage, the strongest act of manliness, is to sacrifice ourselves for others in a totally nonviolent struggle for justice. To be a 35 man is to suffer to others. God help us to be men! ■ ■ ■

New immigrants from Mexico helped make Hispanic-Americans the fastest growing minority group in America during the 1960s and 1970s. By 1980 Mexicans and Mexican-Americans made up about 60 percent of the nation's 14.6 million Hispanics. They were followed in numbers by Puerto Ricans and Cubans. While lumped together on census forms, Hispanics reflected a wide variety of cultures. The diversity is evident in the different names used to describe them: the most commonly used term was *Hispanic*, but many people of Spanish descent preferred to describe themselves as *Latino*. Others identified with their native country: Cuban, Puerto Rican, Dominican. Some Mexican-Americans used the term *Chicano*. "A Chicano," observed the journalist Ruben Salazar, "is a Mexican-American with a non-Anglo image of himself."

Hispanics developed different strategies for adapting to American society. Mexican immigration was circular, made up of poor workers who traveled back and forth between the United States and Mexico in search of better jobs. Immigrants from South and Central America tended to be middle class or professionals who either fled their homeland because of political instability or were attracted to America by the dream of a better life. These immigrants were often downwardly mobile, abandoning high-status jobs at home for menial work in the United States. When Fidel Castro assumed power in Cuba and began nationalizing industry, the professional and middle class fled to the United States and created a thriving community in Miami, Florida. In 1979 Cuban-Americans had the highest median family income of all Hispanic groups, although they still lagged behind white non-Hispanics. In 1979 more than one-third of Puerto Rican families had no workers in the household, earned less than any other ethnic group on the mainland, and had the highest school-dropout rate of all ethnic groups.

During the 1970s Hispanic intellectuals and labor leaders rejected traditional notions of the "melting pot" and espoused a militant message of cultural pluralism. In 1972 Rodolfo Acuna, who established a pioneering Chicano Studies Program at the California State University at Northbridge, published *Occupied America: The Chicano's Struggle Toward Liberation*. Acuna claimed that America was a "European term of occupation and colonization," and he advised Chicanos to resist integration and "captivity." In Denver Rodolfo "Corky" Gonzales, a former boxer and Democratic party official, rejected conventional reform politics and established a separate organization, the *Crusade for Justice*. In addition to calling for better housing and greater economic opportunity, the crusade openly discussed declaring its independence from the United States. In New Mexico the Federal Alliance of Land Grants, a militant separatist group, attempted to reclaim land, water, and grazing rights that had been usurped by Anglos. At the same time, Chicano student leaders in the Southwest demanded educational reform and helped establish Ethnic Studies programs at a handful of universities.

The nationalist sentiment of the Chicano movement found expression in literature and the arts. In 1970 Richard Vasquez's *Chicano* (1970) told the story of the immigrant experience through the lives of three generations of a family. In *Barrio Boy* (1971), Ernesto Galarza shared the personal story of his family's move from Mexico. Corky Gonzales wove Mexican history and immigrant anguish into his moving poem "I Am Joaquin" (1967). The late 1960s and 1970s witnessed an explosion in Chicano journals, periodicals, and publishing houses. Chicano songwriters criticized Anglo treatment of Mexicans and celebrated ethnic pride. *Viva la Causa—Songs and Sounds from the Delano Strike* (1966) used music and oral history to document the struggle for union recognition.

Many Hispanic leaders hoped that the emergence of an extensive Spanish-language communications media would help build a greater sense of community. By 1980 nearly two-thirds of Hispanics had access to Spanish media. Spanish International Network (SIN) included 101 TV stations and produced a wide range of programs—news shows, soap operas, sports, comedy, variety, and public affairs. "SIN has managed to provide a communications outlet never available before," said a spokesman for the National Puerto Rican Forum. "Through the news programs, Hispanic groups are learning about each other. This will have a great impact on our political power formation."

Dramatic increases in immigration following passage of the 1965 Immigration Reform Act contributed to a growing assertiveness among Asian-Americans. In the twenty years following the 1965 act, the Asian population in the United States soared from 1 million to 5 million—nearly four times as many Asians entered the country during that period as had emigrated in the previous one hundred years. Before 1965 New York's Chinatown never had a population of more than ten thousand people; twenty years later it had become the home of one hundred thousand. During the same time period the Korean and Indian population in the United States jumped from ten thousand to more than five hundred thousand.

Unlike the impoverished and often illiterate laborers who had once flocked to American shores, many of the new Asian migrants came from middle-class backgrounds and had professional or technical skills. The educated middle class in such countries as India, the Philippines, and Korea realized that they could have better lives by finding employment in the United States. "Wages in Manila are barely enough to answer for my family's needs," said a Philippine immigrant. "I must go abroad to better my chances." By 1974 Asian immigrants made up nearly one of five practicing physicians in the United States. The percentage was even higher in large urban areas. In some hospitals in New York City Asian immigrants made up more than 80 percent of staff doctors.

Searching for an identity in a society that viewed race in terms of black and white, Asian-Americans convinced the U.S. Census Bureau to list Asian as a racial category on the 1980 census form. At the same time, third-generation Japanese Americans, the Sansei, pressured Washington to establish a commission to investigate the internment of their parents during World War II. They also encouraged these parents, the Nisei, to speak out about their wartime experiences. In July 1980 the Commission on Wartime Relocation and Internment of Citizens recommended that the government issue a formal apology for the internment and provide $20,000 in compensation for each survivor. Congress accepted the recommendation and enacted it into law in 1988.

The Modern Gay-Rights Movement

Along with other groups, homosexuals challenged prevailing ideas about their place in society. While small gay-rights organizations such as the Mattachine Society and the Daughters of Bilitis had been fighting for civil rights for years, the modern gay-rights movement was born on Friday night, June 27, 1969, when a group of Manhattan police officers raided the Stonewall Inn, a gay bar in the heart of Greenwich Village. Such raids, and the police abuse that frequently followed, were routine affairs. Not this time. As one reporter noted, "Limp wrists were forgotten. Beer cans and bottles were heaved at the windows and a rain of coins descended on the cops."

The Stonewall riot ignited a nationwide grass-roots "liberation" movement among gay men and women. Using confrontation tactics borrowed from the civil-rights movement and the rhetoric of revolution employed by the New Left, the gay-rights movement achieved a number of victories during the decade. The number of gay organizations in America grew from less than fifty to more than one thousand. In many large cities gays and lesbians created support networks, newspapers, bars, and travel clubs. In less than a decade, noted an observer, American society had witnessed "an explosion of things gay." The gay-rights movement received a psychological boost in 1973 when the American Psychiatric Association reversed a century-old policy and stopped listing homosexuality as a mental disorder.

Though thirty-two states continued to designate homosexual practices as crimes, eighteen states eliminated sodomy laws that barred sexual acts between consenting adults. Many cities approved ordinances prohibiting job, credit, and other discrimination on the basis of sexual preferences. In Congress two dozen sponsors introduced an amendment to the Civil Rights Act of 1964 adding homosexuals to the list of groups that may not be discriminated against in public accommodations and employment. Many corporations enacted a policy of nondiscrimination on the basis of sexual orientation in hiring and promotion. In 1975 the San Francisco School Board voted unanimously to revise the school system's family-life curriculum to acknowledge homosexual lifestyles. "Gays felt some of the references reflected negatively on them," said one administrator. "They were right."

PRIMARY SOURCE

11.2 | *A Radical Manifesto, 1969*

The Stonewall riots radicalized many gay activists who saw a clear link between their cause and the plight of other oppressed groups in the United States. This "radical manifesto," issued in August 1969, captures the anger and frustration felt by many gay leaders. It also reveals their desire to build political alliances with other minority groups.

A Radical Manifesto—The Homophile Movement Must Be Radicalized! *(August 28, 1969)*

1) We see the persecution of homosexuality as part of a general attempt to oppress all minorities and keep them powerless. Our fate is linked with these minorities; if
5   the detention camps are filled tomorrow with blacks, hippies and other radicals, we will not escape that fate, all our attempts to dissociate ourselves from them notwithstanding. A common struggle, however, will bring common triumph.

2) Therefore we declare our support as homosexuals or bisexuals for the struggles of the black, the feminist, the Spanish-American, the Indian, the Hippie, the
10 Young, the Student, and other victims of oppression and prejudice.

*NACHO was a coalition of about 24 gay groups. Its approach was similar to that of the NAACP.

3) We call upon these groups to lend us their support and encourage their presence with NACHO* and the homophile movement at large.

4) Our enemies, an implacable, repressive governmental system; much of organized religion, business and medicine, will not be moved by appeasement or appeals to reason and justice, but only by power and force.

5) We regard established heterosexual standards of morality as immoral and refuse to condone them by demanding an equality which is merely the common yoke of sexual repression.

6) We declare that homosexuals, as individuals and members of the greater community, must develop homosexual ethics and esthetics independent of, and without reference to, the mores imposed upon heterosexuality.

7) We demand the removal of all restrictions on sex between consenting persons of any sex, of any orientation, of any age, anywhere, whether for money or not, and for the removal of all censorship.

8) We call upon the churches to sanction homosexual liaisons when called upon to do so by the parties concerned.

9) We call upon the homophile movement to be more honestly concerned with youth rather than trying to promote a mythical, non-existent "good public image."

10) The homophile movement must totally reject the insane war in Viet Nam and refuse to encourage complicity in the war and support of the war machine, which may well be turned against us. We oppose any attempts by the movement to obtain security clearances for homosexuals, since these contribute to the war machine.

11) The homophile movement must engage in continuous political struggle on all fronts.

12) We must open the eyes of homosexuals on this continent to the increasingly repressive nature of our society and to the realizations that Chicago may await us tomorrow. ■ ■ ■

The Women's Movement

Each of these groups—African-Americans, American Indians, Hispanics and Asian-Americans, and homosexuals—initiated significant changes in American society during the 1970s. But it was the women's liberation movement that emerged as the largest and most powerful social movement of the decade. "There never has been a movement of social change that has affected so many people so quickly," said feminist Betty Friedan, whose book *The Feminine Mystique* (1963) had helped launch the movement. "The women's movement is everywhere—in sports, churches, offices, homes, languages. It has moved into society as a whole."

The women's movement began with two major wings. One group of feminists, led primarily by older professional women, sought to achieve change by working within the political system. The National Organization for Women (NOW) best exemplified this reform impulse. Formed in 1966 to lobby the government on behalf of issues of special concern to women, and modeled after the National Association for the Advancement of Colored People, NOW announced that its purpose was to "take action to bring women into full participation in the mainstream of American society now, exercising all the privileges and responsibilities thereof in truly equal partnership with men." NOW called for an equal rights amendment to the Constitution, which it believed would help women win other benefits: equal employment, maternity leave, federally subsidized child care support, and the right to choose abortion.

Younger feminist leaders by and large rejected NOW's moderate approach and advocated bolder measures. Many had worked with the Student Nonviolent Coordinating Committee during the Freedom Summer of 1964 or in one of the student protest movements, where they had shaped their beliefs about politics and protest. Like others in the New Left, these women's liberationists, or radical feminists, distrusted establishment political tactics and instead sought ways to change American culture and to build a society based on participatory democracy. Irreverent and eager to challenge prevailing beliefs, they used the tactics of mass protest, direct action, and political theater characteristic of the civil-rights struggles. While some African-American feminists joined these predominately white groups, many believed that their white counterparts underplayed the importance of race. In response, in 1973 nearly four hundred black feminists founded the National Black Feminist Organization.

The feminist movement won a number of impressive victories in the courts and legislatures during the 1970s. New York Democratic congresswoman Bella Abzug declared 1972 "a watershed year. We put sex discrimination provisions into everything." In 1972 Congress passed Title IX of the Higher Education Act, which banned discrimination "on the basis of sex" in "any education program or activity receiving federal financial assistance." The legislation set the stage for an explosion in women's athletics later in the decade. Also in 1972 Congress passed and sent to the states a constitutional amendment banning discrimination on the basis of sex. By the end of the year all fifty states had enacted legislation to prevent sex discrimination in employment. Federal and state laws protecting victims of domestic violence and rape were strengthened. Before 1974, when Congress passed the Equal Credit Opportunity Act, married women were routinely denied credit cards in their own names.

The women's movement helped precipitate a revolution in family law. As demands for divorce increased, many state legislatures liberalized their statutes in an attempt to reduce the acrimony and shame associated with the divorce process. In 1970 California adopted the nation's first "no-fault" divorce law, which allowed a couple to initiate proceedings without first proving that someone was responsible for the break-up of the marriage. Within five years all but five states adopted the principle of no-fault divorce.

Rally for Women's Rights, 1970

During the 1960s, a new generation of women, born after World War II, came of age in America, and many refused to accept the traditional roles of women as wives and mothers. Inspired by Betty Friedan's 1963 book, *The Feminine Mystique,* they sought self-fulfillment through work and higher education. Once in the work force, however, they found male domination of the most lucrative jobs nearly impossible to penetrate. Founded in 1966, the National Organization for Women (NOW) brought women together for the purpose of fighting state and national laws, as well as stereotypes, that prevented women from being equal to men in American society. Lobbying Congress and organizing mass rallies, activist women demanded greater representation of women in employment, equal pay for equal work, and a whole range of social goals that included repeal of antiabortion statutes and easier divorce legislation.

Then most dramatic change came in the area of reproductive rights. In a number of states women fought to give doctors more power to perform abortion. A few states revised their statutes. On January 22, 1973, the Supreme Court declared in the landmark case *Roe* v. *Wade* that a woman had a constitutional right to an abortion. Writing for the majority, Justice Lewis Blackmun asserted that the Fourteenth Amendment, which prohibited states from denying "liberty" to anyone without "due process," established a "right of privacy" that was "broad enough to encompass a woman's decision whether or not to terminate the pregnancy." The Court stated that during the first trimester the decision to abort a fetus should be left to the discretion of a woman and her doctor. Over the next three months, up until the point of fetal viability, the state could establish some limits on the right to an abortion. In the final trimester the government could prohibit an abortion except where necessary to preserve the mother's life or health.

After the United Nations declared 1975 International Women's Year, feminists in the United States convinced Congress to allocate $5 million for a national women's conference to "promote equality between men and women." More than two thousand women, elected at special community meetings, traveled to the conference in Houston, Texas, in 1977. Included among the delegates were three first ladies—Rosalyn Carter, Betty Ford, and Lady Bird Johnson. Over the next few days delegates adopted "The National Plan of Action," affirming support for the ERA and addressing the needs of battered, minority, and poor women. The most controversial plank called for the elimination of discrimination based on sexual orientation and preference. When the plank passed, lesbian delegates released hundreds of pink and yellow balloons exclaiming, "We Are Everywhere."

There were also signs of change in American culture. Feminists created battered women's shelters across the country. Thousands of volunteers and social workers, rallying behind the motto "We will not be beaten," pushed for social and legal reforms. A feminist magazine, *Ms.*, attracted a large national circulation, and the proportion of women entering professional and graduate schools rose dramatically. By 1974 nearly one thousand colleges and universities offered Women's Studies courses. By the 1980s, 25 percent of new graduates of law, medical, and business schools were women, up from only 5 percent in the late 1960s.

Perhaps the most important accomplishment was the development of the women's health movement. What started as hippie "free clinics" in the 1960s soon grew into a national movement in the 1970s as female health activists disseminated biological knowledge, questioned doctors' control over reproductive decisions, and conducted "self-help gynecology" seminars. The publication of the popular *Our Bodies, Ourselves* (1973) marked an important shift in the women's movement. By emphasizing biological difference, the movement now underscored the central paradox of postwar feminism: how to achieve equality while also honoring the differences between men and women.

During the 1970s the pollster Daniel Yankelovich reported a "wide and deep acceptance" of women's liberation. In 1970, 50 percent of college freshman and 30 percent of women agreed that "the activities of married women are best confined to the home and the family." Five years later only 30 percent of men and less than 20 percent of women took that position. "Women's liberation has changed the lives of many Americans and the ways they look at family, job and sexual equality," *Reader's Digest* concluded in 1976. Over two-thirds of the college women whom the magazine questioned agreed that "the idea that a woman's place is in the home is nonsense."

Changing attitudes found expression in popular culture. Television viewers watched as the "perfect family" comedies of the 1950s and 1960s were replaced by new shows that dramatized the ambiguity of family and work. The *Mary Tyler Moore Show* featured an over-thirty career woman. Other popular television shows—Valerie Harper's *Rhoda* and Diana Riggs's *Diana*—presented strong, independent, and resourceful women. *Maude* starred a loud, opinionated feminist who decided to have an abortion in middle age. Male chauvinism was dealt a major blow in 1973 when fifty-five-year-old former Wimbledon tennis star Bobby Riggs, a self-avowed sexist, challenged the top woman's player, Billie Jean King, to a match. "You insist that top woman players provide a brand of tennis comparable to men's. I challenge you to prove it. I contend that you not only cannot beat a top male player, but that you can't beat me, a tired old man." Millions of Americans watched the match on television as King dismantled Riggs, winning in three straight sets. In 1976 journalist Barbara Walters broke through the glass ceiling at ABC, becoming the highest paid television anchor and the first woman to cohost the evening news.

The change in attitudes toward women accelerated the movement of women into the workplace. By the end of the 1970s women made up 41 percent of the labor force. Over 40 percent of working women were single, widowed, or divorced. Perhaps the greatest change took place among young women of child-bearing age. In the past women had joined the work force either before or after raising a family. By 1980 more than 50 percent of all mothers with children were in the work force. Most employers segregated jobs into "men's" and "women's" work, which concentrated 80 percent of women workers in just a handful of positions—secretary, waitress, sales clerk—that offered low pay, little security, and no chance for advancement. Women made up only 2.7 percent of the directors of major corporations and 16 percent of the professions.

Discrimination in the job market was particularly hard on single women with children. During the 1970s the number of women heading families with children increased by 72 percent. A large proportion, as many as 33 percent, of their households fell below the poverty line. By 1980, 66 percent of all adults who the government classified as poor were women. This new phenomenon, which sociologists called the "feminization of poverty," hit black women hardest of all. While the number of white families headed by women increased only marginally during the 1970s, the number of black families headed by women skyrocketed to 47 percent by 1980. Thirty-three percent of all black children were born to teenage mothers, and 55 percent of all black babies were born out of wedlock. In inner-city ghettos the figure often climbed above 70 percent, and 67 percent of all black families living in poverty were headed by women.

Saving the Environment

The environmental movement gained broad appeal during the 1970s. The birth of the modern environmental movement dated to the publication in 1962 of marine biologist Rachel Carson's book *Silent Spring*, which documented evidence that the widely used insecticide DDT was killing birds, fish, and other animals that ate insects. Sufficiently concentrated, DDT also posed significant health risks to humans. Chemical companies that manufactured DDT ridiculed Carson's book, but her eloquence and evidence won numerous allies. In 1972 the government banned the sale of DDT.

Highly publicized disasters contributed to public concern about the costs of a technological society. When people living in the Love Canal housing development near Niagara Falls, New York, reported abnormally high rates of illness, miscarriages, and birth defects, investigators learned that the community had been built on top of an underground chemical waste disposal site. In March 1979 a frightening accident at the Three Mile Island nuclear power plant in Pennsylvania heightened public concern about the safety of nuclear power and led to calls for tighter regulation of the industry.

The government responded with several pieces of legislation. In 1971 Congress created the cabinet-level Environmental Protection Agency to focus government efforts to protect the environment. Congress also passed legislation expanding the government's regulatory powers. The Clean Water Act (1972) and National Air Quality Standards Act (1970) strengthened controls against water and air pollution. The Resource Recovery Act (1970) provided $453 million for resource recovery and recycling systems. The National Environmental Policy Act

Nuclear Accident at Three Mile Island Few Americans had ever heard of Three Mile Island, a nuclear energy plant built along the Susquehanna River in rural Pennsylvania, until March 28, 1979. On that day, a small valve leading to one of the plant's reactor cores stuck open, causing cooling water to escape and allowing the reactor core to start melting. As a result, radioactivity shot into the atmosphere and the plant declared a stage-one emergency. The governor ordered residents to remain in their homes, closed the schools, and encouraged pregnant women and families with small children to leave the area. The plant claimed to have the situation under control and crews were sent out to check the radiation level surrounding the plant, but for several days the community's residents, along with the rest of America, waited anxiously. Five days after the accident, Jimmy and Rosalynn Carter toured the plant, calming the immediate fear of a complete core meltdown, but people were now more aware of the possibility of future accidents at the nation's nuclear power plants, and the intensity of the antinuclear movement increased.

(1969) required the government to consider the impact of government programs on the environment. "The nineteen-seventies absolutely must be the years when America pays its debt to the past by reclaiming the purity of its air, its waters, and our living environment," President Nixon declared in signing the act into law.

Uneasiness about the state of the environment persisted and found expression in the popular culture of the 1970s. In best-selling books like Hal Lindsey's *Late Great Planet Earth* (1970), scientists were heard to predict the end of global supplies of oil and other natural resources. A popular movie, *The China Syndrome* (1979), portrayed a fictitious nuclear power plant in which incompetence and greed threatened to lead to a nuclear meltdown. Others, like *Soylent Green* (1973), envisioned a world in which technological development and overpopulation had exhausted the earth's natural resources. Providing clear evidence of a broad-based, diverse support for environmentalism was the success of the first annual Earth Day celebration on April 22, 1970. Twenty million people gathered in local events across the country to hear speeches and see exhibits and demonstrations promoting environmental awareness in what the *Christian Science Monitor* called "the largest expression of public concern in history over what is happening to the environment."

The Conservative Response

In 1925 after famed attorney Clarence Darrow made a monkey out of William Jennings Bryan in the Scopes trial, fundamentalists repudiated mainstream America, withdrawing from public life. The journalist H. L. Mencken observed, however, that conservative Christianity is a "fire still burning on a far-flung hill, and it may begin to roar again at any moment." It did so in the 1970s.

The decade witnessed a dramatic increase in the number of self-identified evangelical Christians who had experienced a "born-again" conversion, believed in a literal interpretation of the Bible, and accepted Jesus Christ as their personal savior. The number of Americans who identified themselves as "born again" increased from 24 percent in 1963 to nearly 40 percent in 1978. More than 45 million—one of every five Americans—considered themselves fundamentalists by the end of the decade. While mainstream church membership dropped between 1965 and 1980, the number of Southern Baptists rose from 10.8 million to 13.6 million.

Many fundamentalists were converted by television preachers who used mass media to advocate a return to traditional values. The three most successful "televangelists"—Jerry Falwell, Pat Robertson, and Jim Bakker—reached an estimated 100 million Americans each week with fire-and-brimstone sermons about the evils of contemporary life. Like traditional conservatives, members of the religious right believed in small government, low taxes, and free enterprise. Unlike the old Right, however, they viewed politics through the prism of morality. America, they preached, confronted a crisis of the spirit brought on by the pervasive influence of "secular humanism," which stressed material well-being and personal gratification over religious conviction and devotion to traditional Christian values.

In the mind of the religious right, the federal government, and the liberals who staffed it, were responsible for America's moral decline. The New Right religious leaders were "very concerned that the Federal Government has intruded in a massive way into such areas that concern them as the family, religion and the home," said Richard Viguerie, the nation's leading conservative fundraiser. Most traumatic were the Supreme Court's decision legalizing abortion, the gay-rights and women's movements, and the Internal Revenue Service's decision to remove the tax-exempt status of private Christian schools. Paul Weyrich, a conservative political strategist, described the battle between the conservative profamily forces and liberals as "the most significant battle of the age-old conflict between good and evil, between the forces of God and the forces against God, that we have seen in our country."

During the 1970s conservative intellectuals began to dominate the public debate, ensuring that conservative ideas would receive respect and attention. With funding from wealthy individuals and foundations, conservative "think tanks" produced mounds of studies advocating the need for smaller government and a return to traditional values. These new organizations provided an intellectual home to a number of prominent "neoconservatives," former liberals who had soured on government activism and who offered substantial intellectual ammunition to those seeking to reverse liberal "excesses." A neoconservative, observed the social critic Irving Kristol, was a liberal who had been mugged by reality.

Neoconservatives charged that many 1960s government programs designed to alleviate poverty and assist the working poor had backfired. "Our efforts to deal with distress themselves increase distress," observed the sociologist Nathan Glazer. In an influential essay "The Limits of Social Policy," Glazer argued that government welfare programs too often preempted the function of family, church, school, and neighborhood organizations and thus perpetuated the social dependency they sought to resolve. "I am increasingly convinced," he wrote, "that some important part of the solution to our social problems lies in traditional practices and traditional restraints."

In addition to New Right disciples and disgruntled former liberals, the conservative revival of the 1970s included millions of Americans angry over rising taxes. "You are the people," declared Howard Jarvis, a seventy-five-year-old curmudgeon who led the crusade for California's Proposition 13 in 1978, "and you will have to take control of the government again or else it is going to control you." Proposition 13, a referendum that voters approved by a 2–1 margin, reduced assessments, limited property taxes to 1 percent of full value, and prevented the easy passage of new taxes. "This isn't just a tax revolt," insisted President Jimmy Carter's pollster Pat Caddell. "It's a revolution against government." The success in California emboldened tax reformers in other parts of the country. A dozen states followed California's lead, though most chose more moderate measures. Only two states—Idaho and Nevada—passed Prop 13 look-alikes.

Two powerful currents carried the tax revolt. First, between 1960 and 1980 federal, state, and local taxes increased from less than 24 percent to more than 30 percent of the gross national product. The burden often fell heaviest on traditional Democratic constituencies—working-class families and elderly people on fixed incomes. Second, while taxes kept rising, Americans were losing faith in government and the way it spent tax dollars. Poll after poll showed a majority of Americans believing that government was wasteful and inefficient. By the 1970s many Democrats expressed their anger by abandoning their party and joining forces with conservatives.

While the tax-cut wildfire spread through the states, Prop 13's congressional cousin—the Kemp-Roth Tax Bill, which called for a one-third slash in federal income taxes—gained converts in Washington. The idea was the brainchild of economist Arthur Laffer, who argued that hefty cuts in corporate and personal tax rates would stimulate investment and encourage production and consumption. Unlike the Keynesian theory that had guided policy makers since the 1930s, Laffer's so-called supply-side theory argued that tax policy should reward the suppliers of wealth, not the consumers of it. By lowering taxes on the wealthiest Americans, the government would provide an incentive for them to reinvest, creating new businesses and more jobs. Even though tax rates would be lower, revenues would actually increase since more people would be paying taxes.

Many economists challenged the underlying assumptions of supply-side theory, but the idea was politically seductive. When conservative Barry Goldwater campaigned for president in 1964 on a platform calling for reduced taxes, he felt compelled to announce what government programs he would eliminate to balance the books. Supply-side theory allowed conservatives to have the best of both worlds—they campaigned as tax reform crusaders but also claimed they would be able to protect popular government entitlements such as social security.

Cultural Crosscurrents

The 1970s were hardly the quiescent, self-indulgent decade that critics have suggested. The decade experienced a bitter conflict over the legacy of the 1960s. On one side stood the champions of the youth culture and the rights revolution; on the other side of the line were traditionalists who resisted the appeals for change. While they fought over many issues, three were central to the conflict: the equal rights amendment, busing to achieve racial integration, and gay rights.

The Battle over the Equal Rights Amendment

In 1972 Congress overwhelmingly approved the Equal Rights Amendment to the Constitution, which declared in simple but powerful language that "equality of rights shall not be denied or abridged . . . on account of sex." Within minutes after the amendment passed the Senate, Hawaii became the first to ratify it. Delaware, Nebraska, and New Hampshire ratified the next day, and on the third day Idaho and Iowa ratified. Twenty-four more states ratified in 1972 and early 1973. Twenty-one of the twenty-two ratifications in those first eight months were achieved with at least a two-thirds majority in both legislative chambers of the various states involved. Throughout the ratification process polls showed that large majorities of the public supported the measure. While responses differed according to the wording of the question, the "average" survey found 57 percent for the ERA, 32 percent opposed, and 11 percent with no opinion.

But the ERA soon fell victim to the social politics of the 1970s and 1980s, as traditionalists tapped into public backlash against the rights revolution and the challenge to traditional gender roles, which the ERA represented. Support for the amendment, though broad, was not deep. Most Americans instinctively expressed support for the abstract notion of rights, even if they were unwilling to accept real changes in women's roles. In surveys more than two-thirds of people who supported the amendment thought that preschool children were likely to suffer if their mothers worked and believed married women should not hold jobs when jobs were scarce and their husbands could support them. Nearly one-half said they would not vote for a qualified woman for president.

The gap between support for rights and conservative attitudes about gender roles provided an opening to opponents of the amendment, who viewed it as a subversion of those roles. Especially for female opponents, the ERA challenged traditional perceptions of woman's proper place as homemaker. Traditionalists found a talented leader in Phyllis Schlafly, the "Sweetheart of the Silent Majority," who campaigned tirelessly against the ERA. Tapping into traditional views of womanhood, she complained that feminists had abandoned their God-given roles of wife and mother in favor of a radical political agenda that was "anti-family, anti-children, and pro-abortion." She charged that the ERA would promote lesbianism, require women to serve in combat roles in the military, and roll back protective legislation that housewives and female workers cherished.

PRIMARY SOURCE

11.3 | *The Power of the Positive Woman*
PHYLLIS SCHLAFLY

Not all women in the 1970s supported the feminist movement and passage of the Equal Rights Amendment. Phyllis Schlafly, a successful lawyer and mother of six, believed feminists were a radical fringe group that did not represent the views of most women. In her book *The Power of the Positive Woman*, published in 1977, Schlafly attacked modern feminism while underlining the virtues of traditional women's roles.

If man is targeted as the enemy, and the ultimate goal of women's liberation is independence from men and the avoidance of pregnancy and its consequences, then lesbianism is logically the highest form in the ritual of women's liberation.

The Positive Woman will never travel that dead-end road. It is self-evident to
5 the Positive Woman that the female body with its baby-producing organs was not
designed by a conspiracy of men but by the Divine Architect of the human race. . . .

The Positive Woman looks upon her femaleness and her fertility as part of
her purpose, her potential, and her power. She rejoices that she has a capability
for creativity that men can never have. . . .

10 The women's liberationists are expending their time and energies erecting a
make-believe world in which they hypothesize that *if* schooling were gender-free,
and *if* the same money were spent on male and female sports programs, and *if*
women were permitted to compete on equal terms, *then* they would prove themselves to be physically equal. Meanwhile, the Positive Woman has put the inerad-
15 icable physical differences into her mental computer, programmed her plan of
action, and is already on the way to personal achievement. . . .

Despite the claims of the women's liberation movement, there are countless
physical differences between men and women. . . . Males have a tendency to color
blindness. Only 5 percent of persons who get gout are female. Boys are born big-
20 ger. Women live longer in most countries of the world, not only in the United
States where we have a hard-driving competitive pace. Women excel in manual
dexterity, verbal skills, and memory recall. . . .

The differences between men and women are also emotional and psychological. Without woman's innate maternal instinct, the human race would have died
25 out centuries ago. . . . Even in the most primitive, uneducated societies, women
have always cared for their newborn babies. . . .

Why? Because caring for a baby serves the natural maternal need of a woman.
Although not nearly so total as the baby's need, the woman's need is nonetheless
real. . . .

30 The woman's liberation movement complains that traditional stereotyped
roles assume that women are "passive" and that men are "aggressive." The anom-
aly is that a woman's most fundamental emotional need is not passive at all, but
active. A woman naturally seeks to love affirmatively and to show that love in an
active way by caring for the object of her affections.

35 For most of American history, powerful cultural norms have established clear
guidelines for male and female behavior. "The sum total of general belief of the
most enlightened of both sexes," a speaker told the 1876 graduating class of
Mount Holyoke College, "appears to be that there is a difference of kind in their
natural endowments and that there is for each an appropriate field of develop-
40 ment and action." Catharine Beecher, the author of a number of influential
advice books in the 1860s and 1870s, urged women to gain the appropriate training for "her distinctive profession as housekeeper, nurse of infants and the sick,
educator of childhood, trainer of servants and ministers of charities." ■ ■ ■

The affirmation of traditional gender roles struck a responsive chord with
conservative men, but it also appealed to many working-class women who felt
estranged from the largely middle-class leadership of the feminist movement.
Homemakers viewed the amendment as another assault on their prestige by

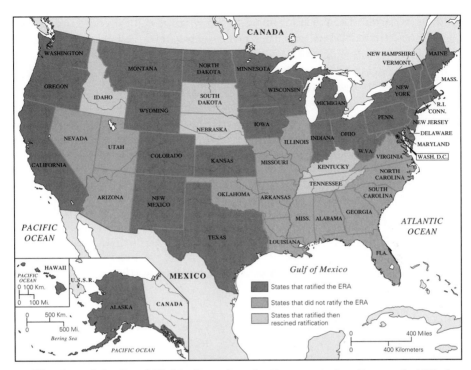

Ratification of the Equal Rights Amendment   First proposed to Congress in 1923, the Equal Rights Amendment called for the equality of rights under the law regardless of sex. With the rise of the women's movement of the late 1960s and early 1970s, the amendment gained new life and passed the House in a 354–24 vote October 12, 1971. On March 22, 1972, the Senate passed the ERA and sent it to the states for ratification. Within one year, the National Organization for Women (NOW) and other women's organizations convinced thirty states to ratify, but then they began to run into stiff opposition from men and women who believed the amendment was too vague and would not protect traditional women's roles as wives and mothers and who were fearful that women would then be eligible for the draft. Over the next six years, the momentum waned and five states rescinded their ratification, while another five ratified it. Despite a congressional extension in 1978, the ERA failed to gain the three states it needed to pass and the amendment died July 1, 1982.

upper-middle-class reformers who shared few of their values or experiences. The cumulative weight of these objections doomed the ERA. On June 30, 1982, the deadline for ratifying the amendment passed with only thirty-five of the required thirty-eight states having ratified: the Equal Rights Amendment was dead.

Busing

Ever since the famous *Brown* v. *Board of Education* decision in 1954, the Supreme Court had called for the desegregation of educational institutions. But it declined to specify remedies or insist on deadlines for implementation, and little progress occurred. Local school boards fiercely resisted local court orders and pleas from activists and parents. Faced with such determined resistance, liberals and civil-rights activists petitioned the Supreme Court to take a more forceful stand on the issue. In two unanimous cases, *Alexander* v. *Holmes County Board of Education* (1969) and *Swann* v. *Charlotte-Mecklenburg Board of Education* (1971), the Supreme Court ordered a quick end to segregation, ruling that cities could be required to bus students if necessary to achieve integration. With the Supreme Court firmly behind busing as a remedy for school segregation, lower courts across the United States followed suit, ordering busing plans in numerous cities.

In 1974 federal judge Arthur Garrity condemned Boston's "systematic program of segregation" affecting all of the city's schools facilities; he called for mandatory busing of seventeen thousand pupils to solve the problem. Garrity divided the Boston school system into eight districts, all of them closely reflecting the systemwide racial makeup: 51 percent white, 36 percent black, and 12 percent other minority groups. Students in grades one through twelve were

Desegregating Schools
Despite Nixon's insistence that integration of schools would take time, the Supreme Court under new Chief Justice Warren Burger, ordered the immediate end of segregation in Mississippi in *Alexander* v. *Holmes County Board of Education (1969)*. *(Carl Mydans LIFE Magazine © Time, Inc.)*

bused strategically within those districts so that individual schools reflected a similar balance.

White residents in South Boston and Charlestown exploded in anger when informed of the plan. Former Congresswoman Louise Day Hicks sounded the alarm. "They shall not take our children from us," she thundered. Opponents created an organization, ROAR (Restore Our Alienated Rights), using as their emblem a large lion pawing a school bus. Busing touched many sensitive nerves. It tapped into deep racial fears and prejudice. "Yes, I'm a racist now," said a white man. "I weren't before that sick judge acted, but I am now. I don't want 'em in my neighborhood. I don't want 'em near my children."

But race alone did not explain the intensity of anger and fear. Class divisions exacerbated the issue as many working-class whites resented the affluent liberals who helped launch the plan but had the luxury of sending their children to private or suburban schools. Traditional distaste of an enlarged and arrogant national government, and of unelected judges, added an additional combustible element to the issue. Opponents of the plans viewed themselves as patriots fighting against

School Busing in Boston   While many northerners approved of the use of *Brown* v. *Board of Education* to desegregate schools in the South, few realized the segregated nature of their own public schools. Because of the gap in wealth that separated urban blacks from suburban whites, students went to school in areas that lacked children of other races. In the case *Swann* v. *Charlotte-Mecklenburg* (1971), the Supreme Court ordered northern schools to use "administratively awkward, inconvenient, and even bizarre" methods to integrate the schools, and on June 21, 1974, Judge W. Arthur Garrity ordered the integration of Boston's public schools by busing students to different areas of town. In the fall, buses took black students from the Roxbury district to South Boston, where they were met by angry parents and hostile students. Throughout the year there were frequent protests and violent confrontations that required authorities to send in police to protect the African-American students.

the federal government. "I served in Korea, I served in Vietnam, and I'll serve in Charlotte if I need to," declared an antibusing activist. Underlying ROAR's hot words and sometimes violent acts was a sense of frustration and desperation of powerless people whose way of life seemed under siege. "We're frightened," said a ROAR founder. "We're locked in. People see their neighborhood threatened, and they're trapped there. What else could that mean but they'll fight back?"

Busing fractured the Democratic Party, turned working-class whites against government schemes for social improvement, and led to massive defections from urban public schools. In the 1974 decision *Milliken* v. *Bradley,* the Supreme Court prohibited the forced transfer of students between city and suburban schools. In many urban areas the decision accelerated "white flight" to the suburbs, leaving urban schools more segregated than they had been before busing. Sixty-six percent of black students in the North and 50 percent in the South attended predominately black schools in 1979. Between 1972 and 1976 nearly twenty thousand white students fled Boston's public school system for private schools or other cities. By 1976 minorities were a majority of Boston's public schools, making them, in the words of journalist J. Anthony Lukas, "the preserve of the black and the poor."

Anita Bryant and the Struggle for Gay Rights

In 1977 Miami's Dade County Council passed an ordinance that banned discrimination in employment and housing based on a person's "affectional or sexual preference." Those who opposed the ordinance immediately went to work to have it repealed and called on singer Anita Bryant to lead the resistance. As a Miss America runner-up, a popular singer billed as "the voice that refreshes," and the symbol of Florida orange juice, Anita Bryant had projected an image of devout wholesomeness for nearly two decades. As president of Save Our Children, she organized a drive that collected more than sixty-six thousand signatures on petitions to force a referendum on the issue. "This is not my battle, it's God's battle," she told a fundraising rally. "Before I yield to this insidious attack on God and His laws," Bryant declared, "I will lead such a crusade to stop it as this country has not seen before."

Besides her objections to homosexuality on religious grounds, Bryant charged that homosexuals preyed on innocent children. She referred to homosexuals as "human garbage" and contended that Miami's antidiscrimination law could protect the right to have "intercourse with beasts." She was often joined on stage at rallies by New Right ministers who preached that homosexuality violated both the laws of God and the laws of nature. "Homosexuality is a sin so rotten, so low, so dirty that even cats and dogs don't practice it," said one minister, concluding that passage of the ordinance "could be the end of the United States of America."

To many of the nation's 20 million homosexuals, the vote—the first of its kind in a major city—was a crucial test of whether the country was willing to extend civil-rights legislation to homosexuals. "Miami is our Selma," said one gay activist. The city's active gay community raised more than $200,000, hired a team of experienced political organizers, and planned for a bruising campaign. "If one group's rights can be taken away, your rights could be next," gay rights activists chanted.

After an intense and bitter campaign, Dade County voters overwhelmingly sided with Bryant, rejecting the ordinance. Gay-rights forces were rebuffed by virtually every voting bloc. Blacks and Jews, traditionally liberal groups, split their vote, while Bryant won enormous support from Dade County's Roman Catholics and religious fundamentalists, as well as from the Cuban community. The vote represented a stunning setback for gay activists, who struggled to put the best face on the Miami debacle. "I think it may be the catalyst we've needed to get the gay community together as a political force," said a local leader. Even before the vote Bryant announced that she would mount a national antihomosexuality campaign. Gay-rights leaders in a number of states vowed to fight her every step of the way. "We have lost a battle," admitted a Washington, D.C., human rights commissioner, "but we certainly have not lost the war."

The struggle over gay rights revealed the anguish of a nation attempting to come to terms with the American paradox. The 1970s witnessed an angry confrontation over the legacy of the 1960s. Inspired by the example of the early civil-rights struggle, many groups on the Left—women, Native Americans, homosexuals—embraced an "empowerment ethic," demanding that the nation live up to the American ideal of equal rights. While these groups achieved some important victories, their challenge to traditional values produced a powerful conservative backlash. Neoconservative intellectuals worried about the unintended consequences of reform, while the religious right reaffirmed deeply held values about gender roles. The political legacy of the 1960s remained unclear, but the cultural impact was distinct and dramatic: the ethic of self-realization, which was so central to the counterculture of the 1960s, seeped into all aspects of 1970s culture.

SELECTED READINGS

▊ Bruce J. Schulman offers the best historical treatment of the decade in *The Seventies* (2001). David Frum offers a critical assessment of the social and cultural changes of the decade in *How We Got Here* (2000), and Stephen Miller argues in *The Seventies Now* (1999) that the decade was not culturally void of importance. Peter Carroll's *It Seemed like Nothing Happened* (1983) is a lively collection of anecdotes about the decade and its frustrations. James Reichley's *Conservatives in an Age of Change* (1981) details the changes in American politics during the Nixon and Ford years, and the dramatic shifts in political and economic power are traced in Bruce Schulman's *The Seventies* (2001). William Berman's *America's Right Turn* (1994) paints a broad picture of the rise of conservatism from Nixon to George Bush. Christopher Lasch's *The Culture of Narcissism* (1978) is an influential description of the Me

Decade. Edwin Schur's *The Awareness Trap* (1976) describes the failure of social change and the rise of "awareness" movements. Robert Kuttner covers the tax revolt in the late 1970s in his definitive work *Revolt of the Haves* (1980).

∎ In *The Declining Significance of Race* (1980), William J. Wilson describes the economic polarization of African-American society. Douglas Glasgow's *The Black Underclass* (1980) charts the black economic decline of the 1970s. Nathan Glazer's *Affirmative Discrimination* (1975) details the controversy around affirmative action. Ronald Formisano explores the opposition to the busing movement in *Boston Against Busing* (1991). J. Anthony Lukas's *Common Ground* (1985) is a moving account of the Boston busing crisis through the eyes of three families.

∎ Ernesto Vigil's *The Crusade for Justice* (1999) explains the development of the Chicano movement through the 1970s. Matt Meier and Feliciano Rivera explore the generational conflicts among Hispanics in *The Chicanos* (1972). *History of Immigration of Asian Americans* (1998), edited by Franklin Ng, contains essays that describe why increasing numbers of Asians migrated to the United States and their steps to create a new life. Paul Smith studies the American Indian Movement through its takeovers at Alcatraz and Wounded Knee in *Like a Hurricane* (1996). Editors Alvin Josephy, Joane Nagel, and Troy Johnson provide fifty primary documents that trace the American Indian activist movement in the last four decades in *Red Power* (2nd ed., 1999). Helen Hertzberg's *The Search for an American Indian Movement* (1971) chronicles the rise of the Red Power movement.

∎ John D'Emilio's *Sexual Politics, Sexual Communities* (2nd ed., 1998) explores the formation of gay identity in the postwar years, and the history of the gay-rights movement is examined in Dudley Clendinen and Adam Nagourney's *Out for Good* (1999). Martin Duberman's *Stonewall* (1993) describes the birth of the modern gay liberation movement.

∎ Sara Evans describes how the women's liberation movement evolved from the civil-rights struggle in *Personal Politics* (1979). Jo Freeman's *The Politics of Women's Liberation* (1979) and Kathleen Berkeley's *The Women's Liberation Movement in America* (1999) provide overviews of the women's movement. Gayle Graham Yates outlines feminist ideology in *What Women Want* (1975). Susan Brownmiller's *In Our Time* (1999) describes the trials and triumphs of the women's movement by describing the work of some of the movements lesser-known activists. Alice Echols explores radical feminism in *Daring to Be Bad* (1989). Susan Hartmann's *From Margin to Mainstream* (1989) has good material on economic discrimination by sex. Joel F. Handler's *We the Poor People* (1997) explores the feminization of poverty.

▮ Rachel Carson's *Silent Spring* (1962) remains the eloquent first word of the environmental movement. Daniel F. Ford describes the nuclear power scare in *Three Mile Island* (1982), while Thomas Raymond Wellock looks at opposition to nuclear energy in California in *Critical Mass* (1998). Samuel P. Hays provides an overview of the movement in *Beauty, Health, and Permanence* (1987). Roderick Nash's *The Rights of Nature* (1989) outlines the environmentalist ethic.

12

America's Crisis of Confidence, 1974–1980

In July 1979, faced with rising oil prices and plummeting public support, President Jimmy Carter scheduled a prime-time televised address to the nation. In a rare display of passion and eloquence, Carter gave a thirty-three-minute sermon that was unlike any speech ever given from the Oval Office. "This is not a message of happiness or reassurance," he declared, "but it is the truth and it is a warning." Convinced that the energy crisis was a symptom of a larger problem, Carter offered the nation his diagnosis of the "crisis of the American spirit." With a sharp voice and his characteristically flashing eyes, the president apologized for his own failures at leadership, confessing that "the gap between our citizens and our government has never been so wide." As a result, Americans had become pessimistic about the future and displayed "a growing disrespect for government and for churches and schools, the news media, and other institutions." The energy crisis, he sermonized, was a trial in which the security and the future of America were at stake. "Energy will be the immediate test of our ability to unite the nation," he said. "On the battlefield of energy, we can win for our nation a new confidence—and we can seize control of our common destiny."

Carter had successfully diagnosed the paradox confronting Americans in the 1970s. In the wake of Vietnam and Watergate, public faith in government declined at the same time that many groups looked to Washington for solutions to pressing social problems. Congress responded by attempting to make the government more responsive to the public will, but most of the reforms it enacted had the opposite impact. For the previous three decades economic growth had sustained American expectations of the future, but stagflation, a new and troubling combination of rising unemployment and soaring inflation, eroded the standard of living of millions of Americans and made them question whether they could pass on a better life to their children. The solution to the urgent issue of energy required a united national response, but the nation had been deeply fractured by debates over Vietnam and race and proved incapable of forging a new consensus. President Carter seemed to understand the paradox, but neither he nor other public leaders offered convincing answers to the questions puzzling most Americans.

Watergate Legacies: The Diffusion of Power

The failure in Vietnam, the Johnson administration's duplicity in explaining it, and the exposure of Nixon's illegal behavior in the Watergate affair combined to erode public faith in the integrity of elected leaders. The journalist Tom Wicker wrote that many Americans had come to look upon their government as "a fountain of lies." "All during Vietnam, the government lied to me," declared the journalist Richard Cohen. "All the time. Watergate didn't help matters any. More lies . . . I've been shaped, formed by lies." A 1976 study revealed 69 percent of respondents felt that "over the last ten years, this country's leaders have consistently lied to the people." Pollster Daniel Yankelovich noted in 1977 that trust in government declined from 80 percent in the late 1950s to about 33 percent in 1976. More than 80 percent of the public expressed distrust in political leaders, 61 percent believed something was morally wrong with the country, while nearly 75 percent felt that they had no impact on Washington decision making.

The new skepticism found expression in the way the media dealt with political leaders. Reporters, believing they had been duped by Lyndon Johnson and Richard Nixon, developed a more assertive and confrontational style, challenging the official version of events. Inspired by the example of Watergate heroes Bob Woodward and Carl Bernstein, many journalists went in search of the next big scandal. "A lot of young reporters today are more likely to ask the right questions of the right people than before Watergate," observed an editor at the *New York Times*. Investigative reporting emerged as a major franchise in many newsrooms, organizing reporting teams and providing them with big budgets. The adversarial style, and the new emphasis on exposing corruption, contributed to growing public distrust of politicians and reinforced the notion that political leaders were corrupt.

In an effort to restore public trust, the nation's political leaders undertook a series of highly visible reforms. Most of the effort was directed at limiting the power of the presidency. In 1973 Congress passed the War Powers Act over President Nixon's veto. The act required a president to "consult with Congress" within forty-eight hours of committing American troops abroad and ordered him to withdraw them within sixty days unless Congress approved the mission. In addition, Congress enjoined the president from undertaking any military action in Vietnam after August 15, 1973.

On the domestic side Congress moved to increase its influence over domestic policy. The Budget and Impoundment Control Act in 1974 streamlined the budgeting process in Congress and created the Congressional Budget Office, which produced an independent analysis of the president's budget each year. Until then Congress had reviewed the annual presidential budget in pieces, adopting spending bills as they came to the floor from the Appropriations Committees without ever stopping to consider their overall fiscal impact. The congressional budget law required Congress to set total spending and revenue limits each year and to stay within them when enacting specific appropriations and tax bills. Senator Sam Ervin, who presided over the congressional hearings on Watergate, called the law "one of the most important pieces of legislation" ever considered by Congress.

Congress also expanded the personal staffs of individual senators and House members, enlarged committee staffs in both houses, and increased the research service of the Library of Congress. Congressional staffs, for example, increased by 41 percent between 1972 and 1978. These steps, though little noticed, represented a significant change in the relationship between the two branches. Congress acquired new capability to evaluate and challenge programs sought by presidents. Increased staff also upset the balance of power in Congress. Since the staff increases were across the board, individual representatives were able to develop expertise and challenge the power of committee chairs.

Recognizing the strength of popular support for reform, congressional leaders agreed to structural changes that greatly diffused authority in the House of Representatives. In the past, the chairmen of the 22 standing committees in the House, a small group of senior legislators, had been able to decide which bills would be considered in their committees. In 1974 House Democrats adopted "the subcommittee bill of rights," which parceled out the power of the original 22 committees to smaller subcommittees. The number of House subcommittees increased from 119 to 148 between 1971 and 1979. Many grew so powerful that they became warring kingdoms. Along with diffusing power, the Democratic majority in both the House and Senate decided in 1974 to require the election of committee chairmen by secret ballot. The significance of this change became apparent the following year when the House caucus removed four veteran chairmen.

While reformers celebrated the changes, many legislators complained that the redistribution of power made it difficult to build coalitions that could pass legislation. "We created a new order but not a new command," complained one reformer. In the past a handful of powerful congressional barons could have huddled and compromised on key legislative proposals and then used the bonds of party loyalty, and the threat of party discipline, to force the rank and file to follow their lead. Under the new system there were no barons, power was dispersed, compromise was difficult to achieve, and party discipline was nearly nonexistent. "Fragmentation," noted the journalist Robert Samuelson: "In a word, that is what has happened to American politics during the past 30 years."

Along with shifting power from the president to Congress and reforming the structure of Congress, legislators moved to limit the influence of money in politics. The Federal Election Campaign Act of 1974 placed caps on the amount of money that individuals could donate to political campaigns and provided some public funding for presidential campaigns. But loopholes in the act allowed new mechanisms of fundraising and donation that actually led to an increase in the flow of private money into elections. Political parties developed direct-mail techniques to solicit huge numbers of small donations that they funneled into important campaigns. Political action committees (PACs) proliferated and dispersed campaign funds. In 1974 there were only 608 PACs; by 1984 the number had soared to over 4,000. Critics charged that well-financed PACs gave powerful interests inordinate influence in Congress. "What is at stake," declared the journalist Elizabeth Drew, "is the idea of representative government, the soul of this country."

The passage of campaign finance laws coincided with broader changes that accentuated the power and influence of PACs. The most significant change was the spiraling cost of campaigning. Congress decided to regulate campaign contributions at the same time that television and sophisticated new computer technology drove up the cost of running for office. PACs also expanded in response to increased government regulation, which exploded in size during the 1970s. In 1940 government at all levels employed 4.2 million people at a cost of a bit more than $20 billion. By 1976 it employed 15 million and spent around $575 billion. This expansion was accompanied by a major increase in the power of government bureaucracies and of the people who ran them. The *Federal Register,* which lists all laws, expanded from 20,036 pages in 1970 to 77,497 pages in 1979. Congress created a host of new regulatory bodies: the Environmental Protection Agency (1970), the Occupational Safety and Health Administration (1970), and the Consumer Product Safety Commission (1972).

The new agencies adopted a more expansive definition of social regulation that went far beyond the economic rules of the New Deal era. In the past federal regulatory bodies had responded to specific complaints of wrongdoing, but the new social regulation was "proactive, emphasizing future compliance to reduce risk and eliminate hazards." During the 1970s the federal government shifted from an "administrative state," in which agencies provided money to states with few strings attached, to a "regulatory state," in which Washington established elaborate rules governing private behavior. "When the government can tell you how much cream to put in ice cream, you have no choice but to influence government," complained a business lobbyist.

In response to the new regulatory state, many corporations and trade associations opened Washington offices, hired Capitol Hill law firms, and retained legions of political consultants to keep track of pending legislation and to develop strategies for promoting favorable policies and killing unfavorable ones. By 1980 nearly 500 corporations had Washington offices, up from 250 in 1970, and the number of lobbyists had tripled. Trade associations opened national headquarters at a rate of one per week, increasing from 1,200 to 1,739 during the decade. "Washington has become a special-interest state," said a government official. "It's like medieval Italy—everyone has his own duchy or kingdom."

If the purpose of campaign finance reform was to limit the influence of special-interest money and restore public confidence in the system, the results failed to express that purpose. Armed with figures made available by new disclosure laws, public-interest groups showed that PACs were not in the charity business. They expected, and often received, something in return for their largess. Polls showed that the vast majority of Americans believed that special interests controlled the system and that Congress and elections were bought by the highest bidder. "If one of the original intentions of campaign finance reforms was to limit the appearance of influence of special interests in the political process, the law has, in practice, had the opposite effect," a Harvard study concluded.

The emergence of special interests further eroded the power of the political parties to forge consensus among competing factions. "The rise of special interests is directly related to the loss of trust that people have had in the traditional political institutions, parties specifically," noted the Republican pollster Richard Wirthlin. The turmoil of the 1960s, especially race riots and the Vietnam War, loosened the loyalties of many Democrats, while Watergate undermined the Republicans' claim to be the party of good government. Interest groups moved in to fill the void, but they had little interest in compromise and consensus. By taking uncompromising positions on sometimes emotional issues, they intentionally polarized debate. "How can you compromise and say, ' I'm going to allow 30,000 publicly funded abortions, but no more'?" asked a congressman. Many interest groups coalesced for the sole purpose of opposing an issue. "It's much easier to wage a campaign against something than for it," said a member of a right-wing group. With limits placed on the amount of money the parties could raise and spend, candidates inevitably turned to special-interest groups to fund their campaigns. In 1972, 17 percent of the money available to House candidates came through their political parties. By 1978 available party money had declined to 4.5 percent. In those six years party contributions to the Democrats fell by 77 percent and to Republicans by 58 percent.

The Politics of Austerity

For most of their history Americans had believed that hard work and talent would be rewarded with upward mobility and greater economic opportunity. They had faith that their innovative spirit and the continent's rich resources would lead to an ever-increasing prosperity for all. Americans, Alexis de Tocqueville wrote as early as 1835, "consider society as a body in a state of improvement." By 1979, however, 55 percent of all Americans believed that "next year will be worse than this year." Nearly 75 percent of Americans polled agreed with the statement "We are fast coming to a turning point in our history. The land of plenty is becoming the land of want."

A host of statistics revealed that the American economy had stalled during the 1970s. During the long postwar boom from 1947 to the mid-1960s, the United States enjoyed average annual productivity increases of 3.2 percent. From 1965 to 1973, however, productivity growth averaged only 2.4 percent annually. By the end of the decade productivity was declining in absolute terms. As inflation exploded to nearly 10 percent and unemployment crept upward, Americans found that their discretionary income declined by 18 percent between 1973 and 1980. The average price of a single-family house more than doubled during the 1970s.

The nation's economic difficulties had many causes. First, an inflationary trend began in the 1960s when President Johnson and Congress decided to expand defense and social spending without asking for higher taxes. Each year high government expenditures stimulated the economy more than taxes slowed it down, creating upward pressure on prices. Inflation, which never exceeded 5 percent between 1955 and 1972 and was often as low as 2 or 3 percent, suddenly exploded to nearly 10 percent by the end of 1973. In 1974 retail prices increased

Discomfort Index   During the 1970s the United States experienced both rising inflation and increasing unemployment. During the 1976 presidential campaign Democrats developed the "discomfort" or "misery" index to measure the public impact of this destructive combination, and to attack their Republican opponents for their poor management of the economy. In 1980, however, Republicans used the same index to highlight Jimmy Carter's economic mismanagement. (Sources: Washington, D.C.: U.S. Government Printing Office, 1981, pp. 238, 263; *Economic Report of the President, 1999; Statistical Abstract of the United States, 1996.*)

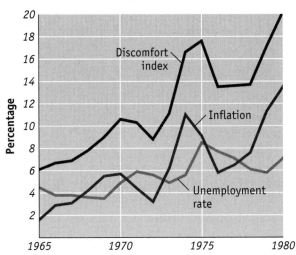

by 11 percent and wholesale prices by 18 percent. "During the 1960s, we fought the pigs," declared Tom Hayden, one of the founders of Students for a Democratic Society. "Now we fight the high price of bacon."

Second, in the 1970s America ran out of "easy oil," a serious challenge to the basic structures of the economy. The nation's expansion in the postwar era depended on the prodigious use of cheap energy. Americans living in sprawling suburban communities enjoyed driving powerful energy-inefficient cars. Large single-family homes offered Americans more living space than people of any other country—but used a great deal of oil to heat in the winter and electricity to cool in summer. And American industry found it cost-efficient to use processes that were energy inefficient as long as energy was cheap.

In the early 1970s political turmoil in the Middle East led to dramatically higher oil prices and undermined the bases of this system. American dependence on cheap foreign oil had increased from 19 percent in 1960 to 30 percent in 1972. What was arguably the most seismic event of the decade came in 1973 when King Faisal of Saudi Arabia, reacting to the latest Israeli-Egyptian war, cut oil production and declared a boycott on shipments to Israel's arms suppliers. The resulting disruption convulsed Europe and produced the first gasoline lines in the United States. According to one scholar, the embargo represented a "watershed, sharply dividing the second half of the twentieth century into two elongated quarter-centuries—the twenty-seven-year period extending from the end of World War Two (the postwar quarter-century) and the other twenty-seven-year period extending from 1973 to the end of the century." America experienced yet another limit on its power.

Third, for the first time since the end of World War II, American business faced stiff competition from other countries. The industrial economies of Western Europe and Japan, finally recovered from the war, began to win an increasing share of international trade. The U.S. share of world trade declined by 16 percent between 1960 and 1970 and dropped another 25 percent during the 1970s. What was even more troubling was that foreign competitors were winning a large share of the rich American market. With exports declining and imports rising, the United States posted its first balance-of-trade deficit in almost a century. The surge in foreign competition offered consumers quality products at lower prices. But it also threatened jobs that had for years offered Americans high wages and dependable employment.

The decline of the American automobile industry provided a clear example. In the 1950s and 1960s U.S. automakers had ruled the domestic market. In the 1970s, with gasoline prices soaring and buying power eroded by inflation, car buyers welcomed affordable, more fuel-efficient imports such as Japan's Toyota and Datsun. Detroit, geared toward producing bulky six-passenger sedans, failed to convert in time, and part of its market drifted away. By 1980 imports had grabbed 34 percent of the U.S. auto market. The United States now imported 3.2 million foreign cars annually, about 60 percent of them from Japan.

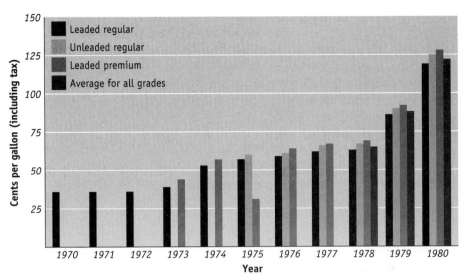

Rising Price of Gasoline   During the Yom Kippur War in October 1973, OPEC ceased exports of oil to the United States because of America's support of Israel. In the 1970s, the United States imported one-third of its oil, most of it from the Middle East, so this embargo created a severe shortage of oil-based products, such as gasoline and home heating oil. While the embargo was lifted in 1974, gasoline prices never returned to their earlier levels. A severe price spike in 1979 and 1980 was again the result of rising tensions in the Middle East, this time caused by the overthrow of the shah in Iran and the taking of American hostages in Lebanon. This second gas crisis forced American consumers to cut back on their driving and encouraged car manufacturers to develop more fuel-efficient automobiles.

In the midst of these crises, political leaders seemed unable to find any solutions. In each of the presidential administrations of the decade there were wild policy swings as leaders and economists sought to understand the profound changes shaking the American economy. Many of the experiments tried were based on short-term thinking; none seemed to improve the nation's economy very much. In combination, they eroded the public's belief that the nation's leaders could manage the economy.

A Time to Heal: The Brief Presidency of Gerald Ford

Gerald Ford did little to restore public confidence in the presidency. Faced with the delicate problem of succeeding Richard Nixon, Gerald Ford tried to present himself as a steady, sober leader whom the public could trust. With his friendly smile and reputation for honesty, Ford enjoyed wide respect. As he took the presidential oath of office on August 9, 1972, the sixty-two-year-old Ford announced that his top priority was to heal "the nation's wounds" and to restore a sense of confidence in government. Initially, the press hailed both the message and the messenger, finding down-to-earth Ford a refreshing break from imperious Nixon. "He's superbly average," observed *U.S. News and World Report*. "He's like Ike. He gives you an impression of solid dependability."

Within a month, however, Ford connected his administration to the Watergate scandal by granting Nixon "a full, free, and absolute pardon . . . for all his offenses against the United States." Ford rightly believed that "it would [have] be[en] virtually impossible for me to direct public attention to anything else" if Nixon had been put on trial. "Public policy demanded that I put Nixon and Watergate behind us as quickly as possible." Although sound public policy, the decision to pardon Nixon produced a political maelstrom. Overnight Ford's approval ratings plunged from 71 to 50 percent.

PRIMARY SOURCE

12.1 | *Pardon of Richard Nixon*
GERALD FORD

When Gerald Ford became president upon the resignation of Nixon, he claimed he had no intention of pardoning Nixon, who still faced possible criminal charges. However, on September 8, 1974, Ford issued a pardon to Nixon, justifying his decision by saying it was to restore peace to a divided nation.

Richard Nixon became the thirty-seventh President of the United States on January 20, 1969, and was re-elected in 1972 for a second term by the electors of forty-nine of the fifty states. His term in office continued until his resignation on August 9, 1974.

5 　　Pursuant to resolutions of the House of Representatives, its Committee on the Judiciary conducted an inquiry and investigation on the impeachment of the President extending over more than eight months. The hearings of the committee and its deliberations, which received wide national publicity over television, radio, and in printed media, resulted in votes adverse to Richard Nixon on rec-
10 ommended Articles of Impeachment.

　　As a result of certain acts or omissions occurring before his resignation from the office of President, Richard Nixon has become liable to possible indictment and trial for offenses against the United States. Whether or not he shall be so prosecuted depends on findings of the appropriate grand jury and on the discre-
15 tion of the authorized prosecutor. Should an indictment ensue, the accused shall then be entitled to a fair trial by an impartial jury, as guaranteed to every individual by the Constitution.

It is believed that a trial of Richard Nixon, if it became necessary, could not fairly begin until a year or more has elapsed. In the meantime, the tranquility to
20 which this nation has been restored by the events of recent weeks could be irreparably lost by the prospects of bringing to trial a former President of the United States. The prospects of such trial will cause prolonged and divisive debate over the propriety of exposing to further punishment and degradation a man who has already paid the unprecedented penalty of relinquishing the high-
25 est elective office in the United States.

NOW, THEREFORE, I, Gerald R. Ford, President of the United States, pursuant to the pardon power conferred upon me by Article II, Section 2, of the Constitution, have granted and by these presents do grant a full, free, and absolute pardon unto Richard Nixon for all offenses against the United States
30 which he, Richard Nixon, has committed or may have committed or taken part in during the period from January 20, 1969, through August 9, 1974.

IN WITNESS WHEREOF, I have hereunto set my hand this 8th day of September in the year of our Lord nineteen hundred seventy-four, and of the independence of the United States of America the 199th. ■ ■ ■

Ford had a hard time overcoming this poor start. His administration failed to develop a consistent approach to the economy. In his first month in office Ford faced a economy in steep decline: prices and unemployment continued to rise, but business was slowing and the gross national product was slipping. Initially Ford sided with conservatives, declared fighting inflation "domestic enemy number one," and called for budget cuts and a tax increase. But as unemployment jumped from 5.8 to 7 percent during the fall, and leading economic indicators signaled a steep recession, Ford switched gears and announced a tax cut to stimulate growth. The president's "flip-flop" on the economy and taxes contributed to a growing public perception that Ford was out of his depth in the White House.

Popular culture reinforced the image of Ford as an "amiable bumbler." Although he was an agile and athletic man, Ford tripped at the front door of the White House, fell on his hands and knees while debarking from a plane, and banged his head against an errant elevator gate. Every week many Americans turned into *Saturday Night Live* to watch comedian Chevy Chase imitate the president's various pratfalls. An Oliphant cartoon depicted Ford tripping down an airplane ramp while Henry Kissinger admonishes him, "I told you not to walk and chew gum at the same time." Most critics saw a clear connection between Ford's physical aerobatics and his intellectual ability. "If he's so dumb, how come he's president?" Chase asked in one of his weekly skits.

On both foreign and domestic issues Ford had to contend with a Congress determined to assert its control over policy. Ford's plan for fiscal austerity also placed him on a collision course with Democrats, who controlled large majorities in both Houses. During his brief term in office Ford vetoed legislation calling for increased spending for federal aid to education and health care. When he refused to approve a federal bailout of New York City, the headline of the *New York Daily News* screamed, "Ford to City—Drop Dead."

Unemployed   During Gerald Ford's fifteen months as president, the United States slipped into its deepest recession since the Great Depression. Unemployment hit 9 percent in 1975, leaving millions of Americans with few options save filing for government relief. This was a choice few people, like this man at an unemployment agency in Cleveland, made easily. *(Seattle/NYT Pictures.)*

In foreign policy Ford continued Nixon's internationalist course. Depending heavily on the advice of Kissinger, Ford traveled to Vladivostok in 1974 to negotiate a new nuclear arms treaty with the Soviets. The Strategic Arms Limitation Talks (SALT) II set equal ceilings on the delivery of strategic weapons. The following summer he signed the Helsinki Accords, which called for peaceful settlements of disputes and greater scientific and economic cooperation between the two countries. Both treaties ran into fierce opposition from conservatives and stalled in Congress. Under attack from his right for appeasing the Soviets, and feeling the need to demonstrate American resolve following the fall of Saigon, Ford took a hard line when Cambodian rebels seized the U.S. merchant ship *Mayaguez* and held its crew hostage. "Let's look ferocious," Kissinger told the White House. Ignoring indications that the Cambodian government was looking for a peaceful solution to the crisis, the administration ordered a daring rescue mission, which resulted in the deaths of a handful of marines. The mission was a military disaster but a public relations coup for the president. The hostages, who had been moved to a different location, had already been released, but the nation applauded Ford's decisive action. "I am very proud of our country and our president today," said a congressman, echoing the feeling of his colleagues.

Jimmy Carter and the New Democrats

The boost in the polls from the *Mayaguez* incident was short-lived: month after month of rising prices and higher unemployment sapped public support for the Ford presidency. Ironically, while the downturn occurred during a Republican administration, it was the Democratic Party that may have paid the greatest political price. Inflation and a growing federal debt eroded public support for government social programs and fractured the Democratic Party.

"Inflation is a great conservatizing issue," noted the journalist George Will. As long as the economic pie was expanding, Americans were more willing to support programs designed to help the less fortunate. With the pie shrinking, and inflation and higher taxes eating away at personal income, people felt less generous with their tax dollars. Americans called for cutting waste from the federal budget, but they were protective of programs that benefited the middle class. Polls recorded the schizophrenia. Large majorities said they thought the federal government was "spending too much money," but a majority of respondents believed that "too little money" was being spent on health, education, and crime fighting.

Public confusion spawned a new type of Democratic politician. In the 1974 congressional elections voters angry about Watergate decided to punish the Republican Party by sending forty-nine new Democrats to the House and four to the Senate, giving them large majorities in both chambers. But many of the gains came from previously Republican suburban areas where voters, and their new representatives, had little taste for new social programs. A clear generational divide emerged in the party as the younger, newly elected representatives distanced themselves from the party's traditional support for expanded social programs and more activist government. Instead, they promised to make government more efficient and responsive, not to address economic grievances or class interests. Nurtured on postwar affluence, these officeholders tended to oppose higher taxes and expanded social programs but were liberal on controversial social issues, such as abortion and gay rights.

On the state level newly elected Democratic governors questioned the faith in expanded government that had guided a previous generation of liberal politicians. "The days of wine and roses are over," proclaimed Hugh Carey of New York. California governor Jerry Brown Jr., a former Jesuit seminarian, sounded like a Republican when he attacked liberal welfare programs. "Sometimes we need fewer programs, less planning, more space to live our lives," he said. "Taxes are too high and the programs they buy don't deliver enough. It's very disturbing when you can't walk the street safely and your money is going for nothing."

The most successful of the new breed of politician was former Georgia governor Jimmy Carter. Many observers saw Carter as a link between Great Society idealism and the economic realities of an age of limits. A Democrat with populist leanings, he was also an engineer with an instinctive aversion to spending and waste. "He's tight as a tick," declared his press secretary Jody Powell. Sensing the opportunity to capitalize on the Watergate affair and public distrust of Washington, Carter decided to run for president in 1976 by campaigning as an outsider who would clean up the mess in Washington.

Beginning his campaign with a name recognition of only 2 percent, Carter took advantage of Democratic Party reforms initiated after 1968 that increased the role of grass-roots activists in the selection process. Carter was able to roll over a number of better-known candidates on the way to a first-ballot victory at the convention. In an effort to reach out to the party's traditional power brokers, whom he had bypassed in the primaries, Carter selected Minnesota senator Walter F. Mondale, a protégé of Hubert Humphrey, as his running mate.

Throughout the primary season Carter skillfully played to the public's conflicting mood. He combined biting attacks on the Washington establishment with uplifting sermons about spiritual renewal. To a public still smarting from Watergate and disenchanted with government, Carter emphasized his rural roots and his lifelong distance from Washington. A Democrat who thought like a Republican, Carter rejected social experimentation and instead emphasized the importance of social efficiency and prudent management of the nation's affairs. A deeply religious man and a self-described born-again Christian, he seemed to offer a religious salve for the nation's wounds, reassuring audiences that they deserved a government as "decent, honest, truthful, fair, compassionate, and as filled with love as our people are." He possessed a visceral appreciation of the sense of betrayal many people felt toward government, and he conveyed a serene confidence in the relevance of old verities. There seemed to be nothing ailing America that could not be solved with a little more democracy. "It's time for the people to run the government," he declared.

In August polls showed Carter leading President Ford by more than 30 percentage points. Not only was Ford burdened by his party's ties to Watergate and by his pardon of Nixon, but he also had to endure a bruising primary fight against conservative Ronald Reagan that left his image muddied and his party deeply split. By early October, however, Democratic mishaps and an effective Republican strategy had eliminated Carter's once-formidable lead. But the legacy of Watergate, continuing bad economic news, and his own lack of charisma were more than Ford could overcome. On election night the Democrats won a narrow victory. Less than 2 percentage points separated the candidates in the popular vote—Carter won 40.8 million votes to Ford's 39.1 million. In the electoral college Carter defeated Ford 297 to 240. It was the narrowest electoral victory since 1916 when Woodrow Wilson defeated Charles Evans Hughes by 23 electoral votes. It was also one of the least compelling, to judge from the turnout. A smaller percentage of Americans voted in 1976 than in any election since 1948. The Democrats, however, maintained large majorities in Congress: a Senate margin of 62–38 and a House lead of 291–142.

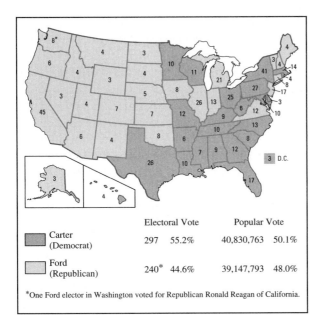

The Election of 1976 Ford's failure to solve the nation's economic problems led to doubts within his own Republican party about his ability to lead the nation, while his opponent, Jimmy Carter of Georgia, emphasized the need for a moral president after years of political corruption unearthed by the Watergate investigations. Fallout from the Watergate era could also be seen in the low voter turnout for the election, as almost half of eligible voters, alienated by the scandal, failed to vote.

		Electoral Vote		Popular Vote	
■	Carter (Democrat)	297	55.2%	40,830,763	50.1%
□	Ford (Republican)	240*	44.6%	39,147,793	48.0%

*One Ford elector in Washington voted for Republican Ronald Reagan of California.

The Democrats' Discontent

In clear contrast to Democratic predecessors John F. Kennedy and Lyndon Johnson, who used their inaugural addresses as clarion calls of American greatness at home and abroad, Carter struck a tone of limits. "We have learned that 'more' is not necessarily 'better,' that even our great nation has its recognized limits, and that we can neither answer all questions nor solve all problems."

Carter sounded new themes, but he failed to develop a strategy for adjusting public expectations, fed by years of prosperity, to the economic reality of an age of limits. The new president faced enormous obstacles in his effort to build a national consensus. His narrow electoral victory provided a shaky foundation for bold proposals. He presided over a party still torn by divisions over Vietnam and civil rights. A resurgent Congress eager to reassert its authority after Watergate, and a public grown cynical about Washington and angry about rising unemployment and high inflation, compounded his difficulties.

Carter began his presidency by raising spending in an effort to put an end to the unemployment generated by Ford's fiscal and monetary restrictions. Unemployment did begin to come down, but only at the cost of another slow rise in inflation that ate into Americans' paychecks. By 1978 the inflation rate had soared to 9 percent, the third highest since 1945 and nearly 3 percentage points above administration predictions. In January 1979 a somber president lectured the nation about the need for fiscal restraint. In keeping with his theme, Carter submitted to Congress a "lean and austere" budget designed to reduce the federal deficit and reduce inflationary pressure. The liberal wing of the Democratic Party revolted, attacking Carter for sacrificing the poor on the altar of austerity. "I'm not going to allow people to go to bed hungry for an austerity program," thundered Speaker of the House Tip O'Neill. Undeterred, Carter maintained that inflation, not unemployment, was the administration's top economic priority.

Most vexing to the president's political fortunes was the gasoline shortage that plagued American consumers in early 1979. By May gasoline lines in California ran as long as five hundred cars, and prices at the pump climbed about a dollar a gallon for the first time. "It's sort of like sex," explained one official. "Everybody's going to get all the gasoline they need, but they're damn sure not going to get all they want." Over the Fourth of July weekend 90 percent of all gas stations in the New York City area were closed, 80 percent in Pennsylvania, and 50 percent in Rhode Island. Polls showed overwhelming disapproval of Carter's handling of the economy.

In foreign policy the president achieved a couple of notable successes. In December 1978 Carter completed the process initiated by Richard Nixon of formally recognizing the People's Republic of China. In March 1979 Carter's persistence and vision produced the most notable success of his administration—the signing of the Camp David Accords, a historic peace treaty between long-standing enemies Egypt and Israel. In the treaty Egypt recognized Israel's right to exist as a sovereign state and Israel promised to return the Sinai Peninsula. President Carter also convinced the Senate, in a very close vote, to ratify a treaty that promised to turn over the Canal Zone to Panama by the year 2000. Carter moved to identify the United States with black African nationalism and to end the "last vestiges of colonialism" in Zimbabwe/Rhodesia and Namibia. Carter chided white South African rulers for apartheid—an official system of segregating non-whites and whites that included removal of blacks to designated homelands, discriminatory wages based on race, and the denial of voting rights, absence of civil liberties, and arbitrary arrests for blacks.

For most of his four years in office, however, Carter struggled unsuccessfully to convince the American public that he could protect America's global interests from an aggressive Soviet Union. The memory of Vietnam haunted the Carter administration's attempts to develop a coherent foreign policy. Since the beginning of the Cold War a commitment to global containment had characterized the Democratic Party's view of the world. Vietnam had called many of those assumptions into question. Unlike World War II, which forged a new consensus, Vietnam divided the party, polarized its leaders, and raised new questions about America's role in the world. The party of Lyndon Johnson, which had expanded America's involvement in Vietnam, defended the military expansion there, and opposed its withdrawal, was also the party of George McGovern, which had cursed the war and called for American withdrawal. As the first postwar Democratic administration, Carter had to pull together the polarized foreign-policy establishment and create a coherent foreign policy.

Camp David Accords Carter's greatest foreign policy achievement was his brokering of a historic peace between Israel and Egypt. In the Camp David Accords, signed by Egyptian president Anwar Sadat (left) and Israeli prime minister Menachem Begin, Israel promised to return all land in the Sinai in return for Egypt's recognition of the Israeli state. Though it did not solve the issue of Palestinian refugees, the Accords did lessen the tensions in the region. (*Jimmy Carter Presidential Library.*)

PRIMARY SOURCE

12.2 | *The Crisis of Confidence*

JIMMY CARTER

As a result of major foreign and domestic problems, President Jimmy Carter's popularity ratings dropped below 30 percent by July 1979. Many American citizens, and some within Carter's own administration, questioned Carter's ability to lead. In a televised address on July 15, 1979, Carter responded to the nation's anxieties and malaise in a speech that examined the nation's "crisis of confidence."

Our people are losing that faith not only in government itself but in the ability as citizens to serve as the ultimate rulers and shapers of our democracy.

As a people we know our past and we are proud of it. Our progress has been part of the living history of America, even the world. We always believed that we were
5 part of a great movement of humanity itself called democracy, involved in the search for freedom, and that belief has always strengthened us in our purpose. But just as we are losing our confidence in the future, we are also beginning to close the door on our past.

In a nation that was proud of hard work, strong families, close-knit commu-
10 nities, and our faith in God, too many of us now tend to worship self-indulgence and consumption. Human identity is no longer defined by what one does, but by what one owns. But we've discovered that owning things and consuming things does not satisfy our longing for meaning. We've learned that piling up material goods cannot fill the emptiness of lives which have no confidence or purpose.

15 The symptoms of this crisis of the American spirit are all around us. For the first time in the history of our country a majority of our people believe that the next five years will be worse than the past five years. Two-thirds of our people do not even vote. The productivity of American workers is actually dropping, and the willingness of Americans to save for the future has fallen below that of all other
20 people in the Western world. As you know, there is a growing disrespect for government and for churches and for schools, the news media, and other institutions. This is not a message of happiness or reassurance, but it is the truth and it is a warning.

These changes did not happen overnight. They've come upon us gradually over the last generation, years that were filled with shocks and tragedy. We were
25 sure that ours was a nation of the ballot, not the bullet, until the murders of John Kennedy and Robert Kennedy and Martin Luther King Jr. We were taught that our armies were always invincible and our causes were always just, only to suffer the agony of Vietnam. We respected the presidency as a place of honor until the shock of Watergate. We remember when the phrase "sound as a dollar" was an
30 expression of absolute dependability, until ten years of inflation began to shrink our dollar and our savings. We believed that our nation's resources were limitless until 1973, when we had to face a growing dependence on foreign oil.

Often you see paralysis and stagnation and drift. You don't like it, and neither do I. What can we do? First of all, we must face the truth, and then we can change
35 our course. We simply must have faith in each other, faith in our ability to govern ourselves, and faith in the future of this nation. Restoring that faith and that confidence to America is now the most important task we face. It is a true challenge of this generation of Americans. . . .

We are at a turning point in our history. There are two paths to choose. One is
40 a path I've warned about tonight, the path that leads to fragmentation and self-interest. Down that road lies a mistaken idea of freedom, the right to grasp for ourselves some advantage over others. That path would be one of constant conflict between narrow interests ending in chaos and immobility. It is a certain route to failure. . . . ■ ■ ■

Carter came to power promising to work for more amicable relations with the Soviet Union and to replace the Nixon-Kissinger commitment to realism with a concern for human rights. "We are now free of that inordinate fear of communism which once led us to embrace any dictator who joined us in our fear," Carter declared. He quickly opened a second round of arms limitations talks (SALT II) with the Soviet Union. One of the most complicated treaties ever negotiated, SALT II for the first time established numerical equality between the United States and the Soviet Union in total strategic nuclear delivery vehicles. But Carter was struggling to extend détente at a time when many Americans were questioning its benefits. Since Nixon and Kissinger had announced their aim of achieving détente, the Soviet Union had repeatedly made clear its continuing support for "liberation" struggles in the Third World. It ordered Cuba to send troops to potential allies in Africa and worked to win influence among Arab nations near the West's supply of oil.

At the end of 1979 a pair of disastrous foreign-policy reverses fixed upon Carter a reputation for insufficient strength and clarity in foreign policy. Early in the year revolutionaries had overthrown the pro-American regime of the shah of Iran and Muslim fundamentalists loyal to religious leader Ayatollah Ruholla Khomeini had gained control of the country. When Carter agreed to let the deposed shah come to the United States for cancer treatment, many Iranians took the act as a direct insult. On November 4, 1979, five hundred young Iranians occupied the American embassy and held fifty Americans hostage. Americans witnessed nightly serenades of "Death to America" from angry demonstrators, while the ailing, seventy-nine-year-old Ayatollah called the United States "the great Satan." "However the crisis ends," *Time* commented, "it seems likely to enhance the impression of American helplessness."

With Carter unable to effect a release by threats or diplomacy, the hostages languished week after week, then month after month. Spending sleepless nights, Carter felt "the same kind of impotence that a powerful person feels when his child is kidnapped." Nightly news broadcasts began to announce the number of days that the hostages had been in captivity and became for many a daily and humiliating reminder of the limits of American power. In April Carter ordered an abortive rescue mission that resulted in the death of 8 soldiers when two helicopters collided during a sandstorm in the desert. Burning helicopters in the desert symbolized America's inability to achieve even so limited an objective as freeing its citizens from the control of a third-rank nation.

As the American hostages entered their eighth week of captivity, another crisis developed. On Christmas Day Soviet troops invaded neighboring Afghanistan, toppling that nation's bumbling puppet regime. The attack represented a bold military operation aimed at ending a tribal rebellion against the Marxist government. The invasion moved Soviet troops to within several hundred miles of the oil-rich and politically unstable Persian Gulf. Vowing to punish the Soviets for their intervention, Carter recalled the American ambassador from Moscow, rallied world opinion against the Soviets, banned American athletes from participating in the Summer Olympics in Moscow, and imposed a politically risky grain embargo.

He also recognized that the Soviet invasion made moot the question of Senate ratification of a SALT agreement. After years of negotiation a frustrated Carter reluctantly requested that the Senate suspend consideration of the SALT II treaty. Carter claimed that the Soviet invasion posed the most serious threat to peace since World War II. In his 1980 State of the Union address, the president proclaimed the Carter Doctrine: "An attempt by any outside force to gain control of the Persian Gulf region will be regarded as an assault on the vital interests of the United States of America, and such an assault will be repelled by use of any means necessary, including military force." In the context of other foreign-policy events of his presidency, his response seemed to many Americans to be a hollow and tardy gesture.

The 1980 Presidential Campaign

Carter seemed helpless in the face of problems both at home and abroad. In late 1979, with inflation soaring into double digits, newly appointed Federal Reserve chairman Paul Volcker applied the monetary brakes. The nation's major banks responded by raising their prime interest rates, first to 13 percent and then to 14.5 percent. With the prime rate reaching all-time highs, the economy began its inevitable slowdown. In October the Dow Jones index of industrial stocks lost nearly one hundred points, auto sales dropped 23 percent compared to the previous year, and rising mortgage rates strangled the housing industry. Abroad the Soviet invasion of Afghanistan was raising fears that the USSR would strike at valuable Middle East oil supplies. Iranian militants continued to "hold America hostage," threatening to put their American captives on trial.

In the face of these crises, observers complained that Carter was aloof and arrogant, incapable of seizing control of the levers of power in Washington. A poor public speaker, he failed to arouse voter passion. "He is a soothing flatterer and a sensible president," noted the *New York Times*, "but not yet a leader, or teacher, even for a quiet time." His own party was in open revolt. With polls showing him leading the president by a 3–1 margin, Massachusetts senator Edward Kennedy, the keeper of the flickering liberal flame, announced that he would challenge Carter for the Democratic nomination. Portraying Carter as a weak and ineffective leader who had abandoned the party's liberal tradition, Kennedy confidently declared, "The only thing that paralyzes us today is the myth that we cannot move."

The American people, however, instinctively rallied around the president during a time of international crisis. Carter watched his job approval rating double to 61 percent in January 1980—the sharpest one-month leap in forty-one years of polling. Capitalizing on his sudden surge of popularity, Carter played the role of national leader by standing above the partisan fray and refusing to campaign. As Kennedy's campaign wilted in the patriotic afterglow, Carter secured his party's nomination on the first ballot.

Believing the president's rise in the polls would be temporary, a revived Republican Party rallied around former Hollywood movie actor turned politician Ronald Reagan, who cruised to victory in the Republican primaries. An effective speaker and master of the media, Reagan articulated a simple but compelling message: love of country, fear of communism, and scorn of government. Preaching what the economist Herbert Stein called the "economics of joy," Reagan repudiated the traditional Republican economic doctrine of tight fiscal policy and balanced budgets and instead preached about the wonders of supply-side economics. Responding to fears that America's stature in the world was in decline, Reagan called for a muscular foreign policy, including huge increases in military spending. Reflecting the influence of the religious right, the GOP platform adopted a plank opposing abortion and the Equal Rights Amendment. In an overture to moderate Republicans, Reagan selected the genial George Bush, a vanquished primary foe and former Central Intelligence Agency head, as his running mate.

PRIMARY SOURCE

12.3 | *New Economic Policies, 1980*
RONALD REAGAN

Plagued by a hurting economy and the Iran hostage situation, Carter faced Republican Ronald Reagan in the 1980 presidential election. Speaking before the International Business Council in Chicago on September 9, 1980, Reagan called for a new economic policy based on supply-side theory, and he promised to deliver one immediately after his inauguration if elected.

W e must first recognize that the problem with the U.S. economy is swollen, inefficient government, needless regulation, too much taxation, too much printing-press money. We don't need any more doses of Carter's eight- or 10-point programs to "fix" or fine tune the economy. For three and one-half years
5 these ill-thought-out initiatives have constantly sapped the healthy vitality of the most productive economic system the world has ever known.

Our country is in a downward cycle of progressive economic deterioration that must be broken if the economy is to recover and move into a vigorous growth cycle in the 1980s.

10 We must move boldly, decisively and quickly to control the runaway growth of Federal spending, to remove the tax disincentives that are throttling the economy, and to reform the regulatory web that is smothering it.

We must have and I am proposing a new strategy for the 1980s.

Only a series of well-planned economic actions, taken so that they complement and reinforce one another, can move our economy forward again.
15

We must keep the rate of growth of government spending at reasonable and prudent levels.

We must reduce personal income tax rates and accelerate and simplify depre-
ciation schedules in an orderly, systematic way to remove disincentives to work,
20 savings, investment, and productivity.

We must review regulations that affect the economy and change them to
encourage economic growth.

We must establish a stable, sound, and predictable monetary policy.

And we must restore confidence by following a consistent national economic
25 policy that does not change from month to month.

I am asked: 'Can we do it all at once?' My answer is: 'We must.' . . .

A fundamental part of my strategy for economic growth is the restoration of
confidence. If our business community is going to invest and build and create
new, well-paying jobs, they must have a future free from arbitrary, government
30 action. They must have confidence that the economic "rules-of-the-game" won't
be changed suddenly or capriciously.

In my administration, a national economic policy will be established, and we
will begin to implement it, within the first 90 days.

Thus, I envision a strategy encompassing many elements—none of which can
35 do the job alone, but all of which together can get it done. This strategy depends
for its success more than anything else on the will of the people to regain control
of their government. . . .

The time has come for the American people to reclaim their dream. Things
don't have to be this way. We can change them. We must change them. Mr.
40 Carter's American tragedy must and can be transcended by the spirit of the
American people, working together.

Let's get America working again.

The time is now.   ■ ■ ■

As the campaign moved into the final weeks, Carter and Reagan were deadlocked. Reagan's acting skills proved decisive in the lone debate held a week
before the election. On debating points the two candidates were evenly matched.
But in the closing remarks Reagan focused public attention on Carter's responsibility for double-digit inflation, the hostages in Iran, and Soviet troops in
Afghanistan. "Are you better off than you were four years ago?" he asked. "Is
America as respected throughout the world as it was?"

On election day Reagan won 489 electoral votes to Carter's 49. In the popular
vote the Republican challenger received 43.9 million votes (50.7 percent) to
Carter's 35.5 million (41 percent). Carter became the first Democrat since Grover
Cleveland in 1888, and the first incumbent since Herbert Hoover in 1932, to be
voted out of the Oval Office. Independent candidate John Anderson, a Republican congressman who bolted his party claiming that it had been hijacked by conservatives, won only 5.7 million popular votes (6.6 percent). The Democrats,
moreover, lost thirty-four House seats and lost control of the Senate as the
Republicans gained twelve seats. Republicans controlled the upper house of Congress for the first time since the days of Dwight Eisenhower. Ominously, 48 percent of eligible voters did not cast ballots, the lowest voter turnout since 1948.

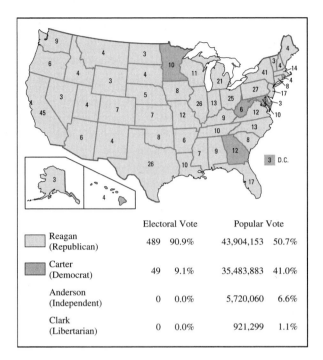

The Election of 1980

While Ronald Reagan won a landslide in the electoral college, the number of popular voters and nonvoters provides a much more complex picture. Only 52.6 percent of eligible voters cast their ballots in the election, giving Reagan only 28 percent of the potential electorate and leading many to question why so many Americans chose not to vote.

	Electoral Vote		Popular Vote	
Reagan (Republican)	489	90.9%	43,904,153	50.7%
Carter (Democrat)	49	9.1%	35,483,883	41.0%
Anderson (Independent)	0	0.0%	5,720,060	6.6%
Clark (Libertarian)	0	0.0%	921,299	1.1%

Most polling experts noted that the election represented "a strong call for moderate change" and that only a fraction of Reagan voters shared his conservative views. The pollster George Gallup concluded, "Examination of political indicators and the views of voters on key issues shows that the Reagan landslide was not so much the result of an ideological shift to the right among the electorate as dissatisfaction with the leadership of the nation and a desire for change." Though Reagan won by a large margin in the electoral college, he captured only 51 percent of the voters, just 3 percent more than Ford had in losing in 1976. Yet because of the electoral college margin and the party's congressional gains, Reagan's election was viewed by many observers as a mandate for conservatism. As Massachusetts Democratic senator Paul Tsongas said, "Basically, the New Deal died yesterday." Reagan's task was to transform appearance into reality.

Reagan's rise to national prominence did, however, highlight the dramatic shift of political power from the more liberal Rust Belt, which extended from Massachusetts down to Delaware and across to Illinois and Michigan, to the conservative Sun Belt—the bottom half of the country extending from North Carolina to southern California. During the previous decade the Sun Belt had accounted for 90 percent of the nation's population growth and by 1980 claimed a majority of Americans. Just three states—California, Texas, and Florida—saw nearly 40 percent of the nation's population growth and controlled nearly 25 percent of the electoral votes needed to win the presidency. Polls showed that Sun

Belt residents were more skeptical about federal power, more resentful of government regulation, and more anti-Soviet than the general voting public. In the South Republicans lured white voters still smarting from the Democrats' support for civil rights during the 1960s. Not surprisingly, the Republican ticket comprised a representative from California and one from Texas.

State	1940	1960	1980	% Increase 1940–1980	% Increase 1960–1980
North Carolina	3,572	4,556	5,874	64.5	28.9
South Carolina	1,900	2,383	3,119	64.2	30.9
Georgia	3,124	3,943	5,464	75.0	38.6
Florida	1,897	4,952	9,740	413.4	96.7
Alabama	2,833	3,267	3,890	37.3	19.1
Mississippi	2,184	2,178	2,521	15.5	15.7
Tennessee	2,916	3,567	4,591	57.5	28.7
Louisiana	2,364	3,257	4,204	77.9	29.1
Arkansas	1,949	1,786	2,286	17.3	28.0
Oklahoma	2,336	2,328	3,025	29.5	29.9
Texas	6,415	9,580	14,228	121.8	48.5
New Mexico	532	951	1,300	144.8	36.7
Arizona	499	1,302	2,718	444.7	108.8
Southern Nevada[a]	16	127	461	2,781.2	263.0
Southern California[b]	3,841	9,399	13,803	259.4	46.9
Total	36,378	53,576	77,224	112.3	44.1
Northeast-Midwest	76,120	96,927	107,986	41.9	11.4
United States	132,165	179,323	226,505	71.4	26.3

[a] Clark County (Las Vegas SMSA)
[b] San Bernadino, Kern, San Luis Obispo, Santa Barbara, Los Angeles, Riverside, Orange, San Diego, Ventura, and Imperial counties

Sun Belt Population, 1940–1980   With the application of air conditioning to American homes after World War II, parts of the country that experienced extreme heat in the summer, the South and Southwest especially, became more inhabitable. These regions, labeled the Sun Belt, were areas of the country that generally lacked strong labor unions and had an abundance of cheap land and labor, leading many corporations to relocate their northern industries. Workers also followed the expanding military industrial complex into the Sun Belt as defense contractors and military bases developed in the region. Different parts of the Sun Belt also experienced tremendous population growth due to the oil boom in the 1970s (Texas, Oklahoma, Louisiana), tourism (Florida and California), and Mexican immigration.

For many conservatives the 1980 election represented the inevitable triumph of Richard Nixon's conservative majority. "Like a great soaking wet shaggy dog, the Silent Majority—banished from the house during the Watergate storms—romped back into the nation's parlor this week and shook itself vigorously," observed the columnist William Safire. Reagan's message of economic and cultural conservatism appealed to Americans grown tired of social experiments and cynical about government power. The 1970s had dealt a number of body blows to American optimism at home and prestige abroad: the resignation of a president, the painful experience of a lost war, the trials of stagflation, and the humiliation of Americans held hostage in Iran. President Carter publicly questioned whether new social and international conditions required Americans to lower their expectations of the future. A majority of Americans, however, found Reagan's reassuring optimism about the future and his slashing attacks on government more appealing. The new president, however, was about to find himself trapped in the paradox of the nation's love/hate relationship with Washington.

SELECTED READINGS

▪ Arthur M. Schlesinger Jr. studies the growth of executive power that presaged Watergate in *The Imperial Presidency* (1973). Bob Woodward, one of the journalists who uncovered the Watergate conspiracy, analyzes the impact of that cover-up on the five subsequent administrations in *Shadow* (1999). Essays examining the causes and consequences of America's erosion of faith in its government have been collected by David Robertson in *Loss of Confidence* (1998). James I. Sundquist's *The Decline and Resurgence of Congress* (1981) tracks the changing balance of power between the two branches of government. Robert Heilbroner and Lester Thurow diagnose the economic ills of the 1970s in *Five Economic Challenges* (1983). John P. Hoerr's tale of America's declining steel industry, *And the Wolf Finally Came* (1988), demonstrates the nation's industrial decline during the decade.

▪ John Robert Greene studies the Ford administration in *The Presidency of Gerald R. Ford* (1995). Bernard Firestone and Alexej Ugrinsky compile lectures from a conference on the Ford administration, including essays by Ford, some of his advisers, and political scientists and historians, in their two-volume *Gerald R. Ford and the Politics of Post-Watergate America* (1992). The story of Ford's ascension to the White House is covered in James Cannon's *Time and Chance* (1993). Ralph Wetterhahn's *The Last Battle* (2001) provides a complete account of the attack and hijacking of the SS *Mayaguez* and the marines sent to rescue it. Jules Witcover's *Marathon* (1977) recounts the 1976 presidential campaign.

▪ On the Carter presidency, see Charles Jones, *The Trusteeship Presidency* (1988); Burton Kaufman, *The Presidency of James Earl Carter, Jr.* (1993); and Gary M. Fink and Hugh Davis Graham, *The Carter Presidency* (1998). Robert

Heilbroner's *An Inquiry into the Human Prospect* (2nd rev. ed, 1991) discusses the energy crisis. William Greider's *Secrets of the Temple* (1987) includes a detailed analysis of economic policy under Carter.

▌ Gaddis Smith's readable *Morality, Reason, and Power* (1987) provides the best overview of Carter's erratic foreign policy, while a defense of Carter's foreign-policy decisions is found in Robert Strong's *Working in the World* (2000). William Quandt describes the Egyptian-Israeli peace accord in *Camp David* (1986). Judith DeMaleissye-Melun details the SALT II negotiations and the breakdown of the relationship between the United States and Soviet Union in *Fall of Detente* (1997). Gabriella Grasselli's *British and American Responses to the Soviet Invasion of Afghanistan* (1996) explains how both nations perceived the Soviet invasion as a threat to western security. Barry Rubin's *Paved with Good Intentions* (1980) covers America's relations with Iran, and Russell Moses evaluates the strategy of the Carter administration and the actions of the Iranian leadership during the hostage crisis in *Freeing the Hostages* (1996).

13

The Reagan Presidency, 1981–1989

In private jets, vintage Gilded Age railcars, and luxury chartered buses, Hollywood celebrities, wealthy industrialists, and powerful political figures descended upon the capital city to join in the celebration of Ronald Reagan's inauguration. Costing $16.3 million, the festivities included a spirited parade, fireworks, and nine official inaugural balls. Throughout the evening black limousines sped tuxedoed men and mink-frocked women to these and other garish parties. Diamond earrings, emeralds, sequins, silk gowns, morning suits, and white ties predominated, signaling a bold departure from the restrained, plebeian style of Reagan's predecessor, Jimmy Carter. Standing in the afterglow of that ostentatious display of wealth, one observer quipped, "It was a far cry from the populist Peanut Special that chugged up from Georgia for the Inauguration four years ago."

During the early afternoon of that unseasonably warm twentieth day of January, Reagan used his inaugural address to evoke a sense of rebirth and new directions. Standing on a podium that, for the first time in the history of the presidency—overlooked the Mall—symbolically facing westward toward the Potomac and the Sun Belt beyond—Reagan called for "an era of national renewal." Abandoning Carter's message of limits, Reagan spoke of a future of endless possibilities led by a "a strong, prosperous America at peace with itself and the world." At home a growing economy would "provide equal opportunities for all Americans with no barriers born of bigotry or discrimination." Abroad the United States would "again be the exemplar of freedom and a beacon of hope for those who do not now have freedom." Reagan told the nation that these grand expectations could be realized only if Americans scaled back the power of the federal government. Americans needed to realize, he declared to the delight of conservatives, that "government is not the solution to our problem; government is the problem."

13.1 | *Inaugural Address*
RONALD REAGAN

Americans witnessed the opulence and style of Hollywood during the presidential inauguration of Ronald Reagan on January 20, 1981. Despite the show-biz atmosphere surrounding the inauguration, Reagan's speech demonstrated his political savvy as he promised "a new beginning" marked by a revised tax system and less government intervention.

The economic ills we suffer have come upon us over several decades. They will not go away in days, weeks, or months, but they will go away. They will go away because we as Americans have the capacity now, as we've had in the past, to do whatever needs to be done to preserve this last and greatest bastion of
5 freedom.

In this present crisis, government is not the solution to our problem; government is the problem. From time to time we've been tempted to believe that society has become too complex to be managed by self-rule, that government by an elite group is superior to government for, by, and of the people. Well, if no one
10 among us is capable of governing himself, then who among us has the capacity to govern someone else? All of us together, in and out of government, must bear the burden. The solutions we seek must be equitable, with no one group singled out to pay a higher price.

We hear much of special interest groups. Well, our concern must be for a spe-
15 cial interest group that has been too long neglected. It knows no sectional boundaries or ethnic and racial divisions, and it crosses political party lines. It is made up of men and women who raise our food, patrol our streets, man our mines and factories, teach our children, keep our homes, and heal us when we're sick—professionals, industrialists, shopkeepers, clerks, cabbies, and truck drivers. They are,
20 in short, "we the people," this breed called Americans.

Well, this administration's objective will be a healthy, vigorous, growing economy that provides equal opportunities for all Americans, with no barriers born of bigotry or discrimination. Putting America back to work means putting all Americans back to work. Ending inflation means freeing all Americans from the
25 terror of runaway living costs. All must share in the productive work of this "new

beginning," and all must share in the bounty of a revived economy. With the idealism and fair play which are the core of our system and our strength, we can have a strong and prosperous America, at peace with itself and the world.

So, as we begin, let us take inventory. We are a nation that has a government—not the other way around. And this makes us special among the nations of the earth. Our government has no power except that granted it by the people. It is time to check and reverse the growth of government, which shows signs of having grown beyond the consent of the governed.

It is my intention to curb the size and influence of the federal establishment and to demand recognition of the distinction between the powers granted to the federal government and those reserved to the states or to the people. All of us need to be reminded that the federal government did not create the states; the states created the federal government.

Now, so there will be no misunderstanding, it's not my intention to do away with government. It is rather to make it work—work with us, not over us; to stand by our side, not ride on our back. Government can and must provide opportunity, not smother it; foster productivity, not stifle it.

If we look to the answer as to why for so many years we achieved so much, prospered as no other people on earth, it was because here in this land we unleashed the energy and individual genius of man to a greater extent than has ever been done before. Freedom and the dignity of the individual have been more available and assured here than in any other place on earth. The price for this freedom at times has been high, but we have never been unwilling to pay that price.

It is no coincidence that our present troubles parallel and are proportionate to the intervention and intrusion in our lives that result from unnecessary and excessive growth of government. It is time for us to realize that we're too great a nation to limit ourselves to small dreams. We're not, as some would have us believe, doomed to an inevitable decline. I do not believe in a fate that will fall on us no matter what we do. I do believe in a fate that will fall on us if we do nothing. So, with all the creative energy at our command, let us begin an era of national renewal. Let us renew our determination, our courage, and our strength. And let us renew our faith and our hope. . . .   ■ ■ ■

The postwar paradox shaped and defined both the Reagan administration and its legacy. At home the new president committed his administration to curbing the size and influence of the federal government by reducing spending and lightening what he called "our punitive tax burden." But his inability to reconcile the public's fears of encroaching federal power with its demand for government programs produced a massive budget deficit. Abroad Reagan spoke eloquently about the nation's commitment to freedom and liberty, but his administration, abandoning Carter's emphasis on human rights, often supported repressive regimes in the Third World. Finally, Reagan's style and leadership inspired the public imagination and raised expectations of government. By the end of his administration the public was placing even greater demands on government.

The Style and Substance of Ronald Reagan

The inaugural address, with its misty patriotism and unrestrained optimism, was vintage Reagan. Born in Dixon, Illinois, in 1911, Reagan graduated from Eureka College and worked briefly as a radio sports announcer before moving to California and signing a contract with Warner Brothers film studio in 1937. Over the next two decades he appeared in fifty-three movies but won little acclaim as an actor. The one exception was his role as George Gipp, Notre Dame's first all-American football player, in the 1940 classic *Knute Rockne, All American.* "Someday, when things are tough, maybe you can ask the boys to go in there and win just one for the Gipper," he pleads in a moving deathbed scene that brought tears to millions of eyes. As president Reagan would repeatedly invoke this phrase to rally the American people or galvanize the Republican faithful.

It was during the postwar years that Reagan underwent a political conversion from a New Deal Democrat of decidedly leftist leanings to a right-wing conservative. But in his youth, according to biographer Edmund Morris, he sought to become a member of the California branch of the American Communist Party. He suffered rejection, however, because leading figures in the party thought the $200-a-week actor was "a flake." Morris saw the conversion as a process involving both personal and political factors. On the personal side, there were the experience of a near-fatal illness, the death of a child by Jane Wyman, Wyman's decision to divorce him, and his fading acting career. On the political side, there were his clash with communist elements within the Screen Actors Guild, and the growing belief that Joseph Stalin's Russia represented the same totalitarian threat as Adolf Hitler's Germany.

These overlapping emotional and ideological traumas shook Reagan to the core and forced him back to first principles, which for him became a rock-ribbed belief in self-reliance and a conviction that government is "them" rather than "us." During the 1950s Reagan became the spokesman for General Electric, traveling everywhere by train because he was afraid to fly, speaking at plants across the country. He emerged from his travels a wealthy man with a practiced modesty, a set speech about limited government, and a muscular anticommunism that would remain the backbone of his message to the American people.

Reagan made his political debut during the 1964 presidential campaign when he delivered a moving television tribute to Barry Goldwater. Columnist David Broder described the performance as the "most successful political debut since William Jennings Bryan electrified the 1896 Democratic Convention with his 'Cross of Gold' speech." Like Bryan's appeal for silver coinage, Reagan pitched an economic panacea. He called for the restoration of the supposed message of the nation's "Founding Fathers that outside of its legitimate functions, government does nothing as well or as economically as the private sector of the economy." The speech established Reagan's conservative credentials and launched his successful bid for governor of California in 1966. After two successful terms Reagan was ready for the national stage.

By all accounts he was intellectually unambitious and notoriously ignorant about the details of policies. The portrait of Reagan that most often emerges from the memoirs written by members of his administration is of a president who was long on decency and determination and short on intellect. Even one of his favorite speechwriters, Peggy Noonan, who deeply admired the president, described his brain as "barren terrain." The Pentagon's Richard Perle thought that Reagan consistently engaged in "intellectual delegation of authority." National security adviser Robert McFarlane once remarked of Reagan to Secretary of State George Shultz, "He knows so little, and accomplishes so much." The president's authorized biographer, who spent countless hours observing Reagan in the Oval Office, described him as "shatteringly banal," "bland," "boring," a man possessed of "encyclopedic ignorance."

Reagan was also one of the most disengaged chief executives in history. "I know that hard work never killed anyone," he once said, "but I figure, why take the chance?" His biographer Lou Cannon observed that Reagan may have been the only president who saw his election as a chance to get some rest. His schedule was designed not to tax him. He read newspapers over breakfast, then went to his office around 9:00, where he fed the squirrels outside in the Rose Garden until his National Security Council (NSC) briefing at 9:30. From 10:00 to 11:00 was personal time to read mail and relax. He ate lunch at noon, napped briefly, and then worked until 5:00, when he retired to the family quarters for an evening of television. He took frequent three-day weekends at Camp David and punctuated the season with many vacations. By one estimate, during his eight-year term he spent an entire year at his California ranch. Reagan spent more time at the movies during his presidency than at anything else. He went to Camp David on 183 weekends, usually watching four or five films on each of these trips.

In his attempt to use the presidency as Theodore Roosevelt's "bully pulpit," Reagan's former career as a professional performer provided immense advantage. Not only did he have an acumen for rousing audiences, but he also could sense how a speech would appear on television. What animated Reagan was a public performance. "Every moment of every public appearance," Chief of Staff Donald Regan recalled, "was scheduled, every word was scripted, every place where Reagan was expected to stand was chalked with toe marks. . . . He had been learning his lines, composing his facial expression, hitting his toe marks for half a century." On the stump as on television, Reagan was a distinctly nonthreatening individual. He never scolded a crowd; his style was always conversational, flavored with humorous and self-deprecating asides. His soft voice made every word fit the natural cadence of his speech. He read smoothly from the TelePrompTer, without miscue. Each gesture was practiced until it appeared genuine and spontaneous.

With his telegenic features and extensive experience in front of a camera, Reagan was ideally suited for politics in a media age. He appealed to values, invoked themes, and identified with myths that were embraced by most Americans. "With Reagan, facts don't determine the case," remarked the journalist Sydney Blumenthal. "Facts don't make his beliefs true. His beliefs give life to facts, which are parables tailored to have a moral." As biographer Garry Wills pointed out, Reagan's upbeat invocation of a simpler America appealed to millions of Americans who believed the same myths and enjoyed having them affirmed.

Despite Reagan's media skills "no previous administration had devoted so many resources to managing the news or approached the task with so much calculation," noted one scholar. The president's advisers, whom James Reston described as "the best public relations team ever to enter the White House," carefully orchestrated media coverage. By controlling access to Reagan, the staff minimized the president's penchant for verbal slips, prevented the press from asking tough questions, and guaranteed that the public saw him in brief visuals that served to enhance his stature. These images, designed around a daily message, allowed the White House to focus public attention on Reagan's accomplishments while ignoring his numerous failures. "So far, he's proving Lincoln was right," observed a veteran reporter. "You can fool all of the people some of the time."

The Reagan Agenda

Reagan was going to need all of his charisma and skill if he was to succeed in lifting the nation's spirits in the winter of 1981. The cost of living had increased by more than 12 percent in 1980, unemployment had risen to 7.4 percent, the prime lending rate was at an astonishing 20 percent, and the government was facing a projected budget deficit of $56 billion. "We've inherited the worst economic mess in 50 years," said Chief of Staff James Baker. The new administration faced reminders of the nation's vulnerability around the world. Russian troops had swarmed over Afghanistan, moving closer to America's strategic oil supplies in the Middle East. Iranian militants had released the hostages after fourteen months of imprisonment, but relations with the former staunch and strategic ally remained tense. The turmoil took its toll on the nation's sense of self-confidence and eroded the public's faith in the president's ability to solve its problems. "The Presidency," noted *Newsweek,* "has in some measure defeated the last five men who have held it—and has persuaded some of the people who served them that it is in danger of becoming a game nobody can win."

At the outset the Reagan administration concentrated on reviving the slumping economy. Announcing his economic recovery plan in February 1981, Reagan promised "to put the nation on a fundamentally different course, a course leading to less inflation, more growth and a brighter future for all of our citizens." The president's economic program consisted of three essential parts. First, embracing the supply-side doctrine of the New Right, Reagan requested a 30 percent reduction in both personal and corporate income taxes over three years. Tax cuts, the administration reasoned, would stimulate the economy by providing incentives for individuals and businesses to work, save, and invest. Second, he planned to cut government spending for social programs by $41.4 billion in fiscal year 1982. Third, he planned to use a tight monetary policy to squeeze inflation out of the economy. Taken together, these proposals would "revitalize economic growth, renew optimism and confidence and rekindle the nation's entrepreneurial instincts and creativity," Reagan said. "The benefits to the average American will be striking."

But in late March 1981, before Reagan could implement his economic program, a would-be assassin shot and seriously wounded the elderly president. Through the ordeal Reagan showed courage and spirit. As he was wheeled into the operating room, he quipped to his wife, Nancy, "Honey, I forgot to duck." In the short run, Reagan's behavior in adversity magnified his popularity and swayed Congress into accepting his radical economic plan. An ABC News–*Washington Post* survey indicated that the president's rating soared 11 points, to 73 percent, immediately following the assassination attempt. "The bullet meant to kill him," observed *Newsweek,* "made him a hero instead, floating above the contentions of politics and the vagaries of good news or bad."

In the long run, however, the assassination drained precious energy from the already diminished president. Reagan came close to dying after the assassination attempt. He lost more than half his blood, and doctors failed to adequately warm his transfusion plasma during a dramatic struggle to save his life. Biographer Morris called the operation "a chilling physiological insult from which he would never fully recover." Weakened by his brush with assassination, Reagan concentrated his diminished mental resources on a few high-priority issues. When threatened by complex questions or conflicting information, Reagan simply "deleted all data that threatened to encumber him," Morris observed.

In May dispirited Democrats joined Republicans in passing a budget resolution that called for deep cuts in many social programs and increased spending for the military. "You close the door on America with the [Reagan budget] bill," Speaker Thomas P. "Tip" O'Neill warned his flock in the hushed last moments of debate. Casting the debate in stark ideological language, Reagan called on Democrats to support his program; those who did not would be defending the "failed policies of the past." After the vote Reagan rejoiced. "The people have been heard," he said. In August Congress rubber-stamped the administration's massive tax cut, providing for across-the-board reductions of 5 percent the first year and an additional 10 percent in each of the succeeding two years.

It was an impressive legislative achievement that earned Reagan the begrudging respect of his critics, who compared his performance to FDR's. "Mr. Reagan has established his goals faster, communicated a greater sense of economic urgency and come forward with more comprehensive proposals than any new president since the first 100 days of Franklin D. Roosevelt," observed the *New York Times.* In many ways, however, Reagan's economic policy failed to address the contradiction inherent in America's view of government. Since the New Deal Americans had come to expect the benefits of the modern welfare state without recognizing the legitimacy of government power. Reagan used the sense of economic emergency to tap into public

Assassination Attempt on President Ronald Reagan   On March 30, 1981, newly inaugurated President Ronald Reagan gave a speech to a building trades conference at the Washington Hilton. Just as he reached his limousine after the speech, 26-year-old John Hinckley Jr. opened fire on the president and his entourage. Of the six bullets Hinckley fired, one hit the president and entered his left lung; one hit Press Secretary James Brady (third from the left) in the forehead, permanently paralyzing him; one hit Secret Service agent Timothy McCarthy (far right) in the chest; and a fourth struck policeman Thomas Delahanty (nearest the umbrella) in the back. Although Reagan joked with his wife Nancy that he "forgot to duck," the president was seriously wounded, and, according to doctors, was close to death when he arrived at the hospital. In 1982, a jury found Hinckley not guilty by reason of insanity and sentenced him to a mental facility.

disenchantment, but he avoided trimming the politically sensitive, middle-class entitlement programs—social security and Medicare—and instead cut programs that directly benefited the poor, such as food stamps, Aid to Families with Dependent Children, school lunches, housing assistance, and Medicaid.

While the public gave the president credit for pushing his legislative program through Congress, it blamed him for the inevitable slowdown that resulted from his tight money policies. By limiting the amount of money in the economy, the Federal Reserve Board, with Reagan's implicit approval, incited a recession by making it difficult for businesses to borrow and expand. In 1982 and 1983 the "Reagan recession" forced some 10 million Americans out of work and the unemployment rate—9.5 percent—stood at its highest rate since 1941. "Main Street U.S.A. is in trouble," said a Senate Democrat looking forward to the 1982 midterm elections, "and they're going to turn to us." The president urged Congress and the American people to "stay the course," predicting that the economy would rebound in 1983. He was right: the gross national product (GNP) increased an impressive 4.3 percent, and unemployment declined to 8 percent.

Attacking the Liberal State

As a presidential candidate, Ronald Reagan pledged to shrink the scope of federal government by returning greater authority and responsibility to the states. The *Federal Register,* which grew to eighty-seven thousand pages in 1980, shrank to a low of forty-seven thousand pages in 1986. One of Reagan's first official acts was to freeze all pending regulations for sixty days to permit additional review; many were later amended or killed. For the remainder of his term all proposed regulations had to be cleared through the Office of Management and Budget.

Anyone who thought that Reagan's tough talk was just bluster was disabused of that notion in August 1981 when members of the Professional Air Traffic Controllers union illegally went on strike. The president ordered the strikers to return to work in forty-eight hours or lose their jobs. Despite the potential hazards to air safety, he made good on his threat and barred the Federal Aviation Administration from rehiring any of the 11,400 fired controllers. His blunt and decisive action dealt a blow to organized labor, already reeling from declining membership, and emboldened the business community to get tough with unions.

He appointed to his cabinet conservatives determined to loosen federal regulation. His secretary of energy, James Edwards, a dentist and an ex-governor of South Carolina who favored unregulated development of nuclear power, planned to eliminate his own department. Secretary of Labor Raymond Donovan was a private construction contractor with few links to organized labor and an advocate of the elimination of several of the labor movement's most cherished federal work-safety regulations.

The most controversial of Reagan's administrators was Secretary of the Interior James G. Watt. Under Watt's leadership the Interior Department opened federal lands to coal and timber production, narrowed the scope of the wilderness preserves, and sought to make 1 million offshore acres with oil potential available for drilling.

Watt believed that after twenty-five years of federal land management it was time to return the use of government land to the public through the deregulation of natural resources. In his first official act as secretary he opened up California's coastline to offshore oil drilling and called a halt to future acquisitions of land for national parks. He remarked to a group of park employees, "There are people who want to bring their motorcycles and snowmobiles right into the middle of Yellowstone national park and our job is to make sure they can." Watt's policies and provocative public statements kept him in the middle of controversy until he finally resigned in 1983.

Paralleling the agencies charged with protecting the environment, many other government agencies created to protect the public welfare now engaged in

Controversial Secretary of the Interior James Watt President Reagan selected individuals for his cabinet that shared his conservative principles, including James G. Watt, the first of three men appointed secretary of the interior during Reagan's administrations. Environmentalists believed interior secretaries should act as trustees of the nation's natural resources and they vehemently opposed the selection of Watt, who had a history of supporting business interests in land development projects. During his two years at the Department of the Interior, Watt cut funding for programs to protect endangered species, opposed increasing the size and number of the national parks and forests, and suggested selling public lands to oil, gas, and mining interests, rejecting the conservationist idea of long-term management of natural resources. As a result, environmentalist groups gathered 1.1 million signatures for a petition demanding Watt's removal and the Senate drafted a resolution to dismiss him, but Watt resigned in 1983 before Congress took action.

efforts to undermine safety standards. The National Highway Traffic Safety Administration decided to save automobile manufacturers money by permitting new cars to carry less substantial (and less safe) bumpers. The Department of Energy and the Nuclear Regulatory Commission ignored mounting evidence of unsafe conditions in the nuclear industry; civilian power plants were seldom penalized for safety violations. The Federal Communications Commission (FCC) cut public-service broadcasting and increased the amount of time that television stations could air commercials. "Television is just another appliance," insisted FCC head Mark Fowler. "It's just a toaster with pictures."

The turbulent history of the savings-and-loan (S&L) industry during the 1980s exemplified the dangers of the Reagan passion for deregulation. Since the depression, S&Ls (called thrifts) had been restricted to using investors' money for low-risk mortgage lending, while banks could offer checking accounts, trust services, and commercial and consumer loans. When interest rates soared in the 1970s, money bled out of the S&Ls and into higher-yielding money market accounts. Conservatives, arguing that deregulation was the key to saving the S&Ls and reviving the banking industry, loosened the rules governing S&L investments at the same time that they increased federal insurance on S&L deposits from $20,000 to $100,000. "This bill is the most important legislation for financial institutions in the last 50 years," President Reagan said in a ceremony announcing the new rules. "All in all, I think we hit the jackpot," he added.

Flush with money from investors trying to turn a quick profit, many S&Ls made risky loans on malls, apartment complexes, and office towers. Opportunists such as Charles Keating, owner of Lincoln Savings, turned their thrifts into giant casinos, using federally insured deposits to bet on high-risk corporate takeovers and junk bonds. It was a game of blackjack that only the consumers could lose. Instead of saving the S&Ls, the legislation provided thrift owners with an incentive to engage in high-risk activity, which led to hundreds of thrifts declaring bankruptcy. The resulting $200 billion taxpayer-financed bailout cost $10 for every man, woman, and child in America.

Reagan Justice

As president, Reagan promised to appoint judges concerned with "protecting the rights of law-abiding citizens," defending "traditional values and the sanctity of human life," and maintaining "judicial restraint." Like many conservatives, he believed that government should relax its efforts to ensure justice and equal opportunity for African-Americans and other minority groups.

To achieve the latter goals, the Reagan administration cut funding for the Equal Employment Opportunity Commission and for the civil-rights division of the Justice Department. In 1981 the Justice Department supported a case brought by Bob Jones University against the Treasury Department, which had refused it tax-exempt status on the grounds that the university discriminated against blacks. Though the Supreme Court in 1983 upheld the Treasury Department, by an 8–1 decision, the administration's support for the university made it abundantly clear that Reagan hoped to turn back the clock on civil rights.

The New Right especially welcomed Reagan's efforts to realign the Supreme Court. In 1981 he appointed conservative Sandra Day O'Connor of Arizona as the first woman to serve on the High Court. When Chief Justice Warren Burger retired in 1986, Reagan elevated William Rehnquist, a strong advocate of law and order, to the position. Reagan offered Rehnquist's open seat to federal judge Antonin Scalia, a rigid advocate of executive power. In 1988 Reagan had sought to replace centrist Louis Powell with conservative Robert Bork, but a coalition of civil-rights and women's groups helped defeat the nomination. The seat was eventually filled by Anthony Kennedy, a Federal Appeals Court judge from California.

The Reagan appointments yielded an aggressive conservative coalition of justices that took command of the court, issuing a series of decisions that reversed the direction of more than three decades of law on criminal procedures, individual liberties, and civil rights. Deciding most major cases by 5–4 margins, the Court ruled that under some circumstances police could submit as evidence confessions coerced from suspected criminals; the Court also curtailed the rights of immigrants to claim political asylum and limited the rights of death row prisoners to challenge the death penalty. In the most significant civil-rights ruling (*Wards Cove* v. *Atonio,* 1987), the justices shifted the burden of proof from those accused of practicing discrimination to its victims. But the justices proved they were not always predictable. One surprise, much to conservatives' dismay, was the Court's decision that burning the American flag was political speech protected by the Constitution.

The 1984 Presidential Campaign

The improving economy of 1983–84 revived Ronald Reagan's popularity. With polls showing the president enjoying a commanding lead against any potential Democratic opponent, many Republican strategists hoped for an electoral landslide that would herald Republican control of the White House for the rest of the century. The Reagan campaign strategy was simple: celebrate the president's identification with peace and prosperity, avoid a debate over specific issues, and identify his Democratic opponent with the "failed policies" of the Carter administration (high taxes, soaring inflation, and vacillating world leadership). Grand expectations were back in style.

PRIMARY SOURCE

13.2 | *1984 Democratic Convention Speech*
GERALDINE FERRARO

Democratic presidential nominee Walter Mondale chose New York representative Geraldine Ferraro as his running mate in 1984. The first woman ever to be nominated for vice president by a major party, Ferraro expressed her desire to leave future generations a better nation in her acceptance speech at the Democratic Convention on July 19.

Ladies and gentlemen of the convention: My name is Geraldine Ferraro. I stand before you to proclaim tonight: America is the land where dreams can come true for all of us. . . .

Tonight, the daughter of a woman whose highest goal was a future for her
5 children talks to our nation's oldest party about a future for us all. Tonight, the daughter of working Americans tells all Americans that the future is within our reach—if we're willing to reach for it. Tonight, the daughter of an immigrant from Italy has been chosen to run for [vice] president in the new land my father came to love. Our faith that we can shape a better future is what the American dream is all
10 about. The promise of our country is that the rules are fair. If you work hard and play by the rules, you can earn your share of America's blessings. . . .

Americans want to live by the same set of rules. But under this administration, the rules are rigged against too many of our people. It isn't right that every year, the share of taxes paid by individual citizens is going up, while the share paid by large
15 corporations is getting smaller and smaller. The rules say: Everyone in our society should contribute their fair share. It isn't right that this year Ronald Reagan will hand the American people a bill for interest on the national debt larger than the entire cost of the federal government under John F. Kennedy. Our parents left us a growing economy. The rules say: We must not leave our kids a mountain of debt.
20 It isn't right that a woman should get paid 59 cents on the dollar for the same work as a man. If you play by the rules, you deserve a fair day's pay for a fair day's work. It isn't right that—that if trends continue—by the year 2000 nearly all of the poor people in America will be women and children. The rules of a decent society say, when you distribute sacrifice in times of austerity, you don't put
25 women and children first.

It isn't right that young people today fear they won't get the Social Security they paid for, and that older Americans fear that they will lose what they have already earned. Social Security is a contract between the last generation and the next, and the rules say: You don't break contracts. We're going to keep faith with
30 older Americans. . . .

It isn't right that young couples question whether to bring children into a world of 50,000 nuclear warheads. That isn't the vision for which Americans have struggled for more than two centuries. And our future doesn't have to be that way.

Change is in the air, just as surely as when John Kennedy beckoned America to
35 a new frontier; when Sally Ride rocketed into space and when Rev. Jesse Jackson ran for the office of president of the United States. By choosing a woman to run for our nation's second highest office, you sent a powerful signal to all Americans. There are no doors we cannot unlock. We will place no limits on achievement. If we can do this, we can do anything. Tonight, we reclaim our dream. We're going to
40 make the rules of American life work fairly for all Americans again. ■ ■ ■

Reagan's challenger, former Vice President Walter Mondale, had won his party's nomination after a bruising primary fight against civil-rights activist Jesse Jackson and Colorado senator Gary Hart. Jackson, a former coworker of Martin Luther King's, became the first African-American to win substantial support in his bid to receive a major-party nomination. Mondale's challenge was to arouse the enthusiasm of the party's traditional constituencies—blacks, Jews, union members, urban residents—while pulling back into the party the "Reagan Democrats," the white middle class that had defected to the Republicans. As a first step in executing his strategy, Mondale tried to demonstrate that he was capable of bold leadership by selecting a woman vice-presidential candidate, former Congresswoman Geraldine Ferraro of New York City. A few weeks later in his acceptance speech at the Democratic National Convention, Mondale tried to prove he was fiscally responsible by proposing to raise taxes to help reduce the deficit.

Riding a wave of personal and organizational confidence, Reagan exhorted voters "to make America great again and let the eagle soar." In his speeches and commercials the president promoted themes of small government, patriotism, and family. "We see an America," he declared, "where every day is independence day, the Fourth of July." He envisioned a future—"a springtime of hope"—with tax rates going "further down, not up"; with budget deficits declared unconstitutional; and with the Soviets being asked to "join us in reducing and, yes, ridding the earth of this awful threat" of nuclear arms. At Republican rallies smothered with balloons and music, the president repeatedly invoked a booming economy and a safer world as evidence of the nation's success under his leadership. "The essence of the Ronald Reagan campaign," ABC reporter Sam Donaldson observed, "is a never-ending string of spectacular picture stories created for television and designed to place the president in the midst of wildly cheering, patriotic Americans. . . . God, patriotism, and Ronald Reagan, that's the essence this campaign is trying to project."

On election day voters returned Reagan to office with 58.8 percent (54,455,075) of the vote and the biggest electoral college vote total in history—525. Mondale received 40.6 percent (37,577,185) of the popular vote and 13 electoral votes. Reagan swept the entire nation except for Minnesota and the District of Columbia. Rarely had America seen so all-encompassing a landslide. In every region, in every age group, in virtually every demographic slice of a heterogeneous nation, the message was clear: "Four More Years." Elderly voters, supposedly beset with fears about the dismantling of social security, gave 61 percent of their votes to the president. Women, for whom Geraldine Ferraro was portrayed as an irresistible symbol, backed Reagan by a 10-point margin. Voters under twenty-five gave 59 percent of their votes to the oldest president ever. And union households, despite union entreaties, awarded nearly 50 percent of their votes to a president who tamed inflation and promised no new taxes. The election, observed *Time* magazine, represented a collective "Thank You" to "a president who had made the country feel good about itself."

There was a stronger class component to the vote in 1984 than in any election since the New Deal era. Reagan, observed a journalist, "was carried to victory by the nation's haves and was decisively rejected by the have-nots." By 1984 a Republican Party increasingly dominated by the upper-middle class and the rich had achieved near parity with the Democratic Party, running just 3 to 5 points behind in most opinion polls of party identification. Like Nixon before him, Rea-

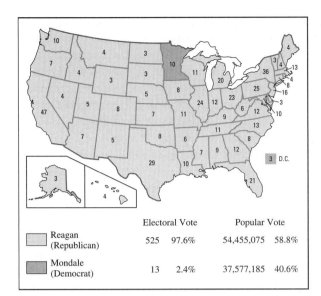

The Election of 1984

Basing his campaign on an improving economy and his tough stand against communism, Reagan easily defeated his Democratic opponent, former vice president Walter Mondale.

	Electoral Vote		Popular Vote	
Reagan (Republican)	525	97.6%	54,455,075	58.8%
Mondale (Democrat)	13	2.4%	37,577,185	40.6%

gan had successfully redefined the legacy of the 1960s, casting the Democrats as the party of arrogant minorities and strident student protesters who were out of touch with mainstream values, while fashioning the Republicans as the party of the "silent majority." A series of focus groups during the decade found that voters viewed the Democrats' emphasis on "fairness" as a code word for "giveaways" to the poor.

Reagan and the Cold War

Reinvigorating the traditional conviction that the United States had a divinely ordained mission to spread American values around the globe, the Reagan administration came to office determined to reassert American power. A classic Cold Warrior, Reagan saw the Soviets at the heart of every international dispute, from revolution in Central America to international terrorism in the Middle East. While the public generally applauded the president's tough rhetoric, it divided on the wisdom of his specific policy experiments. Like previous postwar presidents, Reagan confronted the paradox of American power: public expectations of American influence often clashed with the reality of international power. Reagan proclaimed the United States a beacon of liberty and freedom around the world, but his excessive fear of communism led the administration to support repressive regimes that shared its opposition to Soviet power.

Most of the president's national security and foreign policy advisers—Secretary of State Alexander Haig, his successor George Shultz, Secretary of Defense Caspar Weinberger, National Security Adviser Richard Allen, and Ambassador to the United Nations Jeane Kirkpatrick—shared his exaggerated fear of Soviet power and his determination to assert American military might. To thwart the Soviets, Reagan called for the largest and most expensive peacetime military buildup in American history. "Defense is not a budget item," Ronald Reagan told his staff; "you spend what you need." Along with accelerating the development of existing weapons systems, both nuclear and conventional, the administration reincarnated programs canceled under Carter, including the trouble-plagued B-1 bomber and the controversial neutron bomb. By 1985 the Pentagon was spending more than $28 million an hour—every hour, seven days a week. Excluding veterans' affairs, the defense budget surged from $157 billion in 1981 to $273 billion in 1986. Corrected for inflation, the increases averaged nearly 7 percent a year.

While strengthening America's strategic arsenal, Reagan declared that the United States stood ready to support anticommunist regimes anywhere in the world. In the Middle East, the Philippines, Chile, South Korea, and Angola, the Reagan administration supported repressive governments if they stood strongly against communism. This approach to world politics was especially clear with regard to South Africa, where the system of apartheid, which brutally excluded nonwhites from basic rights, threatened to provoke civil war. Committed to working with the South African whites-only government, the administration abandoned Carter's efforts to force change and adopted a policy known as "constructive engagement." Reagan resisted all calls by liberal and human rights groups to join other countries in coercing the government of South Africa into dismantling apartheid. South Africa, he believed, was a bulwark against the spread of communism. Congress repudiated his policy in 1986, demanding that Reagan take bold steps, including the imposition of economic sanctions, against the South African government.

The New Arms Race

Reagan entered office with a deep-seated distaste for arms control. He also made no attempt to hide his ignorance of basic arms control issues. He acknowledged that he did not understand "throw-weight" (the lifting power of a missile), believed that cruise missiles could be used only defensively, and was unaware that most Soviet missiles were land based. What he was certain of, however, was that the United States had disarmed during the 1970s while the USSR had gained a nuclear superiority. He planned to subject arms control to a period of "benign neglect" while the United States went about the business of "rearming."

Accordingly, Reagan took a tough position in negotiations with the Soviets. As a goal for the intermediate nuclear forces (INF) talks, initiated by the Carter administration to address the nuclear balance of power in Europe, Reagan embraced the "zero option" whereby the Soviet Union would agree to dismantle its six hundred intermediate-range missiles in Europe and Asia while the United States would agree only to deploy no new medium-range missiles. In the separate Strategic Arms Reduction Talks, the president proposed a one-third cut in nuclear warheads. The reductions, however, were structured in such a manner that the Soviet Union would have had to destroy a disproportionate share of its heavy land-based missiles. The proposals angered the Soviets, who grew increasingly distrustful of Reagan and his leading advisers.

U.S.–Soviet relations were already tense when in September 1983 a Soviet interceptor aircraft shot down a Korean Airlines plane, killing all 269 people on board, after the Boeing 747 strayed into Soviet airspace on a flight from Anchorage to Seoul. American intelligence suggested the tragedy was the result of confusion and incompetence on the part of Soviet military officials who believed the civilian airliner was a spy plane, but Reagan used the incident to bolster his contention that the USSR was an "evil empire." Moscow, angered by Reagan's moralistic condemnation and frustrated with the stalemate on arms control, feared the United States was preparing for war. For the first time since the Cuban missile crisis, Moscow sent a *Molinya* (Flash) message to its stations in western capitals, telling its agents to secure staff and premises against imminent attack. "The international situation," declared Politburo member Grigory Romanov, "is white hot, thoroughly white hot." "The world situation is now slipping towards a very dangerous precipice," Soviet foreign minister Andrei Gromyko warned.

Soviet diplomats also walked out of the INF talks. The walkout left the superpowers for the first time in fourteen years with no ongoing arms control talks. The United States responded by deploying new missiles in West Germany, Britain, and Italy. The USSR moved new rockets into Czechoslovakia and East Germany. "The second cold war has begun," shrilled an Italian newspaper.

Reagan's opposition to arms control and his tough Cold War rhetoric revived the nascent peace movement. A nationwide poll in the spring of 1982 showed that 57 percent of the respondents favored an immediate freeze on the testing, production, and deployment of nuclear weapons. A wide variety of religious and academic leaders were questioning the wisdom of the administration's policies. "Cease this madness," implored George Kennan, the father of containment. The American Catholic bishops prepared a pastoral letter on the moral and theological dimensions of nuclear deterrence. The message of the letter was clear: "We must continually say no to the idea of nuclear war."

The threat of global annihilation also seeped into the realm of popular culture. Americans crowded into movie theaters in 1983 to watch *War Games,* which showed a teenage computer hacker accidentally launching a nuclear war. (Computer: "Shall we play a game?" Teenager: "Let's play Thermonuclear War.") In 1984 over 100 million people anxiously watched a docudrama, *The Day After,* that portrayed the effects of nuclear war on Kansas. Editorial columns and cartoons grasped at the implications of a renewed arms race. In one particularly poignant cartoon, a musclebound genie—symbolizing nuclear energy—emerges from a missile-shaped bottle. A puny, yet defiant Ronald Reagan, whip in hand, fecklessly directs the hulking figure to return from whence it came. With a sinister grin stretching from ear to ear, the genie arrogantly responds, "You gotta be kidding, fella." This cartoon joined countless other expressions of powerlessness in the face of a nuclear world and of anxiety about an unknown future.

Reagan tried to defuse the growing calls for arms limitation by proposing a space-based antiballistic-missile defensive shield that would use laser beams to destroy incoming missiles. In March 1983 Reagan gave a nationally televised speech on "peace and national security," most of it a standard review of the Soviet military buildup and of Soviet and Cuban intelligence efforts in Central America. Near the end of the speech he proposed his defensive shield, the Strategic Defense Initiative (SDI)—a bold pitch that had never even been discussed by the National Security Council. In a memorable passage Reagan called on "the scientific community in our country, those who gave us nuclear weapons, to turn their great talents to the cause of mankind and world peace, to give us the means of rendering these nuclear weapons impotent and obsolete."

"Star Wars Plan to Zap Red Nukes," read the banner headline in the *New York Post* the day after Reagan's speech. Nicknamed "Star Wars" by the media, SDI reflected the administration's belief that improbable technological solutions could solve complex political problems. The administration's top military scientist, however, pointed out that the defensive system could be overcome by Soviet weapons unless it was coupled with an offensive arms control agreement. "With unconstrained proliferation" of Soviet warheads, he said, "no defensive system will work." Despite the criticism, the administration pushed forward, spending $17 billion on SDI between 1983 and 1989.

Reagan's idea of building a space-based system for making the United States invulnerable to nuclear attack had many roots. As was often the case with Reagan, the original idea was probably planted by a Hollywood movie, *Murder in the Air* (1940), featuring Reagan as Secret Service agent "Brass" Bancroft. In the movie Bancroft thwarts a spy trying to steal the "inertia projector," which could shoot planes out of the sky from a distance before they could bomb the United States. A 1979 visit to the headquarters of the North American Aerospace Defense Command at Cheyenne Mountain, Wyoming, compounded Reagan's uneasiness about national defense. He was shocked to learn that the United States was helpless when a missile was launched. "We have spent all that money and have all that equipment and there is nothing we can do to prevent a nuclear missile from hitting us," he reflected. A hardcore group of conservative scholars and scientists helped keep the idea alive, providing Reagan with intellectual support for his celluloid fantasy.

The initial Soviet response was hostile. "All attempts at achieving military superiority over the USSR are futile," Yuri Andropov responded four days after Reagan's announcement. The Kremlin chief denounced the administration's military strategy as "not just irresponsible," but "insane." SDI scared the European allies, who suddenly realized that a defensive shield over the United States would leave them uniquely vulnerable to a Soviet nuclear arsenal that might have no other target.

By 1984, however, a number of developments were pushing Moscow and Washington closer together. Concerned about a possible backlash against his policies in the upcoming presidential campaign, Reagan called for a "constructive working relationship" with the Kremlin. He claimed that the massive military buildup during his first three years in office allowed the United States to negotiate from a position of strength. At the same time, a new leader, who seemed readier than his predecessors to renew détente with the United States, assumed leadership in the Soviet Union. Mikhail Gorbachev, at fifty-four the youngest head of the Soviet Communist party since Joseph Stalin, came to power determined to reform Soviet society. At home he advocated *perestroika,* or "restructuring," to relax government economic and social control. Abroad he advocated a new policy of *glasnost,* or "openness."

Hoping to avoid an expensive arms race, Gorbachev declared a moratorium on deployment of medium-range missiles in Europe and asked the United States to do the same. He began shifting government rubles away from the military, publicly assailed the failures of the socialist economy, and promised economic and political reform. The next year at the Communist party congress he renounced the doctrine of fundamental conflict between socialism and capitalism, calling for global cooperation to avoid nuclear and ecological disaster. For the rest of his tenure he made news practically every few months with another bold reform in the areas of *perestroika, glasnost,* and arms control. He made it clear he wanted out of Afghanistan, his country's Vietnam-like quagmire.

The result of these developments was a series of four Reagan-Gorbachev summits. In 1986 the two leaders met at Reykjavik, Iceland, and agreed on a first step toward cutting strategic nuclear forces in half. Gorbachev wanted to go further, calling for the complete elimination of all nuclear weapons, but he insisted that the United States also abandon SDI, something Reagan refused to do. The following year the United States and the Soviet Union agreed to the INF treaty, which for the first time called for the destruction of existing missiles and allowed for on-site inspections to verify compliance. In December Gorbachev traveled to Washington to sign the treaty in a warm ceremony with Reagan. While in the United States, the Soviet leader announced a unilateral reduction in Soviet military forces.

By the time Reagan left office, he and his counterpart in the Kremlin had toasted each other as "Ronnie and Mikhail." Opinion polls reported Americans feeling friendlier toward the Soviet Union than at any time since the end of World War II. When a reporter asked Reagan in 1987 if he still thought the Soviet Union was an evil empire, he responded, "No, I was talking about another time, another era." The thaw in U.S.–Soviet relations angered hardliners. Conservative leader Howard Phillips called Reagan a "useful idiot for Soviet propaganda."

The Cold War in Central America

Before and during *glasnost* Reagan's Cold War views shaped his approach to radical insurgencies in Latin America. Ignoring the complex social and political conditions that fostered revolution in the region, Reagan believed Moscow was to

Reagan in Moscow   The thawing of Cold War tensions between the United States and the Soviet Union was evident in the signing of the Intermediate Nuclear Forces Treaty in December 1987, which eliminated intermediate-range nuclear missiles. This goodwill between the nations grew with Reagan's historic visit to Moscow in May 1988. Reagan and Mikhail Gorbachev toured Red Square and developed a cordial personal relationship. *(Wide World Photos, Inc.)*

blame for most of the trouble. "Let us not delude ourselves," he advised the American people. "The Soviet Union underlies all the unrest that is going on. If they weren't engaged in this game of dominos, there wouldn't be any hot spots in the world." For Reagan and his advisers, any leftist victory in Latin America would threaten the possibility of another Cuba that could serve as a staging ground for Soviet expansion in the Western Hemisphere. Communist control of Nicaragua, White House communications director Patrick Buchanan warned, "would lead, as night follows day, to loss of central America," and "if Central America goes the way of Nicaragua, they will be in San Diego." The administration also worried that communist gains could produce a flood of political refugees pouring over the U.S. border.

Memories of the Vietnam War were never far from the minds of Reagan and his advisers when developing their strategy for the Caribbean. During his 1980 presidential campaign Reagan had referred to Vietnam as a "noble cause," an altruistic attempt to help a "small country newly free from colonial rule" defend itself against a "totalitarian neighbor bent on conquest." Like many of his conservative supporters, the president believed that the "liberal media," antiwar protesters, and incompetent Washington bureaucrats were responsible for America's defeat because they forced the military to fight with "one hand tied behind their backs." Alexander Haig argued that the war could have been won at any of several junctures if American leaders had been willing to "apply the full range of American power to bring about a successful outcome." The one concrete lesson Reagan learned, however, was that it was impossible to commit U.S. troops to a protracted war that lacked the support of the American people.

The new conservative revisionism of Vietnam found its way into the popular culture of the decade. Beginning in 1982 Hollywood produced a series of action films in which a handful of American veterans returned to Vietnam, often to free prisoners of war, and along the way managed to win the war and teach the Vietnamese a lesson about U.S. military power. In two major *Rambo* (1982, 1985) movies the superhuman Sylvester Stallone managed to knife, shoot, electrocute, or blow up a large number of Vietcong and their Russian overlords. In addition to battling these foes, Rambo had to contend with a cowardly Congress, an unpatriotic media, and antiwar protesters who fought "a war against all the soldiers returning."

Since the administration viewed relations with Central America as an extension of the superpower conflict, it relied heavily on military aid and covert warfare to prop up friendly regimes and help overthrow unfriendly ones. In El Salvador, a poor country where 2 percent of the people controlled nearly all of the wealth, a coalition of leftist guerrillas had been attempting to topple the government. Reagan, convinced that rebels against the established regime represented Soviet influence, spent nearly $5 billion providing military and economic aid to the government.

The army used the arms to wage a fierce campaign of repression against civilians suspected of sympathizing with the rebels or agitating for social change. Between 1979 and 1985 army "death squads" killed as many as forty thousand peasants, teachers, union organizers, and church workers. On one day, December 11, 1981, troops systematically slaughtered nine hundred people in the town of El Mozote, raping women before shooting them and burning children alive. The Reagan administration, however, considered unfriendly communists more of a threat than friendly thugs. A few weeks after the attack Reagan certified that El Salvador was making "a concerted and significant effort" to protect human rights. In 1984 the moderate Jose Napoleon Duarte won a popular election and opened talks with rebel leaders, but the bloody civil war continued.

In Nicaragua Reagan committed the United States to overthrowing the Marxist-led Sandinistas who overthrew repressive dictator Anastasio Somoza in 1979. Beginning in 1982 the Central Intelligence Agency (CIA) organized, trained, and financed the contras, a guerrilla army based in Honduras and Costa Rica. Infiltrating Nicaragua, the contras sabotaged bridges, oil facilities, and crops. The CIA offered them training in how to assassinate and kidnap political leaders. Reagan praised the contras as "the moral equivalent of our Founding Fathers," but Congress, and the public, disagreed. In December 1982 Congress, fearful of getting the nation involved in "another Vietnam," halted military aid to the contras for one year. In October 1984 the House passed the Boland Amendment, which forbade any direct aid to the contras.

Meanwhile, Reagan's fear of communism in the Caribbean found an outlet in the tiny nation of Grenada, a 133-square-mile island whose principal export was medical students. In 1983 when a leftist government friendly with Cuba assumed power in Grenada, Reagan ordered 6,000 marines to invade the island and install a pro-American government. The administration claimed the invasion was necessary to protect American students living on the island and to stop the construction of an airfield that would allegedly serve Cuban and Soviet interests. Critics asserted that the students were never in danger and the airfield was being built to boost the island's ailing tourist industry. World opinion condemned the invasion, but the first successful assertion of American military might since Vietnam renewed pride and confidence among millions of Americans.

The Threat of International Terrorism

The Reagan administration came to office convinced that during the 1970s, while Washington was seeking friendship and trade with Moscow, the USSR was conspiring with terrorists of every stripe to disrupt or overthrow governments friendly to the United States. Secretary of State Haig accused the Soviets of "training, funding and equipping" the forces of worldwide terrorism.

The threat of terrorism was greatest in the Middle East, where, despite the Israeli-Egyptian treaty, peace proved elusive. In 1983 Israeli forces attacked Palestine Liberation Organization (PLO) strongholds in southern Lebanon on Israel's northern border. The United States arranged for a withdrawal of both Israeli and PLO troops from Beirut and sent 2,000 marines into the region as part of an international peacekeeping force. In October 1983 a radical Shïite Muslim terrorist drove a truck loaded with explosives into the U.S. Marines barracks near the Beirut airport. The explosion killed 241 marines. While insisting that the marines in Lebanon had been "central to our credibility on a global scale," Reagan quietly withdrew the remaining troops.

The bombing of the barracks heralded a broader campaign of terror launched by radical Middle East groups. In 1985 terrorist attacks in the Middle East and Europe claimed the lives of more than 900 civilians, including 23 Americans. In June 1985 American television captured the ordeal of the 135 passengers aboard TWA flight 847. Hijacked over Greece, they endured seventeen nightmarish days of captivity before being released. A few months later, in October, PLO agents seized an Italian cruise ship, the *Achille Lauro,* and murdered a wheelchair-bound American passenger. "You can run but you can't hide," Reagan warned. In 1986 when Libyan agents were implicated in the bombing of a Berlin nightclub frequented by American soldiers, Reagan, calling Libyan leader Muammar Qaddafi the "mad dog of the Middle East," ordered a retaliatory air attack. The raid killed an estimated 37 Libyans, including Qaddafi's infant daughter.

Americans applauded the flexing of U.S. military muscle, but the cycle of terrorism escalated. In December 1988 a Pan Am jet en route from London to New York crashed near Lockerbie, Scotland, killing all 259 aboard, including numerous Americans. Investigators found conclusive evidence that a bomb had been hidden in the baggage section.

Having come to office in 1980 on a groundswell of public outrage over Iran's seizure of American hostages, Reagan proudly emphasized that he would never negotiate with terrorists. "The United States gives terrorists no rewards," he said in June 1985. "We make no concessions. We make no deals." But while talking tough, Reagan was negotiating behind the scenes with Iran to secure the release of American hostages taken in Beirut. A few months earlier the president had approved a plan hatched by his national security adviser Robert McFarlane and CIA head William Casey. American agents would secretly try to curry favor with the radical regime in Iran by selling them high-tech U.S. arms, which they needed in their ongoing war against Iraq. The secretaries of defense and state had vigorously objected to the idea, dismissing it as "almost too absurd to comment on." The president, however, moved by the pleas of hostages' families to do something to bring their loved ones home, had approved the secret sale of state-of-the-art anti-tank missiles to Iran.

The plot had an added twist: U.S. operatives overcharged Iran for the weapons and diverted some of the profits to fund the contras in Nicaragua. The operation was carried out by NSC aide Oliver North, who used various middlemen to funnel millions of dollars illegally to the contras and was in clear violation of the Boland Amendment, which expressly forbade aid to the contras. The flow of money continued through the early autumn of 1986 before a Lebanese news magazine exposed the scheme. At first the administration denied that it had violated its own policy by offering incentives for the release of the hostages. Over the next few months, however, reporters exposed the sordid details of the arms sales and the funneling of money to the contras.

Oliver North Being Sworn in at the Iran-Contra Hearings In 1984, the National Security Council put their military aide, Lieutenant Colonel Oliver North, in charge of providing the contras with anything they needed to fight the leftist Sandinistas in Nicaragua. According to Congress's Boland Amendment, this activity could not be funded by money from the CIA or Department of Defense, so North turned to private sources. In January 1986, North began siphoning money from a deal to sell weapons to Iran in exchange for American hostages to continue his work. After the story of the arms deal with Iran became public in November 1986, Attorney General Edwin Meese verified that millions from those sales had gone to the contras. A congressional joint investigative committee then conducted its own investigation, holding forty days of public hearings in the summer of 1987. An unapologetic Oliver North appeared before the committee in July and explained his role in the affair. The congressional committee reported in November that the president ultimately bore responsibility for the actions of his administration, but it found no solid proof that he knew about the transfer of funds. In May 1989, North was tried and convicted of obstructing Congress, but the conviction was later overturned. North became a hero for conservatives— an American patriot working to stop communism in Latin America any way he could.

13.3 | *Iran-Contra Testimony*

Oliver North

In 1986 as rumors spread through Washington that the United States had traded arms with Iran for the release of American hostages and then used the money from that transaction to support the contras, Reagan denied the allegations. However, in July 1987 the person most directly involved in the deals, Lieutenant Colonel Oliver "Ollie" North, testified before a joint congressional hearing and admitted that such dealings had occurred.

It is also difficult to comprehend that my work at the NSC [National Security Council]—all of which was approved and carried out in the best interests of our country—has led to two massive parallel investigations staffed by over 200 people. It is mind-boggling to me that one of those investigations is criminal and
5 that some here have attempted to criminalize policy differences between coequal branches of government and the executive's conduct of foreign affairs.

I believe it is inevitable that the Congress will in the end blame the executive branch, but I suggest to you that it is the Congress which must accept at least some of the blame in the Nicaraguan freedom fighters matter. Plain and simple, the Con-
10 gress is to blame because of the fickle, vacillating, unpredictable, on-again, off-again policy toward the Nicaraguan Democratic Resistance—the so-called Contras. I do not believe that the support of the Nicaraguan freedom fighters can be treated as the passage of a budget. I suppose that if the budget doesn't get passed on time again this year, it will be inevitably another extension of another month or
15 two. But the Contras, the Nicaraguan freedom fighters, are people—living, breathing young men and women who have had to suffer a desperate struggle for liberty with sporadic and confusing support from the United States of America.

Armies need food and consistent help. They need a flow of money, of arms, clothing, and medical supplies. The Congress of the United States left soldiers in
20 the field unsupported and vulnerable to their communist enemies. When the executive branch did everything possible within the law to prevent them from being wiped out by Moscow's surrogates in Havana and Managua, you then had this investigation to blame the problem on the executive branch. It does not make sense to me.
25 In my opinion, these hearings have caused serious damage to our national interest. Our adversaries laugh at us and our friends recoil in horror. I suppose it would be one thing if the intelligence committees wanted to hear all this in private and thereafter pass laws which in the view of Congress make for better policies or better functioning government. But to hold them publicly for the whole
30 world to see strikes me as very harmful. Not only does it embarrass our friends and allies with whom we have worked, many of whom have helped us in various programs, but must also make them very wary of helping us again. . . . ■ ■ ■

The scandal, which consumed Reagan's final two years in office, damaged the president's reputation as an effective leader. A congressional committee charged that the president had abdicated his "moral and legal responsibility to take care that the laws be faithfully executed," but stopped short of accusing him of intentionally breaking the law. Far more damaging was the report of independent counsel Lawrence E. Walsh, who concluded that the White House had successfully constructed a "firewall" to protect the president, allowing lower-level officials—North along with NSC officials Robert McFarlane and John Poindexter—to take the blame for an illegal policy approved by the president. Walsh, however, never found conclusive evidence that linked Reagan directly to the illegal activities. And although troubled by the Iran-contra affair, the public, as with other scandals that plagued the Reagan administration, did not blame the president himself. Polls showed declining support for the administration and renewed questions about the president's casual leadership style, but Reagan remained immensely popular when he left office.

The Reagan Legacy

At a farewell party at the White House in January 1989, Reagan recited the data showing how much the country and the world had changed for the better during the 1980s, and he concluded, "All in all, I must say, not bad for a fellow who couldn't get his facts straight and worked four hours a day." Supporters argued that Reagan's economic policies produced a remarkable period of sustained growth. Between 1983 and 1990 unemployment fell to 5.2 percent, the economy grew by 33 percent, 19 million new jobs were created, and inflation remained stable at less than 4 percent. Conservatives spoke proudly of the "Reagan Revolution," which cut back the size of government, slashed taxes, and promoted economic growth.

Critics concede that Reagan steered public policy in a different direction, but they tend to focus on the underside of the administration's policies. His domestic policies imposed undue hardship on the poor and had little to do with the economic recovery. His income-tax cut proved illusory for all except the wealthiest Americans. By the end of Reagan's administration the average family was actually paying more in taxes than in 1980, thanks in large part to a sharp increase in social security taxes and hikes in state and local taxes. The GNP grew an average of 2.6 percent annually under Reagan, compared with 3 percent under Carter and an average of 3.4 percent under the previous four presidents.

The same polarized debate shapes discussion of Reagan's foreign policy. Reagan's supporters contend that his tough rhetoric and increased military spending not only pushed the Soviets to the bargaining table, but also forced them to accept American terms. Reagan's Star Wars proposal, by forcing the Russians to face the prospect of a crippling arms race, hastened the demise of the Soviet system. McFarlane wrote that countering SDI would have "required a substantial increase in Soviet expenditures for strategic forces at a time when the overall [Soviet] budget was stretched to the limit." Critics challenge the notion that Reagan ended the Cold War: the Soviet Union, they assert, collapsed under the weight of America's bipartisan policy of containment, dating back to the Truman Doctrine and the Marshall Plan, and under the weight of communism's inherent instability.

It is difficult to reach conclusive answers on these questions. Until historians know more about the inner workings of Kremlin decision makers, it will be impossible to assess all the forces that contributed to Moscow's new openness to the West. Certainly Reagan's strident rhetoric and massive arms buildup intensified Cold War tensions, while many of his policies, especially those toward Latin America, overestimated Soviet influence and underplayed the role of local forces. Much to his credit, however, Reagan appreciated the need to soften his hard line with the Soviets, embracing Gorbachev and the new Soviet *glasnost*.

Perhaps Reagan's chief legacy was a ballooning federal deficit. Reagan's inability to reconcile his tax-cutting policies with his spending priorities, especially the massive military increases, caused the federal deficit to soar. By the time Reagan left office, the federal government was spending $206 billion more per year than it was receiving in tax revenues. In just eight years the national debt rose from $908.5 billion to nearly $2.7 trillion. The mountain of red ink may have inadvertently furthered Reagan's agenda since it focused public attention on cutting spending and dashed liberal hopes of funding new social programs.

One legacy transcends dispute, however. Reagan's skillful use of television changed the style of presidential leadership. "Television in modern politics has been as revolutionary as the development of printing in the time of Gutenberg," the journalist Teddy White observed. Television forced politicians to articulate themes that could appeal to a broad spectrum of the electorate at the same time that it personalized politics by allowing leaders to bypass parties and build a direct relationship with voters. President Reagan was a master craftsman of the new technology. Leaving the details of governing to aides, Reagan concentrated on the symbolic aspects of his presidency. Using television to emphasize resilient themes of self-help, individualism, and limited government, he rarely discussed specific policies.

While Reagan restored respect for the presidency, he heightened expectations of what it could accomplish. Reagan's media savvy helped boost his personal popularity to record levels. Polls showed his approval rating at 68 percent in his final month in office—the highest ever recorded for a departing president. Reagan's appeal rubbed off on the rest of Washington. In 1980 only 22 percent of people polled said they could trust government "most of the time." After eight years of Republican rule the percentage had increased to 38 percent, and nearly 50 percent said they favored increased government spending. Reagan came to office preaching a message of limited government and individual initiative. The paradox was that his success over the next eight years increased public faith in

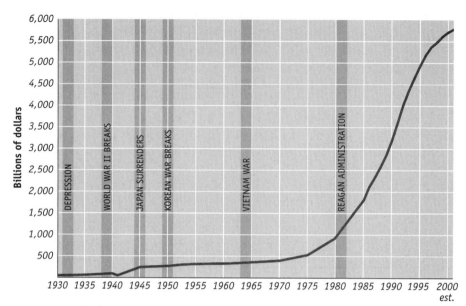

The National Debt, 1930–2000   Ending a trend of static or slightly rising national debt, the Reagan era saw the deficit more than triple from $908 billion in 1980 to $2.7 trillion at the end of 1989 as Congress and the president refused to raise taxes or cut popular programs. This trend continued into the nineties and beyond (the data for 1999–2000 are estimations). (Sources: *Historical Statistics of the United States* and *Statistical Abstract of the United States,* relevant years; *Economic Indicators,* Council of Economic Advisors; U.S. Government Printing Office, Washington, D.C., 1999.)

government at the same time that his massive deficits crippled Washington's ability to respond to demands for greater services. It would be left to Reagan's successors to reconcile the contradiction.

SELECTED READINGS

▪ The writing available on the 1980s is unusually polarized, but there are nonetheless some broad surveys of the period. Samuel Freedman's *The Inheritance* (1996) provides a good sense of the mood of many early Reagan voters. Michael Schaller offers the first historical work on the 1980s in *Reckoning with Reagan* (1992).

▪ Most of the historical treatments of Reagan's presidency are sharply critical. In *Dutch* (1999), Edmund Morris, Reagan's authorized biographer, produces an idiosyncratic but useful portrait of the president. Gary Wills's *Reagan's America: Innocents at Home* (1987) is the classic treatment. Lou Cannon's *President Reagan: The Role of a Lifetime* (rev. ed., 2000) stresses the theatricality in Reagan's presidency. Mark Hertsgaard's *On Bended Knee* (1988) castigates the press for glorifying Reagan. Haynes Johnson provides an overview of the country in *Sleepwalking Through History* (1991). Sidney Blumenthal and Thomas Edsall collect a series of essays on Reagan's presidency in *The Reagan Legacy* (1988).

▌ Charles Murray outlines the major economic theories of the Reagan administration in *Losing Ground* (2nd ed., 1995). William Greider takes the Reagan economists to task in *The Education of David Stockman and Other Americans* (1982). Martin Carnoy's *A New Social Contract* (1983) is a socialist critique of Reagan's policies. Lester Thurow's *Zero-Sum Society* (1980) is valuable for understanding the economics of the 1980s. The successes and failures of Reagan's economic policies are assessed in John Sloan's *The Reagan Effect* (1999).

▌ E. J. Dionne's *Why Americans Hate Politics* (1991) captures the political mood of the 1984 campaign and the dilemma faced by the Democratic Party. Peter Goldman and Tony Fuller's *The Quest for the Presidency, 1984* (1985) recounts the strategies and actions of the two campaigners. Jack Germond and Jules Witcover express cynicism over Reagan's campaign of images in *Wake Us When It's Over* (1985).

▌ Richard Melanson argues in *Reconstructing Consensus* (1991) that the overarching foreign-policy goal of the Reagan administration was to rebuild the Cold War consensus destroyed during the Vietnam War. In *Buildup* (1992), Daniel Wirls stresses the importance of domestic politics in Reagan's foreign policy, and Frances Fitzgerald explains how Reagan spent billions for Star Wars with public approval in *Way Out There in the Blue* (2000). Strobe Talbott surveys the escalation of the arms race in *Deadly Gambit* (1984). Seweryn Bialer and Michael Mandelbaum address the emerging détente between the superpowers in *Gorbachev's Russia and American Foreign Policy* (1988).

▌ Broad introductions to Reagan's Central American policies include Walter LaFeber's *Inevitable Revolutions* (1984); Kenneth Coleman and George Herring's *The Central American Crisis* (1985); and Cynthia Arnson's *Crossroads* (2nd ed., 1994). Robert Pastor surveys America's relations with Nicaragua in *Condemned to Repetition* (1987). The Nicaraguan operation fed directly into the Iran-contra scandal, which is covered by Jane Hunter et al. in *The Iran-Contra Connection* (1987). Bob Woodward reviews Reagan's secret operations in *Veil: The Secret Wars of the CIA* (1987).

14

The Culture Wars, 1980–1992

Jerry Falwell, founder of the Moral Majority, claimed that God instructed him to bring together "the good people of America" in a Christian crusade against pornography, sex education, and abortion. Abandoning traditional fundamentalist disdain for mainstream politics, Falwell decided in the late 1970s that it was no longer possible for Christians to stay out of politics. To spread the word, Falwell combined old-time religion with the most sophisticated computer technology, targeting potential contributors and lobbying for political candidates who shared his conservative views. "Get them saved, baptized, and registered," Falwell advised his ministerial colleagues.

Abandoning any pretense of nonpartisanship, Falwell became a regular visitor at the Reagan White House, prayed at Republican meetings, and helped draft the party's 1984 platform. He called Ronald Reagan and Vice President George Bush "God's chosen instrument for the regeneration of the country." With access to Washington, religious fundamentalists and other conservatives were strategically positioned to wage a war against social liberalism and secular humanism: to restore the moral authority of the family, reestablish appropriate gender roles, and reassert American nationalism.

The legacy of the 1960s was at the heart of the culture wars of the 1980s. The social turmoil of the 1960s exposed the tension between the nation's postwar faith in economic growth and its fidelity to traditional values. But prosperity helped produce a new middle class that challenged the existing morality, placing a new emphasis on self-fulfillment and personal gratification. The conflict between individual expression and moral righteousness, which had deep roots in the nation's past, found expression in the 1980s in battles over family values, abortion, gay rights, and immigration restriction. At the heart of the conflict were competing views of the meaning of American identity. Conservatives stressed cultural nationalism, emphasizing the existence of a singular American cultural tradition and a shared national identity. Many liberals, however, spoke a language of cultural diversity, highlighting the persistence of unique traditions, underscoring the importance of difference, and articulating a vision of a multicultural America.

The Politics of Family Values

Activist fundamentalists exerted increasing political influence throughout Reagan's two terms in office. Having played an influential role in the election of 1980, the Moral Majority again figured significantly in Reagan's landslide victory over Walter Mondale in 1984. By 1989 popular televangelists Jim and Tammy Faye Bakker, Jimmy Swaggert, Jerry Falwell, Pat Robertson, and Oral Roberts had launched over 1,300 religious radio stations and more than 330 Christian ministries on television. In addition to these enterprises, Christians boasted a $1 billion book industry that offered instruction on how to be a better Christian, how to raise children, and how religion could cure an ailing nation.

The televangelists owed their success to their ability to combine all the elements that most characterized the Reagan era: money, morality, conservatism, entertainment, and religious and patriotic symbolism. But a less tangible, deeply embedded sense of anxiety infused the country's political culture and also fed into the revitalization of the New Christian Right. Ronald Reagan strove to give clear articulation to this inchoate sense of unease when he remarked at a prayer breakfast in 1984: "The truth is, politics and morality are inseparable. And as morality's foundation is religion, religion and politics are necessarily related." Although he allowed the consequences of challenging that truth to remain ambiguous, the president concluded, "We need religion as a guide."

PRIMARY SOURCE

14.1 | *Return to Traditional Religious Values*
JERRY FALWELL

The Reverend Jerry Falwell, recognizing the anxieties felt by many Americans who opposed the political and social changes of the 1960s and 1970s, founded the Moral Majority in 1979. In his 1980 work *Listen America!* Falwell encouraged citizens to help him in his quest to return America to its moral traditions by transforming the political climate.

We must reverse the trend America finds herself in today. Young people between the ages of twenty-five and forty have been born and reared in a different world than Americans of years past. The television set has been their primary baby-sitter. From the television set they have learned situation ethics and
5 immorality—they have learned a loss of respect for human life. They have learned to disrespect the family as God has established it. They have been educated in a public-school system that is permeated with secular humanism. They have been taught that the Bible is just another book of literature. They have been taught that there are no absolutes in our world today. They have been introduced
10 to the drug culture. They have been reared by the family and by the public school in a society that is greatly void of discipline and character-building. These same young people have been reared under the influence of a government that has taught them socialism and welfarism. They have been taught to believe that the world owes them a living whether they work or not.
15   I believe that America was built on integrity, on faith in God, and on hard work. I do not believe that anyone has ever been successful in life without being willing to add that last ingredient—diligence or hard work. We now have second- and third-generation welfare recipients. Welfare is not always wrong. There are those who do need welfare, but we have reared a generation that understands nei-
20 ther the dignity nor the importance of work.
Every American who looks at the facts must share a deep concern and burden for our country. We are not unduly concerned when we say that there are some very dark clouds on America's horizon. I am not a pessimist, but it is indeed a time for truth. If Americans will face the truth, our nation can be turned around
25 and can be saved from the evils and the destruction that have fallen upon every other nation that has turned its back on God.
There is no excuse for what is happening in our country. We must, from the highest office in the land right down to the shoe shine boy in the airport, have a return to biblical basics. If the Congress of our United States will take its stand on
30 that which is right and wrong, and if our President, our judiciary system, and our state and local leaders will take their stand on holy living, we can turn this country around.
I personally feel that the home and the family are still held in reverence by the vast majority of the American public. I believe there is still a vast number of Ameri-
35 cans who love their country, are patriotic, and are willing to sacrifice for her. I remember that time when it was positive to be patriotic, and as far as I am concerned, it still is. I remember as a boy, when the flag was raised, everyone stood proudly and put his hand upon his heart and pledged allegiance with gratitude. I remember when the band struck up "The Stars and Stripes Forever," we stood and
40 goose pimples would run all over me. I remember when I was in elementary school during World War II, when every report from the other shores meant something to us. We were not out demonstrating against our boys who were dying in Europe and Asia. We were praying for them and thanking God for them and buying war bonds to help pay for the materials and artillery they needed to fight and win and come back.
45   I believe that Americans want to see this country come back to basics, back to values, back to biblical morality, back to sensibility, and back to patriotism.

Americans are looking for leadership and guidance. It is fair to ask the question, "If 84 percent of the American people still believe in morality, why is America
50 having such internal problems?" We must look for the answer to the highest places in every level of government. We have a lack of leadership in America. But Americans have been lax in voting in and out of office the right and the wrong people.

My responsibility as a preacher of the Gospel is one of influence, not of control,
55 and that is the responsibility of each individual citizen. Through the ballot box Americans must provide for strong moral leadership at every level. If our country will get back on the track in sensibility and moral sanity, the crises that I have herein mentioned will work out in the course of time and with God's blessings.

It is now time to take a stand on certain moral issues, and we can only stand if we
60 have leaders. We must stand against the Equal Rights Amendment, the feminist revolution, and the homosexual revolution. We must have a revival in this country. . . .

As a preacher of the Gospel, I not only believe in prayer and preaching, I also believe in good citizenship. If a labor union in America has the right to organize and improve its working conditions, then I believe that the churches and the pastors, the
65 priests, and the rabbis of America have a responsibility, not just the right, to see to it that the moral climate and conscience of Americans is such that this nation can be healed inwardly. If it is healed inwardly, then it will heal itself outwardly. . . .

Americans have been silent much too long. We have stood by and watched as American power and influence have been systematically weakened in every
70 sphere of the world.

We are not a perfect nation, but we are still a free nation because we have the blessing of God upon us. We must continue to follow in a path that will ensure that blessing. . . .

Let us never forget that as our Constitution declares, we are endowed by our
75 Creator with certain inalienable rights. It is only as we abide by those laws established by our Creator that He will continue to bless us with these rights. We are endowed our rights to freedom and liberty and the pursuit of happiness by the God who created man to be free and equal.

The hope of reversing the trends of decay in our republic now lies with the
80 Christian public in America. We cannot expect help from the liberals. They certainly are not going to call our nation back to righteousness and neither are the pornographers, the smut peddlers, and those who are corrupting our youth. Moral Americans must be willing to put their reputations, their fortunes, and their very lives on the line for this great nation of ours. Would that we had the courage of our
85 forefathers who knew the great responsibility that freedom carries with it. . . .

Our Founding Fathers separated church and state in function, but never intended to establish a government void of God. As is evidenced by our Constitution, good people in America must exert an influence and provide a conscience and climate of morality in which it is difficult to go wrong, not difficult for peo-
90 ple to go right in America.

I am positive in my belief regarding the Constitution that God led in the development of that document, and as a result, we here in America have enjoyed 204 years of unparalleled freedom. The most positive people in the world are

people who believe the Bible to be the Word of God. The Bible contains a positive
95 message. It is a message written by 40 men over a period of approximately 1,500
years under divine inspiration. It is God's message of love, redemption, and deliv-
erance for a fallen race. What could be more positive than the message of
redemption in the Bible? But God will force Himself upon no man. Each individual American must make His choice. . . .
100   Americans must no longer linger in ignorance and apathy. We cannot be
silent about the sins that are destroying this nation. The choice is ours. We must
turn America around or prepare for inevitable destruction. I am listening to the
sounds that threaten to take away our liberties in America. And I have listened to
God's admonitions and His direction—the only hopes of saving America. Are
105 you listening too?   ■ ■ ■

The New Right, and particularly religious, conservatives believed the message
was clear: the root of America's social problems could be traced to the decline of
the traditional family. Social changes over the previous few decades—the
increased presence of women in the work force, the heightened visibility of abortion and divorce, and the breakdown of the double standard for male and female
behavior—had placed severe strain on the ideal two-parent family. During the
1980s a rising divorce rate accompanied soaring numbers of illegitimate births,
which doubled between 1975 and 1986. By the middle of the decade more than
two-thirds of all young wives worked outside the home, whereas less than one-
half had done so in 1973.

Conservatives blamed social liberalism, inflation, and declining moral standards for such troubles. In 1987 the Reagan administration released the "White
House Task Force Report on the Family," alleging that family life had been
"frayed by the abrasive experiments of two liberal decades." New Right political
strategist Paul Weyrich described the contest between the conservative profamily
forces and liberals as "the most significant battle of the age-old conflict between
good and evil, between the forces of God and the forces against God, that we have
seen in our country."

The pernicious influence of popular culture became a primary focal point for
conservatives throughout the 1980s. For many critics liberals had transformed
mass culture, which had helped mold reassuring images of consensus in the
1950s, into a subversive technology that eroded support for traditional values.
Music, television, and film, they contended, emphasized sexual intimacy outside
of marriage, violence, and profanity. "Television is undermining the Judeo-
Christian values you hold dear and work hard to teach your children." Calling for
a return to "traditional values," the religious right organized in local communities to challenge the teaching of evolution, ban books that ran counter to religious teachings, oppose sex education, and reinstate school prayer. Sparked in
part by the highly publicized "textbook wars" in Kanawha County, West Virginia,
during the last half of the 1970s, the censorship furor quickened during the
1980s. One 1981 survey estimated that 20 percent of the country's school districts and 30 percent of school libraries had their literature and textbooks chal-

lenged. By 1985 the number of censorship efforts increased by 37 percent and included overt demonstrations in forty-six states.

Some of the challenges made their way into the courts. Two of the most publicized court cases involving censorship erupted in Alabama and Tennessee. Led by Pat Robertson's National Legal Foundation, the evangelical plaintiffs claimed that Alabama's State Board of Education violated the establishment clause of the First Amendment by actively encouraging students to embrace "secular humanism," a "religion" that contradicted Christian teachings. Meanwhile, in Tennessee a federal judge considered the expulsion of students by the Hawkins County School District for refusing to read books they deemed "anti-Christian" to be a violation of their free exercise of religion. After initial victories in district courts, two circuit appeals courts overturned the earlier decisions. While liberals claimed a victory for diversity, ecumenism, and critical thinking, conservative evangelicals bemoaned the sanction of what they considered to be the teaching of evolution, feminism, socialism, and godless atheism.

Conservatives also applied the notion of embattled traditional values to the problem of urban poverty. The Heritage Foundation's Robert Rector contended that "the primary cause of black poverty" derived not from an inequitable distribution of wealth or persistent racism, but from "disintegration of the family." Others blamed child poverty and juvenile deviance on single-parent homes and particularly on the absence of strong male figures. Antifeminist icon Phyllis Schlafly argued in 1986 that there existed a "two-class American society." However, she rejected class analyses that spoke of the increasing disparity between rich and poor. Instead, Schlafly differentiated society's haves and have-nots in terms of whether families instilled proper values of industry, thrift, and diligence in their children.

PRIMARY SOURCE

14.2 | *Letter to Yale Freshmen, 1981*
A. BARTLETT GIAMATTI

In remarks to Yale University students on August 31, 1981, university president A. Bartlett Giamatti challenged the growing influence of Jerry Falwell's Moral Majority. Championing the importance of a liberal education and the pluralism of American society, Giamatti described the Moral Majority as a coercive organization attempting to destroy civil liberties in America.

A self-proclaimed "Moral Majority," and its satellite or client groups, cunning in the use of a native blend of old intimidation and new technology, threaten the values I have named. Angry at change, rigid in the application of chauvinistic

slogans, absolutistic in morality, they threaten through political pressure of pub-
5 lic denunciation whoever dares to disagree with their authoritarian positions.
Using television, direct mail and economic boycott, they would sweep before
them anyone who holds a different opinion. . . .

What disgusts me so much about the "morality" seeping out of the ground
around our feet is that it would deny the legitimacy of differentness. We should all
10 be dismayed with the shredding of the spiritual fabric of our society, with the urging
to selfishness and discrimination all around us. We should be concerned that so
much of our political and religious leadership acts intimidated for the moment and
will not say with clarity that this most recent denial of the legitimacy of differentness
is a radical assault on the very pluralism—of peoples, political beliefs, values, forms
15 of merit and systems of religion—our country was founded to welcome and foster.

Pluralism is not relativism. It does not mean the denial of absolutes or the
absence of standards. Pluralism is not code for anything. It signals the recognition that people of different ethnic groups and races and adherents of various
religious and political and personal beliefs have a right to coexist as equals under
20 the law and have an obligation to forge the freedoms they enjoy into a coherent,
civilized and vigilant whole. . . .

These efforts to deny others the freedom to be themselves wish for a closed
society, a form of community similar to a vast, airless bunker. That is not the kind
of community you have come to and that has been waiting to welcome you. Yale
25 is a diverse, open place, receptive to people from throughout our society, and it
must and will remain so. It is a university community given to the competition of
ideas and of merit, devoted to excellence and dedicated to the belief that freedom
of choice, speech, and creed is essential to the quest for truth that constitutes its
mission. Those who wish such a place to teach only their version of the "right"
30 values and "correct" views misunderstand completely the free market of ideas
that is a great university; they misapprehend the extent to which the university
serves the country best when it is a cauldron of competing ideas and not a neatly
arranged platter of received opinions.

You will find, if Yale is at all successful, much that is different here. Revel in that
35 diversity. Whether different idea or person, connect with it in order to understand it.
Female and male, Christian and Jew, black, white, brown and yellow, you must find,
as we all must, what binds us together, in common hope and need, not what divides
us. You may or may not come all to love one another, but to be part of the best of this
place you must have the moral courage to respect one another. This is not a com-
40 munity that will tolerate the sexism, the racism, the anti-Semitism, the bigotry about
ethnic groups, the hysterical rejection of others, the closing off and closing in, that is
now in the air. The spirit that sends hate mail, paints swastikas on walls, burns
crosses, bans books—vandalizes minds—has no place here. We must, and we will,
maintain at Yale a spirit that is tolerant, respectful and candid, for that spirit is the
45 form of order essential to sustain the freedom of the mind inquiring. ■ ■ ■

Meanwhile, many liberals tried to redefine the debate over "family values" by
focusing on economic issues—child care, tax credits for working families with children—that would lessen the financial burdens weighing on most Americans. Lib-

erals also preached about the importance of individual rights and warned against unwarranted government intrusion into the lives of private citizens. In 1980 television producer Norman Lear founded the People for the American Way to provide a political counterweight to the New Right. "First and foremost among our shared values is a celebration of diversity and respect for the beliefs of others," he declared. People for the American Way entered the fray by providing the legal teams that represented the schools in both Alabama's and Tennessee's textbook wars.

Politics, no less than morality, shaped the debate over family values. Republican leaders used the family appeal to demonstrate compassion and rebut criticism that their party was concerned only with protecting the interests of the rich and powerful. "It's important to our party and our country that we talk as Republicans about the proper role for government to play in assisting families," declared a Republican governor. For Democrats eager to overcome the public perception that they catered to the poor and to special-interest groups, appeals to family issues allowed them to side with the struggles of the middle class. "The Democratic Party will be successful in recapturing the White House when it is successful in capturing the issue of family," noted a prominent Democrat.

Abortion

Debates over family values turned inevitably into a clash over abortion. The legalization of abortion following the Supreme Court's decision in *Roe* v. *Wade* (1973) created a new and highly focused setting for confrontation by opponents: the hundreds of abortion clinics scattered throughout the United States, in shopping centers, office buildings, and residential neighborhoods. Initially, "prolife" organizers picketed and organized prayer vigils outside clinics. In January 1986 Randall Terry, age thirty, a born-again Christian, signaled the formalization of a more militant activism in the movement when he founded Operation Rescue. Over the next two years Terry organized tightly controlled blockades to prevent women from entering abortion clinics. "These acts of civil disobedience," he wrote, "are designed to save lives by preventing abortionists from entering their death chambers, and to dramatize for the American people the horrors of the abortion holocaust." Elsewhere demonstrators posed as patients, entered clinics, and then splattered red paint in waiting rooms, ignited stink bombs, or bound themselves to examining tables.

Even more frighteningly, the number of bomb threats and actual bombings at clinics soared. The Federal Bureau of Alcohol, Tobacco, and Firearms reported thirty bombings between May 1982 and January 1985. Twenty-four occurred in 1984 alone. Three bombs ripped through Florida abortion clinics on Christmas morning 1984 and another in early January 1985. One of the people involved claimed that the bombings were "a gift to Jesus on his birthday." John Burt, another antiabortion activist, remarked, "I don't approve of the bombings, but I'm glad the killing has stopped and the clinics have closed." "It's warfare," he continued. "We're literally in a war between good and evil."

Debate over Abortion   As the Religious Right grew in political importance, so did the issue of a woman's right to an abortion, legalized by the 1973 Supreme Court decision in *Roe v. Wade*. Prolife organizations held rallies and protested in front of abortion clinics, emphasizing that abortion was a form of infanticide. Though prochoice advocates had the support of the courts, they continued to challenge the arguments made by prolife advocates, pressing a woman's right to choose, as seen in this protest in Boston. *(Evan Richman/The Boston Globe. Republished with permission of Globe Newspaper Company, Inc.)*

Although most mainstream prolife advocates sought to distance themselves from political violence, they continued to picket clinics. In January 1985 antiabortion activists organized a large demonstration called the March for Life to mark the twelfth anniversary of *Roe* v. *Wade*. Bundled up to fend off the winter cold, they marched in front of the Supreme Court carrying American flags and chanting their resistance to the landmark decision. The opponents of abortion and birth control found an ally in the White House. To a crowd of over seventy thousand people milling about the Washington Monument, Reagan gave his assurance that "I feel a great sense of solidarity with all of you."

In addition to providing verbal support to the cause of ending legal abortion, the president persuaded Congress to bar most public funding for birth control and to stop Medicare from funding abortions for poor women. An administration measure provided funding for religiously oriented "chastity clinics" where counselors advised teenage girls and women to "just say no" to avoid pregnancy. Opponents realized, however, that the Supreme Court held the key to the abortion issue. "The bishops have understood that ultimately the battle over abortion is going to be played out at the state level," said a church official. "And abortion has become the vehicle for the church utilizing grass-roots politics in a way it had never engaged in before."

The moral position of religious conservatives meshed with the political strategy of Republican operatives determined to use social issues to fracture the Democratic coalition. "There is a real feeling among blue-collar Catholics that the Democratic Party has been spending its time chasing women, blacks and gays and ignoring everyone else," noted a Catholic writer. "Abortion serves as a symbol for that sense of abandonment as well as for the perception that traditional values are declining."

Among activists the debate over abortion revolved around different conceptions of motherhood. Abortion opponents believed in traditional sex roles and saw motherhood as a woman's highest mission in life. Viewing the conflict as a clash between "nurturance" and "selfish individualism," they considered abortion one more assault on the last bastion of human tenderness in a cold and uncaring world. "We've accepted abortion because we're a very materialistic society and there is less time for caring," observed an antiabortion activist in Fargo, North Dakota.

Prochoice activists, in contrast, believed that motherhood was only one of the many roles that women played. Only by addressing the gender inequalities that prevented women from competing equally against men, they argued, could American society support families. Feminists considered the option of having an abortion to be indispensable; as the responsibility for children devolved to women, so must the choice as to when to bear them. Along with supporting a host of political and economic reforms—paid parental leave, flexible hours, child-care facilities—feminists trumpeted the value of individual liberty over government interference. Observed Planned Parenthood president Faye Wattleton, "The fundamental principles of individual privacy are under the most serious assault since the days of McCarthyism."

Activists on both sides represented a small proportion of opinions, however. Polls showed a public torn between the extremes of the abortion debate: overwhelming opposition to an absolute ban on abortion but discomfort with an absolute right to abortion. The public debate, however, obscured opportunity for consensus as both sides used powerful symbols to rally support for their cause. In 1984 antiabortion activists produced a graphic videotape, *The Silent Scream,* which showed abortion "from the point of view of the unborn child." The film gained a wide audience after President Reagan endorsed it during the March for Life in January 1985. In response, prochoice advocates often displayed coat hangers—grim reminders of the illegal and unsafe abortions that had taken place before the Supreme Court ruling.

Class and religious beliefs served as the fault lines in the abortion debate. Polls showed that higher-income earners, people with a college degree, and the self-employed proved more likely to support a woman's right to choose. Only one-fourth of blacks and Latinos favored abortion, compared to more than one-third of Anglos. Surprisingly, women and men divided equally on the issue. But people who deemed religion as "very important" in their lives opposed abortion by an overwhelming 2-1 margin.

Surveys revealed a considerable regional variation on abortion issues. People along the Pacific coast and in New England favored the termination of pregnancies more than did other Americans. Smaller rural areas in the Deep South and Midwest registered markedly higher rates of opposition than the national average. Those who supported abortion rights often did not attend church services, lived near major metropolitan areas, and held liberal views on other family values issues such as gay rights. Those opposed to abortion more frequently expressed concern that the nation was in a state of moral decline, believed that a woman's place was in the home, and regularly attended religious services.

AIDS and the Struggle for Gay Rights

Perhaps with the exception of abortion, few subjects during the 1980s generated more raw emotion than homosexuality. The gay-rights movement, born at the Stonewall Inn in 1969, continued to gain momentum during the 1970s. Homosexuals flooded into cities such as San Francisco and New York and established a variety of support organizations. Between 1974 and 1978 more than twenty thousand homosexuals moved to San Francisco, many of them living in the city's Castro District. In response to the growing visibility of the gay community, a number of states repealed their sodomy statutes and a few enacted legislation preventing discrimination based on sexual orientation.

The movement took a tragic turn in 1981 when doctors in San Francisco and New York began reporting that young homosexual men were dying from a rare disease initially called Kaposi's sarcoma. As panic spread through the gay community, researchers at the Centers for Disease Control (CDC) discovered the villain: a deadly virus spread by bodily fluid that rendered the victim's immune system helpless against opportunistic infections. They renamed the mysterious disease acquired immune deficiency syndrome (AIDS).

Initially the majority of AIDS victims were homosexual men infected through sexual contact. During the 1970s many gay men associated freedom with sexual promiscuity. "The belief that was handed to me was that sex was liberating and more sex was more liberating," observed the activist Michael Callen. "[Being gay] was tied to the right to have sex." As the death toll mounted, gay leaders organized to educate the public and to pressure government to find a cure. In New York the Gay Men's Health Center spearheaded the effort, raising millions of dollars, offering services to the sick, and lobbying Washington. The Human Rights Campaign Fund, founded in 1980, raised millions of dollars to support gay-friendly politicians. The pressure produced tangible results. By the end of the decade 21 states and 130 municipalities offered gays and lesbians some form of legal protection against discrimination.

At the same time, radical groups such as the AIDS Coalition to Unleash Power, or ACT UP, founded in 1987 to protest a lack of commitment to finding a cure for AIDS, rattled politicians and drug companies with their colorful demonstrations. ACT UP's slogan, "Silence = Death," underscoring a pink triangle on black, became a trademark for late-1980s uncivil disobedience. Accompanied by chants such as "Out of the closets and into the streets!" its members picketed meetings of the Food and Drug Administration, disrupted Catholic Masses to protest church policies on AIDS, and chained themselves to the doors of major drug companies to protest high drug prices.

The AIDS crisis produced an outflow of gay literature and art. In 1987 the Names Project began sewing quilts for each victim who succumbed to AIDS. In a highly publicized event in 1992 the AIDS quilt—now incorporating thousands of individual panels—was unfolded in front of the Washington Monument. "It's a way for people to say, 'This person was here and won't be forgotten,' " said the quilt's creator. Hollywood addressed the crisis in a movie, *Longtime Companion* (1990), which followed eight gay men and one female friend through the history of the disease. New York photographer Nan Goldin's exhibition "Witnesses: Against Our Vanishing" offered a collection of work created "to celebrate the indomitable spirit of our community, to prove that our way of life still exists, that we are being killed by AIDS but our sensibility could not be killed off." Gay writers' works, such as Larry Kramer's *The Normal Heart* (1985) and journalist Randy Shilts's *And the Band Played On* (1987), raised public awareness about the disease and about gay life. Gay playwright Tony Kushner's drama *Angels in America* (1992) earned a Pulitzer Prize for its depiction of gay life in the 1980s.

Conservatives reacted with horror, viewing gay rights as unnatural, contrary to God's will, and hostile to the traditional family. The gay-rights movement represented "the most vicious attack on traditional family values that our society has seen in the history of our republic," declared a conservative congressman. White House adviser Pat Buchanan suggested that AIDS was God's revenge for violating natural law. "The poor homosexuals. They have declared war on nature and now nature is exacting an awful retribution."

PRIMARY SOURCE

14.3 | *AIDS Testimony*
RYAN WHITE

The emergence of HIV in the early 1980s shocked Americans and led to widespread fear of contact with an infected person. Even though most of the early victims of AIDS were homosexuals and intravenous drug users, blood transfusions exposed thousands of hemophiliacs to the virus. On March 3, 1988, Ryan White, a hemophiliac diagnosed with HIV at age thirteen, braved the stigma society attached to the disease and testified before the Presidential Commission on AIDS, where he described the discrimination he faced as a carrier of the disease.

Reflecting on the AIDS Quilt on the Mall in Washington, D.C. The AIDS epidemic struck the city of San Francisco earlier than most of the nation's regions, and it was there that the idea for a tribute to those killed by the virus was born. In June 1987, friends and loved ones gathered to discuss ways to honor the growing number of AIDS victims and provide a visual display that would force the nation to recognize the devastating effects of the disease on families and entire communities. The group decided to create quilt panels, each 3 feet by 6 feet in length, decorated with images that commemorated the lives of those whom they had lost. On October 11, 1987, organizers displayed the quilt for the first time on the national mall during a march for lesbian and gay rights. At that time, there were nineteen hundred panels, but a subsequent four-month national tour of the quilt captured the attention of people across the country who began contributing their own panels. Parts of the quilt continued to tour the country and other nations as the AIDS death toll continued to rise and the number of panels submitted grew. In October 1996, the quilt stretched the entire length of the mall, providing an emotional example of the epidemic's human cost.

Thank you, commissioners. My name is Ryan White. I am sixteen years old. I have hemophilia, and I have AIDS. When I was three days old, the doctors told my parents I was a severe hemophiliac, meaning my blood does not clot. Lucky for me, there was a product just approved by the Food and Drug Administration. It was
5 called Factor VIII, which contains the clotting agent found in blood.

While I was growing up, I had many bleeds—or hemorrhages—in my joints which make it very painful. Twice a week I would receive injections or IV's of Factor VIII which clotted the blood and then broke it down. A bleed occurs from a broken blood vessel or vein. The blood then had nowhere to go, so it would swell up in a joint. You could compare it to trying to pour a quart of milk into a pint-sized container of milk.

The first five to six years of my life were spent in and out of the hospital. All in all I led a pretty normal life.

Most recently my battle has been against AIDS and the discrimination surrounding it. On December 17, 1984, I had surgery to remove two inches of my left lung due to pneumonia. After two hours of surgery, the doctors told my mother I had AIDS. I contracted AIDS through my Factor VIII which is made from blood. When I came out of surgery, I was on a respirator and had a tube in my left lung. I spent Christmas and the next thirty days in the hospital. A lot of my time was spent searching, thinking, and planning my life.

I came face to face with death at thirteen years old. I was diagnosed with AIDS, a killer. Doctors told me I'm not contagious. Given six months to live and being the fighter that I am, I set high goals for myself. It was my decision to live a normal life, go to school, be with my friends, and enjoy day-to-day activities. It was not going to be easy.

The school I was going to said they had no guidelines for a person with AIDS. The school board, my teachers, and my principal voted to keep me out of the classroom even after the guidelines were set by the ISTH [International Society of Thrombosis and Hemostasis, a nonprofit organization that focuses on blood disorders], for fear of someone getting AIDS from me by casual contact. Rumors of sneezing, kissing, tears, sweat, and saliva spreading AIDS caused people to panic.

We began a series of court battles for nine months, while I was attending classes by telephone. Eventually, I won the right to attend school, but the prejudice was still there. Listening to medical facts was not enough. People wanted 100 percent guarantees. There are no 100 percent guarantees in life, but concessions were made by Mom and me to help ease the fear. We decided to meet everyone halfway—separate rest rooms, no gym, separate drinking fountains, disposable eating utensils—even though we knew AIDS was not spread through casual contact. Nevertheless, parents of twenty students started their own school. They were still not convinced.

Because of the lack of education on AIDS, discrimination, fear, panic, and lies surrounded me: one, I became the target of Ryan White jokes; two, lies about me biting people; three, spitting on vegetables and cookies; four, urinating on bathroom walls; five, some restaurants threw away my dishes; six, my school locker was vandalized inside and folders were marked "fag" and other obscenities. I was labeled a troublemaker, my mom an unfit mother, and I was not welcome anywhere. People would get up and leave so they would not have to sit anywhere near me. Even at church, people would not shake my hand. . . .

It was difficult at times to handle, but I tried to ignore the injustice, because I knew the people were wrong. My family and I held no hatred for those people, because we realized they were victims of their own ignorance. We had great faith that, with patience, understanding, and education, my family and I could be helpful in changing their minds and attitudes around.

55 Financial hardships were rough on us, even though Mom had a good job at GM. The more I was sick, the more work she had to miss. Bills became impossible to pay. My sister, Andrea, was a championship roller skater who had to sacrifice, too. There was no money for her lessons and travel. AIDS can destroy a family if you let it, but luckily for my sister and me, Mom taught us to keep going, don't

60 give up, be proud of who you are, and never feel sorry for yourself.

After two-and-a-half years of declining health, two attacks of pneumocystis, shingles, a rare form of whooping cough, and liver problems, I faced fighting chills, fevers, coughing, tiredness, and vomiting. I was very ill and being tutored at home. The desire to move into a bigger house, to avoid living AIDS daily, and a

65 dream to be accepted by a community and school became possible and a reality with a movie about my life, *The Ryan White Story.*

My life is better now. At the end of the school year, my family and I decided to move to Cicero, Indiana. We did a lot of hoping and praying that the community would welcome us, and they did. For the first time in three years, we feel we have

70 a home, a supportive school, and lots of friends. The communities of Cicero, Atlanta, Arcadia, and Noblesville, Indiana, are now what we call home. I'm feeling great.

I am a normal, happy teenager again. I have a learner's permit [to drive]. I attend sports functions and dances. My studies are important to me. I made the

75 honor role just recently, with two A's and two B's. I'm just one of the kids, and all because the students at Hamilton Heights High School listened to the facts, educated their parents and themselves, and believed in me. I believe in myself as I look forward to graduating from Hamilton Heights High School in 1991. Hamilton Heights High School is proof that AIDS education in schools works. ■ ■ ■

Scientists, including Surgeon General Dr. C. Everett Koop, urged Reagan to endorse a "safe-sex" program to combat AIDS. Koop described his remedy as "one, abstinence; two, monogamy; three, condoms." But the president, bowing to conservative pressure and personally uncomfortable dealing with questions of sexuality, shied away from personal involvement in the crisis. The administration barred the CDC from funding organizations that dealt explicitly with sex, homosexuality, or drug use. Not even the death of movie star, and Reagan friend, Rock Hudson in 1985 inspired the administration to make combating the disease a top priority.

As long as the disease appeared confined to minority populations, the public remained largely apathetic. "If it spreads to the general public, it would be a medical crisis, demanding immediate government response," said one observer. Polls showed that the public remained deeply ambivalent about gay and lesbian rights. An overwhelming majority believed that homosexuals should enjoy equal access to jobs and health care. Yet the same majority opposed gay marriages and felt that gays should not be able to adopt children. Nearly one-half considered homosexuality "unacceptable" behavior and a threat to the family.

Research on the AIDS epidemic continued even though the American people divided over the issue and the Reagan administration remained apprehensive. Dr. Mathilde Krim, who also contributed to the passage of the National Cancer Act of 1971, became an early advocate of consciousness-raising. In 1983 she founded the AIDS Medical Foundation and in 1985 merged it with the National AIDS Research Foundation in Los Angeles. The resulting American Foundation for AIDS Research played an integral role in lobbying for funds to conduct research into the growing problem. Krim also led the effort to make homosexuality and AIDS a part of the public discourse and to discourage the stigmatization of the disease's victims.

Because of the painfully poor understanding of AIDS and the means through which it spread, most commentators defined the disease as a "homosexual problem." As this notion gained currency, a wave of reaction stemmed the liberalization of attitudes toward gays. In March 1986 the Supreme Court delivered a stunning 5–4 decision in *Bowers* v. *Hardwick* that upheld Georgia's antisodomy laws, which proscribed private homosexual acts between consenting adults. The decision dealt a devastating blow to gay rights. Chief Justice Warren Burger's concurring opinion demonstrated the deep-seated conflict over public and private morality. "To hold that the act of homosexual sodomy is somehow protected as a fundamental right," he averred, "would be to cast aside millennia of moral teaching." "Depriving individuals of the right to choose for themselves how to conduct their intimate relationships," Justice Harry Blackmun fired back in his dissenting opinion, "poses a far greater threat to the values most deeply [ingrained] in our Nation's history than tolerance of nonconformity could ever do." Only in 1996, with a 6–3 decision in *Romer* v. *Evans*, would the Supreme Court recognize the illegality of laws that discriminated against homosexuals.

By the end of the 1980s the AIDS epidemic had spread far beyond gay men. Thanks to grass-roots organizing and public education, the number of new AIDS cases among homosexuals had stabilized. In 1987, 50 percent of the deaths from AIDS in the United States were among intravenous drug users and their sexual partners, a group that was 90 percent African-American and Hispanic. Overall, blacks contracted human immunodeficiency virus (HIV), the precursor to AIDS, at a rate three times higher than whites. For Hispanics the infection rate exceeded that of whites by two times. An even more harrowing revelation came when researchers discovered that the disease also spread more rapidly among children than adults.

The World Health Organization divided the AIDS epidemic into three distinct phases: the silent period (1970–1981), the initial discovery (1981–1985), and the worldwide mobilization (1985–). By 1992 HIV infected 12.9 million people worldwide, with most of its victims living in poorer nations that lacked the resources to mount effective campaigns to stem its spread. Sub-Saharan Africa, with 10 percent of the world's population, claimed 68 percent of the total HIV population (8.8 million). Scientists estimated that in sub-Saharan urban areas as many as 50 percent of all adults, including 20 percent of pregnant women, were infected—the vast majority through heterosexual contact.

Black, Brown, and Yellow

The massive wave of immigrants that flooded American cities after 1965 raised new questions about the nation's racial and ethnic identity. "The nation is rapidly moving toward a multiethnic future," *Newsweek* reported in 1992. "Asians, Hispanics, Caribbean islanders, and many other immigrant groups compose a diverse and changing social mosaic that cannot be described by the old vocabulary of race relations."

The immigration rate of the 1980s eclipsed the previous high set during the century's first decade as the new immigrants, mostly from Asia, Central and South America, and the Caribbean, sought a new life in the United States. According to the Census Bureau, the nation absorbed 8.9 million legal immigrants—and, by most estimates, at least 2 million illegal ones—during the 1980s. By the early 1990s over 1 million new legal immigrants were arriving in the United States every year, accounting for almost one-half of U.S. population growth.

Most of these immigrants settled in large cities in a handful of states—New York, Illinois, and New Jersey, as well as Florida, Texas, and California. One of every three new immigrants entered the United States through California, making the nation's most populous state its unofficial Ellis Island. By 1990 the population of Los Angeles, the nation's second-largest city, was one-third foreign born. Los Angeles was also home to the second-largest Spanish-speaking population (after Mexico City) of any city on the North American continent. New York's foreign-born population, like that of Los Angeles, also approached 35 percent of its total populace in 1990, a level the city had last reached in 1910.

Most Americans saw and heard daily reminders of the cultural impact of the new waves of immigrants. A complex chorus of foreign languages filled urban streets. In Miami 75 percent of residents spoke a language other than English at home, and in New York City the figure was 40 percent, and of these, 50 percent could not speak fluent English. In kitchens across the country salsa replaced ketchup as America's favorite condiment. In music such Hispanic artists as Los Lobos, the Miami Sound Machine, and Lisa Lisa topped the billboards with hit songs. Many white artists tried assimilating new cultural impulses into their music. David Byrne injected Talking Heads music with African, Latin, and other rhythms. Peter Gabriel and Paul Simon found similar success with African rhythms.

The new diversity provided fertile ground for bigotry. "The more diversity and burgeoning minority groups we have," the National Conference of Christians and Jews observed, "the more prejudice we must overcome." Blacks, Hispanics, and Asians often felt as much animosity toward each other as they did toward whites. In Florida Hispanics and blacks, who had once considered themselves allies against the white power structure, battled each other for jobs and scarce resources. In many cities African-Americans and Korean immigrants engaged in heated confrontations. At the root of the conflict, exacerbated by language and cultural differences, was resentment of Korean immigrants' success in running small businesses in economically depressed black neighborhoods.

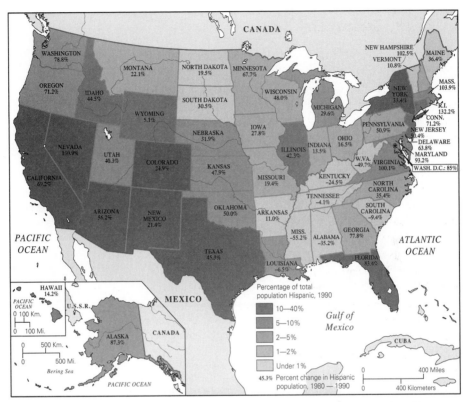

Growth of Hispanic Population in the 1980s   For the first time in American history, the majority of immigrants came from countries outside of Europe. The Hispanic population claimed the largest percentage of new immigrants. This influx altered the social and cultural dynamics of cities and states across the nation, just as previous waves of immigration had done.

Acclaimed director Spike Lee captured this climate in satirical fashion in his movie *Do the Right Thing* (1989). A Korean shopkeeper in Brooklyn averts a confrontation with black residents of the neighborhood by shouting in desperation, "Me no white. Me no white. Me black."

The Los Angeles riots following the Rodney King trial in April 1992 were the most visible demonstration of this new tension. The riots commenced after a mostly white jury in a Los Angeles suburb acquitted four white police officers accused of savagely beating an African-American motorist, Rodney King, after stopping him for a traffic violation. The jury arrived at the verdict despite the existence of a videotape showing the officers delivering numerous blows to a seemingly defenseless King.

Shortly after the verdicts were announced, African-Americans in South-central Los Angeles erupted in the deadliest urban riot in over a century. They were soon joined by Latinos who were shocked by the verdict. As the violence

Video of the Rodney King Beating   On March 3, 1991, Rodney King failed to stop when a Los Angeles police car signaled him to pull over, beginning a chase in which speeds reached an estimated 100 mph. When police finally stopped the car, they pulled King out and began beating him—according to the officers, because he showed signs that he might try to get off the ground and run. On the balcony of a building that faced the highway, George Holliday videotaped the incident. The next day Holliday gave the tape to an L.A. news station, which aired it. The video shows the police hitting King with their batons fifty-six times and kicking him six times—all within two minutes. King suffered eleven skull fractures, along with brain and kidney damage, yet officers, not knowing they had been recorded, failed to mention the injuries in their report. On May 15, four white officers identified in the video were charged with use of excessive force and assault with a deadly weapon. The judge moved the trial from L.A. to suburban Simi Valley, where a jury acquitted the officers on April 29, 1992. The verdict angered African-Americans in Los Angeles and touched off six days of rioting in south central L.A. Later in the year, the officers were arraigned on federal charges, and two were convicted in 1993.

unfolded, a unique pattern emerged: the riots were multiethnic, and they were not confined to a limited area. Latinos made up more than one-half of the first five thousand people arrested, and buildings from West Los Angeles to Korea-town, to Santa Monica, were burned. "The riots were not carried out against Blacks or Whites, they were carried out against the Latino and Asian communities by the Blacks," the Mexican-American newspaper *La Prensa* claimed. "Faced with nearly a million and a half Latinos taking over the inner city, Blacks revolted, rioted and looted." According to an African-American commentator, the clash should "shatter, perhaps for good, one of the most enduring myths of our time: The myth of black-brown solidarity."

By the time the riots ended three days later, fifty-eight people lay dead, over eight hundred buildings had been destroyed, and thousands more had been damaged or looted. President Bush's initial response was to blame the riots on failed liberal social programs from the 1960s. When that explanation failed to convince people or reassure the nation, Bush traveled to the riot area and promised more federal aid for a "Weed and Seed" program offering financial incentives to companies willing to invest in the inner cities, programs for disadvantaged children, and a massive buildup of the police and criminal justice system. Critics complained that the emphasis was on the "weed" rather than the "seed." Nearly 80 percent of the $500 million was earmarked for beefed-up police presence.

The Backlash Against Multiculturalism

Many white Americans complained about new immigrants stealing jobs from native workers, worried about the cohesiveness of American culture, and questioned its ability to absorb and assimilate so many different cultural influences. "Is it really wise to allow the immigration of people who find it so difficult and painful to assimilate into the American majority?" asked conservative journalist Peter Brimelow. In Miami bumper stickers appeared declaring, "Will the last American out of Miami please take the flag?" After years of debate on how to control illegal immigration, Congress in 1986 passed the Immigration Reform and Control Act. It offered legal status to undocumented aliens who had lived and worked in the United States but imposed fines on employers who hired new undocumented workers.

Critics also complained that immigrants imposed a heavy financial burden on local governments. On average immigrant-headed households included more school-age children than native households, were poorer, received more welfare, and, since they owned less property, paid less in taxes. Local governments provided many of the services immigrants needed, yet the federal government collected most of their tax dollars. "At the federal level, it appears that immigrants are a fiscal plus," noted a sociologist. "They pay more in taxes than they use in services. It's the local governments that are most adversely affected." By one estimate each illegal immigrant household in California consumed on average $1,178 more in public services than it contributed in taxes. When multiplied by the estimated 2 million undocumented aliens in the state, the figure amounted to a significant drain on public resources. If averaged out across the nation, the net burden would be much lower, between $166 and $226 per native household.

Fears about the swelling foreign-language populations produced a powerful "English-only" movement. "The language of American government is English," said a Connecticut Republican. "The language of American business is English. We are not a dual-language society." In 1986 California spearheaded the drive for "English only" by voting overwhelmingly for a referendum outlawing bilingualism and defending "English as a unifying force in the United States." Representatives of

Hispanic groups condemned the movement as "fundamentally racist in character," but before the end of the decade seventeen other states had joined California in passing English-only laws. "Language," *The Economist* noted, "symbolizes the United States' fear that the foreign body within its borders is growing too big ever to be digested."

The debate over American identity found expression on college campuses as students attempted to "increase sensitivity" to racial and cultural diversity in the university community. At Stanford reformers fought to change the Western Civilization curriculum, which they claimed presented a "male, Eurocentric" view of the world. Many universities accommodated the pressure to diversify by expanding the range of programs in disciplines such as Women's Studies, African-American Studies, Hispanic Studies, and Gay Studies. In 1987 Allan Bloom led the conservative counterattack on changes in American higher education with his book *The Closing of the American Mind*. Subtitled *How Higher Education Has Failed Democracy and Impoverished the Souls of Today's Students*, the book asserted the primacy of "the great books" of western civilization. "You can't talk about Chaucer without someone saying 'What's the woman's perspective?', 'What about the Third World perspective?' " he lamented. Bloom's volume remained at the top of the *New York Times* best-seller list for seven weeks, selling more than 1 million copies.

Historical experience suggests that concerns about immigrants' failing to assimilate were misplaced; similar fears about past waves of immigrants proved unfounded. The public has always looked favorably on past generations of immigrants and unfavorably on contemporary migrants. In the nineteenth century Americans complained about the "lazy and hard-drinking Irish" who were "polluting" the cities; later waves of newcomers from Italy and Eastern Europe confronted similarly hostile attitudes. Over time, however, those groups became acculturated and now swell the mainstream that fears the addition of new migrants from Mexico, Iran, and Haiti. Strident affirmations of identity actually masked the degree to which ethnic differences grew less overt—higher education, consumerism, movies and television, professional sports, and popular culture worked to make Americans more alike, whatever their ethnic origins.

The rising rate of intermarriage between ethnic groups, especially Asian-Americans and non-Asians, also suggested that ethnic differences were softening over time. In the 1980s more than 50 percent of all Japanese-Americans, and 40 percent of Chinese-Americans, married outside their ethnic group. As in the past, these relationships often resulted in families that blended cultural traditions. Weddings might incorporate symbolism and rituals from cultures of both the husband and the wife; children had the opportunity to develop fluency in two languages; the patterns of everyday life, from cuisine to entertainment, reflected the accommodation of two heritages. No matter what particular balance families struck, they reflected in microcosm the vitality of a dynamic American identity that drew its strength from diversity.

The conservative reassertion of cultural nationalism took place during a decade of profound social changes and nearly unprecedented immigration. The contrast highlighted the conflict between American ideals and social realities and exposed another dimension of the American paradox. But the cultural conflict paled in comparison to the striking disparity between rich and poor that would come to characterize the United States of the 1980s. The realization of the great American paradox, of poverty amid tremendous affluence, would enter popular consciousness to a degree unrivaled since the 1960s.

SELECTED READINGS

▌ William Martin's *With God on Our Side* (1996) describes the changing politics of the religious right. Clyde Wilcox studies the leaders of the religious right in *God's Warriors* (1992), while Burton Yale Pines looks at the cultural appeal of fundamentalism in *Back to Basics* (1982). Sidney Blumenthal's *The Rise of the Counter-Establishment* (1986) chronicles the emergence of the neoconservatives. Michael Lind, a defector from the conservative camp, critiques the New Right in *Up from Conservatism* (1996).

▌ Leslie Reagan reconstructs the situation for women before *Roe* v. *Wade* in *When Abortion Was a Crime* (1997). Rosalind Petchesky explains the philosophical and legal conflicts surrounding abortion in *Abortion and Women's Choice* (1990). The definitive discussion of the political campaign over abortion is found in Kristin Luker's *Abortion and the Politics of Motherhood* (1985). Editor Rickie Solinger compiles a prorights look at the abortion debate from the 1950s through the 1990s in *Abortion Wars* (1998). A social history of the antiabortion campaign since the decision in *Roe* is provided by Kerry Jacoby in *Souls, Bodies, Spirits* (1998).

▌ Eric Marcus's *Making History: The Struggle for Gay and Lesbian Equal Rights* (1992) delivers a broad overview of the gay liberation movement. John Manuel Androite in *Victory Deferred* (1999) chronicles the impact of AIDS and the impact on the gay community as people stepped forward to protest government inaction. The growth of the gay community in San Francisco and the devastating effect of the AIDS epidemic are evoked through oral interviews collected by Benjamin Shepard in *White Nights and Ascending Shadows* (1997). The reasons the government bureaucracies failed to respond quickly to the AIDS crisis are analyzed in Sandra Panem and Samuel Thier's *The AIDS Bureaucracy* (1988).

▌ David Reimers's *Still the Golden Door* (2nd ed., 1994) is a good starting point for material on immigration. Thomas Espenshade's *The Fourth Wave* (1985) describes the "New Asian" immigrants in California, while James Cockcroft's *Outlaws in the Promised Land* (1986) looks at the immigration experience of Hispanics. David Gutierrez examines how Mexican immigrants have defined their political and cultural identities in America in *Walls and Mirrors* (1995). Peter Brimelow's *Alien Nation* (1995) offers a pessimistic analysis of the new wave of immigration. Raymond Tatalovich's, *Nativism Reborn?* (1995) studies the underlying factors that provoked agitation to make English the nation's official language.

▌ Nancy Abelmann and John Lie examine the conflict between blacks and Koreans that led to significant damage to Korean-American businesses in the L.A. riots in *Blue Dreams* (1995). The essays collected by Robert Gooding-Williams in *Reading Rodney King/Reading Urban Uprising* (1993) explore the connection between the Rodney King incident and the L.A. riots. James Delk's *Fires and Furies* (1995) chronicles how the riots unfolded.

15

The Triumph of Consumerism, 1980–1992

New York City's real estate tycoon Donald Trump emerged as the most glaring symbol of a decade that celebrated ruthless competition and extravagant wealth. "There is no one my age who has accomplished more," he boasted after building the palatial Trump Tower skyscraper on fashionable Fifth Avenue. "Everyone can't be the best." With his empire estimated at more than $3 billion in 1987, Trump lived like a modern-day Gatsby, replete with a fleet of private jets, a $29 million yacht, a 110-room mansion in Florida, and a 10-acre, 45-room weekend getaway estate in Connecticut. With his name plastered on almost every building he owned and his face appearing on the cover of news magazines and daily gossip tabloids, Trump became one of the most recognizable men in America. He was, *Newsweek* reported, "the latest of a breed unique to the decade: the businessman who becomes larger than life, like a star athlete or popular actor."

During the 1980s Americans abandoned the previous decade's emphasis on limits and austerity and instead celebrated the culture of consumerism. "The man in the street, the little guy, digs the limo, the helicopter, the 727," Trump told a reporter. The Reagan administration preached the wonders of free enterprise, promising that the pursuit of private wealth would enhance the public welfare.

The celebration of money, however, failed to live up to expectations. During a decade of ostentatious displays of wealth, the specter of an intractable poverty became the decade's quintessential paradox. Instead of bringing Americans closer together, the pursuit of profit divided the nation: rich and poor, city and suburb, black and white.

The Money Culture

Ronald and Nancy Reagan epitomized the new money culture of the 1980s. "The marriage of economic wealth and political power has been solemnized anew," *The New Republic* reported in the wake of the House's passage of Reagan's tax cut in 1981. Heralding the advent of a "New Gilded Age," the magazine argued, "Under the Reagan dispensation, shame is banished, greed enshrined, and the political supremacy of private wealth celebrated."

The public seemed enthralled by the air of unembarrassed extravagance that the Reagans championed. They set the tone for the decade with a lavish inaugural celebration that included two nights of show-business performances, an $800,000 fireworks display, and nine inaugural balls. Once in the White House, First Lady Nancy Reagan unapologetically spent $209,508 for new White House china—a Lenox pattern with a raised gold presidential seal—while her husband was busy cutting welfare rolls. "Wealth is back in style," a journalist noted in 1981. "The Reagans are setting a lifestyle so different from the hide-it-under-a-bushel attitude of the Carters. The feeling now is that if you have it, why not enjoy it?"

The real nexus of the money culture, however, was Wall Street. Passage of the 1981 tax law combined with the Reagan Justice Department's relaxed attitude toward enforcement of antitrust statutes produced a "merger mania" on Wall Street. Many of the nation's largest corporations, including R. J. Reynolds, Nabisco, Walt Disney, and Federated Department Stores, were the objects of leveraged buyouts. Between 1984 and 1987 Wall Street executed twenty-one mergers valued at over $1 billion each. The money culture created lucrative opportunities for the battalions of bankers, investors, and venture capitalists who made money out of money. Among the very highest rollers was Ivan Boesky, who worked eighteen-hour days behind a three hundred-line phone bank and made a fortune orchestrating merger deals. "Greed is all right," he told a cheering University of California at Berkeley Business School audience in 1986. "Everybody should be a little bit greedy."

PRIMARY SOURCE

15.1 | *Commencement Address, 1986*
IVAN BOESKY

Ivan Boesky embodied the quest for money and extravagant living witnessed in the 1980s. In a graduation speech on May 18, 1986, at the Berkeley Business School, Boesky described the privileges and obligations of wealth.

I am pleased to stand here before you and tell you I am working class. My father was a Russian immigrant Jew, and I am here to tell you, dear students, you will

be running this nation's enterprises. I urge you to do so in a manner that will enhance the mantle *businessman* with dignity and honor. Since it is your charge
5 to administer, do so as aggressively and as promptly as possible. Do not be patient. Be restless. Do not be orderly because that's the way it's done. Be anxious to be heard. Demonstrate the virtues of those who, in many cases, founded the businesses that will be employing you. Dare to stretch, imagine, create, and then market your skills. Be entrepreneurial in spirit. Earn positions of leadership and
10 earn your right to remain in those positions.

I urge you, as a part of your mission, to seek wealth. It's all right. Does anyone disagree with that? No! But do it in a virtuous and honest way, the purer the process gathering in that way, it is one of the surest ways to having a voice in the system. Having wealth, if you aim high, can allow you to be what you want to
15 become in this great land. You could be more of a person who would make a difference. As you accumulate wealth and power, you must remain God fearing and responsible to the system that has given you this opportunity. Be respectful of the history of your people and your nation. Give back to the system with humility, and don't take yourself too seriously.

20 You know, I think of my own circumstance, and my father was one of six children whose brother took a Russian army officer's overshoe one winter day. For that act the family was going to be persecuted and killed and therefore [my father] came to America and began the process of working and supporting his family, and a mere few years later, here I am. So it wasn't my fault; my history had
25 a lot to do with it. Don't be too certain as you progress that it's your fault either. Be thankful for all those who laid down their paths and their futures for you.

Beware of a society that sorely needs retraining to keep up with modern technology and thereby is currently losing so many citizens to hopeless ghettoes. Let your American dream reflect itself in a way that will make it more possible for all
30 Americans to be able to dream. Let your wealth redound to needy institutions that are organized to stamp out bigotry, to increase jobs, reconcile Christian and Jew, white, black, Jew, and Arab—institutions that will unify people and keep us a free society. As businessmen and women, we must be missionaries with financial clout. To enter business to create goods and services, the successful are given
35 money as a reward. The businessmen of today have the responsibility of nobility of old to look after our cultural institutions, the arts and sciences, politics. Do not be narrow in your sense of who you are as a custodian of the nation's affairs. This land is your land, and you have all the common obligation to be uncommon and enlightened in your stewardship. With the privilege of wealth and power comes
40 enormous obligations. As I look out at this audience and this class, I see a significant diversity of background, a splendid array of colors and cultures. You are the noble trustees of the future of this country, and I do salute you. . . .   ■ ■ ■

Greed, however, soon landed Boesky in jail. In late 1986 he pleaded guilty to using confidential information about corporate takeovers to trade stocks illegally. In 1987 *Fortune* magazine named him "Crook of the Year." Boesky was far from the only lawbreaker. Between 1977 and 1989 Michael Milken raised more than $100 billion in funds for American business. In 1987 alone he earned more than $550 million in commissions. He later confessed to defrauding investors and rigging the bond market.

The emphasis on making money was a manifestation of the aging of the baby-boom generation—the 76 million men and women born from 1946 through 1964 who were entering high-earning, high-spending adulthood at the start of the 1980s. By mid-decade a new social category had emerged on the American scene. *Newsweek* magazine called 1984 "The Year of the Yuppie," an acronym for young urban professional. Yuppies aspired to become investment bankers, not social workers. "Much of the energy and optimism and passion of the '60s," *Newsweek* observed, "seems to have been turned inward, on lives, careers, apartments and dinners." As one observer noted, contrasting the difference between two generations of young people, "Hippies were interested in karma; yuppies prefer cars."

No longer committed to social justice, yuppies opted for "networking." In 1985, for example, one-third of the entire senior class at Yale sought jobs as financial analysts at First Boston Corporation. When college freshmen were asked in the late 1960s about personal goals, roughly 80 percent listed "develop[ing] a meaningful

Wall Street Americans, fascinated with the accumulation of wealth in the eighties, saw Wall Street as the heart of the new money culture. Junk bond pioneers and corporate raiders like Michael Milken and Ivan Boesky personified the qualities Americans respected: they were aggressive, risk-takers who succeeded in making quick profits which they spent to sustain their lavish lifestyles.

philosophy of life" and only about 40 percent listed being "well off financially." By 1985, 71 percent listed being well off financially and only 43 percent mentioned having a philosophy of life. Politically, yuppies blended an infatuation with wealth, conspicuous consumption, and economic conservatism with more liberal positions on social issues regarding the environment, abortion, and homosexuality. However, their first loyalty was to material comfort and social status. "The name of the game," declared *The Yuppie Handbook* (1984), "is the best—buying it, owning it, using it, eating it, wearing it, growing it, cooking it, driving it, doing whatever with it."

Evidence of a new culture of consumerism was everywhere. Awards of law and business degrees climbed through the mid-1980s. *Money* magazine watched as its circulation soared from 800,000 in 1980 to 1.85 million in 1987. Chrysler chief Lee Iacocca's self-serving autobiography, appropriately titled *Iacocca* (1984), sold more than 2 million copies in hardcover. He made special appearances on the popular television show *Miami Vice,* received five hundred fan letters a week, and wrote a weekly newspaper column. In 1984 and 1985 he ranked as among the ten most admired men in America—the first businessman to make the list since 1958. Victor Kiam joined the business-celebrity ranks with his television commercials for Remington electric shavers. "I liked the shavers so much I bought the company," he told audiences.

Even television preachers who pleaded for a return to traditional cultural values reinforced the message that wealth was a symbol of virtue. Their prosperity theology stressed that faith would bring both material gain and eternal salvation. "You sow it, God will grow it," Oral Roberts told his flock. In other words, God needed seed money in order to solve your problems. "Instead of preaching for a better people or a better world," noted a critic, television preachers "pander to the worst excesses of consumerism." Robert Schuller called his church "a shopping center for God" and told audiences that "God wants you to succeed." Many of the preachers lived extravagant lifestyles with luxury houses, cars, and airplanes. Before being sent to prison for defrauding investors, Jim Bakker owned six houses, including one with gold-plated bathroom fixtures and an air-conditioned doghouse.

Popular writers fed the public's fascination with the excesses of wealth. In *People Like Us* (1988), Hollywood producer turned writer Dominick Dunne chronicled the status-crazed world of the superrich, where tycoons fight for party invitations, fly to Paris for lunch, and spend millions on the latest fashions. Jay McInerney's *Bright Lights, Big City* (1984) detailed the cocaine-snorting adventures of a pleasure-seeking yuppie who bounces from one Manhattan party to the next. Bret Easton Ellis's *Less than Zero* (1985) looked at the empty lives of Southern California's spoiled adolescents with money.

Television and movies reinforced the Reagan-era infatuation with wealth and status. *Dallas,* the most successful prime-time soap opera of the decade, chronicled the wealth, infidelities, and outrageous behavior of Texas oilman J. R. Ewing. Robin Leach's *Lifestyles of the Rich and Famous* took viewers on shopping trips along exclusive Rodeo Drive and into the homes of the wealthy before ending with Leach's trademark sign-off: "May you have caviar wishes and champagne dreams." In Oliver Stone's film *Wall Street* (1987), Michael Douglas, playing Gordon Gekko, a ruthless corporate raider who relies on inside information to make his deals, tells stockbrokers: "Greed, for lack of a better word, is good. Greed is right. Greed works."

Conservatives failed to appreciate the paradox of preaching traditional values while also celebrating the triumph of consumerism. The celebration of wealth often distorted national priorities, creating the self-satisfied and selfish society they cursed from the pulpit. African-American theologian and social critic Cornel West expressed concern about the "unintended cultural consequences" of America's culture of wealth. He bemoaned "a spiritual impoverishment in which the dominant conception of the good life consists of gaining access to power, pleasure, and property, sometimes by any means." These manifestations of the market culture impinged on the influence of older civic institutions—families, places of worship, and local communities. "Is it a mere accident that nonmarket values like loyalty, commitment, service, care, concern—even tenderness—can hardly gain a secure foothold?" he asked.

The MTV Generation

Technological changes during the 1980s aided advertisers in their efforts to reach high-spending consumers. Over the decade cable television grew from a presence in less than 20 percent of homes to a place in 56.4 percent of television homes. By the end of the decade the average television household received more than twenty-seven channels. As viewers' choices grew, and the three broadcast networks lost their automatic grip on the audience, the spoils went increasingly to the programmer who could cater to a special interest and offer advertisers a small but well-targeted cluster of consumers.

At the cutting edge of this new TV environment, music television, known from the start as MTV, inspired a revolution in television broadcasting. "Ladies and Gentlemen," intoned a baritone voice at 12:01 A.M. on August 1, 1981, "Rock and roll!" MTV showed music videos around the clock, interrupted only by ads and bits of connective patter from "veejays." From the beginning MTV was designed to appeal to young adults with lots of disposable income. "It was meant to drive a 55-year-old person crazy," said chairman Tom Freston. But that was simply MTV's shrewd twist on the key selling strategy of the decade: "narrow casting," or "niche" marketing designed to "superserve" a narrowly defined viewer or reader or customer. In addition to MTV, networks pitched ads to children (Nickelodeon), to African-Americans (Black Entertainment Television), to news junkies (CNN), and to women between ages eighteen to forty-nine (Lifetime). Viewers willing to subscribe to "pay" services that charged an extra fee could choose all-sports, all-weather, all-movies, all-Spanish, all-sex, and more.

Television was the most dramatic, but not the only, example of the culture's rearrangement into niches. Consumers could choose from hundreds of specialized magazines, among them twenty-nine new automotive magazines, twenty-five devoted to computers, nine food journals, thirteen gay magazines, and five bridal magazines. The splintering of the media reinforced, and was fed by, a splintering of the consumer market. Retailing saw a proliferation of stores that sold only coffee or only socks, for example. Within department stores merchandise was increasingly fractured into miniature enclaves sorted according to designer.

The success of MTV and other forms of niche marketing contributed to the fragmentation of public culture. During the 1940s and 1950s many technological changes helped create a sense of community and a more national culture. The advent of television, with just three networks, combined with the burgeoning of long-distance telephone service, the construction of interstate highways, and the expansion of air travel, helped shrink distance and bring people closer together. Until the explosion in cable television and the proliferation of new networks, most of the viewing public watched the same television shows. As recently as the 1970s more than one-third of U.S. homes tuned in weekly to watch *All in the Family*. "Television in the old days made it a smaller community," said producer Norman Lear. In the 1980s, however, technology was transforming the "mass culture" into endless "niche cultures." With so many shows to choose from, the audience splintered into smaller subsets of viewers. Studies showed, for example, that blacks and whites watched completely different shows.

The Hourglass Society

The public focus on the money culture during the Reagan era obscured the social reality affecting most Americans. Society in the 1980s assumed the appearance of an hourglass: bulging on the extremes and thin in the middle. "There are more and more affluent people, and more and more poor people," said Martin Holler, a Methodist minister who ran a food bank in Wichita, Kansas. "More people who have much more than they have ever had, and more people with nothing."

The number of millionaires doubled during the decade. The net worth of the four hundred richest Americans nearly tripled. By the end of the decade the top 1 percent of families owned 42 percent of the net wealth of all U.S. families, including 60 percent of all corporate stock and 80 percent of all family-owned trusts. The richest 20 percent of the population increased its share of total income from 7.8 to 44.3 percent between 1973 and 1990. Conversely, the bottom 20 percent of the population's share of aggregate income declined from 16.4 to 4.6 percent during the same period. Stated another way, the richest 2.5 million people had nearly as much income as the 100 million Americans with the lowest incomes.

The flurry of business mergers and acquisitions gave a handful of corporations increasing control over decision making in the private economy. The largest two hundred industrial corporations controlled roughly 60 percent of the assets of all industrial corporations, up from less than 50 percent in the early 1950s. And despite the continuing celebration of "people's capitalism," the percentage of American households owning at least one share of stock fell from 25 percent in 1977 to 19 percent in 1983, while the wealthiest 1 percent of all American households controlled nearly 60 percent of all corporate stock.

While the rich got richer, the poor got poorer. The government classified about 26.1 million people as poor in 1979, 11.7 percent of the total population. By 1990 the number of poor had reached 33.6 million, or 13.5 percent of the country. The aggregate numbers masked a major transformation in the nature of poverty. Increased spending on programs such as social security and Medicare dramatically improved the lot of the elderly and handicapped. The bulk of the poorest segment of the population after 1980 therefore consisted of single mothers, young children, and young minority men with little education and few job skills.

A marked jump in out-of-wedlock births, which doubled between 1975 and 1986, and female-headed households, which did the same between 1970 and 1989, contributed to the feminization of poverty. By 1989 one of every four births in the United States was to an unwed woman. The feminization of poverty was also disproportionately black. By the early 1990s, 26 percent of all children under eighteen lived with a single parent, with more than 60 percent of black children falling into that category. "With the exception of drugs and crime, the biggest crisis facing the black community today is the plight of the single mother," declared a publication by the National Association for the Advancement of Colored People (NAACP).

Not surprisingly, the rise in one-parent families contributed to an epidemic of child poverty. "Two out of three poor adults are women," reported one study, and women headed "half of all poor families" in the United States. In addition, over 50 percent of the children in female-headed households were poor and disproportionally black and Hispanic. While child poverty had decreased from 27 to 15 percent between 1960 and 1974, it expanded to 21 percent by 1986. More than 40 percent of black and 38 percent of Hispanic children were poor.

By virtually any measure the problems of society's poorest worsened during the 1980s. High interest rates for construction coupled with tax law changes sharply cut commercial production of low-cost rental housing, leaving a shortage of affordable housing for low-income people. For many the only choice was the streets. At any given time during the decade, between 250,00 and 400,000 Americans were homeless. "Get off the subway in any American city," said the head of the National Coalition for Low Income Housing, "and you are stepping over people who live on the streets." Most of the homeless were unskilled workers, the chronically mentally ill, and women fleeing abusive spouses. Most had already been living in poverty before becoming homeless. When Reagan's budget measures reduced funds available for shelters for homeless people, cities and states could not respond to the crisis. One homeless Vietnam veteran described the conditions in one of New York's homeless shelters as "rat infested, roach infested, drug infested, filth infested, garbage everywhere, and little children play-ing in the stairs. Innocent people, women, children," he continued, "boxed in by their misery."

Conditions on some of the nation's 278 Indian reservations, where half of the nation's estimated 1.5 million Native Americans lived, were just as grim. The unemployment rate on the Pine Ridge reservation in South Dakota averaged nearly 80 percent. Although four times the size of Rhode Island, Pine Ridge offered few commercial services—there were no banks, hardware stores, or cloth-ing shops. The infant mortality rate ran five times the national average. By some estimates between 80 and 90 percent of the adult residents were alcoholics, and alcoholic-related diseases were the most common cause of death. Fifty percent of all crimes by adults on the reservation were linked to alcohol, but the Indian Health Service, the federal agency responsible for Indian health care, allocated only 3 percent of its budget to alcoholism treatment.

As some members of the middle class fell into poverty and others acquired wealth, the middle class shrank. According to some estimates, the middle class—families making between $20,000 and $60,000—dwindled from 53 percent of the nation in 1973 to 49 percent in 1985. After doubling between 1947 and 1973, median family income stagnated. In 1985 the average middle-class family earned less money than it did in 1973. Hardest hit were younger families, who feared that the American dream of rising prosperity would pass them by.

Homelessness   During the 1980s the wealthiest 1 percent of the American population saw a dramatic rise in their average incomes, while the poorest segments of society saw a decline in income. Increasing numbers of families were reported to be homeless in America, along with former psychiatric patients and drug users. (*Wide World Photos, Inc.*)

The Poverty Debate

Despite the social reality of a growing population of poor, many Americans clung to their vision of a classless society where everyone had the opportunity to succeed. How, then, could the contrast between affluence and poverty be explained? In the influential *Wealth and Poverty* (1981), George Gilder blamed the federal government, and Lyndon Johnson's war on poverty, for "erod[ing] work and family and thus keep[ing] poor people poor." Gilder argued that, in a classic case of unintended consequences, unemployment compensation promoted unemployment, affirmative action prevented African-Americans from realizing their full potential through competition, and welfare promoted dependency by discouraging the development of a healthy work ethic.

Gilder was joined by social scientist Charles Murray, whose best-selling *Losing Ground* (1984) became the conservative policy bible of the 1980s. Focusing primarily on Aid to Families with Dependent Children (AFDC), a public assistance program created during the New Deal and expanded during the 1960s and 1970s, Murray contended that welfare actually fostered dependency. Liberals, he charged, failed to realize that social inequality was a necessary part of capitalism. "Some people are better than others," he contended. "They deserve more of society's rewards, of which money is only one small part." No less influential were the claims that poverty and crime increased because of the expansion of welfare and that the number of female-headed black families increased because AFDC payments discouraged marriage.

Critics complained that Reagan, and the conservative intellectuals who provided the justification for his policies, oversimplified a complex problem, blaming the poor themselves for their own plight. They charged that poverty increased because the economy worsened after 1973. Real wages declined, productivity dropped, inflation soared, and unemployment rose. Reagan's policies accelerated the increase in homelessness, hunger, child poverty, and unemployment brought on by the larger economic crises of the 1970s and 1980s. The president's policies made the problem worse by redistributing income upward to those who needed it the least. His tax cuts offered the largest breaks to the wealthy. Meanwhile, regressive social security taxes, which taxed only the first $45,000 on income and wages, more than tripled over the decade. The result was that only the top 10 percent of the population received a significant net tax cut between 1977 and 1988; most of the other 90 percent paid a higher share of their incomes to Washington. At the extremes, the richest 1 percent got a net tax savings of 25 percent; the poorest 10 percent of workers saw 20 percent more of their incomes swallowed by taxes.

At the same time, Congress approved severe budgetary cuts in social programs that benefited the poor. In 1985 AFDC payments were down by $4.8 million, child nutrition support dropped by $5.2 billion, food stamps were cut by $6.8 billion, and low-income energy assistance plummeted by some $700 million. Extended unemployment insurance benefits coverage fell from 78 to 39 percent, and Reagan ended the Comprehensive Employment Training Program, an initiative that had employed 306,000 people. Liberals were especially critical of the administration's decision to cut federal subsidies to build or rehabilitate low-income housing from $32 billion to $7 billion. Although programs for low-income Americans accounted for one-tenth of the federal budget, they amounted to one-third of the total cuts in Reagan's 1987 budget. In *Rachel and Her Children* (1988), the journalist Jonathan Kozol suggested that the actions and behavior of the poor were not the only ones tested by poverty. "What of the behavior of a president who tells us that there is no hunger in the land," he queried, "while children die of diarrhea caused by malnutrition, or because their mothers were malnourished—both the consequence, at least in part, of policies he has advanced?"

The reasons for the growing disparity between wealth and poverty, however, went beyond the administration's policies and reflected deeper currents of change in American society. Most of the new jobs created during the decade were lower-paying service jobs. By 1985 there were more people flipping hamburgers at McDonalds for minimum wage than working in steel manufacturing—one of the cornerstones of America's industrial might. Between 1979 and 1984 six of ten jobs added to the U.S. labor market paid $7,000 a year or less. Most were in the service sector, as home health-care attendants, salesclerks, food servers, janitors, or office clerks. Besides low pay, these jobs offered few pension or health-care benefits, were often part-time or temporary, and held out few opportunities for promotion. As a result, real hourly wages declined 0.5 percent per year from 1982 to 1987.

In another classic case of unintended consequences, public and private efforts at urban renewal often exacerbated the problems of inner-city residents. In an attempt to revitalize crumbling downtown areas, city governments lured new high-tech industries to build office towers in areas where abandoned factories had once stood. In a parallel fashion, yuppies initiated a process of "gentrification," buying and renovating old homes in once-depressed neighborhoods. Federally subsidized expressways and commuter trains piped other highly educated workers into the city center during the day and out to bedroom communities at night. Together, these changes increased the cost of living in the cities, devastated the tax base that supported education and social services, and forced the poor into ever-smaller pockets of destitution.

Meanwhile, the marketplace underwent a process economists termed *globalization*. Rather than relying on domestic production for domestic consumption, American businesses more aggressively extended into the international market. Many domestic manufacturers moved their plants to underdeveloped countries in order to take advantage of the cheap labor they supplied. No less dramatic was the penetration of foreign goods in the American economy. Even as American corporations globalized, they found themselves challenged by an influx of foreign-manufactured goods. By the 1970s the United States began running exorbitant trade deficits as it imported more products than it exported. Japanese and

German corporations bought out American industries, and the steel and automotive sectors suffered tremendous decline.

In the rural regions of the South and Midwest automation revolutionized farm labor. The era of the independent small producer had been in decline for decades. But the last vestiges of independent family-owned operations suffered even more as they failed to compete in an international market. During the 1980s, after several robust decades of growth, farm prices fell, land values depreciated, and real interest rates remained high. Farm income had been slashed to one-third its value in the years between 1980 and 1985. Bank foreclosures followed in the wake of many farm families' attempts to produce more by taking loans to invest in more seed, stock, fertilizer, equipment, and land. By mid-decade unemployment in the Midwest was twice that of the nation at large. In the wake of these disasters, corporations bought up the land, consolidated production, and introduced fewer labor-intensive production technologies.

Finally, during the decade the number of union members declined from 24 million to less than 20 million, a 16 percent drop at a time when the work force expanded by 20 percent. At their peak during World War II, unions had represented 35 percent of the work force; by 1990, however, unions represented only 16 percent of the nation's 100 million workers. The decline was the result of intense global competition, renewed anti-union activity by management, and declining public support for unions. More than 10 million industrial jobs, many of them unionized, were lost primarily due to lower-wage foreign competition. The decline of once-powerful unions contributed to lower pay and less job security for millions of American workers and the erosion of real income for many living in the middle class. When unions represented a larger portion of the work force, they put forward a larger social agenda that benefited union and nonunion workers, such as social security, occupational safety, and health care. By the end of the decade, however, opponents effectively painted union members as agents for special interests, thus minimizing their bargaining power.

While conditions restricted the opportunity for most people to make money, expenses for basic necessities soared during the decade. A typical family home in 1984 absorbed 44 percent of the median family's yearly income, compared with 21 percent in 1973. Buying the average-priced car cost twenty-three weeks of pay in 1988. Ten years earlier it had cost eighteen weeks of pay.

American Apartheid

The celebration of wealth reinforced the ideal of America as a classless society united by a common commitment to prosperity. The social reality, however, revealed a nation deeply divided by class and racial conflict. In 1968 the Kerner Commission, appointed by President Lyndon Johnson to study the causes of racial rioting, had warned that the country was moving toward a bifurcated society, one white, one black, and neither equal to the other. By 1990 African-

Americans were more segregated than they had been before the civil-rights struggles of the 1960s. The sociologist Douglas Massey used the term *hypersegregation* to describe the profound level of racial segregation existing in major metropolitan areas in the United States. The metropolitan areas he studied—Baltimore, Chicago, Gary, Cleveland, Detroit, Los Angeles, Milwaukee, Newark, Philadelphia, and St. Louis—contained roughly one-quarter of the African-American population of the United States.

The dramatic movement of the white middle class from the central city to outlying suburbs exacerbated the growing physical disparity between the races. During the 1970s St. Louis, Cleveland, Pittsburgh, and Detroit lost more than 20 percent of their population. During the same period Philadelphia, Chicago, and New York City saw population drop by more than 10 percent. The movement of the white middle class to the suburbs accounted for much of the population loss. Between 1960 and 1990 the white population of New York fell by half. Between 1990 and 1995 both New York and Los Angeles lost more than 1 million native-born residents, even as their populations increased by roughly the same numbers with immigrants. The jobs followed the middle class to the suburbs. Between 1947 and 1982 factory employment in Chicago declined 59 percent, but surrounding Cook County experienced a 131 percent increase.

While much of the nation prospered during the 1980s, inner-city neighborhoods fell deeper into poverty and despair. Suburbanization, and the complex of public transportation and highways that made it viable, left behind decaying urban centers populated by poor blacks and recent immigrants. Between 1970 and 1985 New York City's minority population increased by more than 12 percent, Philadelphia's by 10 percent, and Detroit's by over 20 percent. By that time nearly 60 percent of all blacks in the United States lived in central cities of metropolitan areas, compared with 25 percent of all whites. In the urban centers of the Snow Belt—New York, Chicago, Detroit, Philadelphia, and Boston—77 percent of blacks lived in the city, but only 28 percent of whites. Poverty rates for inner cities soared from 12.7 to 19 percent during the decade. "In Chicago, there are neighborhoods where you can count up the number of bank branches and retailers that have closed up and five liquor stores have taken their place," observed a scholar. "You can clearly see neighborhoods shifting from working-class to hard-core poverty."

The physical distance between the races produced a growing trend toward racial segregation in the public schools. In the Northeast one-half of all African-American students attended schools where minorities made up 90 percent of the student body. In 1954 when the Supreme Court issued its decision in *Brown,* one in ten public school students was nonwhite; by 1990 the figure was one in three. Between 1975 and 1990 the percentage of white students in Philadelphia public schools dropped from 32 to 23. The drop was more dramatic in California: Pasadena saw its white student population plummet from 40 percent to 19 percent; Los Angeles, from 40 percent to 13 percent. "With more than 80 percent minority population, there's not much you can do," said a spokesman for New York City's public schools. The growth of Hispanic and Asian communities complicated the problem of desegregation. Urban classrooms in the 1980s, observed the *Boston Globe,* "are a sea of black and brown faces interrupted only by the occasional white child." Only the South, home of the highest proportion of blacks and site of the most ambitious desegregation plans, showed signs of progress.

The federal courts played the biggest role in slowing down desegregation. In *Milliken* v. *Bradley* (1974), the Supreme Court barred lawmakers from including the suburbs in metropolitanwide desegregation plans. The Reagan administration, however, believed the government should end its involvement in race-mixing in the schools. "The remedies we have been leaning on for a long time no longer serve a very useful purpose," declared a Reagan Justice Department official, which filed only three desegregation cases in its first seven years. By comparison, in 1966 alone the Johnson administration had filed thirty cases. "School districts no longer felt the hot breath of the Justice Department on their backs," complained a civil-rights attorney.

By now, many black leaders had lost enthusiasm for desegregation, frustrated over the slow pace of change and skeptical of the premise that blacks needed to attend school with whites to learn. Many civil-rights activists stressed the problem of class segregation: the white and black middle classes either moved to the suburbs or sent their children to private schools in the city. With the local tax base eroding, urban public schools lacked the resources to provide a quality education to their students. Numerous studies showed that minority schools were poorly equipped and had less experienced teachers, lower test scores, and a higher dropout rate.

Because of declining population, the cities saw their political power, both at the state and the federal levels, diminish. Reapportionment resulted in a dramatic decline in urban representation, especially in areas with large minority populations. In New York growing suburban communities such as Nassau and Suffolk Counties had as many representatives in the state legislature and the House of Representatives as did Manhattan and the Bronx. In both the state house and Congress urban influence waned at just the time that city leaders were forced to deal with overwhelming problems of homelessness, AIDS, and crime. As a consequence, state and federal resources shifted away from the city and toward the suburbs. In 1978 direct federal funding to cities equaled $10.2 billion, or about 16 percent of city revenues. In 1984 direct federal aid to cities had declined to $7 billion in inflation-adjusted terms, or 10 percent of city revenues.

The physical distance between city and suburb contributed to a growing racial divide in America on a number of issues. A poll commissioned by the NAACP Legal Defense and Educational Fund in January 1989 found that blacks and whites were "worlds apart" in their perception of race relations. Most whites believed that blacks were treated equally in America, while large numbers of blacks disagreed. Blacks, by an overwhelming majority, supported larger government with many services; whites preferred smaller government with fewer services. The ideological gap between blacks and whites created "wedge issues" that allowed Republicans to focus on taxation, welfare spending, and the general role of government in ways that split the Democratic coalition along racial lines. "Direct appeals to racial prejudice may no longer be acceptable in American politics, but race, in an indirect and sometimes subliminal way, remains a strong undercurrent in presidential politics and a driving force in the battle today between Republicans and Democrats," concluded the journalist Thomas Edsall.

During the 1980s Americans engaged in an angry culture war over issues such as abortion, gay rights, and immigration, but they formed a broad consensus in support of the new consumerism. Everyone from the president to Hollywood producers to religious preachers praised the healing power of prosperity. After the slow-growing 1970s, expectations ran high that economic growth would end the scourge of poverty, guarantee opportunity to all citizens, and help bring Americans closer together. Once again, however, expectations clashed with social realities. In a classic example of the American paradox, the "culture of greed" that pervaded the decade produced a greater gap between rich and poor, increased the number of homeless and poor, and widened the racial divide in America.

SELECTED READINGS

▌ James Steward's *Den of Thieves* is an account of the shady dealings in the financial markets during the 1980s. Connie Bruck's *The Predators' Ball* (1988) details the world of the junk bond traders. Allan Murray's *Showdown at Gucci Gulch* (1987) explains the influence such financiers had on government during the decade. Nicolaus Mills's *Culture in an Age of Money* (1990) criticizes the influence of corporations and wealth on American culture during the 1980s. Barbara Ehrenreich studies the insecurities over wealth and status that preoccupied much of the middle class in her *Fear of Falling* (1989).

▌ Kevin Phillips attacks the growth of economic inequality in the 1980s in *The Politics of Rich and Poor* (1990). Thomas Edsall explains the political motivations for attacking the poor in *The New Politics of Inequality* (1984). Leslie Dunbar analyzes the impact of Reagan's economic policies on minorities in *Minority Report* (1984), while William Julius Wilson's *The Truly Disadvantaged* (1987) studies the effects of Reaganomics in the inner cities. The war on welfare is exposed in Michael Katz's *The Undeserving Poor* (1989).

16

The End of the Cold War, 1988–1992

S ince construction in 1961, the Berlin Wall stood as a harsh physical emblem of the Cold War. The harrowing images of barbed wire and watchtowers, vast minefields, snarling patrol dogs, and well-armed sentries served as a stark reminder of a divided Berlin, of two Germanys, and of a world separated East from West. But shortly after midnight on November 9, 1989, East Germany's communist government yielded to growing demands for freedom, and increased pressure from the reform-minded Soviet leader Mikhail Gorbachev, by opening the Berlin Wall, thereby symbolically raising the Iron Curtain and elevating hopes for an end to the Cold War.

Thousands of people on both sides of the wall gathered to celebrate the moment. "We are all Germans," the crowd shouted. People danced in the streets and cars honked their horns as hammer-wielding Berliners climbed atop the wall to pound away at its concrete surface. "I want to go across. We have waited for this so long," exclaimed a West Berlin resident who was fighting back tears. Jubilant Germans hung a banner on the wall: "Stalin is Dead, Europe lives." At Checkpoint Charlie, which separated the American and Soviet zones, small groups of Berliners walked across the white line that had divided East and West for forty years. The police made no attempt to stifle the celebrations or to block the movement from East to West. "They just let us go," said a shocked East Berlin woman as she set foot on western soil. "I can't believe it."

The unfilled promises of the Reagan administration haunted the presidency of George Bush. When he assumed the reins of power in 1989, Bush confronted a world transformed by the dissolution of the Soviet Union and the end of the Cold War. The threat of a superpower conflict receded, but Iraq's Saddam Hussein reminded Americans that the post–Cold War

Fall of the Berlin Wall A symbolic reminder of the division between East and West Berlin came crashing down in November 1989. As Berliners from both sides of the divide celebrated, people poured freely through the opening for the first time in decades. (*Wide World Photos, Inc.*)

world was not devoid of danger. While President Bush successfully rallied world opinion and American military might in the Gulf War, he failed to exercise similar leadership in confronting the American paradox of rising expectations. He faced a difficult problem: Ronald Reagan had bequeathed to his successor a federal government crippled by massive deficits and a public demanding increased spending on education, health, and the environment. Over the next four years Bush struggled to develop a consistent message that would satisfy public expectations of government without raising taxes. He failed. In 1992 the voters rejected Bush in favor of the tempered liberalism of Arkansas governor Bill Clinton.

The Search for Reagan's Successor

Since the Twenty-second Amendment to the Constitution barred Reagan from seeking a third term, the GOP faced the difficult task of choosing a candidate who would continue his policies. The logical choice was George Bush, who had served as Reagan's loyal vice president for the previous eight years. Bush, however, was not conservative enough for many party members, who instead rallied around two formidable primary opponents: televangelist Pat Robertson and Kansas senator Robert Dole. After a slow start Bush gathered both endorsements and votes in securing the nomination.

Polls showed that most Republicans supported Bush because of his close association with the popular president, but in many ways he was a very different politician. Reagan was a conservative ideologue who understood the power of television and the importance of using symbols and rhetoric to sway voters. Bush was a political pragmatist, uncomfortable with the media and shy about articulating broad themes. As a result, most Republicans, and a majority of Americans, lacked a clear image of Bush. Was he a moderate who disguised his views out of loyalty to Reagan? Or was he a true Reagan disciple who could be trusted to fulfill the conservative agenda?

Bush's career had done little to clarify his ideological leanings, and his success had depended on an ability to skirt the party's ideological divisions. The son of a wealthy New England family, Bush joined the navy in 1942, earning the Distinguished Flying Cross after his plane was shot down in the South Pacific. Bush returned home after the war, graduated from Yale University, and moved to Midland, Texas, where he used family connections to make millions in the booming oil business. In 1964 he ran for the Senate as a "Goldwater Republican" who opposed the Civil Rights Act of 1964. He lost the election, but two years later, campaigning as a moderate, he earned a seat in Congress. Over the next few years he established his independence, voting for a controversial open-housing bill. "A man should not have a door slammed in his face because he is a Negro or speaks with a Latin American accent," he told a hostile white audience.

During the 1970s as conservatives were regaining a foothold in the party, Bush served in a number of appointive posts, including director of the Central Intelligence Agency (CIA). However, when he campaigned for the presidency in 1980, it was as a moderate; at one point he dismissed Reagan's recovery plan as "voodoo economics." Bush then spent the next eight years defending those same policies, often selling them to a skeptical Congress. "I'm for Mr. Reagan—blindly," he said in an awkward moment in 1984.

Bush faced a difficult political balancing act. Though Reagan remained as popular as ever, the same could not be said for the Republican Party or for the conservative ideas that had allowed him to gain power. In 1989 pollsters found that 55 percent of Americans believed the nation was on the "wrong track"; only 36 percent said it was on the "right track." A series of public scandals on Wall Street, combined with embarrassing revelations that former Reagan aides had used their government connections to reap millions as lobbyists and consultants, eroded Republicans' claims that they cared for "common people." Most Americans viewed the Republican Party as the captive of special interests that catered to the wealthy.

By the end of the decade organized opposition to Reagan's antigovernment message showed new signs of life, complicating Bush's political task. Membership in the ten largest environmental groups, including the Sierra Club and the World Wildlife Fund, increased from 3.3 million in 1985 to 7.2 million in 1990. Their growth reflected widespread public support for the environment. A 1990 poll revealed that 74 percent of Americans believed that "protecting the environment is so important that requirements and standards cannot be too high, and continuing environmental improvements must be made regardless of cost." Labor made gains by recruiting public workers and by recruiting members in the growing service sector of the economy. Between 1980 and 1992 the Service Employees International Union, for example, increased its membership by four hundred thousand.

In his acceptance speech at the Republican convention in July 1988, Bush tried to articulate a message that would retain the loyalty of Reagan conservatives without alienating the growing number of moderates. In an effort to energize the party's conservative faithful, Bush promised to continue the fight against terrorism abroad and big government at home. The centerpiece of the speech was a dramatic and carefully scripted promise not to raise taxes. "Read my lips," he said. "No new taxes." The vice president also appealed to moderates by emphasizing his support for education and the environment. In a move that puzzled observers, and many of his closest advisers, Bush picked the untested and lightly regarded Dan Quayle, a conservative senator from Indiana, as his running mate.

The Democrats had a difficult time finding a nominee to challenge Bush. The party's front-runner, Colorado senator Gary Hart, quit the race after reporters disclosed that he was having an affair with a woman other than his wife. Michael Dukakis, the Greek-American governor of Massachusetts, moved to fill the void created by Hart's absence. Dukakis and Hart shared a belief that the Democratic Party had moved too far to the left since the 1960s. Dukakis warned that the party should "break with the past." During the primaries Dukakis bragged about his success in creating jobs and lowering taxes in his home state, a success labeled "Massachusetts miracle." He promised "good jobs at good wages," clean air, child care, and increased federal support for education, but he never suggested how the additional spending would affect the deficit.

Dukakis faced a spirited challenge from African-American civil-rights leader Jesse Jackson, who appealed to the party's traditional liberal base. Trying to stitch together "a quilt" of mutual interests among poor and working-class whites, blacks and Hispanics, Jackson called for increased government spending for social programs to help the poor and working class. He combined old-fashioned liberalism with a powerful social message. Traveling to the poorest inner-city neighborhoods, he told children to stay in school, shun drugs, vote, and respect themselves and each other.

Jackson won some important primaries, but in the end Dukakis's moderate message and well-oiled organization won more. Nominated at the Democratic convention in August, Dukakis tried to skirt the sensitive social issues that had divided the party since the 1960s by declaring that the campaign was about "competence, not ideology." To underscore his new centrist message, he chose conservative Texas senator Lloyd Bentsen as his running mate.

The fall contest between Dukakis and Bush degenerated into one of the most negative campaigns in modern times. With polls showing the Republican ticket trailing Dukakis by more than 20 points, Bush campaign manager Lee Atwater convinced the vice president that the only way he could win was to tar the Democrats with the stigma of social liberalism, to turn the campaign into a battle for the cultural legacy of the 1960s. On cue, the Bush campaign concentrated on convincing the public that Dukakis was soft on crime, unpatriotic and weak on defense, and antagonistic to family values. Dukakis's membership in the American Civil Liberties Union (ACLU) became a device for highlighting the candidate's secularism, and the governor's opposition to requiring school children to recite the Pledge of Allegiance became shorthand for questioning Dukakis's patriotism.

The Republicans realized that their success depended on maintaining the support of the white middle class. While appealing to their fears of big government and high taxes, Bush also exploited racial tensions. Bush's most effective advertisement told voters about Willie Horton, an African-American who had raped a white woman while on leave from a Massachusetts prison while Dukakis was governor. "Dukakis furlough program," the announcer says as the camera shows hardened inmates streaming through a revolving door. Many escaped and "many are at large," he intones; now Dukakis "says he wants to do for America what he's done for Massachusetts." Commentators were shocked by the blatant racial appeal. "This is not racism in a sheet and a hood," noted journalist Tom Wicker; "it is race consciousness in a white as well as a blue collar." Republican strategists, however, understood the political potential of mining Americas' deep racial divide. "If I can make Willie Horton a household name," said Bush's campaign manager Lee Atwater, "we'll win the election."

Dukakis responded defensively to these potent ideological charges. While Bush appealed to the values of the white middle class, Dukakis tried to connect to their pocketbooks. He traveled the country offering detailed proposals for student aid, health care, and a jobs program. "In effect," noted the *New York Times,* "Mr. Dukakis is trying to bury the Pledge of Allegiance and his A.C.L.U. membership card under a mound of policy." Bush responded that "competence makes the trains run on time but doesn't know where they're going. . . . The truth is, this election is about the beliefs we share, the values that we honor and the principles we hold dear." By late October Gallup reported a "stunning turnaround" in the polls.

On election day Bush became the first sitting vice president since Martin Van Buren in 1836 to be elected directly to the presidency. Bush won 53.4 percent of the popular vote and carried forty states with 426 electoral votes. Dukakis won only ten states and the District of Columbia for a total of 112 electoral votes and 45.6 percent of the popular vote. The Democrats, however, managed to increase their margins in Congress, where they held an 89-vote advantage in the House and 56 of 100 seats in the Senate.

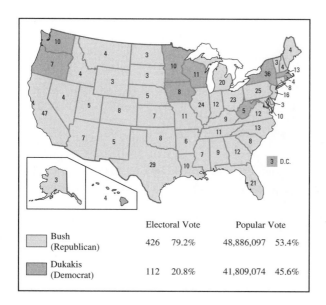

The Election of 1988 As vice president under Reagan, George Bush promised to continue the peace and prosperity he helped to create. At the same time he attacked his opponent, Massachusetts Governor Michael Dukakis, for releasing prisoners on furloughs, which left them free to commit greater crimes.

	Electoral Vote		Popular Vote	
Bush (Republican)	426	79.2%	48,886,097	53.4%
Dukakis (Democrat)	112	20.8%	41,809,074	45.6%

1989: The Year of Miracles

In 1989 as Bush was settling into office, Lech Walesa, a Polish shipyard electrician, led the Solidarity trade union movement in a series of strikes that crippled Poland's Soviet-controlled government. Gorbachev refused to use the military to quell the uprising, and he instructed the puppet regime to negotiate with the reformers. The result was an agreement to hold free elections in 1990—the first free elections in Poland in sixty-eight years. The winds of revolution blew rapidly from Poland to other Soviet-bloc countries. In Hungary reformers adopted a new constitution, called for elections, and disbanded the Communist party. In Czechoslovakia playwright and populist Václav Havel helped orchestrate a "velvet revolution" that resulted in the resignation of the Soviet-installed regime and free elections that carried Havel to the presidency. The most dramatic events were occurring in East Germany. On November 9 the Communist party announced that residents of East Berlin were free to leave the country. The Berlin Wall, the ultimate symbol of Cold War division, had suddenly been rendered irrelevant.

The revolutionary fervor was not confined to communist regimes in Eastern Europe but soon swept into the Soviet Union itself. The Baltic states—Estonia, Latvia, and Lithuania—had lived under Soviet rule since 1939 when Joseph Stalin seized control as part of the Nazi-Soviet pact. In December 1989 the Lithuanian Communist party formally broke ties with the Soviet Union. The following year Lithuania and Latvia declared their independence. Meanwhile, in March 1989 the Soviet Union held its first free elections since 1917. Hundreds of party officials went down in defeat.

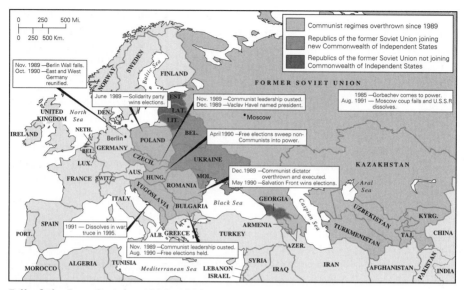

Fall of the Iron Curtain, 1989–1992 To promote economic advancement at home, Soviet premier Mikhail Gorbachev understood the necessity of normalizing international relations. Promising more openness (*glasnost*) for Eastern Europe, Gorbachev announced in December 1988 that hundreds of thousands of Soviet troops would be pulled from the region and emphasized the need for each nation to form their own political ideology. After fifty years of repressive communist rule, Eastern Europeans saw this as a chance for complete independence. Poland initiated the change in June 1989 when the people rejected the Communist party in national elections. After Poland, the rest of Eastern Europe quickly followed suit, with Romania and Czechoslovakia ousting their communist regimes in 1989. The most memorable of the 1989 revolutions occurred in East Germany, when the Berlin Wall fell. By early 1992, the movement for independence had consumed the former Soviet Union, leading to the creation of independent nations, loosely joined in the Commonwealth of Independent States.

All of these changes were too much for party hard-liners in the Soviet hierarchy; they staged a coup in August 1991. With Gorbachev held under house arrest, a defiant Boris Yeltsin, the newly elected chairman of the Russian parliament, thwarted the coup by rallying protesters and facing down the powerful Russian army. Gorbachev survived the failed coup, but Yeltsin emerged as the most powerful force for reform. By the end of the year Russia proclaimed its independence from Soviet control and, along with Ukraine and Byelorussia (now Belarus), formed the Commonwealth of Independent States. On Christmas Day 1991 a weary Gorbachev resigned as president of the Union of Soviet Socialist Republics that had ceased to exist.

Throughout the year the United States played the role of a cheering but cautious spectator. Bush and Secretary of State James A. Baker III, a fellow Texan, watched from the sidelines as the startling events in Europe and the Soviet Union unfolded. The United States found itself in an awkward position: since the beginning of the Cold War it had provided rhetorical support for prodemocracy movements in the Soviet bloc, but at the moment when the democracy movements were succeeding, U.S. leaders offered only tepid praise. Why? The administration did not want to undermine relations with Gorbachev by appearing to exploit his troubles. Moreover, U.S. policy makers feared instability in the region. Who would control the powerful Soviet nuclear arsenal if the nation fragmented into a number of small, independent republics? "Whatever the course, however long the process took, and whatever its outcome," Bush later reflected, "I wanted to see stable, and above all peaceful, change."

The unraveling of the Soviet Union offered an opportunity to continue the progress in arms control that had begun in the final years of the Reagan administration. In 1989 Bush announced that it was time to "move beyond containment" by integrating the Soviet Union into "the community of nations." The following year the North Atlantic Treaty Organization (NATO) and the Warsaw Pact agreed to the biggest weapons cut in history. The Accord on Conventional Forces in Europe slashed the Warsaw Pact's weapons by more than 50 percent and NATO's by 10 percent. With the Soviet threat diminished, the Pentagon announced the largest U.S. troop cut in Europe since 1948, with an initial pullback of 40,000 personnel. Bush and Gorbachev signed agreements to open trade, expand cultural exchanges, and reduce chemical weapons. The two leaders signed the Strategic Arms Reduction Talks (START I) treaty, which cut their countries' strategic nuclear forces in half—an agreement that had seemed unimaginable just a few years earlier. Two years later Bush and Yeltsin came to terms on a START II agreement that called for further cuts and for the elimination of deadly multiple-warhead intercontinental missiles by the year 2003. The Cold War was over.

The New World Order

President Bush declared that the end of the Cold War heralded a "new world order" in which the United States was the only superpower, the rule of law had to govern relations between nations, and the powerful had to protect the weak. In some ways this optimism seemed justified. In a globe no longer dominated by Cold War confrontations, the prospect for resolving local disputes brightened. In South Africa U.S.–imposed economic sanctions pressured newly elected President Frederik W. de Klerk to dismantle apartheid, by which whites had dominated the black majority for forty-two years. Along with lifting the government's ban on antiapartheid organizations, de Klerk freed African National Conference deputy president Nelson Mandela, seventy-one, who was serving the twenty-seventh year of a life prison term. A symbol of resistance to apartheid, Mandela showed that imprisonment had not tempered his commitment to black majority rule. "Power! Power! Africa is ours!" he chanted in his first public appearance following his release. In April 1994 Mandela easily won election as South Africa's first black president.

In Latin America the end of the Cold War coincided with the demise of a number of authoritarian regimes. In Chile General Augusto Pinochet, the last military dictator in South America, turned over power to the elected president, Patricio Aylwin. In Brazil Fernando Collor de Mello took office as the first directly elected president since a 1964 military coup. In Haiti a leftist Roman Catholic priest, Father Jean-Bertrand Aristide, swept that nation's first fully free democratic election for president. Elsewhere in Latin America shaky experiments in democracy showed signs of growing stability. In Nicaragua newspaper publisher Violeta Barrios de Chamorro defeated Marxist president Daniel Ortega in a peaceful election, ending a decade of leftist Sandinista rule. In El Salvador the moderate government and opposition leaders signed a peace treaty early in 1992. The treaty provided for expansive reforms and ended the twelve-year civil war that had left 75,000 dead.

With the threat of Soviet influence in the region diminished, the Bush administration focused its attention on international drug sales, which the president referred to as "the gravest domestic threat facing our nation today." Though many nations were implicated in the drug trade, the administration identified Panamanian dictator General Manuel Noriega as the worst outlaw. During the 1980s American officials ignored Noriega's notorious cocaine trading because he was a CIA informer viewed as an ally in the larger battle to prevent communist infiltration. With that threat removed, American officials decided to move against him, cutting off aid and freezing Panamanian assets in the United States. When Noriega nullified the results of free elections in Panama, Bush urged the Panamanian people to overthrow him. The revolt failed to materialize, and soon after, when soldiers loyal to Noriega killed an American marine, Bush launched Operation Just Cause. On December 20, 1989, more than 22,000 U.S. troops, backed by gunships and fighter planes, invaded Panama in the largest military operation since the Vietnam War. After two days of intense fighting, Noriega's resistance crumbled and he sought asylum at the Vatican's diplomatic mission in Panama City. On January 3, 1990, he surrendered and was flown to Florida, where he faced trial for drug-related crimes and became the first former or current head of state to be convicted by an American jury.

The end of the Cold War also improved relations in the Middle East. No longer fearing Soviet influence in the region, and less concerned about offending Israel, the United States applied pressure on both Palestinian head Yasir Arafat and Israeli leader Yitzhak Rabin to work toward stability. Secretary Baker engaged in a new round of shuttle diplomacy, traveling to the Middle East eight times in 1991 to arrange negotiations in 1992. After more than a year of secret discussions, Arafat and Rabin traveled to Washington in September 1993 to sign a declaration of principles that allowed for eventual Palestinian self-rule in the Gaza Strip and the West bank.

Only China seemed to buck the trend toward greater openness in the post–Cold War era. Bush, who had served briefly as ambassador to China under Richard Nixon, came to office confident that he understood Chinese leaders and could help promote closer economic ties while also encouraging the aging Chinese leadership to enact democratic reforms. His plan suffered a stunning setback in the spring of 1989 when the Chinese army brutally crushed a prodemocracy demonstration in Beijing's Tiananmen Square, killing an estimated four to eight hundred young men and women. A wave of repression, arrests, and public executions followed. The assault, covered extensively by American television, outraged the public and exposed an underlying tension in America's attitude toward the post–Cold War world: Should the United States emphasize its moral leadership by taking action against nations that failed to live up to American

Protest in Tiananmen Square, June 5, 1989   Demands for reform in China simmered just below the surface until Hu Yaobang, former general secretary of the Chinese Communist Party and free speech sympathizer, died in April 1989. University students across the country held peaceful demonstrations in memory of Hu Yaobang, and in Beijing the actions turned into an opportunity to demand greater freedom. Demonstrations continued, and on May 13, students began a hunger strike in Tiananmen Square, despite the government's order to stop the demonstrations and the declaration of martial law. In early June, the government sent troops into the square to remove the protesters, ordering them to use all force necessary. On June 5, a journalist captured this scene of a lone civilian momentarily barring the progress of the tanks in the square, becoming a symbol to people around the world of the tenacious desire for reform in China. It is unclear what happened to the man in the photograph after onlookers pulled him out of the way of the tanks, but soldiers killed and wounded thousands during the several days it took to clear the square. The protest did not bring immediate change but rather a crackdown by the Chinese government, which arrested and executed an untold number of prodemocracy activists in the months following the demonstrations.

standards of human rights, or should it restrict itself to more practical questions of national security?

An unusual coalition of liberals and conservatives wanted the administration to punish China for its repression by imposing economic sanctions and denying it special trading privileges that promoted economic relations. Many business groups, however, warned that sanctions would be counterproductive since they would alienate China, thereby limiting American influence and allowing Europeans to capture the lucrative and expanding Chinese market. Bush waffled on the question. Three days after the massacre he suspended military sales to China and declared that normal relations could not be established until Chinese leaders "recognize the validity of the prodemocracy movement." Within weeks, however, he sent his national security adviser to China and began a gradual move toward normal relations.

War with Iraq

On August 2, 1990, elite Iraqi army troops smashed across the border of Kuwait and roared down a six-lane superhighway for Kuwait City, 80 miles away. Residents of the Kuwaiti capital city were awakened by blasts of rockets and gunfire. "Hurry to our aid," pleaded a voice over state radio. Then the transmitter went dead. Iraqi leader Saddam Hussein, who had just ended a bloody eight-year war with neighboring Iran, justified the invasion by claiming that Kuwait had been illegally carved away from Iraq by British imperial agents in the 1920s. The justification masked a more pressing concern, however. Hussein had nearly bankrupted his country in his war with Iran and now needed Kuwait's huge oil reserves to pay the bills.

President Bush saw the invasion as a direct challenge to U.S. leadership in the post–Cold War world. "This must be reversed," he announced after learning of the attack. His advisers spelled out how the invasion threatened American interests in the region: it would give the unpredictable Hussein control over vast quantities of valuable Kuwaiti oil reserves. Hussein could use the oil revenue to develop nuclear weapons to intimidate American allies in the region, especially Israel and Saudi Arabia. Over the next few months, in an impressive display of international diplomacy, Bush rallied world opinion against "Saddam." The UN Security Council passed resolutions to impose economic sanctions against Iraq in an effort to force it out of Kuwait. In November, after Hussein showed no signs of retreat, the Security Council authorized use of force for the first time since the Korean War, giving Hussein a deadline of January 15, 1991, to pull out of Kuwait or face military action.

To underscore the U.S. commitment, Bush sent thousands of American troops to the Persian Gulf region as part of an international force. By the end of August cargo planes, flying as many as three hundred missions a day, had shuttled 72,000 military personnel and 100,000 tons of military cargo to the gulf. By January the multinational troop strength reached 690,000 troops, representing twenty-eight nations.

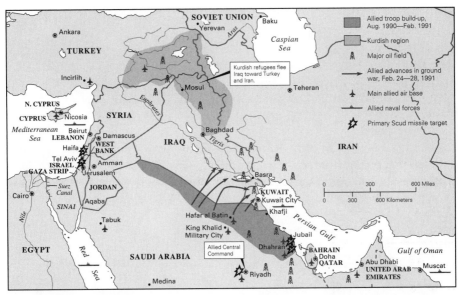

The Gulf War   Beginning with a six-week war in January 1991, Allied forces attacked targets across Iraq and then sent in ground troops under the leadership of General H. Norman Schwarzkopf. Within three days of the ground assault's commencement, Iraqi soldiers were in full retreat or surrender. The war resulted in the dismembering of the Iraqi army, the liberation of Kuwait, and the movement of Kurdish refugees toward Turkey and Iran.

PRIMARY SOURCE

16.1 | *Congress Debates War or Peace with Iraq*

In January 1991 President Bush asked Congress to approve a joint resolution allowing the use of American troops to repel the Iraqi invasion of Kuwait. The debate in Congress, which lasted three days, reflected the division among American citizens on the issue of American military intervention. Supporters of the resolution in Congress, most of them Republicans, argued that force had to be used to return peace to the region; Democrats insisted that economic sanctions, meant to punish Iraq until it left Kuwait, should be given more time to prove their effectiveness.

Voices in Favor of War with Iraq

(Representative Robert H. Michel, R-Illinois) I speak from the prejudice of being a combat veteran of World War II. And those of our generation know from bloody experience that unchecked aggression against a small nation is a prelude
5   to an international disaster.

Saddam Hussein today has more planes and tanks and, frankly, men under arms, than Hitler had at the time when Prime Minister Chamberlain came back

Impact of War After Iraq's invasion of Kuwait on August 2, 1990, President Bush deployed more than 400,000 troops to Saudi Arabia in an attempt to force Iraq's withdrawal from its neighbor. Each American soldier sent to the Gulf left behind family and friends, as was the case with Army Specialist Hollie Vallance, seen here saying goodbye to her husband and seven-week-old daughter. (© *Allen Horne, Courtesy of the Columbus Ledger, Columbus, Georgia.*)

from Munich with that miserable piece of paper—peace in our time. I'll never forget that replay of that movie in my life.

10   And I have an obligation, I guess, coming from that generation, to transmit those thoughts I had at the time to the younger generation who didn't experience what we did. Saddam Hussein not only invaded Kuwait, he occupied, terrorized, murdered civilians, systematically looted and turned a peaceful nation into a waste-land of horror. He seeks control over one of the world's vital resources, and he ulti-

15 mately seeks to make himself the unchallenged anti-Western dictator of the Mideast.
    Either we stop him now, and stop him permanently, or we won't stop him at all.

(*Senator Orrin G. Hatch, R-Utah*) Unless Saddam Hussein believes that the threat of war is real, he will not budge. I think we've learned that. The only way to avoid war, in my opinion in this particular situation, is to be prepared to go to

20 war and to show that our resolve is for real. . . . Our actions should be decisive.

(*Senator William V. Roth Jr., R-Delaware*) One can only imagine what devas-tating consequence would fall should his dominance be allowed in the oil-rich

Middle East. And this is the second reason why he must be stopped. When I speak of the danger that would result from his control of this region, I'm not talking
25 about consequences to major oil companies—quite simply, I'm talking about jobs. I'm talking about the raw material of human endeavor.

Oil runs the economy of the world. It fuels our factories, heats our homes. Carries our products from manufacture to market. It's as basic to the economy as water is to life. And the free trade of international supplies is critical, not only for
30 the industrial democracies, but the fragile third world nations that depend on this precious resource even more than we do.

Any attempt to disrupt these supplies will send a devastating quake to these economies, lengthening unemployment lines, boosting inflation in the industrial democracies and crushing the economies of developing countries where day to
35 day existence depends on imported energy sources.

Voices in Dissent

(Senator George J. Mitchell, D-Maine) This is not a debate about whether force should ever be used. No one proposes to rule out the use of force; we cannot and should not rule it out. The question is should war be truly a last resort when all
40 other means fail or should we start with war, before other means have been fully and fairly exhausted.

This is not a debate about American objectives in the current crisis. There is broad agreement in the Senate that Iraq must fully and unconditionally withdraw its forces from Kuwait. The issue is how best to achieve that goal. Most Americans
45 and most members of Congress, myself included, supported the President's initial decision to deploy American forces to Saudi Arabia to deter further Iraqi aggression. We supported the President's effort in marshaling international diplomatic pressure and the most comprehensive embargo in history against Iraq.

Despite the fact that his own policy of international economic sanctions was
50 having a significant effect upon the Iraqi economy, the President, without explanation, abandoned that approach and instead adopted a policy based first and foremost upon the use of American military force. As a result, this country has been placed on a course toward war. This has upset the balance of the President's initial policy, the balance between resources and responsibility, between interest
55 and risk, between patience and strength.

(Senator Paul D. Wellstone, D-Minnesota) I never thought that the first time I would have an opportunity to speak in this chamber the topic would be such a grave topic—life and death, whether or not to go to war, to ask America's men and women, so many of them so young, to risk life and limb, to unleash a tremendous destructive
60 power on a foreign country and a far away people. This is the most momentous decision that any political leader would ever have to make and decide we must.

And let no one doubt that the Congress has the responsibility to make this decision. The Constitution is unambiguous on this point: Congress declares the war, not the President.
65 The policies that I am afraid the Administration is pursuing, the rush to war that I am afraid is so much of what is now happening in our country and the

world, will not create a new order, Mr. President, it will create a new world disorder. What kind of victory will it be? What kind of victory will it be if we unleash forces of fanaticism in the Middle East and a chronically unstable region becomes
70 even more unstable further jeopardizing Israel's security?

Some causes are worth fighting for, some causes are worth fighting for. This cause is not worth fighting for right now. We must stay the course with economic sanctions, continue the pressure, continue the squeeze, move forward on the diplomatic front and Mr. President, we must not, we must not rush to war.

75 *(Senator Edward M. Kennedy, D-Massachusetts)* I urge the Senate to vote for peace, not war. Now is not the time for war. I reject the argument that says Congress must support the President, right or wrong. We have our own responsibility to do what is right, and I believe that war today is wrong.

War is not the only option left to us in the Persian Gulf. . . . Sanctions and
80 diplomacy may still achieve our objectives, and Congress has the responsibility to insure that all peaceful options are exhausted before resort to war. . . .

Let there be no mistake about the cost of war. We have arrayed an impressive international coalition against Iraq, but when the bullets start flying, 90 percent of the casualties will be Americans. It is hardly a surprise that so many other
85 nations are willing to fight to the last American to achieve the goals of the United Nations. It is not their sons and daughters who will do the dying. . . .

Not a single American life should be sacrificed in a war for the price of oil. Not a single drop of American blood should be spilled because American automobiles burn too many drops of oil a mile; not a single American soldier should
90 lose his life in the Persian Gulf because America has no energy policy worthy of the name to reduce our dependence on foreign oil. ■■■

While rallying international opinion against Iraq, Bush confronted the difficult task of convincing the American people to go to war to expel Hussein from Kuwait. The administration faced an uphill battle. Polls showed a majority of Americans opposed; most wanted to continue relying on economic sanctions even if they failed to prod the Iraqis out of Kuwait. In January as the deadline for military action approached, the Senate and the House vigorously debated a joint resolution that would authorize the use of military force. Opponents urged the president to give the economic sanctions more time to force Iraq out, and they warned of the bloody cost of a drawn-out ground war against Hussein's large army. Many doubted that the invasion represented a threat to American interests. "All that's happened is that one nasty little country invaded a littler but just as nasty country," declared an influential senator. In the end, however, strong lobbying from the administration and a unified Republican Party pushed the resolution through the Senate by a narrow 52–47 margin and in the House by a more comfortable 250–183 margin.

Armed with congressional approval and sustained by strong international support, the president started the war on January 16 with a massive and sustained air assault. For nearly six weeks three thousand daily sorties pounded Iraqi troops, supply depots, and command and communications targets. On February 23 the allies under the command of U.S. general H. Norman Schwarzkopf launched a ground offensive that forced Iraqi troops out of Kuwait in less than one hundred hours. Iraqi soldiers surrendered in droves. U.S. forces lost only 184, compared with nearly 100,000 Iraqi deaths, most of them casualties of the bombing. On February 27 coalition forces liberated Kuwait and the president called off the attack, leaving a vanquished but defiant Saddam Hussein in power.

The Pentagon, still scarred from the media's critical coverage of the Vietnam War, imposed tough new restrictions on the press covering the war. On the ground in Saudi Arabia the military forced reporters to travel with escorts and exercised control over all reports from the gulf. According to a *New York Times* reporter, the Pentagon's tight controls, coupled with the media's limited access to independent information, essentially turned each journalist into "an unpaid employee of the Department of Defense." At televised press conferences military spokesman talked directly to the American people, bypassing the media filter. The briefings, commented a military spokesman, were "the most significant part of the whole operation [because] for the first time ever . . . the American people were getting their information from the government—not from the press."

Despite their reservations about the war, Americans instinctively rallied around the troops once the fighting began. Unlike during coverage of Vietnam, Americans saw virtually no blood or death on their television screens. The victory produced an outpouring of patriotism and renewed faith in the military and its leaders that had been tarnished since Vietnam. It made heroes of military leaders, especially Schwarzkopf and Colin Powell, the first African-American to serve as chairman of the Joint Chiefs of Staff. "By God, we've licked the Vietnam syndrome once and for all," Bush told a national television audience. The president reaped much of the credit for the operation. His approval rating shot to 89 percent—the highest ever recorded for a president up to that time.

Problems on the Home Front

Ironically, Bush's success in the Gulf War may have contributed to his political problems at home, which had begun soon after he took office. With the Cold War over, and with no clear foreign threat to distract them, Americans focused more attention on a stagnant economy. "We did not realize how much we had been leaning on the Berlin Wall until we tore it down," said one White House aide. While the president scored high marks for his adroit handling of the international scene, he never articulated a clear domestic agenda.

After only a few weeks in office he angered voters and enraged conservatives by disavowing his "no new taxes" pledge. "I've started going into the numbers, finally," Bush said referring to the federal deficit, "and they're enormous." In 1990 Bush agreed to a deficit-reduction compromise with congressional Democrats that included $133 billion in new taxes. Reversing the Reagan-era tax policies, the new legislation increased the top bracket from 27 percent to 31 percent, removed some exemptions used by high-income people, and increased "sin taxes" on cigarettes and alcohol. Most observers agreed with the decision to raise taxes, but few were convinced that Bush only learned after the election of the need to do so. The *New York Post*'s front page screamed the reaction—"READ MY LIPS: I LIED."

The deficit package failed to stem the fiscal hemorrhaging. The federal deficit continued its upward spiral to $290 billion in 1992, with forecasters predicting it would rise to $331 billion in 1993. The government was spending $200 billion per year—15 percent of all spending—to pay interest on debt. The added spending weighed down the rest of the economy, which after seven booming years began to sputter. While the gross national product increased at an anemic 2.2 percent, unemployment crept upward, housing starts dropped, and consumer confidence hit new lows. By 1992 Bush's approval rating sagged to 34 percent, with fewer than 20 percent of the public approving his handling of the economy. Voters clamored for the president to take decisive action to revive the ailing economy, but Bush and his advisers decided to take a hands-off approach. "I don't think it's the end of the world even if we have a recession," said Treasury secretary Nicholas Brady. "We'll pull out of it again. No big deal."

Polls showed that Americans wanted more government involvement not only in economic matters but also in issues ranging from education to health care, but the president's hands were tied by the huge budget deficit left over from the Reagan years. Bush did sign one meaningful piece of legislation—the Americans with Disabilities Act (1990), which prohibited discrimination against the 40 million Americans who suffered from mental or physical disabilities.

Bush's handling of environmental issues underscored the difficult task he faced in trying to hold together a political coalition of moderates and conservatives during tough economic times. During the 1988 campaign Bush broke with Reagan's harsh approach to the environment, promising to be "the environmental president" who would champion tough new regulations to protect clean water and air and preserve public lands. Once in office, however, the president retreated when conservatives within the administration, led by Vice President Quayle, complained that new environmental initiatives would undermine American business competitiveness.

The debate sharpened in March 1989 when the giant oil tanker *Exxon Valdez* ran aground in Prince William Sound, Alaska, spilling 10.8 million gallons of crude oil, spoiling the pristine coastline, and killing wildlife. Environmentalists called for an end to Alaskan oil drilling, but Bush disagreed, saying the oil production was essential to meet the nation's energy needs. In the Pacific Northwest environmentalists clashed with loggers and timber companies over whether to preserve the delicate ecosystems of old-growth forest and their endangered inhabitant—the northern spotted owl. Once again Bush sided with business interests, saying that maintaining jobs and profits was a higher priority than preserving the environment. Environmentalists achieved a minor victory in 1990 when Bush signed a moderately progressive Clean Air Act, which forced gradual cutbacks on emissions from cars and power plants.

Many scientists were frustrated when the administration refused to join international efforts to control chlorofluorocarbon gases that eroded the Earth's ozone layer, to aid developing nations in developing alternative energy sources, and to slow the depletion of rain forests in South America and Asia. In 1992 the president attended a UN–sponsored "Earth Summit" in Rio de Janeiro, Brazil, but he refused to sign a sweeping, but nonbinding, resolution pledging the nation's support for biodiversity.

The Bush administration proved unresponsive to a growing chorus of complaints about environmental racism. In communities across the nation local organizers charged that companies and government institutions placed landfills and hazardous-waste sites dangerously close to low-income, largely minority, neighborhoods. They claimed that proximity to waste dumps produced more cases of asthma and cancer than occurred elsewhere. As evidence of their claims, environmentalists and civil-rights activists cited studies revealing that more than one-half of all African-Americans lived near a toxic-waste site, and that the government treated polluters in minority areas less severely than it did those in white communities.

The abortion issue also complicated Bush's delicate political balancing act. In 1989 a divided Supreme Court upheld a Missouri law that restricted abortion (*Webster* v. *Reproductive Health Services*). The law banned public facilities from performing abortions that were not necessary to save the mother's life, and the Court's decision seemed a step toward outlawing all abortions. Justice Harry Blackmun, who had written the original decision in *Roe* v. *Wade* (1973) sanctioning abortion, dissented: "The signs are evident and very ominous, and a chill wind blows."

The decision, which encouraged other states to pass more restrictions on abortion, enraged many moderate Republicans. Polls showed a widening political gender gap as many women, including many Republicans, feared that more Republican judicial appointments could tip the Court's balance away from abortion rights. The justices calmed fears somewhat in 1992 when they struck down a Pennsylvania law restricting abortion because the law placed "undue burden" on women. More importantly, the majority stated that it was reluctant to overturn *Roe,* saying the effort would cause "profound and unnecessary damage to the Court's legitimacy, and to the nation's commitment to the rule of law." That 5–4 decision, however, continued to underscore the precarious legal position of abortion rights.

The Anita Hill–Clarence Thomas Hearings

Bush unintentionally widened the gender gap when he replaced the retiring liberal justice Thurgood Marshall, the only African-American on the Court, with Clarence Thomas, a black conservative federal judge who had once served as head of Reagan's Equal Employment Opportunity Commission (EEOC). Born in the small town of Pin Point, Georgia, Thomas was raised by his grandparents, attended Catholic schools, and went on to earn a law degree from Yale. An outspoken critic of affirmative action, he used his position on the EEOC to weaken government enforcement of laws banning discrimination based on race, age, and sex.

Civil-rights and liberal groups howled in protest. The Congressional Black Caucus publicly opposed Thomas, claiming that his views were out of the mainstream and that he lacked the judicial and intellectual qualifications to serve on the Court. With media attention focused on Thomas's biography, emphasizing how he worked his way up from poverty to a successful career as a judge, most Americans, including a majority of African-Americans, supported the nomination. It seemed certain until University of Oklahoma law professor Anita Hill stepped forward to charge that Thomas had sexually harassed her when he was her boss at the EEOC. Thomas, she claimed, had repeatedly asked her on dates, bragged about his sexual ability, and made explicit references to pornography. "On several occasions Thomas told me graphically of his own sexual prowess," she said.

Conservatives on the Senate Judiciary Committee successfully transformed Hill from victim to villain, characterizing her as part of a liberal conspiracy to sink the nomination. Thomas angrily denounced the charges, claiming it was "a travesty" that such "sleaze" should be "displayed in prime time to an entire nation." Polls revealed that a majority of African-Americans believed white racism was at the heart of Hill's charges: she was being used by white racists determined to block the appointment of a black man to such a powerful position. Thomas manipulated these feelings by denouncing the televised Senate confirmation hearings as "a high-tech lynching for uppity blacks who in any way deign to think for themselves." This time, he said, he was being lynched by the United States Senate rather than being "hung from a tree."

Although many wavering senators believed Hill's testimony and voted against Thomas, his nomination survived by a 52–48 vote—the narrowest margin for a Supreme Court nominee in the twentieth century. But the public debate over Hill's charges raised awareness about sexual harassment in the workplace. Polls showed that 40 percent of women claimed they had been sexually harassed and 50 percent of men admitted to engaging in sexually aggressive behavior at work. In newspapers and magazines, around dinner tables, and in corporate boardrooms and on factory floors, Americans debated the hearings and tried to understand the meaning of sexual harassment. "Everybody's talking about this," said a corporate manager. "All levels, men, women, everybody."

Politically, the affair alienated many moderate women who were outraged by the way many senators dismissed and mocked Hill, and they were angered by the administration's unwavering support for Thomas. "Women will remember where they were when Anita Hill began speaking," declared feminist Naomi Wolf. After the Senate, made up of ninety-eight men and two women, voted in favor of Thomas's nomination, a small group of women demonstrated on the steps of the

Anita Hill at the Clarence Thomas Confirmation Hearing   When Thurgood Marshall announced he was retiring from the Supreme Court on June 27, 1991, President Bush immediately nominated federal appeals court judge Clarence Thomas, a conservative forty-three-year-old African-American. Thomas faced opposition from civil rights organizations who disapproved of Thomas's stand on affirmative action and by women's groups who worried about his antiabortion position. At Thomas's Senate confirmation hearings, however, the expected opposition was overshadowed by the surprising accusations raised by one of Thomas's former subordinates at the EEOC, Anita Hill. Hill claimed Thomas sexually harassed her after she refused to see him socially. While the Senate confirmed Thomas in a 52–48 decision, Anita Hill's testimony made Americans aware of sexual harassment's impact on the workplace and led many to call for guidelines that defined proper behavior and speech in the office.

Capitol, chanting, "We'll remember in November." A leader of the National Organization for Women declared, "Women across this country saw in a visceral way that we are not there and they don't represent us."

The 1992 Presidential Campaign

Already politically vulnerable because of the struggling economy and low job approval, Bush had to fend off a revolt of angry conservatives in the Republican primaries. As the election season opened, former Reagan speechwriter Patrick Buchanan scored a surprising victory in the Iowa caucus by attacking Bush as a captive of the Washington establishment who had lost touch with voters. The fiery conservative forced the president to endure a long primary season of punishing verbal assaults. Bush won all thirty-three primaries, but Buchanan took his challenge all the way to the Republican National Convention. The president secured the nomination, but not before Buchanan polarized the party and alienated many voters by calling for a "cultural war" in America.

Politically weaker than in 1988, Bush also faced a more formidable Democratic challenger in former Arkansas governor Bill Clinton. Born in 1946 in Hope, Arkansas, Clinton attended Georgetown University and went to Oxford on a Rhodes scholarship before returning to graduate from Yale Law School. In 1978, at the age of thirty-two, he won election as governor of Arkansas. A party moderate, Clinton appealed to fellow baby boomers by casting himself as a "new Democrat" who understood the concerns of the struggling middle class. Campaigning as a cultural conservative, he professed his support for capital punishment and promised to "end welfare as we know it," to make the streets safer and the schools better, and to provide "basic health care to all Americans." For traditional Democrats he offered a message of economic populism, promising to raise taxes on the wealthy and fight to preserve popular social programs.

A charismatic personality and spellbinding speaker, Clinton emerged as the front runner from a crowded pack of Democratic contenders. The road to the nomination, however, was strewn with questions about marital infidelity and draft dodging. Throughout his public career Clinton had been shadowed by rumors and accusations of extramarital affairs. The issue came to the surface in 1992 when Gennifer Flowers announced that she had been Clinton's mistress for years—and produced taped phone conversations to prove it. In a televised interview with his wife, Hillary Rodham Clinton, at his side, Clinton acknowledged problems in their marriage but denied Flowers's charges. Reporters also questioned Clinton about conflicting statements concerning how he managed to avoid the draft during the Vietnam War and whether he had smoked marijuana as a student. According to his biographer David Maraniss, Clinton "played the draft like a chess player," managing to avoid both the army and the Reserve Officers' Training Corps. He was less adroit, however, at explaining his actions to reporters. Clinton's often evasive and unconvincing answers led to questions about whether he possessed the strength of character to be a good president.

The lingering doubts did not prevent him from winning the nomination earlier than any Democrat in more than two decades. At the party's convention in New York City, Clinton underscored the new Democrat theme by choosing fellow baby-boom southerner Al Gore, a senator from Tennessee, as his running mate. "There's a little Bubba in both of us," Clinton said.

The fall race was complicated by the presence of an unpredictable third-party candidate, Texas billionaire Ross Perot. With a down-to-earth manner and a history of remarkable success in business, Perot tapped into public discontent with government and Washington by promising to balance the budget and cut the deficit. His position on most other issues remained a mystery, but by July he was leading both Clinton and Bush in the polls when he abruptly decided to leave the race. He returned just as unexpectedly in October, with only one month left, largely in the role of spoiler.

While Perot was on sabbatical from the campaign, Clinton moved to secure his followers and take the lead in the polls by focusing attention on the concerns of middle-class voters. In the first minute of his acceptance speech to the Democratic National Convention, Clinton said he was seeking the presidency "in the name of all the people who do the work, pay the taxes, raise the kids, and play by the rules, in the name of the hard-working Americans who make up our forgotten middle class." "I am a product of that middle class," Clinton declared, "and when I am president you will be forgotten no more."

He promised to "focus like a laser beam" on economic issues. A sign hanging in his campaign office summed up the Democratic strategy: "It's the economy, stupid." Clinton also proved an effective and unconventional campaigner, chatting with young voters on MTV, taking calls on the popular *Larry King Show,* and playing the saxophone and discussing public policy with late-night talk-show host Arsenio Hall. While Clinton climbed in the polls, Bush floundered. His greatest successes had been in dealing with Iraq and Russia, but with the Cold War fading out of mind, the public showed little interest in foreign policy and instead directed its anger at the administration for the sluggish economy.

Voters rewarded Clinton on election night by giving him 43 percent of the popular vote, compared to 37.4 percent for Bush. Clinton's margin in the electoral college was far more decisive. He won thirty-one states and 370 electoral votes. The public registered its disenchantment with both parties by giving Perot a bigger share of the vote—18.9 percent—than it had any third-party candidate since Teddy Roosevelt scored 27.4 percent in 1912. The Democrats retained control of both houses of Congress. Voters sent six women to the Senate and forty-eight to the House of Representatives. California became the first state to elect two women senators—Barbara Boxer and Dianne Feinstein—and Illinois elected the first African-American woman, Carol Moseley Braun, to the upper chamber. Observers triumphantly called 1992 "the year of the woman."

In the short run, although Republicans took credit for ending the Cold War, it was the Democrats who reaped the political benefits. The break-up of the Soviet Union removed anticommunism from among the arsenal of weapons conservatives had used to undermine support for Democrats. Diminished fear of Soviet power also shifted public attention away from international issues, where Bush had strong credentials, and toward domestic problems, which favored Clinton. In

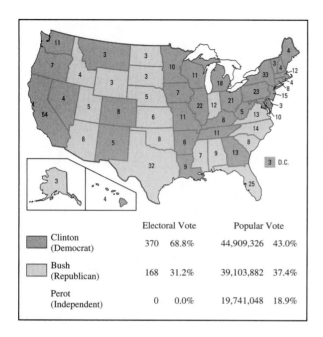

	Electoral Vote		Popular Vote	
Clinton (Democrat)	370	68.8%	44,909,326	43.0%
Bush (Republican)	168	31.2%	39,103,882	37.4%
Perot (Independent)	0	0.0%	19,741,048	18.9%

The Election of 1992 Despite George Bush's victory in Operation Desert Storm, the stagnant economy and his broken pledge not to raise taxes made him vulnerable to attacks by Democrat Bill Clinton who pledged to work for national health care, welfare reform, and a stronger economy. Dissatisfaction with Bush even spilled over into the third party of H. Ross Perot who did not win any electoral votes in November, but who did gain 18.9 percent of the popular vote—the largest third party showing since the Bull Moose Party in 1912.

the end, the Bush administration was trapped by the paradox of rising expectations and the reality of a crippling budget deficit. When Bush tried to reconcile the contradiction by raising taxes, he incurred the wrath of party conservatives, who accused him of abandoning the Reagan legacy. Bill Clinton and the Democrats pounced on the divided Republicans, but the question remained: Could the new administration square the circle of the American paradox?

SELECTED READINGS

▪ Bruce Buchanan's *Renewing Presidential Politics* (1996) covers the 1988 campaign. Penn Kimball's *Keep Hope Alive!* (1992) studies Jesse Jackson's Democratic challenge. Paul Taylor's *See How They Run* (1990) discusses the negative television ads of the campaign. The first comprehensive history of the Bush administration is John Greene's *The Presidency of George Bush* (1999).

▪ There has been extensive material published on the end of the Cold War. Don Oberdorfer's *From the Cold War to a New Era* (1998) is a good introduction. Thomas G. Patterson's *On Every Front* (1992) details the American response to events in Russia. In *Hang Separately* (2000), Leon Sigal argues that the United States could have done more to create agreements with the collapsing Soviet Union to reduce the nuclear arsenal. Francis Fukuyama's *The End of History and the Last Man* (1992) is an early and influential discussion of the post–Cold War world.

▋ Robert Tucker and David C. Hendricksen's *The Imperial Temptation* (1992) studies the emerging debates in American foreign policy after the Cold War. An overview of the foreign policy of George Bush is given in Meena Bose and Rosanna Perotti's *From Cold War to the New World Order* (2002). Edward Flanagan tells the story of Operation Just Cause in *Battle for Panama* (1994). Editors Ramon Myers, David Shambaugh, and Michel Oksenberg evaluate American policy toward China and Taiwan during the Bush and Clinton administrations in *Making China Policy* (2001).

▋ *Triumph Without Victory* (1992), published by *U.S. News and World Report*, is the best early history of Operation Desert Storm. Stephen R. Graubard's *Mr. Bush's War* (1992) discusses the behavior of the media during the war. Martin Yant's *Desert Mirage* (1991) is a sharply critical history of the war. Alberto Bin's *Desert Storm: A Forgotten War* (1998) discusses the dubious legacy of the conflict.

▋ Charles Kolb describes the formidable political struggle Bush faced while trying to create his domestic agenda in *White House Daze* (1993). Arlene S. Skolnick's *Embattled Paradise* (1991) discusses the recession and budget crisis. Michael Meeropol's *Surrender* (1998) recounts how George Bush, and Bill Clinton after him, struggled to balance the budget. Roger Rosenblatt's *Life Itself* (1992) covers the abortion debate. Susan Faludi describes the growing gender gap in *Backlash* (1991). The debate over the impact of the Anita Hill–Clarence Thomas hearings on race and gender issues is examined by editor Geneva Smitherman in *African American Women Speak Out on Anita Hill–Clarence Thomas* (1995) and by Jane Flax in *The American Dream in Black and White* (1998).

▋ John Hohenberg's *The Bill Clinton Story* (1994) details the 1992 Democratic campaign. Editors Marion Just, Montague Kern, and Dean Alger examine how citizens used the information provided by mass media to establish their voter preference in *Crosstalk* (1995). Elizabeth Cook et al.'s *The Year of the Woman* (1994) studies the myths about and realities of the 1992 election.

17

The Clinton Presidency, 1993–2001

On January 7, 1999, a cold, drizzly day in Washington, Chief Justice of the Supreme Court William Rehnquist, dressed in gold-striped black robes, entered the majestic nineteenth-century Senate chamber. The room was hushed, the galleries were packed, and the one hundred senators were seated at rapt attention as the sergeant at arms opened the proceedings. "All persons are commanded to keep silence, on pain of imprisonment, while the House of Representatives is exhibiting to the Senate of the United States articles of impeachment against William Jefferson Clinton."

It was a historic event: the first impeachment trial of an elected U.S. president and only the second such trial in history. The House of Representatives had forwarded two charges against Clinton, the first two-term Democratic president since Franklin Roosevelt. The charges alleged that he had lied under oath and obstructed justice in an effort to hide his affair with Monica Lewinsky, a twenty-two-year-old former White House intern. Under the Constitution, if two-thirds of the Senate, or sixty-seven senators, voted for conviction on either of the two articles of impeachment, Clinton would be removed from office and Vice President Al Gore sworn in to replace him.

After days of listening to Republican prosecutors from the House and to the president's defense lawyers, the senators closed the doors, turned off the television cameras, and deliberated. At the end of the fourth day of closed-door meetings, the doors opened and curious onlookers packed the galleries and filled the aisles to hear the verdict. "Senators, how say you? Is the respondent, William Jefferson Clinton, guilty or not guilty?" Rehnquist asked after a clerk read the first charge of perjury. As the clerk called each senator's name, each stood to announce his or her verdict. Ten Republicans joined a united Democratic Party in declaring the president "not guilty," making the final count 45–55. On the obstruction of justice charge, five GOP senators crossed over, resulting in a 50–50 vote. Clinton "hereby is acquitted of the charges," the chief justice proclaimed.

A subdued Clinton emerged from the Oval Office two hours later to apologize to the American people: "I want to say again to the American people how profoundly sorry I am for what I said and did to trigger these events and the great burden they have imposed on the Congress and the American people." The president could take solace, however, from the fact that neither of the two articles of impeachment attracted even a simple majority of senators' votes, and both fell far short of the two-thirds majority needed to convict and expel the president.

The trial opened a window onto the conflicting social currents of post–Cold War America. Clinton came to office attempting to construct a new vital center to respond to the American paradox. He planned to focus public expectations on incremental reforms, to preach the healing power of economic growth both at home and abroad, and to blur ideological lines by borrowing from both liberals and conservatives. But the president's personal behavior pushed the culture wars to the center of American politics. The scandal, kept alive by a steady diet of salacious details from the Internet and twenty-four-hour news programs, frustrated the president's supporters and emboldened his critics. Clinton remained personally

Lewinsky Affair After Clinton's confession of "a relationship with Ms. Lewinsky that was not appropriate" the House Judiciary Committee began its investigation of the affair. Meanwhile, the scandal set off a media frenzy as the affair became the most visible topic on news shows, the Internet, and in political cartoons. *(By permission of Mike Luckovich and Creators Syndicate.)*

popular throughout the scandal, but his actions helped to intensify partisan divisions, contribute to erosion of public faith in the institutions of government, and prevent him from creating an enduring political coalition.

The Clinton Agenda

As the first Democrat to occupy the White House in twelve years, Clinton set a new tone for his administration by calling for "a government that looks like America." True to his word, he appointed a number of women and minorities to top administration posts, including the first woman attorney general, Janet Reno. Donna Shalala, chancellor of the University of Wisconsin, became secretary of Health and Human Services; attorney Hazel O'Leary accepted the post of secretary of energy. Clinton appointed women to head the Environmental Protection Agency and the Council of Economic Advisors and to serve as U.S. trade representative. Ron Brown, an African-American and former head of the Democratic Party, served as secretary of commerce. Reflecting the growing political prominence of Hispanic voters, the president appointed Henry Cisneros, the mayor of San Antonio, Texas, as head of Housing and Urban Development and Federico Peña, a former mayor of Denver, Colorado, to run the Department of Transportation. Of Clinton's 182 judicial appointees, 32 percent were women, 20 percent were black, and 7 percent were Hispanic, far higher percentages than those of any other president.

Clinton fulfilled his promise to focus intensely on the economy. During the campaign Clinton called for increased government spending for education, health, and the environment and a tax cut for the middle class. Reducing the federal deficit was not a high priority. But even before he took office, Clinton began reconsidering his priorities. In December Federal Reserve Board chairman Alan Greenspan convinced the president-elect that reducing the deficit would have a greater long-term impact on the economy than would a modest program of tax cuts and spending increases. Greenspan's advice directly contradicted the economic philosophy of John Maynard Keynes, which had guided the Democrats since the days of Franklin D. Roosevelt. Keynes had argued that deficits were good because they added money to the economy, which translated into more jobs and increased production. Clinton, however, accepted the new logic, which claimed that deficits drained capital from the private sector, pushed up interest rates, and strangled the economy.

In February the president submitted an ambitious economic plan to Congress calling for a combination of spending cuts and tax increases to reduce the deficit. Both liberals and conservatives took aim at the plan. Liberals objected because it contained only one ambitious new social program—a national service corps by which college students could pay off federal education loans through community work. Conservatives opposed the tax hikes, which raised the top rate from 31 to

36 percent. After months of haggling, most Democrats fell in line with the president's proposal and it passed the House by a 1-vote margin. In an ominous warning of partisan confrontations to come, not a single House Republican voted for the Clinton program. It passed the Senate by a more comfortable margin.

Even before he submitted his economic package to Congress, Clinton created a political firestorm by proposing to lift the long-standing ban on homosexuals in the military. During the campaign Clinton had lobbied aggressively for gay votes, and once in office he moved on a number of fronts to open opportunities for homosexuals. He ended the federal policy of treating gays as security risks and invited gay activists to the White House for the first time. But his proposal to end discrimination in the military angered the Pentagon and aroused conservative opposition. Months of acrimonious public debate forced Clinton to retreat and agree to an unworkable "don't ask, don't tell" policy that angered both gay-rights groups and conservatives. The debate over gays in the military was a political disaster for the new administration: it distracted public attention from Clinton's economic program and allowed conservatives to typecast the president as a social liberal, while the outcome disillusioned many of Clinton's liberal supporters.

After passage of his economic program, Clinton concentrated his energies on passing a complex health care proposal. In 1993 more than 37 million Americans lacked medical insurance and millions more feared losing coverage. While coverage remained spotty, costs continued to escalate. From 1980 to 1992 Medicare and Medicaid payments ballooned from $48 billion to $196 billion and expanded from 8 percent to 14 percent of the federal budget. Shortly after the election the president asked the first lady, Hillary Rodham Clinton, to set up a health care task force. She called the plan "the Social Security Act of this generation, the reform that would establish the identity of the Democratic Party and be the defining legislation for generations to come." In September 1993 the administration unveiled its plan, which would set up government-regulated state and local health alliances to guarantee Americans medical and dental coverage and an array of preventive services. The plan proposed to limit Medicare and Medicaid payments, cap premiums, and foster competition among providers.

Initially, polls showed a large majority of Americans in favor of the new plan and many prominent members of Congress welcomed the initiative. Five months later, however, the plan was dead. What happened? Business leaders and Republicans launched a successful campaign to convince the public that the plan was too costly and the president too liberal. A coalition of conservative opponents paid more than $15 million to air a series of devastating television commercials featuring "Harry and Louise," two ordinary Americans fearful of creeping government intervention in the health care marketplace.

But it was not just pressure from conservatives that killed the legislation. The plan was immensely complicated, running nearly 1,350 pages. Utah Republican senator Bob Bennett called it "incredibly bloated, complex, unresponsive [and] incomprehensible." It was also far too ambitious, especially given the president's slim victory, the Democrats' small majorities in Congress, and the public's lack of faith in government's ability to solve social problems. "We made the error of try- ing to do too much, took too long, and ended up achieving nothing," the presi- dent admitted.

More bad news followed the failure of the health care proposal: Congress asked a special prosecutor to investigate whether the Clintons had been involved in financial wrongdoing stemming from a bad land deal in which they invested in the 1970s. The investigation into the "Whitewater" development venture in northern Arkansas focused on whether the Clintons had received favorable treat- ment and been forgiven loans after the failure of the project. During the investi- gation Vincent Foster, Hillary Clinton's former law partner and counsel to the president, committed suicide. Numerous investigators attributed Foster's suicide to severe depression, but conservatives spun wild yarns, even going so far as to suggest that the White House had tried to silence him. Around the same time new reports surfaced that Arkansas state troopers had procured women for Clin- ton when he was governor. Together the questions over the land deal and the reports of womanizing tapped into larger public doubts about the president's character. By 1994 there were more news stories on Whitewater than on all facets of Clinton's domestic agenda combined.

The first lady emerged as a lightning rod for conservatives. Hillary Clinton remained overwhelmingly popular among women, minority groups, and the rest of the traditional Democratic base. She wrote a popular book on children's issues, *It Takes a Village* (1996), and she impressed observers with her diplomatic skill and political savvy on solo travels to China, South Asia, South America, Bosnia, Greece, and Turkey. She also found herself at the center of White House controversies, from Whitewater to the failure of health care reform. Within a few years her unfavorable rating jumped to nearly 40 percent, nearly 10 points above her favorable rating.

The failure of the health reform package, controversy over the measure to allow gays in the military, and the drumbeat of charges over Whitewater eroded public support for the Clinton presidency. After two years in office Clinton had the lowest poll ratings of any president since Watergate. Energized Republi- cans, led by Georgia firebrand Newt Gingrich of the House, pounced on the helpless Democrats in the 1994 midterm elections. Nearly three hundred Republican congressional candidates signed a ten-point Contract with Amer- ica, a political wish list polished by consultants and tested in focus groups, pledging to trim government waste, cap welfare payments, raise military spending, and lower taxes. Gingrich's goal was to nationalize the congressional election. Republicans had scored well in recent presidential elections, and con- tested for control of the Senate, but the Democrats' patronage power made it difficult to dislodge them from the House. By making each congressional race a referendum on Clinton, the Republicans hoped to tap into the conservative mood of the nation by transforming local races into referendums on national issues.

PRIMARY SOURCE

17.1 | *The Contract with America, 1994*

Seeking to reclaim power from Congressional Democrats in the 1994 midterm elections, Republicans created a comprehensive plan for improving America and winning voters. Written by House Republicans, specifically Georgia's Newt Gingrich and Texas's Dick Armey, the Contract with America stated the principles and intentions of Republicans in an election year and served as a foundation for legislation after their stunning November victory.

The Contract

As Republican Members of the House of Representatives and as citizens seeking to join that body, we propose not just to change its policies, but even more important, to restore the bonds of trust between the people and their elected representatives.

5   That is why, in this era of official evasion and posturing, we offer instead a detailed agenda for national renewal, a written commitment with no fine print.

     This year's election offers the chance, after four decades of one-party control, to bring to the House a new majority that will transform the way Congress works. That historic change would be the end of government that is too big, too intru-
10 sive, and too easy with the public's money. It can be the beginning of a Congress that respects the values and shares the faith of the American family.

     Like Lincoln, our first Republican president, we intend to act "with firmness in the right, as God gives us to see the right." To restore accountability to Congress. To end its cycle of scandal and disgrace. To make us all proud again of the
15 way free people govern themselves.

     On the first day of the 104th Congress, the new Republican majority will immediately pass the following major reforms, aimed at restoring the faith and trust of the American people in their government:

20   ■ FIRST, require all laws that apply to the rest of the country also apply equally to the Congress;

  ■ SECOND, select a major, independent auditing firm to conduct a comprehensive audit of Congress for waste, fraud or abuse;

25   ■ THIRD, cut the number of House committees, and cut committee staff by one-third;

  ■ FOURTH, limit the terms of all committee chairs;

  ■ FIFTH, ban the casting of proxy votes in committee;

30   ■ SIXTH, require committee meetings to be open to the public;

  ■ SEVENTH, require a three-fifths majority vote to pass a tax increase;

■ EIGHTH, guarantee an honest accounting of our Federal Budget by implementing zero base-line budgeting. ■ ■ ■

On election day Republicans made major gains, seizing control of both houses for the first time in forty years and defeating thirty-five incumbent Democrats. "We got our butts kicked," said the chairman of the Democratic National Committee. The election solidified Republican dominance over the South. For the first time since Reconstruction, the Republicans controlled a majority of southern governorships, senators, and congressional seats. Southerners held most leadership positions in the party. The incoming speaker of the House, Newt Gingrich, hailed from Georgia, while the new Republican whip in the Senate, Trent Lott, was from Mississippi. In addition, the Grand Old Party controlled two southern state legislative houses—the North Carolina house and the Florida senate—for the first time since Reconstruction.

Moving to the Center

Clinton responded to the Republican triumph by moving to the center, professing liberal goals even as he co-opted Republican themes of small government and private initiative. By acting independently of both Republicans and Democrats, Clinton planned to occupy the high middle ground of American politics. Clinton adviser Dick Morris called the strategy "triangulation." The approach represented Clinton's response to the American paradox: he would give rhetorical support to public expectations of activist government, while also paying homage to public fears of federal power.

Clinton's first move was to accept the Republican goal of balancing the budget in ten years or less. "The era of Big Government is over," he announced in Reaganesque language. White House liberals fought against the move, and many congressional Democrats complained afterward that the president lacked a clear ideological compass. The president embraced other conservative proposals as well, including a crime bill that would put one hundred thousand new police on the streets and mandatory sentences for criminals convicted three times of felonies.

It was welfare reform, however, that was at the center of Clinton's new strategy. True to the terms of the Contract with America, congressional Republicans passed the Personal Responsibility and Work Opportunity Reconciliation Act. Clinton objected to the original legislation, but later signed a bill that maintained its central features. The 1996 welfare reform bill, which Clinton called a "new social bargain with the poor," eliminated the federal guarantee of welfare as an entitlement. The bill replaced welfare with a program that collapsed nearly forty federal programs, including Aid to Families with Dependent Children (AFDC), into five block grants to the states, giving the states authority to develop their own plans. The most striking provision of the new bill declared that the head of every family on assistance had to work within two years or the family would lose its benefits.

While promising to end welfare as it had been known, Clinton also pledged to "make work pay" by aiding the working poor. "We're spending more on social policy, not less," said an administration official. "But we're spending it in a completely different way. We've radically expanded help to working folks." The administration's most important initiative, the earned-income tax credit, provided low-wage workers with cash bonuses of nearly $4,000. For someone leaving welfare for work, the program turned a job that paid $6.50 an hour into one that paid about $8.35 an hour. Nearly one-half of all beneficiaries were either black or Hispanic. The price tag for the program, $30 billion a year, was double what Washington had paid for AFDC at its peak. "It's the largest anti-poverty program since the Great Society," noted an analyst. Because the program was aimed at workers, it proved more popular than other antipoverty initiatives.

While embracing Republican themes, the president also tried to stigmatize that party's leadership as extremists. Newly elected House Speaker Newt Gingrich played directly into Clinton's hands, misinterpreting the public mood: Americans wanted smaller government and lower taxes, but they did not want popular programs cut. Clinton understood the contradiction and exploited it brilliantly, promising to cut the deficit and protect middle-class social programs. As part of an assault on the "welfare state," Republicans announced plans to cut projected spending on Medicare by $270 billion over five years. Gingrich shocked senior Americans who depended on the program by stating that Medicare should "wither on the vine." At the same time that he was attacking Medicare, Gingrich was pushing a tax cut for the wealthy through Congress.

When Clinton vetoed their budget and spending bills, the Republicans refused to pass the customary stopgap measures to keep the government operating. "I won't yield to these threats," Clinton told the nation. "I'm determined to balance the budget, but I won't be forced into signing a budget that violates our values, not today or tomorrow, not ever." An angry public blamed the Republicans for the resulting shutdown of "nonessential" federal facilities and services. By March 1995, barely two months after Republicans took control of Congress, polls showed nearly six in ten Americans agreeing that Republicans "will go too far in helping the rich and cutting needed government services that benefit average Americans as well as the poor."

While moving to the right on many economic issues, the president adopted a more liberal stance on the environment. Many conservation groups had high hopes for the new administration: during the 1992 campaign Clinton had criticized George Bush's probusiness approach, and once in office Clinton appointed environmental activists to key White House posts. Environmentalists expected the administration to fight for an energy tax hike, an upgrade of the Clean Water Act, the Endangered Species Act, and a renewal of the Superfund toxic waste cleanup law. For Clinton, however, the environment was a much lower priority than his plans for economic and health care reform, so he refused to expend valuable political capital, and the measures failed to pass. In 1994 a conservation group gave the president a "D" grade for his work on the environment.

When the new Republican Congress threatened to "roll back" twenty-five years of bipartisan legislation, however, Clinton made protection of the environment a top priority. "The freedom to breathe clean air, drink safe water, pass a safe world to our children are liberties we dare not take for granted," he told audiences as he promised to veto any Republican attempts to weaken environmental regulations. Clinton found himself on the right side of public opinion. By 1995, 88 percent of the public considered the environment to be either "very important" or "one of the most important problems facing the country."

While Clinton had mixed results with ambitious proposals, he succeeded in promoting a series of smaller, often symbolic, initiatives aimed at middle-class Americans. The administration expanded the student loan program and streamlined procedures for gaining mortgage loans from the Federal Housing Administration. He successfully persuaded Congress to pass legislation requiring that manufacturers insert "V-chips" in televisions, thereby allowing parents to block violent or sexually explicit programming. Clinton brokered an agreement by the television industry to voluntarily devise a ratings system. The president opposed a constitutional amendment on school prayer but supported religious expression in schools. "He was saying yes and saying no at the same time," said a White House adviser. "He was stealing the center, creating the center."

Winning a Second Term: The 1996 Campaign

By 1996 the president's effort to rebuild public support by co-opting Republican issues of welfare reform and crime and balancing the budget while protecting the environment had been remarkably successful. Aided by an expanding economy and declining unemployment, Clinton watched his job approval rating soar to over 60 percent—the highest rating of his presidency. Polls showed that many voters were willing to set aside concerns about Clinton's character in favor of their satisfaction with the humming economy—and their general perception that the country was headed in the right direction.

Republicans chose Kansas senator Robert Dole to challenge Clinton in the 1996 presidential contest. Dole, a seventy-three-year-old veteran of World War II and the oldest man ever to seek the presidency, failed to excite voters, despite a series of self-consciously dramatic gestures. In one of the most memorable campaign moments, Dole resigned from the Senate after three decades in Congress. He also put forth an ambitious 15 percent across-the-board tax-cut plan. In an effort to reach out to younger voters, he chose former Buffalo Bills quarterback and ex-congressman Jack Kemp as his running mate. When all else failed, Dole tried to exploit the "character" issue in the final weeks of the campaign. Nothing seemed to work.

Dole offered himself as a bridge to an older era of strong values and national pride. "Let me be the bridge to an America that only the unknowing call myth," he told cheering Republicans. Clinton countered, using the same metaphor,

Republican Leaders of the House and Senate in 1994   The controversies that developed during Clinton's first two years in office revived the Republican Party and contributed to a sound rejection of Democrats in the 1994 elections. Republicans gained eight seats in the Senate and fifty-two seats in the House of Representatives, providing the party with potent majorities in both houses. The new Speaker of the House, Newt Gingrich (left), saw the Republican victories as confirmation of the public's support for the party's campaign promises, published as the *Contract with America.* During 1995 Gingrich, with the support of Senate majority leader Bob Dole (right), worked diligently to keep Republicans focused on the passage of the *Contract's* basic tenets into law.

offering himself as a bridge "to the 21st century, wide enough and strong enough to take us to America's best days."

On election day Clinton became the first Democrat since Franklin Roosevelt to win a second term as president. Victories in thirty states and the District of Columbia gave him 375 electoral votes. Dole and Jack Kemp carried fourteen states, primarily in the solid Republican South and the mountain states of the West, with a combined 129 electoral votes. Ross Perot, the Texas billionaire who ran on the ticket of the Reform Party, finished a distant third, drawing roughly one-half of the 19 percent of the vote he had won in 1992. "They have affirmed our cause and told us to go forward," Clinton said of the voters. But the election hardly represented a clear mandate. Clinton failed to produce coattails for other Democrats as the Republicans retained control of the House and gained a few seats in the Senate. In a troublesome note on the character issue, more than one-half of all voters, even many who voted for him, told pollsters that the president was neither honest nor trustworthy.

There was another important subtext to the campaign: it revealed how the cold pursuit of cash had overwhelmed the nation's fragile campaign finance system, frustrating years of reform efforts. After Watergate Congress passed a series of laws designed to limit the corrupting influence of big money in politics. The new legislation limited individual contributions and established reporting requirements. Over the years candidates had developed skillful ways to bypass the reforms. Perhaps the biggest loophole was "soft money," contributions designed to help the parties but not individual candidates.

In 1996 soft-money contributions exceeded $261 million, dwarfing the $60 million federal campaign limit for presidential candidates. The Republican Party raised $138.2 million; the Democrats hauled in $123.9 million. Taking a direct interest in soliciting soft money, the president showered supporters and fundraisers with presidential perks, such as state dinner invitations, seats aboard Air Force One, tickets to the White House movie theater, and golf outings with the president. Republican Dole complained about Clinton's tactics while mimicking his methods. "What was once a loophole in the campaign laws has become a four-lane highway full of Brinks trucks," observed *Newsweek*. The abuses led to calls for new reforms, but Congress, whose members coveted soft money themselves, was uncertain about how to stem the flow of money into campaigns.

The New Internationalism

As the first president elected after the end of the Cold War, Clinton faced a variety of new and complex questions. As the only remaining superpower, what relationship should the United States have to the rest of the world? Many Americans celebrated the end of the Cold War, viewing it as a victory for the American ideals of freedom and democracy. But how would the nation define its vital interests in the post–Cold War era? How would it balance its commitment to American ideals with the realities of global politics?

For all of the peril of the Cold War, it had provided policy makers with a framework, though often a narrow one, for interpreting world events and for calculating the national interest. The United States had a grand concept—containment—to guide its approach to the world. As Harry Angstrom, a character in John Updike's *Rabbit at Rest* (1990), reflects: "I miss it, the cold war. It gave you a reason to get up in the morning." The Clinton administration did not attempt to articulate a new framework for U.S. foreign policy in the post–Cold War era. "It is going to be a less ordered world because you don't have the discipline of the Cold War," noted a State Department official.

The United States emerged from the Cold War as the world's only superpower, but whether the nation was prepared to bear the new burdens of internationalism remained unclear. Clinton presided over a party that was still deeply divided over the "lessons of Vietnam," uncertain how to define and defend American strategic interests. The president hoped the end of the Cold War would allow him to devote most of his attention to domestic issues. He chose Warren Christopher, a detail-oriented lawyer who distrusted grand schemes and stressed the limits of American power to serve as secretary of state. Foreign affairs were not high on the agenda for either Congress or the media. Many younger members of Congress, especially New Right Republicans, were more jingoistic than internationalist. The *New York Times* columnist Tom Friedman said their motto could be summed up as "Stupid and proud of it," or "Dumb as we wanna be." This crowd, he wrote, "favors everything from nonpayment of UN dues to further cuts in foreign aid, to outright isolationism." At the same time, network television news, where most American learned about events in the world, cut back on foreign coverage to allow more time for stories on sex and scandal that scored higher ratings.

Clinton developed a centrist response to the conflict between America's global interests and its isolationist leanings. He appealed to America's sense of mission, but exercised restraint in the actual use of power. Without a grand strategy,

Handshake Affirming the Oslo Accords   The Oslo Accords, officially known as the "Declaration of Principles," were the result of secret negotiations in Norway between Israel and the Palestinian Liberation Organization (PLO) to try to create a foundation on which long-term peace between the two peoples could be established. Hosted by President Clinton, Israeli prime minister Yitzhak Rabin (left) and PLO chairman Yasir Arafat (right) signed the accords at the White House on September 13, 1993, and concluded the ceremony with a handshake. The accords called for the removal of Israeli troops from the Gaza Strip and West Bank and required Arafat to renounce terrorism and diplomatically recognize Israel. The accords served as the basis for further negotiations through the rest of the nineties, despite intermittent resumption of violence in the region.

the administration appeared to lurch from one international crisis to another. The first occurred in the Horn of Africa, the northeast region of the continent, where many nations—Ethiopia, Sudan, and Somalia among them—had been suffering from drought, famine, and intermittent civil war. The situation grew grave in 1992 as fighting among rival factions threatened to cut off relief supplies to Somalia, leaving millions to starve. Pushed to respond by public reaction to television pictures of emaciated children, Bush had ordered nearly 30,000 troops to Somalia on a humanitarian mission to restore order and secure relief efforts. Initially, Operation Restore Hope succeeded, but before long the rival clans tired of the U.S. presence and began putting up resistance.

Clinton inherited a complex problem. U.S. troops could not guarantee the flow of supplies without fighting the clans, but engaging the rival factions risked getting America bogged down in a quagmire. Without seeking approval from Congress, Clinton left nearly 9,000 troops in Somalia and expanded their mission to include taking on the local clans. In October 1993, 18 U.S. Army Rangers died in a bloody firefight with a gang of Somalis. A horrified nation watched television video of an American soldier being dragged through the streets of Mogadishu to the cheers of local crowds. The journalist David Halberstam called the incident "a major league CNN-era disaster." Clinton quickly retreated, withdrawing the remaining America forces. "Gosh, I miss the Cold War," Clinton remarked after learning that American soldiers had been killed. The fiasco soured relations between the United States and the United Nations and reinforced congressional opposition to peacekeeping missions. "Creeping multilateralism died on the streets of Mogadishu," blustered Kentucky's Republican senator Mitch McConnell.

The administration used the threat of military force more successfully closer to home in Haiti. In 1991 a band of military leaders overthrew the elected leader, Jean-Bertrand Aristide. The Clinton administration organized an international effort to restore Aristide, applying diplomatic pressure and convincing the United Nations to impose economic sanctions. The military regime showed no interest in giving up power voluntarily until Clinton decided to flex his military muscle, threatening to use the marines to expel the junta. With American warships looming off the coast, Haiti's military leaders backed down and allowed Aristide to return to power.

While uncertain about the use of military force in the post–Cold war era, the Clinton administration made economic policy a centerpiece of its approach to the world. The president described the United States as "a big corporation competing in the global marketplace." Clinton, who came to office complaining that President Bush had placed commerce about human rights, quickly switched gears, arguing that capitalism would promote freedom and democracy. In 1994 Clinton fought a tough legislative battle to win congressional approval of the North American Free Trade Agreement negotiated during the Bush presidency. The agreement gradually abolished nearly all trade barriers among the United States, Mexico, and Canada. Opponents, led by organized labor, feared the agreement would mean the loss of high-paying jobs in the

United States as businesses moved to take advantage of cheap labor in Mexico. "The sucking sound you hear is all the jobs heading south of the border," declared vanquished presidential candidate Ross Perot. Clinton argued the contrary, contending the legislation would increase prosperity for all three countries and diminish the flow of illegal immigrants from Mexico. Later that year Clinton won another key free-trade battle when the administration convinced Congress to approve the General Agreement on Tariffs and Trade, which allowed the United States to participate in a new worldwide trade agreement that would reduce tariffs over ten years. "We have put our economic competitiveness at the heart of our foreign policy," Clinton boasted in his 1994 budget message.

While fighting for free trade in the hemisphere, the administration fought to open new markets to American goods. The president created a new agency—the National Economic Council—to coordinate domestic and foreign economic policies. In 1994 the United States made its peace with Vietnam by lifting a trade embargo and normalizing relations. American companies, which had been barred from doing business in Vietnam, rushed into the country. Within hours of the announcement, Pepsi tried to get a jump-start on its arch-rival Coke by distributing over forty thousand free cans of its soft drink to the Vietnamese.

During the 1992 campaign Clinton had criticized Bush for not punishing China for its human-rights violations. Once in office, however, the president changed his tune. Emphasizing the importance of China as a trading partner, Clinton approved China's most-favored-nation status, which gave it the same privileges as America's closest allies, despite that nation's continued crackdown on dissent.

Russia remained a major worry for the administration. The transition from communism to capitalism left the Russian economy in shambles. A collapse in its domestic market would send shock waves around the world. To help prop up the Russian economy, the administration developed a $4.5 billion aid package to facilitate reform efforts and sustain Russia's currency, the ruble. At the same time, the administration worked closely with Russian counterparts to reduce stockpiles of nuclear weapons. The issue was especially urgent now that control of the nuclear weapons had shifted from Moscow to local commanders in the various republics. In 1994 the United States signed the U.S.–Russian–Ukraine Trilateral Statement and Annex, which led to the destruction of all nuclear weapons in Ukraine. Later that month Russian president Boris Yeltsin and Bill Clinton agreed to "detarget" U.S. and Russian strategic missiles—programming them all to land in the ocean. Of course, they could be reprogrammed in minutes, but the agreement represented an important psychological milestone. There were also fewer missiles to launch, thanks to the successful implementation of the Strategic Arms Reduction Talks (START I and START II) treaties negotiated by the Bush administration.

The president learned, however, that there were limits to the power of capitalism to transform foreign government. Old trouble spots, including the Middle East and Iraq, proved immune to economic incentives. In some countries economic assistance and the opening of markets failed to produce the expected reforms. Russia received enormous sums of international aid, but refused to phase out arms shipments to rogue nations. Many Third World nations suspiciously viewed globalization as a rich country's game where the rules were rigged to favor industrialized nations. In an age of globalization money could move around the globe with the flick of a few computer keys. The new international system transferred authority from local political leaders to a handful of powerful institutional investors.

Trouble Spots: Iraq and Yugoslavia

The end of the Cold War accelerated Yugoslavia's splintering into rival ethnic factions. For most of the Cold War era the strong leadership of Josip Broz Tito managed to balance the unstable coalition of Catholic Croatians, Eastern Orthodox Serbs, and Muslims that made up the Yugoslav nation. Tito's death in 1980, combined with the dissolution of the Soviet Union and the independence fever that swept through Eastern Europe, shattered the peace. In 1991 Yugoslavia's provinces of Slovenia, Croatia, and Bosnia-Herzegovina proclaimed their independence. The move infuriated the Serb-dominated federal government in Belgrade, headed by President Slobodan Milosević. Determined to create a "Greater Serbia," Milosević launched military attacks against Croats and Muslims living in areas dominated by ethnic Serbs. In Bosnia-Herzegovina Serbs shelled the capital of Sarejevo and murdered, raped, and imprisoned Muslims in a vicious campaign of "ethnic cleansing." By the end of 1992 more than 150,000 people had died.

The war produced confusion in Washington. Should the United States intervene? Were American national interests at stake in a conflict that was enormously complex and local, involving generations of ethnic rivalries? Any action also threatened the warm relations with Russia, which maintained close ties with the Serbs. Yet liberal and humanitarian groups argued that the United States had a moral responsibility to stop the genocide. But despite gruesome televised pictures of atrocities, the American public did not want to risk U.S. troops. Torn between a humanitarian desire to help and a public fearful of intervention, the administration waffled. Secretary of State Warren Christopher described Bosnia as the "problem from hell." The president sent confusing signals: "I will not let Sarajevo fall," he told Congress. Then he added, "Don't take that as an absolute."

The situation took a dramatic turn in February 1994 when a mortar shell exploded in Sarajevo's open market, killing sixty-eight people and injuring more than two hundred. A few days later the president delivered an ultimatum to the Serbs: either pull back all tanks and artillery from a 12.4-mile free zone around the city or risk assault from members of the North Atlantic Treaty Organization (NATO). Later that month NATO planes shot down Serb jets that violated the no-fly zone. It was the first time in the alliance's history that NATO planes had seen combat.

Division of Yugoslavia   By 1990, Yugoslavia suffered from a heavy foreign debt, inflation, and unemployment, but nothing was more divisive than the growing nationalism and ethnic conflict long suppressed by communist dictators who were swept out of office in 1989. In the spring of 1990, multiparty elections in Slovenia and Croatia resulted in the victory of parties that supported independence, and later the same year similar results occurred in Macedonia and Bosnia-Herzegovina elections. When Serbian leaders blocked the election of a Croatian to the federal presidency in June 1991, Croatia declared its independence, followed by the other three by the end of the year. Bosnia immediately exploded into ethnic violence as Muslims, Croats, and Serbs sought to purge the country of each other. Montenegro and Serbia joined together in April 1992 under the leadership of Serbian Slobodan Milosević, who used his military to support ethnic cleansing and attempted to force the breakaway nations into accepting a resumption of a unified Yugoslavia, actions which led to international intervention in the region for the rest of the nineties.

The exercise of force brought all the parties to the negotiating table in 1995. Under heavy pressure from the United States, the presidents of Bosnia, Croatia, and Serbia signed a peace agreement that solved territorial differences and brought an end to hostilities. As part of the agreement Clinton committed American troops to Bosnia as part of a multinational force to keep the peace. The move stirred up considerable controversy, especially among conservatives who opposed using American troops as part of a multinational force and who argued that American national security was not at stake. Clinton remained resolute. "We stood for peace in Bosnia," he told the nation in 1996.

Boxed in by NATO troops in Bosnia, Milosević turned his war machine against the province of Kosovo, where ethnic Albanians were struggling for independence. When Serb troops embarked on another campaign of ethnic cleansing, this time in Kosovo, NATO tried to negotiate a peaceful settlement. The Albanian Kosovars reluctantly accepted the terms of an agreement that gave them political autonomy within Serbia. But the Serbs remained defiant, refusing to sign the treaty and stepping up their campaign against innocent civilians. In March 1999 the United States and the NATO allies decided to use force to challenge the Serbs. In the clearest statement of American policy in the region, President Clinton told a skeptical public that Kosovo represented a vital interest that the United States had to defend. If Serb aggression was not stopped, he maintained, the violence could spread to other parts of Europe, destabilizing NATO and risking a wider war. In addition to the strategic issues, the president claimed that the United States had a moral and humanitarian responsibility to stop the bloodshed. Within hours U.S. warplanes, backed by cruise missiles and aircraft from other NATO allies, initiated a massive bombing campaign against the Serbs in Kosovo and Serbia itself. In May, after eighty days of intense bombardment that decimated the army and destroyed the country's fragile infrastructure, Milosević relented to NATO demands and withdrew his forces from Kosovo.

Milosević was fighting another battle at home, where disgruntled Serbian workers were feeling the pain of the UN bombing campaign and tough international economic sanctions. In September 2000 they turned out in massive numbers to vote for the leader of an opposition party. When Milosević tried tampering with the results, calling for a new election, the opposition took to the streets, organizing strikes and peaceful demonstrations to shut the country down. Within days as many as a half-million protesters were in the streets of Belgrade, seizing control of the parliament and the nationally owned television station. With his government in tatters and his own life in jeopardy, Milosević stepped down, ending thirteen years of tyrannical rule.

In attempting to define American national interests in the post–Cold War world, the Clinton administration was forced to revisit the lingering threat posed by Saddam Hussein. Following his crushing defeat at the hands of the allies, the Bush administration assumed that opposition forces would mobilize to overthrow Hussein. Instead, the cagey leader emerged from defeat as powerful as ever, crushing potential adversaries, threatening to destabilize the region, and playing a game of cat and mouse with UN inspectors assigned to root out his secret stockpiles of chemical and nuclear weapons. When Hussein made threatening moves toward Kuwait in 1994, the Clinton administration deployed 54,000 troops and more warplanes to the gulf. Two years later U.S. air units struck Iraqi missile targets when Iraqi troops intensified their anti-insurgent operations in the northern part of the country.

As Hussein grew more intransigent, the U.S. position hardened. The change reflected the more hawkish views of Secretary of State Madeline Albright, who took over from the retiring Warren Christopher in 1997. The first woman to serve as the nation's top diplomat, Albright possessed a generational mindset different from that of the baby-boomer Clinton. Born a diplomat's daughter in Prague, Czechoslovakia, in 1937, she fled Nazi occupation with her family and spent most of World War II living in London. "Some people's historical context is Vietnam; mine is Munich," she told reporters. "For me, America truly is the indispensable nation." For Albright, Hussein seemed the reincarnation of Adolf

Hitler, and she was determined not to go down the failed path of appeasement. When Hussein refused to cooperate with weapons inspectors, Albright urged the president to take dramatic action. In December 1998 the United States and Britain launched the largest bombardment of Iraq since the end of the Gulf War, unleashing cruise missiles as well as fighters and bombers. The U.S. military declared the attack a success, but Hussein remained defiant.

Impeachment

At the same time that Clinton was attacking Iraq, he was fighting a battle at home to keep his job as president. In December 1998 he became only the second president in U.S. history to be impeached by the House and, in January, tried in the Senate. The year-long drama that led up to the trial and consumed much of the nation's attention centered on an affair between Clinton and former White House intern Monica Lewinsky. When charges surfaced, a defiant president denied having had sexual relations with "that woman." After he made the same denials in a civil case, and to a grand jury, Kenneth Starr, the special prosecutor in the case, recommended that the president be impeached and removed from office for "high crimes and misdemeanors." To support his conclusion, he delivered a steamy report to the House detailing the affair and offering eleven potential grounds for impeachment.

PRIMARY SOURCE

17.2 | *Apology to the Nation*
BILL CLINTON

Threatened by a subpoena, Clinton appeared before Starr's grand jury, via closed circuit television, to answer questions concerning his testimony in the Paula Jones sexual harassment case and admit to an affair with Monica Lewinsky. That evening, August 17, 1998, Clinton addressed the national television audience concerning the affair. The speech Clinton ultimately gave was less apologetic than the original draft, leaving room for debate as to which version would have been more successful and less politically damaging.

Original Draft

My fellow Americans:

No one who is not in my position can understand the remorse I feel today. Since I was very young, I have had a profound reverence for this office I hold. I've

been honored that you, the people, have entrusted it to me. I am proud of what
5 we have accomplished together.

But in this case, I have fallen short of what you should expect from a president. I have failed my own religious faith and values. I have let too many people
down. I take full responsibility for my actions—for hurting my wife and daughter, for hurting Monica Lewinsky and her family, for hurting friends and staff,
10 and for hurting the country I love. None of this ever should have happened.

I never should have had any sexual contact with Monica Lewinsky, but I did.
I should have acknowledged that I was wrong months ago, but I didn't. I thought
I was shielding my family, but I know in the end, for Hillary and Chelsea, delay
has only brought more pain. Their forgiveness and love, expressed so often as we
15 sat alone together this weekend, means more than I can ever say.

What I did was wrong—and there is no excuse for it. I do want to assure you, as
I told the Grand Jury under oath, that I did nothing to obstruct this investigation.

Finally, I also want to apologize to all of you, my fellow citizens. I hope you
can find it in your heart to accept that apology. I pledge to you that I will make
20 every effort of mind and spirit to earn your confidence again, to be worthy of this
office, and to finish the work on which we have made such remarkable progress
in the past six years.

God bless you, and good night.

Delivered Speech

Good evening.

This afternoon in this room, from this chair, I testified before the Office of
Independent Counsel and the grand jury. I answered their questions truthfully,
including questions about my private life—questions no American citizen would
5 ever want to answer. Still, I must take complete responsibility for all my actions,
both public and private. And that is why I am speaking to you tonight.

As you know, in a deposition in January, I was asked questions about my relationship with Monica Lewinsky. While my answers were legally accurate, I did
not volunteer information. Indeed, I did have a relationship with Ms. Lewinsky
10 that was not appropriate. In fact, it was wrong. It constituted a critical lapse in
judgment and a personal failure on my part for which I am solely and completely
responsible. But I told the grand jury today—and I say to you now—that at no
time did I ask anyone to lie, to hide or destroy evidence, or to take any other
unlawful action.

15 I know that my public comments and my silence about this matter gave a
false impression. I misled people, including even my wife. I deeply regret that. I
can only tell you I was motivated by many factors. First, by a desire to protect
myself from the embarrassment of my own conduct.

I was also very concerned about protecting my family. The fact that these
20 questions were being asked in a politically inspired lawsuit, which has since been
dismissed, was a consideration, too.

In addition, I had real and serious concerns about an independent counsel
investigation that began with private business dealings twenty years ago—deal-

ings, I might add, about which an independent federal agency found no evidence
25 of any wrongdoing by me or my wife over two years ago. The independent counsel investigation moved on to my staff and friends, then into my private life. And now the investigation itself is under investigation.

This has gone on too long, cost too much, and hurt too many innocent people. Now, this matter is between me, the two people I love most—my wife and
30 our daughter—and our God.

I must put it right, and I am prepared to do whatever it takes to do so. Nothing is more important to me personally. But it is private, and I intend to reclaim my family life for my family. It's nobody's business but ours. Even presidents have private lives. It is time to stop the pursuit of personal destruction and the prying
35 into private lives and get on with our national life.

Our country has been distracted by this matter for too long, and I take my responsibility for my part in all of this. That is all I can do. Now it is time—in fact, it is past time—to move on. We have important work to do, real opportunities to seize, real problems to solve, real security matters to face.

40   And so tonight, I ask you to turn away from the spectacle of the past seven months, to repair the fabric of our national discourse, and to return our attention to all the challenges and all the promise of the next American century.

Thank you for watching, and good night.   ■ ■ ■

The reaction to the Starr Report exposed deep ideological and partisan divisions in Congress. The debate over impeachment transformed into a larger cultural war between liberals and conservatives over the legacy of the 1960s. Many conservatives viewed Clinton as a reflection of the moral laxity and self-indulgence of the baby-boom generation. Impeaching the president, declared a prominent conservative, would "kill off the lax morality of the sixties." For liberals, however, Clinton was being punished for continuing the liberal reforms of the 1960s, expanding the power of government, and challenging the establishment. "The president is guilty of being a populist leader who opened up government and access to power," thundered California Congresswoman Maxine Waters.

While Congress debated the legacy of the 1960s, the president's attorneys raised a number of specific objections to the proceeding. Having an affair with an intern and then lying about it was wrong, they contended, but it did not rise to the level of an impeachable offense. Unlike Richard Nixon's actions in Watergate, Clinton's behavior did not represent a threat to the institutions of government. Moreover, they charged, the issue was being pushed by a highly partisan special prosecutor who seemed driven to destroy the president. House Republicans, however, were determined to press forward. After weeks of public hearings the Judiciary Committee voted to send formal changes to the House, which in turn approved two charges—perjury and obstruction of justice—and sent them on to the Senate for trial.

In 1999 the Senate rang in the New Year by putting the president on trial. Over the next few weeks the senators listened to often-repetitive charges and countercharges by the House prosecutors, also called managers, and the White House defense team. The thirteen prosecutors, all Republicans, had to convince sixty-seven of one hundred Senators both that the president's offenses were criminal and that they merited his removal from office. Bill Clinton had "violated the rule of law and thereby broken his covenant with the American people," declared Henry Hyde (R-Ill.), the chief prosecutor. When the final votes were counted, the Senate failed to muster a majority on either count and fell far short of the constitutionally mandated two-thirds needed to convict the president.

In the end, everyone came out of the affair with tarnished reputations. The president enjoyed high job approval ratings throughout the investigation, but the public gave him low marks for honesty and integrity. The GOP's pugnaciously partisan pursuit of impeachment backfired. The Republicans lost a handful of congressional seats in the midterm 1998 elections, and that, in turn, led Speaker Newt Gingrich to resign. Republicans also appeared hypocritical when reports showed that some who condemned Clinton's behavior had checkered pasts of their own. Louisiana's Robert Livingston, for example, a harsh critic of the president's behavior whom Republicans chose to succeed Gingrich as House Speaker, was forced to resign his seat after confessing that he had "on occasion strayed from my marriage."

The media's obsession with the affair, and all its sordid details, came in for its share of criticism. There was a time when reporters did not think the private lives of presidents were relevant. Journalists kept silent about President John Kennedy's late-night trysts in the White House. The rules started to change in the 1970s when reporters exposed the relationship between powerful House Ways and Means Committee chairman Wilbur Mills (a Democrat from Arkansas) and stripper Fanne Foxe. In 1987 Gary Hart was forced to abandon his campaign for the presidency when journalists staked out his house and discovered him having an affair. By the time Monica Lewinsky entered the discussion, there seemed to be no rules. The advent of the Internet, twenty-four-hour cable television shows, and bombastic talk radio created new outlets for information. Congress posted on the Internet the Starr Report, which contained graphic descriptions of semen-stained dresses, kinky acts with cigars, and oral sex. Many Americans expressed alarm at the coarseness of the public discourse, but news programs and talk shows that delved into the steamy sex escapade scored high ratings.

The Clinton Legacy

Unprecedented prosperity helped Clinton weather the impeachment controversy. The Dow Jones Industrial Average soared from 3,241 when he took office in 1993 to over 10,000 by the time he left eight years later. The economy created 22.5 million new jobs, violent crime dropped by 30 percent, and teen pregnancies dipped 18 percent. The president's supporters insisted that he deserved some of the credit for the success, arguing that his 1993 budget plan, approved without a single Republican vote, created the foundation for the new economy.

It may be difficult to know whether Clinton deserved credit for the economy, but he certainly exercised a powerful influence on his own party. "He modernized the Democratic party for the information age," said a leading Democrat. "He made it competitive again in national politics, and it became a model for center-left parties all over the world." Polls showed that the public gave the Democrats the edge on economic growth, fiscal responsibility, and general fairness. He developed an approach that returned the white middle class to the party, forcing Democrats to shed their liberal skin. He often split with traditional Democrats on free-trade policies, welfare overhaul, and crime. He supported the death penalty and a balanced budget. "The Democratic Party brand used to stand for a lot of things—labor unions, big spenders, soft on crime," said an administration official. "Bill Clinton fundamentally repositioned the Democratic Party."

Clinton also managed to articulate a constructive view of government during conservative times. The president believed that before people would trust activist government, they first had to believe that government was under control. "Roosevelt saved capitalism from itself," Clinton told aides early in his administration. "Our mission is to save government from its own excesses so it can again be a progressive force." Compelled to deal with a Republican Congress, Clinton tried to use a smaller but still activist government to assist individuals to compete in the new economy. He increased funding for education, launched an initiative to broaden health care for uninsured children, and dramatically increased government spending for the working poor.

Even the president's detractors were forced to recognize his considerable political skills. He often outmaneuvered his opponents and frustrated his liberal allies by co-opting conservative positions on issues from crime to welfare. "I believe that Clinton is the best tactical politician, certainly of my lifetime," said his former nemesis House Speaker Newt Gingrich.

Clinton became the first president to contend with the relentless exposure of a competitive twenty-four-hour news cycle and the real-time universe of the Internet. His youth and style made the modern presidency more accessible and approachable. He answered questions on MTV about his underwear and talked about "causing pain" in his marriage. He blended Hollywood and government, blurring the boundaries between the public and private. In his role of celebrity-in-chief he invited the same scrutiny about his private life that Hollywood stars face. "At a time when people lost interest in big public questions, we've riveted our attention on the X-rated soap opera of the Clinton presidency," observed the scholar Michael Sandel.

The battle over Clinton's legacy symbolized the nation's continuing struggle with the cultural impact of the 1960s. Clinton may have forged a centrist coalition on policy, but his personal behavior produced a backlash on the issue of values. For many conservative Americans Clinton came to represent the worst that the 1960s generation had to offer. "Why do you hate Clinton so much?" an interviewer asked a conservative. "His policies have not been particularly radical." "I hate him because he's a womanizing, Elvis-loving, non-inhaling, truth-shading, war-protesting, draft-dodging, abortion-protecting, gay-promoting, gun-hating baby boomer. That's why." Ironically, Clinton's personal behavior angered and alienated the same middle-class voters to whom his policies were designed to appeal.

"Baby Boomers" Bill and Hillary Clinton   One of the reasons that both the President and the First Lady were so controversial was that many Americans viewed them as symbols of the baby boom generation that came to maturity in the 1990s. Clinton won election as a centrist candidate and he often supported conservative legislation like welfare reform. But in style and temperament, both he and Hillary reflected the values of the 60s generation. Here, they enjoy one of the favorite activities of aging boomers: a morning jog.

SELECTED READINGS

▌ There have been several character studies of Bill Clinton. David Maraniss's *First in His Class* (1996) is the leading biography of the president. Charles F. Allen's *The Comeback Kid* (1992) and Jim Moore's *Clinton: Young Man in a Hurry* (1992) both detail Clinton's political career. Editor Steven Schier joins with a dozen other political scientists to explore Clinton's domestic and foreign policies and how he redefined the executive position in *The Postmodern Presidency* (2000). William Berman's *From the Center to the Edge* (2001) focuses on the origins and evolution of Clinton' programs and analyzes his successes and failures.

▌ Bob Woodward's *Agenda* (1994) is a detailed study of Clinton's first years in office. Steven Beckner focuses on Alan Greenspan's impact on the economy of the 1990s in *Back from the Brink* (1999). The fate of Clinton's health care reform initiative and the legacy of the health care debate are discussed in Theda Skocpol's *Boomerang* (1996). Gregory M. Herek's *Out in Force* (1996) chronicles the debate over homosexuals in the military. Jim McDougal's

Arkansas Mischief (1998) explores the real-estate dealings and partisan wrangling that led to the Whitewater scandal.

▌ Charles Jones looks at Clinton's early initiatives that were thwarted by Congress and how Gingrich miscalculated Republican power in *Clinton and Congress* (1999). James A. Thurber's *Remaking Congress* (1995) covers the 1994 congressional elections. Newt Gingrich's *Contract with America* (1994) outlines the ambitions of the "Republican Revolution." *Washington Post* staff reporter Peter Baker presents a behind-the-scenes look at the events that led to impeachment hearings and the subsequent trial of the president in *The Breach* (2000). Marvin Kalb analyzes the media's role in the proceedings in *One Scandalous Story* (2001).

▌ David Halberstam's *War in a Time of Peace* (2001) analyzes the foreign policy of Bush and Clinton and how the end of the Cold War required changes in executive tasks. William Hyland examines the early failures of Clinton's foreign policy and his ability to learn from these mistakes and reinvent his policy in *Clinton's World* (1999). The American response in Somalia, Haiti, and Bosnia is described in Lester Brune's *The United States and Post–Cold War Interventions* (1999). Wayne Bert outlines the struggle to create a policy concerning the Bosnian conflict in *The Reluctant Superpower* (1997). Daniel Byman and Matthew Waxman argue in *Confronting Iraq* (2000) that American pressure on Iraq has been successful in the years since the Gulf War. Essays edited by Ramon Myers, David Shambaugh, and Michel Oksenbergied evaluate the formation and execution of American policy toward China and Taiwan in *Making China Policy* (2001). Thomas Lippman's *Madeleine Albright and the New American Diplomacy* (2000) analyzes Albright's struggle to redefine national security in an era of globalization.

On August 23, 1995, Bill Gates, the often reclusive founder and chief executive officer (CEO) of computer software giant Microsoft, kicked off the sale of the much-anticipated Windows 95 software at a large party at the company's Redmond, Washington, headquarters. The party capped a worldwide megamarketing blitz for an $89 piece of software that Gates promised would help revolutionize the computer industry. Along with offering increased speed and a redesigned interface, the software included a controversial "bundling" of its Microsoft Network on-line service. "Microsoft is celebrating its 20th anniversary this year," Gates said to the crowd of two thousand five hundred people gathered under a packed circus tent and the thousands more watching by satellite hookup in forty-three cities around the world. "Its original vision for a computer on every desk and in every home is slowly coming true."

The highlight of the evening was a standup comedy routine between Gates and late-night-television host Jay Leno. "Windows 95 is so easy, even a talk-show host can figure it out," Gates said in an awkward attempt at humor. But it was Leno who stole the show, often poking fun at the multibillionaire Gates. "This man is so successful," Leno said, "his chauffeur is Ross Perot."

Afterward the crowd danced to the music of the Rolling Stones hit "Start Me Up," played with hundreds of helium-filled balloons, rode a miniature Ferris wheel, and sang an off-key version of "Auld Lang Syne."

The successful launch of Windows 95 made Gates the wealthiest man in the world at the same time that it spurred the computer revolution of the 1990s. The widespread use of personal computers (PCs) and the rise of the World Wide Web formed the foundation of a communications revolution that promised to transform American business and leisure. *The Economist* asserted that the Web represented "a change even more far-reaching than the harnessing of electrical power a century ago." This information society propelled the economy to new heights as high-tech firms produced a surge on Wall Street.

But neither the information society nor the burgeoning prosperity could resolve the American paradox. The new prosperity filled government coffers with added tax revenue, allowing both Washington and many states to balance their budgets after years of living in the red, but it failed to mend deep social divisions in America. The debate over popular culture, the persistence of racial conflict, and the rise of domestic terrorism revealed a wide gulf between American ideals and social realities. The paradox found full expression in the 2000 presidential election, which celebrated the fruits of prosperity while highlighting profound cultural differences.

The Computer Revolution and the Information Society

Scientists launched the first phase of the computer revolution in 1946 when they turned the switch to start up the mammoth Electronic Numerical Integrator and Calculator. This mainframe computer weighed 30 tons, filled an enormous room at the University of Pennsylvania, consumed 150,000 watts of power, and used 18,000 vacuum tubes. The machine required so much power it was rumored that when the scientists turned it on, the lights in the city of Philadelphia dimmed. Over the next twenty years businesses adopted mainframe computers to handle basic tasks such as automating payroll, billing, and inventory controls.

In the 1970s a diverse collection of tinkerers working in garages in the San Francisco Bay Area were responsible for the second phase of the computing revolution—the birth of the personal computer. In 1977 two young entrepreneurs, Steve Wozniak and Steve Jobs, used a new microprocessor chip to assemble the first Apple II computer. This user-friendly and relatively inexpensive machine, which was made up of a keyboard and an external disk drive, would become the prototype of every desktop machine. By 1981 more than twenty thousand customers were using Apple II computers. The new product inspired fierce loyalty among its original buyers and had the opportunity to dominate the computer market. But Apple made a critical mistake: it refused to license its operating system, thus making it impossible for other computer makers and software writers to develop compatible systems. Apple was soon eclipsed by International Business Machines (IBM), which introduced its own PC in 1981. By 1985 the company had sold more than 6 million machines, primarily to its business customers.

Pressed by demand, IBM decided to outsource its operating system and its microprocessor. The decision was a bonanza for two young companies. One was Intel, a small Silicon Valley company that had created the first microprocessor, an integrated circuit that put the power of a mainframe on a single chip. The microchip was to the modern information economy what the combustion engine was to the earlier industrialization of society. The other company was Microsoft, founded by Bill Gates in 1975, which provided software for the PC. Since IBM used open architecture, Microsoft and Intel were able to provide the software and microprocessors to "Big Blue" as well as to the dozens of IBM "clones." As the PC market boomed during the 1980s and 1990s, Intel and Microsoft reaped enormous profits and their CEOs became international celebrities. In 1997 *Time* magazine selected Andrew Grove of Intel as its "Man of the Year." By that time Bill Gates had emerged as the wealthiest person and most recognizable businessman in the world.

The shift from the mainframe to the PC during the 1980s was made possible by tremendous advances in technology. For example, Intel built its Pentium microprocessor on a piece of silicon the size of a thumbnail. The overall effect of two decades of steady increases in the capacity of microprocessors was to drive down prices and put tremendous computing power in the hands of the average citizen. With a PC, individuals could enhance and speed up their performance of personal and business tasks using word processors, spreadsheets, and personal databases. In 1983 *Time,* instead of naming its usual "Man of the Year," named the computer the "Machine of the Year." By the mid-1990s more than 90 percent of all businesses in the United States relied on the personal computer for essential functions. More than one-third of families had a PC at home. In 1995, for the first time, the amount of money spent on PCs exceeded that spent on televisions.

The Birth of the World Wide Web

The third phase of the computer revolution began with the birth of the Internet. Founded in the late 1960s by Defense Department scientists trying to develop a decentralized communications system that could survive a nuclear war, the Internet created a set of standards, or protocols, that enabled thousands of independent computer networks to communicate. The real explosion in Internet use took place during the early 1990s with the development of the World Wide Web, whereby almost any user with a telephone line and a modem could log onto a worldwide computer communications network. By 1997 about 100 million people around the globe used the Internet; by 2000 that number had soared to 327 million, with Americans making up about 40 percent of total users.

The Web was the central character in a larger unfolding drama—the explosion in digital communications technology made it possible to convert text, sound, graphics, and moving images into coded digital messages. People could transmit those messages quickly and efficiently over wired and wireless networks. The Internet was the chief product of the new technology, but it was not alone. Cell phones, once a toy of the rich, became a standard feature in the workplace, as did fax machines and wireless modems.

"This is the Kitty Hawk era of electronic commerce," an Internet entrepreneur boasted. The Internet empowered individuals by putting vast amounts of unfiltered information at their fingertips. In medicine patients used the Internet to find out about new treatments, breaking the monopoly that physicians had once had on medical information. In business the sharing of electronic documents flattened hierarchies and gave lower-level employees access to huge amounts of information previously the purview of managers. Investors could bypass stockbrokers and plan retirement benefits on-line. By allowing people to communicate effortlessly across thousands of miles, the Internet gave rise to the "virtual corporation," in which employees and managers were located in different places. Politicians used the Internet to circumvent the traditional media and communicate their message directly to voters. In 1999 Republican Steve Forbes became the first presidential aspirant to announce his candidacy on the Internet.

For millions of Americans the Web helped break down cultural and geographic borders by creating virtual communities of shared interests. America Online, the largest Internet provider in the United States, saw its membership soar to over 10 million by 1999. More than three-quarters of its subscribers used anonymous chatrooms to meet people with similar interests. People from all over the globe joined together in virtual town halls to discuss issues of mutual interest. Teenagers in San Diego could discuss music with peers in Boston and Washington; a senior citizen in Texas mourning the death of a loved one could commiserate with someone in Florida; a cancer patient in San Francisco could share treatment ideas with doctors in New York.

The technology also promised to reconfigure the consumer society, providing buyers with new options and increased power. Although mail-order catalogs had existed since the nineteenth century, a local merchant had the advantage of being the only store within driving range. Now with the Web, virtual stores were only seconds away, and they were open twenty-four hours a day. "The Internet is nothing less than a revolution in commerce," gloated *Business Week*. Buyers could compare prices and products on-line. New virtual stores, such as amazon.com, grabbed a foothold in the book market by allowing customers to order books from the privacy of their homes. Three years after its launch, amazon.com had 2.25 million worldwide customers and sales that reached $350 million in 1999.

E-mail emerged as the most visible and commonly used feature of the new information society. By 1999 Americans sent 2.2 billion messages a day, compared with 293 million pieces of first-class mail. Nearly every college and university in the country provided some form of e-mail access for its faculty, staff, and students. Between 70 and 80 percent of university faculty used e-mail to communicate with their colleagues. E-mail changed the workplace, allowing employees to conduct business from the road and from home. As is often the case with new technologies, e-mail produced a few unintended consequences. Prosecutors in a number of high-profile cases were able to retrieve old, often erased, e-mail messages and use them as evidence in court. The special prosecutors in the Iran-contra and Lewinsky affairs used e-mail to document their cases. "Everyone has got to be aware that whatever they put in their E-mail could be retrieved and used against them," advised an attorney.

The information revolution raised new questions and forced Americans to confront old problems. How should government balance the right to free speech on the Web with parents' interest in limiting their children's exposure to indecent material? Religious and conservative groups pressured Congress to pass legislation that would limit access to the Web by banning indecent material. Libertarian and civil-liberty groups opposed any effort to limit the free flow of information. In 1996 Congress passed, and the president signed, the Communications Decency Act, which criminalized on-line communications that were "obscene, lewd, lascivious, filthy or indecent, with intent to annoy, abuse, threaten or harass another person." The Supreme Court ruled the law an unconstitutional infringement of freedom of speech, but Congress responded by passing a less restrictive law, the Child Online Protection Act (1998). The new legislation required all commercial Web sites—even those not in the pornography business—to use special services to protect children from material deemed "harmful to minors."

Many people also worried that the nation's reliance on computers would produce "technological segregation," aggravating the gap between the educational haves and have-nots. Households with incomes of $75,000 or above were twenty times more likely to use the Internet than were those with incomes of $20,000 or less. The higher-income households were nine times more likely to own a computer. Whites were 39 percent more likely than African-Americans, and 43 percent more likely than Hispanics, to have access to the Internet. "The digital divide is real, it is growing, and it is very divisive to the progress of the country," warned an observer.

A few critics pointed out that Internet chatrooms and customized newsgroups encouraged people to limit their exposure to like-minded people. Software, which allowed people to customize the information they received, resulted in what one journalist called "The Daily Me"—a personalized view of the world filtered to allow exposure only to individuals with similar interests and ideas. Though the Internet was in some ways very social, increasing people's capacity to form new bonds and social relations, it also limited the possibilities of debate and discussion of opposing points of view, breeding a high-tech form of social and intellectual isolation.

The Web also created new headaches for people trying to protect sensitive information. So-called hackers, ranging from curious teenagers to malicious governments, used their Internet expertise to gain access to privileged information. U.S. corporations spent millions of dollars developing "firewalls" to keep out "poachers." U.S. military computers were the most common target for mischievous computer operators. The problem, said former chief of the Central Intelligence Agency (CIA) James Woolsey, represented "the toughest national security question facing the U.S."

The issue of where to draw the line between consumer rights and creator's ownership in the digital age emerged in 1999 when Shawn Fanning, a nineteen-year-old student at Northeastern University, created "Napster," a program that allowed users to swap copyrighted music over the Internet. The recording industry sued, claiming that Napster facilitated music piracy. The heavy metal band Metallica called Napster an "insidious and ongoing thievery scheme." Napster fans retaliated, hacking the message "LEAVE NAPSTER ALONE" onto the band's Web site. In 2001 the courts sided with the recording industry, ordering Napster to bar copyrighted songs from its network.

PRIMARY **SOURCE**

18.1 | *On Napster*

LARS ULRICH (METALLICA)

While Napster allowed Internet users to trade music on-line, many in the music industry argued that this activity infringed on copyright laws and consequently sued Napster. As the case made its way through the legal system, Lars Ulrich, drummer for the band Metallica, testified before the Senate Judiciary Committee on July 11, 2000, concerning copyright issues and the Internet.

Mr. Chairman, Senator Leahy, Members of the Committee, my name is Lars Ulrich. I was born in Denmark. In 1980, as a teenager, my parents and I came to America. I started a band named Metallica in 1981 with my best friend James Hetfield. By 1983 we had released our first record, and by 1985 we

5 were no longer living below the poverty line. Since then, we've been very fortunate to achieve a great level of success in the music business throughout the world. It's the classic American dream come true. I'm very honored to be here in this country, and to appear in front of the Senate Judiciary Committee today. Earlier this year, while completing work on a song for the movie *Mis-*

10 *sion Impossible 2,* we were startled to hear reports that a work-in-progress version was already being played on some U.S radio stations. We traced the source of this leak to a corporation called Napster. Additionally, we learned that all of our previously recorded copyrighted songs were, via Napster, available for anyone around the world to download from the Internet in a digital

15 for-mat known as MP3. As you are probably aware, we became the first artists to sue Napster, and have been quite vocal about it as well. That's undoubtedly

why you invited me to this hearing. We have many issues with Napster. First and foremost: Napster hijacked our music without asking. They never sought our permission—our catalog of music simply became available as free down-
20 loads on the Napster system. I don't have a problem with any artist voluntarily distributing his or her songs through any means the artist elects—at no cost to the consumer, if that's what the artist wants. But just like a carpenter who crafts a table gets to decide whether to keep it, sell it or give it away, shouldn't we have the same options? My band authored the music which is Napster's
25 lifeblood. We should decide what happens to it, not Napster—a company with no rights in our recordings, which never invested a penny in Metallica's music or had anything to do with its creation. The choice has been taken away from us. What about the users of Napster, the music consumers? It's like each of them won one of those contests where you get turned loose in a store for five
30 minutes and get to keep everything you can load into your shopping cart. With Napster, though, there's no time limit and everyone's a winner—except the artist. Every song by every artist is available for download at no cost and, of course, with no payment to the artist, the songwriter or the copyright holder. If you're not fortunate enough to own a computer, there's only one way to
35 assemble a music collection the equivalent of a Napster user's: theft. Walk into a record store, grab what you want and walk out. The difference is that the familiar phrase a computer user hears, "File's done," is replaced by another familiar phrase—"You're under arrest." . . .   ■ ■ ■

A high-profile Justice Department suit against software giant Microsoft raised another troubling question: How relevant were the nation's century-old antitrust laws in dealing with the new digital economy? In 1997 the federal government and twenty state attorneys general claimed that Microsoft had unfairly limited competition by bundling its Internet browser with its popular Windows software. "To take one product as a condition of buying another monopoly product is not only a violation of the court order, it's also just wrong," said Attorney General Janet Reno. A defiant Microsoft rejected the government's charge. Claiming that its browser was an integrated part of its windows operating system, Microsoft contended that antiquated antitrust laws punished innovation and success in the digital age. In early 1999, after a seventy-eight-day trial, a U.S. District Court ruled that Microsoft had abused its Windows monopoly to crush upstart com-petitors and had illegally tied its browser to the monopoly Windows operating system. The judge ordered Microsoft split into two companies, one centered on the operating system and another on the applications software, such as Microsoft Office.

In 2001, after a series of legal appeals, the two sides reached a compromise. The government dropped its charges in exchange for Microsoft's promise to allow Windows users access to the software of rival companies. A handful of states, however, refused to accept the compromise. "This agreement may not be good enough to protect consumers against misuse of monopoly, to prevent returns to violations of the law and to restore competition in this industry," said Connecticut attorney general Richard Blumenthal.

Wall Street Boom

The surge in computer-related industry helped revive the U.S. economy during the 1990s. By the end of the decade the gross domestic product, discounted for inflation, was growing at an annual rate of 4 percent and unemployment had fallen to a quarter-century low of 4.7 percent. The output of goods or services per hour of work (known as productivity) had risen 2 percent, well above its

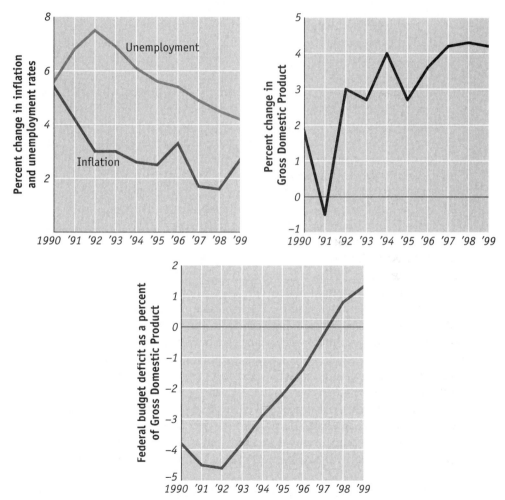

The Economic Boom of the 1990s During the 1990s, Americans enjoyed the longest sustained period of economic growth since the end of the Second World War. Inflation remained steady, unemployment declined, and the Gross Domestic Product rose. Beginning in 1998, the government also had a rosier economic outlook as the federal budget managed a surplus. (Sources: *New York Times,* "News of the Week in Review," May 3, 1998, Copyright © 1998 by the New York Times Co. Reprinted by permission. Bureau of Labor Statistics; *Statistical Abstract of the United States, 1999; Economic Report of the President, 1999;* Bureau of Economic Analysis; Budget of the United States, 2001.)

historically slow annual growth trend of 1 percent since the early 1970s. All the while, inflation had fallen to less than 2 percent.

The information revolution was the cornerstone of the new prosperity, accounting for 45 percent of industrial growth. From 1987 to 1994 the U.S. software industry grew 117 percent in real terms, while the rest of the economy grew only 17 percent. By the end of the decade computer companies based in and around Silicon Valley possessed a market value of $450 billion. By comparison, the auto companies and suppliers of Detroit—the cornerstone of America's previous industrial revolution—were worth about $100 billion. The U.S. software industry accounted for three-fourths of the world market, and nine of the world's ten biggest software companies were located in the United States.

The nation watched as a new generation of computer moguls made millions from new inventions and rising stock prices. When *Forbes* magazine put together its 1990 list of the four hundred richest Americans, Microsoft chief executive Bill Gates was worth $2.5 billion. By 1998 he was worth $85 billion, equal to the wealth of at least one-third of the entire U.S. population. He lived in a house that cost $100 million and covered 66,000 square feet, including a 3,900-square-foot natatorium, a 2,500-square-foot exercise pavilion, a theater, a reception hall, a security building, an underground garage, and a mailroom. Much of his wealth was produced by the soaring price of Microsoft stock, which rose 38,000 percent between 1986 and 1998. By the end of the decade high-tech industry captains held most of the places on *Fortune*'s list of wealthiest people. Of the first five, only one had not made his fortune in a computer-related field.

Wall Street was the most visible sign of the new prosperity. Between 1992 and 1998 the Dow Jones Industrial Average increased fourfold. The New York and NASDAQ Stock Exchanges added over $4 trillion in value—the largest single accumulation of wealth in history. The wealthiest Americans benefited the most from the rising price of stocks. Between 1990 and 1998 the average net worth of the four hundred wealthiest Americans climbed from $680 million to $1.8 billion. During the same time the average compensation for corporate CEOs rose from $1.9 million to $7.8 million, with most of the gain coming in the form of stock options.

In fact, the stock-market boom even reached the middle class. With the tide rising rapidly for more than a decade, stock assets accounted for a larger share of household wealth than ever before: 24.2 percent in mid-1998. Much of the growth resulted from the creation of mutual funds—large investment groups that bought shares in a variety of stocks and bonds to limit risk. In 1980 only 6 percent of U.S. households had mutual funds accounts for stocks or bonds. By 1997 the share had leaped to 37 percent, with a colossal pool of capital approaching $5 trillion. Most of the money for mutual funds came from special retirement funds—401(k) accounts—that allowed workers to have their contributions matched by employers. By 1998 more than 25 million workers had $1 trillion invested in their 401(k) accounts.

From Wall Street to Main Street

The postwar paradox rested on the assumption that prosperity—produced with limited government intervention—would uplift the poor, provide the middle class with more leisure, and narrow the gap between rich and poor. "Rising tides would lift all boats" became a familiar refrain. The reality, however, proved more complicated. For one thing, the computer revolution seduced Americans into working longer hours. According to some estimates, the average American in the 1990s worked 164 more hours per year than in 1970—the equivalent of an additional month. One reason for the expanded hours was that technology virtually erased the boundaries between work and leisure, allowing employers to expect workers to be accessible and productive any hour, any day. A more compelling reason was that many people worked extra jobs to sustain their earning power. In 1979, 4.9 percent of U.S. workers reported working more than one job during the same workweek. By 1995 the percentage was up to 6.4 percent. Virtually all of this increase occurred among women, who represented nearly half of all multiple-job holders. In many families both husband and wife were working full-time for wages. From 1969 to 1996 the proportion of full-time working wives in married households with children rose from 17 percent to 39 percent. In households with no children it soared from 42 percent to 60 percent.

Though American families were working more hours, they were not experiencing a significant increase in living standard. Between 1989 and 1998, for example, the bottom fifth of wage earners saw their average incomes grow less than 1 percent—an $85 rise—over a decade. "To the extent that the typical American family has been able to hold its ground, the most important factor has been the large increase in the hours worked by family members," a major study of U.S. work patterns concluded in 1999. "Were it not for the extra hours of work provided by working wives, the average income of these families would have fallen in the 1990s." In addition, despite low unemployment rates, the average hourly wage, $7.88, adjusted for inflation, had not increased in thirty years.

Nevertheless, many people benefited from the booming economy. The poor did not get poorer in the 1990s. Their family incomes rose slightly, the number below the poverty rate fell somewhat, and the average pay for low-wage jobs increased. Minorities, especially African-Americans, showed real economic gains. In 1989, 30.8 percent of blacks qualified as poor. By 1997, 26.5 percent did. Moreover, incomes for African-American households jumped 16.8 percent, or $3,600, between 1992 and 1999—nearly three times more than incomes for the nation as a whole. By 1998 a record 66.6 percent of households owned their own home and a large number of the new homeowners were members of minority groups and immigrants, groups traditionally shut out of the housing market.

Yet while the poor were advancing by inches, the well-to-do were bounding ahead by miles. In 1990 a corporate CEO earned 85 times as much as the average factory worker; in 1997 he or she made 324 times more. The information society's demand for educated, high-tech workers contributed to the income gap.

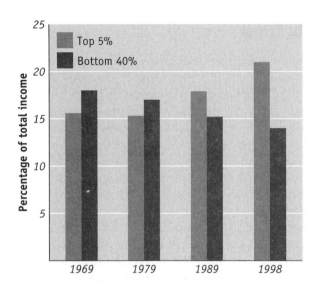

Growing Disparity in the Wealth of the Nation's Families After 1979, the yearly income of the wealthiest 5 percent of the nation's families grew rapidly, far outreaching the more modest progress in wealth experienced by the rest of the American population. While prices continued to rise in the 1980s and 1990s, wages for the poorest 20 percent remained stagnant, middle-income households saw an increase of 10 percent over the two decades, and the top 5 percent saw incomes that climbed an average of 150 percent in twenty years. By 1998, the gap between the top 5 percent and the poorest 20 percent was greater than at any time since the Great Depression.

The new technology placed greater demands on people who worked with their heads, not their hands. The government classified six of every ten jobs created in the 1990s as managerial, professional, or technical. Most of the new job growth took place in industries, such as finance, engineering, data processing, consulting, and education, that employed a large number of college graduates. In 1990 college graduates earned 52 percent more than high-school graduates; in 1997 they earned 62 percent more.

The transition to an information economy created considerable instability in the job marketplace. The 1990s witnessed an increase in the number of workers who, although still earning, had been displaced from their former jobs. At a time of low unemployment, almost 30 percent of those employed were not in regular full-time jobs. Many worked as day laborers, held temporary jobs, or acted as independent contractors. The share of workers employed by agencies that supplied temporary workers doubled between 1989 and 1997. The vast majority of these workers were married women. One estimate for 1995 placed the total number of contingent workers (part-time, temporary, and contract workers) at close to 35 million—28 percent of the civilian labor force.

Despite low interest rates and strong job growth, the number of individuals filing for bankruptcy reached 1.3 million in 1998, up an astonishing 93 percent during the decade. Roughly one out of every seventy-five households filed for personal bankruptcy in 1998. Why? Especially among low-income households, the desire for new consumer products outpaced income; encouraged by credit card companies that begged people to use their cards, people spent more money than they had. In addition, cultural attitudes about bankruptcy had changed. The moral stigma had disappeared, making it easier for people to take the risk of debt that might become unmanageable.

The Politics of Prosperity

By 1998 the combination of a healthy, growing economy, fiscal restraint, and the end of the Cold War had solved the budget crisis that had plagued Washington since the early Reagan years. Years of low inflation cut the government's cost of borrowing and held down spending on programs such as social security and Medicare. At the same time, the strong economy and stock market generated a rising tide of tax payments. In 1992 the annual deficit soared to $290 billion, an all-time high, leading politicians of both parties to warn that the United States was destined to leave its children a mountain of debt. By 1998 the federal government reported a $70 billion surplus for fiscal year 1998—the first in three decades—and projected a $4.4 trillion surplus over the next fifteen years.

For the first time in decades politicians had an opportunity to debate how to spend new revenue. The Clinton administration called for devoting the extra revenue to needed social spending. The president called on Congress to reserve 62 percent of the long-term surplus money for social security; 15 percent for Medicare; 11 percent for "universal" investment accounts that would provide workers with money for retirement savings; and 11 percent for a range of activities in education, defense, and research. Congressional conservatives called for limited spending on defense and social security and advocated giving most of the money back to the public through large tax cuts.

Most of the states, which had been financially strapped for the previous two decades, benefited from the healthy economy. California, home of many thriving high-tech companies, projected a $4.4 billion surplus by 2000. A handful of other states—New York, Indiana, Alaska, Minnesota, North Carolina, and New Jersey—were operating more than $1 billion in the black. Unlike Washington, where spending decisions were marked by partisan wrangling, most states started spending the surpluses for tax and debt relief, education funding, infrastructure upgrades, health care, programs for children, and other projects. Education was the big winner, with average projections nationwide up more than 7 percent, nearly double the average rate of state budget increases.

Economists pointed out, however, that while the deficit had been eliminated, the United States still faced a mountain of debt, which was the cumulative amount of money the U.S. Treasury owed its creditors. As of 1999 the debt stood at $5.4 trillion, one-third of it owed to foreign investors. According to the Congressional Budget Office, 15.2 percent of all federal outlays were to pay interest on the debt, a total of $245 billion annually.

Sex, Violence, and the Culture Wars

Even though prosperity helped turn red ink into black, it did little to mute the continuing debate over cultural values. During the 1990s the debate over popular culture represented part of the continuing clash over the legacy of the 1960s. The defenders of traditional values blamed television for promoting alternative values, claiming that the depiction of sex and violence contributed to the decline of the family, lower test scores, and school violence.

Since the television networks needed to reach the broadest possible audience, they often tried to avoid controversial issues that would alienate potential viewers. During the 1980s and 1990s the competition from new cable networks forced the three majors—ABC, CBS, NBC—to experiment with new programs. These three networks, which had accounted for 90 percent of prime-time viewing in the 1970s, watched their audience share dip to 47 percent in 1998. By that time more than 75 percent of U.S households received dozens of channels via cable or satellite dishes. The technology allowed new networks—FOX, CNN, Warner Brothers—to compete with the majors for prime-time ratings. In an effort to attract back viewers, ABC, NBC, and CBS relaxed rules limiting the airing of explicit sex and violence. "In a cluttering environment where there are so many more media, you have to be more explicit and daring to stand out," observed a television executive. Meanwhile, the courts placed severe limits on the ability of the Federal Communications Commission to regulate shows that aired after 8:00 P.M.

The scramble for viewers, and the looser regulations, gave adventurous producers the opportunity to experiment with different themes and ideas. The *Ellen DeGeneres Show* featured an episode in which its central character, a lesbian, "came out of the closet." ABC executives slapped *Ellen* with a parental warning label and eventually canceled the show because of poor ratings. But by the end of the decade more than a half-dozen prime-time shows featured gay characters. Television also attempted to tackle controversial social issues, from spousal abuse to teen pregnancy. The star of NBC's *The John Larroquette Show* played a recovering alcoholic; *Beverly Hills, 90210* featured a character dealing with drug addiction; an episode of *Murder One* dealt with three women who had been raped by their doctor. Issues featured on the evening news regularly turned up as plots in drama series such as *NYPD Blue* and *The Practice*.

The most common competitive approach, however, was to lure in viewers with sex and violence. One study found that a sexual act or reference occurred every four minutes on average during prime time. *Dawson's Creek,* a popular weekly TV drama about a group of teenagers in the fictional small town of Capeside, Massachusetts, made recurring themes out of teenage sex and parental adultery. Daytime television was dominated by racey talk shows on which guests openly described their sex lives and their family feuds. A study by the American Psychological Association concluded that the typical child, watching twenty-seven hours of TV a week, would see eight thousand murders and one hundred thousand acts of violence from age three to age twelve.

According to one media critic, the United States in the 1990s was in "the midst of a veritable Renaissance of Vulgarity, a gross-out of historic proportions." Reality TV shows revealed footage of employees photocopying their private parts. Millions of Americans tuned in every week to catch the latest crisis in the lives of MTV's *Real World* or to view the latest challenge facing the characters

The "Coming Out" of TV's *Ellen* Ellen DeGeneres, star of the comedy show *Ellen,* made television history in the spring of 1997 when her title character finally proclaimed, after several years of viewer speculation, that she was gay. Not only did the character Ellen announce to the world her sexuality, but Ellen DeGeneres the actor also "came out" publicly. Although the network cancelled the show a year later as the result of plummeting ratings, *Ellen* destroyed the television taboo that had prevented discussion of homosexuality on television's major networks in prime time. The show paved the way for future comedies and dramas that wanted to explore the lives of gay and lesbian characters.

in the CBS hit *Survivor.* USA Network premiered a late-night quiz show, *Strip Poker,* in which attractive young men and women removed successive layers of clothes. HBO's series *Sex in the City* followed the lives of four young women who openly discussed every aspect of their sexual desires and habits.

Many Americans reacted in horror, arguing that mass culture was responsible for producing a generation of "selfish, dishonest, sexually promiscuous, and violent" children. "In these shows," former Secretary of Education William Bennett complained about daytime television, "indecent exposure is celebrated as a virtue." Parental groups were especially concerned about violence. "These patterns teach children that violence is desirable, necessary, and painless," said a critic. A 1996 poll showed that two-thirds of the public believed TV shows contributed to such social problems as violence, divorce, teen pregnancy, and the decline of family values. In 1996 Congress responded to the pressure by passing the Telecommunications Reform Act. Primarily aimed at the deregulation of TV, cable, and telephone services, the act required that manufacturers install parental control devices, called V-chips, into all new model televisions. Major distributors, including Wal-Mart and Blockbuster Video, exercised their own form of censorship, refusing to stock materials they considered indecent.

Critics also blamed television for producing lower standardized test scores, noting that since the early 1960s, when television became a daily habit for children, average scores for high-school students taking the Scholastic Aptitude Test (SAT), the broadest measure of academic ability, plunged from 478 to 424 on the verbal exam and from 502 to 466 in mathematics. "Is television a cause of the SAT-score decline? Yes, we think it is," a committee of educators concluded. "Television has become surrogate parent, substitute teacher." A handful of social scientists claimed that television viewing was responsible for declining public trust and growing public apathy.

A rash of school shootings in 1998 and 1999 intensified the public debate over violence on television. The most deadly attack took place in April 1999 at Columbine High School in Littleton, Colorado. During the final week of classes two disgruntled and heavily armed students killed twelve classmates and a popular teacher, and planted thirty pipe bombs and other explosives, before taking their own lives. Polls showed that a majority of Americans held Hollywood and television executives "at least partially" to blame for the killings, claiming that they helped create a culture that made violence acceptable. A minority found fault with the nation's lax guns laws, which allowed young people easy access to such powerful weapons.

Hip-Hop Nation

Parents also worried about the appeal of new musical styles, especially hip-hop, among the young. Created by black artists on the mean streets of New York and Los Angeles, hip-hop used repetitive samples of other musical tracks as background for the rhythmic poetry of rap singers. "We're marketing black culture to white people," claimed Rap artist Dr. Dre. In the past African-American artists had softened their image to appeal to mainstream America. Hip-hop took a different approach, accentuating race and highlighting issues of the urban underclass. "Forget about watering down," claimed the cofounder of the group Public Enemy. "I think there's dehydration. Not only are we not going to add water, we're going to take water out." In 1998 rap surpassed country music as the nation's top-selling format. "Hip-hop is the rebellious voice of the youth," boasted rapper Jay-Z. "It's what people want to hear." By the end of the decade suburban whites purchased more than 70 percent of hip-hop albums.

Hip-hop was not only popular; it was also controversial. Its glorification of violence, relentless promotion of sex, and derogatory treatment of homosexuals and women appealed to many suburban white youth, but these same attitudes angered parents, the police, and many civic-minded groups. Police organizations complained about the song "Cop Killer," which included the lyrics "I'm 'bout to bust some shots off/I'm 'bout to dust some cops off" and the chant "Die, Die, Die Pig, Die!"

Not all hip-hop artists promoted sex and violence. Artists such as DMX and Master P avoided controversy by writing songs that examined the pathologies of the black community but avoided encouraging social activism. Madison Avenue and Hollywood tried to tame hip-hop, making it less rebellious. Hollywood featured hip-hop artists Ice Cube, Queen Latifah, and Will Smith in movie releases. Designer Tommy Hilfiger turned an inner-city clothing style—oversized shirts and baggy, drooping pants—into a $1 billion business, and advertising firms used a toned-down version of rap to sell a number of products to young people.

American culture may have been controversial, but it sold, both at home and around the world. During the 1990s popular culture emerged as America's biggest export. By 1996 international sales of software and entertainment products totaled $60.2 billion, more than any other industry. The explosion in sales was spurred by the collapse of the Iron Curtain, rising prosperity, and the proliferation of TV sets, videocassette recorders, stereos, personal computers, and satellite dishes. American corporations moved aggressively to tap into the new markets. The Blockbuster Entertainment video chain opened two thousand outlets in twenty-six foreign countries during the decade; Tower Records operated seventy stores in fifteen countries.

Foreigners were not only viewing and listening to U.S. culture—they were also eating American food, reading U.S. magazines, and wearing designer clothes produced in America. *Reader's Digest* circulated in nineteen languages; its forty-eight international editions, with a combined circulation of 28 million, dwarfed its U.S. circulation of 14.7 million. *Cosmopolitan* billed itself as the world's best-selling women's magazine, with international sales of 4.5 million from thirty-six foreign editions. Right behind it was *Playboy,* with sixteen international editions and a readership of 5 million. McDonald's restaurants were opening at a rate of six a day around the world. American fashion—baggy jeans and baseball caps—became the global teenage uniform. Globalization, an observer noted, had an "American face: It wears Mickey Mouse ears, it eats Big Macs, it drinks Coke or Pepsi and it does its computing on an IBM or Apple laptop, using Windows 98, with an Intel Pentium II processor and a network link from Cisco Systems."

Race and American Justice

Sustained prosperity failed to bridge the gap between the races, however. The disparity in world-views between blacks and whites became clear during the murder trial of former star African-American football player O. J. Simpson, who was charged in the 1994 murder of his ex-wife Nicole Brown Simpson and a friend, Ronald Goldman, at her posh Beverly Hills home.

The ensuing televised trial, which lasted for nine months, transfixed the public, breathing new life into struggling cable news shows and tabloid newspapers desperate to attract an audience. "Everyone loves a good murder," said an *Esquire* writer about what was billed as the "Trial of the Century." There had been other famous trials in this century, but never before could Americans sit in their living

McDonald's Goes to China   American corporations expanded their overseas activities in the nineties, stretching into regions of the globe that just a few years earlier would have been off-limits to the United States because of the constraints of the Cold War. American goods poured into the Soviet Union after the collapse of communism and even became readily available in the communist stronghold of China. McDonald's, the epitome of America's passion for fast food, infiltrated the Chinese market with the opening of their first store in 1992 in Beijing. Serving American-style hamburgers as well as Chinese favorites, Mai Dan Lau (McDonald's in Chinese) proved so popular that by 1998 China had almost two hundred McDonald's, all sporting the golden arches in front.

rooms watching the courtroom drama unfold. At night they tuned into their favorite talk show to listen as experts debated the significance of the day's events. Reporters speculated about every possible angle, from O. J.'s motive to the psychological impact of the murder on Nicole Simpson's dog. Most of the lead players in the drama, and a few minor ones, eventually signed multimillion-dollar book deals. A few became television celebrities.

The prosecutors charged that Simpson murdered Nicole and Goldman, who had dropped in unexpectedly, in a jealous rage. Painting Simpson as obsessed with Nicole and prone to violence, they walked the jury through a trail of DNA evidence that they contended led directly to Simpson. African-American defense attorney Johnnie Cochran responded by arguing that the DNA evidence was contaminated and that Simpson was being framed by a racist policeman, Mark Fuhrman. Cochran, in his closing argument, played the "race card," exhorting jurors to "do the right thing" and set Simpson free as a message to the world against racism and police misconduct.

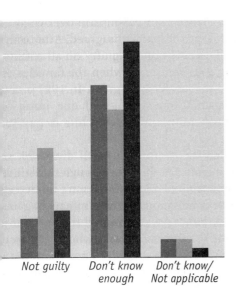

Not guilty   Don't know   Don't know/
              enough   Not applicable

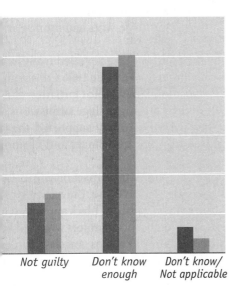

Not guilty   Don't know   Don't know/
              enough   Not applicable

Race Divide in the O.J. Simpson Decision On October 3, 1995, a jury of nine African-Americans, two whites, and one Hispanic found O.J. Simpson, an African-American football star, not guilty of the murder of O.J.'s ex-wife Nicole Brown Simpson and her friend Ronald Goldman, both white. For many Americans, the case highlighted the racial divide that separated white and black Americans, as defense attorneys argued that white police officer Mark Fuhrman and other white officers had intentionally sought to frame O.J. for the murders. According to Simpson's attorney Johnnie Cochran, "Race plays a part of everything in America," and polls conducted a month after Simpson's arrest seemed to prove Cochran right. While gender did not seem to be a factor in peoples' judgment of Simpson's guilt or innocence, nearly twice as many whites thought Simpson was guilty, while African-Americans surveyed were three times as likely to proclaim Simpson not guilty. It is important to note the number of individuals surveyed who had yet to develop an opinion on the subject.

led his voice to the debate. "We have talked at each other and about for a long time. It's high time we all began talking with each other," d graduates at the University of California at San Diego. That same n established a national commission on race issues and spoke out in rmative action.

ioned with liberal remedies, many African-Americans turned to black for answers. Membership in the Nation of Islam and other Black

Most experts found the evidence against Si
of nine blacks, two whites, and one Hispanic c
of deliberation they delivered a verdict of not
over Simpson's guilt or innocence continued
filed civil charges against the former football
up of nine whites, one Hispanic, one Asiar
African heritage found Simpson guilty and or
damages.

The Simpson trials exposed the continuin
showed that blacks and whites looked at the ca
large majorities African-Americans believed in
that the American justice system intentionally
and that rogue cops, like Mark Fuhrman, ofter
distrust of the police was so intense that even b
believed that much of the evidence was taint
observed one writer. Nearly 75 percent of whir
vincing, rejected the suggestion that race play
prosecution, and assumed Simpson's guilt. Per
tice was the final victim of the trial. Blacks an
one thing: there was a different justice for thos
did not.

The racial divide exposed by the Simpson
ing controversy over affirmative action. In Nov
54–46 percent margin, passed Proposition 209
preference based on race and sex in determinir
and employment by the state. Men overwheln
percent), while women disapproved (52 perce
in large numbers.

The ban on affirmative action had a drama
to colleges and universities in the state. In 1S
Berkeley reported a 57 percent drop in the numl
cent decline in the number of Hispanic high-scl
for admission. For the University of Californic
percent for African-American students and 33
students.

As other states mimicked California, the t
over racial preferences. Critics of affirmative
among them, contended that quotas underm
"an enlargement of self-doubt" by creating th
could not earn their positions. Robert L. Woc
candidate, contended that affirmative action
determination and personal responsibility th
for the stability of the black community." Pi
affirmative action helped open the doors c
women, increasing their representation in the

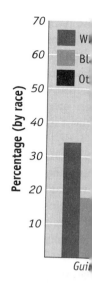

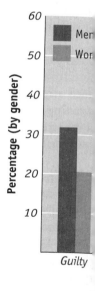

Clinton a
each othe
Clinton to
year Clint
favor of a

Disillu
nationalis

Muslim groups swelled, and Malcolm X reemerged as the decade's leading African-American figure. Traditional African dress—colorful West African fabric, beads, and leather medallions with outlines of Africa—became popular in many black communities. In 1995 Nation of Islam leader Louis Farrakan organized a "million man march" on Washington to "declare to the Government of America and the world that we are ready to take our place as the head of our families and our communities and that we, as Black men, are ready to take responsibility for being the maintainers of our women and children and the builders of our communities." At the same time, Afrocentrism, which argued that black people possessed a distinctive set of cultural values and practices, became popular on some university campuses. Independent schools emphasizing an Afrocentric curriculum popped up in many major cities.

The Many Shades of Color in America

Hispanics and Asians were dramatically altering a nation that had defined race in terms of black and white. Fueled by massive immigration and high birthrates, the nation's Hispanic population jumped by 38 percent during the decade, from 22.4 million to 35.3 million, while the overall population increased by only 9 percent. Demographers were predicting that Latinos would become the nation's largest minority by 2005, making up 25 percent of the U.S. population. If the African-American civil-rights slogan was "We shall overcome," claimed the editor of a bilingual magazine, the Latino motto will be "We shall overwhelm."

The growing numbers of Latinos caught the attention of business leaders and politicians. In 1995 American corporations, led by Procter & Gamble, AT&T, and Sears, spent more than $1 billion on Spanish-language advertising. The concentration of Latino voters in a handful of key electoral states—New York, California, Texas, Illinois, and Florida—magnified their political power. Mobilized to political action during the 1990s by efforts in California to restrict immigrant rights, Latino voting jumped 27 percent between 1994 and 1998. During that same time period the number of Latino officeholders statewide increased from 460 to 789.

Close proximity, and the constant movement between borders, produced a blend of Mexican and American cultures. Banda music, for example, which became a huge fad in Southern California in the 1990s, was an innovative mix of rock, salsa, country-western, and *norteño*—the traditional folk music of northern Mexico. The music was neither Mexican nor American, but rather a mixture of the two. Many Dominican entrepreneurs owned bodegas (neighborhood grocery stores) in both New York City and Santo Domingo. They shipped merchandise back and forth and often commuted between stores. Farm workers from Mexico traveled to the United States for the summer home-construction season in Texas and California, but they worked the rest of the year closer to home.

By 2000 Asian-Americans made up only 4 percent of the population, but they represented 5.4 percent of all college students, making them the only racial group whose percentage of students was above their proportion of the national population. One in four undergraduates at Stanford was Asian; one in five at Harvard, Northwestern, and the University of Pennsylvania. In California, where nearly 40 percent of Asians lived, they were the largest racial group among undergraduates at the University of California at Berkeley, at Los Angeles, and at Riverside. At many of these universities Asian clubs organized around race rather than ethnicity. At Los Angeles, for example, about one-half of the sixty-five Asian-American student organizations were pan-Asian.

Although sharing a common identity as minorities in America, blacks, Latinos, and Asians did not always agree on a common agenda. They collaborated on mutual interests, such as defending affirmative action, fighting against police brutality, and seeking more government spending on education. In 1999 the National Latino Media Council, the National Association for the Advancement of Colored People, American Indians in Films and Television, and the National Asian-Pacific American Media united to demand greater minority representation in the major TV networks' programs. But African-Americans often opposed the efforts of Latinos to receive tax breaks for minority-owned businesses or federal money to help students from disadvantaged backgrounds to attend college. Some blacks joined whites in opposing immigration out of fear that immigrants would take away citizens' jobs. In the 1980s organized labor and segments of the black community supported tough immigration laws intended to reduce the influx of legal Hispanic immigrants. In 1994 a narrow majority of black voters in California supported Proposition 187, which would have barred any sort of state assistance to illegal aliens. Many Hispanic leaders, in turn, complained that blacks were overrepresented in the federal government, where they made up 17 percent of the civil work force, compared to 6 percent for Hispanics.

Terrorism American Style

In the aftermath of the Gulf War many American officials worried that Iraq would attempt to retaliate by slipping chemical or biological weapons into the United States. In 1990 the CIA warned that Iraq could use "special forces, civilian-government agents or foreign terrorists to hand-deliver biological or chemical agents clandestinely." Preparing for the possibility, Congress passed the Defense Against Weapons of Mass Destruction Act (1996), which aided local governments in planning for a possible attack. The army and marine corps created special task forces to respond to germ or gas threats, and many cities organized drills to train emergency relief workers.

While the nation braced for a possible biological or chemical attack, international terrorists used more traditional methods in their campaign of fear. In February 1993 five people died and more than one thousand were injured when a bomb exploded in New York City's World Trade Center. Federal agents traced the bombing to a group of radical Muslims in New York. The same group, it turned out, planned to blow up New York landmarks, including UN headquarters and the George Washington Bridge. American targets outside the United Sates also found themselves vulnerable to attack. In 1996 a truck bomb exploded next to a military barracks in Saudi Arabia, killing 19 U.S. servicemen. Two years later simultaneous bombs exploded in a crowded street in Nairobi, Kenya, and 450 miles away in front of the U.S. embassy in Tanzania. The chief suspect in these bombings was an extremist Saudi millionaire named Osama bin Laden, who called on Muslims to declare war against Americans. The bombs, said *Newsweek,* offered a dramatic but simple message: "Don't forget the world's superpower still has enemies, secret, violent and determined."

Not all the terrorists were foreign extremists: alienated Americans were among the most violent and determined enemies. On April 19, 1995, Gulf War veteran Timothy McVeigh parked a rented Ryder truck packed with a mixture of ammonium nitrate and fuel oil in front of the Alfred P. Murrah Federal Building in Oklahoma City. At 9:02 A.M. the bomb exploded, and the blue-orange fireball ripped through the building, collapsing all nine floors on the building's north side. The blast killed 168 people, including 19 children. The first reaction of many Americans was to blame overseas terrorists. But this act of terrorism was homegrown. Prosecutors in the case disclosed that McVeigh was motivated by a paranoid hatred of the U.S. government.

The decade also witnessed a rise in "hate crimes" targeted specifically against minorities. In 1998 Matthew Shepard, a twenty-one-year-old openly gay student at the University of Wyoming, was lured from a bar and driven to a remote area where he was tied to a fence, pistol-whipped, and left exposed to die. The same year in Jasper, Texas, three white supremacists tied African-American James Byrd to the back of their pickup truck, dragging him to his death. In the South a number of African-American churches were bombed, while New England experienced a wave of synagogue desecrations.

Following the devastation in Oklahoma City, federal and local law enforcement agencies cracked down on radical right-wing armed militias and "patriot" groups, which had grown in numbers since the mid-1980s. To aid in the crackdown, Congress and the White House nearly tripled the counterterrorism budget of the Federal Bureau of Investigation (FBI) between 1994 and 1999, allowing the bureau to add 350 new agents to domestic terrorism cases. The added resources did little to stem the growth of militia groups. According to some sources, the number of militia and patriot organizations increased by 6 percent during the decade to 858 identifiable groups, including 380 that were armed with semiautomatic weapons. While not all the groups practiced violence, most shared some variation of the view that a sinister cabal of Jews and environmentalists were seeking world domination, usually under the auspices of the United Nations.

Many radical right-wing groups used the Internet to reach potential members and promote their paranoid fantasies. The Internet had the advantage of

Oklahoma City Memorial   Five years after Timothy McVeigh detonated a bomb in front of the Alfred P. Murrah Federal Building, the Oklahoma City Memorial was dedicated on April 19, 2000, on the site of the tragedy. The memorial includes a reflecting pool, a tree that survived the blast, and a museum dedicated to understanding terrorism. The most moving scene at the memorial is that of the 168 empty chairs, each inscribed with the name of a victim, which cover the ground where the building once stood.

preserving the anonymity of militia members, as sites did not have to disclose who their operators were or where they were located. By 1999 more than 250 Web sites, chatrooms, and mailing lists promoted the radical right cause. On the U.S. Militia site arms-loving home shoppers could buy everything from explosives to computer mousepads to bumper stickers that said, "Have You Cleaned Your Assault Weapon Today?"

Militia groups were but one manifestation of a larger culture of conspiracy. Surveys showed more than three-quarters of Americans believed that President John Kennedy had been the victim of a massive conspiracy, not of a crazed and lone gunman as a government investigation had shown. Filmmaker Oliver Stone popularized the conspiracy theory in his blockbuster movie *JFK,* which speculated that Lyndon Johnson and the military had backed the assassination. One of the most popular television shows of the decade, the *X-Files,* tapped into the popular fascination with imagined conspiracies. The show featured two FBI agents struggling to disentangle a giant government conspiracy involving alien/human hybridization. "The truth is out there," the announcer intoned.

Why the proliferation of conspiracy theories? Intense public mistrust of government and the media played a role. Real conspiracies in connection with Vietnam, Watergate, and Iran-contra did little to boost public confidence and provided cynics with ample evidence that Washington was capable of deceit. The explosion in Internet use, coupled with the fragmenting of mass culture, produced an environment in which anyone could manipulate facts with no accountability to distinguish between reasoned argument and outrageous opinion. The Internet also provided virtual communities where people could find mutual support for theories about the death of Vincent Foster, the planned UN takeover of America, or other conspiratorial threats. In the end, conspiracy theories abounded because they offered simplistic and coherent explanations for complex and often incoherent events.

The Perils of Prosperity: Suburban Sprawl

The prosperity of the 1990s not only failed to solve old problems; it also created new ones. By the end of the decade the Sierra Club identified sprawl, defined as "low-density, automobile-dependent development," as the chief environmental problem facing the nation. Between 1992 and 1997 Americans developed about 3.2 million acres of open land every year, nearly double the rate during the 1980s. In 1920 there were about ten people living on every acre of land in America's cities and suburbs; by 1990 there were only four. The result was a human-made suburban landscape composed of strip malls and cookie-cutter residential areas. Sprawl eroded about 50 acres of valuable farmland every hour. "Where Old Macdonald had a farm, a hamburger joint now stands," noted *The Economist.*

One of the most annoying features of sprawl was traffic congestion. In 1990 Americans owned 180 million cars and light trucks. By 1997 the fleet was up to 200 million. With relatively few new roads to travel on, the extra cars inevitably caused more traffic jams. The expansion of stores, fast-food restaurants, and housing developments added to the congestion. Between 1982 and 2000 the U.S. population grew by 20 percent, but the amount of time Americans spent in traffic increased by a staggering 236 percent. Atlanta led the nation in the average distance its commuters traveled each day to work, 36.5 miles round-trip. Seattle residents spent an average of fifty-nine hours per year stuck in traffic, the sixth highest in the nation. "We moved to the suburbs to get lawns and a country setting," complained an environmentalist. "Now we find we are sitting in traffic going to work and going to get a quart of milk."

While Americans embraced the idea of a single home in the suburbs as the fulfillment of the American dream, they often resented the consequences of unlimited growth. Polls revealed that the vast majority of Americans associated the suburbs with better schools, low crime, and convenient shopping. Critics charged that antisprawl advocates who had already purchased their ideal home in the suburbs wanted to deny others the same opportunity. "What's the difference between an environmentalist and a developer?" asked a popular joke. "The environmentalist already has his house in the mountains."

The fractured nature of American local government made sprawl difficult to control. Metropolitan areas in the United States were often divided into dozens of smaller administrative units that made the decisions about whether to permit building. In 1998 voters in local communities across the nation approved 173 referendums designed either to limit regional growth or preserve open space. By a 2–1 margin voters in New Jersey agreed to pay $100 million over ten years to buy 1 million acres of open space. In 1999 the Clinton administration launched a "livability agenda," which called for the creation of a $9.5 billion fund for state and local governments to buy undeveloped land. Since the federal government encouraged the growth by building highways and roads, providing federally guaranteed mortgages, and offering a strong tax incentive for people to purchase a home, Clinton argued that Washington had a responsibility to help solve the problem.

The 2000 Presidential Election

Prosperity provided the backdrop to the first presidential election of the new millennium. The Democrats rallied around Vice President Al Gore, who promised to sustain the Clinton-era economic growth. In August at the party's convention in Los Angeles, Gore launched his "prosperity and progress" campaign, promising increased federal spending on health care, social security, and education. Striking a populist pose, Gore promised middle-class taxpayers that he would fight for "the people" and against "the powerful" special interests. Walking a political tightrope, Gore clung to Clinton's success while distancing himself from the president's scandals. "I stand here tonight as my own man," he told cheering delegates. As his running mate, Gore selected Joseph Lieberman, a centrist senator from Connecticut, who became the first Jewish-American nominated by a major party.

Republican leaders, eager to win back the White House, threw their support and money behind Texas governor George W. Bush, the oldest son of the former president. After stumbling in the primaries against Vietnam War hero Senator John McCain of Arizona, Bush regained his footing and captured his party's nomination. With federal coffers overflowing with revenue, Bush promised the nation "prosperity with a purpose." Calling for a "compassionate conservatism," the Republican nominee solidified his conservative base by advocating a massive tax cut while at the same time reaching out to independents with pledges to fund increased social spending for education and health care. Above all, he vowed to return honor and dignity to the White House. Ahead in the polls, and confident of victory, Bush chose the uncharismatic former Secretary of Defense Richard Cheney as his running mate.

Bush watched his once-sizable lead in the polls evaporate through the summer and fall. For the final two months of the campaign the two contestants remained locked in a tight race. Bush hammered away at the vice president's integrity, while Gore raised questions about Bush's stature and experience. Three presidential debates in October did little to break the logjam. Voters found Gore more knowledgeable on issues, but they felt that Bush appeared more relaxed and personable. While Gore and Bush battled each other, consumer advocate Ralph Nader, running on the Green party platform, mocked both candidates. Nader relished the role of spoiler, threatening to siphon enough votes in key states—California, Michigan, Oregon, and Washington—to deny Gore a victory.

On election night Gore clung to a small margin in the popular vote, but with Florida and its critical 25 electoral votes too close to call, the election remained deadlocked. After a series of counts and recounts, Florida's Republican secretary of state certified Bush the winner on November 27—more than two weeks after the election. But the campaign did not end there: Gore contested the results, claiming that many ballots remained uncounted or improperly counted, effectively disfranchising thousands of voters. Republicans accused Gore of trying to steal the election; Democrats attacked Republicans for thwarting the "will of the people." The nation braced for a constitutional crisis. On December 12, after weeks of legal maneuvering, a deeply divided Supreme Court ended the historic impasse. In a controversial 5–4 ruling in the case of *Bush* v. *Gore*, the justices blocked further manual recounts, which effectively named George Bush the winner. Bush became only the fourth president, and the first since 1888, to take office having lost the popular vote.

PRIMARY SOURCE

18.2 | *Bush* v. *Gore*
      | SUPREME COURT

With the presidential election depending on a ruling in the *Bush* v. *Gore* case, the Supreme Court ordered the manual recount of Florida votes to end on December 12, 2000. The controversial nature of the case, resulting in a 5–4 split among the justices, was evident in the *per curiam* and dissenting opinions.

From the Per Curiam Opinion

The Supreme Court of Florida has said that the legislature intended the State's electors to "participate fully in the federal electoral process" . . . as provided in 3 U.S.C. 5.

That statute, in turn, requires that any controversy or contest that is designed
5 to lead to a conclusive selection of electors be completed by December 12. That date is upon us, and there is no recount procedure in place under the State Supreme Court's order that comports with minimal constitutional standards.

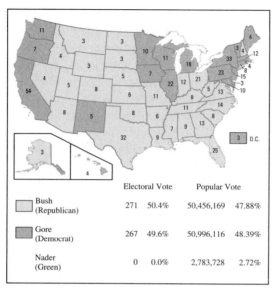

	Electoral Vote		Popular Vote	
Bush (Republican)	271	50.4%	50,456,169	47.88%
Gore (Democrat)	267	49.6%	50,996,116	48.39%
Nader (Green)	0	0.0%	2,783,728	2.72%

The Election of 2000   Early on the evening of the election (November 7), most of the major media outlets proclaimed Al Gore and his running mate, Joseph Lieberman, winners in Florida, but as the night wore on and votes from the panhandle of the state trickled in, journalists had to recant. By morning, George Bush, if he held Florida, was the presidential victor, but his lead was so minimal that Gore did not publicly concede that he had lost the election. Questions concerning the Florida votes, especially the ballots discarded for improper marks, led to a month-long debate over whether the disputed ballots should be counted by hand, leaving the fate of the election undecided. On December 12, the Supreme Court ruled 5–4 against the manual recount and Gore accepted defeat, despite the fact that he had won the majority of popular votes.

  Because it is evident that any recount seeking to meet the December 12 date will be unconstitutional for the reasons we have discussed, we reverse the judg-
10 ment of the Supreme Court of Florida ordering a recount to proceed. Seven Justices of the Court agree that there are constitutional problems with the recount ordered by the Florida Supreme Court that demand a remedy. . . . The only disagreement is as to the remedy.

  Because the Florida Supreme Court has said that the Florida Legislature
15 intended to obtain the safe-harbor benefits of 3 U.S.C. 5, Justice Breyer's proposed remedy remanding to the Florida Supreme Court for its ordering of a constitutionally proper contest until December 18—contemplates action in violation of the Florida election code, and hence could not be part of an "appropriate" order. . . .

From Chief Justice Rehnquist, with Whom Justice Scalia and Justice Thomas Join, Concurring

In most cases, comity and respect for federalism compel us to defer to the decisions of state courts on issues of state law. That practice reflects our understanding that the decisions of state courts are definitive pronouncements of the will of the States as sovereigns. . . . Of course, in ordinary cases, the distribution of powers among the branches of a State's government raises no questions of federal constitutional law, subject to the requirement that the government be republican in character. . . . But there are a few exceptional cases in which the Constitution imposes a duty or confers a power on a particular branch of a State's government. This is one of them."

From Justice Stevens, with Whom Justice Ginsburg and Justice Breyer Join, Dissenting

When questions arise about the meaning of state laws, including election laws, it is our settled practice to accept the opinions of the highest courts of the States as providing the final answers. On rare occasions, however, either federal statutes or the Federal Constitution may require federal judicial intervention in state elections. This is not such an occasion. The federal questions that ultimately emerged in this case are not substantial. . . .

From Justice Breyer's Dissent

The Court was wrong to take this case. It was wrong to grant a stay. It should now vacate that stay and permit the Florida Supreme Court to decide whether the recount should resume.

The political implications of this case for the country are momentous. But the federal legal questions presented, with one exception, are insubstantial. . . . The majority justifies stopping the recount entirely on the ground that there is no more time. In particular, the majority relies on the lack of time for the Secretary to review and approve equipment needed to separate undervotes. But the majority reaches this conclusion in the absence of *any* record evidence that the recount could not have been completed in the time allowed by the Florida Supreme Court. . . . Of course, it is too late for any such recount to take place by December 12, the date by which election disputes must be decided if a State is to take advantage of the safe harbor provisions of 3 U.S.C. 5.

Whether there is time to conduct a recount prior to December 18, when the electors are scheduled to meet, is a matter for the state courts to determine. . . . Halting the manual recount, and thus ensuring that the uncounted legal votes will not be counted under any standard, this Court crafts a remedy out of proportion to the asserted harm. And that remedy harms the very fairness interests the Court is attempting to protect. The manual recount would itself redress a problem of unequal treatment of ballots. . . . I fear that in order to bring this agonizingly long election process to a definitive conclusion, we have not adequately attended to that necessary "check upon our own exercise of power," "our own sense of self-restraint." . . . What it does today, the Court should have left undone. I would repair the damage done as best we now can, by permitting the Florida recount to continue under uniform standards. I respectfully dissent."

From Justice Souter's Dissent, with Whom Justices Breyer, Stevens, and Ginsburg Join

If this Court had allowed the State to follow the course indicated by the opinions of its own Supreme Court, it is entirely possible that there would ultimately have been no issue requiring our review, and political tension could have worked itself out in the Congress following the procedure provided in 3 U.S.C.
5 15. The case being before us, however, its resolution by the majority is another erroneous decision. . . .

As will be clear, I am in substantial agreement with the dissenting opinions of Justice Stevens, Justice Ginsburg and Justice Breyer. I write separately only to say how straightforward the issues before us really are. . . . In deciding what to do
10 about this, we should take account of the fact that electoral votes are due to be cast in six days. I would therefore remand the case to the courts of Florida with instructions to establish uniform standards for evaluating the several types of ballots that have prompted differing treatments, to be applied within and among counties when passing on such identical ballots in any further recounting (or
15 successive recounting) that the courts might order.

Unlike the majority, I see no warrant for this Court to assume that Florida could not possibly comply with this requirement before the date set for the meeting of electors, December 18. ■ ■ ■

The election revealed that unprecedented prosperity had failed to mute deep social divisions in America. The public remained deeply troubled by the election outcome, the winner lacked a clear mandate, the Senate was split 50–50, and Republicans held only a razor-thin majority in the House. Included among the new class of senators was New York's Hillary Rodham Clinton, who became the only first lady in history to seek and win elective office.

Analysis of voting results revealed that Democrats had done well in urban areas and that Republicans had won majorities in suburban and rural areas. By race, African-Americans gave 95 percent of their votes to Gore; whites preferred Bush. By gender, women favored Democrats; men leaned toward the Republicans. Finally, by religion, regular churchgoers voted Republican; infrequent churchgoers supported Democrats. The election revealed, observed the journalist Andrew Sullivan, "that America is currently two nations, as culturally and politically alien as they are geographically distinct."

SELECTED READINGS

■ Arthur M. Schlesinger Jr.'s *The Disuniting of America* (1991) is a good discussion about the conflicts and tensions of 1990s American society. Robert Bellah et al. discuss the continuing presence of a national culture in *The Good Society* (1991). Haynes Johnson examines the prosperity of the decades as well as the culture's darker side in *The Best of Times* (2001). Currently, the best sources for discussion about trends in American culture and politics are periodicals—which are a useful and timely source of commentary for any period. See, for example, *The Atlantic Monthly, Business Week, Congressional Quarterly, The Economist* (London), *Fortune, Harper's Magazine, Monthly Labor Review, The New Republic, National Review, The Nation, The New Leader, New York Times Magazine, The Progressive, U.S. News and World Report,* and *The Utne Reader.*

▪ Michael Williams's *A History of Computing Technology* (1997) describes the development of the modern computer. In *The Politics of Cyberspace* (1997), Chris Toulouse and Timothy W. Luke explore the emerging information age. Art Wolinsky traces the development of the Internet as a communication tool from its military beginnings to its use in everyday life in *The History of the Internet and the World Wide Web* (1999). Thomas L. Friedman's *The Lexus and the Olive Tree* (1999) discusses the impact of globalization on American society.

▪ Patricia Albjerg-Graham's *SOS: Sustain Our Schools* (1992) studies the crisis in education. Alex Kotlowitz's *There Are No Children Here* (1991) is a searing depiction of urban poverty and violence in the 1990s. Harreel Rodgers discusses the impact on poverty as a result of changes in welfare laws in the late 1990s in *American Poverty in a New Era of Reform* (2000). Juliet B. Schor's *The Overworked American* (1993) and *The Overspent American* (1998) both study the shrinking leisure time of Americans in the 1990s. Andres Duany, Jeff Speck, and Elizabeth Plater-Zyberk assess the impact of suburban sprawl on the economy, the environment, and society in *Suburban Nation* (2000).

▪ Popular culture in the 1990s has been exhaustively studied in popular books, though often without much historical perspective. Neal Gabler's *Life: The Movie* (1999) contains an excellent analysis of how entertainment has infiltrated and conquered reality. Gini Graham Scott explores the influence and impact of talk shows on society in *Can We Talk?* (1996). Lawrence M. Friedman's *The Horizontal Society* (1999) explores the democratization of modern popular culture. Chuck D, a twenty-year veteran of the rap-music industry, describes this musical movement and its impact on America culture in *Fight the Power* (1997).

▪ Richard J. Herrnstein and Charles Murray's *The Bell Curve* (1996), though still hotly debated, is emblematic of the debate over affirmative action. Editor Evelyn Hu-DeHart provides essays that examine the impact of globalization on recent Asian immigrants in *Across the Pacific* (1999). Robert Suro's *Strangers Among Us* (1998) investigates the history of the Latino community in America and the challenges its growth presents for the future. Richard Abanes's *American Militias: Rebellion, Racism, and Religion* (1996) and Philip Lamy's *Millennium Rage* (1996) are both good introductions to the antigovernment groups of the 1990s.

The Challenges of the New Century

The distinctive Twin Towers of the World Trade Center had been a landmark of Manhattan's skyline since their construction in 1973. The 110-story Towers, the tallest buildings in North America, served as home to some of the world's largest financial services firms, and the surrounding area of restaurants and stores resembled a small city, providing services for the twenty-five thousand people who worked in the two skyscrapers.

On the morning of September 11, 2001, Aaron Goldsmith, a Columbia University student and part-time employee of the investment bank Lehman Brothers, was sitting at his desk on the fortieth floor of Tower One. At 8:48 he felt a powerful tremor. "Everything shook," he recalled. "The lights dimmed." As he rushed out of the building, Goldsmith learned that an American Airlines plane loaded with passengers had smashed into the upper floors of the building. By the time Goldsmith had climbed down forty flights of stairs, a second plane plowed into the upper floors of Tower Two. As the rest of the nation looked on in horror, the intense heat from the burning jet fuel melted the steel frame of Tower Two, forcing it to collapse in on itself. A few minutes later Tower One crumbled, sending a choking gray cloud billowing through the canyons of Lower Manhattan. "The screaming was just horrendous," recalled a witness. Thousands of victims were crushed, including hundreds of New York firefighters and police who had rushed into the building to rescue office workers trapped in the inferno. In a matter of minutes the once-majestic towers had been reduced to a heap of twisted metal and the area around the World Trade Center resembled a desert after a terrible sandstorm.

The attacks on the World Trade Center were part of a well-coordinated terrorist assault on the symbols of American economic and military might. A third hijacked plane smashed into the western part of the Pentagon. A fourth plane, possibly headed to the Capitol building or the White

House, crashed in a field in western Pennsylvania after passengers rushed the cockpit.

The repercussions of the attack spread across the nation. The White House, the Pentagon, and the Capitol were evacuated. The Federal Aviation Administration halted all air traffic across the United States and diverted all international flights to Canada. The government closed the borders with Canada and Mexico and shut down most federal buildings across the country. Major skyscrapers and a variety of other potential terrorist targets, ranging from Florida's Disney World to the Sears Tower in Chicago, were evacuated. Global financial markets plunged into chaos. "IT'S WAR!" screamed the headline of the *New York Daily News*.

The attacks confronted the young Bush administration with a major international crisis. Many observers believed that the threat of global terrorism would usher in a new era in international relations, reshuffling old alliances, and reaffirming others, in a struggle that would be as defining as the Cold War. "You recognize that something's changed forever in the way that the United States thinks about its security," observed national security adviser Condoleezza Rice. President George Bush proclaimed that the United States was engaged in the "first war of the 21st century." The attacks forced the nation to confront new challenges, but they also raised old concerns about the American paradox.

The Bush Presidency

George Bush turned to veterans of previous Republican administrations to staff his White House. Three members of the Bush inner circle had served under President Gerald Ford: Vice President Dick Cheney, Secretary of the Treasury Paul O'Neill, and Secretary of Defense Donald Rumsfeld. From his father's administration, Bush chose General Colin Powell for secretary of state, the first African-American to serve in that post. Another African-American, former Stanford University professor Condoleezza Rice, served as national security adviser. Senate Democrats blocked the nomination of conservative Hispanic commentator Linda Chavez as labor secretary, but they failed to defeat other conservative appointments, most notably former Senator John Ashcroft as attorney general and former Attorney General of Colorado Gale Norton as interior secretary.

Despite the narrowness of his victory, Bush moved aggressively to pass key elements of his agenda. First on the list was a $1.6 trillion, ten-year tax-cut package. The president's original proposal passed the Republican-dominated House, but ran into trouble in the Senate, where moderates trimmed roughly

$450 billion from the original proposal and added more spending than the president wanted. Passage of the trimmed-down tax cut, the largest since 1981, represented a major legislative victory for the new administration.

The intensely partisan debates over the tax cuts, and the president's unwillingness to give more ground to Senate Democrats, cast the new administration in a decidedly conservative light. The president's hard line on politically sensitive environmental issues contributed to the perception that he was trying to secure his conservative base in the early days of his administration. The president angered environmentalists when he retreated on his campaign pledge to regulate carbon dioxide emissions from power plants. He also announced that the United States would abandon the 1997 Kyoto Protocol, which required developed countries to reduce greenhouse gas emissions. When he pushed to allow oil drilling in the Arctic National Wildlife Refuge, many critics, including moderate Republicans, complained that the president had abandoned his pledge to be a "compassionate conservative."

In May the administration suffered a serious blow when Vermont Republican senator James Jeffords announced that he was bolting the Republican Party and becoming an Independent. Jeffords, who often voted with Democrats, charged that the administration had moved too far to the right, ignoring the advice of moderates, especially on the environment and education. The move switched control of the Senate to the Democrats and produced legislative gridlock on Capitol Hill. Throughout the summer Democrats and Republicans bickered over campaign finance reform, a patient's bill of rights, and education reform. An odd coalition of liberals and conservatives opposed Bush's effort to help religious, or "faith-based," groups obtain federal funds. Liberals claimed that such funding violated the constitutional separation of church and state, while religious conservatives worried that the government would try to influence their message. By the end of the summer Bush's approval rating had dropped more than 10 points, to around 50 percent in most surveys.

The political agenda switched dramatically on September 11. The president was in Florida speaking to schoolchildren when he received word of the terrorist attacks. He boarded Air Force One but did not return immediately to Washington. Warned of a possible assassination plot, the Secret Service ordered the plane to an air force base in Nebraska. Returning later that night to the White House, a somber president told the nation that the United States would hunt down and punish those responsible for the "evil, despicable acts of terror." A few days later in a televised speech before a joint session of Congress, Bush told Americans to prepare for a "lengthy campaign unlike any other we have ever seen." The goal, he said, was to find, stop, and defeat "every terrorist group of global reach." The United States would make no distinction between those who carried out the hijackings and those who harbored and supported them, he said.

PRIMARY **SOURCE**

Epilogue | *Declaration of War on Terrorism*
GEORGE BUSH

In a televised message on September 20, 2001, President Bush addressed the nation before a joint session of Congress and proclaimed war on terrorism in retaliation for the attacks on the World Trade Center Towers and the Pentagon.

On September the 11th, enemies of freedom committed an act of war against our country. Americans have known wars—but for the past 136 years, they have been wars on foreign soil, except for one Sunday in 1941. Americans have known the casualties of war—but not at the center of a great city on a peaceful
5 morning. Americans have known surprise attacks—but never before on thousands of civilians. All of this was brought upon us in a single day—and night fell on a different world, a world where freedom itself is under attack.

Americans have many questions tonight. Americans are asking: Who attacked our country? The evidence we have gathered all points to a collection of loosely
10 affiliated terrorist organizations known as al Qaeda. They are the same murderers indicted for bombing American embassies in Tanzania and Kenya, and responsible for bombing the USS *Cole*.

Al Qaeda is to terror what the mafia is to crime. But its goal is not making money; its goal is remaking the world—and imposing its radical beliefs on peo-
15 ple everywhere.

The terrorists practice a fringe form of Islamic extremism that has been rejected by Muslim scholars and the vast majority of Muslim clerics—a fringe movement that perverts the peaceful teachings of Islam. The terrorists' direc- tive commands them to kill Christians and Jews, to kill all Americans, and
20 to make no distinction among military and civilians, including women and children.

This group and its leader—a person named Osama bin Laden—are linked to many other organizations in different countries, including the Egyptian Islamic Jihad and the Islamic Movement of Uzbekistan. There are thousands
25 of these terrorists in more than 60 countries. They are recruited from their own nations and neighborhoods and brought to camps in places like Afghanistan, where they are trained in the tactics of terror. They are sent back to their homes or sent to hide in countries around the world to plot evil and destruction.

30 The leadership of al Qaeda has great influence in Afghanistan and supports the Taliban regime in controlling most of that country. In Afghanistan, we see al Qaeda's vision for the world.

Afghanistan's people have been brutalized—many are starving and many have fled. Women are not allowed to attend school. You can be jailed for owning
35 a television. Religion can be practiced only as their leaders dictate. A man can be jailed in Afghanistan if his beard is not long enough.

The United States respects the people of Afghanistan—after all, we are cur- rently its largest source of humanitarian aid—but we condemn the Taliban regime. (Applause.) It is not only repressing its own people, it is threatening peo-
40 ple everywhere by sponsoring and sheltering and supplying terrorists. By aiding and abetting murder, the Taliban regime is committing murder.

And tonight, the United States of America makes the following demands on the Taliban: Deliver to United States authorities all the leaders of al Qaeda who hide in your land. (Applause.) Release all foreign nationals, including American
45 citizens, you have unjustly imprisoned. Protect foreign journalists, diplomats and aid workers in your country. Close immediately and permanently every terrorist training camp in Afghanistan, and hand over every terrorist, and every person in their support structure, to appropriate authorities. (Applause.) Give the United States full access to terrorist training camps, so we can make sure they are no
50 longer operating.

These demands are not open to negotiation or discussion. (Applause.) The Taliban must act, and act immediately. They will hand over the terrorists, or they will share in their fate.

I also want to speak tonight directly to Muslims throughout the world. We
55 respect your faith. It's practiced freely by many millions of Americans, and by millions more in countries that America counts as friends. Its teachings are good and peaceful, and those who commit evil in the name of Allah blaspheme the name of Allah. (Applause.) The terrorists are traitors to their own faith, trying, in

effect, to hijack Islam itself. The enemy of America is not our many Muslim
60   friends; it is not our many Arab friends. Our enemy is a radical network of terrorists, and every government that supports them. (Applause.)

Our war on terror begins with al Qaeda, but it does not end there. It will not
end until every terrorist group of global reach has been found, stopped and
defeated. (Applause.)

65   Americans are asking, why do they hate us? They hate what we see right here
in this chamber—a democratically elected government. Their leaders are self-
appointed. They hate our freedoms—our freedom of religion, our freedom of
speech, our freedom to vote and assemble and disagree with each other.

They want to overthrow existing governments in many Muslim countries, such
70   as Egypt, Saudi Arabia, and Jordan. They want to drive Israel out of the Middle
East. They want to drive Christians and Jews out of vast regions of Asia and Africa.

These terrorists kill not merely to end lives, but to disrupt and end a way of life.
With every atrocity, they hope that America grows fearful, retreating from the world
and forsaking our friends. They stand against us, because we stand in their way.

75   We are not deceived by their pretenses to piety. We have seen their kind
before. They are the heirs of all the murderous ideologies of the 20th century. By
sacrificing human life to serve their radical visions—by abandoning every value
except the will to power—they follow in the path of fascism, and Nazism, and
totalitarianism. And they will follow that path all the way, to where it ends: in his-
80   tory's unmarked grave of discarded lies. (Applause.) . . .   ■ ■ ■

Blowback

Intelligence experts suspected that only Saudi billionaire Osama bin Laden possessed the resources to pull off such a daring and complicated operation. Craft-
ing a public image in the Islamic world as the leader of a religious struggle on
behalf of the poor and the dispossessed, bin Laden led a worldwide network of
supporters known in Arabic as al Qaeda ("The Base"). Dubbed "Terror, Inc.,"
al Qaeda represented a new form of terrorist threat. Although it lacked a clear
hierarchy, no lieutenants or generals, al Qaeda maintained the sort of discipline
found in well-trained armies. "It's a completely new phenomenon," said a British
intelligence official. "You could call it disorganized-organized terrorism."

Ironically, the United States had supported bin Laden during the 1980s when
both were fighting to expel the Soviet Union from Afghanistan. The Central
Intelligence Agency (CIA) spent nearly $500 million a year to arm and train the
Afghan rebels fighting the Soviets. In 1985, with the Soviets making major
gains on the battlefield, the CIA provided the rebels with stinger surface-to-air
missiles. The new weapons, which allowed the Afghans to shoot down hundreds of Soviet planes, marked a decisive turning point in the war. The United
States considered its support of the insurgents one of the most successful examples of counterterrorism. But in a classic case of "blowback," the victory came
back to haunt America. The Afghan jihad, or "holy war," fired the radical Arab

imagination. With the fall of the Soviet Union, many of the rebels turned their anger against the world's only remaining superpower—their former patron, the United States. "This is an insane instance of the chickens coming home to roost," said one U.S. diplomat in neighboring Pakistan. "You can't plug billions of dollars into an anti-Communist jihad, accept participation from all over the world and ignore the consequences. But we did."

The key turning point came in 1990 when the United States sent troops to Saudi Arabia during the Gulf War. Bin Laden denounced the "occupation" of the Arab Holy Land by "American crusader forces," which he described as "the latest and greatest aggression" against the Islamic world since the death of the prophet Muhammad in 632. The following year bin Laden fled Saudi Arabia, moving first to Afghanistan and then to Sudan, where he financed several terrorist training camps and orchestrated attacks on American interests, including the 1993 attack on the World Trade Center. In 1996 Sudan expelled bin Laden and most of his supporters after the United States mounted political and diplomatic pressure. He moved back to Afghanistan, where he provided financial support to the radical Taliban leaders who were fighting against the Northern Alliance for control of the capital of Kabul.

Hiding in mountain retreats, and protected by his Taliban hosts, bin Laden in 1998 coordinated the bombings of U.S. embassies in Tanzania and Kenya, killing more than 220. The United States responded to the attacks by bombing training camps in Afghanistan and a factory in Sudan that was suspected of producing chemical weapons. The Clinton administration warned the Taliban government that it risked further retaliation if it continued to give safe haven to bin Laden. Taliban leaders refused to turn him over, and the al Qaeda network continued its destructive ways. In October 2000 the USS *Cole,* a destroyer making a refueling stop in Yemen, was nearly sunk when a small boat loaded with explosives slammed into its side. "The destroyer represented the capital of the West," bin Laden said, "and the small boat represented Muhammad."

"We Are All Soldiers Now"

President Bush declared war on terrorism the day that the hijackers slammed the commercial airliners into the World Trade Center and the Pentagon, but the actual military response did not begin until early October. In the weeks leading up to the military assault, the administration froze the assets of organizations suspected of supporting terrorists and built an impressive international coalition to bolster military action in Afghanistan. Included in the coalition were a number of Arab states, especially neighboring Pakistan, whose support was necessary to gather intelligence and to provide bases for the United States to launch air strikes. More importantly, the administration hoped that an alliance with other Arab states would blunt bin Laden's effort to characterize the war as a battle between the Christian West and the Muslim East.

American military technology and superior air power proved no match for the poorly equipped Taliban fighters. On October 7 the United States and Britain launched a series of punishing air strikes using long-range bombers and cruise missiles. The air campaign weakened the Taliban regime and allowed the opposition Northern Alliance forces to gain control of the capital, Kabul, in November. While U.S. special forces joined the hunt for Osama bin Laden in a series of cave complexes near Tora Bora, U.S. planes continued their relentless bombing of suspected Taliban positions in the south. On December 6, Taliban forces surrendered the southern city of Kandahar, their last stronghold. Pockets of Taliban forces remained in Afghanistan, launching hit-and-run attacks against western troops, but they had lost control of major cities and transportation routes. Critics hailed the American campaign as "a masterpiece of military creativity and finesse," but it ended without the capture of Osama bin Laden or the leaders of the Taliban government.

The war imposed additional hardship on the Central Asian nation of 22 million people that over the previous two decades had contended with Soviet invasion, civil war, hunger, drought, and the rise of the radical Taliban militia. More than 4 million people had already fled. "A humanitarian crisis of stunning proportions is unfolding in Afghanistan," the United Nations warned at the beginning of the war. Those most at risk were women and children "with a fragile grip on survival." Once again many innocent civilians were caught in the crossfire. "I don't know Osama. Why when things happen in the east, the west or the north of the world, do the problems have to come here and hit straight at the people of Afghanistan?" asked Farida, a forty-year-old widow and mother of four in Kabul.

The need to sustain a broad coalition to fight the war complicated America's relationship with its closest ally in the region—Israel. Needing to keep moderate Arab friends on board, the Bush administration publicly endorsed the creation of a Palestinian state. The announcement shocked Israeli leaders, who feared that the United States was rewarding terrorism. Prime Minister Ariel Sharon compared America's actions to those of Britain and France in 1938 when they allowed Nazi Germany to take over part of Czechoslovakia in exchange for Adolf Hitler's promise of peace—a promise that was quickly broken. "Do not try to placate the Arabs at Israel's expense," he blustered. "We are not Czechoslovakia."

The war on terrorism blurred the line between combatant and civilians. With thousands of militants bent on waging a holy war with the United States, the nation braced for more attacks at home. Hours after the air attack bin Laden issued a chilling video celebrating the attacks on New York and Washington as "America struck by almighty God in its vital organs." He threatened further terrorist attacks. "I swear to God that America will not live in peace before peace reigns in Palestine and before all the army of infidels departs the land of Muhammad."

When an employee of American Media, a tabloid publisher in the Florida town of Boca Raton, died from exposure to anthrax, the nation assumed that bin Laden and his network had unleashed the biological attack. Concern about biological terrorism heightened a few weeks later when thirty-one workers on

Capitol Hill were exposed to anthrax spores from a contaminated letter sent to the office of Senate majority leader Tom Daschle. Public health officials were caught off-guard by the realization that anthrax seeped through the sealed letters and contaminated postal facilities in Washington and New York. The postmaster general announced that he could not guarantee the safety of the mail. "We are all soldiers now," Bush told the nation.

The Paradox of Power

The September 11 terrorist attacks led to a major reordering of priorities for the new Bush administration. Having won election by promising to shrink the Washington bureaucracy and limit government spending, Bush presided over an expansion of federal power unseen since the days of Lyndon Johnson's Great Society. Within the first few weeks of the crisis the president approved $55 billion in federal spending, including a massive federal relief package for New York. The president abandoned traditional conservative faith in deregulation and orchestrated a federal bailout of the airlines.

Most surprising of all, Bush became the first president since Jimmy Carter to create a new cabinet-level agency. Nine days after the attack the president appointed Pennsylvania's Republican governor Tom Ridge to serve as new homeland security coordinator. Trying to balance his conservative instincts with the heightened public expectations, the president gave the new antiterrorism czar a broad mandate but little authority. The executive order creating the office used the word *coordinate* more than thirty times but never used the word *command* or *control.* Facing the daunting task of coordinating over forty government agencies and a bewildering mass of overlapping jurisdictions, Ridge lacked the power to issue orders or control budgets.

In June 2002, Bush responded to criticism that the homeland security czar lacked the authority to deal with the security threat facing the nation by calling for the creation of a new department of homeland security, which would include 169,000 employees from eight existing Cabinet departments and a budget of $37.4 billion. The proposal represented the largest reorganization of the federal government since Harry Truman signed the National Security Act of 1947. "Our government must be reorganized to deal more effectively with the new threats of the twenty-first century," the president said in an eleven-minute television address.

The administration showed less restraint in flexing federal police power. Fear that a network of "sleeper agents" was operating in the United States, preparing a future attack, led to a dramatic expansion of federal law enforcement power. In the first few months after the attack the Federal Bureau of Investigation arrested over one thousand suspects, moved them to unknown locations, and monitored their communications with their lawyers. In addition, the president signed an executive order allowing foreigners accused of terrorism to be tried in military tribunals. Attorney General John Ashcroft said the policy was intended to stop inmates who had been involved in terrorism from passing messages to confederates through lawyers, their assistants, or translators "for the purpose of continuing terrorist activities." But critics asked how far the government would go in attempting to balance its need to protect the national welfare with its responsibility to protect civil liberties. "We call ourselves a nation of laws," a defense attorney said, "and the test of a nation of laws is whether it adheres to them in times of stress."

In response to the crisis, the nation experienced a revival of patriotism, a new assertion of civic nationalism. Charitable donations to victims soared, stores sold out of flags, and people waited in long lines to donate blood. The American public rallied around the president, giving him the highest sustained approval ratings since Franklin Roosevelt. Students, whose predecessors had provided the backbone of the peace movement during the 1960s, expressed overwhelming support for the military action in Afghanistan. Revealing a sea change in student opinion, nearly 80 percent of Harvard undergraduates supported the air strikes and 75 percent said they "trust the military to do the right thing."

For a brief period the language of national unity replaced the rhetoric of cultural pluralism. "I was watching when the second plane crashed," remarked Laura Ovalle, a Mexican immigrant living in Texas. "I'm 100 percent Mexican, but I'm 200 percent proud of living in the United States." Tony Morgan, an African-American who worked at Ground Zero, said, "I'm American 100 percent, but I haven't always been proud of what America has done." A gay computer programmer in Houston was struck by the inclusiveness of the new unity. "There was media coverage of gay families, gay pilots and gay heroes," he said. "The red cross responded without blinking that it would honor gay and lesbian relationships when determining who would be provided assistance."

While African-Americans supported the war effort, many feared that debate over social problems would be stifled by calls for national unity. "The country will now put money into cleaning out terrorists, money that it couldn't find for schools for black children, or for jobs and opportunities," observed the psychiatrist James P. Comer. Without condoning terrorism, many blacks understood the resentment many Arab nations felt toward America's sense of racial superiority. "Many black families are in pain and are profoundly affected by these tragedies," observed an African Methodist Episcopal bishop. "At the same time, you have a strain of concern that says our country's foreign policy treats Arabs the same way its domestic policy has historically treated blacks." African-American congresswoman Barbara Lee of California received death threats when she cast the only vote against legislation allowing the president "to use all necessary and appropriate force" against the terrorists.

The conflict between nationalism and pluralism was especially painful for Muslims and Arab-Americans. Like everyone else, they grieved the loss of friends and colleagues, supported the war effort, and raised money for victims' families. But since all the known hijackers were Arabs, most Americans looked at members of that community with added suspicion. Polls showed that most groups, including African-Americans, favored some form of racial profiling of Arabs. For the most part, however, the public heeded President Bush's plea for tolerance and incidents of bias were kept to a minimum. Some Japanese-Americans, who had been herded into internment camps during World War II, expressed sympathy for the plight of Arabs. "I know how the people being called terrorists are feeling, what it's like when people think you're guilty just because of your looks," reflected Sumi Shimatsu, who spent time in an internment camp as a child. "I remember when the only good Jap was a dead Jap."

President Bush's "new type of war" on terrorism touched off a familiar fight over government secrecy. The administration argued that changing technology required the Pentagon to clamp down on information about military movements. In an age of instant communications and twenty-four-hour news channels, news traveled around the world in seconds, raising the possibility that crucial details about American military maneuvers could fall into the wrong hands. Bush laid out ground rules two days after the September 11 attacks: "Let me condition the press this way: Any sources and methods of intelligence will remain guarded in secret."

While circumstances have changed since 1945, the nation continues to struggle with the same paradox that defined much of its history in the last century. Will popular attitudes toward government prove capable of reconciling the demands for greater services with the traditional fear of federal power? How will society adjust to the influence of its diverse population while maintaining its sense of common identity? Can the government protect the national interest abroad without sacrificing democracy at home? The answers to those questions may prove elusive, but Americans will continue their search for a better society. "The idea of the search is what holds us together," noted the historian Daniel Boorstin. "The quest is the enduring American experiment. The meaning is in the seeking."

Credits

Text credits

P. 10: "The Sources of Soviet Conduct" by George Keenan reprinted by permission of *Foreign Affairs* (July, 1947). Copyright 1947 by the Council on Foreign Relations, Inc. P. 20: Henry Wallace letter to Truman from *The American Experiment: A History of the United States,* by Steve Gillon and Cathy Matson, pp. 1089–1090. Boston, MA: Houghton Mifflin Company. P. 22: The Truman Doctrine. Courtesy of the U.S. Historical Documents Archive. P. 43: Acceptance Speech by President Harry S. Truman at the Democratic National Convention, Philadelphia, July 15, 1948. P. 56: Excerpts from "NSC-68: A Report to the National Security Council," April 14, 1950, from *Foreign Relations Of The United States: 1950,* I, pp. 237–92. P. 72: Senator Joseph McCarthy Launches a "Final, All-Out Battle" Against Communist Sympathizers in the United States and Senator Margaret Chase Smith Warns Against Those Who Use "Fear, Ignorance, Bigotry, and Smear (Tactics)" for Political Gain. P. 92: "Here is Text of Graham's Wednesday Night Sermon" by Billy Graham from the *Charlotte Observer,* September 25, 1958, p. 6A. Reprinted with permission from The Charlotte Observer. Copyright owned by The Charlotte Observer. P. 99: "A Young $10 Billion Power: The US Teen-age Consumer Has Become a Major Factor in the Nation's Economy" from *Life,* August 31, 1959, pp. 78–84. Copyright © 1959 Time Inc. Reprinted by permission. P. 103: "What TV Is Doing To America" from *U.S. News & World Report,* September 2, 1955, pp. 36–50. Copyright © 1955 U.S. News & World Report, L.P. Reprinted with permission. P. 111: Excerpts from "The Fund Broadcast" speech by Richard M. Nixon, September 23, 1952. Reprinted by permission of the Estate of Richard Nixon. P. 127: Dwight D. Eisenhower, Decision Not to Intervene at Dien Bien Phu (1954). P. 128: "The Domino Theory" by Dwight D. Eisenhower from *Public Papers Of The Presidents Of The United States: Dwight D. Eisenhower,* 1954 (Washington, DC: Government Printing Office, 1958), pp. 381–390. P. 148: From *By The Bomb's Early Light: American Thought and Culture at the Dawn of the Atomic Age,* by Paul Boyer, pp. 310–311. Reprinted by permission of the author. P. 149: "Signs of Times in Atomic Age" from *Life,* February 27, 1950. Copyright 1950 Time Inc. Reprinted by permission. P. 163: "Statement of Purpose" from Student Nonviolent Coordinating Committee, 1960. Reprinted by permission of Martin Luther King, Jr. Papers Project c/o Stanford University. P. 176: Letters between President Diem to President Kennedy, 1961. P. 191: Text of Barry Goldwater's 1964 speech at the 28th Republican National Convention, accepting the nomination for President. P. 204: "The Gulf of Tonkin Resolution, 1964" from *Department Of State Bulletin,* Vol. 51, No. 1313 (August 24, 1964), p. 268. P. 205: "Memorandum for the President from George Ball" from *The Pentagon Papers,* Senator Gravel Edition, Volume IV, pp. 615–619. Boston, MA: Beacon Press. P. 219: "Port Huron Statement" by Tom Hayden, 1962. Reprinted by permission of the author. P. 221: "Sproul Hall Steps" by Mario Savio from December 2, 1964. Reprinted by permission. P. 226: "Appendix A, The Sharon Statement" from *The Other Side Of The Sixties: Young Americans for Freedom and the Rise of Conservative Politics,* by John A. Andrews III, pp. 221–222. Reprinted by permission. P. 232: "The Black Revolution" by Malcolm X from *Malcolm X Speaks.* Copyright © 1965, 1989 by Betty Shabazz and Pathfinder Press. Reprinted by permission. P. 254: President Richard M. Nixon Address on Vietnam to American Public, November 3, 1969. P. 271: "The Smoking Gun" by Richard Nixon, June 23, 1972 from Hearings Before The Committee On The Judiciary, House Of Representatives, 93rd Congress, 2nd Session (Washington, DC: Government Printing Office, 1974), pp. 512–514. P. 287: TM/© 2002 the Cesar E. Chavez Foundation by CMG Worldwide www.cmgww.com. Reprinted by permission. P. 291: Excerpt from *The Gay Militants* by Donn Teal. Copyright © 1995. New York: St. Martin's Press. P. 301: From *The Power Of The Positive Woman* by Phyllis Schlafly. Reprinted by permission of the author. P. 318: Proclamation of Pardon by Gerald R. Ford. P. 325: President Jimmy Carter Addresses the "Crisis of Confidence" Affecting the "Heart and Soul and Spirit" of the Nation. P. 328: From Ronald Reagan speech delivered before the International Business Council, September 9, 1980 in

Vital Speeches Of The Day, October 1, 1980, pp. 738–741. Reprinted by permission. P. 336: Reprinted with the permission of Simon & Schuster from *Speaking My Mind* by Ronald Reagan. Copyright © 1989 by Ronald W. Reagan. P. 346: Excerpt from Geraldine Ferraro's speech at the Democratic National Convention, 1984. Reprinted with permission of the Associated Press. P. 359: From Oliver North's Statement before a joint session of the Senate Select Committee on Secret Military Assistance to Iran and the Nicaraguan Opposition and House Select Committee to Investigate Covert Arms Transactions with Iran on July 9, 1987. P. 365: From *Listen America* by Jerry Falwell, copyright © 1980 by Jerry Falwell. Used by permission of Doubleday, a division of Random House, Inc. P. 369: Text of A. Bartlett Giamatti Letter to Yale Freshmen as appeared in the *New York Times,* September 6, 1981, p. 25. Copyright © 1981. Reprinted by permission of the Estate of A. Bartlett Giamatti. P. 375: Excerpt from March 3, 1988 testimony by Ryan White before the Presidential Commission on AIDS. P. 388: Excerpt from Ivan Boesky speech to Berkeley Business School graduating class, May 18, 1986. P. 413: President Bush asks Congress for a resolution authorizing military force against Iraq from *The American Experiment: A History Of The United States* by Steve Gillon and Cathy Matson, pp. 1297–1299. Boston, MA: Houghton Mifflin Company. P. 431: Source: Rep. Newt Gingrich, Rep. Dick Armey, and the House Republicans, *The Contract With America,* 1994. Reprinted by permission of Republican National Committee. P. 443: The Original Draft of President Bill Clinton's Apology to the American People for His "Improper Relationship" with Monica Lewinsky & The Speech He Ultimately Gave. P. 455: Portions of the statement by Lars Ulrich before the Senate Judiciary Committee reprinted with the permission of Lars Ulrich. P. 475: Excerpts from the U.S. Supreme Court Decision, December 13, 2000. P. 483: Address to a Joint Session of Congress and the American People, United States Capitol, Washington, D.C. September 20, 2001.

Maps and Figures credits

P. 18, Map 1.2: From *A Preponderance Of Power: National Security, The Truman Administration,* by Melvyn P. Leffler, p. 66. Copyright © 1992. Palo Alto, CA: Stanford University Press. P. 174, Map 7.1: From *Grand Expectations: The United States,* 1945–1974, by James T. Patterson, p. 503. Copyright © 1996. New York: Oxford University Press. P. 468, Figure 18.3: "Simpson Guilty Polls, 7/11–12/94" from the *New York Times,* January 1, 1995. Copyright © 1995 by The New York Times Co. Reprinted by permission. P. 460, Figure 18.2: "The Growth of Inequality" from the *New York Times,* January 1, 1989. Copyright © 1989 by The New York Times Co. Reprinted by permission.

Photo credits

P. 17: U.S. Army, courtesy Harry S. Truman Library. P. 19: Harry S. Truman Library. P. 27: Courtesy of the American Red Cross Museum. All rights reserved in all countries. P. 28: Abbie Rowe, National Park Service, courtesy Harry S. Truman Library. P. 37: ©United Mine Workers Archive. P. 40: ©AP/Wide World Photos. P. 47: © Bettmann/CORBIS. P. 49: © Bettmann/CORBIS. P. 63: © Bettmann/CORBIS. P. 64: © Bettmann/CORBIS. P. 67: ©AP/Wide World Photos. P. 68: © Bettmann/CORBIS. P. 78: Courtesy D.C. Public Library. P. 84: © Bettmann/CORBIS. P. 91: © Bettmann/CORBIS. P. 93: © Gjon Mili/Timepix. P. 96: © Richard Cummins/CORBIS. P. 98: ©AP/Wide World Photos. P. 111: © Bettmann/CORBIS. P. 143: ©Dan Weiner, courtesy Sandra Weiner. P. 146: ©Sovfoto. P. 159: John Fitzgerald Kennedy Library. P. 162: © Bettmann/CORBIS. P. 166: © Charles Moore/StockPhoto.com. P. 168: © Bettmann/CORBIS. P. 172: Photo No. Dx65-105:135 in the John F. Kennedy Library. P. 173: ©AP/Wide World Photos. P. 180: ©AP/Wide World Photos. P. 195: ©AP/Wide World Photos. P. 199: © Bettmann/CORBIS. P. 211: ©AP/Wide World Photos. p. 216: ©John Dominis/The Image Works. p. 222: Courtesy of University Archives, Bancroft Library, University of California, Berkeley. p. 229: © Bud Lee/Timepix. p. 239: LBJ Library Photo by Jack Kightlinger. p. 247: ©John Filo. p. 261: Nixon Presidential Materials Project, National Archives and Record Administration. p. 265: ©Paul Fusco/ Magnum Photos. p. 275: Nixon Presidential Materials Project, National Archives and Record Administration. P. 286: Owen Luck Photographer. P. 287: © 1976 George Ballis/Take Stock. P. 294: © Bettmann/CORBIS. P. 297: © J. Atlan/Corbis Sygma. P. 304: Carl Mydans/Timepix. P. 305: ©1974 Ira Wyman. P. 320: ©The New York Times. P. 325: Courtesy Jimmy Carter Library. P. 342: ©AP/Wide World

Photos. P. 344: ©Wilson McLean/The Newborn Group. P. 354: ©AP/Wide World Photos. P. 358: © Bettmann/CORBIS. P. 372: Republished with permission of Globe Newspaper Company, Inc., from *The Boston Globe,* ©circa 1973. P. 376: ©AP/Wide World Photos. P. 382: © Getty Images. P. 390 © Ed Eckstein/CORBIS. P. 395: ©AP/Wide World Photos. P. 403: ©AP/Wide World Photos. P. 411: ©AP/Wide World Photos. P. 414: ©Allen Horne, Columbus Ledger-The Enquirer Newspaper. P. 421: © Bettmann/CORBIS. P. 435: ©Scott Ferrell. P. 437: ©AP/Wide World Photos. P. 448: ©AP/Wide World Photos. P. 463: Courtesy Photofest. P. 466: © Julia Waterlow; Eye . Ubiquitous/CORBIS. P. 472: © Steve Liss/Timepix. P. 483: ©AP/Wide World Photos.

Cartoon credits

P. 77: Library of Congress. P. 121: "Don't Be Afraid—I Can Always Pull You Back"—from <u>Herblock's Special For Today,</u> (Simon & Schuster, 1958). P. 259: Library of Congress. P. 427: By permission of Mike Luckovich and Creators Syndicate.

Index